Michigan's Fiscal and Economic Structure

Michigan's
Fiscal and Economic Structure

Harvey E. Brazer, *Editor*
Deborah S. Laren, *Assistant Editor*

Ann Arbor
The University of Michigan Press

Published in the United States of America by
The University of Michigan Press and simultaneously
in Rexdale, Canada, by John Wiley & Sons Canada, Limited
Manufactured in the United States of America

Library of Congress Cataloging in Publication Data
Main entry under title:

Michigan's fiscal and economic structure.

Includes bibliographic references.
1. Finance, Public—Michigan—Addresses, essays, lectures. 2. Michigan—Economic conditions—Addresses, essays, lectures. I. Brazer, Harvey Elliot, 1922– . II. Laren, Deborah S.
HJ505.M5 336.774 81-22028
ISBN 0-472-10022-X AACR2
ISBN 0-472-08027-X (pbk.)

Camera-ready copy provided by the editors.

Paperback ISBN: 978-0-472-75046-7

Acknowledgments

I am deeply grateful to all of my colleagues who made the production of this volume possible. My greatest debt is to Robin Barlow and Edward M. Gramlich, who served diligently and cheerfully with me on the study's editorial review committee. They read and offered constructively critical comments on drafts of all of the chapters. These chapters in their final versions owe much to the insightful acumen of Professors Barlow and Gramlich.

We have been aided in our endeavors by the cooperation of many people in Lansing, East Lansing, Ann Arbor, Detroit, and Holland, Michigan. Their contributions are acknowledged in appropriate notes by individual authors. Donna Smallwood of the Department of Economics of The University of Michigan has been ever ready with assistance whenever we have been baffled by the intricacies of dealing with university administrative procedures.

I would also like to thank Patricia Berdan, Mary Gick, Maureen Jones, and Colleen Smeekens for the invaluable secretarial and administrative assistance they provided to the project. Special thanks are due to Margo MacInnes and Richard Meisler for their editorial and technical assistance and to Michael Canjar, R. E. Canjar, Michael Flynn, and Matthew Lynes for their work on the tables in this volume.

Finally, and most importantly, I wish to acknowledge the enormous contribution to the project of Deborah Swift Laren. Her title of assistant editor hardly begins to do credit to that contribution. It is, in fact, impossible to imagine that this volume could have come to fruition without her unstinting energy, patience, and skill. All of us who have been involved in the study are most appreciative of her efforts.

Harvey E. Brazer

Editorial Review Committee

Contributors

Patrick M. Barkey, Graduate Student, Department of Economics, The University of Michigan

Robin Barlow, Professor, Department of Economics, and Director, Center for Research on Economic Development, The University of Michigan

Raleigh Barlowe, Professor Emeritus, Department of Resource Development, Michigan State University

Lawrence E. Blume, Assistant Professor, Department of Economics, The University of Michigan

Harvey E. Brazer, Professor, Department of Economics, The University of Michigan

Robert J. Cline, Associate Professor, Department of Economics and Business, Hope College

B. Michael Conboy, Staff Consultant, Institute of Science and Technology, The University of Michigan

Jack S. Connell, Jr., Undergraduate Student, Department of Economics, The University of Michigan

Paul N. Courant, Associate Professor, Department of Economics, and Associate Research Scientist, Institute of Public Policy Studies, The University of Michigan

Joan P. Crary, Assistant Research Scientist, Department of Economics, The University of Michigan

John G. Cross, Professor, Department of Economics, and Associate Research Scientist, Mental Health Research Institute, The University of Michigan

Ronald C. Fisher, Associate Professor, Department of Economics, Michigan State University

John Goddeeris, Assistant Professor, Department of Economics, Michigan State University

Edward M. Gramlich, Professor, Department of Economics, and Director, Institute of Public Policy Studies, The University of Michigan

Jesse Hall, Research Associate, Institute of Science and Technology, The University of Michigan

George E. Johnson, Professor, Department of Economics, and Research Scientist, Institute of Public Policy Studies, The University of Michigan

Janet E. Kohlhase, Assistant Professor, Department of Economics, Michigan State University

Mordechai E. Kreinin, Professor, Department of Economics, Michigan State University

Marian Krzyzowski, Senior Research Associate, Institute of Science and Technology, The University of Michigan

John P. Laitner, Associate Professor, Department of Economics, The University of Michigan

Deborah S. Laren, Research Associate, Institute of Public Policy Studies, The University of Michigan

Paul L. Menchik, Associate Professor, Department of Economics, Michigan State University

Richard C. Porter, Professor, Department of Economics, and Research Scientist, Center for Research on Economic Development, The University of Michigan

Cynthia Rence, Assistant Professor, Department of Economics, Michigan State University

Daniel L. Rubinfeld, Associate Professor of Economics and Law, The University of Michigan

Frank P. Stafford, Professor, Department of Economics, The University of Michigan

Daniel B. Suits, Professor, Department of Economics, Michigan State University

Frank Yu-Hsieh Sung, Graduate Student, Institute of Public Policy Studies, The University of Michigan

Ann R. Thomas, Assistant Professor of Business Economics, Graduate School of Business Administration, The University of Michigan

Wilbur R. Thompson, Professor, Department of Economics, Wayne State University

Robert W. Vishny, Graduate Student, Department of Economics, Massachusetts Institute of Technology

Mary Walz, Undergraduate Student, Department of Economics, The University of Michigan

Barbara Weinstein, Graduate Student, Department of Economics, The University of Michigan

James E. Wheeler, Professor of Accounting and Chairman, Accounting Faculty, Graduate School of Business Administration, The University of Michigan

Gary L. Wolfram, Assistant Professor of Economics, Department of Social Sciences, The University of Michigan-Dearborn

Michael Wolkoff, Assistant Professor, Department of Political Science, University of Rochester

Gary C. Woodard, Graduate Student, Institute of Public Policy Studies, The University of Michigan

Preface

During 1980 it became apparent to most observers that the State of Michigan was passing through a period of difficult economic adjustment. Further, it seemed clear that the adjustment was more basic than the typical cyclical movements that had characterized the economy of the State of Michigan in the post–World War II era. With an economy heavily concentrated in durable goods production, particularly in the production of motor vehicles, sharp cyclical movements in economic activity had been "standard" over the last decades. The Iranian crisis of 1979 may have sharply precipitated many of the issues, and certain longtime domestic government policies were clearly responsible for aspects of the problem, but many analysts also believed that international competition and changing consumer tastes had permanently changed the near monopoly of domestic motor vehicle manufacturers and the labor unions that had so effectively represented industry workers. Whatever the causes, economic activity in Michigan was in recession, and the costs of doing business in the state, particularly in the heavily populated southeastern section, were perceived to be "uninviting" to industry. Previous attempts at diversifying the state's economy had been largely unsuccessful (perhaps unnecessary), but this time the full recovery of the automobile industry was in some doubt.

These events—high unemployment and low economic activity—put considerable fiscal pressure on the state budget and simultaneously raised considerable interest in tax reduction. The citizens of the State of Michigan were actively participating in the ongoing debate regarding the size and role of government, state as well as federal.

As President of the state's flagship public university, I asked myself what helpful role The University of Michigan might play in helping the citizens of the state deal effectively with these challenges. Clearly The University of Michigan was not a key actor in the decisions that would have to be made. These roles were appropriately reserved for the governor, the state legislature, industry, labor, and consumer groups. There were areas, however, where I felt that the university's faculty had special expertise which might be employed to inform the debate on many issues. As I thought further about the issue, I became convinced that The University of Michigan should do what it could to take a responsible part in these developments. At the same time, it was important that our role be an appropriate one which spoke to the special strength that a university might possess in dealing with such matters.

I discussed these issues with my colleagues on the President's Council of State Colleges and Universities and with many leaders in both the public and private sectors. Everyone with whom I spoke encouraged me to proceed. Many suggested that a failure of the university to respond would be irresponsible. As a result, The University of Michigan undertook a number of initiatives designed to bring faculty expertise to bear on some of the economic and social challenges facing the State of Michigan. The study presented here is the outcome of one of those initiatives.

As an economist with a longtime interest in the State of Michigan's economy, I was impressed that the tax reform/reduction debate in our state often displayed a less-than-full understanding of the state's tax structure. On investigation, I discovered that the last comprehensive study of the state's fiscal system was completed over two decades ago. I decided, therefore, to ask Professor Harvey E. Brazer of our Department of Economics, a nationally recognized expert in the area of state and local finance, if he would consider directing a comprehensive review of the state fiscal system. Further, since the debate was ongoing, I asked that the review be completed within six to nine months.

Professor Brazer's response was enthusiastic, with the understanding that he and his faculty colleagues be granted full and complete autonomy in the design of the work and the content of the result. The outcome of this agreement is contained in this book.

Although The University of Michigan provided the bulk of the financial support for this study—exclusively from income on undesignated private gifts—important additional support was provided by Michigan State University and Wayne State University. For this I want to express my special thanks to President Cecil Mackey of Michigan State University and President Thomas N. Bonner of Wayne State University. Our joint hope and expectation is that the material presented here will be of service both to the citizens of the State of Michigan and to the world of scholarship.

Harold T. Shapiro
President
The University of Michigan

Contents

Chapter 1

Introduction

by

Harvey E. Brazer

The University of Michigan

THE NEED FOR THE STUDY

Throughout the period since World War II the State of Michigan has faced severe fiscal difficulties in each of the recessions that has occurred. Typically the recessions have been deeper and more prolonged in Michigan than nationally as output of automotive products fell much more sharply than total industrial production. The declines in industrial output in the nation from 1969 to 1970, 1973 to 1975, and 1979 to 1980, for example, were respectively, 3 percent, 9 percent, and (March, 1979 to July, 1980) 9 percent, whereas the reductions in output of automotive products amounted to 16, 18, and 31 percent (37 percent to May, 1980). Clearly, Michigan's heavy reliance on the auto industry has been the principal factor responsible for the very wide amplitude of fluctuations in its economy. It promises, given the enormous increase in fuel prices since early 1979 and the inroads into the auto market by the Japanese, a slow rate of growth into the foreseeable future.

Michigan's fiscal problems, as well as those of its major cities, are inextricably linked to its economic problems. The past fifteen years have witnessed vast changes in the state's tax system, an enormous expansion of federal aid, and the introduction of such fiscal innovations as the Budget Stabilization Fund. Nevertheless, the fiscal crisis of 1980 was very reminiscent of that of 1959. Inevitably, in recessions as severe as those experienced in Michigan, revenues fall off while expenditure demands increase, particularly in response to the inflation that accompanied the recessions of the 1970s and that continues to plague us. During such recessions there has often been strong, sometimes effective, pressure to increase tax rates. On the other hand, as the economy recovers and revenues rise, new programs become increasingly difficult to resist. Thus a ratchet-like process tends to function in a way that exacerbates the problems presented by recurrent recessions and ensures the periodic appearance of fiscal crises.

It follows, therefore, that a study of the state's fiscal structure that may point the way towards improvements in that structure must be coupled with a study of the economy of the state. The last time this kind of effort was undertaken was in 1957-58. At the invitation of a legislative committee drawn from the taxation committee of the House of Representatives and headed by Representative Rollo G. Conlin, a comprehensive volume entitled, Michigan Tax Study Staff Papers, was prepared and published.[1] That study included an analysis of the state's economy as well as, in much more detail, its fiscal system. This earlier study was inspired by circumstances very similar in many ways to those that prevailed toward the end of 1980, when President Harold T. Shapiro of The University of Michigan took the initiative in launching the present study. In the late 1950s the Michigan economy was in difficult straits, in part because of a national recession, but also because of the losses in employment opportunities brought about by the continuing process of decentralization of the automotive industry, automation, and changes in the product mix involved in military procurement programs. Then, as now, there was major concern in the state about the desirability of achieving greater diversification in the economy and accelerating growth. Twenty-three years later workers are being replaced by machines in a new era of robotics and "high technology." We have learned to live without major dependence on defense contracts, but diversification to a degree that would make the economy less vulnerable to wide fluctuations in demand for trucks, autos, and the tools and equipment used in their production still eludes us.

The severity of the state's fiscal problems in 1958 is

evidenced by the $77.5 million General Fund-General Purpose Budget deficit,[2] almost 20 percent of total G.F.-G.P. expenditures for that year. In 1979-80, the revenue shortfall was $669 million,[3] some 14 percent of budgeted expenditures. And for fiscal 1981, expenditures are likely to be cut back by about $400 million from the level of $4.9 billion in the governor's budget for this year.[4] Thus in these terms as well, Michigan's circumstances appear to have changed little in more than twenty years.

We have, however, seen major changes in the structure of the tax system and in budgetary patterns. Twenty years ago one could unequivocally characterize the state and local tax system in Michigan as an unholy mess. But in 1967 a flat-rate modestly progressive personal income tax was enacted. It now yields one-third more revenue than the second most productive tax, the general sales tax. In 1973 the introduction of the Homestead Property Tax Credit, or "Circuit Breaker," provided substantial property tax relief, now amounting to over one-sixth of residential property tax liabilities. In 1974, the voters favored a constitutional amendment that excludes food purchased for home consumption and prescription drugs from the sales tax base, thus rendering the tax far less regressive than it had been. Thus, the tax system that had been found to be steeply regressive as of 1956[5] is now probably proportional or nearly so, with most taxpayers bearing state and local taxes which, as a proportion of income, vary within a rather narrow range.

The state has also come a long way in its efforts to improve the tax climate for business. Corporations are no longer distinguished, for tax purposes, from other forms of business organization, and the Single Business Tax of 1975, a modified value-added tax, replaced the corporate income tax, the franchise tax (Annual Corporate Privilege Fee), elements of the intangibles tax, the local property tax on business inventories, and four other minor levies. The legislature has authorized the issue of local industrial and commercial development bonds and property tax abatements on new and renovated industrial facilities. The extent to which business carries the impact of state-local taxes in Michigan has been dramatically reduced since 1957. In that year the proportion of these taxes paid by business was estimated to be 40 percent. By 1977 it was down to 28 percent,[6] a proportion lower than that found in thirty-two of the states. And in 1980 the laws relating to Unemployment Insurance and Workmen's Compensation were amended to ease their burdens on employers in Michigan.

The system of intergovernmental fiscal relations within the state has been thoroughly overhauled as well. State revenue sharing with the municipalities is now a major element of this system and the state's role in equalizing fiscal capacity among school districts has been greatly enhanced. The taxing powers of the cities have been substantially increased since 1967 when they were authorized to levy a uniform income tax.[7]

Thus, on the revenue side of state and local budgets the broad picture suggests that we have achieved a more rational, far more equitable tax system that rests broadly on income, consumption, and wealth, principally in the form of real property. It is a system that, as of 1979, absorbed 12.4 percent of personal income received in the state, compared with 8.6 percent in 1957.[8] And it is one which, perhaps because it has been so much revised in recent years, seems both little understood and subject to much complaint.

In per capita constant dollar terms between 1957 and 1979, expenditures of state and local governments in Michigan almost doubled, while increasing some 50 percent faster than personal income.[9] Fully a quarter of the increase was accounted for by public welfare programs, principally Medicaid, more than a fifth by local schools, and a tenth each by higher education and health and hospitals. The very large increase in federal aid, more than six-fold in real terms, still left some $500 per capita in 1979 dollars to be financed from state-local taxes and nontax revenues. Thus the revenue system has been under continuing pressure and, as we have noted, tends to produce less than the desired level of receipts during periodically recurring recessions.

OBJECTIVES OF THE STUDY

The executive and legislative branches of government in Michigan have achieved a great deal of improvement in the state's fiscal system in recent years. Except for some obvious intense interest in reducing property tax liabilities it is difficult to imagine that there is now either a strong demand or justification for major changes in the tax structure. Nor does there appear to be a widespread feeling that budgetary outlays are either excessively high or low.[10] There is, however, general concern about the state's ability to achieve the diversification of its economic base that is needed to attain a more stable economy and, at the same time, a more rapid rate of growth and the increased job opportunities associated with it. The long term fiscal viability of the City of Detroit is a closely related major problem that must be solved if the state as a whole is to be on firm ground. Thus, although a great deal has been accomplished, these and other vexing issues remain unsolved. Intelligent, rational discussion of policies relating to these and other fiscal and economic problems must begin with a thorough understanding of the relevant facts.

Thus the first goal of this study is to present an objective picture of the state's revenue system, its public expenditures, and its economy. Our second objective recognizes that even if one views the fiscal system as a whole as being in relatively good shape there are, nevertheless, bound to be important ways in which it can be improved, important flaws that may be removed. We shall, therefore, attempt to point up the system's deficiencies and explore alternative means of eliminating or ameliorating them. We shall pose and attempt to answer such questions as: What are the consequences for equity and efficiency of the present approach to state-local financing of elementary and secondary education and what are the merits of alternative approaches? What are the sources of dissatisfaction with the local property tax and what are the most appealing means for responding to it? What is the appropriate role of the state in the effort to diversify the economy and accelerate its growth and how can that role be pursued effectively? What may be the consequences of a continuing decline in the 'real' budget of the state; that is, what is likely to happen to public service delivery if expenditures are cut? And, in connection with each of the major taxes, what changes may be indicated in order to improve equity and efficiency and/or facilitate compliance and administration? These broad questions are, of course, only illustrative. Obviously, many more will be raised.

SCOPE OF THE STUDY

Following this introduction, the first substantive chapter presents a general overview of the public sector in Michigan, looking at the budget as a whole and at the overall structure of revenues and expenditures, in terms of historical development and interstate comparisons. Chapter 3 is a descriptive analysis of the Michigan economy. It examines trends in employment and income and offers forecasts for the five years to 1985. The next chapter examines the levels of labor costs in Michigan, by industry, skill classification, and region, and compares these costs with those in competing states and nations. It deals both with wage rates and fringe benefits and attempts to measure the influence of various forces on Michigan's labor costs. Chapter 5 offers a description and analysis of labor costs in the form of social insurance programs, including Old Age Security, Health and Disability Insurance (OASHDI), Unemployment Insurance, and Workmen's Compensation.

There then follow three chapters dealing with, in turn, the United States' comparative advantage in the closely interrelated auto and steel industries; the auto industry in Michigan, North America, and Japan, and prospects for manufacturing in general and automotive manufacturing in Michigan in particular; and an analysis of the causes and consequences of industrial location, a chapter focusing mainly on the factors identified as important in locational decisions and on the efficacy of alternative public policies designed to influence those decisions. Recognizing their possible importance in the future of the Michigan economy, Chapter 9 discusses "high technology" industries, their definition, and analyses of Michigan's past and present experience with them and their potential for growth in the state.

In the next two chapters the authors present a description and analysis of tax abatement as an incentive to industrial location under Michigan's Public Acts 198 and 255 (Chapter 10), and industrial and economic development bond financing as an instrument for attracting new industry and commerce (Chapter 11).

Discussion of the state's fiscal system begins with Chapter 12, which is on the budget and the provision of public services. This chapter examines trends in budget outlays in the decade to 1982, looks at the consequences, by function, of budgetary increases and cuts, and analyzes budgetary implications of intergovernmental fiscal relations and constitutional constraints, as well as a number of related issues.

Fiscal relations between the state and its nonschool local jurisdictions are the subject of Chapter 13, while Chapter 14 deals with the state's role in the financing of elementary and secondary education.

In view of the importance of the initiative referendum for fiscal policy in Michigan, we present an analysis of voter participation through referenda (Chapter 15).

The next nine chapters focus on the state-local tax system in Michigan, beginning with the local property tax and alternatives for property tax relief and continuing with detailed descriptions and analyses of the personal income tax, the sales and use taxes, the intangibles tax, the inheritance tax, the Single Business Tax, taxes on beer, wine, and liquor and operations of the Liquor Control Commission, and ending with a chapter on "all other" state taxes. Chapter 25 examines actual and potential recourse to user charges as revenue sources for the state and for local jurisdictions.

Michigan's natural resources have been important in the past in shaping the state's economy and they promise, given wise management, to play a major role in the future. Chapter 26 is on the taxation and public management of natural resources. It is concerned particularly with the taxation of oil, gas, iron ore, and copper, the management and taxation of forests, and the operation of the state park system.

Gambling as a source of revenue is the subject of Chapter 27. It deals with the existing sources of gambling revenue--the state lottery and horse racing--and analyzes the issues involved in the extension of legal gambling to casinos and off-track betting.

Detroit's fiscal crisis in 1981 highlights the question of whether or not our principal cities are fiscally viable entities. In Chapter 28 this question and related issues are analyzed in detail, with a view toward clearly defining the problem and its sources and, in the process, pointing the way toward alternative approaches to ameliorating the fiscal position of our cities.

Agriculture in Michigan has long been subject to a variety of special tax provisions inspired by the recognition of the industry's special problems. The impact of state and local taxation on agriculture is weighed in Chapter 29 and various features of the law are evaluated.

Finally, the study concludes with a chapter that presents a summary of major findings and provides a set of alternative policy directions for fiscal equity, efficiency and economic growth and stability.

NOTES, CHAPTER 1

[1]Legislative Committee, House of Representatives, Michigan Tax Study Staff Papers, Lansing, 1958.

[2]Harvey E. Brazer, "Michigan's Fiscal Outlook, Wayne State University Law Review, 1965, p.431.

[3]Estimate from Senate Fiscal Agency.

[4]Evidence of the state's fiscal difficulties is found in the downgrading of Michigan's bond rating, by Moody's Investors Service from AA to A, in the fall of 1980. Michigan is one of six states with a bond rating below AA. Citizens Research Council of Michigan, Council Comments, no. 921, November 11, 1980.

[5]R.A. Musgrave and Darwin W. Daicoff, "Who Pays the Michigan Taxes?," Michigan Tax Study: Staff Papers, pp. 138-9.

[6]Advisory Commission on Intergovernmental Relations, Significant Features of Fiscal Federalism, 1979-80 (Washington, 1980), p. 68. As corrected, the reference cited shows a figure of 23 percent for 1977.

[7]Detroit's income tax was introduced in 1961.

[8]See Chapter 2, this volume.

[9]See Chapter 2, this volume.

[10]See Paul Courant, Edward M. Gramlich and Daniel Rubinfeld, "Why Voters Support Tax Limitation Amendments: The Michigan Case," National Tax Journal, March 1980, p. 33.

Chapter 2

The Public Sector: An Overview

by

Harvey E. Brazer, Deborah S. Laren, and Mary Walz

The University of Michigan

The purpose of this chapter is to offer a general, broad picture of the state's fiscal system. We begin with a discussion of the state's budget, proceed to state and local governmental expenditures, and then to the revenue system.

THE STATE BUDGET

When one speaks of "the Budget" in Michigan reference is commonly to the Budget Message of the Governor, a slim volume outlining in summary fashion the highlights of the state's plans for expenditures of the various state departments and agencies and a forecast of revenues by source. An appendix offers a forecast for the economy and the revenue outlook prepared by the Department of Management and Budget. This document is normally presented to the legislature in late January or early February. For details on the planned use of budgeted funds one may turn to the Executive Budget, a two-inch thick tome resembling a telephone book. Appropriations bills and, when needed, tax bills, follow closely the presentation of the budget and are designed to implement the budget plan. Each house in the legislature relies for assistance in budgetary matters on its Fiscal Agency, which serves as a group of staff advisors on matters of budgetary and economic policy.

Confusion may arise when one speaks of "the Budget" because the state's constitution and statutes earmark certain revenues to separate funds, designed, generally, to avoid co-mingling of receipts designated for one specific purpose with other receipts. Thus for fiscal year 1982 total net receipts of all state government funds is projected at $10.9 billion. This sum is apportioned among fourteen separate funds, the largest of which is the General Fund, at $8.2 billion, of which $5.0 billion is available for the General Fund-General Purpose Budget, and $3.2 billion is earmarked for "Special Purpose" use by continuing statutory allocation. The other large funds are the Transportation ($1.6 billion), School Aid ($1.8 billion), Lottery ($0.6 billion), and Employment Security ($0.1 billion) Funds. Principal earmarked receipts not included in the General Fund-General Purpose revenues are all but a small portion of federal aid, three-quarters of sales tax receipts, motor fuel and vehicle license taxes, legislatively determined portions of income, single business, cigarette, liquor, and horse race wagering taxes, and a wide variety of nontax revenues.[1]

Nevertheless, although it accounts for something less than half of all state revenues and expenditures, the General Fund-General Purpose Budget tends to be seen as "the Budget." Appropriations for the state share of welfare programs and medicaid, higher education, mental and public health, corrections, state police, grants to the School Aid Fund, and support of the judicial, legislative, and executive branches of state government are supported by this fund. It is the fund over which the legislature exercises fullest discretion on a year-to-year basis, and its condition is generally seen as a measure of the state's fiscal health. However, because of changes from time to time in the Constitution and because of statutory changes affecting the allocation of revenues among funds, comparability over time with respect to growth or fluctuations in GF-GP expenditures, revenues, deficit, or surplus is very difficult to achieve. The problem of intertemporal comparability is rendered still more complex by the existence of inter-fund transfers.[2] But it is possible to obtain some general impressions with respect to both the rate of growth in this fund and the deficits or surpluses realized.[3]

A decade ago, in fiscal year 1972, GF-GP expenditures

amounted to $1,999 million.[4] Expenditures for 1981 are estimated at $4,496 million and the governor's recommendation for fiscal 1982 calls for spending $4,851 million. For the decade as a whole the rate of growth was 9.3 percent per year. But almost all of this growth occurred before 1980 and the movement of expenditures has tended to be highly responsive, with a lag of about a year, to fluctuations in the Michigan economy. Thus the rate of growth was 12.3 percent from 1972 to 1975, very low in response to the recession of 1974-75, then it picked up to 12.9 percent between 1977 and 1980. It dropped to 0.8 percent for the years 1980 to 1982.

Quite a different picture is seen, however, if allowance is made for inflation.[5] In terms of dollars of constant purchasing power GF-GP expenditures rose only from $1,999 million in 1972 to $2,310 million in 1982, at the rate of 1.5 percent per year. And the years 1980 to 1982 register a sharp decline, at 5.4 percent per year, from the peak level attained in 1980 of $2,581 million. Going back further, to 1977, we find a growth rate for the latest five years of only 0.4 percent.

A variety of influences has converged to reduce growth in state expenditures, including a decline in elementary and secondary school enrollments, a reduction in the number of students attending four-year public institutions of higher education, and a continuing reduction in in-patient treatment of the mentally ill. But perhaps the strongest and most compelling influences are the constitutional requirement that the budget be balanced each year[6] and the recession-induced very slow growth in revenues from 1979 to 1981. Since fiscal 1972 current revenue receipts have fallen short of planned expenditures[7] in three years, 1975, 1976, and 1980, each of which was a year of deep recession in Michigan. In 1975 the revenue shortfall was made up by using $205 million of the balance that had been accumulated in the General Fund out of prior years' surpluses and by Executive Orders of the governor[8] cutting expenditures below appropriations by $110 million, thus funding a "deficit" of $315 million.[9] If we include in the definition of deficit various accounting "adjustments" (such as, for example, the accrual of taxes from the next fiscal year), the deficit in fiscal year 1975 would be placed at about $505 million. For 1976 the deficit was down to $98 million. In that year an Executive Order[10] reduced the GF-GP outlays by $124 million and the General Fund balance was increased by $26 million. In this year also, over $100 million was borrowed from other funds and numerous accounting adjustments, including the three month extension of the fiscal year, were made to balance the budget. Finally, 1980 was, in terms of the absolute size of the year's GF-GP deficit, by far the worst on record.[11] In that year the General Fund balance was drawn down $29 million, the Budget Stabilization Fund (BSF) was stripped of its balance of $264 million, and an Executive Order cut expenditures by $98 million.[12] "Mandated lapses" in expenditures, agreements between the executive and legislative branches, reduced expenditures by another $61 million. And to get through the year over $200 million was realized by borrowing from other funds and by a variety of accounting adjustments. Thus the deficit, using the more inclusive definition, neared $700 million.

Until 1977 (fiscal 1978) only two "regular" means were available for meeting an impending GF-GP deficit: (1) the beginning year fund balance, if any, and (2) an Executive Order issued by the governor and approved by the appropriations committees of the legislature, to reduce appropriations below the levels enacted for the year. In 1977 Governor Milliken proposed[13] the establishment of a Budget Stabilization Fund. The legislature responded with a statute that implements the essence of the governor's proposal.[14] The first of its main features provides that, in years during which personal income in the state, net of transfer payments and adjusted for the change in the Detroit consumer price index, increases by more than two percent over the previous year, a transfer to the BSF is to be made.

The transfer is to be in an amount equal to the percentage above two percent multiplied by total GF-GP revenue in the fiscal year ending during the current calendar year. The effect is, roughly, to limit growth in GF-GP expenditures to two percent per year plus the rate of inflation given by the Detroit CPI. It should, therefore, dampen the "ratchet" effect on expenditures (noted in Chapter 1) that stems from the state's highly volatile economy.

When, on the other hand, the annual growth rate falls below zero, an amount equal to this percentage rate of decline in adjusted income multiplied by the current year's GF-GP revenue may be transferred from the BSF to the General Fund, up to the amount of the GF-GP deficit.[15]

The timing of the legislation bringing the BSF into being was highly appropriate, in that 1977 and 1978 were years of economic expansion. Thus in fiscal 1978 and 1979 transfers to the new fund from the General Fund amounted to $108.7 million and $104.1 million. Interest earned added $28.3 million, to bring the BSF balance to $241.1 million by September 30, 1979. By the beginning of fiscal 1980 the Michigan economy was well launched into a deep recession and in that year the BSF contributed, as noted above, $264 million to the General Fund. Interest accruals during 1980 and 1981 left some $16 million for support of the 1981 GF-GP budget, and by the end of 1981 it is expected that the BSF balance will be zero.[16]

The BSF obviously can be an effective instrument for dealing with Michigan's recurrent fiscal crises. If it has proven to be less than adequate the source of the difficulty lies in the fact that the recession that began in 1979 came only two years after the fund's establishment and it has been exceptionally severe and prolonged. Another potential problem arises under the present circumstances in which GF-GP expenditures for fiscal 1982 are expected to be 10 to 15 percent below those of 1980 in real terms. And yet if "adjusted personal income" in calendar 1982 exceeds that of 1981 by more than 2 percent, it is quite possible that a

PER CAPITA GENERAL EXPENDITURES OF MICHIGAN LOCAL GOVERNMENTS, SELECTED YEARS, 1957 TO 1979
(in 1979 dollars)
(percentage of personal income shown in parentheses)

FUNCTION	ALL LOCAL GOV'TS		COUNTIES	MUNICIPALITIES	TOWNSHIPS	SPECIAL DISTRICTS	SCHOOL DISTRICTS
TOTAL							
1957	558.6	(8.1)	91.6	183.2	12.5	4.2	267.1
1962	654.5	(10.0)	122.3	195.1	13.7	6.3	317.5
1967	761.1	(9.9)	127.4	197.3	14.4	6.1	413.4
1972	925.8	(12.5)	179.4	248.3	19.8	12.1	466.8
1975	957.8	(12.3)	171.9	267.1	17.4	11.3	490.1
1976	1001.4	(13.3)	188.0	276.0	22.0	15.0	501.3
1977	1007.4	(12.8)	197.4	272.8	21.1	16.1	499.9
1978	997.9	(12.1)	175.0	302.5	27.3	16.3	482.3
1979	1028.8	(12.2)	206.4	293.1	28.7	18.6	481.8
Education							
1957	261.7	(3.8)	0.7	0.0	0.0	0.0	261.0
1962	308.0	(4.7)	1.8	0.0	0.0	0.0	306.3
1967	398.9	(5.2)	0.0	0.0	0.1	0.0	398.8
1972	448.3	(6.0)	0.0	0.2	0.1	0.0	448.1
1975	469.6	(6.1)	0.0	0.0	0.0	0.0	469.6
1976	481.7	(6.3)	0.0	0.2	0.0	0.0	481.5
1977	480.7	(6.1)	0.1	0.0	0.0	0.0	480.6
1978	465.6	(5.6)	0.0	0.0	0.0	0.0	465.6
1979	465.5	(5.5)	0.0	0.0	0.0	0.0	465.5
Highways							
1957	71.5	(1.0)	36.1	32.5	2.9	0.0	0.0
1962	64.9	(1.0)	36.3	26.1	2.5	0.0	0.0
1967	63.2	(0.8)	36.0	24.7	2.5	0.0	0.0
1972	65.7	(0.9)	37.9	24.8	3.0	0.0	0.0
1975	64.4	(0.8)	35.3	26.7	2.5	0.0	0.0
1976	65.5	(0.9)	37.5	26.2	1.8	0.0	0.0
1977	65.8	(0.8)	36.1	27.0	2.6	0.0	0.0
1978	60.2	(0.7)	29.2	29.1	2.0	0.0	0.0
1979	69.0	(0.8)	38.0	29.0	1.9	0.0	0.0
Public Welfare							
1957	15.3	(0.2)	11.0	4.2	0.1	0.0	0.0
1962	30.0	(0.5)	19.9	10.1	0.1	0.0	0.0
1967	25.3	(0.3)	21.5	3.8	0.1	0.0	0.0
1972	26.5	(0.4)	25.8	0.7	0.1	0.0	0.0
1975	26.0	(0.3)	25.9	0.1	0.0	0.0	0.0
1976	28.0	(0.4)	27.9	0.1	0.0	0.0	0.0
1977	29.2	(0.4)	29.1	0.1	0.0	0.0	0.0
1978	23.4	(0.3)	23.2	0.2	0.0	0.0	0.0
1979	26.1	(0.3)	26.0	0.1	0.0	0.0	0.0

TABLE 2.1 (continued)

FUNCTION	ALL LOCAL GOV'TS		COUNTIES	MUNICIPALITIES	TOWNSHIPS	SPECIAL DISTRICTS	SCHOOL DISTRICTS
Police and Fire							
1957	43.8	(0.6)	2.8	38.7	2.2	0.0	0.0
1962	45.8	(0.7)	3.1	39.6	3.1	0.0	0.0
1967	50.4	(0.7)	3.3	43.7	3.4	0.0	0.0
1972	66.0	(0.9)	6.3	55.4	4.3	0.0	0.0
1975	72.0	(0.9)	6.0	60.8	5.1	0.0	0.0
1976	74.5	(1.0)	7.3	62.1	5.0	0.0	0.0
1977	79.0	(1.0)	7.8	64.2	7.0	0.0	0.0
1978	88.0	(1.1)	7.4	73.0	7.6	0.0	0.0
1979	83.1	(1.0)	8.9	66.0	8.2	0.0	0.0
Health and Hospitals							
1957	39.7	(0.6)	16.8	20.5	0.5	2.3	0.0
1962	46.4	(0.7)	21.8	20.2	0.1	4.3	0.0
1967	48.1	(0.6)	21.3	21.1	0.0	3.3	0.0
1972	60.6	(0.8)	26.6	25.7	0.1	8.2	0.0
1975	64.2	(0.8)	29.8	27.5	0.0	6.9	0.0
1976	73.5	(1.0)	34.0	28.7	0.0	10.7	0.0
1977	76.5	(1.0)	35.1	29.1	0.0	12.2	0.0
1978	73.9	(0.9)	32.9	26.3	0.0	14.6	0.0
1979	82.3	(1.0)	39.3	27.9	0.1	14.9	0.0
Interest on Debt							
1957	11.6	(0.2)	0.3	5.0	0.1	0.1	6.1
1962	20.4	(0.3)	1.8	7.0	0.2	0.1	11.2
1967	25.4	(0.3)	3.4	6.8	0.3	0.3	14.6
1972	37.7	(0.5)	6.8	11.1	0.9	0.2	18.7
1975	41.4	(0.5)	8.3	11.8	0.5	0.3	20.5
1976	44.4	(0.6)	10.8	12.7	0.6	0.6	19.8
1977	42.2	(0.5)	10.0	12.1	0.3	0.6	19.3
1978	39.4	(0.5)	10.5	11.5	0.2	0.5	16.7
1979	36.9	(0.4)	9.9	9.8	0.3	0.6	16.3
All Other							
1957	115.0	(1.7)	23.9	82.3	6.7	1.8	0.0
1962	139.0	(2.1)	37.6	92.1	7.7	1.9	0.0
1967	149.8	(2.0)	41.9	97.2	8.0	2.5	0.0
1972	221.4	(3.0)	76.0	130.4	11.3	3.7	0.0
1975	220.2	(2.9)	66.6	140.2	9.3	4.1	0.0
1976	233.8	(3.1)	70.5	146.0	14.6	3.7	0.0
1977	234.0	(3.0)	79.2	140.3	11.2	3.3	0.0
1978	247.4	(3.0)	71.8	162.4	17.5	1.2	0.0
1979	265.9	(3.2)	84.3	160.3	18.2	3.1	0.0

NOTES:

1) Data may not add to totals due to rounding.
2) Date are for fiscal years ending nearest to June 30.
3) Zero figures may represent actual zero values or values that round to zero given the number of significant digits used.
4) Values of the population as of July 1 of the year in which the fiscal year begins are used to obtain per capita values (e.g., July 1, 1978 population values used to obtain fiscal year 1979 per capita values.)
5) Values of personal income for the calendar year in which the fiscal year begins are used to convert dollar values to percentages of personal income.
6) The GNP deflator for state and local governments, (transformed, with 1979 equal to 1), was used to convert the data to 1979 dollars.

SOURCES:

Bureau of the Census, 1957, 1962, 1967, and 1972 Census of Governments.
Bureau of the Census, Governmental Finances in 1974-75, 1975-76, 1976-77, 1977-78, 1978-79.
Population data from Bureau of the Census, Current Population Reports, series P-25.
Personal income data from Dept. of Commerce, Survey of Current Business.

substantial transfer to the BSF may be required even though anticipated revenues for fiscal 1983 will not permit 1983 expenditures (in dollars of constant purchasing power) to regain the level of 1978, let alone 1980. At the same time, when the economy is well into recovery and growing rapidly, the provisions of Public Act 76 may require a transfer to the BSF that is far below the amount needed to constrain unsustainable program expansion.

STATE AND LOCAL PUBLIC EXPENDITURES

We turn now to a broad examination of state and local expenditures. We are concerned, first, with the within-Michigan picture for growth over time, and the distribution of direct expenditures [17] between the state on the one hand and its local jurisdictions on the other, and among functional categories. From this internal view we then move to a comparison among Michigan, seven other states, and the nation as a whole.

Expenditures in Michigan

Local. In Table 2.1 we present per capita expenditures, by function, for selected years between 1957 and 1979, for all of Michigan's 83 counties, 531 municipalities, 1,245 townships, 168 special districts, and 606 school districts, expressed in 1979 dollars.[18] We observe that the late 1950s and the decade of the 1960s were years of rapid expansion in expenditures at the local level. Per capita outlays of $559 in 1957 rose to $926 by 1972 and by only an additional hundred dollars to 1979. The rate of growth between 1957 and 1972 was 3.4 percent, followed by a rate of 1.5 percent to 1979, and less than 1 percent between 1976 and 1979. As a proportion of personal income in the state, local expenditures increased from 8.1 to 12.5 percent by 1972 and have since fallen back to just over 12 percent.

Growth rates have been very uneven among the various kinds of local jurisdictions. Compared with an overall increase in twenty-two years of 84 percent for all local jurisdictions, the real per capita expenditures of the counties and townships have gone up by about 130 percent, those of the municipalities by only 60 percent, while for school districts the rise has been 80 percent and for special districts an enormous 340 percent, due in large part to their rapid proliferation. Thus, school districts have accounted for a constant proportion of total local expenditures, while the counties' share has increased, largely at the expense of the cities and villages.

Education, mainly elementary and secondary, but including the community colleges as well, is, of course, the most costly of all local functions. It accounted for 45 to 47 percent of total local expenditures throughout the period under review. The relative importance of local streets and highways, on the other hand, was halved, from 13 to less than 7 percent. All other functions have changed little in terms of their shares of total outlays.

What we find, then, for the years since 1957, is rapid growth through the 1960s, very slow growth in the last decade, especially during its latter half, and few major changes in the distribution of expenditures, among either functions or types of jurisdictions.

<u>State</u>. Expenditures of the State of Michigan, expressed in per capita dollars of constant (1979) purchasing power, for the years 1957 to 1979, by function, are shown in Table 2.2. We note, first, that total outlays for all purposes [19] have precisely doubled in twenty-two years, for an annual rate of growth of 3.2 percent, only slightly higher than the rate for local expenditures. As we have observed with respect to growth in the GF-GP Budget and in local expenditures, however, here too we see a far lower rate of increase in the last few years than earlier in the period. It was 3.4 percent from 1957 to 1972, but only 2.1 percent from 1975 to 1979.

Total state expenditures consist of intergovernmental transfers, in the form of a wide variety of payments to local jurisdictions, over half of which go to school districts and most of the rest to other local jurisdictions

TABLE 2.2

PER CAPITA GENERAL EXPENDITURES OF MICHIGAN STATE GOVERNMENT, SELECTED YEARS, 1957 TO 1979

(in 1979 dollars)

FUNCTION	1979	1978	1977	1976	1975	1972	1967	1962	1957
TOTAL	1019	994	977	924	938	848	695	562	510
Intergov'tal	372	365	364	312	322	303	269	219	207
Direct	647	627	613	612	616	545	426	343	303
-education	171	176	166	168	171	162	169	93	85
-public welfare	231	223	226	228	211	177	64	38	40
-health and hospitals	73	63	60	54	54	49	46	38	38
-highways and other transportation	48	45	53	59	60	67	80	112	84
-police	9	9	8	8	8	7	5	4	4
-corrections	17	17	15	12	10	10	8	8	8
-natural resources	18	18	17	17	17	16	13	11	12
-gen. cont. and fin. admin.	22	21	20	18	17	16	11	9	8
-interest on debt	17	14	13	13	10	11	9	10	6
-other	40	41	35	34	57	29	20	18	17

NOTES:
1) 1957 data for local schools, health and hospitals, and public welfare were adjusted marginally to permit consistent definitions over time.
2) See notes for Table 2.1.

SOURCES:
See sources for Table 2.1.

for streets and highways, general government support, public welfare, and health and hospitals,[20] and direct expenditures for programs that are administered by departments and agencies of the state. State transfers to local governments, having less than doubled since 1957, now comprise 37 percent of total outlays, compared with 41 percent then.

There are several major changes to be observed in the relative importance of the various categories of direct state expenditures.[21] The largest of these changes involves public welfare, consisting mainly of the federal-state financed Aid to Families with Dependent Children, Medicaid, and Supplementary Security Income, and state-financed General Assistance. In terms of 1979 dollars this function cost $40 per capita in 1957, some 8 percent of total and 13 percent of direct general expenditures. These proportions had not changed appreciably by 1967, but by 1972 they had reached 21 and 32 percent, respectively, and, by 1979, 23 and 36 percent. Welfare costs amounted to 0.6 percent of personal income in the state in 1957 and 2.7 percent in 1979. About 40 percent of these costs are paid by the Federal Government through matching grants-in-aid.

The second largest change is in the transportation function, mainly highways and related structures but excluding state aid for local streets, highways, and mass transit. In constant dollars per capita expenditures under this heading have fallen from $84 in 1957 to $48 in 1979. Its relative importance has dropped sharply, from 28 percent of total direct expenditures to only 7 percent.

Direct expenditures of the state for education flow largely to four-year colleges and universities, with the remainder being spent on the administrative functions of the Department of Education and the State Board of Education. Education ranked first in terms of per capita outlays in 1957 and is second to public welfare, at $171 in 1979, double the level of the earlier year. Throughout the period under review direct expenditure on education has accounted for an almost constant 26 to 28 percent of direct and 16 to 17 percent of total expenditures.

Other major functions, including health and hospitals, corrections, and police have grown at about the same pace as total expenditures. On the other hand, expenditures for "General Control and Financial Administration," which includes the Legislature, the Judiciary, the Office of the Governor, Management and Budget, and Treasury, rose at a rate half again as high as total expenditures, while the "Natural Resources" category grew little more than half as rapidly.

State expenditures increased rapidly as a proportion of income received in the state through the latter years of the 1950s and the decade of the '60s, with the total rising from 7.4 to 11.4 percent of income between 1957 and 1972 and direct expenditures going from 4.4 to 7.3 percent. But since 1972 there has been only a slight rise in these proportions.

Thus, in general, we observe that over the period of twenty-two years to 1979 overall state expenditures per capita in real terms roughly doubled, rising from approximately 7 to 12 percent of personal income. Clearly, this part of the public sector has grown substantially relative to the economy as a whole, but growth in these terms appears to have stopped and, since 1977, even turned negative. The other major changes we observe are the large increases in the relative importance of public welfare and the decline in the transportation category.

Michigan Compared with Other States

It is obviously of interest to compare expenditures in their various dimensions in Michigan with those in contiguous or "competing" states. Because of large differences among the states in the allocation among levels of government of jurisdictional responsibility for several important functions, meaningful inter-state comparisons must be carried out using combined state and local expenditures.

We have standardized for population size by expressing expenditure levels in per capita values. But per capita expenditures should be viewed only as spending for inputs; they provide only the roughest indication of quantity and quality of services provided.

In Table 2.3 we present per capita state-local expenditures expressed in 1979 dollars, for Michigan, the neighboring states of Illinois, Indiana, and Ohio, and New York, Pennsylvania, and California, and the United States as a whole, for the years 1957, 1967, 1977, and 1979. Table 2.4 shows expenditures for these states and years as a percentage of personal income received.

For total expenditures per capita we find that Michigan is, and has been since 1957, at a level about 10 to 12 percent above the U.S. average and higher than that average as well for each of the major functional categories except highways and corrections. By far and away the largest difference is found with respect to public welfare where, for 1979 and 1977 the difference between Michigan and the U.S. is about $70 per capita, or 36 to 39 percent of the U.S. level. This represents a major change since 1957 and 1967, when the Michigan level was substantially below the national average.

With respect to the eight states subject to comparison, there are four, New York, California, Michigan, and Wisconsin, that spend at a higher level than the U.S. average, while Indiana, Ohio, Pennsylvania and Illinois are below that average. Among these states Michigan ranks third for total expenditures; second to Wisconsin for higher education[22]; second to New York for local schools; third, following New York and California, for public welfare; second to New York for health and hospitals; and third, after Wisconsin and Illinois, for highways.

Michigan therefore, is, as it has been for several decades, a relatively high spending state. The principal changes in its relative position have involved public welfare and higher education.[23] Relatively high levels of

TABLE 2.3
PER CAPITA DIRECT EXPENDITURES OF STATE AND LOCAL GOVERNMENTS, SELECTED STATES AND YEARS, 1957 TO 1979
(in 1979 dollars)
(state proportion shown in parentheses)

FUNCTION	U.S.	CA.	ILL.	IND.	MICH.	N.Y.	OHIO	PA.	WISC.
TOTAL									
1979	1494(.38)	1679(.31)	1438(.39)	1124(.38)	1676(.39)	1964(.26)	1294(.36)	1352(.40)	1629(.35)
1977	1478(.37)	1761(.30)	1486(.40)	1103(.37)	1600(.38)	2025(.22)	1282(.33)	1364(.45)	1560(.34)
1967	1118(.37)	1547(.32)	981(.35)	969(.36)	1195(.36)	1471(.25)	918(.32)	936(.41)	1248(.33)
1957	779(.34)	1074(.27)	744(.29)	676(.35)	862(.35)	967(.21)	728(.29)	639(.35)	786(.21)
EDUCATION									
1979	554(.26)	591(.20)	532(.22)	501(.33)	643(.27)	605(.19)	509(.25)	480(.22)	647(.28)
1977	564(.26)	667(.22)	550(.21)	504(.31)	634(.26)	638(.17)	529(.21)	485(.23)	632(.29)
1967	460(.25)	562(.20)	407(.23)	501(.31)	577(.29)	549(.17)	394(.20)	393(.21)	552(.36)
1957	276(.17)	405(.18)	261(.13)	297(.25)	352(.24)	293(.05)	268(.11)	232(.12)	261(.17)
-Higher Education									
1979	138(.82)	161(.62)	115(.71)	140(1.0)	168(.82)	112(.58)	122(.93)	69(.84)	196(.77)
1977	141(.81)	200(.65)	125(.73)	140(.99)	163(.81)	111(.58)	126(.78)	71(.84)	192(.81)
1967	107(.87)	141(.69)	90(.91)	142(.99)	170(.88)	90(.71)	91(.81)	48(.94)	193(.92)
1957	42(.90)	82(.78)	34(.93)	73(1.0)	84(.96)	19(.61)	36(.80)	15(1.0)	39(.98)
-Local Schools									
1979	382(.01)	403(.00)	376(.01)	330(.00)	436(.00)	438(.00)	366(.00)	360(.00)	417(.00)
1977	388(.01)	438(.00)	392(.00)	337(.00)	432(.00)	475(.00)	382(.00)	360(.01)	407(.00)
1967	331(.01)	400(.01)	300(.00)	337(.00)	381(.00)	421(.00)	294(.00)	308(.02)	330(.00)
1957	225(.02)	309(.00)	220(.00)	216(.00)	258(.00)	264(.00)	226(.00)	204(.02)	209(.00)
-Libraries and Other									
1979	34(.82)	27(.69)	41(.81)	31(.75)	39(.85)	56(.86)	21(.72)	51(.93)	35(.79)
1977	35(.82)	29(.66)	34(.76)	28(.76)	39(.86)	51(.84)	21(.74)	54(.92)	33(.77)
1967	23(.73)	21(.54)	18(.69)	22(.72)	26(.77)	37(.74)	9(.56)	37(.90)	29(.75)
1957	10(.54)	16(.35)	7(.45)	7(.33)	10(.43)	10(.44)	6(.28)	13(.73)	12(.43)
PUBLIC WELFARE									
1979	185(.71)	273(.55)	207(.96)	105(.61)	257(.90)	301(.13)	152(.73)	224(.87)	242(.60)
1977	187(.66)	279(.51)	216(.96)	103(.57)	255(.89)	345(.02)	144(.72)	233(.88)	237(.57)
1967	98(.52)	205(.32)	86(.79)	42(.09)	90(.72)	142(.05)	80(.57)	74(.81)	96(.39)
1957	71(.51)	100(.02)	66(.66)	46(.08)	56(.71)	81(.01)	65(.43)	49(.76)	69(.06)
HEALTH AND HOSPITALS									
1979	129(.49)	141(.30)	89(.52)	118(.45)	156(.47)	182(.47(	121(.56)	94(.62)	124(.36)
1977	125(.49)	132(.29)	104(.57)	106(.44)	135(.44)	186(.44)	116(.48)	98(.68)	109(.39)
1967	80(.51)	98(.36)	74(.66)	77(.49)	95(.49)	145(.42)	53(.48)	53(.82)	75(.42)
1957	56(.52)	78(.38)	46(.59)	45(.58)	77(.49)	96(.49)	44(.52)	46(.84)	53(.34)
HIGHWAYS									
1979	130(.60)	80(.43)	127(.55)	112(.60)	115(.40)	113(.45)	102(.53)	89(.62)	163(.33)
1977	125(.60)	83(.45)	147(.62)	108(.58)	115(.44)	95(.39)	101(.51)	113(.72)	155(.36)
1967	167(.68)	168(.62)	128(.56)	142(.66)	143(.55)	143(.57)	157(.66)	146(.79)	210(.31)
1957	151(.62)	157(.67)	142(.45)	122(.62)	156(.54)	131(.46)	150(.58)	110(.65)	178(.30)
OTHER TRANSPORTATION									
1979	15(.17)	18(.00)	12(.14)	7(.14)	9(.27)	23(.11)	6(.00)	7(.07)	9(.34)
1977	13(.19)	16(.00)	10(.16)	6(.21)	11(.21)	21(.12)	8(.00)	9(.04)	7(.21)
1967	11(.20)	16(.10)	9(.23)	7(.33)	13(.09)	18(.10)	7(.00)	7(.15)	12(.19)

[illegible]	[illegible]	[illegible]	[illegible]	34(.22)	68(.14)	79(.08)	44(.10)	49(.22)	53(.08)
1977	57(.15)	78(.15)	70(.09)	37(.20)	63(.13)	84(.07)	46(.11)	49(.24)	53(.07)
1967	37(.14)	56(.15)	41(.10)	24(.20)	38(.14)	64(.08)	28(.10)	32(.18)	37(.09)
1957	28(.12)	42(.12)	32(.06)	21(.21)	32(.12)	46(.05)	25(.09)	27(.16)	29(.06)
FIRE									
1979	24(.00)	33(.00)	26(.00)	18(.00)	25(.00)	32(.00)	22(.00)	14(.00)	23(.00)
1977	24(.00)	36(.00)	27(.00)	19(.00)	24(.00)	33(.00)	22(.00)	14(.00)	24(.00)
1967	18(.00)	29(.00)	17(.00)	15(.00)	19(.00)	29(.00)	15(.00)	11(.00)	22(.00)
1957	16(.00)	25(.00)	15(.00)	15(.00)	16(.00)	25(.00)	15(.00)	12(.00)	20(.00)
CORRECTIONS									
1979	25(.65)	38(.41)	21(.68)	16(.76)	26(.66)	34(.58)	17(.70)	19(.46)	22(.77)
1977	24(.63)	39(.42)	17(.64)	14(.72)	24(.64)	31(.55)	17(.73)	20(.50)	20(.77)
1967	14(.66)	28(.51)	11(.80)	8(.78)	12(.69)	20(.46)	10(.70)	13(.65)	14(.80)
1957	9(.71)	21(.53)	9(.72)	7(.80)	12(.68)	9(.80)	8(.77)	7(.64)	9(.70)
SEWERS AND SANITATION									
1979	54(.03)	52(.02)	69(.01)	39(.01)	66(.00)	77(.02)	67(.23)	54(.01)	54(.02)
1977	51(.03)	45(.02)	61(.01)	35(.01)	49(.00)	77(.03)	55(.24)	48(.02)	53(.02)
1967	30(.00)	29(.00)	33(.00)	27(.00)	32(.00)	40(.00)	36(.00)	29(.00)	49(.00)
1957	28(.00)	27(.00)	34(.00)	29(.00)	29(.00)	41(.00)	39(.00)	33(.00)	47(.00)
REC. AND NAT. RES.									
1979	49(.45)	81(.36)	42(.27)	32(.52)	51(.35)	39(.36)	29(.36)	28(.50)	49(.41)
1977	49(.46)	83(.34)	43(.25)	31(.54)	46(.36)	38(.33)	28(.33)	29(.54)	47(.39)
1967	44(.50)	126(.53)	34(.33)	26(.50)	35(.38)	37(.35)	23(.43)	25(.56)	48(.46)
1957	32(.48)	73(.35)	30(.29)	19(.54)	30(.39)	40(.56)	17(.41)	16(.47)	37(.45)
HOUSING AND URBAN DEV.									
1979	22(.05)	24(.03)	22(.02)	10(.02)	14(.05)	47(.07)	24(.01)	24(.01)	10(.04)
1977	18(.05)	17(.02)	17(.02)	11(.02)	12(.04)	47(.14)	20(.01)	18(.00)	11(.02)
1967	18(.02)	11(.05)	22(.01)	10(.00)	11(.00)	38(.01)	18(.00)	24(.00)	7(.00)
1957	10(.00)	6(.00)	18(.00)	2(.00)	3(.00)	33(.01)	5(.00)	12(.00)	2(.00)
GEN. CONT. AND FIN. ADMIN.									
1979	63(.38)	80(.28)	60(.33)	43(.32)	73(.30)	82(.56)	51(.31)	52(.35)	72(.34)
1977	58(.37)	83(.28)	53(.35)	40(.36)	62(.32)	65(.36)	46(.34)	53(.39)	54(.37)
1967	40(.35)	60(.31)	36(.32)	29(.34)	38(.29)	55(.38)	30(.24)	34(.33)	44(.41)
1957	33(.31)	50(.31)	29(.27)	28(.28)	32(.26)	47(.31)	32(.30)	32(.28)	32(.24)
INTEREST ON GEN. DEBT									
1979	60(.45)	35(.43)	56(.47)	29(.17)	54(.31)	143(.59)	44(.41)	81(.37)	49(.46)
1977	61(.44)	36(.42)	51(.40)	27(.23)	52(.26)	175(.54)	44(.42)	85(.45)	43(.44)
1967	36(.34)	43(.45)	35(.25)	25(.37)	34(.26)	65(.34)	28(.26)	40(.32)	29(.24)
1957	21(.32)	19(.32)	24(.30)	15(.55)	17(.34)	41(.28)	20(.30)	26(.34)	9(.00)
OTHER									
1979	128(.39)	159(.49)	106(.44)	61(.32)	121(.32)	207(.24)	106(.22)	136(.31)	110(.44)
1977	123(.39)	167(.44)	119(.38)	62(.33)	120(.30)	190(.26)	105(.29)	110(.42)	114(.28)
1967	67(.43)	118(.49)	48(.33)	37(.33)	57(.36)	127(.40)	39(.27)	56(.46)	54(.29)
1957	38(.42)	55(.34)	26(.42)	28(.56)	45(.39)	57(.36)	35(.28)	33(.44)	38(.30)

NOTES:
1) See notes for Tables 2.2 and 2.1.

SOURCES:

Bureau of the Census, 1957, 1967, and 1977 *Census of Governments*.
Bureau of the Census, *Governmental Finances in 1978-79*.
For sources of population data and deflator series see sources for Table 2.1.

TABLE 2.4
STATE AND LOCAL DIRECT EXPENDITURES AS A PERCENTAGE OF PERSONAL INCOME
SELECTED STATES AND YEARS, 1957 TO 1979
(State proportion shown in parentheses)

FUNCTION	U.S.	CA.	ILL.	IND.	MICH.	N.Y.	OHIO	PA.	WISC.
TOTAL									
1979	19.1(.38)	18.8(.31)	16.1(.39)	14.6(.38)	19.7(.39)	23.9(.26)	16.4(.36)	17.5(.40)	21.6(.35)
1977	19.9(.37)	21.0(.30)	17.5(.40)	15.2(.37)	20.3(.38)	25.1(.22)	17.2(.33)	18.3(.45)	22.1(.34)
1967	16.1(.37)	18.9(.32)	11.8(.35)	13.5(.36)	15.6(.36)	17.7(.25)	12.8(.32)	13.5(.41)	17.9(.33)
1957	12.5(.34)	13.8(.27)	9.7(.29)	10.8(.35)	12.5(.35)	12.4(.21)	10.4(.29)	9.8(.35)	13.2(.21)
EDUCATION									
1979	7.1(.26)	6.6(.20)	6.0(.22)	6.5(.33)	7.6(.27)	7.4(.19)	6.5(.25)	6.2(.22)	8.6(.28)
1977	7.6(.26)	7.9(.22)	6.5(.21)	7.0(.31)	8.1(.26)	7.9(.17)	7.1(.21)	6.5(.23)	8.9(.29)
1967	6.6(.25)	6.9(.20)	4.9(.23)	7.0(.31)	7.5(.29)	6.6(.17)	5.5(.20)	5.7(.21)	7.9(.36)
1957	4.4(.17)	5.2(.18)	3.4(.13)	4.8(.25)	5.1(.24)	3.8(.05)	3.8(.11)	3.6(.12)	4.4(.17)
-Higher Education									
1979	1.8(.82)	1.8(.62)	1.3(.71)	1.8(1.0)	2.0(.82)	1.4(.58)	1.6(.93)	0.9(.84)	2.6(.77)
1977	1.9(.81)	2.4(.65)	1.5(.73)	1.9(.99)	2.1(.81)	1.4(.58)	1.7(.78)	1.0(.84)	2.7(.81)
1967	1.5(.87)	1.7(.69)	1.1(.91)	2.0(.99)	2.2(.88)	1.1(.71)	1.3(.81)	0.7(.94)	2.8(.92)
1957	0.7(.90)	1.0(.78)	0.4(.93)	1.2(1.0)	1.2(.96)	0.2(.61)	0.5(.80)	0.2(1.0)	0.7(.98)
-Local Schools									
1979	4.9(.01)	4.5(.00)	4.2(.01)	4.3(.00)	5.1(.00)	5.3(.00)	4.6(.00)	4.7(.00)	5.5(.00)
1977	5.2(.01)	5.2(.00)	4.6(.00)	4.6(.00)	5.5(.00)	5.9(.00)	5.1(.00)	4.8(.01)	5.8(.00)
1967	4.8(.01)	4.9(.01)	3.6(.00)	4.7(.00)	5.0(.00)	5.1(.00)	4.1(.00)	4.4(.02)	4.7(.00)
1957	3.6(.02)	4.0(.00)	2.9(.00)	3.5(.00)	3.7(.00)	3.4(.00)	3.2(.00)	3.1(.02)	3.5(.00)
-Libraries and Other									
1979	0.4(.82)	0.3(.69)	0.5(.81)	0.4(.75)	0.5(.85)	0.7(.86)	0.3(.72)	0.7(.93)	0.5(.79)
1977	0.5(.82)	0.3(.66)	0.4(.76)	0.4(.76)	0.5(.86)	0.6(.84)	0.3(.74)	0.7(.92)	0.5(.77)
1967	0.3(.73)	0.3(.54)	0.2(.69)	0.3(.72)	0.3(.77)	0.4(.74)	0.1(.56)	0.5(.90)	0.4(.75)
1957	0.2(.54)	0.2(.35)	0.1(.45)	0.1(.33)	0.1(.43)	0.1(.44)	0.1(.28)	0.2(.73)	0.2(.43)
PUBLIC WELFARE									
1979	2.4(.71)	3.1(.55)	2.3(.96)	1.4(.61)	3.0(.90)	3.7(.13)	1.9(.73)	2.9(.87)	3.2(.60)
1977	2.5(.66)	3.3(.51)	2.3(.96)	1.4(.61)	3.0(.90)	3.7(.13)	1.9(.73)	2.9(.87)	3.2(.60)
1967	1.4(.52)	2.5(.32)	1.0(.79)	0.6(.09)	1.2(.72)	1.7(.05)	1.1(.57)	1.1(.81)	1.4(.39)
1957	1.1(.51)	1.3(.02)	0.9(.66)	0.7(.08)	0.8(.71)	1.0(.01)	0.9(.43)	0.7(.76)	1.2(.06)
HEALTH AND HOSPITALS									
1979	1.7(.49)	1.6(.30)	1.0(.52)	1.5(.45)	1.8(.47)	2.2(.47)	1.5(.56)	1.2(.62)	1.7(.36)
1977	1.7(.49)	1.6(.29)	1.2(.57)	1.5(.44)	1.7(.44)	2.3(.44)	1.6(.48)	1.3(.68)	1.5(.39)
1967	1.1(.51)	1.2(.36)	0.9(.66)	1.1(.49)	1.2(.49)	1.7(.42)	0.7(.48)	0.8(.82)	1.1(.42)
1957	0.9(.52)	1.0(.38)	0.6(.59)	0.7(.58)	1.1(.49)	1.2(.49)	0.6(.52)	0.7(.84)	0.9(.34)
HIGHWAYS									
1979	1.7(.60)	0.9(.43)	1.4(.55)	1.5(.60)	1.4(.40)	1.4(.45)	1.3(.53)	1.2(.62)	2.2(.33)
1977	1.7(.60)	1.0(.45)	1.7(.62)	1.5(.58)	1.5(.44)	1.2(.39)	1.4(.51)	1.5(.72)	2.2(.36)
1967	2.4(.68)	2.1(.62)	1.5(.56)	2.0(.66)	1.9(.55)	1.7(.57)	2.2(.66)	2.1(.79)	3.0(.31)
1957	2.4(.62)	2.0(.67)	1.9(.45)	2.0(.62)	2.3(.54)	1.7(.46)	2.2(.58)	1.7(.65)	3.0(.30)
OTHER TRANSPORTATION									
1979	0.2(.17)	0.2(.00)	0.1(.14)	0.1(.14)	0.1(.27)	0.3(.11)	0.1(.00)	0.1(.07)	0.1(.34)
1977	0.2(.19)	0.2(.00)	0.1(.16)	0.1(.21)	0.1(.21)	0.3(.12)	0.1(.00)	0.1(.04)	0.1(.21)
1967	0.2(.20)	0.2(.10)	0.1(.23)	0.1(.33)	0.2(.09)	0.2(.10)	0.1(.00)	0.1(.15)	0.2(.19)

[illegible]	[illegible]	[illegible]	0.8(.10)	0.4(.22)	0.8(.14)	1.0(.08)	0.6(.10)	0.6(.22)	0.7(.08)
1977	0.8(.15)	0.9(.15)	0.8(.09)	0.5(.20)	0.8(.13)	1.0(.07)	0.6(.11)	0.7(.24)	0.8(.07)
1967	0.5(.14)	0.7(.15)	0.5(.10)	0.3(.20)	0.5(.14)	0.8(.08)	0.4(.10)	0.5(.18)	0.5(.09)
1957	0.5(.12)	0.5(.12)	0.4(.06)	0.3(.21)	0.5(.12)	0.6(.05)	0.4(.09)	0.4(.16)	0.5(.06)
FIRE									
1979	0.3(.00)	0.4(.00)	0.3(.00)	0.2(.00)	0.3(.00)	0.4(.00)	0.3(.00)	0.2(.00)	0.3(.00)
1977	0.3(.00)	0.4(.00)	0.3(.00)	0.3(.00)	0.3(.00)	0.4(.00)	0.3(.00)	0.2(.00)	0.3(.00)
1967	0.3(.00)	0.3(.00)	0.2(.00)	0.2(.00)	0.2(.00)	0.3(.00)	0.2(.00)	0.2(.00)	0.3(.00)
1957	0.2(.00)	0.3(.00)	0.2(.00)	0.2(.00)	0.2(.00)	0.3(.00)	0.2(.00)	0.2(.00)	0.3(.00)
CORRECTIONS									
1979	0.3(.65)	0.4(.41)	0.2(.68)	0.2(.76)	0.3(.66)	0.4(.58)	0.2(.70)	0.3(.46)	0.3(.77)
1977	0.3(.63)	0.5(.42)	0.2(.64)	0.2(.72)	0.3(.64)	0.4(.55)	0.2(.73)	0.3(.50)	0.3(.77)
1967	0.2(.66)	0.3(.51)	0.1(.80)	0.1(.78)	0.2(.69)	0.2(.46)	0.1(.70)	0.2(.65)	0.2(.80)
1957	0.1(.71)	0.3(.53)	0.1(.72)	0.1(.80)	0.2(.68)	0.1(.80)	0.1(.77)	0.1(.64)	0.1(.70)
SEWERS AND SANITATION									
1979	0.7(.03)	0.6(.02)	0.8(.01)	0.5(.01)	0.8(.00)	0.9(.02)	0.9(.23)	0.7(.01)	0.7(.02)
1977	0.7(.03)	0.5(.02)	0.7(.01)	0.5(.01)	0.6(.00)	1.0(.03)	0.7(.24)	0.6(.02)	0.8(.02)
1967	0.4(.00)	0.4(.00)	0.4(.00)	0.4(.00)	0.4(.00)	0.5(.00)	0.5(.00)	0.4(.00)	0.7(.00)
1957	0.4(.00)	0.4(.00)	0.4(.00)	0.5(.00)	0.4(.00)	0.5(.00)	0.6(.00)	0.5(.00)	0.8(.00)
REC. AND NAT. RES.									
1979	0.6(.45)	0.9(.36)	0.5(.27)	0.4(.52)	0.6(.35)	0.5(.36)	0.4(.36)	0.4(.50)	0.6(.41)
1977	0.7(.46)	1.0(.34)	0.5(.25)	0.4(.54)	0.6(.36)	0.5(.33)	0.4(.33)	0.4(.54)	0.7(.39)
1967	0.6(.50)	1.5(.53)	0.4(.33)	0.4(.50)	0.5(.38)	0.5(.35)	0.3(.43)	0.4(.56)	0.7(.46)
1957	0.5(.48)	0.9(.35)	0.4(.29)	0.3(.54)	0.4(.39)	0.5(.56)	0.3(.41)	0.2(.47)	0.6(.45)
HOUSING AND URBAN DEV.									
1979	0.3(.05)	0.3(.03)	0.2(.02)	0.1(.02)	0.2(.05)	0.6(.07)	0.3(.01)	0.3(.01)	0.1(.04)
1977	0.2(.05)	0.2(.02)	0.2(.02)	0.1(.02)	0.2(.04)	0.6(.14)	0.3(.01)	0.2(.00)	0.1(.02)
1967	0.3(.02)	0.1(.05)	0.3(.01)	0.1(.00)	0.1(.00)	0.5(.01)	0.2(.00)	0.4(.00)	0.1(.00)
1957	0.2(.00)	0.1(.00)	0.2(.00)	0.0(.00)	0.0(.00)	0.4(.01)	0.1(.00)	0.2(.00)	0.0(.00)
GEN. CONT. AND FIN. ADMIN.									
1979	0.8(.38)	0.9(.28)	0.7(.33)	0.6(.32)	0.9(.30)	1.0(.56)	0.6(.31)	0.7(.35)	1.0(.34)
1977	0.8(.37)	1.0(.28)	0.6(.35)	0.5(.36)	0.8(.32)	0.8(.36)	0.6(.34)	0.7(.39)	0.8(.37)
1967	0.6(.35)	0.7(.31)	0.4(.32)	0.4(.34)	0.5(.29)	0.7(.38)	0.4(.24)	0.5(.33)	0.6(.41)
1957	0.5(.31)	0.6(.31)	0.4(.27)	0.5(.28)	0.5(.26)	0.6(.31)	0.5(.30)	0.5(.28)	0.5(.24)
INTEREST ON GEN. DEBT									
1979	0.8(.45)	0.4(.43)	0.6(.47)	0.4(.17)	0.6(.31)	1.7(.59)	0.6(.41)	1.0(.37)	0.7(.46)
1977	0.8(.44)	0.4(.42)	0.6(.40)	0.4(.23)	0.7(.26)	2.2(.54)	0.6(.42)	1.1(.45)	0.6(.44)
1967	0.5(.34)	0.5(.45)	0.4(.25)	0.3(.37)	0.4(.26)	0.8(.34)	0.4(.26)	0.6(.32)	0.4(.24)
1957	0.3(.32)	0.2(.32)	0.3(.30)	0.2(.55)	0.3(.34)	0.5(.28)	0.3(.30)	0.4(.34)	0.2(.00)
OTHER									
1979	1.6(.39)	1.8(.49)	1.1(.44)	0.8(.32)	1.4(.32)	2.5(.24)	1.3(.22)	1.7(.31)	1.4(.44)
1977	1.6(.39)	2.0(.44)	1.3(.38)	0.9(.33)	1.6(.30)	2.3(.26)	1.4(.29)	1.4(.42)	1.6(.28)
1967	1.0(.43)	1.4(.49)	0.6(.33)	0.5(.33)	0.8(.36)	1.5(.40)	0.6(.27)	0.8(.46)	0.8(.29)
1957	0.6(.42)	0.7(.34)	0.3(.42)	0.4(.56)	0.7(.39)	0.8(.36)	0.5(.28)	0.5(.44)	0.6(.30)

NOTES:

1) The figures for total expenditures are net of intergovernmental transactions between the states and their local governments.

2) See the notes for Tables 2.2 and 2.1.

SOURCES:

See sources for Table 2.3.
For source of personal income data see sources for Table 2.1.

expenditure for welfare may be attributable to large caseloads, high benefit payments, or both. For AFDC, in June of 1979 the payment per recipient in the U.S. was $87.42, the average for the eight states was $97.88, while Wisconsin, at $119.72 and New York, at $118.80, were slightly higher than Michigan's $116.43. Indiana, paying $65.08 per recipient, lagged far behind Ohio's $77.75 and Illinois' $83.68. During the same month 10.2 million in the U.S., 4.7 percent of the total population received AFDC benefits. Among the eight states Indiana was almost incredibly low at 2.7 percent; California, Illinois, and New York were at about 6 percent; Ohio, Pennsylvania and Wisconsin lay between 4 and 5 percent; and Michigan was the outlier at 6.9 percent, the second highest in the nation. Thus it would appear that Michigan's welfare rolls offer relatively easy access[24] and benefit payments per recipient are appreciably higher only in Alaska and Hawaii.[25]

Medicaid is the other major component of public welfare expenditures. The proportion of the population that receives benefits varies widely among the states, as does the amount of payment per beneficiary.[26] For the U.S. as a whole, during the second quarter of 1978 (latest data available) an average of 3.9 percent of the population were recipients of medicaid benefits, the average amount of which was $184.30. For the eight states the ranges were from 1.9 percent in Indiana to 6.4 percent in Illinois, and from $130 in Illinois to $364 per recipient in New York. In terms of both of these measures Michigan, at 4.4 percent and $192, was somewhat above the national average. Among the eight states Michigan was only slightly above the average for proportion of the population receiving benefits and over $20 below the average in terms of monthly amount paid per recipient. Thus, in contrast to AFDC, Michigan, under Medicaid, does not appear to be "out of line," unless comparisons are restricted to the contiguous states of Indiana, Ohio, and Illinois, where either benefit levels, proportion of the population served, or both, are very low.

Public expenditures for higher education depend in part on the costs per student of the programs offered, but they depend as well on the proportion of the population attending colleges or universities, the share of students taken by private institutions, and the distribution of students between public two-year colleges and the more costly four-year colleges and universities. Michigan, Illinois, New York, and Wisconsin all enroll about 5.5 percent of their populations in colleges and universities, just above the national average. California is, at 7.6 percent, very much higher, while Indiana, Ohio, and Pennsylvania are well below the mean at 4.1 to 4.3 percent.[27] In Michigan, like California and Wisconsin, close to 90 percent of all students are enrolled in public institutions, contrasted with between one-half and three-quarters in each of the other five states. Despite a very high proportion of its population in public colleges, however, California keeps its outlays below those of Michigan and Wisconsin, in part at least, by relying heavily on two year colleges. They account for more than 70 percent of that state's public higher education enrollment, contrasted with only 36 percent in Wisconsin and 45 percent (the U.S. average) in Michigan. These facts alone, therefore, are sufficient to explain the comparatively high per capita outlays for higher education in California, Michigan, and Wisconsin of $161, $168, and $196, contrasted with only $69 in Pennsylvania and a range of $112 (New York) to $140 (Indiana) for the other four states.

It is, of course, difficult to sort out cause and effect in analysis of differences among states in expenditures for public welfare, higher education, or other functions. Easy access to either welfare rolls or public college enrollment may make for large numbers of beneficiaries and students, and high benefit payments may induce larger numbers to seek them. But the reverse may be true as well; large numbers of people wishing to attend college may induce the public authorities to provide access, and large numbers of eligible welfare recipients may bring successful political action to raise benefits. Deeper insights require substantially more detailed analysis of the components of public programs than can be undertaken in this overview.[28]

The states differ widely in their capacities to support public services, capacities that may be at least roughly approximated by income received by their residents. In Table 2.4 we present state-local expenditures as a proportion of income. Here we observe that in 1979 Michigan government spending from all sources, including federal aid, amounted to 19.7 percent of income received in the state, not much higher than the national average of 19.1 percent, but well above the levels for Indiana (14.6), Illinois (16.1), and Ohio (16.4). The 19.7 percent figure for 1979 is more than half again as high as the 12.5 percent of 1957. It is, however, 3 percent below 1977.

Michigan devotes a somewhat larger than average proportion of its income to state-local public services for each of the major functions other than highways. The difference between Michigan and the national average has moved down in the major area of education and sharply upward in the case of public welfare since 1967. For education we find that expenditures for local schools were about 3 percent above the average, at 3.7 percent of income in 1957, and, at 5.1 percent, they are still some 3 percent higher than average. The big drop relative to the nation is seen in higher education. The Michigan and national proportions were 1.2 and 0.7 percent in 1957, whereas in 1979 they were 2.0 and 1.8 percent, only 10 percent higher in Michigan as opposed to over 70 percent higher in 1957.

In contrast, public welfare outlays took 0.8 percent of income in Michigan in 1957 and 1.1 percent nationally, but by 1979 Michigan's 3 percent of income was 25 percent higher than the U.S. average, with the change in relative position coming almost entirely during the 1967-77 decade.

Among the eight states subject to comparison here one may observe a fairly consistent pattern. Michigan tends to devote more of its income to state-local services, in total and for most functions, than each of the states other than New York and Wisconsin, while Indiana, Illinois, and Ohio generally are the most frugal.

STATE AND LOCAL REVENUES

We turn now to a parallel overview of state-local revenues. First we take up the highlights of major developments in Michigan's tax system, then move on to describe local and state revenue sources in Michigan. The chapter concludes with a brief comparative analysis of state-local revenues in Michigan and other states.

Highlights of Legislative History

The story of the evolution of Michigan's tax system from territorial days to 1957 has been told elsewhere.[29] By 1957 state-local tax receipts amounted to $1,371 million, distributed among sources as follows:[30]

Local Property Tax		$622 million
State Taxes-		
Sales	308	
Use	20	
Excises on Cigarettes, Beer, Wine, and Liquor	35	
Business Activities	64	
Franchise	47	
Insurance Premiums	18	
Motor Fuels	133	
Motor Vehicles	66	
Intangibles	24	
Inheritance	11	
Other	22	749
Total Tax Receipts		$1,371

This tax structure is easily characterized as one that was made up mainly of the property, general sales and other consumption taxes, the highway-user taxes, and two separate and uncoordinated business taxes. "Hodgepodge" is as good a term as any to describe it. And, as one would expect, it was found to be highly regressive in its incidence.[31]

The effort to achieve major tax reform was launched with the publication in 1959 of <u>The Report of the Citizens' Advisory Committee to the Michigan Tax Study</u>. The objectives sought by the committee were:

(1) "A tax structure greatly improved in terms of equity";
(2) "A tax structure that will be conducive to economic growth";
(3) "A tax structure which will provide enough potential revenue to enable the Legislature, if it chooses, to liquidate the state's mounting deficit within a reasonable period of time, to finance existing and even expanded needs, and to extend increasing aid to the hard-pressed subordinate governmental units"; and
(4) "A tax program that is rational, flexible and relatively simple to administer."[32]

The committee's principal recommendations involved the introduction of a graduated personal income tax and a corporate income tax, exemption of machinery and equipment under the property tax, sales tax relief aimed at reducing the regressivity of that tax, and broadening of the base of the sales tax. The main components of the committee's program were endorsed by Governor G. Mennen Williams in early 1959[33], by Governor John B. Swainson[34] in 1962, and by Governor George Romney in 1963.[35] On several occasions tax reform measures were passed in the House of Representatives, but each time the bills were blocked in the Senate.

Between 1957 and 1967 the only important innovation on the tax scene in Michigan was the adoption by the City of Detroit of a personal and corporate income tax in 1961.

Finally, however, under the leadership of Governor Romney, tax reform was enacted by the Legislature in the fall of 1967. Its components were: a personal income tax based on the federal concept of "adjusted gross income," with a per taxpayer, spouse, and dependent exemption of $1,200 and a flat rate of 2.6 percent; a corporate income tax at the rate of 5.6 percent (7 percent for financial institutions); and repeal of the Business Activities Tax (a form of value added tax).[36]

By the end of the decade of the 1960s, with a balanced income-sales-property tax system in place, attention of the governor and the legislature turned to revision of school financing, property tax relief, and efforts to make the tax structure more appealing to business.

The temporary income tax rate increases of 1971, to 3.9 percent for individuals and 7.8 percent for corporations, were made permanent in 1972. In November of 1972 the voters turned down a proposed constitutional amendment that would have eliminated the property tax as a source of basic school operating revenues and replaced it with state funding of a uniform state-wide finance program. But the governor's office and the legislature, under the leadership of Senator Gilbert E. Bursley, persisted. In 1973 the "Bursley Act" was passed. It provided for minimum levels of support for K-12 public education and encouraged local school districts to help themselves.[37]

In the same legislative session Public Act 20 was approved. It introduced the Homestead Property Tax Credit, commonly known as the "circuit-breaker." It provided for a credit against income tax due, or a refund if none were payable, equal to 60 percent of the difference between the property tax paid on a principal residence ("homestead") and 3.5 percent of the taxpayer's total income. For renters 17 percent of gross rent was deemed to be property tax. And for those 65 years of age and over 100 percent of tax paid in excess of 3.5 percent of income was to be rebated.[38] The maximum credit was set at $500. This maximum has since been raised to $1,200, but other major features of the Homestead Credit remain unchanged.

The same act also increased the personal exemption under the income tax to $1,500. Business concerns were allowed a credit of 25 percent of the amount paid in property taxes on inventories, the rate of the credit to increase annually over a period of years.

Further property tax relief was provided for qualifying firms in 1974 under Public Act 198, which permits the exemption of the value of certain improvements in the case of rehabilitation of obsolete plants or half of the value of new plants for a period of up to 12 years.[39]

In November of 1974 a constitutional amendment was adopted by popular referendum that exempts food purchases for home consumption and prescription drugs from the sales tax.

The movement to reform the Michigan tax structure continued in 1975. A modified value added tax, labeled the Single Business Tax, was enacted.[40] Its title derived from the fact that it replaced eight taxes on business enterprises--the franchise (ACPF), corporate income, and financial institutions taxes, the privilege fees on domestic insurance companies, domestic building and loan and savings and loan companies, and federal savings and loan companies, the business intangibles tax, and the local property tax on inventories. At the same time the personal income tax rate was increased to its present level of 4.6 percent.

In November of 1978 another constitutional amendment, "Headlee," was adopted by popular referendum. This amendment contained two major provisions: 1) state taxes are prohibited from rising above a constant percentage of state personal income, and 2) should the assessed value of a jurisdiction (excluding new construction) increase at a faster rate than the consumer price index, compensating reductions in millage rates must be made. Overrides of both these provisions are possible. In fact, however, neither of these provisions appears to have presented much of a constraint.[41] Several other efforts to cut property taxes by constitutional amendment have failed.

Apart from changes in detail, the tax system of the state and its local jurisdictions is in 1981 essentially what it was by the beginning of 1976. The contrast wrought in less than 20 years may be seen by comparing the tabulation presented above with the following summary of tax receipts for fiscal year 1980:[42]

Local Property Tax		$4,030* million
State Taxes-		
Sales	1,504	
Use	232	
Personal Income	2,293*	
SBT	1,076	
Excises on Cigarettes Beer, Wine, and Liquor	236	
Insurance Premiums	149	
Motor Fuels	477	
Motor Vehicles	236	
Intangibles	42	
Inheritance	50	
Other	219	6,514*
Total Tax Receipts		$10,544

*$381 million added to personal income tax and deducted from property tax so as to reflect the Homestead Property Tax Credit as a reduction in property tax rather than income tax, as the state accounts for it.

Most striking in this comparison are the rise of the income tax from nothing to close to 40 percent of state tax receipts, the drop in the relative role of consumption taxes, and the decline of the property tax from 45 percent of total state-local tax receipts to 38 percent.

General Appraisal of the Tax System

Among the major consequences of the changes in the Michigan tax system that have taken place since 1957 is a large reduction in the extent to which the state and its local subdivisions rely on taxes with an "initial impact" on business.[43] The Advisory Commission on Intergovernmental Relations has estimated that, in 1957, 40 percent of all state-local taxes levied in Michigan were imposed on business. This was not a great deal higher than the U.S. average of about 37 percent. In this respect Michigan ranked (highest to lowest) eighth among forty-eight states, or fifth, if Texas and Louisiana with huge severance taxes and West Virginia, with its gross receipts tax that ACIR chooses to treat as a business rather than a sales tax, are not counted. By 1977 the proportion of taxes paid initially by business was down to an average foı the U.S. of 31 percent, while in Michigan it had been cut by more than a quarter to 28 percent. And Michigan now ranks thirtieth among the 50 states, twenty-sixth if Alaska, Texas, Louisiana, and West Virginia are omitted. Most significant perhaps, is the fact that in this respect Michigan ranks below Illinois, Indiana, New York, Ohio, Pennsylvania, and California.

Toward the end of 1975, on the basis of ACIR "Fiscal Reform Criteria," John Shannon proposed "A Preliminary 'Report Card' on the 50 State-Local Fiscal Systems."[44] The states were "scored" on the basis of fourteen tests falling under the four headings of "Revenue Balance," "Tax Equity," "Effective Property Tax Administration," and "Fiscal Equalization" among local jurisdictions through state aid or centralization of fiscal responsibility.[45] Under the first of these criteria Michigan scored twenty-four out of a possible thirty and ranked eighteenth from the top. Under equity it scored a "perfect 30." On quality of property tax administration most states rated a low score, the mean being six. Michigan ranked fifth, with only four states having county assessment systems and close state supervision doing better. And, finally, in the matter of fiscal equalization, out of an assigned possible total of sixty Michigan scored twenty-nine and ranked fifteenth. When all four criteria are put together Michigan ranks second only to Hawaii, whose rating is suspect because it is so highly centralized in fiscal matters.

Obviously reasonable observers may disagree on the selection of criteria by which to judge the quality of a tax system and on the weights attached to them. Nevertheless, Shannon's criteria are certainly not unreasonable. Moreover, the data used in the analysis were all drawn from the years 1971 to 1974, so that Michigan's 1975 reforms were not taken into account. For whatever the "tests'" value, the fact remains that Michigan does score far higher, at ninety-nine, than all of the other states in the eight-state group of neighboring or competing states. Among these states California and Wisconsin were the only other ones that scored over seventy-five.

A third aspect of the tax system that is frequently examined is the way in which it distributes taxes among those who ultimately bear them, that is, the incidence of the tax system. The most recent study of the incidence of Michigan's state and local taxes is that of Donald M. Peppard, Jr. and Douglas B. Roberts.[46] These authors, using 1970 tax data and reasonable, widely accepted assumptions about tax shifting, found the system to be highly regressive, taking a declining share of income as income rises, ranging from about 15 percent at under $5,000 of income down to 4 to 4.5 percent at over $25,000.

Peppard and Roberts quite properly take account of the extent to which taxes are shifted to residents of other states. They also recognize that income, property, and sales taxes are deductible for federal income tax purposes. This is standard practice and it is appropriate to reduce the taxes assigned to each income group by the extent to which such taxes reduce federal income tax. But, given the progressivity of the federal rate structure, it is almost inevitable that this procedure will ensure a regressive estimate of incidence for state-local taxes. As a general rule, under the graduation in the federal income tax rate structure, any state-local tax system that is less progressive than this rate structure will be found to be regressive.

It seems to us not worthwhile to devote the large amount of time and resources that it would take to update the Peppard-Roberts study. We expect that changes in the Michigan tax law since 1970, including especially the exemption of food and prescription drugs under the sales tax, the increase in the rate and exemptions under the personal income tax, and the introduction of the property tax circuit-breaker have reduced the regressivity of the system appreciably. And, of course, so will the recently enacted dramatic cuts in federal income tax rates. We are

TABLE 2.5

PER CAPITA GENERAL REVENUES OF MICHIGAN LOCAL GOVERNMENTS, SELECTED YEARS, 1957 TO 1979
(in 1979 dollars)
(Percentage of personal income shown in parentheses)

SOURCE	ALL LOCAL GOV'TS		COUNTIES	MUNICIPALITIES	TOWNSHIPS	SPECIAL DISTRICTS	SCHOOL DISTRICTS
TOTAL							
1957	540.5	(7.8)	102.5	173.9	13.6	16.1	247.3
1962	610.5	(9.4)	118.9	186.9	16.7	5.9	282.2
1967	727.7	(9.6)	123.0	201.1	17.6	8.0	378.0
1972	906.0	(12.1)	151.5	267.5	29.2	16.1	470.7
1975	947.8	(12.2)	174.1	273.3	31.4	13.6	465.7
1976	992.0	(12.9)	180.9	291.0	31.0	18.8	470.7
1977	1031.7	(13.1)	188.7	306.4	30.3	18.6	487.6
1978	1028.1	(12.4)	181.3	310.6	34.2	24.6	477.3
1979	1041.6	(12.3)	204.0	298.6	36.8	28.1	473.9
Property Tax							
1957	260.1	(3.8)	49.3	89.2	3.4	1.2	117.0
1962	315.3	(4.9)	56.4	94.1	5.7	1.2	158.0
1967	304.7	(4.0)	48.4	78.6	5.8	0.9	170.8
1972	375.1	(5.0)	43.9	87.3	12.1	1.0	230.1
1975	369.0	(4.8)	41.9	77.9	9.4	0.9	238.9
1976	383.6	(5.0)	43.0	79.8	10.2	0.8	250.0
1977	371.9	(4.7)	43.6	76.5	10.6	0.8	240.4
1978	365.4	(4.4)	40.9	73.3	11.0	0.4	240.0
1979	363.3	(4.3)	42.2	70.9	11.2	1.3	237.7
Other Taxes							
1957	6.1	(0.0)	0.5	4.9	0.8	0.0	0.0
1962	3.9	(0.0)	0.5	2.7	0.7	0.0	0.0
1967	20.7	(0.3)	0.7	19.2	0.7	0.0	0.1
1972	33.6	(0.5)	1.5	31.2	0.7	0.0	0.1
1975	28.9	(0.3)	1.4	26.5	0.6	0.0	0.3
1976	29.7	(0.4)	1.4	27.2	0.7	0.0	0.4
1977	33.3	(0.4)	1.7	30.2	0.7	0.0	0.6
1978	34.5	(0.4)	2.0	30.5	0.9	0.0	1.0
1979	33.8	(0.4)	2.1	30.0	1.0	0.0	0.6

Current Charges And Miscellaneous							
1957	72.7	(1.1)	13.3	40.5	1.8	14.7	15.2
1962	90.7	(1.4)	15.2	46.1	2.7	4.5	22.3
1967	120.6	(1.6)	20.2	56.6	3.7	6.8	33.3
1972	157.8	(2.1)	38.1	68.6	7.5	9.2	36.3
1975	171.8	(2.2)	37.9	74.2	10.0	8.4	41.3
1976	172.1	(2.2)	39.7	73.6	8.8	11.7	38.4
1977	179.7	(2.3)	41.5	73.3	6.9	12.7	45.4
1978	169.7	(2.1)	36.3	73.5	7.7	15.6	36.6
1979	192.0	(2.3)	49.1	73.5	10.6	18.0	40.7
Federal Aid							
1957	3.4	(0.0)	0.1	1.2	0.0	0.1	2.0
1962	6.9	(0.1)	0.1	5.5	0.2	0.0	1.1
1967	15.7	(0.2)	1.2	11.1	0.1	0.1	3.4
1972	46.5	(0.6)	7.3	33.1	0.2	5.7	5.9
1975	71.1	(0.9)	16.1	42.7	2.3	2.5	7.4
1976	101.2	(1.3)	24.7	61.6	2.4	4.4	8.1
1977	102.0	(1.3)	28.5	59.3	2.9	3.3	8.0
1978	111.0	(1.3)	26.8	63.2	4.4	5.1	11.4
1979	111.1	(1.3)	35.1	56.9	3.9	5.4	9.7
State Aid							
1957	198.2	(2.9)	39.3	38.1	7.6	0.1	113.1
1962	193.7	(3.0)	46.7	38.5	7.4	0.2	100.8
1967	266.0	(3.5)	52.5	35.6	7.3	0.2	170.4
1972	293.0	(3.9)	60.7	47.3	8.7	0.2	176.0
1975	307.0	(4.0)	76.8	52.0	9.1	1.8	177.8
1976	305.4	(4.0)	72.1	48.8	8.9	1.9	173.8
1977	344.8	(4.4)	73.4	67.1	9.2	1.8	193.2
1978	347.5	(4.2)	75.3	70.1	10.2	3.5	188.3
1979	341.4	(4.0)	75.5	67.3	10.1	3.4	185.2

NOTES:

1) "Other taxes" includes $25.3 of income taxes in 1972, $21.2 of income taxes in 1975, $21.7 in 1976, $24.0 in 1979 (all figures in constant dollars per capita).
2) See notes for Table 2.1.

SOURCES:
See sources for Table 2.1.

confident that Michigan's state-local tax system is reasonably equitable, given the constraints under which the state and its local subdivisions must function. It remains relevant to examine alternatives for change in terms of their relative incidence, but further efforts to measure "absolute" incidence do not seem to us to promise rewards commensurate with their costs.

Revenues in Michigan

Local. Revenues of all local governments, expressed in per capita dollars of constant purchasing power, are shown in Table 2.5 for selected years from 1957 to 1979. Because of the balanced budget constraint under which local jurisdictions must function, the distribution of revenues among kinds of local units and over time follows very closely the pattern observed with respect to expenditures (Table 2.1).

Property taxes are seen to have increased in real terms between 1957 and 1962 at the rate of 3.9 percent per year. In the next five years they fell by about $11 per capita, and then rose rapidly, at the rate of 4.2 percent, between 1967 and 1972. But since 1972 per capita property tax receipts have not kept pace with inflation.[47] Moreover, the actual decline in net property tax liabilities has been substantially larger than is suggested in the table because the effects of the circuit-breaker after 1972 are not taken into account here. After deduction of the amount of the circuit-breaker we find that the property tax now takes less than 4 percent of personal income, compared with 5 percent as early as 1962 and again as recently as 1975.[48]

"Other" taxes consist mainly of municipal income taxes, now levied by Detroit and fifteen other cities, and Detroit's tax on public utility services. They were not significant revenue sources until after 1962 when the Detroit levy entered the picture, but in recent years in the aggregate they have been contributing over 8 percent of total tax receipts, almost all of it going to the cities.

Per capita real property tax receipts have declined substantially for the counties, municipalities, and special districts of the state for the period since 1957. For the townships and school districts, however, they have more than doubled between 1957 and 1979, even after allowing for population increase and inflation. It is, essentially, the school districts, whose share of the property tax has grown from 45 percent of the total in 1957 to 65 percent in 1979, that have accounted for the great bulk of the increase in property taxes in current dollars.

It is interesting to observe that current charges for services, admissions, and so forth, have grown in per capita real terms far more rapidly than tax receipts. And each of the types of local jurisdiction has shared in this growth.

The importance of federal and state aid is clearly apparent in the lower panels of Table 2.5. Whereas in 1957 together they provided less money than the property tax, as of 1979 they amounted to $452 per capita, compared with $397 from all local taxes. Having been quite insignificant in 1957, federal assistance is now especially important for the municipalities and counties. On the other hand, state aid is of greatest importance for schools, for which it provides 39 percent of revenue from all sources, a decline from 46 percent in 1957.

The general picture that emerges is one in which we see total revenues in recent years at levels substantially higher than they were twenty years ago. During the decade of the 1970s they more than kept up with inflation. In the latter half of this decade, however, they declined relative to personal income received in the state.

State. Tables 2.6 and 2.7 present tax and nontax receipts of the state in per capita real terms and as a percentage of personal income received. Over the period 1957 to 1980 as a whole clearly tax receipts have increased more rapidly than the price level as they have absorbed a proportion of income that has gone up from under five to seven percent. Closer examination of the data reveals that this growth has been

TABLE 2.6

PER CAPITA MICHIGAN STATE GOVERNMENT REVENUES, SELECTED YEARS, 1957 TO 1980
(in 1979 dollars)

SOURCE	1980	1979	1978	1977	1976	1975	1972	1967	1962	1957
TAX REVENUE	590	656	652	619	511	505	573	420	361	329
General Sales	148	161	165	156	127	150	165	168	153	132
Use	19	25	25	23	18	20	20	19	12	9
Selective Sales	38	40	42	42	39	44	53	52	34	26
-alcoholic beverage	9	10	11	10	10	12	13	16	5	3
-tobacco	14	15	17	18	19	20	24	21	18	12
-insurance	12	12	12	10	7	9	10	10	8	8
-parimutuels	3	3	3	3	4	4	5	5	3	3
Individual Income	191	212	203	187	153	122	136	0	0	0
*Corporation Income	91	108	110	101	45	32	53	35	24	27
*Other Corpor. Taxes	1	1	1	1	22	24	27	30	22	20
Motor Fuels	47	55	53	55	55	57	56	52	55	58
Vehicle Licenses	25	27	23	23	22	24	30	28	26	30
Other License Taxes	9	7	10	8	7	8	9	7	8	8
Intangibles	4	4	4	3	7	7	7	13	11	10
Utility Property	9	9	11	12	10	10	10	9	9	4
Inheritance and Gift	5	5	6	7	5	5	6	6	5	5
Other Taxes	4	2	1	1	1	1	0	0	0	0

NON-TAX REVENUE	N.A.	416	408	396	348	371	317	253	173	132
Federal Intergov'tal	N.A.	259	261	261	260	236	198	147	97	58
Current Charges	N.A.	83	81	76	73	70	75	62	42	34
Liquor Monopoly	6	9	6	6	8	12	13	14	14	19
Lottery	21	19	17	15	12	9	0	0	0	0
Miscellaneous	N.A.	45	44	38	33	44	32	31	20	21

NOTES:

*1) Following the Census classification, the Business Activities Tax and the Single Business Tax are infelicitously grouped here under corporation income taxes. The Annual Privilege Fee is classified under other corporation taxes.
2) Lottery revenues include profits, interest earned, and unclaimed prizes.
3) Liquor monopoly revenues are the contributions of the Liquor Control Commission to the General Fund, exclusive of taxes and license fees. These figures are on a cash, not an accrual basis.
4) Amounts collected in 1979 and 1980 from the "Alcoholism Tax" were added to the Census figures for selective sales taxes on alcoholic beverages.
5) See notes for Table 2.1.

SOURCES:
Bureau of the Census, State Government Tax Collections in 1975, ...1976, ...1977, ...1978, ...1979, ...1980.
Lottery revenues obtained from the Michigan Bureau of State Lottery.
Liquor monopoly revenues obtained from Annual Financial Report of the Liquor Control Commission, various years, and Budget Message of the Governor, for fiscal years 1981 and 1982.
See also the sources for Table 2.1.

TABLE 2.7

MICHIGAN STATE GOVERNMENT REVENUES, SELECTED YEARS, 1957 TO 1980
(As a percentage of personal income)

SOURCE	1980	1979	1978	1977	1976	1975	1972	1967	1962	1957
TAX REVENUE	6.9	7.7	7.9	7.9	6.7	6.5	7.7	5.5	5.6	4.8
General Sales	1.7	1.9	2.0	2.0	1.7	1.9	2.2	2.2	2.4	1.9
Use	0.2	0.3	0.3	0.3	0.2	0.3	0.3	0.3	0.2	0.1
Selective Sales	0.4	0.5	0.5	0.5	0.5	0.6	0.7	0.7	0.5	0.4
-alcoholic beverage	0.1	0.1	0.1	0.1	0.1	0.2	0.2	0.2	0.1	0.0
-tobacco	0.2	0.2	0.2	0.2	0.2	0.3	0.3	0.3	0.3	0.2
-insurance	0.1	0.1	0.1	0.1	0.1	0.1	0.1	0.1	0.1	0.1
-parimutuels	0.0	0.0	0.0	0.0	0.0	0.1	0.1	0.1	0.0	0.0
Individual Income	2.2	2.5	2.5	2.4	2.0	1.6	1.8	0.0	0.0	0.0
*Corporation Income	1.1	1.3	1.3	1.3	0.6	0.4	0.7	0.5	0.4	0.4
*Other Corpor. Taxes	0.0	0.0	0.0	0.0	0.3	0.3	0.4	0.4	0.3	0.3
Motor Fuels	0.6	0.7	0.6	0.7	0.7	0.7	0.8	0.7	0.8	0.8
Vehicle Licenses	0.3	0.3	0.3	0.3	0.1	0.3	0.4	0.4	0.4	0.4
Other License Taxes	0.1	0.1	0.1	0.1	0.1	0.1	0.1	0.1	0.1	0.1
Intangibles	0.0	0.0	0.0	0.0	0.1	0.1	0.1	0.2	0.2	0.1
Utility Property	0.1	0.1	0.1	0.1	0.1	0.1	0.1	0.1	0.1	0.1
Inheritance and Gift	0.1	0.1	0.1	0.1	0.1	0.1	0.1	0.1	0.1	0.1
Other Taxes	0.1	0.0	0.0	0.0	0.0	0.0	0.0	0.0	0.0	0.0

NON-TAX REVENUE	N.A.	4.9	4.9	5.0	5.0	4.8	4.2	3.3	2.7	1.9
Federal Intergov'tal	N.A.	3.1	3.2	3.3	3.4	3.0	2.7	2.0	1.5	0.8
Local Intergov'tal	N.A.	0.1	0.1	0.1	0.1	0.1	0.1	0.1	0.1	0.2
Current Charges	N.A.	1.0	1.0	1.0	1.0	0.9	1.0	0.8	0.6	0.5
Liquor Monopoly	0.1	0.1	0.1	0.1	0.1	0.2	0.2	0.2	0.2	0.3
Lottery	0.3	0.2	0.2	0.2	0.2	0.1	0.0	0.0	0.0	0.0
Miscellaneous	N.A.	0.4	0.4	0.3	0.3	0.4	0.3	0.3	0.2	0.1

NOTES:
*1) See notes for Tables 2.1 and 2.6. (See note *1 of Table 2.6 for definitions of "Corporation Income" and "Other Corporate Taxes".)

SOURCES:
See sources for Tables 2.1 and 2.6.

TABLE 2.8

PER CAPITA GENERAL REVENUES OF STATE AND LOCAL GOVERNMENTS, SELECTED STATES AND YEARS, 1957 TO 1979

(in 1979 dollars, state proportion shown in parentheses)

SOURCE	U.S.	CA.	ILL.	IND.	MICH.	N.Y.	OHIO	PA.	WISC.
TOTAL									
1979	1,573(.60)	1,770(.63)	1,520(.56)	1,235(.63)	1,755(.60)	2,112(.52)	1,295(.56)	1,431(.62)	1,693(.66)
1977	1,545(.58)	1,960(.55)	1,489(.57)	1,204(.63)	1,666(.60)	2,175(.51)	1,222(.53)	1,376(.61)	1,591(.66)
1967	1,093(.56)	1,476(.52)	973(.48)	1,000(.57)	1,120(.59)	1,473(.51)	884(.49)	911(.56)	1,169(.63)
1957	736(.52)	1,050(.51)	716(.42)	602(.50)	771(.56)	918(.39)	657(.48)	640(.56)	750(.52)
FEDERAL AID									
1979	344(.73)	368(.74)	308(.67)	234(.73)	370(.70)	456(.74)	276(.70)	295(.75)	343(.82)
1977	338(.73)	399(.78)	294(.73)	219(.76)	363(.72)	415(.75)	249(.72)	306(.72)	316(.81)
1967	184(.89)	281(.92)	132(.85)	123(.92)	164(.90)	164(.83)	128(.88)	133(.84)	144(.95)
1957	74(.91)	112(.93)	50(.95)	41(.95)	61(.94)	51(.89)	53(.90)	41(.93)	54(.98)
OWN SOURCES									
1979	1,229(.56)	1,402(.60)	1,212(.53)	1,002(.61)	1,384(.57)	1,656(.45)	1,019(.52)	1,137(.58)	1,350(.61)
1977	1,206(.54)	1,561(.50)	1,195(.52)	985(.60)	1,303(.57)	1,759(.46)	973(.49)	1,070(.58)	1,275(.63)
1967	908(.50)	1,196(.42)	841(.43)	877(.52)	955(.53)	1,309(.47)	757(.42)	778(.52)	1,025(.58)
1957	662(.48)	938(.46)	666(.38)	561(.47)	710(.52)	867(.36)	605(.45)	599(.53)	696(.48)
OWN TAXES									
1979	942(.61)	1,076(.68)	998(.56)	751(.66)	1,053(.62)	1,362(.48)	768(.56)	919(.63)	1,029(.68)
1977	953(.57)	1,288(.53)	1,000(.55)	763(.63)	1,020(.61)	1,454(.48)	736(.53)	893(.62)	1,020(.67)
1967	731(.52)	979(.45)	707(.45)	694(.52)	750(.56)	1,100(.48)	590(.44)	653(.55)	853(.61)
1957	556(.50)	795(.49)	589(.40)	464(.47)	595(.55)	747(.39)	500(.48)	524(.55)	604(.50)
-Property									
1979	298(.04)	271(.10)	349(.00)	247(.02)	377(.03)	479(.00)	260(.05)	229(.02)	349(.06)
1977	339(.03)	543(.04)	368(.00)	277(.02)	382(.04)	521(.00)	278(.04)	233(.03)	352(.07)
1967	312(.03)	504(.05)	346(.00)	337(.02)	329(.07)	433(.02)	305(.04)	219(.00)	356(.07)
1957	248(.03)	376(.07)	305(.00)	255(.04)	274(.05)	356(.00)	240(.04)	175(.00)	312(.07)
-Gen. Sales And Use									
1979	213(.85)	309(.82)	238(.82)	243(1.0)	185(1.0)	255(.57)	146(.91)	161(1.0)	175(1.0)
1977	197(.85)	283(.82)	232(.82)	228(1.0)	180(1.0)	254(.57)	135(.92)	150(1.0)	168(1.0)
1967	121(.88)	175(.76)	172(.90)	142(1.0)	188(1.0)	141(.56)	83(1.0)	128(1.0)	55(1.0)
1957	78(.84)	182(.80)	116(.87)	90(1.0)	140(1.0)	81(.00)	84(1.0)	56(1.0)	0(---)
-Selective Sales And Use									
1979	81(.80)	64(.70)	105(.75)	33(.97)	43(.93)	97(.71)	74(.99)	78(.97)	53(.96)
1977	81(.83)	64(.77)	103(.78)	28(.96)	46(.91)	110(.73)	66(.98)	80(.96)	54(1.0)
1967	67(.88)	49(.87)	82(.10)	35(1.0)	52(1.0)	105(.71)	52(1.0)	55(.98)	55(1.0)
1957	50(.86)	36(.92)	58(.81)	26(1.0)	27(1.0)	72(.83)	50(.98)	42(.95)	39(1.0)
-Individual Income									
1979	169(.88)	213(1.0)	155(1.0)	120(.92)	236(.90)	364(.78)	146(.55)	205(.64)	294(1.0)
1977	158(.87)	195(1.0)	147(1.0)	112(1.0)	211(.89)	379(.77)	127(.53)	191(.61)	288(1.0)
1967	70(.84)	63(1.0)	0(---)	75(1.0)	17(.00)	242(.82)	27(.00)	46(.00)	207(1.0)
1957	34(.89)	34(1.0)	0(---)	0(---)	0(---)	95(1.0)	19(.00)	27(.00)	94(1.0)
-Corporate Income									
1979	56(1.0)	106(1.0)	44(1.0)	24(1.0)	108(1.0)	69(1.0)	47(1.0)	73(1.0)	70(1.0)
1977	50(1.0)	89(1.0)	40(1.0)	19(1.0)	101(1.0)	84(1.0)	34(1.0)	66(1.0)	63(1.0)
1967	27(1.0)	57(1.0)	0(---)	7(1.0)	35(1.0)	58(1.0)	0(---)	49(1.0)	58(1.0)
1957	19(1.0)	40(1.0)	0(---)	0(---)	27(1.0)	50(1.0)	0(---)	48(1.0)	48(1.0)

-Corporate License Taxes									
1979	6(1.0)	0(---)	3(1.0)	1(1.0)	1(1.0)	0(---)	9(1.0)	22(1.0)	0(---)
1977	6(1.0)	0(---)	3(1.0)	0(---)	1(1.0)	0(---)	14(1.0)	21(1.0)	1(1.0)
1967	7(1.0)	0(---)	2(1.0)	0(---)	30(1.0)	1(1.0)	15(1.0)	15(1.0)	1(1.0)
1957	8(1.0)	0(---)	2(1.0)	1(1.0)	21(1.0)	1(1.0)	0(---)	42(1.0)	0(---)
-Highway User Taxes									
-motor fuels									
1979	46(.99)	40(1.0)	39(.96)	51(1.0)	55(1.0)	29(.99)	39(1.0)	45(1.0)	39(1.0)
1977	50(.99)	44(1.0)	42(1.0)	57(1.0)	55(1.0)	34(.99)	43(1.0)	49(1.0)	43(1.0)
1967	58(.99)	69(1.0)	40(1.0)	61(1.0)	53(1.0)	36(1.0)	62(1.0)	58(1.0)	61(1.0)
1957	55(.99)	70(1.0)	44(1.0)	50(1.0)	57(1.0)	27(1.0)	51(1.0)	53(1.0)	55(1.0)
-motor vehicle license									
1979	24(.93)	18(1.0)	36(.81)	19(1.0)	27(1.0)	19(.89)	28(.91)	25(1.0)	20(1.0)
1977	25(.92)	19(1.0)	40(.85)	20(1.0)	23(1.0)	21(.88)	23(.85)	26(1.0)	23(1.0)
1967	27(.94)	26(1.0)	39(.81)	23(1.0)	28(1.0)	27(.98)	29(.99)	20(1.0)	32(1.0)
1957	27(.93)	25(1.0)	40(.77)	26(.97)	30(1.0)	25(.99)	33(1.0)	22(1.0)	32(1.0)
-Other Taxes									
1979	50(.74)	55(.53)	29(.66)	13(.85)	20(.70)	49(.80)	19(.58)	81(.49)	30(.87)
1977	47(.74)	52(.56)	26(.62)	22(.59)	21(.71)	51(.82)	17(.59)	77(.51)	28(.86)
1967	42(.76)	36(.64)	26(.58)	15(.93)	18(.78)	57(.86)	18(.56)	62(.50)	28(.79)
1957	38(.71)	31(.61)	24(.42)	16(.75)	19(.68)	40(.75)	23(.61)	59(.47)	25(.64)
CURRENT CHARGES									
1979	181(.38)	202(.31)	137(.35)	190(.46)	222(.37)	182(.23)	166(.46)	125(.40)	219(.38)
1977	169(.39)	179(.32)	128(.35)	177(.50)	197(.38)	182(.26)	154(.39)	115(.40)	185(.45)
1967	126(.40)	132(.26)	97(.35)	154(.50)	145(.43)	160(.39)	120(.39)	89(.37)	115(.51)
1957	73(.33)	82(.23)	52(.18)	81(.47)	81(.42)	91(.19)	75(.31)	52(.40)	60(.39)
MISCELLANEOUS									
1979	106(.48)	125(.40)	77(.43)	61(.46)	110(.52)	112(.49)	85(.32)	93(.37)	102(.45)
1977	85(.47)	93(.39)	67(.48)	45(.49)	85(.49)	123(.52)	83(.31)	62(.35)	70(.40)
1967	53(.38)	85(.35)	38(.24)	28(.50)	60(.37)	49(.35)	47(.19)	36(.31)	57(.35)
1957	33(.42)	62(.35)	25(.28)	16(.44)	33(.24)	29(.31)	30(.17)	23(.26)	34(.24)

NOTES:

1) The figures for total revenue are net of intergovernmental transactions between the States and their local governments.
2) For 1957 and 1967, again using the Census classification, Michigan's "Business Activities Tax" is grouped under corporate income taxes. The Single Business Tax is also so classified. See note *1 of Table 2.6. Michigan's "Annual Corporation Privilege Fee" is classified under corporate license taxes.
3) Three of the states used in the comparisons, Michigan, Ohio, and Pennsylvania, also obtain revenues from the profits of the state liquor monopolies. Such revenues are examined in detail in Chapter 23. Michigan revenues from this source are also shown in Tables 2.6 and 2.7 of this chapter.
4) See notes for Table 2.1.

SOURCES:
See sources for Table 2.1 and 2.3.

TABLE 2.9
GENERAL REVENUES OF STATE AND LOCAL GOVERNMENTS AS A PERCENTAGE OF PERSONAL INCOME
SELECTED STATES AND YEARS, 1957 TO 1979

SOURCE	U.S.	CA.	ILL.	IND.	MICH.	N.Y.	OHIO	PA.	WISC.
TOTAL									
1979	20.1(.60)	19.8(.63)	17.1(.56)	16.1(.63)	20.7(.60)	25.7(.52)	16.5(.56)	18.5(.62)	22.5(.66)
1977	20.7(.58)	23.3(.55)	17.5(.57)	16.6(.63)	21.1(.60)	26.9(.51)	16.4(.53)	18.5(.61)	22.5(.66)
1967	15.7(.56)	18.1(.52)	11.7(.48)	13.9(.57)	14.6(.59)	17.7(.51)	12.4(.49)	13.1(.56)	16.8(.63)
1957	11.8(.52)	13.5(.51)	9.4(.42)	9.6(.50)	11.2(.56)	11.8(.39)	9.4(.48)	9.9(.56)	12.6(.52)
FEDERAL AID									
1979	4.4(.73)	4.1(.74)	3.5(.67)	3.0(.73)	4.4(.70)	5.5(.74)	3.5(.70)	3.8(.75)	4.6(.82)
1977	4.5(.73)	4.8(.78)	3.5(.73)	3.0(.76)	4.6(.72)	5.1(.75)	3.3(.72)	4.1(.72)	4.5(.81)
1967	2.6(.89)	3.4(.92)	1.6(.85)	1.7(.92)	2.1(.90)	2.0(.83)	1.8(.88)	1.9(.84)	2.1(.95)
1957	1.2(.91)	1.4(.93)	0.6(.95)	0.7(.95)	0.9(.94)	0.7(.89)	0.8(.90)	0.6(.93)	0.9(.98)
OWN SOURCES									
1979	15.7(.56)	15.7(.60)	13.6(.53)	13.0(.61)	16.3(.57)	20.1(.45)	13.0(.52)	14.7(.58)	17.9(.61)
1977	16.2(.54)	18.6(.50)	14.1(.52)	13.6(.60)	16.5(.57)	21.8(.46)	13.1(.49)	14.4(.58)	18.0(.63)
1967	13.1(.50)	14.6(.42)	10.1(.43)	12.2(.52)	12.5(.53)	15.7(.47)	10.6(.42)	11.2(.52)	14.7(.58)
1957	10.6(.48)	12.0(.46)	8.7(.38)	9.0(.47)	10.3(.52)	11.1(.36)	8.7(.45)	9.2(.53)	11.7(.48)
OWN TAXES									
1979	12.0(.61)	12.1(.68)	11.2(.56)	9.8(.66)	12.4(.62)	16.6(.48)	9.8(.56)	11.9(.63)	13.7(.68)
1977	12.8(.57)	15.3(.53)	11.8(.55)	10.5(.63)	12.9(.61)	18.0(.48)	9.9(.53)	12.0(.62)	14.4(.67)
1967	10.5(.52)	12.0(.45)	8.5(.45)	9.7(.52)	9.8(.56)	13.2(.48)	8.2(.44)	9.4(.55)	12.3(.61)
1957	8.9(.50)	10.2(.49)	7.7(.40)	7.4(.47)	8.6(.55)	9.6(.39)	7.2(.48)	8.1(.55)	10.1(.50)
-Property									
1979	3.8(.04)	3.0(.10)	3.9(.00)	3.2(.02)	4.4(.03)	5.8(.00)	3.3(.05)	3.0(.02)	4.6(.06)
1977	4.5(.03)	6.5(.04)	4.3(.00)	3.8(.02)	4.9(.04)	6.5(.00)	3.7(.04)	3.1(.03)	5.0(.07)
1967	4.5(.03)	6.2(.05)	4.2(.00)	4.7(.02)	4.3(.07)	5.2(.02)	4.3(.04)	3.2(.00)	5.1(.07)
1957	4.0(.03)	4.8(.07)	4.0(.00)	4.1(.04)	4.0(.05)	4.6(.00)	3.4(.04)	2.7(.00)	5.2(.07)
-Gen. Sales And Use									
1979	2.7(.85)	3.5(.82)	2.7(.82)	3.2(1.0)	2.2(1.0)	3.1(.57)	1.9(.91)	2.1(1.0)	2.3(1.0)
1977	2.6(.85)	3.4(.82)	2.7(.82)	3.2(1.0)	2.3(1.0)	3.1(.57)	1.8(.92)	2.0(1.0)	2.4(1.0)
1967	1.7(.88)	2.1(.76)	2.1(.90)	2.0(1.0)	2.5(1.0)	1.7(.56)	1.2(1.0)	1.8(1.0)	0.8(1.0)
1957	1.2(.84)	2.3(.80)	1.5(.87)	1.4(1.0)	2.0(1.0)	1.0(.00)	1.2(1.0)	1.9(1.0)	0.0(---)
-Selective Sales And Use									
1979	1.0(.80)	0.7(.70)	1.2(.75)	0.4(.97)	0.5(.93)	1.1(.71)	0.9(.99)	1.0(.97)	0.7(.96)
1977	1.1(.83)	0.8(.77)	1.2(.78)	0.4(.96)	0.6(.91)	1.4(.73)	0.9(.98)	1.0(.96)	0.8(1.0)
1967	1.0(.88)	0.9(.87)	1.0(1.0)	0.4(1.0)	0.7(1.0)	1.3(.71)	0.7(1.0)	0.8(.98)	0.8(1.0)
1957	0.8(.86)	0.6(.92)	0.7(.81)	0.4(1.0)	0.4(1.0)	1.0(.83)	0.7(.98)	0.7(.95)	0.7(1.0)
-Individual Income									
1979	2.2(.88)	2.4(1.0)	1.7(1.0)	1.6(.92)	2.8(.90)	4.4(.78)	1.9(.55)	2.7(.64)	3.9(1.0)
1977	2.1(.87)	2.3(1.0)	1.7(1.0)	1.5(1.0)	2.7(.89)	4.7(.77)	1.7(.53)	2.6(.61)	4.1(1.0)
1967	1.0(.84)	0.8(1.0)	0.0(---)	1.0(1.0)	0.2(.00)	2.9(.82)	0.4(.00)	0.7(.00)	3.0(1.0)
1957	0.5(.89)	0.4(1.0)	0.0(---)	0.0(---)	0.0(---)	1.2(1.0)	0.3(.00)	0.4(.00)	1.6(1.0)

-Corporate Income									
1979	0.7(1.0)	1.2(1.0)	0.5(1.0)	0.3(1.0)	1.3(1.0)	0.8(1.0)	0.6(1.0)	0.9(1.0)	0.9(1.0)
1977	0.7(1.0)	1.1(1.0)	0.5(1.0)	0.3(1.0)	1.3(1.0)	1.0(1.0)	0.5(1.0)	0.9(1.0)	0.9(1.0)
1967	0.4(1.0)	0.7(1.0)	0.0(---)	0.1(1.0)	0.5(1.0)	0.7(1.0)	0.0(---)	0.7(1.0)	0.8(1.0)
1957	0.3(1.0)	0.5(1.0)	0.0(---)	0.0(---)	0.4(1.0)	0.6(1.0)	0.0(---)	0.7(1.0)	0.8(1.0)
-Corporate License Taxes									
1979	0.1(1.0)	0.0(---)	0.0(---)	0.0(---)	0.0(---)	0.0(---)	0.1(1.0)	0.3(1.0)	0.0(---)
1977	0.1(1.0)	0.0(---)	0.0(---)	0.0(---)	0.0(---)	0.0(---)	0.2(1.0)	0.3(1.0)	0.0(---)
1967	0.1(1.0)	0.0(---)	0.0(---)	0.0(---)	0.4(1.0)	0.0(---)	0.2(1.0)	0.2(1.0)	0.0(---)
1957	0.1(1.0)	0.0(---)	0.0(---)	0.0(---)	0.3(1.0)	0.0(---)	0.0(---)	0.6(1.0)	0.0(---)
-Highway User Taxes									
-motor fuels									
1979	0.6(.99)	0.5(1.0)	0.4(.96)	0.7(1.0)	0.7(1.0)	0.4(.99)	0.5(1.0)	0.6(1.0)	0.5(1.0)
1977	0.7(.99)	0.5(1.0)	0.5(1.0)	0.8(1.0)	0.7(1.0)	0.4(.99)	0.6(1.0)	0.7(1.0)	0.6(1.0)
1967	0.8(.99)	0.8(1.0)	0.5(1.0)	0.9(1.0)	0.7(1.0)	0.4(1.0)	0.9(1.0)	0.8(1.0)	0.9(1.0)
1957	0.9(.99)	0.9(1.0)	0.6(1.0)	0.8(1.0)	0.8(1.0)	0.3(1.0)	0.7(1.0)	0.8(1.0)	0.9(1.0)
-motor vehicle license									
1979	0.3(.93)	0.2(1.0)	0.4(.81)	0.2(1.0)	0.3(1.0)	0.2(.89)	0.4(.91)	0.3(1.0)	0.3(1.0)
1977	0.3(.92)	0.2(1.0)	0.5(.85)	0.3(1.0)	0.3(1.0)	0.3(.88)	0.3(.85)	0.3(1.0)	0.3(1.0)
1967	0.4(.94)	0.3(1.0)	0.5(.81)	0.3(1.0)	0.4(1.0)	0.3(.98)	0.4(.99)	0.3(1.0)	0.5(1.0)
1957	0.4(.93)	0.3(1.0)	0.5(.77)	0.4(.97)	0.4(1.0)	0.3(.99)	0.5(1.0)	0.3(1.0)	0.5(1.0)
-Other Taxes									
1979	0.6(.74)	0.6(.53)	0.3(.66)	0.2(.85)	0.2(.70)	0.6(.80)	0.2(.58)	1.0(.49)	0.4(.87)
1977	0.6(.74)	0.6(.56)	0.3(.62)	0.3(.59)	0.3(.71)	0.6(.82)	0.2(.59)	1.0(.51)	0.4(.86)
1967	0.6(.76)	0.4(.64)	0.3(.58)	0.2(.93)	0.7(.78)	0.7(.86)	0.3(.58)	0.9(.50)	0.4(.79)
1957	0.6(.71)	0.4(.61)	0.3(.42)	0.3(.75)	0.3(.68)	0.5(.75)	0.1(.61)	0.9(.47)	0.4(.64)
CURRENT CHARGES									
1979	2.3(.38)	2.3(.31)	1.5(.35)	2.5(.46)	2.6(.37)	2.2(.23)	2.1(.46)	1.6(.40)	2.9(.38)
1977	2.3(.39)	2.1(.32)	1.5(.35)	2.4(.50)	2.5(.38)	2.3(.26)	2.1(.39)	1.5(.40)	2.6(.45)
1967	1.8(.40)	1.6(.26)	1.2(.35)	2.1(.50)	1.9(.43)	1.9(.39)	1.7(.39)	1.3(.37)	1.7(.51)
1957	1.2(.33)	1.0(.23)	0.7(.18)	1.3(.47)	1.2(.42)	1.2(.19)	1.1(.31)	0.8(.40)	1.0(.39)
MISCELLANEOUS									
1979	1.4(.48)	1.4(.40)	0.9(.43)	0.8(.46)	1.2(.52)	1.4(.49)	1.1(.32)	1.2(.37)	1.4(.45)
1977	1.1(.47)	1.1(.39)	0.8(.48)	0.7(.49)	1.1(.49)	1.5(.52)	1.2(.31)	0.8(.35)	1.0(.40)
1967	0.8(.38)	1.0(.35)	0.4(.24)	0.3(.50)	0.8(.37)	0.6(.35)	0.6(.19)	0.5(.31)	0.8(.35)
1957	0.5(.42)	0.8(.35)	0.3(.28)	0.3(.44)	0.5(.24)	0.4(.31)	0.4(.17)	0.4(.26)	0.6(.24)

NOTES:
1) See notes for Tables 2.1 and 2.8.

SOURCES:
See sources for Tables 2.1 and 2.3.

far from steady. The decline between 1972 and 1975 reflects both the recession of 1974-75 and the exemption of food and drugs under the sales tax after the end of calendar year 1974. Similarly, the sharp decline between fiscal 1979 and 1980, both as a percentage of income and per capita, reflects the severe recession of 1979-80 and the sensitivity to economic fluctuations of the present Michigan tax system.

The trend over time in sales tax receipts is influenced strongly by the increase in the rate from three to four percent in 1961 and the food and drug exemption effective in 1975. Since 1975 per capita growth in sales tax revenues has been virtually nil.

The income tax, on the other hand, has increased in per capita real terms, but this increase is largely a reflection of the increase in the rate from the initial 2.6 percent of 1967-68 to 3.9 percent in 1971-72 and to 4.6 percent in 1974-75. Growth since 1972 has been understated because the state treats the circuit-breaker as a reduction in income tax receipts.

Michigan Compared with Other States

One may observe in Tables 2.8 and 2.9 how Michigan fares with respect to state and local revenues relative to the nation as a whole and the same group of states used in our discussion of expenditures.

Both total revenues from all sources and tax receipts in Michigan are about 10 to 12 percent higher per capita than they are in the nation as a whole. And this relationship has been roughly stable throughout the period under review. Michigan's total revenues and tax receipts are higher than those of each of the other seven states save New York and California. California had been consistently higher than Michigan, and still is, with respect to taxes alone and revenue from its own sources, but the effects of Proposition 13 may be seen in the steep decline in revenues experienced in that state between 1977 and 1979.

Michigan receives more federal aid than the average

state and more than each of the states subject to comparison other than New York. For 1957 and 1967 Michigan received less than the national average in federal aid, but we have been 8 to 10 percent above that average in more recent years.

Per capita tax revenues are higher in California and New York than in Michigan, over 25 percent lower in Indiana and Ohio, $124 per capita lower in Pennsylvania, and $55 and $24 lower in Illinois and Wisconsin. State-local taxes in Michigan take 12.4 percent of personal income, slightly more than the 12 percent national average, appreciably less than in Wisconsin and New York, but above the levels for each of the other five states.

Further perusal of Tables 2.8 and 2.9 makes it appear that most of the difference between Michigan and the average for all states in per capita tax revenues is attributable to the property tax. When account is taken of the circuit breaker, however, the difference due to the property tax declines from $79 out of $111 to $44.

Michigan's sales tax is lighter in its impact in both per capita terms and relative to income than is the sales tax in the U.S. as a whole, California, Illinois, Indiana, and New York. On the other hand the individual income tax yield exceeds the U.S. average by $67 per capita and exceeds that of all but New York and Wisconsin within the eight-state group.

The data presented in these tables is supportive of the appraisal drawn from John Shannon's analysis that is discussed earlier in this chapter. Michigan's revenue system can be described as reasonably well balanced, but sensitive to economic fluctuations, and, while yields have been increasing in current dollars, they have not kept up with recent years' rapid rate of inflation. For the period under review as a whole clearly taxes in Michigan, as in the nation as a whole, have taken an increasing share of income. But since the mid-seventies the trend seems to have turned downward, most sharply in such states as California and New

York, where taxes relative to income had been extremely high.

NOTES, CHAPTER 2

[1]State of Michigan, _Budget Message of the Governor for Fiscal Year 1982_ (Lansing, 1981), p. 74.

[2]Following and fully understanding these transfers is a task requiring intimate acquaintance with the details of an arcane accounting system.

[3]See Chapter 12 for further discussion of the complexities of the state government's accounting procedures.

[4]Data on General Fund-General Purpose expenditures, appropriations, and recommendations are from _Budget Message of the Governor_, various years.

[5]Using the Department of Commerce, Bureau of Economic Analysis' "implicit price deflator" for state and local government purchases of goods and services, as presented in _Economic Report of the President, 1981_, p. 237 and, for 1981 and 1982, projected by the authors.

[6]_The Constitution of the State of Michigan, 1963_, Article V, Section 20. More accurately the Constitution requires the avoidance of a cumulative deficit. That is, prior years' surplus may count as current year revenue, so that receipts for any one year need not equal expenditures.

[7]Legislative appropriations.

[8]1974-11 and 1975-2. We are indebted to Theodore A. Ferris of the Senate Fiscal Agency for assistance in compiling information regarding General Fund adjustments, etc.

[9]We use here an _ex ante_ concept of the deficit: the change in the balance of the General Fund plus the amount of cuts in expenditures which took place by Executive Order. This definition provides a measure of the deficit that _would_ have existed had expenditures not had to be cut back because of a shortfall in revenues. _Ex post_, of course, there can be no deficit.

[10]1975-12.

[11]The $78 million deficit of 1959, at 21 percent of GF-GP expenditures, was substantially larger in relative terms.

[12]1980-3.

[13]Budget Message, 1977-78, pp. 4-5.

[14]Public Act 76 of 1977.

[15]The Act (Section 4) also provides for additional modest withdrawals from the BSF in calendar quarters when the unemployment rate exceeds 8 percent. These withdrawals, equal to 2.5 or 5.0 percent of the fund balance, must be used for specified job-creating purposes.

[16]Theodore A. Ferris of the Senate Fiscal Agency and the State Treasurer's Office are the sources of the data used here.

[17]Direct expenditures are those involving the provisions of services and the distribution of transfer payments to individuals. They exclude intergovernmental transfers, so that the expenditure amounts presented are independent of the source of financing.

[18]We use the GNP deflator for state and local governments to convert current dollars to constant dollars for all categories of expenditure. This index, however, is more appropriate for some categories than for others. For example, as the cost of construction is one component in this deflator, it clearly is not an appropriate deflator to use to convert the value of transfer payments. While we recognize this shortcoming in the use of this deflator, we do feel that an analysis which looked at the value of expenditures over time in current dollars would have far more shortcomings. We also feel that given that we have chosen to deflate all categories of expenditure by the same index, the GNP deflator for state and local governments is the best choice among the various deflators that are available.

[19]Other than utility, insurance trust, and liquor store revenues.

[20]State aid for local schools is discussed in detail in Chapter 14; for aid to other local jurisdictions see Chapter 13.

[21]As noted in the sources for our tables, most of our analysis is based on data from the Bureau of the Census. Differences between Census classifications and those of the state government may result in some variance between the figures we use and those available directly from the state government.

[22]It is of interest to note that in 1957 per capita expenditures for higher education in Michigan were fully double the U.S. average, compared with 22 percent above the average by 1979.

[23]See Chapter 12 of this volume for a more complete analysis of Michigan state government expenditures on welfare and higher education.

[24]Rather than having relatively lenient eligibility criteria compared to other states, Michigan may simply have more people who meet the eligibility requirements.

[25]U.S. Department of Health, Education, and Welfare, Social Security Administration, Social Security Bulletin, December 1979, 42, No.12.

[26]Data are from U.S. Department of Health and Human Services, Healthcare Financing Administration, Medicaid Management Reports (1981). They are for average monthly amounts and numbers of beneficiaries for the months of April through June, 1978.

[27]Enrollment from National Center for Education Statistics, Fall Enrollment, 1979, August, 1980. Population estimates as of July 1, 1979 from Bureau of the Census, Series P-25, Population Estimates and Projections.

[28]See Chapter 12 of this volume.

[29]Michigan Tax Study Staff Papers (Lansing, 1958), pp. 25-37.

[30]Michigan Tax Study Staff Papers, pp. 36-37.

[31]See R. A. Musgrave and D. W. Daicoff, "Who Pays The Michigan Taxes?," in Michigan Tax Study Staff Papers.

[32]The Report of the Citizens' Advisory Committee to the Michigan Tax Study (Lansing, 1958), pp. 3-4.

[33]1959 Michigan Journal of the Senate, 1: 98-106.

[34]Message to the Seventy-First Michigan Legislature, January 16, 1962.

[35]Message of Governor George Romney to the Seventy-Second Michigan Legislature, Special Session, September 12, 1963.

[36]Public Act 281 of 1967.

[37]Public Act 101 of 1973. See Chapter 14 for a detailed discussion of the Bursley Act and subsequent developments.

[38]For elderly people the 3.5 percent threshold was reduced to 0 at income below $3,000, 1 percent at $3,000 to $4,000, 2 percent at $4,000 to $5,000, and 3 percent for income of $5,000 to $6,000.

[39]Public Act 198 and related legislation are discussed in detail in Chapter 10.

[40]Public Act 19 of 1975.

[41]See Gramlich and Woodard, Chapter 15 of this volume.

[42]Property tax receipts shown are as estimated by the State Tax Commission. State tax receipts are as reported in Department of Management and Budget, State of Michigan Annual Financial Report, Fiscal Year Ended September 30, 1980, p. 97. Value of the Homestead Tax Credit is as reported in the Budget Message, fiscal year 1982, p.43.

[43]The term is defined and the estimates used in the text are provided in Advisory Commission on Intergovernmental Relations, Regional Growth: Interstate Tax Competition (Washington, 1981), Appendix. Table A-2 of this Appendix has been revised since publication and the revised estimates are used here.

[44]Paper prepared for the School Finance Conference Sponsored by the Ford Foundation, December 9, 1975 (mimeo).

[45]Space does not permit detailed description of the "tests." Suffice it to say here that revenue balance refers to reliance on each of the income, property, and sales taxes for 20 to 30 percent of state-local tax revenue: equity requires a progressive personal income tax, food exemption (or credit) under the sales tax, and a property tax circuit-breaker; quality of property tax administration is judged by the narrowness of measures of dispersion of assessment ratios and conformity of local assessments to state law; fiscal equalization is measured by whether or not the state carries the nonfederal portion of public welfare costs, has an adequate school finance equalization plan, and has an equalizing revenue sharing plan.

[46]Donald M. Peppard, Jr. and Douglas B. Roberts, Net Fiscal Incidence in Michigan: Who Pays and Who Benefits? (East Lansing, 1977).

[47]As measured by the GNP deflator for state and local government purchases.

[48]See Chapters 16 and 17 of this volume for further discussion of the effects of the circuit-breaker.

Chapter 3

The Michigan Economy

by

Joan P. Crary and Patrick M. Barkey

The University of Michigan

INTRODUCTION

Recently, for the third time in the past twenty-five years, Michigan has experienced an entire year of unemployment rates in excess of ten percent while the national unemployment rate remained well below ten percent. This has prompted a need to reexamine the Michigan economy in order to understand just what it is about the economic structure of this state which causes it to suffer so much whenever the national economy experiences anything more than a mild recession. Although the 1980 recession was officially declared the briefest on record by the National Bureau of Economic Research, the unemployment rate in Michigan averaged 12.7 percent for 1980, hardly an indication that brief national recessions are any less painful for Michigan than are longer ones such as the 1974-75 recession.

The purpose of this chapter is to examine the present structure of the Michigan economy and changes in it over the past decade. We will focus on income and the composition of employment in Michigan with an emphasis on manufacturing and the auto industry. We begin with a discussion of the status of the economy in 1980, followed by a comparison of employment and income the United states and Michigan as well as among other states in the Great Lakes region. We will conclude by considering some alternative projections for income and employment in Michigan over the period 1981-85 designed to highlight the influence of the domestic auto industry on the Michigan economy.

THE MICHIGAN ECONOMY IN 1980

In 1980 Michigan was in the midst of a recession which had begun in the second half of 1979, well before the slowdown was felt nationally. The downturn was sufficiently severe to prompt comparisons to the 1974-75 period which has been billed nationally as the worst recession since the Great Depression. Although significant differences exist, such comparisons have been a useful way to put the economic conditions of 1980 in perspective and to underscore areas of major concern.

The declines in employment suffered in both the 1974-75 and 1980 recessions follow the same pattern, with employment in the manufacturing sector of the economy experiencing substantial losses. Table 3.1 summarizes the changes in employment and real income that occurred in Michigan during both recessionary periods. Employment in motor vehicle assembly (SIC 371) led the declines in manufacturing in 1974-75 and 1980. Losses in motor vehicle employment accounted for 40.9 and 44.1 percent of the manufacturing employment declines in the respective periods. The nonmanufacturing and government sectors have remained the least sensitive to cyclical downturns in economic activity.

The declines in motor vehicle employment in Michigan during both recessions were part of a general weakness in the entire domestic auto industry. Domestic auto production, as measured by real gross auto product, fell for the third year in a row in 1980 for a total decline of 23.8 percent since its 1977 peak, with nearly three-quarters of the total decline coming in 1980. Not only was there an absolute decline in auto output, but real gross auto product declined as a share of real gross national product over the same period, from a peak value of 3.7 percent in 1977 to a low of 2.6 percent in 1980. A comparable decline in auto production occurred during the 1974-75 recession as auto output fell 23.1 percent. However, nationally the decline in other sectors was more severe in the 1974-75 recession than in 1980 so the auto product share of real GNP fell from

TABLE 3.1

EMPLOYMENT, INCOME, INFLATION, AND UNEMPLOYMENT IN THE 1974-75 AND 1980 RECESSIONS, MICHIGAN

	1974-75 Recession	1980 Recession
Employment and Income		
Percent change, peak to trough[1]		
Employment		
Total	-5.1	-5.5
Wage and Salary	-4.5	-5.0
Manufacturing	-16.5	-14.6
Durable	-18.3	-15.6
Motor Vehicle	-19.9	-18.6
Nondurable	-8.9	-10.3
Nonmanufacturing	-1.9	-2.0
Government	3.6	1.0
Income		
Per Capita Income (1967 dollars)	-5.7	-11.5
Inflation and Unemployment		
Annual Percent Change in Detroit CPI, trough year	7.5	15.9
Unemployment Rate, trough year	12.5	12.7

Note: [1]The trough year for the 1974-75 recession was 1975; the trough year for the 1980 recession is assumed to be 1980. For those series which did not experience a decline in the trough year, the "peak" year used in the calculations is the year preceding the trough.

Source: Michigan Employment Security Commission; U. S. Department of Labor, Bureau of Labor Statistics; and U. S. Department of Commerce, Bureau of Economic Analysis.

a high of 3.7 percent in 1973 to a low of 2.8 percent in 1975.

Although the aggregate nonmanufacturing sector was less affected by the recent downturn in economic activity, some subsectors exhibited significant declines in employment in 1980. Employment in contract construction declined 15.5 percent while employment in the distributive industries, which include wholesale and retail trade as well as transportation, communication and public utilities, declined 3.6 percent. For both of these sectors 1980 was the first year of decline in the current business cycle. During the 1974-75 recession employment in contract construction fell 19.0 percent from 1973 to 1975 while employment in the distributive industries declined 2.0 percent.

Employment in both the service and government sectors of the Michigan economy grew during 1980. The increase in service employment at 2.6 percent was two percentage points higher than the 1975 increase while the 1.1 percent increase in government employment in 1980 was less than one-third of the 1975 increase.

Even though some sectors of the state economy fared better in 1979-80 than in 1974-75, the decline in total employment (see Table 3.1) was somewhat worse in the more recent period. As a result, the growth in personal income in 1980 (5.3 percent) was slightly less than the growth in 1975 (5.6 percent). In both periods of recession the rate of inflation, as measured by the Detroit consumer price index, exceeded the gains in personal income, but the rate of inflation in 1980 (15.9 percent) was more than double the rate of inflation in 1975 (7.5 percent). While the argument can be made that the consumer price index overstates the rate of inflation, the difference between the rate of increase in income and the rate of increase in prices, however measured, shows Michigan residents had substantially less real income in 1980 than in 1979.

Michigan's performance in the recent recession resembled that of the downturn of 1974-75 not only in its severity but also in its timing. This can be seen from Figure 3.1, which plots the path of wage and salary employment, expressed as a percentage of its pre-1975 peak value, for the period 1972-80. For comparison, the paths for the U.S. and the states (excluding Michigan) in the East North Central region (Illinois, Indiana, Michigan, Ohio, and Wisconsin) are also presented. It can be seen that total employment in all three areas fell in 1975, but that unlike the others, Michigan's employment growth had slowed to zero a full year ahead of the 1975 decline. The 1975 recession, the employment figures would indicate, was more severe in Michigan than elsewhere, with employment falling more rapidly in the downswing, and rising more rapidly, in relative terms, in the recovery. The same general pattern seems to be emerging in the current cycle, except that U.S. total employment only suffered a slowdown in growth in 1980, whereas the employment in Michigan and the other East North Central states actually fell--by 5 percent and 1.4 percent, respectively--between 1979 and 1980. As in 1974, the growth in wage and salary employment in Michigan fell off a full year ahead of the national slowdown.

While the similarities in Michigan between the two major recessions of the last decade are numerous, the performance of the national economy through each of these downturns has been markedly different. Moreover, the factors that historically have caused the cycles in the Michigan economy to be more extreme than their national counterparts remain important, as the experience of the recent recession has painfully reminded us. While these facts alone justify a closer examination of the composition of employment in the state economy, there is also concern that in the longer run, the state's employment mix may ill suit it to participate fully in future economic growth. We therefore turn to a closer examination of the composition of Michigan's employment, and attempt to identify the trends in employment growth that may dictate the state's future economic performance.

FIGURE 3.1
WAGE AND SALARY EMPLOYMENT AS PERCENTAGE
OF ITS PRE-1975 PEAK 1972-80

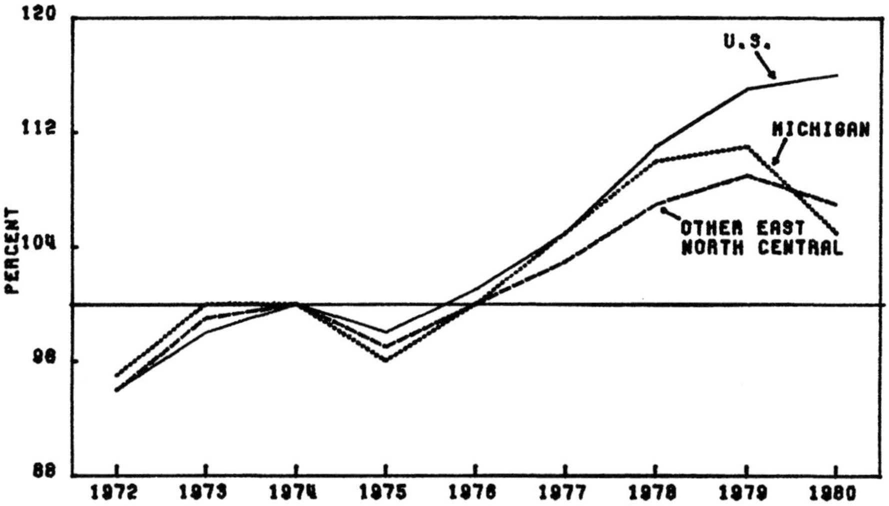

SOURCE: U.S. DEPT. OF LABOR, BUREAU OF LABOR STATISTICS AND
MICHIGAN EMPLOYMENT SECURITY COMMISSION.

FIGURE 3.2
DURABLE MANUFACTURING EMPLOYMENT AS PERCENTAGE
OF ITS PRE-1975 PEAK 1972-80

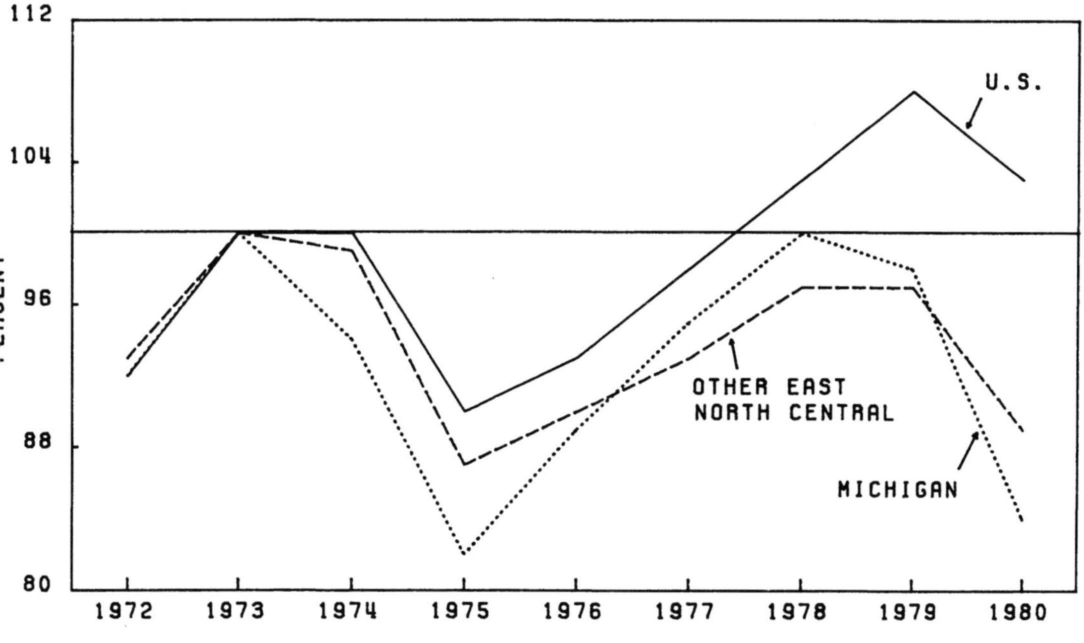

SOURCE: U.S. DEPT. OF LABOR, BUREAU OF LABOR AND STATISTICS AND
MICHIGAN EMPLOYMENT SECURITY COMMISSION.

Trends in Wage and Salary Employment

The growth in wage and salary jobs[1] that has been experienced in the U.S. since 1972 has not been distributed evenly over the geographic regions. Wage and salary employment in the East North Central region has grown at an average annual rate of 1.5 percent, while the nation's growth has been 2.6 percent. Employment growth since 1972 has been even more sluggish in Michigan, where the figure was 1.3 percent. In light of these differences it is not surprising that three of the East North Central states (Ohio, Illinois, and Michigan) rank among the top six states in the U.S. in their rate of population net out-migration over the period 1970-79. The recent decade's pattern of slow growth in employment and population in the East North Central region reflects the maturity of its industrial base as well as the leveling off in demand for the products it produces. We now examine the composition of employment in more detail.

The U.S., Michigan and other East North Central states have all experienced a steady decline in the fraction of total employment attributable to manufacturing industries, which has been largely balanced by growth in private manufacturing employment. This can be seen from Table 3.2 which presents the breakdown of total employment between manufacturing, private nonmanufacturing, and government sectors for selected years 1972-80. Throughout the period, however, employment in the East North Central region, particularly in the State of Michigan, has been more concentrated in manufacturing industries than the national average. Twenty-nine percent of the total Michigan employment in 1980 was in manufacturing--the lowest the figure has been in over forty years--yet it was still seven percentage points higher than the corresponding national figure. The concentration of Michigan employment in the slow growth manufacturing industries contributes significantly to the state's slow growth in total employment.

FIGURE 3.3
NONDURABLE MANUFACTURING EMPLOYMENT AS PERCENTAGE
OF ITS PRE-1975 PEAK 1972-80

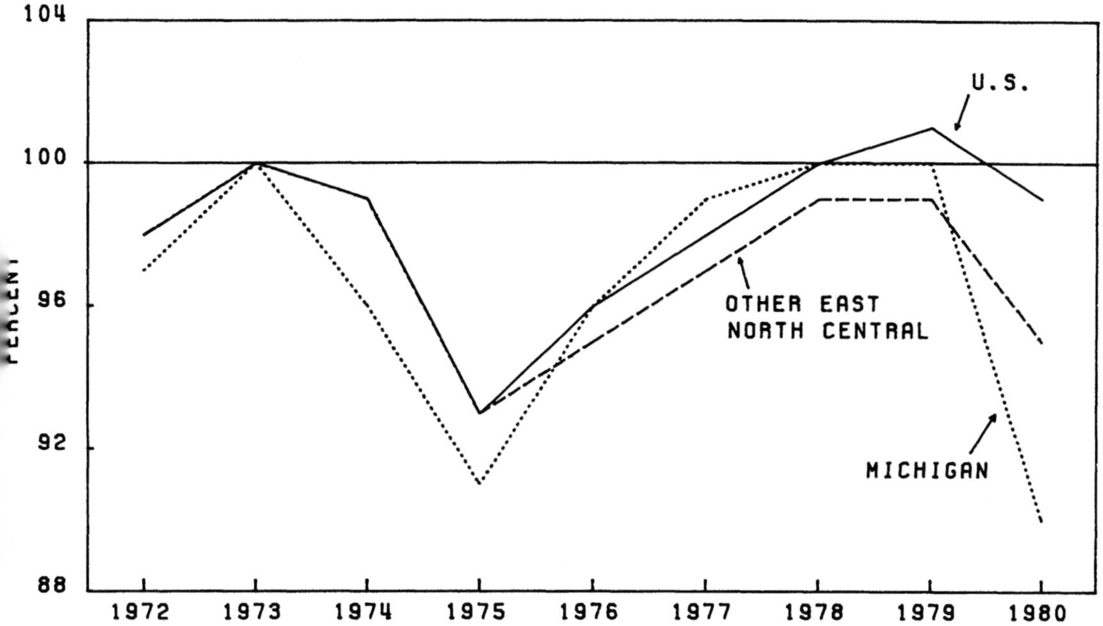

SOURCE: U.S. DEPT. OF LABOR, BUREAU OF LABOR STATISTICS AND MICHIGAN EMPLOYMENT SECURITY COMMISSION.

TABLE 3.2
COMPOSITION OF WAGE AND SALARY EMPLOYMENT, U.S., MICHIGAN AND OTHER EAST NORTH CENTRAL STATES, SELECTED YEARS, 1972-80

REGION	SECTOR	FRACTION OF WAGE AND SALARY EMPLOYMENT					PERCENT CHANGE 1972-80
		1972	1974	1976	1978	1980	
U.S.	Manufacturing	0.26	0.26	0.24	0.24	0.22	-15.4%
	Nonmanufacturing	0.56	0.56	0.57	0.58	0.60	7.1
	Government	0.18	0.18	0.19	0.18	0.18	0.0
Michigan	Manufacturing	0.35	0.34	0.32	0.33	0.29	-17.1%
	Nonmanufacturing	0.48	0.49	0.50	0.50	0.52	8.3
	Government	0.17	0.17	0.18	0.17	0.18	5.9
Other East North Central States	Manufacturing	0.33	0.32	0.30	0.30	0.28	-15.1%
	Nonmanufacturing	0.52	0.52	0.54	0.55	0.56	7.7
	Government	0.15	0.15	0.16	0.15	0.16	6.7

Source: U.S. Department of Labor, Bureau of Labor Statistics and Michigan Employment Security Commision.

Manufacturing Employment

Since the manufacturing sector of the state economy is large relative to the nation, we will examine it in more detail. Table 3.3 reports the breakdown of total manufacturing employment into durables and nondurables for the U.S., Michigan and other East North Central states for selected years 1972-80. For all three areas the durable and nondurable shares have been stable over time, but the differences between the areas are striking. Compared to the nation, manufacturing employment in the East North Central states, especially Michigan, is much more concentrated in durables. Indeed, in 1980, Michigan's durable share was twenty percentage points higher than the U.S.'s share, while the other East North Central states were almost ten percentage points higher in durable manufacturing.

An even more dramatic illustration of the uniqueness of the Michigan economy is obtained by comparing the employment shares of manufacturing that are attributable to the manufacture of motor vehicles (SIC 371), as is done in Table 3.3. From these figures emerges perhaps the single most important fact concerning the state economy: in 1980 Michigan manufacturing employment was fully eight times more concentrated in motor vehicles than the nation, while in the other East North Central states' economies motor vehicle assembly was only slightly more dominant when compared to the U.S. Indeed, if one were to simply remove motor vehicle employment from the figures used to calculate the durable and nondurable shares, the composition of Michigan's nonvehicle manufacturing employment would much more closely resemble that of the other East North Central states.[2] Michigan's nonvehicle durable employment was 71 percent of nonvehicle manufacturing in 1979, while in the U.S. and other East North Central states the figures were 59 and 68 percent, respectively.

Although the manufacturing sector of the Michigan economy accounts for no more than one-third of total employment, it is the dominant procyclical factor in the movements of total employment through the course of the business cycle. This can be seen in a number of ways. One is to simply compare the drop in manufacturing employment with the decline in total employment in a recession period. On this basis, the drop in manufacturing employment was 83.6 percent of the downturn in total employment in 1979-80; durable manufacturing alone was 71.8 percent. Alternatively, one can consider a longer period and examine the extent to which variations in manufacturing employment can statistically explain the variations in total employment. From 1960 to 1980, changes in Michigan manufacturing employment accounted for 93.8 percent of the variation of total employment.[3] In the U.S. and the other East North Central states, the figures were 84.8 percent and 98.2 percent, respectively. Thus, much of the economic well-being of the state, or lack thereof, can be traced to the health of the manufacturing sector.

Finally, we can look at the paths of employment in manufacturing, durables and nondurables, expressed as a percentage of their respective pre-1975 recession peaks, for the U.S., Michigan and the other East North Central states, for the years 1972-80. These are presented in Figures 3.2 and 3.3. From these graphs one can recognize a pattern similar to that of the total employment paths presented above, but markedly more pronounced. For both durables and nondurables, the employment paths for Michigan are greater in amplitude than those for the other East North Central states, (which are in turn greater than those for the U.S.). Indeed, Figure 3.2 tells much of the story of why the recessions of 1975 and 1980 were especially severe in the state. Michigan durable employment, upon which the state's total employment closely follows, fell in both years to less that 82 percent of its 1973 level. The path of nondurables over the period examined exhibits the same pattern, with Michigan employment falling earlier and faster in economic downturns, and with above average growth in the recoveries.

The differences in the composition of durable

FIGURE 3.4
DISTRIBUTION OF DURABLE
MANUFACTURING EMPLOYMENT U.S. 1980

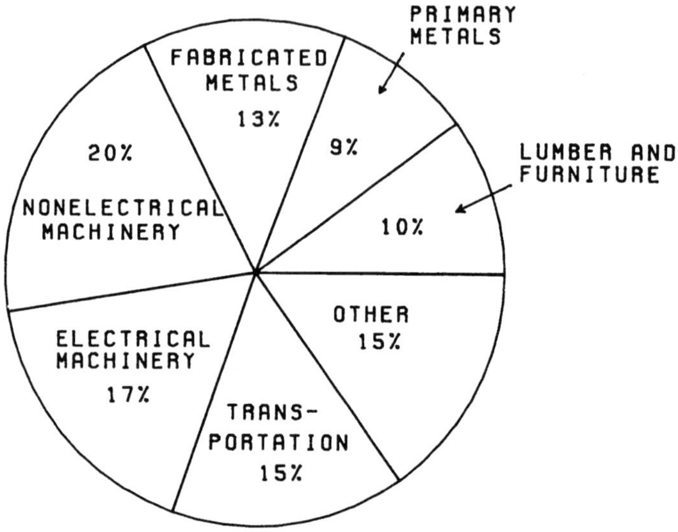

FIGURE 3.5
DISTRIBUTION OF DURABLE MANUFACTURING
EMPLOYMENT MICHIGAN 1980

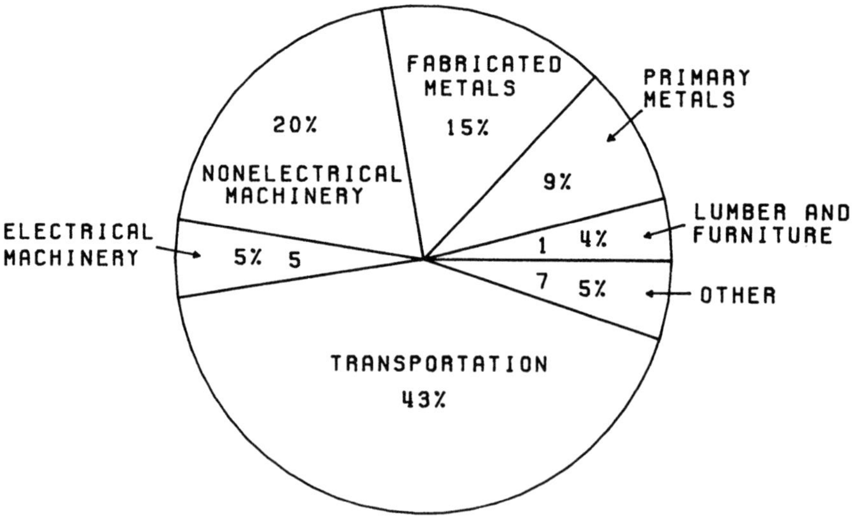

SOURCE: U.S. DEPT. OF LABOR, BUREAU OF LABOR STATISTICS AND MICHIGAN EMPLOYMENT SECURITY COMMISSION.

FIGURE 3.6
DISTRIBUTION OF DURABLE MANUFACTURING EMPLOYMENT OTHER E. NO. CENTRAL STATES 1979

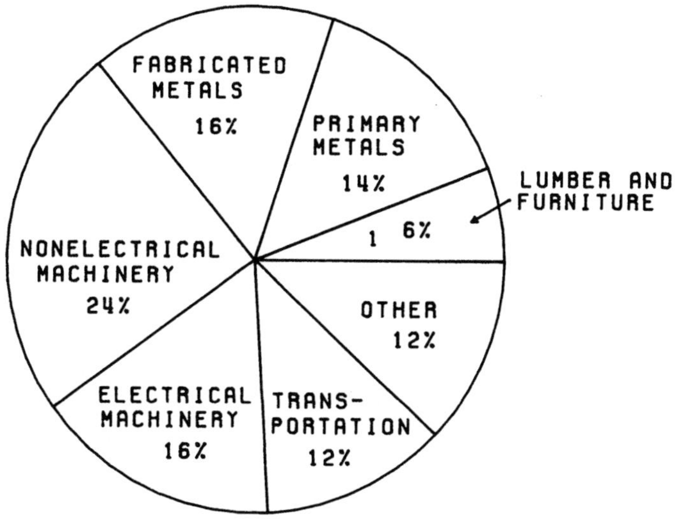

SOURCE: U.S. DEPT. OF LABOR, BUREAU OF LABOR STATISTICS AND MICHIGAN EMPLOYMENT SECURITY COMMISSION.

TABLE 3.3
COMPOSITION OF MANUFACTURING EMPLOYMENT,
U.S., MICHIGAN, AND OTHER EAST NORTH CENTRAL STATES,
SELECTED YEARS, 1972-80

REGION	SECTOR	FRACTION OF MANUFACTURING EMPLOYMENT					PERCENT CHANGE 1972-80
		1972	1974	1976	1978	1980	
U.S.	Durable	0.57	0.59	0.58	0.60	0.60	5.2%
	(Vehicles)	(0.04)	(0.04)	(0.04)	(.05)	(0.04)	0.0
	Nondurable	0.42	0.41	0.42	0.40	0.40	-4.7
Michigan	Durable	0.80	0.81	0.80	0.81	0.80	0.0
	(Vehicles)	(0.34)	(0.33)	(0.34)	(0.35)	(0.33)	-2.9
	Nondurable	0.20	0.19	0.20	0.19	0.20	0.0
Other East North Central States	Durable	0.69	0.70	0.69	0.70	0.69	0.0
	(Vehicles)	(0.06)	(0.06)	(0.06)	(0.06)	(N/A)	N/A
	Nondurable	0.31	0.30	0.31	0.30	0.31	0.0

Source: U.S. Department of Labor, Bureau of Labor Statistics and Michigan Employment Security Commission.

manufacturing employment between Michigan and both the U.S. and other East North Central states are striking, as Figures 3.4 through 3.6 illustrate. The figures clearly show the overwhelming dominance of transportation equipment in the Michigan durable manufacturing economy: of the 43 percent transportation share in Michigan, 41.5 percentage points are attributable to motor vehicle manufacturing, whereas for the U.S. and other East North Central states the figures are 6.3 and 8.8 percentage points, respectively. Michigan's domination by motor vehicles comes at the expense of electrical machinery, lumber and furniture and other durables, which include stone and glass products, instruments and miscellaneous manufactures. What is not apparent from Figure 3.5 is the number of firms within classifications other than transportation equipment that are directly affiliated with the automotive industry. Automotive stampings and the manufacture of wheels fall under fabricated metals, whereas pistons and valves are nonelectrical machinery and automotive foundries are classified under primary metals, to name but a few examples. At the four digit SIC code level, the Michigan Employment Security Commission (MESC) recently classified thirty-four industries as "motor vehicle related," only four of which were included under SIC 371, motor vehicle assembly.[4] A survey of the firms in these industries administered by the MESC revealed that in March 1979 fully 55 percent of Michigan's manufacturing employment was motor vehicle related, whereas the figure for the U.S. was only 11 percent. As might be expected, 62 percent of durable goods manufacturing employment was motor vehicle related, but also more than 21 percent of employment in the nondurable sector fell under the vehicle related classification. This means that the Michigan durable goods manufacturing industry is even more cyclically sensitive than its heavy imbalance towards transportation equipment manufacture would indicate, since so many of the goods that are inputs to the vehicle assembly process are manufactured in the state.

Nonmanufacturing Employment

Much of the growth in national employment in the last decade is attributable to private nonmanufacturing. From 1960 to 1980 the average annual percentage growth in nonmanufacturing employment was 3.2 percent, 0.6 percentage points above the growth rate of wage and salary employment. Over the same period Michigan's average annual growth in nonmanufacturing was 2.7 percent, considerably lower than the national figure but 1.2 percentage points higher than the state's average rate of growth in wage and salary employment. The number of new jobs created in nonmanufacturing in the U.S. from 1972 to 1980 was 76.2 percent of the total increase in jobs in all sectors, while the fractions of total new jobs that were attributable to increases in nonmanufacturing employment in Michigan and the other East North Central states over the same period were even higher, at 96.8 percent and 88.8 respectively.

In addition to enjoying stronger growth than their respective manufacturing counterparts, employment in nonmanufacturing industries for the state, regional and national economies is generally less sensitive to the fluctuations of the business cycle, with the notable exception of contract construction, a highly cyclical component of the nonmanufacturing sector. Figure 3.7 illustrates this point, where nonmanufacturing employment, expressed as a percentage of its pre-1974 recession peak, is plotted for the U.S., Michigan and the other East North Central states for the 1972-80 period. From the figure, one can see that through both the 1974-75 and 1980 recession, nonmanufacturing employment in the U.S. has never declined, although its growth from 1974 to 1975 was almost zero. The East North Central states show slightly more fluctuation, particularly Michigan, where nonmanufacturing employment slipped by 2.0 percent in 1980. Over half of this 1980 decline in the state was attributable to a dip in contract construction employment.

FIGURE 3.7
NONMANUFACTURING EMPLOYMENT AS PERCENTAGE
OF ITS PRE-1975 PEAK 1972-80

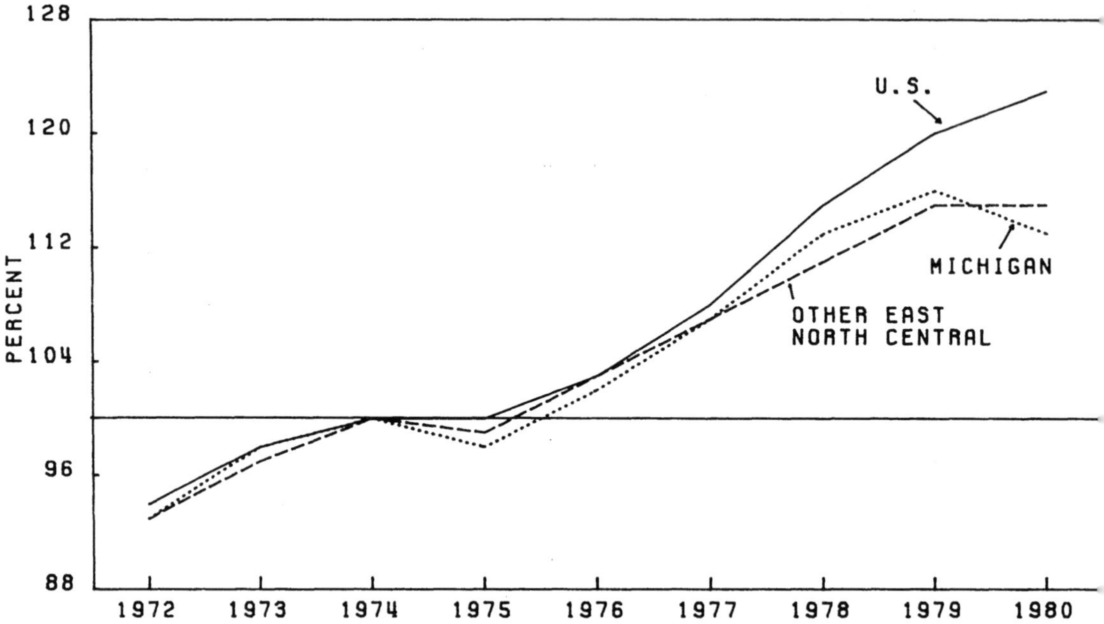

FIGURE 3.8
GOVERNMENT EMPLOYMENT AS PERCENTAGE
OF ITS PRE-1975 PEAK 1972-80

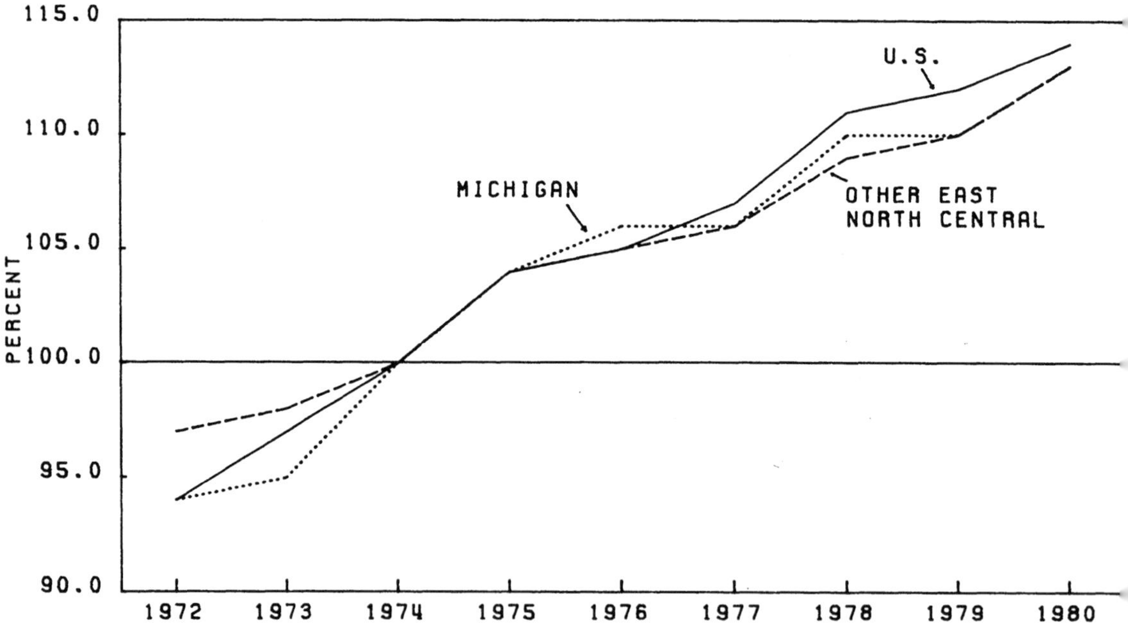

SOURCE: U.S. DEPT. OF LABOR, BUREAU OF LABOR STATISTICS AND MICHIGAN EMPLOYMENT SECURITY COMMISSION.

Government Employment

Of the three employment categories, manufacturing, private nonmanufacturing and government, only in government employment has Michigan's growth kept pace with that of the nation. Up to 1980, in both Michigan and the U.S., government employment grew at a 3.3 percent average annual rate, while in the other East North Central states the growth rate was 3.1 percent. In both the state and the nation over the past two decades, state and local government employment have experienced the most rapid growth, although growth in the local sector has ebbed considerably in recent years, especially in Michigan. An examination of Figure 3.8, which gives total government employment for the 1972-80 period as a percentage of its 1974 value for the three areas, reveals the government employment sector to be remarkably insensitive to the fluctuations in economic activity along the business cycle. Government employment growth in Michigan was steady in the midst of the 1974-75 and 1980 recessions, and was slowest during periods when the other sectors of the state economy realized substantial growth. The employment paths for the U.S. and the other East North Central states show even less deviation from a steady upward trend.

The Michigan economy over the past decade has experienced the same pattern of slow trend growth in total employment that most of the other states in the Great Lakes region have experienced. The state economy, however, has been markedly more sensitive to fluctuations in economic activity along the business cycle, largely due to its relative imbalance towards durable goods manufacturing especially in motor vehicles related industries. We have seen that much of the variation in the state's total employment can be accounted for by the swings in employment in the durable goods sector, and the amplitude of the employment oscillations in that sector have historically been large. Finally, the domination of employment in the state economy by durable goods manufacturing industries may adversely affect the outlook for future employment growth, since over the last decade the relative labor requirements of this sector have been shrinking.

TRENDS IN PER CAPITA INCOME

The dominance of the Michigan economy by high-wage, durable goods industries has produced historically a higher per capita income in the state than the national average. Table 3.4 shows per capita personal income data for the U.S., the East North Central region and the individual states within the region for 1970-80. The average income per capita for the East North Central states was consistently higher than the U.S. average for the entire decade. The ranking within the East North Central states from highest per capita income to lowest was Illinois, Michigan, Ohio, Indiana, and Wisconsin.[5] Illinois and Michigan have remained consistently above the national average in per capita income while Indiana and Wisconsin have remained consistently below. Ohio has shifted back and forth with per capita income below the national average in four of the last eleven years, and three out of the last five.

Ohio, Indiana, and Wisconsin have per capita incomes which are lower than the average for the region while Illinois and Michigan have incomes which are higher. Notable exceptions occur for Michigan in trough years. In 1970 and 1975 Michigan's per capita income fell below the regional average. In 1980 the Michigan figure remained above the average for the East North Central states but the difference narrowed to $76 per person from $285 in 1979.

Table 3.4 also presents average annual rates of growth in per capita incomes for the periods 1970-75, 1975-80 and 1970-80. Income growth in Wisconsin exceeded the national average for the decade; income growth in Michigan matched the national average while the other states lagged behind. Income growth in the first half of the decade lagged behind growth in the second half due in part to lower inflation

TABLE 3.4
PER CAPITA PERSONAL INCOME, U.S. and EAST NORTH CENTRAL STATES, 1970-80
(dollars)

YEAR	U.S.	EAST NORTH CENTRAL	MICHIGAN	ILLINOIS	INDIANA	OHIO	WISCONSIN
1970	3893	4050	4041	4446	3709	3949	3712
1971	4132	4318	4371	4744	3974	4153	3945
1972	4493	4679	4804	5075	4314	4512	4266
1973	4981	5225	5341	5687	4935	4990	4754
1974	5428	5649	5687	6216	5228	5433	5183
1975	5861	6049	6008	6734	5612	5771	5616
1976	6401	6677	6760	7308	6250	6411	6087
1977	7043	7417	7604	8049	6940	7091	6823
1978	7854	8224	8514	8887	7701	7836	7555
1979	8773	9118	9403	9799	8570	8715	8484
1980	9458	9771	9847	10658	8978	9398	9254
AVERAGE ANNUAL RATES OF GROWTH (percent)							
1970-80	9.3	9.2	9.3	9.1	9.2	9.1	9.6
1970-75	8.5	8.4	8.3	8.7	8.6	7.9	8.6
1975-80	10.0	10.1	10.4	9.6	9.9	10.2	10.5

Source: U.S. Department of Commerce, Bureau of Economic Analysis.

TABLE 3.5
PER CAPITA PERSONAL INCOME, UNITED STATES AND MICHIGAN, 1970-80
(1967 dollars)

YEAR	U.S.		MICHIGAN	
	Level	Percent Change From Previous Year	Level	Percent Change From Previous Year
1970	3347	--	3440	--
1971	3408	1.8	3595	4.5
1972	3587	5.3	3807	5.9
1973	3743	4.3	3973	4.4
1974	3673	-1.9	3815	-4.0
1975	3634	-1.1	3747	-1.8
1976	3754	3.3	4001	6.8
1977	3879	3.3	4215	5.4
1978	4015	3.5	4387	4.1
1979	4035	0.5	4298	-2.0
1980	3832	-5.0	3883	-9.7

Source: U.S. Department of Commerce, Bureau of Economic Analysis and U.S. Department of Labor, Bureau of Labor Statistics.

rates during the earlier part of the seventies. During the period 1970-75 income growth in Michigan and Ohio lagged behind the national average while the other three states ran slightly ahead. From 1975 to 1980 growth of per capita income in Michigan, Ohio, and Wisconsin exceeded the national average while Illinois and Indiana trailed.

Nominal income data do not give a complete picture of the relative well-being of different regions, because the rate of inflation can vary from place to place. Appropriate price series for each state are not readily available so Table 3.5 compares real per capita income for the U.S. and Michigan only. The U.S. and Detroit consumer price indices were used to deflate the national and Michigan data, respectively. On a constant dollar basis Michigan per capita income continues to exceed the national average throughout the decade. However, Michigan real per capita income grows more rapidly during periods of recovery and declines more sharply during downswings so the spread between the Michigan figure and the national average in 1980 was the smallest in the entire decade. It remains to be seen whether the gap will widen again in the future.

ALTERNATIVE FORECASTS OF EMPLOYMENT AND INCOME IN MICHIGAN, 1981-85

It is extremely difficult, if not impossible, to predict five years into the future with any reasonable level of accuracy. Rather than attempt such a task we will try to bracket future employment and income in Michigan by considering a pessimistic outlook and an optimistic outlook for the state.[6] Clearly, the state's well-being depends on the condition of the national economy. Periods of boom or bust in the national economy will carry the Michigan economy along. However, our basic concern is the impact of the state's economic structure on employment and income in Michigan, so both the pessimistic outlook and the optimistic outlook will be conditional forecasts of the state economy based on a trend national outlook in which real gross national product is assumed to grow at an average annual rate of 3.2 percent. Thus, the state economy is assumed to be operating within a national environment which is experiencing modest, steady growth.

Because the motor vehicle industry dominates the state economy, the major difference between the two conditional forecasts is the share of real GNP which is attributed to the domestic auto industry, as measured by real gross auto product. In the pessimistic alternative we assumed real gross auto product will remain 2.6 percent of real GNP. This share was both a cyclical and historical low when it occurred in 1980. In the optimistic alternative we assumed real gross auto product would rise to a peak of 3.7 percent of real GNP in three years as it did in the recovery after the 1974-75 recession, and then remain at this level for the remaining two years of the forecast.

We will consider the pessimistic outlook first followed by the optimistic outlook.

<u>The Pessimistic Alternative</u>

It should be noted first that although real gross auto product is assumed to be a flat 2.6 percent of real GNP, this does not imply real gross auto product will remain constant. For auto output to remain a fixed share of total output it must grow at the same rate as the aggregate, an average of 3.2 percent per year. However, even after five years this rate of growth would be insufficient to return the level of auto output to its pre-recession peak of 50.7 billion 1972 dollars which occurred in 1977. In fact, in this scenario auto output would remain more than 10 percent below its previous peak even by 1985.

Several factors could contribute to a relatively weak outlook for the domestic auto industry in the context of normal growth of GNP. Rising gasoline prices could deter new car purchases. Sustained high interest rates could force many consumers to delay or avoid purchasing a new car. Continued strong competition from foreign cars could also keep demand for domestic cars sluggish even though total demand strengthened.

Table 3.6 presents a summary of the more pessimistic outlook. Since auto output fails to attain pre-recession levels nationally, it is not surprising that employment in motor vehicle manufacturing in Michigan also fails to attain complete recovery. Although the average annual rate of growth in motor vehicle employment from 1980 to 1985 is 2.1 percent, the level of employment in 1985 still falls 40,000 jobs short of the 1978 peak.

Because motor vehicle manufacturing so heavily dominates manufacturing in Michigan, even though nonvehicle manufacturing employment grows more rapidly over the five-year period than does motor vehicle employment, the average rate of growth for total manufacturing employment is 2.8 percent, leaving a deficit of 25,000 jobs between the 1985 level and the 1978 peak.

Recovering from the dip which occurred in 1980, nonmanufacturing employment grows steadily through 1985 averaging 2.1 percent growth per year. Although some weakness in construction persists during the early part of the forecast, it is offset by growth in both the distributive and service industries. In this scenario increases in nonmanufacturing employment represent 60 percent of the wage and salary jobs added between 1980 and 1985.

To complete the employment outlook, government employment shows a modest decline between 1980 and 1985 as fiscal conservatism at the federal level necessitates some reductions at all three levels of government. Although the reduction averages less than one percent per year, it is sufficient to reduce the share of government employment in wage and salary employment to slightly more than 16 percent which is one to two percentage points lower than the share which persisted during the latter half of the 1970s.

Combining the three sectors yields total wage and salary employment which grows at an average 1.9 percent per

TABLE 3.6
THE MICHIGAN ECONOMY, PESSIMISTIC OUTLOOK

	1980	1981	1982	1983	1984	1985	AVERAGE ANNUAL GROWTH RATE 1980-1985 (percent)
Employment (thousands)							
Wage and Salary	3454	3472	3505	3593	3694	3786	1.9
Manufacturing	1007	1016	1030	1071	1118	1154	2.8
Nonmanufacturing	1819	1839	1864	1915	1968	2020	2.1
Government	628	617	611	607	608	612	-0.5
Per Capita Income (dollars)	9847	10827	11642	12782	14029	15290	9.2
Per Capita Income(1972 dollars)	3883	3889	3824	3863	3921	3957	0.4
Addenda:							
Gross Auto Product (billions of 1972 dollars)	38.6	39.8	40.5	43.8	45.2	45.2	3.2
Gross Auto Product as a Share of GNP	.026	.026	.026	.026	.026	.026	0

Source: U.S. Dept. of Labor, Bureau of Labor Statistics; U.S. Dept. of Commerce, Bureau of Economic Analysis; Michigan Employment Security Commission; and Research Seminar in Quantitative Economics, University of Michigan.

year. This is only half the rate of growth which occurred following the 1974-75 recession. Consequently, it takes until 1984 for wage and salary employment to surpass its pre-recession peak level.

A relatively weak employment picture yields only moderate growth in per capita income, an average of 9.2 percent per year. Although this rate of growth is more than a percentage point below the average rate of growth for the 1975-80 period, it is consistent with the average for the entire decade of the 1970s. Once an adjustment has been made for inflation, growth in real per capita income averages a mere 0.4 percent per year. This represents about half the rate of increase which occurred during the last half of the 1970s and suggests that Michigan residents would hardly be able to do much more than maintain their standard of living.

While the pessimistic alternative is not a disaster scenario, it does leave room for substantial improvement. Given the current status of the domestic auto industry, it is unlikely that Michigan would be able to match the economic performance of the post-1974-75 recovery. However, since some improvement in the domestic auto outlook can be anticipated, we will examine a scenario in which auto output's share of total output resembles the most recent recovery period to establish an upper limit for the employment and income outlook in Michigan.

The Optimistic Alternative

During the recovery following the 1974-75 recession real gross auto product rose from a cyclical low of 2.8 percent of real GNP to a peak of 3.7 percent. For our optimistic scenario we have assumed auto output would increase from a low of 2.6 percent of real GNP in 1980 to 3.7 percent in 1983, following a path similar to that of the post-1975 recovery, and would remain at 3.7 percent of real output, an historic high, for 1984-85. Table 3.7 presents summary data for the optimistic alternative. It should be noted that with these assumptions real gross auto product

TABLE 3.7
THE MICHIGAN ECONOMY, OPTIMISTIC OUTLOOK

	1980	1981	1982	1983	1984	1985	AVERAGE ANNUAL GROWTH RATE 1980-85 (percent)	IMPROVEMENT FROM PESSIMISTIC OUTLOOK IN 1985 (percent)
Employment (thousands)								
Wage and Salary	3454	3488	3575	3687	3790	3882	2.4	2.5
Manufacturing	1007	1030	1085	1142	1188	1228	4.0	6.4
Nonmanufacturing	1819	1840	1876	1932	1987	2035	2.3	0.7
Government	628	618	614	613	615	619	-0.3	1.1
Per Capita Income (dollars)	9847	10889	11901	13138	14416	15705	9.8	2.7
Per Capita Income(1972 dollars)	3883	3911	3902	3948	3985	3997	0.6	1.0
Addenda:								
Gross Auto Product (billions of 1972 dollars)	38.6	43.4	54.3	60.1	62.2	64.1	10.7	41.8
Gross Auto Product as a Share of GNP	.026	.029	.035	.037	.037	.037	7.3	42.2

Source: U.S. Dept. of Labor, Bureau of Labor Statistics; U.S. Dept. of Commerce, Bureau of Economic Analysis; Michigan Employment Security Commission; and Research Seminar in Quantitative Economics, University of Michigan.

exceeds its pre-recession peak in 1982, and by 1985 auto output is almost 42 percent greater than in the pessimistic alternative. Lower interest rates, lower demand for foreign cars, or lower relative prices for domestic cars could all contribute to stronger growth in the domestic automotive sector.

The brighter domestic auto outlook strengthens the entire Michigan economy with primary emphasis in motor vehicle manufacturing and secondary improvement in other sectors. Employment in motor vehicle manufacturing grows at an average annual rate of 6.1 percent yielding by 1985 an additional 80,000 jobs over the pessimistic alternative. In contrast to the other scenario, motor vehicle employment exceeds its previous peak in 1984.

When compared to the pessimistic alternative, some of the gain in manufacturing employment in motor vehicles is offset by slightly slower growth in nonvehicle manufacturing. This is consistent with the implicit underlying national economy. Since total national output is assumed to be the same for both alternatives, if auto output is stronger in one, other areas must be weaker. However, somewhat weaker nonvehicle manufacturing in conjunction with much stronger vehicle manufacturing yields a net improvement over the other scenario of 74,000 jobs in 1985. Total manufacturing employment also exceeds its previous peak in 1984.

Additional strength in the manufacturing sector stimulates the nonmanufacturing and government sectors as well, but the improvement is much less dramatic. Non-manufacturing employment grows at an average annual rate of 2.3 percent. By 1985 employment in this sector is 15,000 jobs higher than in the other alternative. Slightly stronger state and local government employment brings an improvement of 7,000 jobs by 1985 in total government employment in Michigan.

Thus, by 1985 total wage and salary employment in the optimistic alternative exceeds that in the pessimistic alternative by 96,000 jobs or 2.5 percent of the wage and salary employment in the pessimistic scenario. One other advantage of the more rapid growth is that wage and salary employment would exceed its pre-recession peak in 1983, a year earlier than in the more pessimistic outlook.

Figures 3.9 and 3.10 summarize the differences between the two alternative forecasts for wage and salary employment and manufacturing employment. In each figure the series are expressed as a percentage of their own peak value prior to the 1980 recession. As was noted above, total employment in the optimistic scenario exceeds its previous peak a year earlier than in the pessimistic outlook, and once both series are beyond pre-recession levels the gap continues to widen.

The differences for manufacturing employment are even more pronounced. In the optimistic scenario the pre-recession peak is surpassed in 1984, while from the graph it appears it would take at least one more year of sustained growth beyond 1985 to achieve the 1978 peak value under the pessimistic scenario.

More rapid growth in employment generates more rapid growth in income yielding average annual growth in per capita income of 9.8 percent. By 1985 this additional growth amounts to $415 more per person than in the more pessimistic outlook. When adjusted for inflation, the additional income per person in 1985 is 40 1972 dollars which is a one percent increase over the more pessimistic alternative.

We do not mean to suggest that the Michigan economy will follow either of these paths over the next five years, but if the national economy were to experience a period of modest growth without the food and oil price shocks of recent years, the path of the Michigan economy could well fall between the two paths presented above. While a healthy national economy plays a large role in Michigan's economic well-being, even a robust national economy will not guarantee a vigorous state economy if the auto industry is

FIGURE 3.9
WAGE AND SALARY EMPLOYMENT AS PERCENTAGE
OF ITS PRE-1980 PEAK MICHIGAN 1976-85

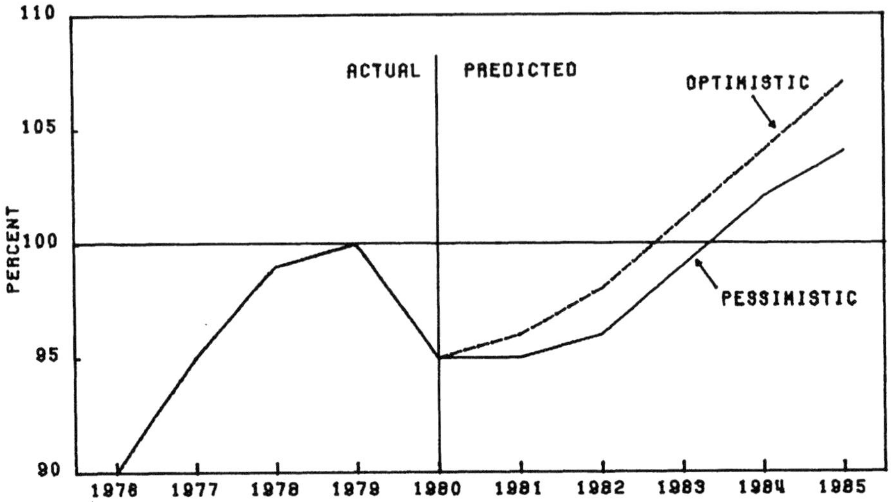

SOURCE: MICHIGAN EMPLOYMENT SECURITY COMMISSION AND RESEARCH SEMINAR IN QUANTITATIVE ECONOMICS, UNIVERSITY OF MICHIGAN.

FIGURE 3.10
MANUFACTURING EMPLOYMENT AS PERCENTAGE
OF ITS PRE-1980 PEAK MICHIGAN 1976-85

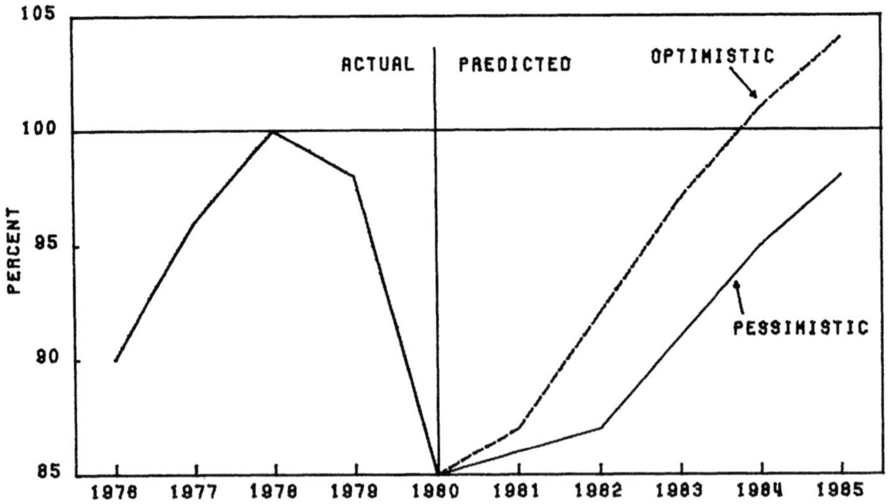

SOURCE: MICHIGAN EMPLOYMENT SECURITY COMMISSION AND RESEARCH SEMINAR IN QUANTITATIVE ECONOMICS, UNIVERSITY OF MICHIGAN.

not healthy as well.

CONCLUDING REMARKS

Michigan, more than any other state in the East North Central region must be concerned about the future of durable manufacturing, and more specifically motor vehicle manufacturing. Historical evidence demonstrates that variations in the state's total employment have closely followed those of manufacturing, especially durable manufacturing, over the past twenty years. This has been unfortunate for Michigan since fluctuations in durable goods demand are strongly procyclical. Michigan is distinct from the rest of the East North Central region and the nation in the importance of its durable manufacturing sector. As a share of total employment, durable manufacturing in Michigan in 1980 was twenty percentage points higher than the corresponding U.S. figure and ten percentage points higher than the rest of the region. In addition, motor vehicle employment dominates the Michigan economy to a degree that is unsurpassed by any other industry for any other comparably sized state; one-third of all Michigan manufacturing employment is accounted for by this single category in addition to numerous jobs under other classifications that are vehicle related.

As a result of the highly procyclical nature of such a major portion of the state's economy, during recession Michigan residents tend to lose ground in terms of real per capita income when compared to the U.S. average, but gains have been made during periods of recovery within the state.

With such a heavy concentration of motor vehicle related manufacturing Michigan cannot depend on general national growth to provide its economic vigor. A range of alternative economic conditions is possible in Michigan during the next five years. We have considered two which rely on moderate national growth and two very different forecasts for the domestic auto industry.

The question remains which alternative is likely to

unfold. Certainly the real possibilities of further oil price shocks, high interest rates, and sustained sales of foreign vehicles would support a less vigorous economy than that implied by the optimistic case.

NOTES, CHAPTER 3

[1]These figures do not include farm workers, the self-employed, domestic workers and unpaid family workers. Thus, little can be said from these figures about the relative importance of agriculture among the various states. Data on income could be used to assess the size of the agricultural sector, however we do not pursue this here.

[2]Of course, this is a rather artificial exercise, since many jobs that are not classified as "motor vehicle assembly" are tied directly to motor vehicle production; body stamping and auto glass manufacture, to name a couple.

[3]The figure cited represents the R^2 statistic for the (descriptive) regression of first differenced wage and salary employment on first differenced manufacturing employment. The regression results are:

$$\Delta \ln \text{WAGE SALARY} = \underset{(0.002)}{0.0184} + \underset{(0.029)}{0.5023}\ \Delta \ln \text{MANUFACTURING}$$

$$R^2 = 0.942 \quad DW = 1.31 \quad F.P. = 1960\text{-}80$$

[4]Michigan Employment Security Commission, Bureau of Research and Statistics, "Motor Vehicle and Related Industries in Michigan," Summer 1981.

[5]Indiana and Wisconsin reversed positions in trough years such as 1970, 1975, and 1980, but in the past Indiana has returned to fourth place once a recovery was underway.

[6]These forecasts were generated using the Michigan Quarterly Econometric Model of the U.S. Economy and the State of Michigan Quarterly Econometric Model from the Research Seminar in Quantitative Economics at The University of Michigan.

Chapter 4

Wage Rates in Michigan Compared with the Rest of the U.S.

by

George E. Johnson

The University of Michigan

INTRODUCTION AND SUMMARY

The future economic climate of Michigan will depend to a very large extent on the degree to which its business firms can compete successfully with those in other states. Since labor compensation represents, in the aggregate, almost 70 percent of the total costs of businesses, the level of wages in Michigan relative to those in other states (and certain other countries) is a major determinant of the state's competitive position.

It is well known that wage rates in Michigan's principal export industry, motor vehicles, are very high. Average hourly earnings for production and nonsupervisory workers in the motor vehicles industry in May 1981 were $10.95, as compared with $7.92 for all manufacturing industries, or 38.3 percent greater. In 1970, average hourly earnings in motor vehicles were $4.23, compared with $3.36 for all manufacturing, or 25.8 percent greater. Thus, wage rates in Michigan's principal industry are relatively high and have been growing over the past decade by about one percentage point per year faster than those in other manufacturing industries.

The primary question asked in this chapter is: How do wages in industries in Michigan other than motor vehicle manufacturing compare with those in other parts of the U.S.? Before examining the relevant data, one can think of reasons why they might be lower than the national average and other reasons why they might be higher. The existence of a very high wage sector (one out of each nine nonagricultural jobs in Michigan was directly in motor vehicles; one in four in durable goods manufacture, much of which deals with supplying the motor vehicle industry) could influence other wages either way. On the one hand, the possibility of obtaining a very high wage job in the auto industry should attract a large supply of labor from other parts of the country. Not all of these persons can, of course, find immediate employment in that industry, so, while they wait, they take jobs in other industries that do not pay such high wages. This would tend to drive down wage rates in these industries below their levels in areas that do not have high wage alternative employment opportunities.

On the other hand, the existence of this very high wage industry may directly influence the wage determination process in nonunion industries. One way in which this happens, which is discussed in some detail in the next section, is that employers may find it necessary to reduce the differential between their wage offers and those of the very high wage sector in order to reduce the turnover of their trained labor force. This hypothesis, which I refer to as the "fallout" model of wage determination, implies that the high wage rates in the very high wage rate sector get passed along, at least in part, to the rest of the labor market.

The answer to the primary question of the chapter is that wage rates in <u>all industries</u> throughout Southeastern Michigan are much higher than those in the rest of the nation. Wage rates in durable and nondurable goods manufacturing industries are very high in the Standard Metropolitan Statistical Areas of Detroit, Ann Arbor, Flint, Lansing, and Saginaw; high relative to the national average in the Bay City, Battle Creek, Jackson, Kalamazoo, and Muskegon SMSAs. Only in Grand Rapids, which has very little employment in the motor vehicle industry, are wage rates similar to the national average. The first five of these SMSAs, which contain two-thirds of Michigan's population, are dominated by the auto industry.

A second finding of the study is that, consistent with what has happened to wage rates in the auto industry, wage rates in Michigan manufacturing have increased substantially during the past decade. Most of this increase was in durable goods industries (including autos), but there was still a substantial widening of the Michigan/U.S. differential in nondurable goods industries. This, like the preceding finding, is consistent with the fallout model.

Wages are also considerably higher in the nonmanufacturing sector in southeastern Michigan than in the U.S. as a whole. Bureau of Labor Statistics indices of pay levels by occupational category are 11 to 17 percent higher in nonmanufacturing industries in Detroit than in the average of 262 SMSAs around the U.S. This is about half the relative wage advantage of workers in manufacturing industries in the Detroit SMSA.

The price levels in Michigan and the Detroit area are not much different from surrounding states and comparable cities. Therefore, the observed high nominal wage levels in southeastern Michigan are high in <u>real</u> terms as well. Although data on fringe benefits are not available on a regional basis, there is reason to believe that fringes as a fraction of take-home pay are on the high side in Michigan. Thus, the high wage rates in Michigan cannot be explained away by high prices or low fringe benefits.

In the next-to-the last section of this chapter I present an analysis of the determination of wages in the thirty-four largest SMSAs in the U.S. (including Detroit) using U.S. Census data on individual workers. This analysis is necessary because it is possible that wages are higher in southeastern Michigan because workers are of higher quality, and the microeconomic data permit an analysis of the effect of location on wages <u>net</u> of the influence of education, labor market experience, sex, race, union status, and other factors that influence wages. The results were consistent with the conclusions from the analysis of aggregate data: wage rates are high in the Detroit area regardless of industry, union status, or any other set of characteristics.

The major qualification to the acceptance of the

fallout model as an explanation of the wage structure in Michigan is the fact that in some other regions it does not seem to work very well. Specifically, there is a great deal of unionization and a very high wage sector in the SMSAs of Cleveland, Buffalo, Pittsburgh, St. Louis and Seattle, but their other wage rates are close to or below the national average. On the other hand, there are very high wage sectors in San Francisco, Oakland, San Jose, and Washington D.C., and the fallout model appears to apply. Given this conflicting evidence, I must point out that the fallout hypothesis has not been proven. There is no question, however, but that wages in most of Michigan are much higher than in the rest of the country.

A FRAMEWORK FOR MEASURING RELATIVE LABOR COSTS

Wage rates and other forms of labor compensation may be considered from two points of view. First, from the point of view of suppliers of labor they are a partial index of the relative attractiveness of living in Michigan. The net real wage of a person with skill level S in area i can be defined as:

$$(4\text{-}1)\quad R_i(S) = (W_i(S)(1-t_i^1) + F_i(S))/P_i,$$

where $W_i(S)$ is the average straight-time wage for skill level S in area i, t_i^1 the individual average tax rate in area i, $F_i(S)$ the hourly value of fringe benefits, and P_i the price level in the area. t_i^1 includes federal taxes (personal income and social security) as well as state and local income taxes, and in more general form it could be made a function of $W_i(S)$, as well as hours worked per year, to reflect income tax progressivity and the discontinuity of the individual social security tax. Variations across areas in sales and property taxes would be reflected in the area price level.

The net real wage in Michigan relative to that in area j for skill level S is then:

$$\text{(4-2)}\quad \frac{R_m(S) = W_m(S)\ P_j\ (1-t_m^1+f_m(S))}{R_j(S) = W_j(S)\ P_m\ (1-t_j^2+f_j(S))}$$

where $f_i(S) = F_i(S)/W_i(S)$ is the ratio of fringe benefits per hour to straight-time hourly earnings. Thus, Michigan is the more attractive relative to other areas from the point of view of workers the higher are its wage level and fringe benefit fraction and the lower are its price level and income tax rate.

The second way to view wage rates and other forms of labor compensation is from the employers' side; they are a partial index of the relative cost of locating (or retaining) a firm in Michigan. The average gross cost to an employer of hiring a unit of the services of a worker with skill level S in area i can be defined as:

$$\text{(4-3)}\quad C_i(S) = W_i(S)(1+t_i^2) + F_i(S) + H_i(S),$$

where t_i^2 is the payroll tax rate (for social security, unemployment insurance, and worker compensation) and $H_i(S)$ is the (appropriately discounted) value of hiring and training costs per worker.

Average gross cost of hiring a unit of labor in Michigan relative to its cost in area j is then:

$$\text{(4-4)}\quad \frac{C_m(S) = W_m(S)\ (1+t_m^2+f_m(S)+h_m(S))}{C_j(S) = W_j(S)\ (1+t_j^2+f_j(S)+h_j(S))}$$

where $h_i(S) = H_i(S)/W_i(S)$ is the ratio of hiring costs to labor compensation. Just as higher relative wages in Michigan make location in the state more desirable to workers, they lower the relative desirability to firms of locating in Michigan. Similarly, higher payroll taxes (t_m^2), fringe benefits (f_m), and hiring costs (h_m) lower the relative desirability of locating in Michigan from the point of view of business firms.

Under what circumstances might we expect wages to vary between regions? Algebraically, how could the ratio of wage rates in Michigan to each other labor market, $W_m(S)/W_j(S)$, be other than one? This is not a purely academic question, for, as I shall show in subsequent sections, wage rates in most of Michigan are much higher than in virtually all other labor market areas of the United States.

On the demand side a high ratio of Michigan to "other" wages implies, holding constant relative payroll taxes, fringe benefits, and hiring costs, that $C_m(S)/C_j(S)$ is greater than one. Unless there is something peculiar to Michigan that makes for lower costs of other factors of production (land, raw materials, public services, etc.), there will be a tendency for firms to leave the state. But if some industries that export to the rest of the country find it profitable to remain in Michigan even with high wages, then certain other industries (like retailing, services, and the like) will also locate in Michigan because of the presence of a market for their products.

On the supply side a high value of $W_m(S)/W_j(S)$ means that, other things equal, Michigan is a relatively desirable place to live and work. If wage rates were free to fall in the face of an excess supply of labor, potential workers would move from other areas until real wages in Michigan equalled real wage rates in other areas. As wages in Michigan fell relative to those in other areas, the price level in Michigan would approach that of other areas--reflecting, ultimately, only differences in transportation costs between sources of raw materials and Michigan, as well as upkeep costs due to meteorological differences.

Suppose, however, as is indeed the case, that the primary export industry in Michigan is organized by a powerful trade union that is able to establish wages for its members that are well above the national average for that skill class. Then there is no guarantee that workers who come to Michigan in search of very high wage jobs will find them. Some of these entrants (who include those who have lost jobs in the high wage sector) will be faced with the option of taking a job in the nonunionized (or weakly unionized) sector at much lower wages or remaining unemployed and waiting for very high wage jobs as they come up.

To the extent that new entrants take jobs in the nonunionized (or nonhigh wage) sector, the existence of a large, very high wage sector, should actually lower wages in the nonunion sector. The reason for this is that, relative prices and other factors held constant, employers that are free to do so can hire workers of a given skill at a lower price than they could in an area that does not hold out the promise to workers of a very high wage job in the future. For example, suppose that a person has the option of taking a job in Atlanta for twenty years at (in constant dollars) $8 per hour. That person also has the option of migrating to Lansing and working at a low wage job for ten years and then a very high wage job for $12 per hour for the remaining ten years of his working life. Obviously, he would prefer the Lansing alternative even if the low wage job paid somewhat less than $8 per hour. (If the discount rate were zero, the equilibrium wage for the low wage job in Lansing would be $4; for a positive but finite discount rate the equilibrium wage in Lansing is between $4 and $8 per hour.)

An additional implication of this scenario is that firms would tend to locate in Michigan if they forecast that they would not have to pay the very high wage levels associated with unionism. If, on the other hand, they perceived that their workers were ripe for union organization, they would locate in other areas.

There are, however, complicating factors to this relatively straightforward story. First, if there is a greater chance of obtaining a very high wage job when one is unemployed than when one is employed, new entrants and those who lose very high wage jobs may decide not to take nonunion jobs in favor of remaining in the queue for very high wage jobs.[1] This possibility is especially likely if unemployed persons receive generous unemployment insurance or other benefits. In this case, the existence of a large very high wage sector would not necessarily depress wage rates in the nonunion sector. However, the <u>highest</u> that the nonunion wage could be, by this argument, is the wage (again, adjusted for price level and other such differences) in completely nonunion areas.

A second complicating factor is what I have called the <u>fallout model</u> of wage determination. Consider a firm that is not represented by a trade union and can thus offer any wage it chooses (equal to or above the statutory minimum wage). Now if it pays a wage equal to, say, that prevailing in nonunion areas (like the $8 in the above numerical example), it can attract a labor force from among those who are waiting for jobs in the very high wage sector. However, as soon as one of its employees is offered a much higher wage (the $12), he will leave. Any specific training or skills picked up by that worker are now lost. The employer then realizes that if he paid a higher wage his employees would expend less time and effort searching for jobs in the very high wage sector. This would result in a lower turnover rate and <u>possibly</u> a lower average gross cost of labor.

An increase in the wage in the very high wage sector might then induce nonunion firms to raise their wage offers in order to minimize their average gross labor costs. This means that, by the fallout model, high union wages may spill over to at least a portion of the nonunion sector.

Two implications follow from this fallout, or wage spillover, scenario. First, since wage rates in the nonunion sector may not adjust to provide jobs for a surplus labor force, there will generally (i.e., in good times as well as bad) be high unemployment rates in areas that have a large very high wage sector. This kind of unemployment cannot be solved by traditional policies that attempt to increase employment in an area of high unemployment, for any expansion of employment will be met by a proportional increase through in-migration in the number of individuals seeking employment. Short of a reduction of the wage in the very high wage sector, the area must "live with" an unemployment rate in excess of the national average.

A second implication of the fallout model is that industries that have the option of locating in a wide variety of areas (as opposed to say, lobster packing, which must locate in New England) will never locate in areas that already have a significant very high wage industry. Even if a firm could be assured that it would not be unionized, it would have to pay a higher wage in an area with a very high wage sector than in an area without one.

ANALYSIS OF AGGREGATE DATA

The very high wage industry in Michigan is, of course, the motor vehicle industry. As seen in Table 4.1, whereas 1.1 percent of total nonagricultural employment in the U.S. as a whole (0.7 percent for the U.S. exclusive of Michigan) was in the motor vehicle industry in 1978, the figure for Michigan was 11 percent. Furthermore, much of Michigan's other durable goods employment was in transportation-related activities.

Part of the reason why the average wage in Michigan manufacturing is so much higher--a full 32 percent (see Table 4.2)--than the U.S. average is that Michigan manufacturing workers are move heavily concentrated in the durable goods sector. In Michigan, 80 percent of manufacturing employment is in durable goods as compared with 60 percent for the U.S. as a whole. Since, for the entire U.S., wages in durable goods are approximately 20 percent higher than wages in nondurable goods manufacturing industries, one would expect the <u>average</u> wage in manufacturing to be higher in Michigan than for the U.S. as a whole merely due to this compositional difference. In fact, wages in Michigan's durable and nondurable goods industries were, respectively, 27 and 26 percent greater than the national average. Thus, about a sixth of the 32 percent differential between Michigan and the rest of the country is accounted for by the relatively high

TABLE 4.1
NONAGRICULTURAL EMPLOYMENT AND WAGES IN THE UNITED STATES, MICHIGAN, AND ELEVEN STANDARD METROPOLITAN STATISTICAL AREAS IN MICHIGAN

AREA	Year	TOTAL EMPLOYMENT (000'S)					% Durable Total	% Trans. Total	AVERAGE HOURLY EARNINGS		
		Nonagri-cultural	Manufac-turing	Durable	Non-durable	Trans-por-tation			Manufac-turing	Durable	Non-durable
U.S.	1965	60765	18062	10405	7656	843[1]	17.1	1.4	2.61	2.79	2.36
	1970	70880	19367	11208	8158	799[1]	15.8	1.1	3.35	3.55	3.08
	1978	85763	20332	12160	8172	977[1]	14.2	1.1	6.17	6.58	5.53
Michigan	1965	2687	1103	889	214	377	33.1	14.0	3.22	3.29	2.90
	1970	3005	1072	855	217	345	31.8	11.5	4.15	4.22	3.78
	1978	3535	1140	914	226	395	25.9	11.1	8.13	8.39	6.95
Ann Arbor	1965	85.3	31.4	28.7	2.7	13.2[1]	33.6	15.5	3.28	3.31	2.79
	1970	101.0	32.6	28.9	3.7	13.3[1]	28.6	13.1	4.25	4.26	4.11
	1978	130.1	42.7	38.6	4.1	21.2	29.7	16.3	8.79	8.96	6.23
Battle Creek	1965	54.9	24.6	14.9	9.7	--	27.1	--	--	--	--
	1970	61.4	25.0	15.4	9.7	--	25.1	--	4.07	3.87	4.40
	1978	66.5	23.7	13.9	9.8	--	20.9	--	8.06	7.49	8.95
Bay City	1965	27.4	11.6	9.4	2.2	4.2	34.3	15.3	2.98	3.08	2.53
	1970	30.0	10.8	8.9	1.9	4.0	30.0	12.5	3.86	3.95	3.47
	1978	36.7	11.4	8.7	2.7	4.4	23.7	12.0	7.63	7.94	6.57
Detroit	1965	1366	576	487	89	231	35.7	16.9	3.39	3.42	3.17
	1970	1502	555	466	89	214	31.0	14.2	4.38	4.43	4.04
	1978	1741	580	486	94	245	27.9	14.1	8.76	8.93	7.77
Flint	1965	151.3	81.2	77.0	4.2	60.7	50.9	40.1	3.59	--	--
	1970	156.3	67.5	63.3	4.2	49.2	40.5	31.5	4.66	--	--
	1978	201.6	87.4	83.1	4.3	63.3	41.3	31.4	8.98	--	--
Grand Rapids	1965	164.5	72.6	54.7	17.9	2.4	33.3	1.5	2.85	--	--
	1970	190.2	71.5	53.4	18.1	2.5	28.1	1.3	3.71	--	--
	1978	247.3	87.4	66.0	21.4	4.2	26.7	1.7	6.62	--	--
Jackson	1965	42.3	18.3	14.9	3.4	5.6[1]	35.2	13.2	3.13	3.04	3.53
	1970	46.1	17.3	14.3	3.0	5.8[1]	31.0	12.6	4.07	3.97	4.53
	1978	52.3	16.7	13.0	3.7	5.2[1]	24.9	9.9	7.11	7.01	7.50
Kalamazoo	1965	63.2	29.6	10.2	16.4	3.0	16.1	4.7	2.86	3.01	2.77
	1970	72.8	27.9	12.6	15.3	3.0	17.3	4.1	3.97	4.17	3.80
	1978	106.4	36.0	17.5	18.5	4.1	16.4	3.9	7.25	7.77	6.64
Lansing	1965	111.3	36.8	33.8	3.0	25.3	30.4	22.7	3.40	3.45	2.74
	1970	130.6	33.9	30.5	3.4	22.4	23.3	17.2	4.34	4.41	3.57
	1978	185.8	42.9	38.0	4.9	27.5	20.4	14.8	8.49	8.84	5.63
Muskegon	1965	47.2	25.9	22.6	3.3	--	47.8	--	3.01	3.01	2.96
	1970	51.4	24.4	21.2	3.3	--	41.2	--	3.78	3.74	4.06
	1978	60.7	22.3	19.1	3.2	--	31.3	--	7.05	7.07	--
Saginaw	1965	63.8	29.8	26.9	2.9	9.6	42.2	15.0	3.28	--	--
	1970	70.2	28.8	25.9	2.9	10.5	36.8	15.0	4.42	--	--
	1978	91.8	37.7	34.8	2.9	15.9	37.9	17.3	9.25	--	--

Notes: [1]Motor Vehicles and Equipment, SIC 371, instead of Transportation and Equipment, SIC 37. In Michigan, employment in SIC 371 composed 96-97% in SIC 37 in 1965, 1970, and 1978.

WAGE RATES IN MANUFACTURING INDUSTRIES FOR SELECTED AREAS RELATIVE TO U.S. AVERAGE, 1978

INDUSTRY	U.S. AVE.	STATE-WIDE MICH.	SMSA DETROIT	NON-DET. MICH.	OHIO	STATE-WIDE ILL-INOIS	SMSA CHI-CAGO	NON-CHI. ILL.	N.Y.	CA.	SMSA LOS ANG.	PA.	N.J.	MO.	TEXAS	GA.
MANUFACTURING	$6.17	1.32	1.42	1.22	1.19	1.10	1.07	1.09	0.99	1.04	0.97	1.03	1.01	1.01	0.95	0.79
Durable Goods	6.58	1.27	1.36	1.18	1.14	1.05	1.01	1.04	1.01	1.00	0.93	1.06	0.96	1.01	0.88	0.85
24. Lumber	5.61	0.90	0.98	0.89	0.86	0.96	1.08	1.00	0.79	1.22	0.89	0.86	0.88	0.68	0.80	0.72
25. Furniture	4.68	1.25	1.48	1.24	1.21	1.18	1.22	1.19	1.06	1.12	1.09	1.13	1.06	1.05	0.88	0.95
33. Primary Metals	8.20	1.09	1.19	0.97	1.07	0.93	0.94	0.94	0.99	0.90	0.79	1.04	0.80	0.93	0.90	0.77
331. Blast Furnaces	9.41	1.13	1.16	0.77	1.00	0.94	0.91	0.93	0.98	0.99	--	0.98	0.75	--	--	--
332. Iron Foundaries	7.24	1.25	1.33	1.22	1.12	0.89	0.94	0.92	1.14	0.84	0.75	0.94	0.80	0.86	--	--
34. Fab. Metal	6.34	1.27	1.30	1.25	1.16	1.08	1.12	1.09	0.98	0.99	0.90	1.02	1.03	1.02	0.93	0.88
342. Cutlery	6.06	1.39	1.53	1.32	1.24	1.05	1.14	1.09	0.85	0.97	0.92	0.89	1.26	1.05	--	--
346. Metal	7.37	1.23	1.24	1.20	1.19	1.10	1.02	1.09	1.11	0.80	0.77	1.08	0.79	--	--	--
35. Machinery	6.76	1.19	1.31	1.07	1.06	1.13	1.04	1.09	0.98	0.98	0.93	1.01	0.98	0.98	0.90	0.82
354. Metal	7.02	1.17	1.31	0.92	1.03	0.98	0.96	0.98	0.95	0.95	0.92	1.02	0.94	--	--	--
36. Elect. Mach.	5.83	1.23	1.00	1.28	1.12	1.01	0.96	1.00	0.98	1.02	0.88	1.05	1.04	0.99	0.89	0.95
37. Trans. Equip.	7.91	1.16	1.17	1.13	1.09	1.03	1.09	1.05	1.05	0.98	0.96	0.96	1.05	1.04	0.87	1.01
371. Motor Vehic.	8.97	1.03	1.04	1.01	1.00	0.94	0.97	0.96	0.97	0.89	0.81	0.92	0.97	0.93	--	--
Nondurable Goods	5.53	1.26	1.40	1.15	1.22	1.17	1.17	1.17	1.00	1.12	1.02	0.97	1.09	1.01	1.09	0.82
20. Food	5.80	1.17	1.29	1.10	1.16	1.16	1.15	1.15	1.04	1.15	1.16	1.02	1.11	1.09	0.91	0.81
22., 23. Text. & App.	4.08	1.93	2.03	1.79	1.11	1.05	1.05	1.05	1.12	1.00	0.98	1.04	1.18	0.92	0.88	0.95
26. Paper	6.52	1.06	1.03	1.06	1.00	0.92	0.86	0.91	0.90	1.13	1.07	0.93	0.87	0.89	0.96	1.07
27. Printing	6.47	1.09	1.35	0.80	1.14	1.11	1.15	1.12	1.24	1.17	1.15	1.04	0.97	1.01	0.87	--
28. Chemicals	7.01	1.11	1.18	1.07	1.00	0.95	0.98	0.96	0.95	1.03	0.96	0.92	1.02	1.02	1.25	0.84

Source: Data from U.S.B.L.S., Employment and Earnings for States and Areas.

concentration of durable goods industries in Michigan.

Table 4.2 also reveals that average wages in overall manufacturing and in its durable and nondurable components are also higher than in comparable states in the New Jersey to Illinois manufacturing belt. The overall manufacturing wage is 11 percent higher than in Ohio, 20 percent higher than in Illinois, 33 percent higher than in New York, and so on. They are similarly higher than these states in all durable goods industries except lumber and all nondurable goods except paper. These numbers confirm the notion that manufacturing labor is extremely expensive in Michigan. They also provide some initial evidence in favor of the fallout model of wage determination. Wage rates are not simply high in the motor vehicle industry; they are significantly higher than the U.S. average in most other manufacturing industries as well.

To some extent the very high wage level in Michigan manufacturing is peculiar to the Detroit SMSA rather than the entire state. The Detroit area accounted for approximately half of both nonagricultural and manufacturing employment in 1978 (slightly less than in 1965 and in 1970), and its wage rates are 15 to 20 percent greater in the three aggregative categories than are wages in the rest of the state. This is confirmed in greater detail in Table 4.1 in which employment and wage data for the other ten SMSAs are reported. (These eleven SMSAs, including Detroit, accounted for 83 percent of total nonagricultural employment in Michigan in 1978.) Wage rates are similar to Detroit in Ann Arbor, Flint, Lansing, and Saginaw; somewhat closer to the national average in Bay City, Battle Creek, Jackson, Kalamazoo, and Muskegon; and much closer in Grand Rapids. It is worth noting that wages in Michigan SMSAs appear to be directly correlated with the extent of employment in the transportation equipment industry.

The trend of the decade of the 1970s was toward a marked widening of the differential between manufacturing wages in Michigan and the U.S. As shown in Table 4.3, from

TABLE 4.3
PERCENTAGE CHANGES IN WAGE RATES IN MANUFACTURING INDUSTRIES IN THE U.S. AND MICHIGAN BETWEEN 1970 AND 1978

INDUSTRY	U.S.	MICHIGAN
MANUFACTURING	84.2	95.9
Durable Goods	85.4	98.8
24. Lumber	89.5	86.7
25. Furniture	69.0	72.2
33. Primary Metals	108.7	108.5
331. Blast Furnaces	126.2	125.5
332. Foundries	94.6	117.0
34. Fab. Metal	79.6	90.8
342. Cutlery	83.6	98.6
35. Machinery	79.3	87.2
354. Metal	70.8	75.6
36. Electrical Machinery	77.7	95.1
37. Transportation Equipment	94.8	107.3
371. Motor Vehicles	102.9	107.4
Nondurable Goods	79.6	83.9
20. Food	83.5	84.1
22., 23. Text. & App.	68.6	113.5
26. Paper	89.5	92.2
27. Printing	65.1	61.9
28. Chemicals	90.0	93.3

1970 to 1978 the overall manufacturing wage in Michigan rose 95.9 percent versus only 84.2 percent in the U.S. as a whole. This means the Michigan/U.S. relative wage increased from 1.24 to 1.32. Most of this increase was in the durable goods sector--98.8 percent in Michigan versus 85.4 for the U.S. as a whole, or an increase in the Michigan/ U.S. relative wage in durable goods from 1.19 to 1.28. Indeed, since the fraction of total durable goods employment located in Michigan is nontrivial (7.5 percent in 1978), it is interesting to calculate the ratio of Michigan wages to those of the U.S. less Michigan. The U.S. durable goods wage rose by only 84.2 percent, and the Michigan/U.S. less Michigan relative wage rose from 1.21 to 1.30. Thus, a large fraction of the problem of very high wages in Michigan has arisen during the past ten years.

The preceding analysis of manufacturing wage rates leaves little doubt that Michigan's relative wage position is extremely high, and it also suggests that the motor vehicle industry is the source of high wages. A further test of the fallout model concerns the level of wages in Michigan nonmanufacturing industries relative to other parts of the country. To perform this test, I examined Bureau of Labor Statistics area wage indices for selected occupations in 1978, and the raw data are shown for forty-six SMSAs in Table 4.4. Detroit is the only Michigan SMSA for which complete data are available, but the 1978 survey also included Saginaw, which like Ann Arbor, Detroit, Flint, and Lansing, is heavily influenced by the motor vehicle industry. The two reported values of the indices for Saginaw were 116 for "all office clerical" (versus 119 for Detroit) and 148 for "all unskilled plant" (versus 131 for Detroit). Thus, the Detroit figures are most likely fairly representative of those five SMSAs that account for approximately two-thirds of total "nonagricultural" employment in Michigan. In 1973-74, the BLS survey also included Muskegon, an area that is not so heavily influenced by motor vehicle manufacturing. Its wage levels were 80 to 85 percent of those in Detroit, or roughly equal to the

RELATIVE PAY LEVELS FOR SELECTED OCCUPATIONS BY INDUSTRY IN SELECTED SMSAS (U.S.=100), 1978

STANDARD METROPOLITAN STATISTICAL AREA	OFFICE/CLERICAL			ELECTRONIC DATA PROCESSING			SKILLED MAINTENANCE		UNSKILLED PLANT		
	All	Mfg	Non-Mfg	All	Mfg	Non-Mfg	All	Mfg	All	Mfg	Non-Mfg
Akron	105	102	103	105	102	-	102	100	124	118	106
Anaheim	106	103	105	110	-	-	98	101	90	91	85
Atlanta	102	-	105	105	-	108	96	93	86	94	86
Baltimore	105	107	104	97	-	97	101	103	93	98	89
Birmingham	93	98	93	96	-	97	89	90	71	85	67
Boston	97	94	99	92	92	93	93	92	89	87	93
Buffalo	98	103	90	95	-	-	109	111	110	112	106
Chattanooga	86	87	85	92	-	-	83	83	84	84	-
Chicago	105	101	107	102	98	104	108	105	121	101	128
Cincinatti	97	96	96	93	-	94	98	97	99	103	89
Cleveland	101	102	100	105	101	107	107	108	110	116	102
Columbus	94	91	97	90	-	93	97	95	95	98	96
Dallas	94	95	94	96	98	95	93	92	78	83	76
Denver	100	99	102	102	-	105	99	98	94	101	94
Detroit	119	129	111	116	118	111	116	117	131	133	117
Greenville	87	83	88	91	-	-	70	70	74	64	-
Hartford	91	93	90	94	-	-	89	90	85	90	79
Houston	103	102	104	104	-	106	103	102	75	90	72
Indianapolis	97	107	92	94	-	88	106	108	107	108	101
Kansas City	98	92	101	100	-	101	106	104	114	115	106
Los Angeles	109	107	109	105	104	105	102	100	97	87	102
Louisville	97	96	96	96	-	-	102	103	100	113	79
Memphis	96	95	98	96	-	100	99	96	76	89	76
Miami	97	88	101	105	-	107	86	-	74	67	78
Milwaukee	94	96	100	103	98	106	107	107	106	107	101
Minneapolis	94	89	97	96	97	94	104	102	113	108	113
Nassau-Suffolk	94	91	95	100	-	102	88	86	88	84	87
Newark	104	101	106	104	103	106	97	95	97	95	102
New Orleans	89	-	90	-	-	-	96	101	72	93	69
New York	103	103	105	109	108	110	98	96	118	94	128
Oklahoma City	94	86	97	91	-	94	87	82	75	77	78
Omaha	95	96	96	-	-	-	97	94	87	101	81
Paterson	97	94	97	98	-	-	88	89	91	83	93
Philadelphia	98	100	95	99	98	99	97	98	106	105	99
Pittsburgh	105	108	102	100	103	94	104	105	104	114	93
Portland, Me.	88	-	89	-	-	-	72	70	99	81	103
Portland, Or.	107	100	111	93	-	94	108	108	121	115	118
Providence	87	85	88	88	-	-	78	78	80	72	85
Richmond	92	93	91	95	-	93	99	100	85	90	81
St.Louis	100	98	100	96	90	102	101	103	106	111	101
Salt Lake City	91	89	93	94	-	96	95	94	93	80	98
San Diego	99	102	97	98	99	96	102	-	94	-	87
San Francisco	111	109	113	102	-	101	118	118	131	122	134
San Jose	109	107	109	114	112	109	109	110	118	-	121
Seattle	111	-	111	97	-	99	111	111	124	120	124
Toledo	106	109	101	97	98	-	106	106	125	118	118
Washington	104	-	107	102	-	103	104	-	79	97	81
Worcester	98	92	97	96	-	99	84	84	95	82	-

Source: U.S.D.O.L., Handbook of Labor Statistics, Bulletin 2070, December 1980, Table 107.

average for all SMSAs in the country.

Given the high level of manufacturing wages in Detroit reported in Table 4.1, it is not surprising that Detroit leads all other SMSAs in the occupational categories for manufacturing industries. The Detroit advantage over the average for the 262 SMSAs is about 30 percent for office and unskilled workers and about 17 percent for data processing and skilled maintenance workers. What is important, however, is the fact that Detroit is also a very high wage area in the nonmanufacturing sector, even though the differential with the rest of the country is only about half its value in manufacturing. This is, again, consistent with the fallout model of wage determination. The motor vehicle industry and its satellites are the very high wage sector, but these high wages are reflected, in part, in other manufacturing industries and also, to a slightly smaller extent, in unrelated industries like retailing, finance and services.

It is possible that wage rates in Michigan are high because prices are higher than elsewhere in the U.S. If this were so, it would refute the hypothesis that wages are artificially inflated due to the existence of a very high wage sector and the subsequent passing along of a portion of these "rents" via the fallout process. Table 4.5 reports a comparable price index for all regions of the U.S. and selected states within each region. The consumer price index in Detroit was six percent higher in 1972 than the national average, and this is roughly the same as in most of the surrounding states in the East North Central region. The Michigan (Detroit) price level is considerably higher than in the South and Southwest--28 percent higher than in Georgia and 19 percent higher than in Arizona. However, the price level differential is not sufficiently large to account for the size of the gap between nominal wages in Michigan manufacturing and in the rest of the nation.

Moreover, much of the difference in price levels between states appears to be caused by the much lower price

TABLE 4.5
PRICE INDICES IN 1972 FOR SELECTED REGIONS AND STATES (U.S.=100)

REGION	PRICE INDEX
East North Central	105
Michigan	106
Ohio	106
Indiana	100
Illinois	107
Wisconsin	104
West North Central	98
Minnesota	98
Middle Atlantic	115
New York	124
Pennsylvania	103
New England	103
Massachusetts	105
South Atlantic	89
Georgia	83
East South Central	88
Alabama	86
West South Central	88
Texas	87
Mountain	88
Arizona	89
Pacific	103
California	104
Washington	105

Source: V. Fuchs, R.Michael, and S. Scott, "A State Price Index," National Bureau of Economic Research Working Paper No. 320, February 1979.

TABLE 4.6
INDICES OF COMPARATIVE COSTS ON AN INTERMEDIATE BUDGET FOR A 4-PERSON FAMILY, 1979

Urban U.S.	100
Metropolitan	102
Non-Metropolitan	91
Northeast	
Boston	119
Buffalo	106
New York	116
Philadelphia	104
Pittsburgh	97
Non-Metropolitan	101
North Central	
Chicago	100
Cincinnati	99
Cleveland	102
Detroit	101
Kansas City	96
Milwaukee	104
Minneapolis	104
St. Louis	97
Non-Metropolitan	92
South	
Atlanta	92
Baltimore	99
Dallas	89
Houston	93
Washington, D.C.	108
Non-Metropolitan	85
West	
Denver	100
Los Angeles	97
San Diego	98
San Francisco	105
Seattle	101
Non-Metropolitan	94

Source: U.S.B.L.S., *Handbook of Labor Statistics*, 1980, Table 154.

levels in rural areas, especially those in the South. Table 4.6 shows comparable cost-of-living indices for several large SMSAs and nonmetropolitan areas (cities with populations between 2,000 and 50,000). The price level in Detroit is only 9 percent higher than that in Atlanta, 13 percent higher than prices in Dallas. It is comparable with other areas in the Midwest and those in the West and much lower than most cities in the Northeast.

Thus, the high wage levels indicated in Tables 4.2 and 4.4 are high in real as well as nominal terms. For example, the average unskilled plant worker in Detroit earns 131/86 = 1.52 of what he/she could earn in Atlanta. By Table 4.6 prices in Detroit are 101/92 = 1.10 of their value in Atlanta, so the average Detroit worker earns 1.52/1.10 = 1.38 in real terms times what an Atlanta worker earns. Put differently, the unskilled Atlantan earns 28 percent less than his/her Detroit counterpart.

The price indices in Table 4.6 take account of variations in local taxes, but neither they nor the various wage indices include fringe benefits. In the aggregate, wages and salaries are only about 75 percent of total labor costs, and fringe benefits (holidays, private retirement programs, insurance, etc.) paid by employers 20 percent of total compensation (slightly more for nonoffice than for office workers and in manufacturing than in nonmanufacturing). Unfortunately, data on variations in the fringe/wage ratio across areas are not available--in particular, its value in Michigan relative to the rest of the country. We do, however, know that fringe benefits as a fraction of total compensation are greater for union than for nonunion workers and for high wage than for low wage workers.[2] Michigan is obviously a high wage state, and the extent of collective bargaining is as high in Michigan as any state in the country (involving 47 percent of production workers versus 36 percent for the entire U.S.).[3] The ratio of fringe benefits to wage rates, f, is about six percentage points higher for union than for nonunion workers, which would imply that average compensation in Michigan relative to the U.S. as a whole may be about a half of one percent higher than the ratio of Michigan to U.S. wage rates.

ANALYSIS OF MICROECONOMIC DATA

It is possible that observed high wage rates in Michigan reflect differences in worker quality. Specifically, workers in Michigan may be inherently better workers than those in most other states and would earn 15-30 percent more than the national average wherever they lived and worked. This hypothesis is obviously inconsistent with the fallout model; although Michigan workers receive a higher average wage than elsewhere, they are, by what I shall call the _quality model_, worth it.

To test this hypothesis it is necessary to have data on the joint distribution of wage rates and individual characteristics of workers by area. The best data set for this purpose is the May Current Population Survey of the U.S. Census, which I use for the years 1973 through 1976 inclusive. This data set permits the identification of all those individuals residing in thirty-four SMSAs, including Detroit. The hourly wage rate for each person in the sample is the ratio of usual weekly earnings divided by usual weekly hours. The sample of full-time workers is split into four groups: a) men paid on a hourly basis; b) hourly women; c) salaried men; and d) salaried women.

To adjust for quality and other factors, I related the (logarithm of the) wage rate of each individual in each of the four groups to a set of skill, race, monopoly and locational variables. These included:

skill

- -years of schooling
- -years of potential labor market experience
- -experience squared

monopoly

- -membership in a trade union
- -holding a public job
- -public employee union member

race

-black
-other nonwhite

locational

-thirty-three "dummy" variables for residence in each SMSA (Detroit the comparison group)

In the full model, as opposed to the basic model, I also included dummy variables for the occupation and industry in which the person holds a job.

The coefficient on each of the thirty-three locational variables can be interpreted as the estimated proportionate difference between the wage rate in that SMSA and its value in Detroit, holding constant education, experience, race, union membership, and public employment.[4] The results for the four groups of full-time workers are shown in Table 4.7. These coefficients may be interpreted as follows: private sector nonunion male hourly workers in the New York SMSA earn approximately 0.109 less than equivalent workers (same education, experience and race) in Detroit. This is the -0.109 coefficient in the first row and first column of Table 4.7. (The exact estimate is 1-exp(-0.109) = 10.3 percent less.) When additional adjustment is made for occupation and industry, New Yorkers earn approximately 0.116 less (exactly 1-exp(0.116) = 11.0 percent less).

The important point is that Detroit wages are still substantially higher than those in most other large metropolitan areas of the U.S., even after adjusting for the other variables that influence individual wages. The SMSAs that are exceptions to this rule include Nassau-Suffolk (which to some extent reflects the fact that persons with unusually high earnings in New York City flee to the suburbs), the District of Columbia (which is dominated by a unique very high wage industry, the federal government), and the San Francisco-Oakland-San Jose area.

The estimates in Table 4.7 do not take account of the impact of unionization on wages, and there is a fairly large union/nonunion differential for hourly workers in the U.S.

ESTIMATED LOGARITHMIC DIFFERENCE BETWEEN WAGE LEVELS IN 34 SMSAs AND DETROIT FOR FULL-TIME HOULY AND SALARIED WORKERS, BY SEX, 1973-76

	HOURLY				SALARIED			
	Men		Women		Men		Women	
	Basic	Full	Basic	Full	Basic	Full	Basic	Full
East								
1. New York	-.109	-.116	.031	-.049	-.144	-.104	-.005	-.015
4. Philadelphia	-.082	-.116	-.071	-.180	-.128	-.117	-.160	-.172
8. Boston	-.103	-.146	-.016	-.020	-.158	-.129	-.077	-.090
9. Nassau-Suffolk	.020	-.033	.008	-.088	-.033	.002	-.046	-.047
10. Pittsburgh	-.183	-.187	-.172	-.129	-.188	-.164	-.172	-.184
15. Newark	-.110	-.124	-.087	-.078	-.094	-.086	-.139	-.140
23. Paterson	-.048	-.085	.010	-.118	.016	.032	-.033	-.025
25. Buffalo	-.161	-.143	-.098	-.149	-.230	-.200	-.264	-.248
Midwest								
3. Chicago	-.009	-.036	.018	-.026	-.056	-.034	-.049	-.066
5. Detroit	.000	.000	.000	.000	.000	.000	.000	.000
11. St. Louis	-.058	-.088	-.096	-.121	-.117	-.120	-.178	-.172
13. Cleveland	-.075	-.097	-.097	-.149	-.081	-.072	-.164	-.160
16. Minneapolis	.000	-.038	-.025	-.087	-.059	-.044	-.137	-.143
20. Milwaukee	-.038	-.051	-.021	-.022	-.089	-.081	-.117	-.135
22. Cincinatti	-.119	-.145	-.096	-.202	-.227	-.209	-.261	-.234
27. Kansas City	-.083	-.107	-.132	-.166	-.192	-.168	-.226	-.211
30. Indianapolis	-.080	-.116	-.068	-.054	-.127	-.124	-.214	-.201
South								
7. District of Columbia	.071	-.012	.003	-.015	.018	.007	-.032	-.135
12. Baltimore	-.070	-.116	-.038	-.050	-.151	-.138	-.150	-.146
14. Houston	-.031	-.120	-.167	-.116	-.060	-.057	-.215	-.216
17. Dallas	-.168	-.202	-.098	-.189	-.115	-.103	-.239	-.218
21. Atlanta	-.073	-.111	-.040	-.142	-.112	-.096	-.126	-.130
26. Miami	-.149	-.179	-.141	-.132	-.285	-.232	-.190	-.179
32. New Orleans	-.115	-.190	-.227	-.144	-.142	-.140	-.290	-.274
33. Tampa	-.249	-.283	-.216	-.264	-.300	-.278	-.308	-.290
West								
2. Los Angeles	-.103	-.109	-.015	-.076	-.115	-.087	-.087	-.050
6. San Fransisco	.024	.020	.034	.061	-.089	-.058	-.044	-.049
18. Seattle	-.066	-.077	-.075	-.094	-.093	-.082	-.169	-.135
19. Anaheim	-.053	-.073	-.060	.004	-.069	-.063	-.120	-.128
24. San Diego	-.089	-.127	-.105	-.079	-.187	-.168	-.158	-.149
28. Denver	-.028	-.083	-.081	-.082	-.144	-.141	-.143	-.133
29. San Bernadino	-.071	-.099	-.146	-.175	-.212	-.059	-.227	-.186
31. San Jose	.011	-.003	.017	.053	-.071	-.076	-.061	-.045
34. Portland	-.067	-.075	-.074	.000	-.182	-.146	-.163	-.131
All SMSAs	-.065	-.091	-.054	-.075	-.106	-.087	-.105	-.106
Inter-Area Variation	.060	.059	.065	.067	.066	.059	.080	.074

From the basic model, the estimated percentage wage advantage of unionized workers is 28.7 percent for hourly males and 20.2 percent for hourly females, but it is 1.9 and 8.1 percent for salaried males and females, respectively. As seen in Table 4.8, hourly workers in Detroit are more likely than the average of the thirty-four SMSAs to be unionized. Thus, for hourly males the average wage in Detroit is 0.287 x (0.73-0.56) = 0.048, or an additional five percent, higher due to unionism than it is for the average of all 34 SMSAs. For hourly females, the average wage is 0.202 x (0.37-0.17) = 0.040 or 4 percent higher. In addition, 53 percent of full-time workers in Detroit are paid on an hourly basis as compared to only 43 percent for all SMSAs.

The estimates of wage rates in Detroit are, like the more aggregative data, consistent with the fallout model of wage determination. There is more unionization in Detroit than in most other cities, and nonunion wages (including the wages of those workers who are paid on a salaried basis) are higher than in most other cities. It would be tempting, therefore, to conclude that this is the end of the story and let matters rest. However, a closer look at Tables 4.7 and 4.8 reveals some facts that do not fit. Specifically, if nonunion wages in Detroit are high because of fallout from the large, unionized high wage sector, we should observe that nonunion wages are high in other highly unionized cities. This is true, as pointed out above, in San Francisco and Washington (where the federal government employment rather than unionism is the driving force). It should <u>also</u> be true in Pittsburgh, Buffalo, St. Louis, Cleveland, Milwaukee and Seattle, for these areas all have high rates of unionization of hourly male workers. However, only Milwaukee has a nonunion wage level in excess of the national average, and Buffalo and Cleveland have very low nonunion wage levels.

Thus, when one takes into account wage rates in other areas, the fallout model does not appear to apply

TABLE 4.8

PERCENTAGE OF PRIVATE AND PUBLIC SECTOR EMPLOYEES WHO ARE UNION MEMBERS BY SMSA, 1973-1976

REGION	PRIVATE HOURLY		TOTAL PRIVATE	FREEMAN-MEDOFF	PUBLIC
	Male	Female			
East					
1. New York	65	46	35	32	66
4. Philadelphia	55	32	29	28	44
8. Boston	38	15	18	17	53
9. Nassau-Suffolk	55	26	29	25	61
10. Pittsburgh	74	30	45	35	36
15. Newark	61	46	33	28	41
23. Paterson	58	38	32	29	31
25. Buffalo	70	25	42	36	47
Midwest					
3. Chicago	64	26	32	28	39
5. Detroit	73	37	40	34	65
11. St. Louis	75	29	38	33	20
13. Cleveland	67	26	36	30	39
16. Minneapolis	57	29	29	24	36
20. Milwaukee	65	28	35	29	53
22. Cincinnati	53	10	28	23	24
27. Kansas City	60	22	31	25	25
30. Indianapolis	59	19	29	26	32
South					
7. D.C.	36	16	16	12	13
12. Baltimore	53	17	27	25	36
14. Houston	32	7	14	14	18
17. Dallas	24	10	11	9	9
21. Atlanta	26	12	11	13	3
26. Miami	29	11	15	16	31
32. New Orleans	39	13	17	16	21
33. Tampa	16	12	9	8	10
West					
2. Los Angeles	48	23	24	23	32
6. San Francisco	68	39	40	33	35
18. Seattle	65	36	37	32	31
19. Anaheim	41	17	20	21	19
24. San Diego	53	17	25	22	31
28. Denver	42	13	19	15	18
29. San Bernadino	59	8	31	25	19
31. San Jose	51	22	25	22	36
34. Portland	62	22	29	25	38
All 34 SMSAs	56	17	28	--	37

TABLE 4.9
MEDIAN ANNUAL EARNINGS IN 1969 OF YEAR-ROUND MALE OPERATIVES IN SELECTED INDUSTRIES IN THE U.S., MICHIGAN, AND FOUR MICHIGAN SMSAs

	ALL U.S. (dollars)	RELATIVE TO U.S.				
		Michigan	Detroit	Flint	Grand Rapids	Lansing
MANUFACTURING	7623	1.15	1.22	1.17	1.05	1.19
Durable Goods	7547	1.16	1.23	1.19	1.07	1.20
Wood & Furniture	5709	1.29	1.48	--	1.50	--
Primary Metals	7928	1.07	1.19	--	1.03	1.14
Fabricated Metals	7270	1.15	1.21	--	1.10	--
Machinery	7762	1.18	1.29	1.13	0.99	1.10
Motor Vehicles	8578	1.05	1.06	1.06	1.00	1.09
Other Transport.	8081	1.10	1.46	--	0.96	--
Non-Durable Goods	7753	1.14	1.18	1.14	1.09	1.15
Food	7070	1.22	1.26	--	1.05	1.29
Apparel	5418	1.46	1.37	--	--	--
Paper	7863	1.11	1.09	--	0.98	--
Chemicals	8488	1.10	1.10	--	0.95	--
NON-MANUFACTURING	6864	1.17	1.28	1.17	1.14	1.18
Transp. & Pub. Uts.	7644	1.11	1.08	--	--	--
Trade	6414	1.19	1.35	1.25	1.20	--

Source: U.S. Census, 1970, Occupational Characteristics, PC(2)-7A, Table 15, and Detailed Characteristics: Michigan, Table 175.

TABLE 4.10
MEDIAN ANNUAL EARNINGS IN 1969 OF YEAR-ROUND MALE WORKERS IN SELECTED OCCUPATIONS IN THE U.S., MICHIGAN, AND FOUR MICHIGAN SMSAs

OCCUPATION	ALL U.S. (dollars)	RELATIVE TO U.S.				
		Michigan	Detroit	Flint	Grand Rapids	Lansing
Accountants	11226	1.11	1.16	1.15	1.04	1.04
Draftsmen & Surveyors	9106	1.31	1.44	1.34	0.99	1.18
Buyers & Sales Mgrs.	11592	1.12	1.21	1.04	1.04	1.02
Managers, Trade	10346	1.16	1.28	1.19	1.14	1.08
Insurance Agents	10509	1.12	1.14	1.23	1.12	1.22
Bank Tellers	5911	1.05	1.13	0.92	0.76	1.23
Bookkeepers	7912	1.20	1.26	1.34	1.14	1.24
Apparel Craftsmen	6934	1.22	1.26	--	1.22	--
Cabinetmakers	7133	1.13	1.31	--	1.08	--
Auto Mechanics	7420	1.23	1.34	1.28	1.17	1.26
Radio & TV Mechs.	7918	1.10	1.23	1.18	1.00	1.03
Compositors & Type Set.	8774	1.13	1.27	1.32	1.01	1.18
Sanitary Engineers	9032	1.23	1.37	1.23	1.08	1.07
Assemblers	7516	1.10	1.10	1.13	1.03	1.14
Laundry Ops.	5661	1.18	1.16	--	--	--
Butchers	7992	1.08	1.15	1.05	1.10	1.08
Bus Drivers	7787	1.11	1.22	--	0.94	--
Truckdrivers	7674	1.20	1.29	1.20	1.20	1.16
Construction Laborers	6199	1.35	1.50	1.50	1.23	1.39
Material Handelers	6436	1.16	1.22	1.30	1.09	1.21
Cleaning Service	5583	1.24	1.34	1.37	1.14	1.17

Source: See Table 4.9.

universally. For this reason I am reluctant to conclude that the fallout hypothesis is <u>the</u> explanation of the high wage levels in southeastern Michigan. In order to have complete confidence in it, I would have to be able to explain why it appears to work in some areas but not in others. This task will require further research.

ANALYSIS OF 1970 CENSUS DATA

A final data set that can be used to estimate the U.S./ Michigan relative wage comes from the 1970 U.S. Census. These data have the advantage of being very extensive. Their disadvantage is that the published data are in terms of annual earnings for 1969 rather than hourly wages. To get around this problem, I confine attention to the annual earning of males who worked 50 to 52 weeks in 1969. Most of these individuals also worked full-time throughout the year, so, except for variations in the normal work week, and in overtime hours, annual labor earnings are a good proxy for relative earnings.

In Table 4.9 the annual earnings of operatives (semi-skilled) in several manufacturing and two nonmanufacturing industries for Michigan as a whole and in the four Michigan SMSAs with population in excess of 250,000 relative to their U.S.-wide values are reported. The relative manufacturing wages are somewhat lower than those for 1970. For example, the overall manufacturing wage in Michigan was 24 percent above the national average; for operatives in 1969 relative earnings in Michigan were only 15 percent above the U.S. average. This probably reflects a greater relative use of skilled labor in Michigan than elsewhere.

Table 4.9 does, however, show that "raw" labor in both manufacturing and nonmanufacturing industries is 15 to 20 percent more expensive in the high-wage section of Michigan, and it is 5 to 10 percent more expensive even in Grand Rapids, the one large SMSA in Michigan that is not characterized by a very high wage level. It is also interesting that operative wages are as high relative to the

U.S. average in nondurable goods and nonmanufacturing industries as they are in durable goods.

Table 4.10 provides the same type of data for a wide range of occupational categories. These results confirm the general impression that the high wage structure in southeastern Michigan is not confined to blue collar unionists in motor vehicles and allied industries. High wages, even for white collar jobs, seem to permeate the economy.

NOTES, CHAPTER 4

[1]For evidence on this point see Lawrence Kahn and Stuart Low, "The Relative Effects of Employment and Unemployed Job Search," Review of Economics and Statistics, forthcoming.

[2]See R. B. Freeman, "The Effect of Trade Unionism on Fringe Benefits," National Bureau of Economic Research, Working Paper No. 292, October 1978.

[3]See R. B. Freeman and J. L. Medoff, "New Estimates of Private Sector Unionism in the U.S.," Industrial and Labor Relations Review, January 1979.

[4]For technical details of the adjustment procedure, see my "Inter-Metropolitan Wage Differentials in the U.S.," mimeo, 1981.

Chapter 5

Costs of Social Insurance Programs

by

Cynthia Rence

Michigan State University

INTRODUCTION[1]

There are three major social insurance programs for which the majority of employers in Michigan and other states are legally required to make contributions: Old Age, Survivors, Disability, and Health Insurance (OASDHI), Unemployment Insurance (UI), and Workers' Compensation (WC). This chapter analyzes interstate differentials in the employer costs of UI and WC, the two state-administered programs. There are many important issues with respect to the adequacy and equity of social insurance benefits; these and other questions regarding social insurance are beyond the scope of this paper.

In recent years there has been a tremendous amount of concern about the high employer costs associated with Michigan's UI and WC programs. Much of the concern centers around the alleged effects of UI and WC costs on plant location decisions: therefore, it is useful to compare Michigan UI and WC costs relative to payrolls with those costs in other states. The next two sections of this chapter will compare Michigan's UI and WC costs with employer costs for a group of competing states. The comparison states which are used are: California, Illinois, Indiana, New York, Ohio, Pennsylvania, and Wisconsin. This chapter examines factors which contribute to the interstate UI and WC cost differentials. In December 1980, both the UI and WC laws in Michigan were amended, and the expected effects of those amendments on Michigan costs are discussed. This chapter explores how UI costs in Michigan could be lowered by changing the experience-rating system for UI taxes, and how WC costs could be lowered while increasing benefits for the severely and totally disabled.

UNEMPLOYMENT INSURANCE

The Unemployment Insurance system in the U.S. is composed of separate state programs with federal standards which were initially set in the 1935 Social Security Act. Unemployment Insurance benefits in the U.S. are financed almost entirely out of taxes paid directly by employers.[2] In this chapter the employer's entire contribution into the UI system is treated as a business cost for the employer, and questions of the incidence of the UI tax are ignored.[3]

The costs of UI for employers vary considerably across states for a number of important reasons. The level and structure of benefits are determined by the different state laws, and eligibility rules vary considerably across states affecting state UI costs. Perhaps the most important source of interstate UI cost differences is the fact that insured unemployment rates vary considerably across states. These sources of interstate cost differences are analyzed in the next section after analyzing the magnitude of the interstate differences. Since the Michigan UI statute was amended in December 1980, it is the costs and characteristics of the old law which will be compared with the group of seven competing states. A later section will examine the potential effects of the new law.

Employer Costs Relative to Payrolls

Employer UI costs are given in Table 5.1 for Michigan and the seven comparison states using tax collection rates which are contributions as a percentage of the total rather than taxable payrolls. Tax collection rates varied for this group of states from 0.79 in Indiana to a high of 1.68 in California in 1978. During 1978 Michigan's tax collection rate was the second highest for this group of states with contributions equal to 1.65 percent of total payrolls, however, the Michigan rate only exceeded the U.S. average by 0.30 percent of total payrolls. Michigan's 1978 rate exceeded the Indiana contributions by only 0.86 percent of total payrolls. Michigan was a relatively high UI cost state in 1978, however, the magnitude of the interstate differences in tax collection rates is actually quite small.

As can be seen in Table 5.1 state UI contribution rates can not be represented solely by a secular trend. Rather, there is a considerable amount of cyclical fluctuation in tax collection rates. State UI tax collections are adjusted to cover the cost of benefits over a period of years rather than on an annual basis. Reserve funds are used by the states to enable them to reduce the year-to-year fluctuations in tax rates. States with high tax collection rates are states which have had high benefit outlays in the past or which expect to have relatively high future benefit outlays. Tax contribution rates rose during the 1970s for this group of eight states, and net reserves in the state UI funds declined considerably for many of these states between the end of 1969 and the end of 1978. Michigan's average tax rate was exceeded by three of the comparison states in the 1960s and only one in the 1970s. Using this group of states one may conclude that Michigan was a relatively high UI cost state in the 1970s, but the Michigan average exceeded the Indiana tax collection rate by substantially less than 1 percent of payroll.

Sources of Difference Among State UI Costs

Two major groups of factors contribute to interstate differences in UI costs: (1) economic factors such as unemployment rates and industry mix, and (2) provisions of state UI laws. Interstate differences in the administration of the UI laws may also have important effects on UI costs. However, it is difficult to measure administrative factors, and no attempt is made in this chapter to examine administrative policies or administrative costs.

States with high levels of unemployment tend to have relatively high benefits which lead to high UI costs. Regressing benefit cost rates on insured unemployment rates (IUR) and a constant term for all fifty states (plus D.C. and Puerto Rico), yields an estimated coefficient on

TABLE 5.1
UNEMPLOYMENT INSURANCE TAX COLLECTION RATES

YEAR	MICHIGAN	AVG.U.S.	CALIFORNIA	ILLINOIS	INDIANA	NEW YORK	OHIO	PENNSYLVANIA	WISCONSIN
1960	1.58	1.17	1.36	1.12	0.75	1.30	0.86	1.79	0.83
1961	1.54	1.23	1.36	1.14	0.66	1.57	0.79	1.88	0.90
1962	1.53	1.39	1.91	1.19	0.75	1.84	1.12	1.89	0.82
1963	1.63	1.35	1.91	1.09	0.69	1.74	1.09	1.79	0.87
1964	1.50	1.27	1.84	0.99	0.66	1.40	1.41	1.83	0.82
1965	1.22	1.18	1.75	0.70	0.60	1.48	1.22	1.78	0.86
1966	1.13	1.07	1.72	0.42	0.64	1.26	1.04	1.62	0.85
1967	0.83	0.89	1.60	0.22	0.60	0.93	0.67	1.42	0.85
1968	0.65	0.77	1.53	0.13	0.54	0.89	0.47	0.83	0.86
1969	0.65	0.70	1.32	0.18	0.51	0.76	0.38	0.72	0.81
1970	0.61	0.65	1.22	0.22	0.45	0.68	0.39	0.66	0.73
1971	0.63	0.65	1.06	0.34	0.41	0.79	0.38	0.69	0.64
1972	1.31	0.85	1.36	0.66	0.50	1.02	0.52	0.77	0.76
1973	1.25	0.98	1.45	1.00	0.55	1.22	0.72	1.04	0.81
1974	1.07	0.94	1.24	0.85	0.51	1.21	0.61	1.14	0.89
1975	1.04	0.90	1.30	0.46	0.49	1.15	0.56	1.18	0.87
1976	1.47	1.16	1.83	0.72	0.74	1.26	0.84	1.20	1.39
1977	1.61	1.27	1.90	1.07	0.73	1.23	1.03	1.22	1.56
1978	1.65	1.35	1.68	1.36	0.79	1.45	1.22	1.48	1.63

Notes: Tax collection rate is contributions collected as a percentage of total payroll in covered employment.

Sources: U.S. Department of Labor, Employment and Training Administration, Handbook of Unemployment Insurance Financial Data 1938-1976, Washington, D.C., 1978

U.S.Department of Labor, Employment and Training Administration, "Unemployment Insurance Program Letter No.32-79; Unemployment Insurance Financial Developments For Calendar Year 1977," Washington, D.C., July, 1979.

U.S. Department of Labor, Employment and Training Administration, "Unemployment Insurance Program Letter 41-80; Unemployment Insurance Financial Developments for Calendar Year 1978," Washington, D.C., July 1980. (Column 15)

IUR = 0.23 for 1976 (standard error = 0.02, R^2 = 0.73), for 1977 a coefficient on IUR = 0.25 (standard error = 0.02, R^2 = 0.80), and for 1978 a coefficient on IUR = 0.32 (standard error = 0.02, R^2 = 0.88).[4] Among the eight states included in Table 5.1, Michigan had the highest IUR between 1970 and 1979 and the second highest tax contribution rate.

Michigan's relatively high employer UI costs are not a result of relatively generous weekly benefit provisions. Table 5.2 shows minimum and maximum weekly benefits for Michigan and the seven comparison states for January 1981 and January 1978. Michigan has a relatively low minimum benefit in both years. Allowing for the maximum dependents' allowance the Michigan 1978 maximum weekly benefit is the fourth highest, and the 1981 maximum benefit is the sixth highest. For an individual without dependents the 1978 and 1981 Michigan maximum benefits are the seventh highest. The Michigan UI program in 1978 had relatively low statutory benefit levels, and it covered workers with higher average wages. Using benefits for a worker earning the state average wage, the ratio of benefits to wages in Michigan only exceeds Indiana benefits.

In addition to weekly benefit levels, potential duration of benefits can affect UI cost differentials. Duration provisions do not appear to be a major source of the high UI costs experienced in Michigan during the 1970s. Table 5.2 also shows statutory provisions concerning potential duration, and average potential duration for 1978 claimants. Michigan's duration provisions are less generous than four of the comparison states, and 1978 potential duration for claimants was less than that in five of the states.

Most private sector nonagricultural wage and salary workers are covered by state UI laws, and federal amendments in 1970 and 1976 require that many previously excluded agricultural and domestic workers are now covered by state UI laws.[5] There is very little variation across states in

TABLE 5.2

UNEMPLOYMENT INSURANCE WEEKLY BENEFITS AND POTENTIAL DURATION

STATE	UNEMPLOYMENT INSURANCE WEEKLY BENEFITS				BENEFITS FOR AVERAGE WAGE WORKER			1978 WEEKS POTENTIAL DURATION		
	Jan. 1981		Jan. 1978		1978 Avg. Weekly Wage	1978 Benefits Of Earned Avg. Wage	Benefits as % of Average Wage	Min.	Max.	Average for Claimants
	Min.	Max.	Min.	Max.						
Michigan	$16-18	$97-136	$16-18	$97-136	$288.96	$97	34	11	26	22.7
California	30	120	30	104	243.15	104	43	12	26	23.7
Illinois	43	142-189	15	116-138	259.54	116	45	26	26	26.0
Indiana	40	84-141	35	74-124	242.65	74	30	4	26	19.4
New York	25	125	25	115	259.47	115	44	26	26	26.0
Ohio	10	136-215	10-16	111-175	255.64	111	43	20	26	25.6
Pennsylvania	35-40	175-183	13-18	143-151	233.96	122	52	30	30	30.0
Wisconsin	31	166	25	135	228.46	114	50	1-13	34	22.1

Notes: All minimums amd maximums are from Significant Provisions. The range of benefits for minimums and maximums is due to dependents' allowances. Average weekly wage is average weekly total wages in covered payroll. Unemployment insurance benefit for 1978 is calculated assuming no dependents. Potential duration minimum and maximum for January 1981 are basically the same as 1978, except that the Pennsylvania schedule is no longer uniform and has a 26 week minimum.

Sources: U.S. Department of Labor, Employment and Training Administration, Significant Provisions of the State Unemployment Insurance Laws, Washington, D.C., January and July 1978, and January 1981.

U.S. Department of Labor, Employment and Training Administration, Handbook of Unemployment Insurance Financial Data 1938-1976, Washington, D.C., 1978.

U.S. Department of Labor, Employment and Training Administration, "Unemployment Insurance Program Letter No. 32-79; Unemployment Insurance Financial Developments for Calendar Year 1977," Washington, D.C., July 1979.

U.S. Department of Labor, Employment and Training Administration, "Unemployment Insurance Financial Developments for Calendar Year 1978," Washington, D.C., July 1980. (Columns 6, 27)

the coverage of UI laws, and it would be quite difficult to attribute interstate variations in costs to differences in coverage.

Although most wage and salary workers are covered by UI laws, many unemployed workers are ineligible for UI benefits. Eligibility rules vary considerably across states, and may contribute to interstate cost differentials. An unemployed individual must have a recent history of employment in a covered job to be eligible for UI benefits. New entrants to the labor force are automatically excluded from all UI programs, and a large portion of reentrants are also excluded. Between 1970 and 1978, an average of 41.5 percent of unemployed individuals in the U.S. were entrants or reentrants.[6]

It is quite likely that one factor contributing to Michigan's relatively high costs is the lenient qualifying formula used for UI as of January 1981. The state UI plans have qualifying requirements in terms of weeks of employment or earnings, and many workers are unable to meet these requirements due to the brevity of their recent employment. Table 5.3 shows qualifying requirements. Seven of the states require a certain level of base-period wages as a condition for receiving minimum UI benefits. The Michigan formula is the least stringent in terms of base period wages.

An unemployed individual who satisfies the base-period requirement may be disqualified from UI benefits if the individual: (1) is unable to work, (2) is not available for work or not seeking work, (3) refuses to accept suitable work, (4) voluntarily quit his or her most recent job without good cause, (5) was discharged for misconduct, or (6) is unemployed due to a labor dispute. Some of the disqualifications differ considerably across states affecting the number of unemployed workers who can receive benefits.

Among the eight states, the New York and Michigan ability and availability for work provisions appear to be the most lenient, because the individual is only required to

TABLE 5.3
QUALIFYING REQUIREMENTS FOR UNEMPLOYMENT INSURANCE ELIGIBILITY
JANUARY 1981

STATE	BASE PERIOD	QUALIFYING WEEKS EMPLOYMENT	BASE PERIOD WAGES FOR MINIMUM BENEFIT	HIGH QUARTER WAGES FOR MINIMUM BENEFIT	QUALIFYING FORMULA
Michigan	last 52 weeks	14 weeks	$350.14	--	14 weeks at $25.01 or more
California	4 quarters ending 4-7 months before claim	--	$900.00	--	$900 in base period
Illinois	4 quarters ending 4-7 months before claim	--	$1400.00	--	$1400, $385 outside high quarter
Indiana	1st 4 of last 5 quarters	--	$1500.00	--	1.25 x high quarter wage, not less than $1500, $900 in last 2 quarters of base period
New York	last 52 weeks	20 weeks	$800.00	--	20 weeks at $40 or more
Ohio	last 52 weeks	20 weeks	$400.00	--	20 weeks at $20 or more
Pennsylvania	1st 4 of last 5 quarters	--	$1320.00	$800.00	$800 high quarter and $1320 base period, with at least 20% of base period wage outside high quarter
Wisconsin	last 52 weeks	15 weeks	--	--	15 weeks, average wage $58.01 or more with one employer

Sources: U.S. Department of Labor, Employment and Training Administration, Significant Provisions of State Unemployment Insurance Laws, Washington, D.C., January 1981.

U.S. Department of Labor, Employment and Training Administration, Comparison of State Unemployment Insurance Laws, Washington, D.C., 1980, Tables 300 and 301.

be available for work similar to the worker's usual occupation. However, it is quite difficult to assess the operational differences in search and availability requirements, because of variations in administrative practices defining "suitable" or "similar" work or "active" search.[7]

Table 5.4 summarizes four types of disqualifications from UI benefits. Workers who voluntarily leave their jobs are treated generously in Michigan. Michigan postpones benefits for thirteen weeks rather than the duration of unemployment, and allowing the long-term unemployed who quit their jobs to receive UI benefits contributes to the relatively high costs of the Michigan program. Michigan's disqualifications for refusal of suitable work and for misconduct discharges are also relatively brief, thereby contributing to relatively higher UI costs in Michigan.

The relatively high UI costs in Michigan cannot be attributed to generous weekly benefit amounts nor to the duration of UI benefits. Michigan's eligibility rules, including the base-period qualifying formula and the disqualifications shown in Table 5.4, are factors contributing to the relatively high UI costs in Michigan. However, the major factor contributing to high UI costs is the high level of unemployment in Michigan.

Expected Effects of December 1980 Statutory Changes

The legislature of Michigan amended the Michigan Employment Security Act, the state's Unemployment Insurance Law, in December 1980.[8] The provisions in these amendments became effective on March 1, 1981, and many of these statutory changes could have substantial effects on Michigan UI costs relative to the seven comparison states.

The eligibility rules existing prior to March 1981 contributed to high UI costs relative to the other states, and many of these rules were changed. The new qualifying requirement for UI benefits stipulates eighteen weeks of covered employment at a weekly wage equal to twenty times

TABLE 5.4
DISQUALIFICATIONS FROM UNEMPLOYMENT INSURANCE BENEFITS
OCTOBER 1980

STATE	REFUSAL OF SUITABLE WORK	VOLUNTARILY LEAVING JOB	MISCONDUCT CHARGE	UNEMPLOYMENT CAUSED BY LABOR DISPUTE
Michigan	6 weeks	13 weeks	13 weeks	S
California	1-9 weeks	D	D	S
Illinois	10 weeks*	12 weeks*	10 weeks*	S
Indiana	D	D	D	S
New York	D	D	D	7 weeks
Ohio	D	D	D	S
Pennsylvania	D	D	D	S
Wisconsin	D	D	3 weeks	S

Notes: Benefits postponed for fixed number of weeks or variable number, duration of unemployment (D), or during unemployment due to labor dispute (S). Many states which postpone benefits for the duration require a minimum amount of earnings or weeks of employment in order to make the individual eligible again for unemployment insurance benefits. These disqualification provisions are more complicated than what is given in this table. The reader is referred to the data source for more complete explanations of the disqualification. Good causes for voluntarily leaving a job are discussed in the data source.

*Illinois requires that some individuals have their benefits postponed for the duration of unemployment rather than for the fixed number of weeks given.

Source: U.S. Department of Labor, Employment and Training Administration, Comparison of State Unemployment Insurance Laws, Washington, D.C., 1980, Tables 401, 402, 404.

the minimum wage, which yields a base-period wage requirement of $1,206 ($3.35 x 20 hours for 18 weeks). This represents a 344 percent increase in the base-period wage requirement, and it makes the Michigan requirement the fourth most stringent rather than the least stringent (see Table 5.3). Unemployed workers who worked less than twenty hours per week during the base period are now required to earn in excess of the minimum wage to qualify for UI in Michigan. The disqualifications for voluntarily leaving a job or a misconduct discharge are now for the duration of unemployment rather than merely postponing benefits for thirteen weeks. The Michigan treatment of these two disqualifications is no longer the most lenient of the eight states, instead Michigan's treatment of these cases is now similar to the majority of the comparison states. These more stringent eligibility rules will decrease the number of people eligible for UI benefits and lower Michigan UI costs.

It should be noted that the December 1980 amendments still allow individuals who refuse suitable work to receive benefits after they are postponed for six weeks. The majority of the comparison states have a more stringent treatment of this disqualification, and it would lower Michigan UI costs if the refusal resulted in a disqualification for the duration of unemployment.

The old benefit formula effective January 1981 set weekly benefits at 60 percent of the claimant's average weekly gross income up to $97, plus dependents' allowances.[9] The 1980 amendments eliminated the dependents' allowances and changed the benefit formula to 70 percent of average weekly net income. The maximum weekly benefit is now set at 58 percent of the state's average weekly wage, which means that the maximum as of March 1981 was $182 ($313.45 x 58 percent).[10] The new minimum benefits are higher as a result of the change in the base-period wage requirement, and the new minimum benefit is about $41 per week.[11] The March 1981 minimum and maximum are similar to those in effect in Illinois, Ohio, and Pennsylvania, and

Michigan is now a relatively high benefit state. If the new provisions had been in effect during 1978, the minimum and maximum benefits would have been approximately $40 and $150. A worker earning the average weekly wage would have been entitled to $150 which would have made Michigan a relatively high benefit state in 1978 rather than a low benefit state, as measured by the gross replacement rate for a worker earning the state's average wage.[12]

The December 1980 statutory changes should on the one hand have the effect of lowering UI costs in Michigan due to the tightening of eligibility rules, but on the other hand the liberalization of the benefit formula should increase costs. The net effect of the 1980 amendments may or may not lead to a decrease in employer UI costs. Prior to the new law Michigan was a high-cost, low-benefit state relative to the comparison states. Michigan will now be a high-benefit state even if it remains a relatively high-cost state. It must be remembered that possibly the most important factor affecting interstate cost differentials is the level of unemployment, and Michigan's high unemployment rate is unlikely to be substantially altered by changing provisions in the state UI law.

Effects of UI Laws on Unemployment Rates

State UI laws do have some effect on levels of unemployment through economic incentives affecting worker and employer behavior. Incentives affecting workers can influence the duration of unemployment and the number of people in the state's labor force. The existence of UI benefits for a firm's laid-off workers and the experience-rating of UI taxes create incentives for a firm to alter its use of temporary layoffs.

An increase in the UI benefits that increases the gross replacement rate (weekly benefits relative to gross weekly wages prior to unemployment) has both income and substitution effects on the unemployed worker's behavior. The net effect of an increase in the replacement rate has been estimated by numerous authors, and a good estimate of the net effect of a ten percent increase in the gross replacement rate is that duration of unemployment increases by about half a week when unemployment rates are relatively low.[13]

For some Michigan workers the new law provides for an increase in benefits from $97 to $182 per week in 1981. Even though unemployment rates in Michigan are currently quite high, this large increase in benefits could induce some laid off workers to stay unemployed longer than they would have at the old benefit level. It is difficult to predict how large this effect will be either in terms of Michigan's unemployment rate or employer UI costs.

The level and potential duration of UI benefits can affect how many workers are in the labor force, because a worker who is eligible for UI benefits has a strong incentive to remain in the labor force and receive those benefits rather than exiting from the labor force. This tends to increase the reported unemployment rate, but it may result in a statistical difference rather than a real change in the magnitude of the state's unemployment problem. A worker who does not have a job and is not eligible for UI benefits may become discouraged about job opportunities and give up searching for a job, in which case he or she would be counted as not in the labor force. The eligible worker, although discouraged, would continue to search in order to meet the state's job-seeking requirement for UI benefits. Both workers would like to have jobs, but the UI recipient is counted as an unemployed worker and the other individual is counted as out of the labor force.

The structure of the UI system affects the costs of temporary layoffs for firms. The existence of UI benefits lowers the firm's costs of laying off a trained employee, because the benefits increase the probability that the worker will be available to be recalled, thus protecting the firm's investment in that worker. The UI tax scheme, on the other hand, is designed to increase the costs of temporary layoffs for firms. The UI tax rate is not uniform; it is based on the employer's past unemployment experience, and temporary layoffs can result in an increase in the firm's tax rate.

Most states, including Michigan, use a reserve ratio formula to experience-rate UI taxes. Each employer has an account to which contributions are added and from which benefits to the firm's former employees are deducted, and the firm's reserve ratio is the balance in the account divided by the firm's annual payroll. Individual firm tax rates vary inversely with the firm's reserve ratio. A perfect experience-rating schedule would involve some increment in the tax rate when the reserve ratio fell and allow for decreases in the tax rate for rising reserve ratios. However, there are maximum tax rates in all states, and many states have nonzero minimum taxes. A firm paying the maximum tax rate, with a low or negative balance in its account, would incur no extra costs in the form of higher UI taxes if it laid off a large number of workers. The more perfect the experience-rating schedule is, the greater the disincentives for firms to layoff workers temporarily. Imperfect experience-rating tends to encourage layoffs, thereby increasing the amount of UI benefits paid and increasing state UI costs. Furthermore, firms that are paying the maximum UI tax ratio do not bear the full costs associated with temporary layoffs of their employees, and they are subsidized by other firms within the state with relatively low unemployment experiences.

The definition of the tax base also has an important effect on experience-rating and the employer incentives created by UI taxes. Because the taxable wage base is subject to a maximum, tax rates as a percent of total payroll have a much lower effective maximum for high-wage employers than the maximum tax as a percent of taxable payroll. UI tax rates and taxable wage bases are shown in Table 5.5 for Michigan and the seven comparison states.

Consider the following example as an illustration of the importance of the tax base in the determination of UI taxes as a percent of total payroll. Suppose three employers have the same reserve ratio in Michigan and each pay the maximum 8.5 percent tax, but one is a construction employer, the second is a service employer, and the third operates a restaurant. Assuming that each pays the average weekly wage rate for their respective industries, their effective tax rates as a percent of total payroll would be approximately: 2.9 percent in construction, 4.6 percent in service, and 8.5 percent for the restaurant.[14] An increase in the taxable wage base would decrease the cross-industry rate differentials and create stronger disincentives for high-wage employers to lay off workers.

Michigan's maximum 8.5 percent tax rate is higher than in any of the comparison states (Table 5.5), yet currently over 40 percent of Michigan's employers pay UI taxes which are less than 2 percent of taxable payroll (see Table 5.6). If the maximum tax rate was less than 8.5 percent, these low-unemployment firms would pay larger taxes, because the rate advantages enjoyed by high-unemployment firms would then be larger than they are presently. Cross industry comparisons of UI costs within Michigan could be made using average tax rates as a percentage of total payrolls, but this data is not available at the present time. The ratio of industry benefits to taxes for major industries would provide some evidence on the magnitude of the cross-industry subsidies within Michigan. A consistent pattern over time of benefit-tax ratios in excess of one would be evidence that an industry is receiving cross-industry subsidies within the state UI system. Benefit-tax ratios for Michigan are not available, however. The subsidies to high-wage, high-unemployment firms could be reduced and the experience-rating of UI taxes would be improved by: (1) lowering the minimum tax rate to zero, (2) raising the maximum tax rate, and (3) increasing the taxable wage base.[15] These changes would create stronger disincentives for employers to use temporary layoffs, and thereby tend to decrease average UI costs in Michigan.

TABLE 5.5
UNEMPLOYMENT INSURANCE TAX BASES AND RATES
JANUARY 1981

STATE	MINIMUM TAX RATE	MAXIMUM TAX RATE	TAXABLE WAGE BASE*	MAXIMUM TAX PAYMENT PER EMPLOYEE
Michigan	1.0%	8.5%	$6000	$510.00
California	.7	4.0	6000	240.00
Illinois	.4	5.3	6500	345.50
Indiana	.3	3.3	6000	198.00
New York	1.5	5.2	6000	312.00
Ohio	.8	4.5	6000	270.00
Pennsylvania	1.75	6.45	6300	406.35
Wisconsin	.5	6.5	6000	390.00

Notes: *Taxable wage base is the maximum annual wage or salary per worker on which the employer taxes are based.

Source: U.S. Department of Labor, Employment and Training Administration, Significant Provisions of State Unemployment Insurance Laws, Washington, D.C., January, 1981.

TABLE 5.6
DISTRIBUTION OF EMPLOYER ACCOUNTS
BY TAX RATE*
MICHIGAN 1980

TAX RATE INTERVAL	NUMBER OF ACCOUNTS	PERCENT OF ACCOUNTS
1.0-1.4	34,998	24.8%
1.5-1.9	21,813	15.5
2.0-2.4	9,533	6.8
2.5-2.9	13,949	9.9
3.0-3.4	6,796	4.8
3.5-3.9	7,849	5.6
4.0-4.4	4,023	2.9
4.5-4.9	3,248	2.3
5.0-5.4	4,654	3.3
5.5-5.9	6,514	4.6
6.0-6.4	4,702	3.3
6.5-6.9	7,782	5.5
7.0-7.4	4,489	3.2
7.5-7.9	1,896	1.3
8.0-8.4	1,142	.8
8.5	7,465	5.3
Total	140,853	100%

Notes: *Tax rates as a percent of taxable payroll.

Source: Michigan, Department of Labor, Michigan Empoyment Security Commission, ES-204 Experience Rating Report Rate Year 1980, Detroit, Michigan.

WORKERS' COMPENSATION

The Workers' Compensation (WC) system in the U.S. is composed of separate state programs without federal standards for those programs. WC insurance is either purchased from a private carrier or a state fund, and some states allow some firms to self-insure. The costs of WC for employers vary considerably across states for a number of reasons including the industrial mix, interstate differences in safety records, and statutory differences in WC programs. The measures of employer WC costs which are used in this chapter are intended to capture interstate differences which result from statutory factors, and sources of interstate cost differences are analyzed after examining the magnitude of the interstate differences. The Michigan WC statute was amended in December 1980; costs and provisions of the old law are compared with the group of seven competing states. A later section examines the expected effects of the new Workers' Compensation law.

Employer Costs Relative to Payrolls

Costs of WC are more difficult to measure than UI employer costs, because unlike UI, Workers' Compensation is not financed solely by taxes paid to the state by employers. The insurance options available to employers vary across states. Some states permit employers with sufficient financial abilities and a good history of paying claims to self-insure, either individually or with group self-insurance. Table 5.7 shows the insurance options available in Michigan and the seven comparison states, and it shows estimated benefits by insurance type for 1978. Self-insurance is by far more common in Michigan than in other states. One proxy for 1978 employer WC costs is given in Table 5.7 using the amount of benefits rather than the amount of insurance premiums as a percent of payroll (the payroll figures are UI covered payroll). Michigan is a relatively high-cost state using this rough measure of WC costs, but Michigan's benefits as a percentage of payroll only exceed Indiana's by 0.8 percent. The lack of data and

TABLE 5.7
WORKER'S COMPENSATION:
INSURANCE ARRANGEMENT AND BENEFITS BY INSURANCE TYPE

STATE	METHODS AVAILABLE				1978 ESTIMATED TOTAL PAYMENTS ($000)	ESTIMATES OF 1978 PAYMENTS ($000)			Self/ Total	Total as % Payroll
	Private Carrier	State Fund	Self-Insurance			Private	State	Self Insurance		
			Individual	Group						
Michigan	X	X	X	X	496987	270700	20437	205850	.41	1.2%
California	X	X	X		1246813	736873	207940	302000	.24	1.3
Illinois	X		X	X	490010	412010	---	78000	.16	.9
Indiana	X		X		89708	75408	---	14300	.16	.4
New York	X	X	X	X	496606	294823	133783	68000	.14	.7
Ohio		X	X		531518	1377	376141	154000	.29	1.2
Pennsylvania	X	X	X		403113	271938	57175	74000	.18	.9
Wisconsin	X		X		123333	101233	---	22100	.18	.7

Notes: X=Method of insurance available in state. Estimates of 1978 payments are for both cash and medical benefits as estmated in the Social Security Bulletin. Total 1978 payments as a percentage of payroll, uses state payroll data for total covered by unemployment insurance.

Source: Chamber of Commerce of the United States, Analysis of Worker's Compensation Laws, Washington, D.C., 1980; Williams, C. Authur and Peter S. Barth, Compendium on Workman's Compensation, National Commission on State Workman's Compensation Laws, Washington, D.C., 1973, pages 257-259; Price, Daniel N., "Workers' Compensation: 1978 Program Update," Social Security Bulletin, Volume 43, Number 10, October 1980, page 8; and U.S. Department of Labor, Employment and Training Administration," Unemployment Insurance Program Letter No. 41-80; Unemployment Insurance Financial Developments for Calendar Year 1978," Washington, D.C., July, 1980 (Column 3).

the variations in WC insurance arrangements make it quite difficult to get reliable measures of average employer costs. The only data available on self-insurers are estimated benefits like those in Table 5.7.

For the purposes of interstate cost comparisons, the best estimates of WC costs as a percentage of payroll are those done by John Burton and his co-authors.[16] Burton makes his cost estimates using insurance manual rates from the National Council on Compensation Insurance (NCCI). NCCI insurance manual rates are used by private carriers to determine insurance premiums, but these are not measures of actual employer costs. Insurance costs also depend upon the employer's accident experience, premium discounts for quantity, dividends, and other factors. Burton has estimated adjusted manual rates which take these factors into consideration. Injury and illness rates vary considerably across industry groups. In order to get measures of interstate cost differentials which are independent of state variations in industry structure, Burton calculates average manual and average adjusted manual rates for three groups of employers in each state. The three groups are: (1) forty-five types of employers accounting for 57 percent of covered payroll, including thirteen manufacturing, seven contracting, and twenty-five other types of firms; (2) twenty-five types of manufacturing employers which are 10 percent of covered payroll; and (3) seventy-nine types of employers accounting for 72 percent of covered payroll, including thirty manufacturing, thirteen contracting, and thirty-six other types of employers. The manual and adjusted manual rates for forty-five, twenty-five, and seventy-nine insurance classes are weighted using the U.S. payroll distribution in order to derive average rates for each state. Burton's average adjusted manual rates are a good measure of interstate differences in costs resulting from variations in statutory WC provisions. However, these rates are not measures of average actual costs (for firms not self-insuring), because average actual costs are a function of the industry mix and payroll distributions in each state.

Adjusted manual rates for 1978 are shown in Table 5.8. Michigan is a relatively high-cost state for all three groups of employers. Michigan's adjusted manual rate for forty-five and seventy-nine types of employers is only exceeded by the California rates. However, the Michigan rates exceed the eight-state means by less than $1 per $100 of payroll.

The group of twenty-five manufacturing employers is particularly interesting for consideration of the effects of interstate WC differentials on plant location decisions. The 1978 average adjusted manual rate for Michigan for the twenty-five employer group is $5.04 per $100 of payroll; this rate is the highest among the eight states and exceeds the Indiana rate by $4.13. However, the Michigan rate exceeds the eight-state mean by only $2.14 per $100 of payroll. The growth rate for the adjusted twenty-five employer manual rate for Michigan exceeds that in the comparison states for the 1962 through 1978 period.

Burton estimated the maximum interstate differential for manufacturing firms in 1965 to be only 1.44 percent of payroll which he estimated to be less than 0.3 percent of total costs.[17] The level of WC costs in many states including Michigan has increased dramatically since 1965, and the interstate differentials have risen at an alarming rate.

<u>Cross-Industry Comparison of Workers' Compensation Costs</u>

The average adjusted manual rates in Table 5.8 provide an overall measure of the interstate cost differentials resulting from differences in WC programs, but adjusted manual rates are not available for a cross-industry comparison. The only data available for analysis of interstate differences by industry are NCCI manual rates. It should be remembered that actual WC insurance premiums may be either greater or less than the manual rates. The manual rates by insurance classifications in Table 5.9

TABLE 5.8
EMPLOYERS' AVERAGE COSTS OF WORKERS' COMPENSATION
(Rates per $100 Payroll)

STATE	1978 Manual Rates			1978 Adjusted Manual Rates			Adjusted Manual Rates 25 Types of Manufacturing Employers					
	45 Types of Employers	25 Types of Manufacturing	79 Types of Employers	45 Types of Employers	25 Types of Manufacturing	79 Types of Employers	1962	1965	1972	1975	Ratio 1978/1962	Ratio 1978/1972
Michigan	2.31	6.14	3.04	1.89	5.04	2.49	1.12	1.17	2.03	3.00	4.51	2.48
California	2.60	5.17	3.24	2.14	4.24	2.66	1.49	2.00	2.07	2.75	2.85	2.05
Illinois	1.69	2.97	2.01	1.38	2.43	1.65	1.02	1.05	1.41	2.09	2.37	1.72
Indiana	.59	1.11	.71	.48	.91	.59	.62	.65	.69	.83	1.47	1.32
New York	2.16	4.68	2.64	1.77	3.84	2.16	n.a.	n.a.	1.89	2.15	n.a.	2.03
Ohio	1.66	2.90	1.98	1.55	2.70	1.84	1.02	1.18	1.40	1.90	2.64	1.93
Pennsylvania	1.43	3.13	n.a.	1.17	2.56	n.a.	.62	.60	.70	1.68	4.11	3.65
Wisconsin	.92	1.85	1.17	.75	1.52	.96	.84	.99	.94	1.11	1.80	1.61
Average All States	1.67	3.49	2.11	1.39	2.90	1.76	.96	1.09	1.39	1.94	2.82	2.10

Note: N.A. means data not available.

Sources: Elson, Martin and John F. Burton, "Workers' Compensation Insurance: Recent Trends in Employer Costs," Monthly Labor Review, Volume 104, Number 3, pages 46-47, March 1981

Burton, John F., "Workers' Compensation Costs for Employers," Research Report of the Interdepartmental Workers' Compensation Task Force, U.S. Department of Labor, Employment Standards Administration, Washington D.C., Volume 3, page 25, 1980.

Watkins, Nancy and John F. Burton, "Employer's Costs of Workman's Compensation," Supplemental Studies for the National Commission on State Workmen's Compensation Laws, Washington, D.C., Volume II, p.235, 1973.

Burton, John F., Interstate Variations in Employers' Costs of Workmen's Compensation: Effect on Plant Location Exemplified in Michigan, Kalamazoo, Michigan: Upjohn Institute for Employment Research, pages 44-45, 1966.

should be viewed with this caveat in mind.

Michigan's manual rates are higher than the seven comparison states in Table 5.9 for seven of the classifications shown. Although there is considerable variation across industries in relative WC costs, Michigan does not have a relatively low manual rate for any of the classifications that are shown. If interstate differences in insurance premiums approach the magnitude of the differences in the manual rates, then firms in many of the businesses shown in Table 5.9 have strong incentives to locate in states like Indiana or Wisconsin rather than Michigan. The differences in manual rates between Michigan and the other five states are much smaller on average, but the manual rates suggest that WC costs may significantly discourage firms in industries such as foundaries or metal goods from locating in Michigan rather than one of these other industrial states. An analysis based on state average data tends to mask the substantial WC cost disadvantage that Michigan has in some industries.

<u>Sources of Differences Among States in Costs</u>

Workers' Compensation programs provide medical benefits, rehabilitation services, and income benefits. There are five kinds of disability income benefits provided: temporary total (TTD), temporary partial (TPD), permanent total (PTD), permanent partial (PPD), and survivors' death benefits. Data for the U.S. for 1974 show that PPD cases were 24.8 percent of the compensable cases, yet they received 62.7 percent of the income benefits.[18] The largest number of cases are temporary total disability cases, meaning that the individual is temporarily unable to work due to a work-related injury. Most of these workers recover from their injuries and are able to return to work, but after the healing period some of the TTD cases become permanent disabilities.

Table 5.10 shows income benefits for total disabilities for 1980. Michigan's minimum benefit is relatively high, but five of the comparison states pay maximum weekly

TABLE 5.9
WORKERS' COMPENSATION MANUAL RATES
PER $100 PAYROLL, 1977

Classification	NCCI Code	7-77 Mich-igan	5-77 Cali-fornia	9-77 Illi-nois	7-76 Indi-ana	7-77 New York	7-77 Ohio	7-77 Pennsyl-vania	4-77 Wiscon-sin
Bakeries	2003	$4.88	$5.07	$3.27	$1.09	$4.79*	$4.285	$3.55	$1.60
Grain Milling	2014	4.54*	9.95	6.58	2.04	7.59	5.195	4.95	3.80
Creameries	2070	3.91	-	3.22	1.35	3.95*	2.975	5.05	1.39
Laundries	2585	7.02	4.57	3.19	1.12	-	5.045	3.05	1.88
Furniture Manufacturing	2883	6.48	8.50	5.88	1.72	4.50	3.935	3.60	3.44
Foundaries	3081	15.39*	14.85	9.67	2.30	7.09	9.785	8.00	3.78
Tool Manufacturing	3113	2.26	-	2.72	.62	2.29	2.035	2.10	1.22
Metal Goods	3400	13.43	8.68	5.73	1.76	8.18	6.655	-	3.89
Machine Goods Manufacturing	3632	6.83	5.36	4.38	.75	3.96	3.035	3.10	1.30
Printing	4299	3.10	2.81	1.81	.47	2.19*	1.465	2.05	1.02
Masonry	5022	7.53	5.85	6.83	1.47	6.01	5.795	3.60	3.26
Plumbing	5183	4.18	5.54	4.57	1.19	4.33	2.765	2.70	2.43
Carpentry	5403	6.95	13.63	9.04	2.27	6.98	5.415	4.40	4.94
Painting	5475	-	9.24	6.91	1.81	7.94*	6.285	2.05	3.11*
Excavation	6217	7.65	6.20	5.89	2.35	5.06*	5.175	5.70	4.59
Salesmen	8742	.63	.74	.56	.20	.53*	.565	.57	.29
Average		6.31	7.21	5.01	1.41	5.61	4.40	3.63	2.62

Notes: *Some states did not have completely comparable positions, but Walzer made an attempt to match positions as closely as possible.

Source: Walzer, Norman, Worker's Compensation: Illinois and Other States, Springfield, Ilinois: Illinois Cities and Villages Municipal Problems Commission, pages 44 and 46, 1977.

TABLE 5.10
WORKERS' COMPENSATION BENEFITS
FOR TOTAL DISABILITY
JANUARY 1980

State	Minimum Weekly Benefit	Maximum Weekly Benefit	Notations
Michigan	$134-$149	$171-$200	Range of benefits because of dependents' allowances. There are provisions for Social Security offsets.
California	$49	$154	Extra $70 weekly during rehabilitation. 50% higher if employers serious willful misconduct or violation of safety order.
Illinois	TTD - $100.90 PTD $132.45	$353.19	TTD up to $124.30 with dependents (minimum). Compensation may be increased 25% for willful safety violation by employer.
Indiana	$50	$130	Benefit is actual weekly wage if less than minimum. Time limit 500 weeks and amount limit $65,000. Additional benefit available from special fund.
New York	TTD - $20 PTD - $30	$215	Beneifit is actual weekly wage if less than minimum. PTD recipients may collect full benefits and wages up to pre-injury wage.
Ohio	TTD - $86 PTD - $129	$258	Benefit is actual weekly wage if less than minimum.
Pennsylvania	$121	$242	Actual wage if less than minimum, but not less than 1/3 state average weekly wage.
Wisconsin	$30	$218	There are provsions for Social Security offsets. Benefits may be reduced 15% for worker's failure to use safety devices.

Notes: Weekly benefits are 66 2/3% of weekly wage up to maximum, except in Ohio where the percentage is higher for the first 12 weeks (70%). Except as noted benefits are either permanent total for life or for duration of TTD.

Source: Chamber of Commerce of the United States, Analysis of Worker's Compensation Laws, Washington, D.C., 1980, pages 45-47.

benefits in excess of the Michigan maximum. Michigan could be considered a relatively low-benefit state for total disabilities, especially when the weekly benefits are compared with Michigan's relatively high wages. Permanent partial benefits are probably a much more important source of Michigan's high WC costs.

Variations in coverage can be a source of interstate WC cost differentials. Michigan excludes high-wage professional athletes and some employers with fewer than three employees. The comparison states exclude some or all domestic workers and casual employees (not in the course of the employer's normal business). Farm labor is excluded from coverage in Indiana. Certain employers of farm labor in New York and Illinois have elective coverage, some employers of farm labor in those states face compulsory coverage provisions.[19] Coverage of farm labor and domestics in Michigan certainly increases WC costs, but it is difficult to assess the importance of this factor.

Michigan and comparison states all cover all occupational diseases arising out of employment, but many of these states require that the onset of the disability be within two or three years after the last occupational exposure to the work-related hazard (except in the case of radiation). The Michigan statute of limitations is more lenient, and only requires that a claim be filed within six months after disablement due to the occupational disease.[20]

Without better data than are available on Workers' Compensation benefits it is impossible to identify the factors which are the largest sources of interstate cost differentials. The National Commission on State Workmen's Compensation Laws issued a set of nineteen essential recommendations for state programs in 1972.[21] One rationale for the recommendations was to reduce interstate differences in employer costs, but unequal rates of improvement in state laws may have contributed to the growth in interstate cost differentials since 1972.

Contested Cases and Judicial Interpretations in Michigan

Workers' Compensation is a form of no-fault insurance purchased by employers which pays benefits to injured workers. One of the advantages of the WC system is that it provides workers with benefits as determined by state statutes, without the delays and legal costs involved in court proceedings. However, a substantial amount of litigation takes place in efforts to determine whether an individual's injury or illness is compensable. Considerable litigation also takes place with regard to the extent of an individual's disability resulting from a compensable injury or illness. Thus, despite the fact that the WC system was designed to avoid litigation, there is a tremendous amount of litigation in Michigan and other states. The ratio of petitions for hearings relative to reported injuries was 0.50 in 1976, and in 1980 the ratio of petitions (37,352) to reported injuries (64,809) was 0.58.[22] This high rate of litigation involves considerable legal fees which can contribute to high employer WC costs.

After determining through a hearing that a case is compensable, some claimants then receive regular weekly income benefits and medical benefits. However, in Michigan, the majority of hearings result in redemption agreements, lump-sum payments terminating the insurance company's liability. In 1980, 43,279 contested cases were disposed of, and 26,123 resulted in redemptions. A large number of cases did not reach the hearing state, 2,323 were voluntarily paid by the insurer after the petition for the hearing, and 11,330 cases were withdrawn or dismissed. Eighty-nine percent of the cases in which hearings were completed ended in redemption agreements.[23]

The Michigan Association of Insurance Companies has referred to Michigan's WC as "a system out of balance," due to the fact that Michigan has relatively high WC costs even though many benefit levels are relatively low in comparison with other states.[24] This association attributed part of this lack of balance to a number of problems, including judicial interpretations, such as the following which have increased employer costs:

"(1) Because of a 1966 Supreme Court decision, Michigan has no effective statute of limitations, thereby clearing the way for claims to be filed which allegedly occurred years ago but which have otherwise been unreported.

(2) Michigan appears to be the only state in which benefits are paid to retirees on a grand scale. Employees voluntarily leaving the Michigan labor market because of advancing age, or, in order to take advantage of retirement programs, can still receive workers' compensation settlements as though they were active members of the work force.

(3) Partially disabled workers in Michigan are entitled to full compensation benefits so long as they do not return to work. This provision encourages employees with minor impairments to remain off the job for an extended period of time.

(4) With the application of minimums, some employees by not working may have higher incomes with their weekly disability benefits than they would if they promptly returned to their jobs and earned their regular wages.

(5) The Michigan Supreme Court ruled that in eye injury cases, workers are to be fully compensated without regard to whether their vision can be restored through the use of prescription classes or not.

(6) The Michigan Supreme Court has ruled that conditions normally associated with the aging process, e.g., arthritis, emphysema, heart disorders, etc., can be compensable in cases where there may be only the very slightest possible work-related connection.

(7) Contrary to the original intent of the law, judicial interpretations have extended benefits to employees injured in the course of social, personal, or recreational activities and without regard to whether they suffered their injuries at or away from the workplace.

(8) And, finally, in 1978 the Michigan Supreme Court ruled that employees can receive compensation for mental disorders which the <u>honestly believe</u> are work-related, even though it can be shown that the conditions are <u>not</u> in any way work-related."[25]

Judicial interpretations can either broaden the class of compensable cases as these examples of Michigan rulings have done, or they might serve to narrow the class of compensable cases. Judicial rulings seem to be an important determinant of employer costs in Michigan, and it is quite likely that they have contributed to rising WC costs in Michigan in recent years.

Expected Effects of December 1980 Statutory Changes

Attempts in Michigan to reform the WC law were unsuccessful for five years before Public Act No. 357 was passed in December 1980.[26] Some administrative provisions of these WC amendments took effect January 1, 1981, but the major provisions affecting benefit amounts and compensability will take effect on January 1, 1982.

The new maximum weekly benefit will be 90 percent of the state average weekly wage. Maximum benefits in Illinois, Ohio, and Pennsylvania are higher percentages of average wages at 133-1/3 percent, 100 percent, and 100 percent respectively.[27] The maximum benefit in Michigan will be similar to other industrial states under the new law, rather than lower. Michigan's benefit calculation formula will be changed to 80 percent of after-tax wages rather than two-thirds of gross wages. The National Council on Compensation Insurance (NCCI) estimates that these two benefit changes will increase income benefits by less than 15 percent.[28]

The minimum benefits in the old Michigan law are relatively high, but the new law eliminates the minimum benefit except for two types of cases. The minimum benefit for death benefits will be 50 percent of the maximum weekly benefit, and scheduled injuries will receive a minimum of 25 percent of the maximum for the number of weeks listed in the schedule. NCCI estimated that this change in the minimum benefit would lower income benefits by approximately 4 percent.[29]

Many of the problems created by judicial interpretations are addressed by the 1980 amendments. The WC reform provides for a cut-off date for filing claims which is two years after an injury or within two years of disability due to an occupational disease. The clause in the old law which made the statute of limitations ineffective was eliminated.

The old law did not contain provisions regarding the payment of WC benefits to individuals who have voluntarily retired. Some estimates of the cost of retiree WC benefits are as high as $100 million annually.[30] The 1980 amendments include a rebuttable presumption that an individual who is no longer employed and is receiving a nondisability government or private pension has not suffered a loss of earnings capacity. This statutory change should lower permanent partial disability benefits, thereby lowering average employer costs.

The 1980 amendments include clauses defining the work relationship of injuries and diseases which will narrow the range of compensable cases. Injuries resulting from social and recreational activities are specifically excluded. Conditions of the aging process, including heart disease and mental illness, must be real and aggravated by employment "in a significant manner" in order to be compensable.

The 1980 amendments also specify that a claimant can not receive both WC and UI benefits from the same employer's accounts at the same time.

It is not possible to determine the magnitude of the savings due to the 1980 changes affecting compensability. Thus, it is impossible to estimate the net effect of the benefit increases and compensability changes. The worst possible outcome appears to be that Michigan will remain a relatively high WC cost state, but become a relatively high-benefit rather than low-benefit state.

<u>Methods of Calculating Permanent Partial Benefits</u>

The majority of WC income benefits are paid to the permanently partially disabled (PPD), and there is a tremendous amount of interstate variation in methods of calculating PPD benefits.[31] Attempts to lower WC costs should involve a thorough review of the Michigan method of determining PPD benefits, due to the magnitude of these benefits. Two classes of work-related impairments can serve as the basis for permanent partial benefits: scheduled losses (impairments) such as the loss of an arm or finger; and nonscheduled losses resulting from causes such as head or back injuries. Most state statutes include schedules for a list of impairments, and these schedules usually specify for each loss a number of weeks of benefits with weekly benefits dependent upon the worker's pre-injury wage rate. Scheduled PPD benefits for Michigan appear to be relatively neither low nor high.[32] However, for states such as Michigan and New York, scheduled benefits, in fact, convey very little about the size of permanent partial benefits, because both Michigan and New York provide wage loss benefits in addition to scheduled permanent partial benefits.

Permanent partial benefits in Michigan are determined on a retrospective basis dependent upon actual earnings losses (after the healing period and after any benefits for scheduled losses are exhausted). The Michigan statute states that permanent partial benefits are a function of the difference between pre-injury earnings and the "average weekly wage which the injured employee is able to earn after the personal injury."[33] As correctly pointed out by John Burton: "This sounds like a loss of earnings capacity approach. Court decisions and actual practice, however, make clear that the basis of benefits is the actual loss of earnings."[34] New York uses an earnings-capacity approach which relies on a prospective assessment of the extent of the earnings loss which the worker is likely to experience during his or her working life. If a work-related injury or disease affects wage-earning capacity after scheduled benefits are exhausted, then a worker in New York receives weekly benefits equal to two-thirds of the difference between pre-injury wages and predicted post-injury wages.[35] In New York, earnings losses are predicted soon after the healing period when the impairment is considered permanent; however, in Michigan actual earnings losses might occur long after the healing period and benefits would be determined at that time.

Although there are many other methods of determining permanent partial benefits, this section will just compare the economic incentives and cost implications of the Michigan and New York methods. After a New York worker's earnings capacity is predicted and WC benefit determined, that worker has a strong incentive to work as permitted by his or her disability in order to supplement the WC income benefits. Permanent partial disability income benefits in New York are not taxed as a result of labor market earnings. The work incentives for disabled workers in Michigan are much weaker. Under the old Michigan statute a PPD claimant who is not employed receives full weekly WC benefits, and if employed that individual's WC benefits are reduced $2 for each $3 of earnings. Although there are no estimates of the labor supply effects of this policy, it is quite likely that a substantial number of workers with relatively minor impairments are discouraged from seeking full-time employment. The relatively high minimum benefits in effect until January 1982 mean that some low-income workers receive higher WC benefits than their pre-injury wages, which gives the low-income disabled worker no incentive to seek work.[36]

The 1980 statutory changes will improve the work incentives for low-income workers in Michigan, because the minimum benefit for partially disabled workers is eliminated. However, the new PPD benefit formula will tax a worker's WC benefits $8 for each $10 increase in after-tax earnings, and this is still a very high tax rate which discourages the disabled from seeking lucrative jobs. The lower the actual earnings of PPD claimants in Michigan, the higher their benefits and the higher the cost of the WC program to employers.

Two workers in Michigan with equal pre-injury earnings could receive equal benefits, despite the fact that one had a major disability and the other a minor disability. Yet the Michigan system for PPD benefits was praised by the National Commission in 1972 because it "has the substantial merit of matching benefits to a worker's actual loss of wages, rather than basing benefits on guesses about future wage loss."[37] The vast number of redemption agreements in Michigan is inconsistent with this wage-loss approach, but more important than the divergence from the wage-loss approach in contested cases are the problems with the actual wage-loss approach for benefit determination in uncontested cases. The work incentives are quite weak in uncontested cases due to the monitoring of wage losses and the high tax on earnings. The Michigan program is currently a high-cost program paying relatively low benefits to the totally or severely disabled while a disproportionate share of benefits are received by workers with relatively minor disabilities. It is unlikely that the benefits for severe disabilities relative to minor cases will improve dramatically unless the actual wage-loss approach is either eliminated or severely altered. An alternative method of PPD benefit determination could allow benefits to the severely disabled to be increased while simultaneously lowering the costs of PPD benefits.

CONCLUSIONS

Michigan was a high-cost state in 1978, relative to the comparison states, in terms of the employer costs of both Unemployment Insurance and Workers' Compensation. Average WC costs in Michigan as measured by adjusted manual rates for manufacturing firms exceeded Indiana's costs by 4.13 percent of payroll, and the combined UI and WC costs for Michigan exceeded Indiana's by 4.99 percent (using WC data for manufacturing employers). The magnitude of the UI cost differentials is probably too small to be a substantial factor influencing plant location decisions. In recent years WC cost differentials have risen rapidly, especially for manufacturing firms. It is quite possible that Workers' Compensation interstate cost differentials have an influence on plant location decisions. The 1977 and 1978 data presented in this chapter suggest that the WC cost disadvantages in Michigan are substantial in many industries.

Michigan's relatively high unemployment rates during the 1970s are probably the most important factor contributing to Michigan's relatively high UI costs. Michigan has been a relatively low Unemployment Insurance benefit state with lenient eligibility rules. The 1980 statutory changes could have a substantial effect on Michigan's UI costs, because benefit amounts were liberalized and eligibility rules were tightened.

The UI tax structure in Michigan provides relatively small cross-industry subsidies within the state. However, Michigan could further reduce the cross-subsidies to high-wage, high-unemployment firms by raising the taxable wage base and widening the range of tax rates. These changes in the UI tax schedule would strengthen the disincentives for employers to temporarily lay off workers and thus tend to lower average UI costs in Michigan.

Michigan has paid relatively low WC benefits for severe disabilities. Permanent partial disability benefits in Michigan include wage loss benefits which are determined by monitoring actual wage losses. This method of determining benefits permits workers with relatively minor disabilities to receive relatively large benefits. The permanent partial benefit calculation method also creates strong work disincentives for many disabled workers. A large proportion of permanent partial cases are contested cases which result in redemption agreements. It is difficult to assess the net effect of this process of litigation and lump-sum settlements on Michigan's WC costs, but the high proportion of lump-sum settlements may encourage workers with minor disabilities to file claims and hearing petitions. Monitoring of wage losses and the widespread use of redemption agreements both tend to give a disproportionate share of benefits to workers in Michigan with relatively minor disabilities. The 1980 statutory changes in the minimum and maximum WC benefits should improve the balance between benefits received in severe and minor cases.

A number of judicial rulings have broadened the class of compensable cases in Michigan, thereby increasing average employer WC costs. The 1980 Workers' Compensation amendments include several provisions which are intended to narrow the range of compensable cases. Lowering the number of compensable cases will help to lower Michigan's WC costs relative to competing states.

In recent years Michigan has been a high-cost, low-benefit state for both Unemployment Insurance and Workers' Compensation. This is certainly not a desirable combination of costs and benefits. The 1980 statutory changes in both programs tighten eligibility requirements, and both sets of amendments raise benefits. It is too early to assess the net effect of these amendments in terms of employer costs in Michigan relative to competing states.

NOTES, CHAPTER 5

[1]Valuable research assistance was provided by Karen Bole and Ruth Beier.

[2]There are also employee taxes in Alabama, Alaska, and New Jersey. U.S. Department of Labor, Employment and Training Administration, Handbook of Unemployment Insurance Financial Data 1938-1976, Washington, D.C. (1978) p. 165.

[3]For a discussion of the incidence of UI taxes see chapter 2 of Daniel S. Hamermesh, Jobless Pay and the Economy. (Baltimore: Johns Hopkins University Press, 1977). By treating all UI taxes as employer costs one gets an upper bound on the effect of UI costs on plant location decisions.

[4]Benefit cost rates are UI benefits paid as a percentage of total payroll in covered employment. IUR equals the average weekly insured unemployment as a percentage of covered employment. The coefficient on IUR = 0.23 means that UI benefits as a percentage of payroll increased, on average, by 0.23 percentage points for each 1 percentage point increase in the IUR. The $R^2 = 0.73$ indicates that 73 percent of the variation across states in benefit cost rates can be explained by using only a constant term and IUR.

Data for regressions from: U.S. Department of Labor, Employment and Training Administration, Handbook of Unemployment Insurance Financial Data 1938-1976,

(Washington, D.C., 1978); U.S. Department of Labor, Employment and Training Administration, "Unemployment Insurance Program Letter No. 32-79; Unemployment Insurance Financial Developments for Calendar Year 1977," (Washington, D.C., July 1979); and U.S. Department of Labor, Employment and Training Administration, "Unemployment Insurance Program Letter NO. 41-80; Unemployment Insurance Financial Developments for Calendar Year 1978," (Washington, D.C., July 1980).

[5]U.S. Department of Labor, Employment and Training Administration, Comparison of State Unemployment Insurance Laws, (Washington, D.C., 1980), Section 1.

[6]Calculated from Employment and Training Report of the President, (Washington, D.C., 1979), p. 275.

[7]U.S. Department of Labor, Employment and Training Administration, Comparison of State Unemployment Insurance Laws, (Washington, D.C., 1980), Table 400 and pp. 4-2 and 4-3.

[8]Information about provisions of the new state law are from Michigan, Amendments to the Michigan Employment Security Act, (Lansing, Michigan, Public Act No. 358, 1980); and Michigan, "Amendments to the Michigan Employment Security Act," (Lansing, Michigan, Mimeograph, January 13, 1981).

[9]U.S. Department of Labor, Employment and Training Administration, Significant Provisions of State Unemployment Insurance Laws, (Washington, D.C., January, 1981).

[10]Michigan, Department of Labor, Michigan Employment Security Commission, Changes in Michigan's Unemployment Compensation Program, (Detroit, Michigan, January 1981).

[11]Ibid.

[12]Minimum and maximum calculated by author using wage data from U.S. Department of Labor, Employment and Training Administration, Handbook of Unemployment Insurance Financial Data 1938-1976, (Washington, D.C., 1978); U.S. Department of Labor, Employment and Training Administration, "Unemployment Insurance Program Letter No. 32-79; Unemployment Insurance Financial Developments for Calendar Year 1977," (Washington, D.C., July 1979); and U.S. Department of Labor, Employment and Training Administration, "Unemployment Insurance Program Letter No. 41-80; Unemployment Insurance Financial Developments for Calendar Year 1978." (Washington, D.C., July 1980).

[13]During periods of high unemployment one would expect the effect on duration of unemployment to be smaller, because a worker is less likely to pass up a job opportunity

for leisure time when jobs are scarce. For an excellent summary of studies in this area see chapter 3 of Daniel S. Hamermesh, Jobless Pay and the Economy, (Baltimore: Johns Hopkins University Press, 1977). The estimate in the text was chosen by Hamermesh.

[14]Tax rates calculated using 1978 average weekly earnings times fifty-two weeks. Wage data from Michigan State University, Graduate School of Business Administration, Michigan Statistical Abstract, (East Lansing, Michigan, 1980), pp. 179-180.

[15]Increasing the tax base without lowering the minimum tax would increase effective tax rates for high-wage, low-unemployment firms. The tax base and minimum rate should both be changed at the same time.

[16]See Burton's publications for details of his methodology. John F. Burton, Interstate Variations in Employers' Costs of Workmen's Compensation: Effect on Plant Location Exemplified in Michigan, (Kalamazoo, Michigan: Upjohn Institute for Employment Research, 1966). John F. Burton, "Workers' Compensation Costs for Employers," Research Report of the Interdepartmental Workers' Compensation Task Force, U.S. Department of Labor, Employment Standards Administration, (Washington, D.C., Volume 3, 1980). Martin W. Elson and John F. Burton, "Workers' Compensation Insurance: Recent Trends in Employer Costs," Monthly Labor Review, Volume 104, Number 3, March 1981. Nancy Watkins and John F. Burton, "Employer's Costs of Workmen's Compensation," Supplemental Studies for The National Commission on State Workmen's Compensation Laws, (Washington, D.C., Volume II, 1973).

[17]John F. Burton, Interstate Variations in Employers' Costs of Workmen's Compensation: Effect on Plant Location Exemplified in Michigan, (Kalamazoo, Michigan: Upjohn Institute for Employment Research, 1966), pp. 44, 45, 72.

[18]Daniel N. Price, "Workers' Compensation Program in the 1970s," Social Security Bulletin, (May 1979) 42: 5.

[19]Chamber of Commerce of the United States, Analysis of Workers' Compensation Laws, (Washington, D.C., 1980), pp. 5-7.

[20]Chamber of Commerce of the United States, Analysis of Workers' Compensation Laws, (Washington, D.C., 1980), pp. 10-12.

[21]National Commission on State Workmen's Compensation Laws, The Report of the National Commission on State Workmen's Compensation Laws, (Washington, D.C., 1972).

[22]Allan H. Hunt, Workers' Compensation in Michigan:

Problems and Prospects, (Kalamazoo, Michigan: Upjohn Institute for Employment Research, 1979), p. 8. 1980 data are from personal communication with the Contested Case Section of the Bureau of Workers' Disability Compensation, Michigan Department of Labor.

[23]Data from personal communication with the Contested Case Section of the Bureau of Workers' Disability Compensation, Michigan Department of Labor.

[24]Machinery and Allied Products Institute, *Workers' Compensation: A System in Need of Reform*, (Washington, D.C.: MAPI, 1980), pp. 75-76.

[25]*Ibid.*, pp. 75-76.

[26]Information about provisions of the new state law are from: Michigan, *Workers' Compensation Act Amendments*, Lansing, Michigan, Public Act No. 357, 1980; and Michigan, "Workers' Compensation Act Amendments," (Lansing, Michigan, Mimeograph, January 1981).

[27]Chamber of Commerce of the United States, *Analysis of Workers' Compensation Laws*, (Washington, D.C., 1980), pp. 15-16.

[28]Michigan, "Workers' Compensation Act Amendments," (Lansing, Michigan, Mimeograph, January 1981).

[29]*Ibid.*

[30]*Ibid.*

[31]National Commission on State Workmen's Compensation Laws, *The Report of the National Commission on State Workmen's Compensation Laws*, (Washington, D.C., 1972), p. 54.

[32]Chamber of Commerce of the United States, *Analysis of Workers' Compensation Laws*, (Washington, D.C., 1979), pp. 22-23, and 1980, pp. 18-19.

[33]Michigan, *Workers' Compensation Act Amendments*, Lansing, Michigan, Public Act No. 357, 1980.

[34]John F. Burton and Wayne Vroman, "Permanent Partial Disability," *Research Report of the Interdepartmental Workers' Compensation Task Force*, U.S. Department of Labor, Employment Standards Administration, (Washington, D.C., 1981) 6: 27.

[35]*Ibid.*, pp. 25-27.

[36]Lump-sum settlements do not have these weak work incentives, because that settlement is unaffected by actual

earnings after the redemption agreement is signed. However, this strengthens the incentives for workers in Michigan with relatively minor injuries to get redemption agreements which involve substantial legal costs.

[37]National Commission on State Workmen's Compensation Laws, The Report of the National Commission on State Workmen's Compensation Laws, (Washington, D.C., 1972), p. 69.

REFERENCES, CHAPTER 5

Barron, John M. and Mellow, Wesley. "Interstate Differences in Unemployment Insurance." National Tax Journal 34 (March 1981).

Becker, Joseph M. Experience Rating in Unemployment Insurance: Virtue or Vice. Kalamazoo, Michigan: Upjohn Institute for Employment Research, 1972.

Becker, Joseph M. Unemployment Benefits: Should There Be a Compulsory Federal Standard?. Washington, D.C.: American Enterprise Institute, 1980.

Blaustein, Saul J. and Kozlowski, Paul J. Interstate Differences in Unemployment Insurance Benefit Costs: A Cross Section Study. Kalamazoo, Michigan: Upjohn Institute for Employment Research, 1978.

Bureau of National Affairs, Inc. Payroll. BNA Policy and Practice Series, Washington, D.C., 1981.

Burton, John F. Interstate Variations in Employers' Costs of Workmen's Compensation: Effect of Plant Location Exemplified in Michigan. Kalamazoo, Michigan: Upjohn Institute for Employment Research, 1966.

Burton, John. "Workers' Compensation Costs for Employers." Research Report of the Interdepartmental Workers' Compensation Task Force, U.S. Department of Labor, Employment Standards Administration, Washington, D.C., Vol. 3, 1980.

Burton, John F. and Vroman, Wayne. "Permanent Partial Disability." Research Report of the Interdepartmental Workers' Compensation Task Force. U.S. Department of Labor, Employment Standards Administration, Washington, D.C., Vol. 6, 1981.

Chamber of Commerce of the United States. Analysis of Workers' Compensation Laws. Washington, D.C. 1979, 1980.

Chamber of Commerce of the United States. Employee Benefits, 1979. Washington, D.C. 1980.

Chelius, James R. Workplace Safety and Health: The Role of Workers' Compensation. Washington, D.C.: American Enterprise Institute, 1977.

Elson, Martin W. and Burton, John F. "Workers' Compensation Insurance: Recent Trends in Employer Costs." Monthly Labor Review 104 (March 1981).

Hamermesh, Daniel S. Jobless Pay and the Economy. Baltimore: Johns Hopkins University Press, 1977.

Hunt, H. Allan. Workers' Compensation in Michigan: Problems and Prospects. Kalamazoo, Michigan: Upjohn Institute for Employment Research, 1979.

Machinery and Allied Products Institute. Workers' Compensation: A System in Need of Reform. Washington, D.C.: MAPI, 1980.

McKean, Eugene C. Unemployment Insurance Costs of the ABC Corporation in Michigan and Nearby States. Kalamazoo, Michigan: Upjohn Institute for Employment Research, 1962.

Michigan, State of. Amendments to the Michigan Employment Security Act. Lansing, Michigan: Public Act No. 358, 1980.

Michigan, State of. "Amendments to the Michigan Employment Security." Lansing, Michigan: Mimeograph, January 13, 1981.

Michigan, State of. Workers' Compensation Act Amendments. Lansing, Michigan: Public Act No. 357, 1980.

Michigan, State of. "Workers' Compensation Act Amendments." Lansing, Michigan: Mimeograph, January 1981.

Michigan, State of. Department of Labor, Michigan Employment Security Commission. Changes in Michigan's Unemployment Compensation Program. Detroit, Michigan: January, 1981.

Michigan, State of. Department of Labor, Michigan Employment Security Commission. ES-204 Experience Rating Report Rate Year 1980. Detroit, Michigan: 1980.

Michigan State University, Graduate School of Business Administration. Michigan Statistical Abstract. East Lansing, Michigan: 1980.

National Commission on State Workmen's Compensation Laws. The Report of the National Commission on State Workmen's Compensation Laws. Washington, D.C.: 1972.

Price, Daniel N. "Workers' Compensation: 1978 Program Update." Social Security Bulletin 43 (October 1980).

Price, Daniel N. "Workers' Compensation Program in the 1970s." Social Security Bulletin 42 (May 1979).

Rejda, George E. Social Insurance and Economic Security. Englewood Cliffs, New Jersey: Prentice-Hall, 1976.

Tinsley, LaVerne C. "Workers' Compensation in 1980: Major Enactments." Monthly Labor Review 104 (March 1981).

U.S. Department of Health, Education, and Welfare. Social Security Administration. Social Security Bulletin, Annual Statistical Supplement. Washington, D.C.: 1975, 1976, 1977-1979.

U.S. Department of Labor. Employment and Training Administration. Comparison of State Unemployment Insurance Laws. Washington, D.C.: 1980.

U.S. Department of Labor. Employment and Training Administration. Handbook of Unemployment Insurance Financial Data 1938-1976. Washington, D.C.: 1978.

U.S. Department of Labor. Employment and Training Administration. "Unemployment Insurance Program Letter No. 32-79; Unemployment Insurance Financial Developments for Calendar Year 1977." Washington, D.C.: July 1979.

U.S. Department of Labor. Employment and Training Administration. "Unemployment Insurance Program Letter No. 41-80; Unemployment Insurance Financial Developments for Calendar year 1978." Washington, D.C.: July 1980.

U.S. Department of Labor. Employment and Training Administration. Significant Provisions of State Unemployment Insurance Laws. Washington, D.C.: January and July 1975-1980, and January 1981.

U.S. President. Employment and Training Report of the President, Washington, D.C.: 1979.

Walzer, Norman. Workers' Compensation: Illinois and Other States. Springfield, Illinois: Illinois Cities and Villages Municipal Problems Commission, 1977.

Watkins, Nancy and Burton, John F. "Employer's Costs of Workmen's Compensation." Supplemental Studies for The National Commission on State Workmen's Compensation Laws, Washington, D.C. Vol. 2, 1973.

Williams, C. Arthur and Barch, Peter S. Compendium on Workmen's Compensation. National Commission on State Workmen's Compensation Laws, Washington, D.C.: 1973.

Chapter 6

United States' Comparative Advantage in Motor Vehicles and Steel

by

Mordechai E. Kreinin

Michigan State University

U.S. INTERNATIONAL TRADE IN MOTOR VEHICLES AND STEEL

Much public attention has been focused in recent years on the deterioration in the U.S. international trade position in two highly visible industries: autos and steel. The decline in exports and the increase in imports has turned the labor unions in these industries from "free traders" to "protectionistic" in their orientation. It led to the following statement, attributed to Nobel Laureate in economics Professor Paul Samuelson:[1]

> The evidence is strong that steel and autos have lost comparative advantage. The burden of proof should go against government's keeping uneconomic business activities alive.

It is easy to document the nature and extent of the problem plaguing the two industries. Table 6.1 presents data underlying the aforementioned public concern. Panel A shows that while the U.S. net trade position in all manufactured products improved during the 1970s, the country's position in the two industries under review deteriorated consistently. Panel B presents U.S. trade in motor vehicles with the three major trading areas. Its main purpose is to enable the interested reader to net out U.S. trade with Canada, which grew in a "balanced fashion," due partly to the U.S.-Canada auto pact. It also shows the precipitous rise in imports from Japan. Finally, the U.S. share in total manufacturing exports of the industrial countries increased slightly at the end of the past decade (Panel C). But its share in the export of autos and steel declined markedly.

This chapter explores one possible cause of the problem

TABLE 6.1
UNITED STATES TRADE IN AUTOS AND STEEL

A. U.S. TRADE POSITION (billions of current dollars)

YEAR	ALL MANUFACTURES			ROAD MOTOR VEHICLES			IRON AND STEEL		
	Exports	Imports	Balance	Exports	Imports	Balance	Exports	Imports	Balance
1963	$13.3	$6.9	$6.4	$1.3	$0.6	$+0.7	$0.5	$0.7	$-0.2
1968	22.4	18.6	3.8	3.3	3.9	-0.6	0.6	2.1	-1.5
1973	42.7	42.5	0.2	6.0	10.1	-4.1	1.3	3.0	-1.7
1977	77.8	74.5	3.1	11.6	17.5	-5.9	1.7	6.0	-4.3
1979	113.5	106.9	6.6	14.7	23.6	-8.9	2.3	7.5	-5.2
1980	138.3	118.8	19.5	14.2	25.7	-11.5	3.1	7.4	-4.3

B. U.S. TRADE IN MOTOR VEHICLES WITH MAIN TRADING PARTNERS (billions of current dollars)

YEAR	CANADA		WESTERN EUROPE		JAPAN	
	U.S. Export	U.S. Import	U.S. Export	U.S. Import	U.S. Export	U.S. Import
1963	0.5	0.0	0.2	0.6	0.0	0.0
1968	2.2	2.2	0.2	1.5	0.0	0.3
1973	4.1	4.9	0.5	3.0	0.1	2.2
1977	7.4	8.3	0.9	3.6	0.1	5.4
1979	8.7	8.0	1.4	5.7	0.2	9.5
1980	7.5	7.5	1.4	6.1	0.2	11.7

C. SHARE OF U.S. EXPORTS IN THE EXPORTS OF THE INDUSTRIAL COUNTRIES (percent)

YEAR	ALL MANUFACTURES	ROAD MOTOR VEHICLES	IRON AND STEEL
1973	14.9	15.9	5.5
1977	14.7	15.1	4.4
1979	14.8	13.6	3.9
1980	15.6	12.3	4.9

Source: General Agreement on Trade and Tariffs, International Trade, Various Issues, Appendix Tables.

afflicting the two "ailing industries": "excessive" increases in labor production costs in the United States. The center of attention is motor vehicles--the mainstay of the Michigan economy. Iron and steel is included for purposes of comparison and analogy, and because steel is a major input into car production.

Following a discussion of the auto industry in Michigan, the chapter compares the behavior of unit labor costs in steel and in motor vehicles to their counterpart in all manufacturing. In each case, the comparison is undertaken both for the United States and for Japan. From it, conclusions are drawn about the U.S. comparative advantage in the two industries. The chapter concludes with an assessment of future prospects.

PERSPECTIVES ON MICHIGAN AND THE AUTO INDUSTRY

Because of their role in the Michigan economy, special importance attaches to international trade in new passenger cars. Figure 6.1 shows total passenger car sales in the United States. Table 6.2 and Figure 6.2 show that imports of new passenger cars grew precipitously since 1977 and approached 30 percent of the U.S. market in 1980. Imports from Germany peaked in 1971 at 771 thousand; and beginning in 1976, Japan took an overwhelming lead among foreign suppliers. Shipments from Japan more than doubled between 1975 and 1979, and that rate of increase placed these imports at the center of public discussion and policy debate. U.S. output of cars declined sharply in the late 1970s (last column of Table 6.2), partly because of domestic economic conditions and in part because of competition from imports. Table 6.3 offers supplementary data on production and trade in passenger cars of each of the major producing nations.[2]

An estimated 950,000 workers are employed in the motor vehicles and parts industry in the United States (with an additional 1.4 million employed in the supplying industries).[3] Of the 778,000 hourly workers, over 250,000,

TABLE 6.2
U.S. TRADE IN NEW PASSENGER AUTOMOBILES
(Thousands of Units)

YEAR	U.S. IMPORTS FROM:			TOTAL U.S. IMPORTS	SHARE OF IMPORTS IN APPARENT[1] CONSUMPTION	U.S. EXPORTS	NET TRADE DEFICIT	U.S. FACTORY SALES
	Canada	West Germany	Japan					
1964	9.0	364.7	16.0	536.7	6.6%	181.7	355.1	7,751.8
1968	500.1	708.0	169.6	1,620.5	16.0%	330.5	1,290.0	8,822.2
1971	802.3	770.8	703.7	2,587.5	24.0%	386.7	2,200.8	8,584.6
1973	871.6	677.5	624.8	2,437.3	21.0%	509.2	1,928.2	9,657.6
1976	825.6	349.8	1,128.9	2,536.7	24.5%	680.7	1,856.1	8,497.6
1977	849.8	423.5	1,341.5	2,790.1	24.7%	697.9	2,002.2	9,198.9
1979	677.0	495.6	1,617.3	3,005.5	28.2%	781.6	2,223.9	8,419.2

Notes: [1]Apparent Consumption is defined as U.S. factory sales plus imports minus exports.

Source: U.S. International Trade Commission, Automotive Trade Statistics 1964-1979, Washington D.C., June 1980 (USITC Publication 1078), Various Tables.

(Thousands of Units)

YEAR	JAPAN			BRAZIL			MEXICO			ARGENTINA		
	Production	Imports	Exports	Production	Imports	Exports	Production	Imports	Exports	Production	Imports	Exports
1975	4,568	45	1,827	524			237		3	186	.165	10
1976	5,028	40	2,539	527			213		4	147	.234	11
1977	5,431	41	2,959	464			188		12	177	.167	4
1978	5,976	55	3,042	535		57[1]	243		26	137		
1979	6,176	64	3,375							250	10	

YEAR	KOREA			ITALY			F.R. GERMANY			FRANCE		
	Production	Imports	Exports	Production	Imports	Exports	Production	Imports	Exports	Production	Imports	Exports
1975	17			1,349	379	661	2,687	769	1,356	2,546	399	1,770
1976	26		.558	1,471	487	696	3,301	854	1,704	2,980	604	1,911
1977	42		5	1,440	478	644	3,567	960	1,833	3,092	575	2,084
1978	86		26	1,509	531	640	3,620	1,069	1,793	3,111	564	2,087
1979			29	1,481	637	648	3,933	NA	1,997	3,220	808	1,698

YEAR	UNITED KINGDOM			UNITED STATES			WESTERN EUROPE	
	Production	Imports	Exports	Production	Imports	Exports	Total Production	
1975	1,268	449	516	6,717	2,075	640	1975	7,850
1976	1,333	534	496	8,498	2,537	680	1976	9,085
1977	1,328	678	475	9,214	2,790	697	1977	9,427
1978	1,223	801	466	9,177	3,025	700	1978	9,513
1979	1,070	1,071	410	8,434	3,006	781	1979	9,704

Notes: [1]Refers to January-August, 1978; Total Annual World Demand for New Passenger Cars in the late 1980s is estimated at 32 MILLION cars.

Sources: World Vehicle Data, 1979, published by Motor Vehicles Manufacturing Association of the U.S., Inc. Individual Country Trade Data Handbooks, 1979.

FIGURE 6.1
PASSENGER CAR SALES IN THE UNITED STATES

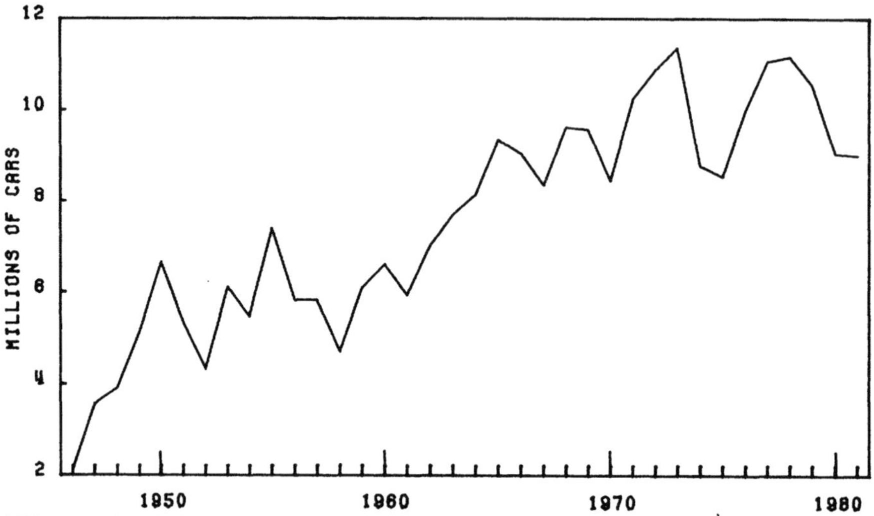

SOURCE: WARD'S AUTOMOTIVE REPORT AND U.S. DEPT. OF COMMERCE, BUREAU OF ECONOMIC ANALYSIS.

FIGURE 6.2
IMPORT SHARE OF U.S. RETAIL MOTOR VEHICLE SALES
(UNITS QUARTERLY DATA)

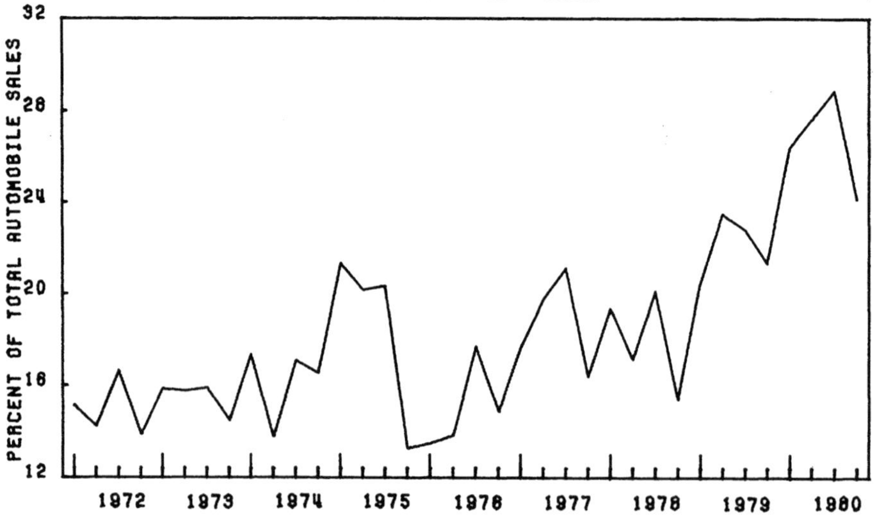

SOURCE: U.S. DEPT. OF COMMERCE, BUREAU OF ECONOMIC ANALYSIS.

Figure 6.3

AUTO, STEEL, AND TIRE PLANT CHANGES 1975—1980

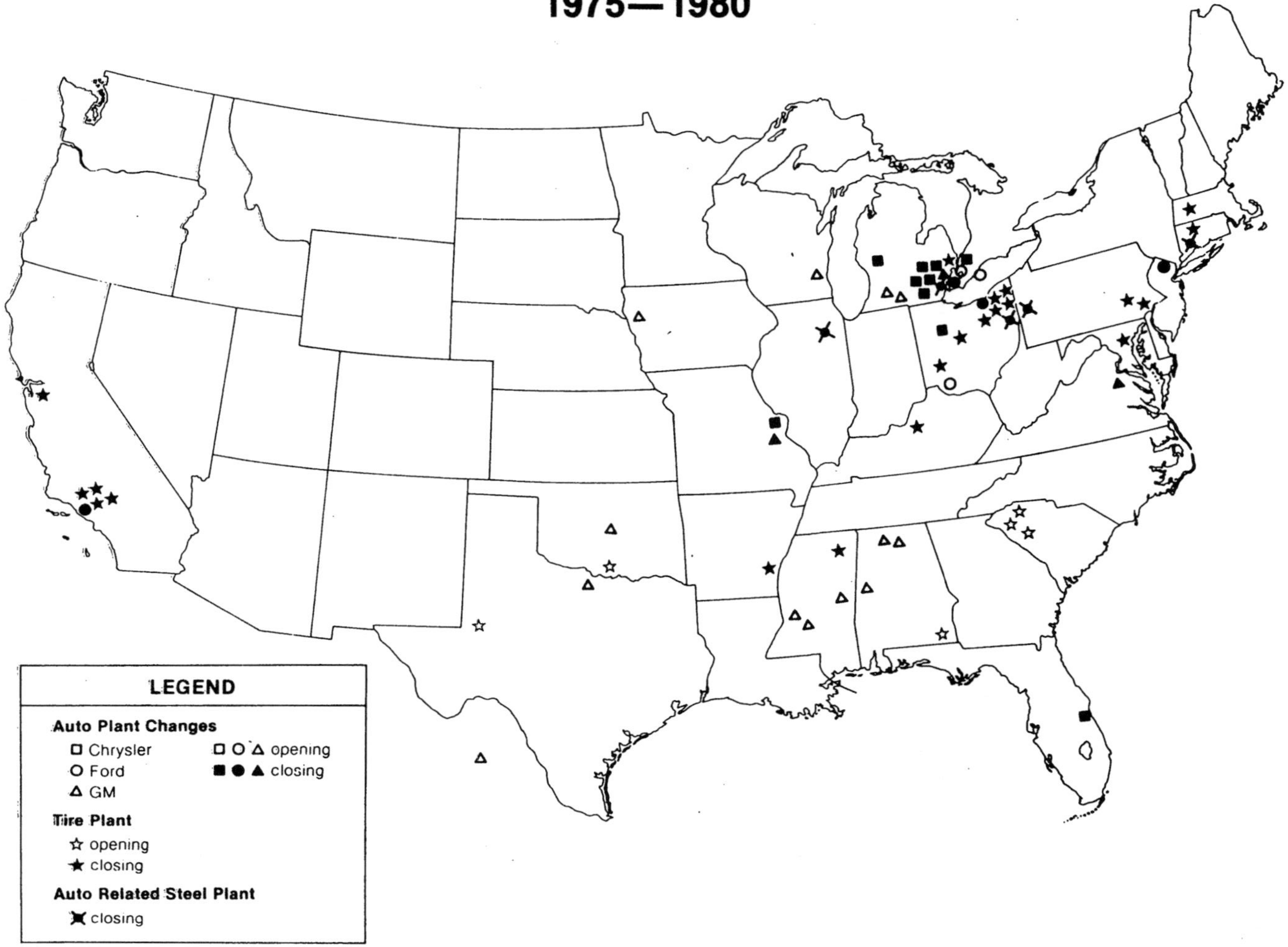

or 32 percent, were on indefinite layoffs in mid-1980, caused by declining production and sales of new cars.

Because of the concentration of automobile plants in Michigan, this state along with Ohio, sustained a heavy impact of auto related unemployment. Figure 6.3 shows auto related plant changes in the 1975-80 period, with numerous plant closings in Michigan (autos) and Ohio (tires). Table 6.4 illustrates the importance of auto employment in five states and ten metropolitan areas.[4] The auto industry layoffs are particularly severe in Flint, Saginaw, and Detroit.

By now it is well established that not all auto layoffs are attributable to import penetration. Much of the depression in the industry is due to domestic economic conditions. Still, competition from imports played an important role in bringing about the present circumstances. What is more, because of a decline in market segmentation, the U.S. ability to compete will loom increasingly important in determining the future course of the industry.

Until the mid-1970s the automobile market was viewed as consisting of two distinct segments: large and small cars, with a rather low substitution elasticity between them. The U.S. manufacturers catered to the first segment, while foreign producers concentrated on the second. Substitution between the two was limited, so that a "reasonable" price differential between large and small cars was sustainable.

But that situation changed dramatically with the sharp rise in the price of gasoline, first in 1974 and secondly in 1979-80 as seen in Figure 6.4. American consumers became highly conscious of fuel efficiency, and a massive switch in consumer taste towards smaller cars was in the making. In other words, there was a shift in demand from large to small cars. American producers were slow to make the change to smaller cars. But they are now in the process of accommodating this change in consumer demand, and new generations of smaller, fuel efficient cars are coming off the U.S. assembly lines. This conversion process requires

FIGURE 6.4
PRICE OF GASOLINE RELATIVE TO ALL ITEMS
(RATIO OF CPI INDEX FOR GASOLINE TO CPI FOR ALL ITEMS)

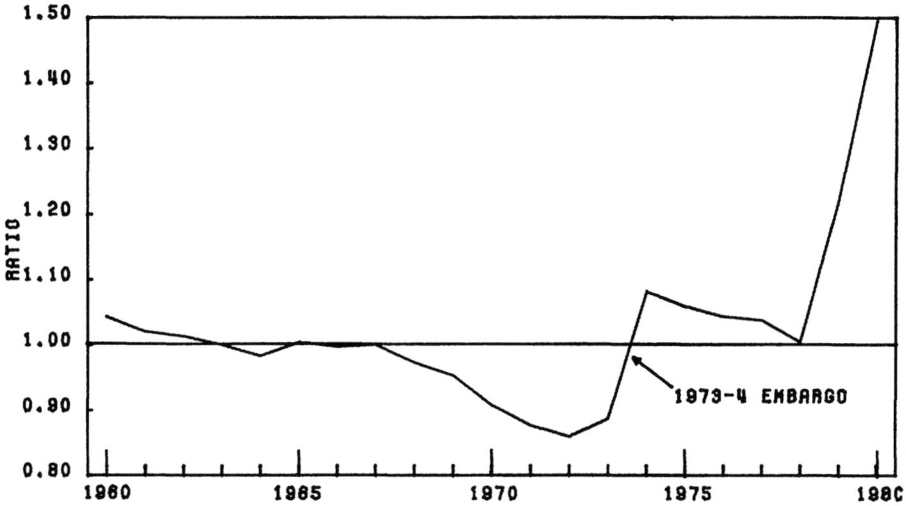

SOURCE: U.S. DEPT. OF LABOR, BUREAU OF LABOR STATISTICS.

FIGURE 6.5
AVERAGE PRODUCTION WORKER COMPENSATION MID-YEAR 1980:
ALL MANUFACTURING AND MOTOR VEHICLES AND EQUIPMENT

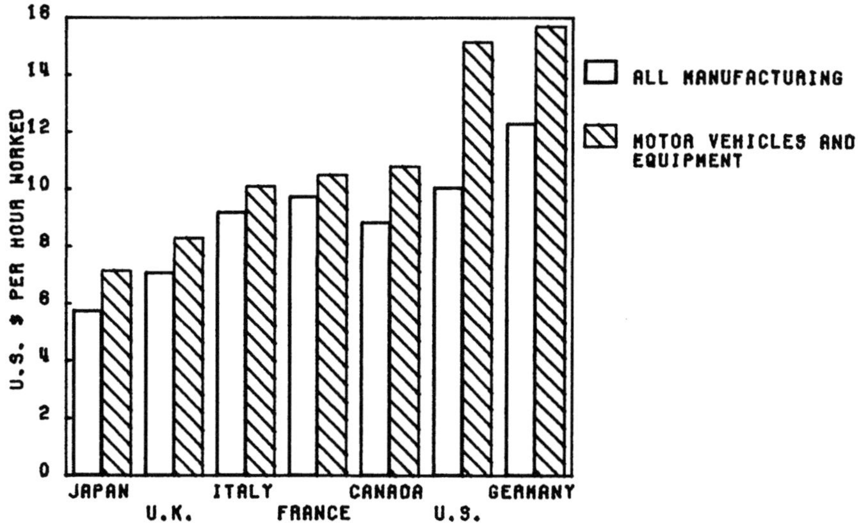

SOURCE: BUREAU OF LABOR STATISTICS, OFFICE OF PRODUCTIVITY AND TECHNOLOGY, NOVEMBER 1980.

TABLE 6.4
AUTO-RELATED EMPLOYMENT BY STATE AND AREA

	NUMBER OF PLANTS	AUTO EMPLOYMENT	AUTO EMPLOYMENT AS PERCENT OF MANUFACTURING EMPLOYMENT	JULY 1980 UNEMPLOYMENT RATE (percent)
STATE				
Michigan	136	365,000	30	14.8
Ohio	51	186,260	13	10.2
Indiana	33	94,300	13	11.3
New York	14	65,100	4	8.1
Illinois	12	38,200	3	9.9
METROPLOITAN AREAS				
Detroit	78	201,000	33	14.6
Flint	16	60,800	69	22.2
Buffalo	7	43,800	30	10.4
Dayton[1]	11	41,800	52	9.6
Cleveland[1]	9	35,900	13	9.2
Ann Arbor	8	32,500	74	9.0
Indianapolis[1]	10	26,700	20	8.8
Saginaw	11	24,400	65	16.8
St. Louis	6	23,700	9	8.6
Anderson	2	23,500	91	20.2

Notes: [1]Rate for county containing the city listed above.

The long run prospects for employment in the industry are far from encouraging even when the long awaited sales pick-up arrives. And that is because of technological innovations in the indusrty and a changeover to small car production. See "Reeling Region" Wall Street Journal, May 26, 1981, p.1.

time, as well as tens of billions in investment dollars.

Barring unforeseen developments on the energy front, the distinction between large U.S. built and small foreign built cars is likely to grow increasingly blurred. And consequently cost-price factors would become of ever rising importance in determining market share. Price has long been the basis for competition <u>within segments</u> of the automobile market; but as the product becomes more homogeneous it is becoming a very important factor in the <u>entire</u> market. Hence this chapter centers attention on labor costs of production.

THE IMPORTANCE OF LABOR COSTS

This is not to deny that the problem of the auto industry is multi-faceted, including quality of the final product, fuel efficiency, and a massive transition of the industry to a new product mix. A comprehensive report on all these and other matters was issued recently by the U.S. Department of Transportation,[5] and the discussion need not be repeated here.

Also, while the present study concentrates on labor cost, there is no denying that other costs also enter price calculations. Material and management costs, as well as inventory control techniques and the clustering of related plants are often cited as examples of Japanese cost advantages. But labor costs are important. They are estimated at 46 percent of all production costs.[6] And references (sometimes fragmentary) to them abound in the literature.

Thus the aforementioned U.S. Department of Transportation Study points out that each one dollar per hour in wage rate translates into one billion dollars cost to the industry. It proceeds to compile a chart, reproduced in Figure 6.5, demonstrating that the ratio of auto industry compensation to compensation in all manufacturing is higher in the United States than in any other country. It is 1.5 in this country compared to under 1.3 in Japan and Germany.

The same study then cites estimates that Japan enjoys a cost advantage over the U.S. in cars landed in this country of anywhere between $1,000 and $1,700 per unit or of 20-25 percent of price. The main factors responsible for this cost differential are: (1) Lower Japanese wage rates: mid-1980 U.S. hourly compensation in the automotive industry was $15--more than double its Japanese counterpart of $7 (converted from the yen at the then existing exchange rate); (2) fewer man-hours required per vehicle, or higher productivity, in Japan; (3) differential costs in management of inventories, materials and components. These advantages are partly offset by freight cost and the 2.9 percent U.S. import duty.

Another recent and often-quoted study estimates the Japanese labor cost advantage over the U.S. at $1,920 per car, half of which is attributable to lower wage rates and the other half to higher productivity in Japan.[7] To that the authors add capital and material cost advantage, and from it they subtract transport costs and import tariff, to arrive at a net advantage of $1,650 per car.

In sum, concentration on labor cost is justified by its overwhelming contribution to total production costs. But there is another equally important reason why it is warranted. Auto producers are truly multinationals. They can shift production of components, parts, or final assembly, around the globe so as to minimize production costs. Labor costs thus becomes a main determinant of plant location. Hence, comparative U.S.-foreign labor costs are of prime importance to future production and employment in this country and in the State of Michigan.

APPROACH

Practically all studies comparing production costs between countries, including those cited above for motor vehicles and earlier ones pertaining to steel, do so at a given point in time (i.e., a recent year) and limit themselves to one industry. The international cost comparison involves at least two elements: (1) labor productivity; and (2) labor compensation, either per hour or per employee. While productivity can be measured in some absolute units (such as the number of hours required to build a vehicle in each country), roughly comparable across countries, labor compensation is estimated in different currencies, and must be converted from one currency to another by the use of the prevailing exchange rate, such as the dollar-yen rate.

Exchange rates of the main industrial countries fluctuate, or float, in response to market conditions. But in many cases, including Japan, the float is "managed" by the central bank, and sometimes it is heavily managed. In the case of the D. Mark, Germany is a member of the European Monetary System, so that the Mark is pegged to six other currencies, and its rate relative to the dollar is affected by conditions in other European countries as well as in Germany. For this and other reasons, the prevailing exchange rate may deviate from the long run equilibrium rate, rendering the comparison of labor compensation inaccurate.

To illustrate the point consider the Abernathy results mentioned above. In it Japanese auto producers are shown to have 25 percent labor cost advantage over their American counterparts in 1980. But suppose Japan had a similar cost advantage in all or most industries. Then clearly the Japanese yen is undervalued.[8] Raising its market value relative to the dollar (or equivalently lowering the value of the dollar relative to the yen) to its equilibrium level would eliminate the cost advantage in auto production.

While international comparisons of a single industry are useful, they do not go far enough. They must be embedded in the total economy. What matters is the cost advantage of a country in one industry relative to its cost advantage in all other manufacturing industries.

In particular, what is necessary is to rank all industries <u>within</u> <u>each</u> country by order of their (labor) production cost: from the lowest to the highest cost industries. This is equivalent to ranking them by comparative advantage. The exchange rate then determines the cut-off points between three types of industries: the export industries (those with lowest cost); the nontraded goods industries; and the import-competing industries. A variant of this approach is employed in the present study, first for the U.S. and then for Japan. Within each country, the behavior of labor cost in motor vehicles and in iron and steel is considered *relative* to their counterpart in the entire manufacturing sector.

However, labor productivity within each country is published in a form of an index; it shows performance relative to some base period. Consequently, labor cost must also be calculated in the same manner. The analysis therefore relies on alternative base periods, prior to the massive deterioration in the U.S. trade position in the two industries. It then observes changes over time from that base. Should the data reveal a rise in the labor cost in one of the industries (or both) far in excess of the national manufacturing average, it can be inferred that the industry moved down in the ranking by comparative advantage, and the Samuelson verdict is validated.

But since the base period is necessarily arbitrary, and because productivity data are notoriously inaccurate (and often unavailable), only broad and consistent trends (over time) can be relied upon to reach a firm conclusion. No meaningful inferences can be made on the basis of a figure pertaining to a single year.

THE IRON AND STEEL INDUSTRY

In a study undertaken two years ago[1] we pieced together data from the Census and Surveys of Manufacturers, the Handbook of Labor Statistics, and other sources to determine the behavior of labor cost in steel over a twenty year period beginning in 1957. Between the years 1957 and 1977, as well as for periods in between, the following results emerge: hourly compensation in iron and steel increased at a rate well above that in all U.S. manufacturing, while labor productivity in iron and steel production increased at a rate slightly below the national manufacturing average. This combination shows that unit labor cost in the U.S. steel industry increased at a rate well above the national average. Clearly the steel industry declined in the ranking of U.S. industries by comparative advantage. The decline started in the early 1960s and intensified in subsequent years.

A new and consistent set of data became available in mid-1980. Compiled by the Bureau of Labor Statistics it shows changes in productivity, labor compensation and unit labor cost between 1964 (=100) and the 1972-80 years, for the five major industrial countries.[10] These data can be collated with equivalent BLS statistics pertaining to all manufacturing in eleven countries (including the above five) for 1950-80.[11]

Throughout the period 1972-80 the growth rate in unit labor cost in the U.S. iron and steel industry was above that for all U.S. manufacturing. What is more, the difference between the two has been on the increase over time. And that for two reasons: labor compensation in steel grew much faster, and labor productivity somewhat slower than in all manufacturing. Table 6.5 shows that between 1964 and 1980 unit labor cost in iron and steel grew by 221 percent compared to only 123 percent growth in the case of all manufacturing. Clearly iron and steel declined in the ranking of U.S. industries over this period, continuing a trend begun during the 1960s. Regardless of the base year, the U.S. is shown to have lost its comparative advantage in steel.

How does this performance compare with that of other countries and especially our main competitor--Japan? Table 6.6 shows that in Japan the unit of labor cost index in iron and steel (1964=100) was considerably below that of all manufacturing in 1972-74; somewhat below in 1975-76; and

TABLE 6.5
INDICES OF LABOR COMPENSATION, PRODUCTIVITY, AND UNIT LABOR COST IN IRON AND STEEL AND ALL MANUFACTURING FOR 1972-80 (1964=100) IN THE UNITED STATES

YEAR	HOURLY COMPENSATION		OUTPUT PER HOUR		UNIT LABOR COST	
	Iron and Steel	All Mfgs.	Iron and Steel	All Mfgs.	Iron and Steel	All Mfgs.
1964	100	100	100	100	100	100
1972	161	153	116	122	138	125
1973	176	165	121	129	145	128
1974	202	182	124	126	163	145
1975	239	204	116	129	206	157
1976	257	220	120	134	215	163
1977	277	238	116	138	239	172
1978	308	258	125	139	246	185
1979	341	283	124	141	276	201
1980	382	312	119	140	321	223

Sources: See notes number 10 and number 11 in the text.

TABLE 6.6

HOURLY COMPENSATION, OUTPUT PER HOUR, AND UNIT LABOR COST IN THE IRON AND STEEL INDUSTRY AND IN ALL MANUFACTURING IN JAPAN (1964=100)

YEAR	HOURLY COMPENSATION		OUTPUT PER HOUR		UNIT LABOR COST	
	Iron and Steel	All Mfgs.	Iron and Steel	All Mfgs.	Iron and Steel	All Mfgs.
1964	100	100	100	100	100	100
1972	277	304	219	221	126	138
1973	342	374	272	246	126	154
1974	456	498	276	257	165	192
1975	550	498	256	267	214	216
1976	583	617	282	292	206	211
1977	645	680	290	318	222	214
1978	686	723	308	339	227	213
1979	712	778	341	367	209	212
1980	725	848	352	390	220	218

Sources: BLS: (a) "International Comparison of Manufacturing Productivity and Labor Costs," Washington D.C., May 20, 1981; (b) "International Comparisons of Productivity and Labor Costs in the Steel Industry," Washington, September 1980.

TABLE 6.6A

1980 INDEX OF UNIT LABOR COST IN IRON AND STEEL AND IN ALL MFGS. IN FIVE COUNTRIES (1964=100)

U.S.A.		France	
Iron & Steel	321	Iron & Steel	341
All Mfgs.	223	All Mfgs.	281
Japan		U.K.	
Iron & Steel	220	Iron & Steel	691
All Mfgs.	218	All Mfgs.	528
Germany			
Iron & Steel	197		
All Mfgs.	215		

somewhat above in 1977-78. By the end year, unit labor cost in iron and steel was roughly in line with its counterpart in the entire Japanese manufacturing sector. Both the index of labor productivity and of labor compensation in iron and steel stood below their counterpart for all manufacturing by roughly the same proportion.

In Germany iron and steel improved its position slightly as the rise in labor compensation in that industry lagged behind the national manufacturing average, while productivity rose in tandem. The French and British situations are similar to that of the U.S. In both countries unit labor cost in iron and steel rose consistently much faster than in all manufacturing because compensation grew faster while productivity rose more slowly in steel. Not available are corresponding statistics for the semi-industrial countries, such as Korea or Brazil, that are gradually acquiring competitive advantage in steel production.

In regard to the U.S. position, the Samuelson verdict appears verified with respect to steel. Using either the mid-1950s or the mid-1960s as a base period, the steel industry slipped in the ranking of industries by comparative advantage, a slippage which began two decades ago. Hourly compensation in steel tripled between 1964 and 1977-78, relative to a 2.5 fold increase in all manufacturers, attesting to the strong position of the USW union. Over the same period labor productivity in steel failed to keep pace with that in all manufactures. These two factors combined to push the unit labor cost index in iron and steel well above that of all manufacturing. In contrast, the Japanese iron and steel industry maintained its rank order among all Japanese manufacturing industries. The fact that in the late 1970s Japanese unit labor cost in iron and steel was around 50 to 60 percent of its American counterpart was due to gradual and prolonged slippage of the industry position in the United States and not to any unusual (exemplary or otherwise) performance in Japan.

MOTOR VEHICLES

In the study mentioned above[12] it was concluded that the position of the U.S. motor vehicle industry did not deteriorate, and may even have improved, relative to all industries during the 1957-67 decade. Table 6.7 provides the data necessary to assess developments between 1967 and 1980. In the first five years, unit labor cost in the motor vehicles industry moved roughly in line with that of the manufacturing sector in general. Between 1972 and 1977 unit labor cost in car production advanced somewhat faster than its counterpart in all manufactures. While productivity in the automobile industry first kept pace with, and then advanced ahead of that in all manufactures, the differential was more than offset by an even greater differential in workers' compensation (namely, wages and fringe benefits), reflecting perhaps the well-known strength of the UAW.

Finally, and most emphatically, in the last three years the difference in unit labor cost between motor vehicles and all manufactures was growing wider. Part of the decline in labor productivity in 1979-80 was undoubtedly cyclical, reflecting the deep depression in the industry and its well-known correlation with labor productivity. But for the most part, the widening gap in unit labor cost was a result of a rapidly increasing differential in labor compensation between the auto industry and all manufacturing.

To some extent, this may have resulted from the cost of living escalator in the UAW contract, coupled with the high rate of inflation in the late 1970s. The Department of Labor estimates that only about 9 million workers are covered by some cost of living clause (COLA). A common COLA provides for a one cent per hour increase for every 0.3 point rise in the Consumer Price Index. But for part of the three year contract negotiated in 1979 the auto workers won an especially lucrative arrangement: a one cent per hour wage increase for every 0.26 point rise in the Consumer Price Index. (The CPI itself accentuates the rate of inflation.) Thus the average GM worker in 1980, when the

TABLE 6.7

INDICES OF HOURLY LABOR COMPENSATION, OUTPUT PER EMPLOYEE AND UNIT LABOR COST IN THE MOTOR VEHICLES INDUSTRY AND IN ALL MANUFACTURING IN THE UNITED STATES (1967=100)

YEAR	COMPENSATION		OUTPUT PER WORKER		UNIT LABOR COST	
	Motor Vehicles	All Mfgs.	Motor Vehicles	All Mfgs.	Motor Vehicles	All Mfgs.
1967	100	100	100	100	100	100
1968	107	107	106	104	101	103
1969	113	115	105	105	108	109
1970	122	122	103	105	119	117
1971	139	130	117	112	119	117
1972	148	137	120	117	123	117
1973	159	147	122	123	130	119
1974	178	162	121	121	148	135
1975	200	182	128	124	156	147
1976	218	196	134	129	162	151
1977	243	212	143	133	170	160
1978	265	230	142	134	187	172
1979	284	252	139	135	205	187
1980	314	279	139[1]	135	227	207

Notes: [1]The statistic in this cell was missing. It was conservatively assumed to remain the same as in 1979 (in line with all manufacturing) although by reason of the severe depression in the industry there is reason to believe that it might have been lower.

All figures are rounded, but calculations were made at the first decimal level.

Because of data constraints, the series for all manufacturing applies to all employees, while that for Motor Vehicles applies only to production workers. However, it was possible to compare the output per hour series for all employees and for production workers in the auto industry throughout the entire period; they are almost identical. Likewise, it was possible to compare the hourly compensation series for all employees and for production workers in "all manufacturing" for the last six years; they are very similar.

Sources: The all manufacturing data are from the BLS, "International Comparisons of Manufacturing Productivity and Labor Costs," May 20, 1981. For autos, the data are from the BLS, "Indices of Output Per Employee (1967=100) in Motor Vehicles and Equipments" and "Estimated Hourly Compensation of Production Workers in the Motor Vehicles and Equipment Industry, 14 countries, 1975-1980," with an adjusted census of manufacturing series going back to 1967.

CPI rose 12.4 percent, received an increase of $1,780 in his annual pay just from the COLA.[13] This component would subside if the rate of inflation declines; or if the contract is renegotiated, either with a different pegging arrangement or an indexation to the GNP Deflator rather than to the CPI.

Clearly, the United States appears to be in the process of losing comparative advantage in motor vehicles. But the process has begun very recently. Unlike steel there is still time to turn the situation around.

It may be asked whether the Japanese car industry gained comparative advantage by moving upward along the Japanese ranking of industries. Table 6.8 presents the relevant indices for Japan covering the 1965-80 years. Although there were periodic deviations in either direction, unit labor cost in the motor vehicles industry moved roughly in line with that for all manufacturing. The exception years were 1977-79 when, due to a (mysterious)[14] precipitous drop in productivity in the auto industry, unit labor costs shot way above those for all manufacturing. But "parity" was restored in 1980. The recent erosion in the U.S. competitive position in motor vehicles is due to unfavorable developments in this country rather than to unusually favorable developments in Japan.[15]

PROSPECTS

It is clear from the data presented above that the U.S. iron and steel industry lost its position in the rank order of industries by comparative advantage due to increases in unit labor costs which far exceeded the average for the entire manufacturing sector. The erosion in its competitive position is deep seated and of long standing.

Import protection of steel through the use of tariffs, quotas, voluntary export restraints, and the trigger price mechanism <u>artificially</u> increases the price of steel in the U.S. above world market levels, and only serves to perpetuate inefficiency. In addition, such restrictions

TABLE 6.8
INDICES OF HOURLY LABOR COMPENSATION, OUTPUT PER EMPLOYEE-HOUR AND UNIT LABOR COST IN MOTOR VEHICLES AND ALL MANUFACTURES FOR JAPAN (1965=100)

YEAR	LABOR COMPENSATION		OUTPUT PER HOUR		UNIT LABOR COST	
	Motor Vehicles	All Mfgs.	Motor Vehicles	All Mfgs.	Motor Vehicles	All Mfgs.
1965	100	100	100	100	100	100
1966	111	110	110	110	101	100
1967	126	124	130	126	96	98
1968	146	144	154	142	95	101
1969	172	171	170	164	101	104
1970	204	203	185	185	110	110
1971	233	235	202	193	115	122
1972	272	271	234	212	116	128
1973	346	333	269	237	129	141
1974	448	438	251	246	178	178
1975	530	513	276	256	192	200
1976	599	550	315	280	190	196
1977	656	606	284	305	231	199
1978	723	644	259	326	279	198
1979	776	693	326	352	238	197
1980	832	755	419	374	199	202

Sources: Data for All Manufactures, from the BLS, "International Comparisons of Manufacturing Productivity and Labor Costs," Washington, May 20, 1981. For the Motor Vehicles Industry: Productivity Index published by Japan's Productivity Center, Productivity Research Institute; and a series from: Kenzo Yukizawa: "Comparative Productivity in the Automobile Industry," Kyoto Institute for Economic Research, Kyoto, Japan March 1977. Compensation series supplied privately through the gracious assistance of the BLS.

undermine the competitive position of industries which use steel as an input. Furthermore, because the degree of dependence on steel input varies from one industry to another a rise in steel prices can distort the ranking of industries by comparative advantage.

A recent study concludes that removal of import restrictions in steel would generate benefits to the steel-using industries (in the form of lower prices) far in excess of the losses to the steel industry itself.[16]

One such steel using industry is automobiles. Since steel is an important input into the motor vehicle industry, comprising nearly one-fifth of the value of the final product, the protection of steel is formally equivalent to a tax on domestically produced automobiles. For every five percent increase in the domestic price of steel above the world market price, the price of domestically produced automobiles increases by one percent (see the Anderson-Kreinin paper cited above for computations).

As for the motor vehicle industry, the erosion in its competitive position is of recent origin. And certain favorable trends are likely to appear on the horizon. First, because of import protection measures in steel, U.S. car producers pay about ten percent more for steel than their Japanese counterparts. But as a part of the drive to increase fuel efficiency, the industry is in the process of switching to lighter materials, such as aluminum.[17] And these are vastly cheaper (40 percent cheaper in the case of aluminum) in the U.S. Secondly, the U.S. manufacturers are in the process of altering their product mix, to accommodate the change in taste towards small cars. To accomplish this the companies are investing massive amounts in new plants and other production facilities. The average age of American plants will decline measurably by 1985. These plants will embody the latest technology (including robots),[18] and contribute to a vast improvement in productivity, an improvement which would be particularly evident once potential scale economies in small car production are fully exploited.[19]

But these favorable trends would not suffice; nor would the temporary "Voluntary Export Restrictions" imposed on Japanese cars. They must be reinforced by deliberate and concerted efforts on the part of labor and management to reduce production costs and halt the rapid escalation in product prices.[20] Compensation may be permitted to advance at a rate higher than the national average only to the extent warranted by a similar differential in productivity growth. Otherwise the motor vehicle industry may go the way of iron and steel. Indeed, it would be highly desirable to reestablish the 1977 relation in unit labor cost between the motor vehicle industry and the national manufacturing average.

At the beginning of the 1980s decade the American automobile industry finds itself at a cross road. Continuation of the 1978-80 trend in unit labor costs could spell severe problems to production and employment in the industry, and may induce the companies to locate new plants outside this country. But this trend is of recent vintage. Once recognized, it could and should be reversed. Samuelson's verdict may yet prove wrong in the case of the motor vehicle industry.

NOTES, CHAPTER 6

[1]See William J. Abernathy, James J. Harbor, and Jay M. Menn, Productivity and Comparative Cost Advantages: Some Estimates for Major Automotive Producers, a mimeographed report to the Department of Transportation, February 13, 1981.

[2]The minor discrepancies between Tables 6.2 and 6.3 are due to differences in sources of data.

[3]In addition, 2.3 million workers are employed by dealers, local purchasers and other auto-related industries, for a total of 4.6 million. For purposes of comparison, total U.S. employment is 98.3 million, and manufacturing employment is estimated at 21 million. (See the following note for source of these figures.)

[4]Table 6.4 is from U.S. Department of Transportation, The U.S. Automobile Industry, 1980 (Washington, January 1981), p. 87.

[5]*The U.S. Automobile Industry, 1980* (Washington, January 1981).

[6]Material costs are about 42 percent of the total. Abernathy et al., *op. cit.*, Table 13.

[7]Abernathy, et al., *Productivity and Comparative Cost Advantages*, tables 11 and 13.

[8]Although there exist various theories concerning the determination of exchange rates, there is little doubt that relative production cost is a most powerful determinant of the long run equilibrium rate.

A study of Japan's exchange rate policy is beyond the scope of this chapter. However, total Japanese international reserves have been rising regularly over the years: from the $3-5 billion range in the late 1960s to the $12-18 billion range in the early and mid-1970s; and to the $21-26 billion range in the late 1970s, reaching $27 billion in January 1981. The dollar-yen exchange rate fluctuated between 270-300 yen = $1 during 1973-77, a range of only 10 percent; and between 210-230 yen to the dollar during 1978 to early 1981, again a range of only 10 percent. It is possible that the yen is undervalued. The above data were compiled from the *International Financial Statistics* of the I.M.F.

[9]R. G. Anderson and M. E. Kreinin, "Labor Cost and U.S. Comparative Advantage in Steel and Motor Vehicles," *The World Economy*, June 1981. While the Anderson-Kreinin article and the present chapter employ the same approach to the problem, there are important differences. The Anderson-Kreinin paper relies on data pieced together from a variety of sources, for five benchmark years between 1957 and 1977. This study is based on a new consistent BLS series of annual data from 1964 to 1978 for steel and from 1967 to 1980 for motor vehicles. Second, this study presents also the comparable data for Japan, while the Anderson-Kreinin study is limited to the United States. A final and rather important difference is that the Anderson-Kreinin study is restricted to a wage index, while the present study uses an index of total labor compensation. There is ample evidence that: a) in the two industries nonwage payments rose faster than wage payments; and b) nonwage payments in the two industries rose much faster than nonwage payments in the manufacturing sector as a whole.

Despite the different sets of statistics employed in the two studies, it is reassuring to note that the results for steel are similar if not identical. In the case of motor vehicles, *roughly* comparable results were obtained for the 1967-77 period. The only difference is that the Anderson-Kreinin study shows some slight gain in comparative advantage in autos, while the present study does not. But this is probably due to the omission of nonwage payments from the Anderson-Kreinin study. But the present study carries the investigation in to the 1977-80 years; and for this later period it shows a dramatic deterioration in the U.S. comparative advantage. Indeed, the steep Japanese penetration of the U.S. market occurred during these years.

[10]"International Comparisons of Productivity in Labor Costs, in the Steel Industry: United States, Japan, France, Germany, United Kingdom; 1964 and 1972-78." Prepared by the U.S. Department of Labor, Bureau of Labor Statistics (BLS), Office of Productivity and Technology, May 1980.

[11]BLS, "International Comparisons of Manufacturing Productivity and Labor Costs Preliminary Measures for 1980" (Washington, D.C., May 20, 1981).

[12]Anderson and Kreinin, "Labor Cost."

[13]"Fizzling COLA," *Wall Street Journal*, August 5, 1981, p.1.

[14]These two figures may also be incorrect.

[15]Unfortunately, I am not in possession of an hourly labor compensation series for the German auto industry, to make possible a similar unit cost analysis. But data on output per hour (namely, labor productivity) do exist for 1962-78. Productivity in the motor vehicles industry advanced roughly in line with that in all manufacturing in 1962-66, somewhat more slowly during 1967-73, and increasingly more slowly in the 1974-78 years. While this may explain the decline in the German competitive position in motor vehicles, no definitive conclusion can be drawn without data on labor compensation. Data compiled from the *German Statistical Yearbook*.

[16]William G. Dewald, et. al., eds., *The Impact of International Trade and Investment on Employment* (Washington: U.S. Department of Labor, 1979). Reviewed in the *Journal of Political Economy*, December 1980, p. 1261.

[17]Abernathy et al., *op. cit.*, Table 5.

[18]It would be interesting to know the extent to which the new machines to be installed in these plants are made in Michigan.

[19]Dewald, *The Impact of International Trade*.

[20]For discussions that emphasize the role of U.S. production costs and car prices in the current sales slump see the *Wall Street Journal*, April 28, 1981; February 18, 1981 (editorial); March 20, 1981 (editorial and an article by Charles Schultz "Against Auto Import Protection"); and April 22, 1981. For a different view see Frank P. Stafford, "The Automobile Industry in North America and Japan," *Economic Outlook USA* (University of Michigan Survey Research Center, spring 1981), pp. 36-38. The two views may be complementary rather than mutually exclusive.

Chapter 7

Automobile Manufacturing in the Great Lakes Region and Japan

by

Frank P. Stafford

The University of Michigan

INTRODUCTION[1]

In the last two decades there has been rapid growth in the level of international trade. This growth has characterized both manufactured goods and primary inputs, such as oil, ores, agricultural products and lumber. In light of an evolving pattern of international trade it seems important to assess the near term and longer term prospects for automobile manufacturing in Michigan and other states in the Great Lakes Region. Since industrial location decisions across countries and among regions within countries are based on relative input costs, such an assessment requires a comparison to other locations in the U.S. and other countries.

The principal approach here is to identify a broad set of conditions which would give rise to certain areas of comparative economic advantage for the Great Lakes Region and to assess the prospects for the central manufacturing industries in Michigan, particularly automobiles. Analysis of the automobile industry in Michigan requires an understanding of input availability and relative prices. Some of the inputs are primary inputs such as water, fuel, and labor. Other are intermediate inputs such as steel, energy, labor with specialized skills, machine tools, and industrial robots.

Another important set of inputs is government provided services such as the transportation system, education and the like. These goods can also be thought of as having a price--namely the tax rates on economic activities which in turn yield revenues to finance the services. Government can be viewed as a provider of intermediate goods to industry.

In this view of government one public sector function is cost-effective provision of support services which facilitate business success. Though harder to assess this is, in a sense, one of the major topics of the other papers in this volume. It does imply that it is not just the level of government as measured, say, by average tax rates, but also the level of government services which facilitate business development that is of concern.

A large government sector which provides services of little value for economic development will certainly discourage business, but there are some interesting effects of government activity on business success. To illustrate, cost-effective provision of public recreation areas can benefit not only the tourist industry but can aid other industries in making a region more attractive to employees. Part of their compensation from residence in a region can be realized in the form of recreational opportunities and some of these may be better provided by public programs. Another function which (national) government can assume is that of economic planning. In market economies this is often referred to as industrial policy. Because many manufactured goods are traded in international markets and because many of our trading partners have industrial policies designed to enhance the growth of selected industries, it is important to understand the nature of these policies in different countries. One of the themes developed in this paper is that Japanese industrial policy deliberately favors their heavy manufacturing industry including automobile manufacturing.

Many discussions of industrial development mention the possible development of "high tech" industries, such as computer manufacturing. It seems important to relate this possible area of industrial development to auto manufacturing since production techniques for automobiles are undergoing a major transformation to computer-assisted processes and robotics. Computer production can be for accounting and information systems or for manufacturing systems. The potential of the former in Michigan relative to other states (such as California or Massachusetts) and relative to other countries (such as Japan) is less certain. In particular, Japan has made a major commitment to the design and production of new generation computers[2] and other "high tech" items such as photocopiers. Computer equipment generally has a very high ratio of value to weight and it seems that there will be increased international specialization of computer manufacturing because shipping costs will not be such an important factor as for automobiles or steel. A computer industry which is based on industrial applications may have much better prospects in Michigan.

There are numerous uncertainties and more conjectured elements here, but it appears that industrial technology is on the verge of a series of dramatic breakthroughs in the design of computer-assisted manufacturing systems, particularly computer-controlled applications of industrial robots. Currently much of the robotics in manufacturing employs electronic readouts on quality control tolerances. Electronic feedback and sensing and computerization of manufacturing plants have great potential to alter manufacturing. The manufacture of robotics and computer assisted manufacturing equipment constitutes an industry in its own right and, importantly, shapes the technology of the industries it serves.

Rapid changes in what may be called the high tech manufacturing industry as applied to automobiles are likely to have important implications for location of all other industries. If there are developments which lead to far greater effectiveness of industrial capital, then the inputs for manufacturing which grow in importance are skilled labor (to build and operate more capital intensive production processes) and raw material inputs. As a consequence, across countries and within countries there will be a shift toward manufacturing in those regions endowed with natural resources and highly skilled labor. In this way production

TABLE 7.1
EMPLOYMENT BY INDUSTRY GROUP,
MARCH 1978 COVERAGE UNDER FICA
(percentage given in parentheses)

INDUSTRY GROUP	MICH.	CALIF.	MASS.	MINN.	N.J.	OHIO	TEXAS
Agricultural Services, Forestry, Fisheries	5,839 (0.2)	48,835 (0.7)	7,231 (0.3)	3,861 (0.3)	6,275 (0.3)	8,401 (0.2)	17,812 (0.5)
Oil and Gas Extraction	3,294 (0.1)	22,060 (0.3)	---	---	69 (0.0)	14,611 (0.4)	130,484 (3.0)
Other Mining, Extraction	9,766 (0.3)	17,640 (0.2)	1,183 (0.1)	14,873 (1.1)	2,685 (0.1)	13,835 (0.4)	38,800 (1.1)
Manufacturing	1,164,433 (39.8)	1,876,483 (25.4)	650,841 (30.9)	367,563 (26.6)	804,754 (33.7)	1,381,842 (37.6)	968,205 (22.2)
Food and Kindred Products	44,600 (1.5)	153,895 (2.1)	27,407 (1.3)	42,984 (3.1)	44,301 (1.9)	67,613 (1.8)	93,166 (2.1)
Lumber and Wood Products	16,049 (0.6)	66,950 (0.9)	5,974 (0.3)	14,607 (1.1)	---	14,813 (0.4)	34,171 (0.8)
Furniture and Fixtures	21,220 (0.7)	55,442 (0.8)	7,930 (0.4)	3,993 (0.3)	10,176 (0.4)	17,342 (0.5)	19,051 (0.6)
Paper	23,767 (0.8)	36,842 (0.5)	30,424 (1.4)	15,869 (1.1)	29,765 (1.2)	36,706 (1.0)	21,341 (0.5)
Printing and Publishing	36,586 (1.2)	110,141 (1.5)	44,784 (2.1)	31,710 (2.3)	47,162 (2.0)	67,724 (1.8)	53,192 (1.2)
Chemicals	34,946 (1.2)	57,899 (0.8)	16,368 (0.8)	6,900 (0.5)	97,706 (4.1)	48,656 (1.3)	69,081 (1.6)
Rubber and Misc. Plastic Products	37,781 (1.3)	67,203 (0.9)	31,836 (1.5)	11,601 (0.8)	39,501 (1.7)	100,259 (2.7)	26,789 (0.6)
Primary Metals	86,521 (3.0)	50,010 (0.7)	14,479 (0.7)	8,236 (0.6)	23,262 (1.0)	149,653 (4.1)	42,993 (1.0)
Fabricated Metals	140,570 (4.8)	143,201 (1.9)	49,542 (2.4)	35,259 (2.5)	56,924 (2.4)	167,797 (4.6)	85,752 (2.0)
Machinery, Except Electrical	155,950 (5.3)	191,021 (2.6)	86,944 (4.1)	71,961 (5.2)	68,298 (2.9)	200,480 (5.5)	129,787 (3.0)
Electric and Electronic Equip.	38,574 (1.3)	247,805 (3.6)	86,213 (4.1)	30,082 (2.2)	80,837 (3.4)	113,197 (3.1)	74,890 (1.7)

Transportation Equipment	331,742 (11.3)	274,176 (3.7)	24,806 (1.2)	8,538 (0.6)	23,114 (1.0)	168,066 (4.6)	67,206 (1.5)
Instruments	11,682 (0.4)	75,463 (1.0)	50,977 (2.4)	15,050 (1.1)	28,958 (1.2)	24,520 (0.7)	17,201 (0.4)
Other Manufacturing	184,445 (6.3)	346,435 (4.7)	173,157 (8.2)	70,464 (5.1)	254,750 (10.7)	205,016 (5.6)	233,585 (5.4)
Contract Construction	119,832 (4.1)	425,500 (5.8)	78,539 (3.7)	74,010 (5.4)	98,765 (3.9)	162,776 (4.4)	426,222 (11.6)
Transportation and Public Utilities	140,518 (4.8)	486,217 (6.6)	111,491 (5.3)	78,504 (5.7)	178,503 (7.5)	196,346 (5.3)	304,470 (7.0)
Wholesale Trade	160,741 (5.5)	497,374 (6.7)	125,180 (5.9)	106,673 (7.7)	200,301 (8.4)	236,799 (6.4)	355,560 (8.2)
Retail Trade	579,918 (19.8)	1,578,412 (21.4)	411,631 (19.6)	306,723 (22.2)	450,397 (18.8)	726,831 (19.8)	943,868 (21.7)
Finance, Insurance, Real Estate	151,786 (5.2)	577,035 (7.8)	145,405 (6.9)	92,794 (6.7)	150,771 (6.3)	199,199 (5.4)	292,400 (6.7)
Services	575,149 (19.7)	1,798,989 (24.4)	567,672 (27.0)	331,462 (24.0)	491,372 (20.8)	725,951 (19.7)	894,901 (20.5)
TOTAL PRIVATE PAYROLL	2,921,639 (100.0)	7,380,631 (100.0)	2,104,767 (100.0)	1,383,339 (100.0)	2,389,711 (100.0)	3,676,465 (100.0)	4,400,522 (100.0)
Civilian Federal Employment	54,121	312,680	57,333	30,819	71,650	90,551	160,094
Ratio of Civilian Federal to Total Private Employment	1.9	4.2	2.7	2.2	3.0	2.5	3.6

costs for high wage countries (such as the U.S.) could be reduced below many lower wage manufacturing locations because of our skilled labor force and natural resource endowment.

In the first section of the paper we will review the current structure of industry in Michigan and provide a comparison with other states including California, Ohio, and New Jersey, and several prefectures in Japan. The second section of the paper will offer comments on the prospects for auto manufacturing in Michigan. The emphasis will be on indicating prospects rather than attempting to forecast the well-being of the industry. Prospects for an industry and success of an industry are not necessarily the same; a region with numerous favorable conditions for a particular industry may fail to have a flourishing industry of that type because of poor managerial decisions, an unfavorable government policy, or many other factors which intervene between potential for an industry and its successful development. In the case of the auto industry governmental factors limiting the industry include our national and international tax policy as it influences international trade patterns.

A summary is provided in the third section. In this section there is a discussion of industrial policy as it affects automobile manufacturing in Japan and the possible need for an industrial policy for automobile manufacturing in the U.S.

THE STRUCTURE OF INDUSTRY IN MICHIGAN AND THE ECONOMIC ENVIRONMENT OF DOMESTIC AUTOMOBILE INDUSTRY

To characterize Michigan industry one could examine capital, sales or employment by industry groups. Regional disaggregations of industry are relatively scarce, but a rather clear picture can be derived by examining employment by industry. Table 7.1 presents data from County Business Patterns, a publication based on payrolls covered by the Federal Insurance Contributions Act. A disadvantage of such

TABLE 7.2

1980 EMPLOYMENT[1] BY INDUSTRY GROUP FOR THREE JAPANESE PREFECTURES

INDUSTRY GROUP	JAPANESE PREFECTURES					
	Aichi		Osaka		Kanagawa	
	number	percent	number	percent	number	percent
Agricultural services, Forestry, Fisheries	8.900	0.4	4,700	0.2	8,200	0.3
Oil and Gas Extraction and Other Mining Extraction	1,800	0.1	700	0.0	1,800	0.1
Manufacturing	855,100	37.6	934,600	31.7	846,600	32.1
Food and Kindred Products	57,100	2.5	53,700	1.8	55,500	2.1
Lumber and Wood Products	17,400	0.8	14,600	0.5	5,700	0.2
Furniture and Fixtures	20,800	0.9	12,400	0.4	8,800	0.3
Paper	15,700	0.7	28,400	1.0	10,600	0.4
Printing and Publishing	27,700	1.2	56,500	1.9	35,700	1.4
Chemicals	25,100	1.1	70,700	2.4	57,300	2.2
Rubber and Miscellaneous Plastic Products	12,800	0.6	13,400	0.5	12,200	0.5
Primary Metal	53,300	2.3	69,600	2.4	50,700	1.9
Fabricated Metal	86,800	3.8	147,100	5.0	70,700	2.7
Machinery except Electrical	81,200	3.6	111,500	3.8	88,600	3.4
Electrical and Electronic Equipment	61,000	2.7	107,300	3.6	208,400	7.9
Transportation Equipment	179,500	7.9	37,300	1.3	131,400	5.0
Instruments	14,400	0.6	15,800	0.5	23,800	0.9
Other Manufacturing	202,300	8.9	196,300	6.7	87,200	3.3
Transportation and Public Utilities	180,700	7.9	261,600	8.9	259,900	9.9
Contract Construction	191,400	8.4	259,000	8.8	235,900	8.9
Wholesale Trade	223,100	9.8	344,600	11.7	192,000	7.3
Retail Trade	257,200	11.3	357,100	12.1	308,500	11.7
Finance, Insurance, and Real Estate	87,500	3.8	156,200	5.3	139,600	5.3
Services	386,500	17.0	531,400	18.0	525,500	19.9
Total Private Payroll	2,273,500	100.0	2,951,100	100.0	2,636,400	100.0

Note: [1]Employees are defined as employed persons 15 years old and older, excluding self-employed and family workers.

a data base is that it excludes government employees, self-employed, farm workers, and domestic service workers. The last two rows of Table 7.1 present data on civilian federal employment. The states selected are designed to provide regional comparisons of states which, like Michigan, have a substantial manufacturing sector. In Table 7.2 are employment data for three prefectures in Japan. There are fifty-six prefectures in Japan and the three included in the table are Aichi, Osaka, and Kanagawa. The Aichi prefecture is the "Michigan" of Japan; it has the heaviest concentration of automobile manufacturing and includes Nagoya. The Osaka prefecture is the "Ohio-Pennsylvania" of Japan; it includes the heaviest concentration of steel production. Finally, the Kanagawa prefecture is the "California-Massachusetts" of Japan; it includes the heaviest concentration of electronic equipment production and also contains a substantial concentration of transportation equipment employment.

The data indicate that, among the states listed, Michigan, with almost 40 percent of its employment in manufacturing, has the highest employment share in manufacturing. Close behind is Ohio (with 38 percent of employment in manufacturing), and New Jersey and Massachusetts both have large manufacturing sectors, accounting for over 30 percent of employment. California, Minnesota, and Texas all have about one-quarter of their employment in manufacturing. The Aichi prefecture of Japan has about 38 percent of its payroll employment (employment excluding self employed and family workers) in manufacturing.

Differences across the states and prefectures in type of manufacturing are much greater than differences in total manufacturing. Michigan has a large share of employment in transportation equipment manufacturing (11.3 percent) and related industries (fabricated metal, 4.8 percent, and primary metal, 3.0 percent). The Aichi prefecture has 7.9 percent of its employment in the transportation equipment industry. Ohio's industry is represented by a greater share of employment in primary metal, rubber products, and electric and electronic equipment. Although Texas, Massachusetts and California are often characterized as high tech states, the share of employment in the industrial category, electric and electronic equipment, is as high as 4 percent only in California and Massachusetts. Of course, given California's large labor force, the absolute scale of "high tech" industry (electronic equipment plus some segment of the machinery, transportation, and instruments industries) sector with an employment of perhaps half a million persons is something on the scale of Michigan's auto industry.

Across the states in Table 7.1, the other industry groups exhibit much smaller variations. A possible exception is oil and gas extraction and associated industry which is highest in Texas. In a sense the top part of Tables 7.1 and 7.2 (agriculture, extractive industries, and manufacturing) represents the different export sectors of each state/prefecture while the lower part of the table (transportation, trade, finance, services) represents support industries which supply nontraded goods used in "domestic" consumption.

The last two rows of Table 7.1 reflect the well-known differences across the states in levels of federal expenditure. Although restricted to civilian federal employment, the states with higher civilian federal employment usually receive larger shares of federal expenditure.

If Michigan's export economy is based on manufacturing to a larger extent than other states, how healthy is U.S. manufacturing generally and how healthy are the manufacturing industries which are predominant in Michigan? Many popular accounts imply that the slow rate of U.S. productivity growth combined with rapid wage growth has led to a slower rate of growth of manufacturing and corresponding economic problems for states such as Michigan,

Ohio, and New Jersey. Productivity growth rates for U.S. manufacturing are presented in Table 7.3. Although the general pattern of productivity growth exhibits a systematic decline, several industries appear to have sustained the higher growth rates of the 1949-65 period. These are food processing, textiles and motor vehicles.

Labor costs depend on both productivity and wage rates. Although productivity in some manufacturing industries has been strong in the last ten to fifteen years, what has happened to wages? Table 7.4 shows that in heavy industry (steel, railroads, motor vehicles) there has been rapid wage growth in the period 1970-79. While general inflation has increased 87 percent over this period, the wage in the motor vehicle industry has increased by 115 percent. Overall, wage growth above the rate of inflation has been about 3 percent in the motor vehicle industry while productivity growth has exceeded 3 percent implying a decline in unit labor costs. This does not mean that the auto industry has no problems in terms of production costs. One problem is that supplier industries (notably primary metals and fabricated metals) have experienced poor productivity growth and rapid wage growth with unit labor costs rising during the 1970s. Further, it is claimed that our international trading partners, notably Japan, have had rapid productivity growth and moderate wage growth.

Recent international comparisons show that during the 1970s, unit labor costs in the U.S. have not risen more rapidly than in other industrialized countries. In making such international comparisons it is necessary to allow for changes in the exchange rate. During the 1970s the decline in the U.S. dollar relative to most other currencies (except the Canadian dollar and the British pound) has meant that unit labor costs converted to U.S. dollars have risen more slowly in the U.S. than in most industrialized countries. These comparisons are presented in Table 7.5. Despite the more rapid rise in foreign unit labor costs (in U.S. dollars) the absolute levels of unit labor costs are

TABLE 7.3
PRODUCTIVITY GROWTH AND VALUE ADDED PER WORKER IN U.S. MANUFACTURING

MANUFACTURING INDUSTRY	AVERAGE ANNUAL PRODUCTIVITY GROWTH (percent)			STANDARDIZED VALUE ADDED PER WORKER HOUR (average=1.00)		
	1949-1965	1966-1973	1974-1978	1949-1965	1966-1973	1974-1978
Food and Kindred Products	3.0	3.1	3.8	1.00	1.03	1.09
Textile Mill Products	5.1	2.5	4.6	0.45	0.58	0.62
Furniture	2.0	1.6	1.2	0.74	0.63	0.62
Petroleum and Coal Products	5.3	3.1	1.6	2.15	2.77	2.71
Chemicals	4.8	4.6	0.6	1.09	1.34	1.37
Primary Metals	1.7	1.1	-2.6	1.57	1.26	1.08
Fabricated Metals	2.3	1.7	0.9	1.00	0.92	0.85
Machinery, except Electrical	1.9	2.1	0.2	1.20	1.05	0.98
Electrical Equipment and Supplies	4.7	4.2	2.1	0.74	0.94	0.99
Motor Vehicles	5.0	3.2	6.0	1.43	1.64	1.85
All Manufacturing	3.0	2.6	1.7	1.00	1.00	1.00

ource: Congressional Budget Office calculations based on data from the Department of Commerce and the Bureau of Labor Statistics. Published in The Productivity Problem: Alternatives for Action, Congressional Budget Office, January, 1981.

TABLE 7.4
PERCENTAGE WAGE CHANGE FOR SELECTED INDUSTRIES, 1970-1979

INDUSTRY	PERCENTAGE CHANGE
Basic Steel	150
Railroads	130
Cigaretts	124
Motor Vehicles	115
Laundries	89
Knitting Mills	83
Clothing Stores	75
Banks	62

Note: In comparison with the above figures, the Consumer Price Index rose 87 percent during 1970-1979.

Source: Bureau of Labor Statistics, Employment and Earnings in the U.S., 1980.

TABLE 7.5

INDEXES OF MANUFACTURING OUTPUT PER HOUR, HOURLY COMPENSATION, UNIT LABOR COSTS, AND RELATED DATA, 1970-79.

	UNITED STATES	CANADA	JAPAN	FRANCE	GERMANY	ITALY	UNITED KINGDOM	BELGUIM	DENMARK'	NETHER-LANDS	SWEDEN	EIGHT EUROPEAN COUNTRIES	TEN FOREIGN COUNTRIES
YEAR	OUTPUT PER HOUR												
1970	105.0	114.7	146.6	121.2	116.1	121.7	110.1	129.5	129.3	134.0	123.5	120.2	125.7
1971	110.5	122.9	152.9	127.6	121.3	125.2	113.9	136.7	138.7	143.0	130.3	126.2	131.7
1972	115.7	128.3	168.0	135.1	128.7	135.3	121.9	152.2	150.7	154.4	138.7	135.0	141.7
1973	118.9	135.0	187.3	142.5	136.4	151.7	128.9	167.8	159.8	170.2	148.9	143.7	152.7
1974	113.0	137.2	195.0	147.3	144.7	159.7	128.6	176.9	165.1	184.3	153.9	149.3	158.7
1975	118.8	133.7	202.9	151.9	151.6	152.9	125.7	186.9	178.0	181.1	151.9	151.5	162.0
1976	124.0	140.2	221.9	164.3	161.3	166.0	129.6	204.4	191.4	204.2	152.9	161.7	173.9
1977	127.7	147.3	241.5	171.7	170.2	167.8	129.1	215.9	195.4	212.5	149.9	166.3	182.1
1978	128.2	151.9	258.0	180.2	176.3	173.0	130.7	227.6	204.0	223.4	158.9	172.2	190.4
1979	129.2	153.7	279.0	188.7	185.5	189.1	132.9	238.1	206.3	232.5	172.0	181.3	201.9
YEAR	HOURLY COMPENSATION												
1970	122.3	124.0	164.0	131.6	133.5	145.7	132.3	131.2	145.0	146.2	130.3	136.2	139.8
1971	129.9	133.5	189.4	147.1	150.9	168.1	151.1	150.2	157.2	167.1	146.4	154.4	158.3
1972	136.6	143.8	218.6	164.0	168.6	192.7	169.8	174.6	176.1	191.5	167.4	173.9	178.4
1973	146.5	158.0	269.2	188.0	191.5	243.9	188.3	202.4	203.4	228.4	183.1	199.0	206.7
1974	161.7	181.9	353.8	226.0	220.8	303.9	232.4	247.1	244.9	272.2	213.5	235.1	250.5
1975	181.1	208.8	414.1	270.4	248.8	391.7	306.4	298.8	291.2	311.3	258.9	279.3	296.4
1976	196.1	238.6	444.0	309.6	266.9	469.2	359.0	334.7	324.5	349.8	310.3	315.2	329.9
1977	212.7	269.1	489.4	352.6	293.2	557.6	399.3	371.9	357.5	379.8	348.3	351.7	366.9
1978	229.9	289.3	520.3	398.1	317.7	639.0	461.3	398.4	394.3	409.1	391.8	391.3	403.0
1979	250.8	317.9	553.2	453.5	338.4	774.8	539.3	432.9	435.8	437.8	422.9	439.3	446.0
YEAR	VALUE OF OF FOREIGN CURRENCY RELATIVE TO THE U.S. DOLLAR												
1970	100.0	103.4	101.1	89.0	109.3	99.5	87.1	100.1	93.1	99.6	99.5	100.3	100.6
1971	100.0	106.8	104.2	89.3	114.7	100.9	88.9	102.4	94.3	103.2	101.1	103.4	103.7
1972	100.0	108.9	119.5	97.5	125.0	106.9	90.9	112.9	100.4	112.2	108.5	111.5	113.0
1973	100.0	107.9	133.7	110.9	150.5	107.3	89.1	128.0	115.9	129.6	118.6	126.8	127.3
1974	100.0	110.3	124.2	102.4	154.4	95.9	85.1	127.8	114.8	134.3	116.5	123.8	123.2
1975	100.0	106.1	122.1	114.9	162.4	95.7	80.0	135.4	121.7	142.8	124.6	127.6	125.2
1976	100.0	109.4	122.2	103.0	158.4	75.2	65.6	128.8	115.5	136.3	118.5	116.5	117.5
1977	100.0	101.5	135.2	100.1	171.7	70.7	63.4	138.7	116.3	146.8	115.5	119.0	121.8
1978	100.0	94.6	173.8	109.3	198.8	73.5	69.7	158.1	126.7	166.7	114.3	131.8	139.2
1979	100.0	92.1	166.0	115.7	217.5	75.1	77.2	169.4	132.7	179.6	120.4	139.9	142.9

YEAR	UNIT LABOR COSTS IN NATIONAL CURRENCY												
1970	116.5	108.1	111.9	108.6	115.0	119.8	120.3	101.4	112.2	109.1	105.5	113.3	111.3
1971	117.6	108.6	123.9	115.2	124.4	134.3	132.7	109.8	113.3	116.9	112.4	122.4	120.2
1972	118.1	112.1	130.1	121.4	130.9	142.4	139.3	114.7	116.8	124.1	120.6	128.8	125.9
1973	123.2	117.0	143.7	132.0	140.4	160.8	146.1	120.7	127.3	134.2	123.0	138.5	135.3
1974	143.1	132.5	181.4	153.4	152.6	190.4	180.8	139.7	148.4	147.7	138.7	157.5	157.8
1975	152.4	156.2	204.1	178.0	164.1	256.2	243.8	159.8	163.6	171.9	170.4	184.4	183.0
1976	158.2	170.2	200.1	188.4	165.5	282.7	277.0	163.7	169.5	171.3	203.0	194.9	189.7
1977	166.6	182.7	202.7	205.3	172.2	332.3	309.2	172.2	182.9	178.7	232.4	211.4	201.5
1978	179.4	190.5	201.7	220.9	180.2	369.5	353.0	175.1	193.3	183.1	246.6	227.2	211.7
1979	194.1	206.9	198.3	240.4	182.4	409.7	405.7	181.8	211.2	188.3	245.9	242.3	220.9
YEAR	UNIT LABOR COSTS IN U.S. DOLLARS												
1970	116.5	111.7	113.1	96.7	125.7	119.2	104.8	101.4	104.4	108.7	105.0	113.6	111.9
1971	117.6	116.1	129.1	102.9	142.7	135.6	117.9	112.4	106.8	120.6	113.6	126.5	124.6
1972	118.1	122.1	155.5	118.4	163.7	152.2	126.7	129.4	117.3	139.2	130.9	143.6	142.2
1973	123.2	126.2	192.1	146.4	211.3	172.5	130.2	154.4	147.6	174.0	145.8	175.6	172.3
1974	143.1	146.2	225.4	157.0	235.6	182.6	153.8	178.5	170.3	198.3	161.5	195.1	194.4
1975	152.4	165.6	249.2	204.6	266.4	245.1	196.9	216.4	199.2	245.4	212.4	235.3	229.1
1976	158.2	186.2	244.5	194.1	262.2	212.5	181.8	210.9	195.8	233.6	240.6	227.1	222.8
1977	166.6	185.5	174.1	205.5	295.8	234.9	196.2	238.9	212.7	262.4	268.5	251.6	245.5
1978	179.4	180.3	350.5	241.5	358.3	271.7	246.2	276.7	245.0	305.3	281.8	299.5	294.7
1979	194.1	190.6	329.1	278.0	396.8	307.8	313.1	308.0	280.3	338.1	296.0	339.0	315.8

Note: [1]Excluding manufacturing handicrafts.

lower in other industrial countries. To illustrate, in mid-year 1980, average hourly motor vehicle production worker compensation, converted to U.S. dollars at prevailing exchange rates, was higher only in Germany (about $16) than in the U.S., where the compensation was about $15. Italy, France and Canada had hourly compensation of about $10-$11 while Japan had hourly compensation of about $7 per hour.

It is worth noting that large private cost differences in production do relate to trade flows. While Japanese auto imports to the U.S. have increased in recent years auto imports from Europe have declined. Similarly, U.S. textile exports have grown and this is consistent with the rapid productivity growth (Table 7.3) combined with moderate wage increases (Table 7.4). In contrast the U.S. steel industry has experienced a declining world market share; the poor productivity performance (Table 7.3) combined with exceptionally large wage increases (Table 7.4) are certainly explanatory factors. It is unlikely that either Japan or Europe has a comparative advantage in steel delivered to the North American market, particularly in light of the impressive developments in taconite and hematite ore processing, access to coal, and water shipment in the Great Lakes Region.[3] Yet the domestic steel industry has experienced a declining market in the 1970s.

The health of the domestic steel industry is of great importance for the automobile industry in Michigan and in other states in the Great Lakes Region. In its current state the steel industry constitutes a source of cost disadvantage rather than what should be an advantage for manufacturing in the U.S. The inherent advantages of the Great Lakes Region for steel production are suggested by the longer term growth of the region as a share of U.S. raw steel production. Specifically, Indiana, Illinois and Michigan have grown from 27 percent of U.S. raw steel production in 1956 to 35 percent in 1978 (Table 7.6).[4]

Major reasons for this intracountry shift in steel production are inherent resource cost advantages in the

TABLE 7.6
GEOGRAPHICAL DISTRIBUTION OF U.S. RAW STEEL PRODUCTION, 1956, 1966, 1976, AND 1978
(percent)

LOCATION	1956	1966	1976	1978
Northeast	38.7	36.0	29.2	28.2
New England, New Jersey, Delaware, Maryland	6.0	6.2	4.6	4.6
New York	5.4	5.8	3.7	3.1
Pennsylvania	27.3	24.0	20.9	20.5
Southeast[1]	7.2	8.1	9.2	9.7
Great Lakes	46.4	46.3	51.5	50.3
Ohio	19.4	17.1	17.5	15.5
Indiana	12.5	13.5	17.3	17.8
Illinois	8.4	8.2	8.6	9.1
Michigan	6.1	7.5	8.1	7.9
Midwest[2]		3.4	4.0	5.7
	7.8			
West[3]		6.4	6.1	6.1
Total United States	100.0	100.0	100.0	100.0

Notes: [1]Includes Alabama, Arkansas, Florida, Georgia, Kentucky, Louisiana, Mississippi, North Carolina, South Carolina, Tennesse, Virginia, and West Virginia

[2]Includes Iowa, Minnesota, Missouri, Nebraska, Oklahoma, and Texas.

[3]Includes Arizona, California, Colorado, Hawaii, Oregon, Utah, and Washington.

Source: Annual Statistical Report: American Iron and Steel Institute, selected years. Figures are rounded. (Reprinted from Crandall, p. 145.)

Great Lakes Regions as well as increased demand as the population center of the U.S. has moved westward. The westward population shift combined with the recent expansion of low cost taconite and hematite plants in Minnesota and Northern Michigan, along with access to low cost coal from the western states with shipping via the Great Lakes through Duluth/Superior, will most likely further expand the longer-run share of the Great Lakes steel market. This will be discussed in greater detail in the second section of the paper.

Much of Michigan's short term economic distress is related to a decline in domestic auto sales. To a substantial extent, this can be described as a shift in demand toward smaller cars as a consumer reaction to rising fuel prices and apprehension over fuel availability. Table 7.7 indicates the relation between the share of the new auto market going to smaller cars and the price of gasoline after adjustment for inflation. The 1978-81 fuel price increases were much greater than the 1972-75 price increases, and the recent shift to smaller cars has been much more dramatic than in the earlier "oil shock." Overall, the response by consumers certainly shatters the old myth that the U.S. automobile market was characterized by an inherent preference for large cars. The real price of gasoline has increased by twenty cents in 1971 dollars (an increase of two-thirds) while the share of the market going to small cars has increased by 100 percent.

Industry plans for a rapid transition to smaller cars were curtailed or at least slowed when real gasoline prices stabilized and slightly declined in 1976-78 and the market share of small car sales fell. An inspection of Table 7.7 seems to suggest that U.S. consumers look at fuel prices on the way to the dealer showrooms and decide on fuel efficiency based on what price prevails at that moment. If short term movements in fuel costs and availability do explain short term sales patterns, it seems that the auto industry should consider this in the design of future

TABLE 7.7

MARKET SHARES OF TOTAL (DOMESTIC AND IMPORT) AUTOMOBILE SALES IN THE U.S. VS. REAL GASOLINE PRICES, 1971-81

YEAR	SMALL CAR SALES AS PERCENTAGE OF TOTAL U.S. AUTO SALES[1] (percent)	REAL PLUS TAX PRICE OF REGULAR GASOLINE[2] (cents/gallon)
1971	17.3	30.0
1972	17.5	28.8
1973	20.1	29.2
1974	20.5	35.5
1975	24.1	35.5
1976	19.8	34.9
1977	21.0	34.7
1978	20.6	33.6
1979	27.9	40.4
1980	33.3	47.5
1981[3]		
January-March	33.7	50.4
April-May	34.2	50.5
January-May	33.9	50.4

Notes: [1]Small cars are defined as "subcompacts" for domestically made cars, and as those with displacement of 1800 c.c. or less for imported cars.

[2]Real gasoline price is the nominal retail price of gasoline plus tax divided by the consumer price index (CPI-U).

[3]1981 import data for small cars is based on import small car market shares for 1980 by make applied to 1981 import car sales by make.

Sources: Small Car Market Shares: Market shares for small domestically produced cars is from *Automotive News 1981 Market Data Book* (April 29, 1981), and various later issues of *Automotive News*. Market Shares for small imported cars were calculated from sales data by model reported in *Ward's Automotive Yearbook* (various issues) for 1971-78 data, and from sales data by model reported in *Automotive News 1981 Market Data Book* and later issues of *Automotive News* for 1979-81.

Real price of gasoline: Nominal price data for regular gasoline is from the Congressional Research Service's *The Energy Factbook* (Washington, D.C.: U.S. Government Printing Office, November 1980), page 293, for 1971-79 data; 1980-81 data is from *Oil and Gas Journal*, various issues.

Consumer price index data (CPI-U) is from the Bureau of Labor Statistics.

capital outlays. In calculating _expected_ returns from investment it is necessary to consider the return from capacity in smaller size cars (such as "commuter" cars or electric cars) based not only on sales at current fuel prices but on sales should fuel prices rise (or fall) substantially in real terms and in light of long design and production lags, particularly in engine manufacturing. To illustrate the point, the production of commuter cars by U.S. manufacturers has been discouraged by the overall share of sales in these size classes during 1981. However, if oil prices soar upward, it is certain that the sales of small displacement engine cars (1,000 cc or less) and electric cars will follow. As a result, it may pay to accept a moderate current return on plant designed for such cars to protect against losses which would occur if oil prices are pushed up by international events.

PROSPECTS FOR AUTOMOBILE MANUFACTURING IN MICHIGAN

Auto manufacturing in Michigan includes not only a large share of the nation's assembly plants, which tend to be more geographically dispersed toward the various regional markets, but also engine and component plants which are often of a scale to serve the entire national market from a single plant. The production of automotive products in Michigan depends on access to both primary inputs of materials (such as coal, iron ore, water) as well as energy and other intermediate goods such as glass, plastics, steel, aluminum, machine tools, industrial robots, specialized industrial computers, and public services.

Because of the current transformation of the U.S. auto industry to new fuel efficient designs and because of the complete obsolescence of many of the older plants, many of the current business decisions are truly fresh decisions on fundamental design and marketing strategy as well as geographic location. The idea here is to consider some of the probable features of the new product designs and production methods and to assess the prospects of the Great

Lakes Region as a location relative to other regions or countries. This obviously cannot be a comprehensive assessment since there is substantial variety in the future state of consumer demand and because there are so many auto components, some of which will have different locational advantages.

Material Inputs

Materials are a very large share of manufacturing costs for autos. They represent about 40 percent of the costs of the mid-1970s (Table 7.8). The transition to smaller (or at least more fuel efficient) cars manufactured with modern, capital-intensive production methods will still make use of many traditional materials despite the search for weight saving substitutes. As designers have remarked, there is no such thing as a cheaper and lighter material which serves the same function in the car. Rather, it is that higher fuel costs lead to greater utilization of more expensive, lighter weight materials. As the industry switches to greater use of light weight materials, the short run price of these lighter weight materials may or may not exceed its long run price. For example, an increased demand for aluminum may push up its short run cost but will lead to greater aluminum production capacity or invite new lighter weight substitutes such as magnesium produced under revolutionary production methods.

To illustrate this point further, rising aluminum prices have motivated research on the potential extraction of magnesium from large scale seawater processing plants.[5] Though magnesium is lighter than aluminum, its current alloys are not as strong. Considering both strength and weight, there is a price ratio at which it is attractive to switch from aluminum to magnesium. This ratio is not necessarily larger than the ratio of specific gravity of aluminum alloy to that of magnesium alloy (about 1.5) because that ratio only defines the weight needed to fill a given size casting; both weight and strength are necessary to define fuel savings. This is because a stronger material

TABLE 7.8
PERCENTAGE DISTRIBUTION OF AUTOMOBILE MANUFACTURING COSTS, MID 1970s

	COST ELEMENT[1]				
	AUTOMOTIVE ASSEMBLY	BODY UNIT	FRAME	ENGINE	TRANS-MISSION
A. Materials[2]	68	38	43	36	34
B. Capital Overhead	2	11	4	7	5
C. Labor	15	38	25	38	39
D. Labor Overhead	5	3	18	9	12
E. Profit Target	10	10	10	10	10
Share of total cost of given cost element for a compact auto	32	40	6	18	4

Notes: [1]Tires and other externally purchased components are excluded as are corporate (administrative, research, marketing and dealer) costs.

[2]Materials number is meant to represent value added at each stage. For automotive assembly, the materials figure is derived from combined data on auto and truck production. Professor Ebner believes that the number greatly overstates the percentage of cost in automotive assembly attributable to materials added at that stage, and that materials probably account for between 30 and 50 percent of the value added in automotive assembly.

Source: Data supplied to Professor Ebner of Boston University by Ford Motor Company. Reprinted in Impact of Trade Policies in the U.S. Automobile Market, Bureau of International Labor Affairs, U.S. Dept. of Labor, Washington D.C., October 1976.

TABLE 7.9
PAST AND PROJECTED MATERIAL CONTENT FOR AVERAGE PASSENGER CAR IN THE U.S., 1975 THROUGH 1990

MATERIAL	1975		1980		1985		1990	
	Pounds	Percent	Pounds	Percent	Pounds	Percent	Pounds	Percent
Cast Iron	625	16	460	15	300	12	250	11
Steel	2420	61	1835	60	1600	63	1300	57
Plactics	170	4	185	6	240	9	300	13
Aluminum	85	2	125	4	150	6	200	9
Copper	40	1	25	1	25	1	20	1
Zinc	50	1	20	1	25	1	20	1
Magnesium	--	--	--	--	5	1	15	1
Other	580	15	430	14	200	--	175	8
Total	3970	100	3080	100	2545	100	2280	100

Source: U.S. Automotive Industry Trends for the 1980s, Arthur Anderson and Company, 1981, and The U.S. Automobile Industry, 1980, U.S. Department of Transportation, January 1981.

requires a thinner casting.

According to current estimates the critical price ratio at which it is worth switching to magnesium is about 1.3.[6] The current price ratio of magnesium to aluminum has been in the range of 1.6. What this implies is that moderate decreases in the price of magnesium relative to aluminum, perhaps the consequence of a bauxite cartel, could lead to a major adoption of magnesium.

The illustration of the possible substitution between aluminum and magnesium suggests some of the reasons for uncertainty about material use in the production of automobiles. With this caveat in mind we turn to a recent study which attempted to survey engineering opinion about types of materials used in automobile manufacturing during the next ten years. The projected material content estimates for 1985 and 1990 are given in Table 7.9, along with the 1975 and 1980 actual use data. The projected material uses cannot resolve the sorts of substitution uncertainties arising from unforeseen input price changes or production innovations, but they are based on a consensus forecast by design engineers in the industry.

These estimates forecast a decline in average weight from about 4,000 pounds per car in 1975 to about 2,300 pounds in 1990. As part of this transition there is materials substitution with a growth of lighter materials such as aluminum and plastics and a decline in materials such as glass and cast iron. Yet iron and iron derivatives will still represent a dominant share of total materials. While in 1975 about 75 percent of the weight is iron or iron derivatives, in 1990 about 70 percent of the weight is projected to be iron or iron derivatives. This small decline in the share of iron is attributable to its low cost and the development of new types of steel.

If iron is to be the primary material for auto manufacturing, the location of the auto industry can be influenced by access to low cost iron and steel products. What are the prospects for the cost of steel in the U.S. and the Great Lakes? According to a recent monograph, the prospects for the U.S. steel industry are not particularly bright.[7] In this study, the three reasons given for problems in the domestic industry are antiquated equipment, high labor costs, and high raw material costs. The first two of these are clearly reflected in our observation of declining productivity in primary metals (Table 7.3), and rapid wage increases in basic steel (Table 7.4).

As Crandall points out it may be cost-effective to live with a substantial share of "antiquated" capital or to modernize old plants rather than rebuild the entire steel industry. This is because capital is not free, and in fact it may be better to use some rather labor intensive methods since there are no alternative uses for the old capital. It seems plausible that the future of investment in the domestic steel industry will probably involve a blend of modernization of existing plants and new construction rather than only new construction.

Costs in the steel industry would certainly be improved by a more realistic wage structure. As Crandall points out, the rapid wage escalation in the 1970s appears to have been occasioned by unwarranted optimism in the industry during the commodity price boom of 1973-74. Another conclusion which Crandall draws is that a major source of cost disadvantage for the domestic industry is in the area of raw materials. While in 1956 the basic materials costs[8] favored the U.S. industry ($50.96 per ton versus $85.43 in Japan), in 1976 the basic materials costs favored Japan. Combined with higher costs in the U.S. it would appear to be a sure formula for higher U.S. steel costs. A flaw in the analysis by Crandall is that he assumes that iron ore costs in the U.S. exceed the world ore costs. This conclusion is reached based on the data presented in Table 7.10.

The problem with the analysis is that it treats what is known as the "Lake Erie price" as though it were a cost. In the U.S., 76 percent of steel production is accounted for by eight firms. Most of these firms either own their own iron

TABLE 7.10
IRON ORE AND METALLURGICAL COAL PRICES IN THE UNITED STATES AND JAPAN, 1956-76
(Dollars per net ton, cost, insurance and freight)

YEAR	COKING COAL		IRON ORE	
	United States	Japan	United States	Japan
1956	9.85	22.14	9.63	16.69
1957	10.77	26.22	10.42	19.69
1958	10.48	19.31	10.61	14.70
1959	10.50	16.33	10.80	12.70
1960	10.56	15.63	11.15	12.88
1961	9.83	15.50	11.78	12.88
1962	9.70	15.35	11.60	12.97
1963	9.35	14.74	11.67	12.32
1964	9.85	14.43	11.88	12.21
1965	9.65	14.27	11.80	12.17
1966	9.82	14.41	11.74	11.91
1967	10.33	14.22	11.91	11.49
1968	10.59	14.40	12.31	11.09
1969	10.76	14.82	12.42	10.56
1970	12.27	18.29	13.05	10.74
1971	15.27	19.41	14.12	10.51
1972	17.68	19.87	15.04	10.37
1973	19.79	21.61	15.48	11.12
1974	34.22	40.71	19.62	13.26
1975	52.66	50.82	23.99	15.15
1976	56.04	53.60	27.62	15.81

Source: Robert W. Crandall, The U.S. Steel Industry in Recurrent Crisis, Brookings Institution, Washington, D.C. 1981. Based on data in U.S. Federal Trade Commission, The United States Steel Industry and its International Rivals: Trends and Factors Determining International Competitiveness (Government Printing Office, 1978), table 3.3, p. 117.

TABLE 7.11
WEIGHTED AVERAGE BILLS FOR INDUSTRIAL SERVICE BY CENSUS REGIONS, 1970, 1979, 1980
(in dollars)

CENSUS REGIONS	January 1, 1980				January 1, 1970[1]		
	150 kW 30,000 kWh	300 kW 60,000 kWh	1,000 kW 200,000 kWh	5,000 kW 1,500,000 kWh	150 kW 30,000 kWh	300 kW 60,000 kWh	1,000 kW 200,000 kWh
New England	1,838	3,553	11,362	76,379	675	1,251	3,775
Middle Atlantic	2,536	5,034	16,261	100,849	827	1,515	4,526
East North Central	1,658	3,183	10,038	61,191	677	1,237	3,603
West North Central	1,421	2,786	8,800	52,764	656	1,208	3,547
South Atlantic	1,590	3,100	10,031	54,337	570	1,033	3,066
East South Central	1,368	2,670	8,205	49,994	504	936	2,736
West South Central	1,360	2,621	8,170	51,683	555	1,002	2,842
Mountain	1,540	2,943	9,040	57,135	588	1,098	3,252
Pacific	1,479	2,904	9,162	68,777	468	835	2,487
Noncontiguous	2,035	3,934	12,438	80,361	696	1,291	3,949
U.S. Average	1,757	3,431	10,910	68,874	648	1,183	3,492

Note: [1]Data not collected in 1970 for 5,000 kW-1,500,000 kWh.

Source: Energy Data Report: Typical Electrical Bills, Januaru 1, 1980. Beverly D. Byrdsong, Office of Coal and Electrical Power Statistics, U.S. Department of Energy, Washington, D.C. 20461.

ore processing plants or purchase their ore on long term contracts. Some small share of output is sold to external buyers, and the price at which this sells probably has little to do with the long run marginal cost of producing iron ore from taconite deposits. This is because development of the taconite/hematite industry is still underway and the current entrants may be earning short run profits. The production of ore pellets was established to supply parent firms in light of the vast reserves and cost advantages of the taconite/hematite processes plus low shipping costs on the Great Lakes. In fact, given these low costs and vast reserves (identified reserves and resources equal to perhaps one-third of total world iron reserves and resources) of iron ore in the Lake Superior Region, a large increase in ore production capacity took place during the 1970s' which does not square with the conclusions of cost disadvantages for raw materials inputs. Quite to the contrary it would seem that low raw materials prices are what has kept the industry alive in light of aging plants and high wage rates. To illustrate the point, while the Lake Erie price was about $32 per ton in 1978, the actual production costs (labor, capital, energy, materials) for ore from Michigan and Minnesota was on the order of $16 per ton.[10] Shipping costs to lower Great Lake ports resulted in a delivered cost of about $20 per ton. Based on OECD data, the 1977 unit value of ore delivered to Japan was $19.25 per ton[11] and 1979 unit value of Brazilian ore delivered to Japan was $24.30 per ton.

If the conclusion of raw material disadvantages for the U.S. were true, then we would expect a migration of the industry to coastal areas (where imported inputs would presumably cost less due to lower transport costs), a prediction contradicted by the steady growth of the Great Lakes' share of domestic steel production (Table 7.6) and the fact that Lake Superior ores are used as far east as Pennsylvania. The growth of western coal shipments to the Great Lakes ports via Duluth/Superior should act to lower the costs of coking coal and is a major factor influencing current and future energy prices in the region and in the U.S. generally. Since coal is the source of more than two-thirds of the energy used in steel production,[12] low cost coal has major cost implications in the U.S. steel industry.[13]

An important factor influencing the price of domestic steel relative to offshore prices is the fact that steel production is a matter of industrial policy in many industrialized as well as developing economies. The share of capacity in which the government has a majority ownership exceeds 50 percent in many countries, including Brazil, France, England, Sweden, Venezuela, and Italy.[14] Substantial government subsidization often accompanies these industries and is not necessarily consistent with an efficient international division of labor. Low private costs of steel, achieved by government policy, also influences the user industries and can lead to unwarranted growth of these industries.

In considering the costs of steel, suppose there is a slight cost advantage or disadvantage to steel production in the U.S. Is a $100 difference either way of great significance for an automobile costing $7,000? The one or two percent difference in the cost of the car is of some importance, but what is of perhaps greater importance is the adaptive strength from having strong supplier industries. If the supplier industry is producing a variety of automotive and nonautomotive products it will be better able to develop new applications of steel as market conditions change. The rapid development of corrosion resistant steels which can be used in light-weight unitized body construction is an important illustration of the adaptability of the domestic steel industry.

From Table 7.9 we know that there are several other key basic materials in auto production as forecast for 1990. Plastics are petroleum derivatives for the most part and, with uniform world oil prices, no major cost differences should arise across countries or regions within the U.S.

Aluminum has a production cost which is determined heavily by electricity costs which favors the Pacific Northwest as the low cost region for aluminum in the U.S.

Electrical Energy

A rather small percent of auto manufacturing costs are for electricity (about one percent of total materials input costs as of 1972).[15] More importantly, a number of intermediate goods for autos such as electric furnace steel are produced with electricity. The monthly bills for large industrial users as of January 1980 are presented in Table 7.11. The "bills" are utility rates since they are standardized by kilowatt hours. To illustrate, the bill of $61,191 for the East North Central for 200,000 kwh in January 1980 translates into a rate of 4.1 cents per kwh. The lowest rates in the country are in the East South Central and in the Pacific Northwest. The South Atlantic region currently has lower rates because of spillover effects of TVA and low cost coal in Kentucky and Tennessee. As demand expands new generating equipment will be added with much higher costs than TVA rates.

In contrast to current industrial rates of four or five cents per kwh in the U.S., rates of about nine cents per kwh characterize Japan[16]. These rates are not much different from those of the Middle Atlantic states. This is not surprising since both Japan and the Middle Atlantic states rely heavily on fuel oil for electricity generation.[17] Rates in Europe are substantially higher than in the U.S. and are more in line with those of Japan. A major source of cost advantage for U.S. manufacturing is our abundance of low sulphur coal. As long as nuclear plants remain very costly to construct, coal will remain a critical input for low cost stationary power sources, and shipping via the Great Lakes will favor the central U.S. as a low cost energy location. Despite a temporary lull in world petroleum price increases we should expect a worldwide increase in the share of petroleum used for mobile power sources and away from petroleum consumption by stationary

TABLE 7.12
INDUSTRIAL WATER RATES BY CITY
IN THE U. S. (JULY 20-24, 1981) AND JAPAN (1978)

CITY	INDUSTRIAL WATER RATE (DOLLARS PER 1,000 CUBIC FEET)
U.S.	
Boston	$7.55
Detroit	2.39
Houston	4.34-8.68
Los Angeles	3.65 (hike to 4.66 pending)
Minneapolis	6.50
Phoenix	2.70-3.20
Pittsburgh	6.88
Tucson:	
winter	6.30
summer	6.30-8.70
JAPAN	
Yokohama	6.39
Nagoya	7.70
Tokyo	5.53
Average in Japan	7.05

Sources: For U.S.: City of Boston Water and Sewer Commission; City of Detroit Water and Sewerage Department; City of Houston Public Works Department, Water Division; City of Los Angeles Water and Power Department; City of Minneapolis Water Works; City of Phoenix Water and Sewers Department; City of Pittsburgh Department of Water; City of Tucson Water and Sewers Department.

For Japan: Statistics Bureau, Prime Minister's Office, *Japan Statistical Yearbook, 1980* (Tokyo: Japan Statistical Association, 1980), p. 397. Data are based on the retail price survey.

sources. Unlike petroleum, there will be a less uniform world coal price because certainly, over the near term, it is more costly to transport than oil, particularly given the large worldwide capital stock in place for transporting oil.

Water

Virtually all manufacturing processes make use of water. Water rates are often the result of public policies designed to ensure availability of water. For this reason it is not necessarily a warranted conclusion that the private water rates will be lower in water abundant regions. This can be seen in Table 7.12. Detroit's industrial water rate is very low, thanks to Lake Huron, but the rate is not much higher in Phoenix or Los Angeles, thanks to pricing below social marginal cost! However, there are some political limits on the extent to which voters will tolerate subsidized water systems and the true economic costs of water for industrial and other uses are ultimately considered as part of the process of supplying water to various users. As population growth in the drier areas of the U.S. continues, the rising water costs will place definite limits on its availability at low cost to the users.

Machine Tools

Machine tools are important intermediate goods for manufacturing and are actively traded in international markets. As indicated in Table 7.13 the U.S. has become a net importer of machine tools between 1972 and 1978 with the largest import growth occurring in U.S.-Japanese trade. What this trade implies is that among industrial economies all have access to a similar level of technology. Because the technology does get embodied in specific plant and equipment there are differentials in the level of obsolescence of existing manufacturing capital.

A major development in manufacturing which has enormous longer run potential is the growing use of industrial robots. The Robot Institute of America defines an

TABLE 7.13
U.S. WORLD IMPORTS AND EXPORTS OF MACHINE TOOLS
CY 1972-78
(thousands)

Imports, value in foreign country;
exports, value at U.S. port

YEAR	METALCUTTING		METALFORMING		TOTAL	
	Imports	Exports	Imports	Exports	Imports	Exports
1972	$ 82,560	$148,329	$31,438	$111,705	$113,998	$260,034
1973	125,974	205,472	41,082	145,063	167,057[1]	350,535
1974	209,098	264,347	61,642	179,468	270,740	443,815
1975	248,147	343,116	69,431	224,528	317,578	567,644
1976	245,321	289,808	72,983	256,725	318,304	546,533
1977	319,249	257,666	81,655	194,398	400,904	452,064
1978	582,165	366,459	133,117	193,741	715,282	560,200

Note: [1]Total does not add due to rounding.

Source: U.S. Department of Commerce, Census Report No. EM 522 (Exports), as reproduced by N.M.T.B.A.
U.S. Department of Commerce, Census Eeport No. IM 146 (Imports), as reproduced by N.M.T.B.A.

Reported in United States-Japan Trade: Issues and Problems, General Accounting Office, Washington, D.C., September 1979.

TABLE 7.14
ROBOTS IN USE BY COUNTRY

COUNTRY	ESTIMATED NUMBER OF ROBOTS AS DEFINED BY RIA	PERCENT OF TOTAL
Japan	10,000	57.0
U.S.	3,250	19.0
Europe		
West Germany	850	5.0
Sweden	600	3.0
Italy	500	3.0
Poland	360	2.0
Norway	200	1.0
England	185	1.0
Finland	130	1.0
Other	1,425	8.0
TOTAL	17,500	100.0

Source: Bache Halsey Stuart Shields, Inc., Institutional Research - Robotics, 1980. Reported in Michigan for Robotics, Office of Economic Development, Michigan Department of Commerce, Lansing, September 1980.

industrial robot as a "...reprogrammable multifunctional manipulator designed to move materials, parts, tools or specialized devices through the variable programmed motions for the performance of a variety of tasks." A major feature of the robot is the reprogramming feature which allows a given production line to handle a variety of product styles. The fact that a robot may be reprogrammed allows a wider range of product types to be produced by the same piece of equipment.

In a sense, industrial robots are an important extension of traditional machine tools; it is just that they can be designed to handle a wider range of activities with a given program and can be reprogrammed. Production involving greater use of robots changes the human task to one of machine design and construction, process monitoring and machine adjustment. As presented in Table 7.14, 57 percent of industrial robots in use in 1979 were in Japan. The greatest increase in the use of industrial robots has been in the U.S. auto industry and many of the new plants and plant conversions underway involve large scale use of robots for spot welding. In the near future we may see a much broader range of application, notably in spray painting and sorting. The use of robots for welding is particularly important in low cost production of unitized body construction which is a weight saving replacement for traditional body assembly techniques based on a frame. Without increased use of robotics, a transition to smaller cars would probably mean a larger share of production costs devoted to labor, a factor which would work against the U.S. industry.

The greatest concentration of industrial robot manufacturers in the U.S. is in Michigan and Ohio (Table 7.15) and the industry is predicted to have an exceedingly high growth rate as suggested by the projections in Table 7.16. The difficulty in projecting the future shape of this industry is accentuated by questions about how quickly sensing and feedback systems can be designed for industrial

TABLE 7.15
INDUSTRIAL ROBOT MANUFACTURERS IN THE U.S.

<u>MICHIGAN</u> Auto-Place, Inc. Charledge Forging Equipment Fraser Automation Gametics, Inc. Hodges-Anatronix ITT Industrial & Automation Systems Livernois Automation Company Planet Corporation Prab Conveyors, Inc./Robot Div. Production Automation Corporation Robogate Systems, Inc. Robomation Corporation Sterling Detroit U.S. Automation Company <u>OHIO</u> Advanced Robotics Corp. Automation Products, Inc. Cincinnati Milacron, Inc. The DeVilbiss Company The Kent Machine Company Nordson Corporation The Rimrock Corporation The Van Epps Design & Development Co., Inc. <u>ILLINOIS</u> Binks Manufacturing Co. General Numeric Corporation Reis Machines	<u>MASSACHUSETTS</u> Automated Parts Removers, Inc. Automatix Incorporated Richard D. Dane Corporation <u>CALIFORNIA</u> Modular Machine Co. Sieko Instruments, Inc <u>CONNECTICUT</u> R & I Manufacturing Co., Inc. Unimation, Inc. <u>NEW YORK</u> ASEA, Inc. Eutectic Corporation <u>FLORIDA</u> IBM Corporation <u>INDIANA</u> Thermwood Corporation <u>PENNSYLVANIA</u> Automation Devices, Inc. <u>WISCONSIN</u> Industrial Automates, Inc.

Source: Robot Institute of America; Office of Economic Development. Reported in <u>Michigan for Robotics</u>.

TABLE 7.16
THE ROBOTICS MARKET

ROBOTS IN USE IN:	1973	1978	1985	ANNUAL GROWTH 1973/1985
United States	800	3,000	50,000	49 %
Japan	1,500	4,000	65,000	49%
West Europe	300	2,000	30,000	47%
Other	200	500	5,000	47%
TOTAL	2,800	9,500	150,000	48 %
ROBOT SHIPMETS				
Units	1,000	4,000	40,000	39.9 %
$1,000/Unit	75	50	25	-9.4%
TOTAL($ Million)	75	200	1,000	26.0 %

Source: <u>Robots and Automated Mail Handling Systems</u>, Predicasts Inc., Report No. GR5. Reported in <u>Michigan for Robotics</u>.

robots (smart robots) and the range of production which can be aided by robots. To illustrate, there are currently underway installations which will use robots for inserting light panel bulbs and television equipped spray painters for automobiles. An important aspect of industrial robots is that their application may spread beyond their initial application and substantially shape all of manufacturing, a change which would have enormous implications for Michigan's economy. If the use of such capital leads to low production costs, the role of Michigan in U.S. manufacturing and world exports could be dramatically increased.

Wages and Productivity in Michigan Industry

As reported elsewhere in this volume (Chapter 4, George E. Johnson), Detroit is one of the highest wage cities in the U.S. These comparisons adjust for differences across cities in the levels of education and job market experience. In part these high wages reflect a highly capital-intensive structure of manufacturing. Michigan has the highest value added per worker of any of the Great Lakes states. Based on 1977 Census of Manufacturing data the value added in manufacturing per production hour was $29.04 in Michigan compared to the Great Lakes average of $23.47 per hour.[18] In comparing different regions, one of the beliefs which the Johnson analysis fails to support is the traditionally observed North-South wage differential. Specifically, for men, the Midwest, the South and the West are high wage regions relative to the East.

While this means that the Michigan wages may not be so high as to hinder the growth of its share of U.S. manufacturing, particularly of iron or steel based products, the wages may lead to manufacturing out of the country. To illustrate, manufacturing wages were about $12 per hour in U.S. manufacturing in 1980 ($15 per hour in motor vehicles and equipment). Wages in Japan were about $6 per hour in all manufacturing ($7 per hour in motor vehicles) and wages in all manufacturing in Italy were $9 per hour ($10 in motor vehicles.)[19] The wage differentials are large enough that they could offset some of the inherent cost advantages of automobile manufacturing in Michigan, particularly if the rate of technological progress and industrial productivity is not healthy.

In assessing wage rates and productivity in the U.S., Michigan and in other countries, it is interesting to note that there are substantial differences in the age structure of the populations in the industrial countries. According to economic models of worker productivity, a worker's effectiveness usually increases not only with formal schooling but also with on-the-job experience and learning. As a result workers aged thirty-five to sixty are viewed as more productive than younger workers.

Because of different birth patterns across industrial countries, the countries differ in the fraction of population over sixty-five and in the peak productivity years. As of 1980, about 12 percent of the U.S. population is sixty-five or older and this is projected to rise moderately by 1990 and fall thereafter. In comparison, Sweden has about 16 percent of its population in this age range (with a modest increase projected for 1990) and Japan has about 8 percent of its population in this age range, with a projected rise throughout the rest of this century (to about 14 percent in 2000 and 18 percent in 2010).[20] Dramatic changes in age composition of the sort projected for Japan can affect the supply of productive labor in potentially important ways. Prior to retirement the older workers are the most productive (in their fifties and early sixties), and from this position of a large contribution as experienced workers they abruptly move to zero labor supply and lay claim to current output under the retirement income arrangements of advanced industrial economies.

Shipping Costs of Final Product

Shipping costs of final product are very important in determining the geographic distribution of market share. Domestic producers often locate final assembly plants to coincide with geographic demand patterns. Data on shipping costs are difficult to obtain because producers regard the information as strategic marketing information.

Industry observers have remarked that shipping costs from Japan about offset the lower wage costs in Japan, but this obviously depends on what part of the North American market one is discussing. California is very different from the East Coast. Table 7.17 indicates that as of the mid-1970s shipping costs amounted to over 20 percent of the list price of East Coast deliveries of medium priced Japanese cars. The data also indicate the much lower cost of shipping from Europe to the East Coast. Perhaps differentials of this sort describe the shipping cost differential from Japan to the West Coast in comparison with the shipping cost from Japan to the East Coast.

A caveat is that large volume shipping can lower shipping costs and that shipping is a part of Japan's industrial policy. As such there are reports that 50 to 80 percent of the capital costs for new ships are covered by government subsidized loans. By such policies the private costs of shipping may diverge substantially from the social or full opportunity costs of shipping.

Taxes and Industrial Policy

If manufacturing in Michigan and other Great Lakes states develops a rapid rate of technical growth in both final goods and supplier industries such as steel and machine tools, one would expect a larger share of the manufacturing industry in Japan and, to some extent, Europe to shift toward items with higher value to weight ratios; products which are less raw material intensive or less costly to ship. This sort of transition has been sketched out in a recent volume by Japan's Ministry of International Trade and Industry.[21]

A part of this transition process may be affected by international trade policies, policies which affect the terms of trade and which are not subject to unilateral control by citizens of the United States, let alone the

TABLE 7.17
INTERNATIONAL TRANSPORT COSTS: SELECTED IMPORTED CARS

MODEL	FREIGHT PER CUBIC FOOT[1]	CUBIC FEET	TOTAL FREIGHT	U.S. LIST PRICE (1975)	PERCENT TRANSPORT COST[2]
Datsun 240-Z	$2.23	229	$667	$6284	11.87%
Datsun 610, 4 dr. sedan	2.23	330	736	4029	22.35
Datsun 1200, sedan	2.23	271	604	2849[3]	26.90
Toyota Corona, 2 dr. hardtop	2.23	356	794	4379	22.15
Toyota Corona, 4 dr. sedan	2.23	358	798	3789	26.68
Ford Capri	0.54	320	173	4117	4.39
Mercedes 280, 4 dr. sedan	0.54	415	224	12576	1.81
V.W. Super Beatle	0.54	339	183	2895	6.75
Volvo 142	0.54	391	211	5625	3.90

Notes: [1]From Japan and Western Europe ports to East Coast (U.S.) ports for autos from Japan and Europe, respectively.

[2]Percent transport cost is expressed as a markup over the foreign price. Percent transport cost = (Total Freight)/(U.S. List Price - Total Freight).

[3]Price of Datsun B-210, the successor to the Datsun 1200 and Price of Datsun 280-Z, the successor to the 240-Z.

Sources: Freight data supplied by Massport Authority, list prices from Automotive News Almanac, 1975.

State of Michigan. Moreover, most industrialized and developing economies have some form of industrial policy which favors the growth and development of selected industries. In our discussion of the steel industry we had occasion to remark on the substantial government involvement in many nations' steel industries.

AN INDUSTRIAL POLICY FOR THE UNITED STATES AUTO INDUSTRY?

Some authors have suggested that government policy has been successful in Japan because there has been less; they didn't attempt to have an elaborate bureaucracy providing detailed supervision of economic activity.[22] It is suggested that, rather, what was provided was a set of more diffuse encouragements--an environment in which the truly successful firms could flourish. Yet once we pass this basic "minimalist" premise, what we discover is that the government has pursued an active program of major subsidies in such forms as selective accelerated depreciation write-offs, subsidies for scrapping obsolete equipment, concentrated government efforts for "strategic" industries (steel, energy, shipping), forcing producers out of low value-added industries by allowing a flow of imports (and by implication, not allowing a flow of imports into other, high value-added industries), and discouraging "nonessential" consumption of petroleum.[23] Among industrial economies Japan has by far the largest share of its energy consumption in its industrial sector. As of 1978, about 58 percent of total energy consumption in Japan was by industry. In contrast, about 40 percent of energy consumption in France, Germany and the U.K. was accounted for by industry.[24]

Popular description of U.S. policy as protectionist doesn't really fit for autos. Research by international trade economists shows that the U.S. had and continues to have low rates of protection for autos.[25] Further, a recent report by the Congressional Budget Office concludes that selective credit allocation by the Japanese government and banks has been an important policy tool for the growth of chosen industries. A similar view is offered by Ryutaro Komiya, who argues that there are two groups of export industries in Japan: one, those industries such as television, motorcycles, and cameras, which were able to stand up by themselves with little government protection or planning; the other, those industries such as steel, chemicals, autos, and shipping, which have received and continue to receive subsidies.[26] One method of subsidization has been the use of selective access to credit.

What all of this amounts to is large-scale government intervention to stimulate favored industries and perhaps favored firms versus other industries and firms not in favor. If such an active program as is described for Japanese manufacturing were even contemplated in North America, it is certain that a majority of economists would rightly object on the grounds that excessive intervention would simply create distortions. It is on such grounds that economists have objected to special aid to agriculture and other sectors of the U.S. economy. The favored sectors flourish, but this occurs at the expense of the nonfavored sectors. Many aspects of what Calder describes for Japan apply to other industrial nations with which we trade.

International Tax Policy

A major source of continuing government-induced distortion, which many researchers have completely overlooked, is the area of international tax policy. Most industrial nations with which we trade and compete rely on a value-added tax or commodity taxes to raise revenues for a substantial share of government finance. This means that, in general, they have a smaller share of government revenue derived from corporate income taxes, or payroll taxes (such as Social Security taxes). The typical level of the value-added tax or tax on manufactured commodities in these countries is about 10-15 percent. Under the provisions of the General Agreement on Tariffs and Trade (GATT) a country may exempt exports from such taxes on the grounds that taxes be placed on goods at destination (location of consumption). Further, these countries impose value-added or commodity taxes on imports on the same principle of taxes based on destination of goods.

In the example of trade between the U.S. and Japan, where Japan relies on commodity taxes which exempt exports but are imposed on imports, the U.S. manufacturers are disadvantaged by our unwillingness to use a similar system.[27] Goods manufactured by Japan and our other trading partners and exempt from their tax upon export are not subject to destination tax of a similar type or magnitude when they arrive in the U.S. Further, our exports are not allowed exemptions from any taxes--corporate income, personal income, or payroll--imposed on producers and workers in these industries.

A standard economic argument is that in such a regime the apparent distortion toward what would appear to be a flood of imports into the U.S. is offset by a change in the exchange rates. Efforts by U.S. consumers to purchase cheap (tax exempt) imports are thwarted because our nontax-exempt goods look less attractive to foreign buyers, and as a result the value of the dollar falls, making imports harder for us to buy. No doubt there are some exchange rate offsets, but it can hardly be claimed that movements in the overall exchange rate would reverse the industry-specific distorting effects of the existing tax system.

Many industrial countries with which we trade, such as Japan, exempt certain commodities from any import tax. Specifically, subsequent to the Tokyo round of trade negotiations, "raw materials" (iron ore, coal, oil) entering Japan are completely exempt from commodity (import) taxes, while manufactured goods are not. What this tax exemption does (along with subsidized ships) is help export oriented industry--manufacturing, in the case of Japan. Raw materials enter Japan tax free and the manufactured goods leave exempt from commodity taxes (and local sales taxes). Manufacturing of export goods therefore expands and draws away domestic inputs (labor force) from the contracting nontraded sectors (domestic services, housing, and so on). Exchange rate adjustments do not offset selective import taxes designed to favor the export sector in Japan.[28]

<u>The Cost of an Industrial Policy?</u>

Industrial policies which favor one sector often have their costs borne in the nonfavored sectors. The price of goods in the export industries of Japan is low compared to goods in their nontraded sector. A naive argument is that this is explained by productivity differences: it is alleged that the rapid growth of productivity in the export sector has led to these lower prices . There are numerous deficiencies in productivity statistics, and in the auto industry many of the productivity statistics are based on final assembly plants; but this is not a good indicator of total productivity in autos, particularly when comparing North America and Japan. In Japan the marketing firms specialize in final stages of production (Toyota has only 47,000 employees), and their industry has realized substantial productivity growth at the assembly stage. However, if the industry comparisons are at lower stages of vertical integration, relatively small differences appear between the two countries. Recent analysis shows that motor vehicles are one of the fastest productivity growth industries in the U.S. (See Table 7.3.)

To finance essential public services and income redistribution in the countries subsidizing exports, there necessarily is a larger relative tax burden on the shrunken nontraded sectors of the economy. Because these are often characterized by inelastic demands, a large share of the tax burden is passed on to their consumers in the form of higher prices. The goods and services in the nontraded sector become a general tax sponge which the government squeezes out to finance essential public services (education, defense, transportation). This leads to other kinds of subsidies to the export sector with even more expensive goods in the nontraded sector than would have been the case without the export-stimulating policies.

Groups which gain in the U.S. are import buyers, and groups which lose here are those in the industrial sector which would have produced the goods that were imported instead. To the extent that labor is mobile within the U.S. it will migrate to the nonmanufacturing, nontraded sector (e.g., the service industry), and in equilibrium there are too many resources in these sectors, the exact opposite of the shortage of resources in the nontraded sector of the export stimulating country. Nonmanufactured and nontraded goods thus become (relatively) cheaper in the U.S. In part, this explains why at official exchange rates our trading partners look exceptionally rich. Yet, if one attempts to buy a set of consumption goods, including the nontraded items, in these same foreign countries, they look far less affluent. Further, this analysis explains the observed tendency for much more rapidly rising prices in the nontraded sector of Japan than in the internationally traded sector. It is certainly consistent with the Wall Street Journal index of living costs in different countries--the price of a Big Mac. Apparently, Tokyo came out on top last year.

The Future

It should not be concluded that the only problem facing Michigan's automobile industry is the international tax system or subsidies to the export sectors of our trading partners. There are many other problems including previously insufficient managerial emphasis on production innovations, labor-management relations, the wage structure between the industrial and nonindustrial sector, and tax and other work disincentives. Recent empirical work indicates that in our central manufacturing and heavy industrial sectors (e.g., autos, steel, railroads) wages have grown more rapidly than in other sectors of our economy during the 1970s. (See Table 7.4.) Although there are certainly important nontax factors influencing production, the U.S. should adopt a tax policy that puts us parallel to our trading partners, and we should discourage them from following policies designed to subsidize particular export sectors.

Based on the analysis of input and shipping costs, my own belief is that we do have a longer run comparative advantage in manufacturing autos and other heavier items, perhaps even great enough to ward off government-subsidized imports. This is because as argued earlier, goods make greater relative use of inputs which are relatively abundant in the United States (coal, oil, iron ore, water) with shipping via the Great Lakes. These are inputs which have become scarce on a worldwide basis subsequent to the Japanese commitment to heavy industry.[29] They remain relatively expensive to transport in terms of their true costs rather than subsidized costs. In the case of autos two important inputs are iron ore and, non-(low sulfur) coal.[30] These are shipped via Duluth/Superior and from other sources on the Great Lakes. This makes the entire Great Lakes Basin a low resource cost region for certain types of manufactured goods. The transition to smaller cars will provide shipping capacity for coal since less will be needed for shipping iron ore. It appears that Good Fortune may have provided us with a sort of shipping subsidy. Of course, having potential cost advantages and exploiting them are not always the same.

Those who have explored the north shore of Lake Superior near Thunder Bay, Ontario know the outline of Sleeping Giant, a portion of the Laurentian Shield visible from thirty miles through the clear summer air. Will our sleeping industrial giant come to life again? This will depend on what course of action we choose. Foolish policy decisions by both the public and private sectors can prevent the development of a proper industrial mix, as can foolish policy decisions by our trading partners. The current international tax policy was established with the U.S. outside the general system of value-added taxes of her trading partners. This was rationalized on the grounds that there was a "dollar shortage" and thus a need to help other countries cope with this shortage. Times have changed. We now have flexible exchange rates, and dollar shortages certainly have little meaning, if they ever did. It was in recognition of a changing world economy that the Nixon administration attempted but did not succeed in establishing a U.S. value-added tax to bring our economy in line with our trading partners.

If we do proceed to put ourselves on a more equal footing with our trading partners, it will take a while to understand and evaluate tax plans, including value-added taxes and tax treatment of raw materials exports. One simple policy would be to limit the extent to which a country can exempt exported goods from taxes of any kind. In the meantime our industrial sector is in an adjustment period and in direct competition with industrial sectors which are subject to more favorable tax treatment of exports. I believe we and our trading partners should move toward establishing an international tax system which does not suffer from modern versions of mercantilism.[31]

The long-run interest of people in Michigan is best served by free trade. Yet, in the case of auto manufacturing, it would be far-fetched to argue that free trade currently exists. Free trade is a two-way street, but our industrial trading partners have numerous tariff and nontariff barriers inhibiting the flow of automotive products. In the case of Japan, there are currently many ways in which the auto industry receives subsidies, particularly for exports. The fact that such goods flow at all has been simplistically interpreted by many as demonstrating that free trade exists.

NOTES, CHAPTER 7

[1]I would like to thank Ned Gramlich and Gary Saxonhouse for helpful comments and suggestions. The opinions expressed in the paper and any errors are my own.

[2]Gene Bylinski, "The Japanese Chip Challenge," Fortune, March 23, 1981, pp. 115-122.

[3]See Terry D. Monson, "The Effects of Domestic and International Competition Upon Michigan's Iron Ore and Steel Industries," Bureau of Industrial Development, School of Business and Engineering Administration, Michigan Technological University, March 1980. He reports that between 1960 and 1976, usable ore production per man year of production labor rose by about 75 percent nationwide and the Great Lakes region accounts for 90 percent of domestic ore (1978).

[4]The Ohio industry accounts for a declining share of domestic production, but most of the decline has occurred in the southern part of Ohio. See Steel at the Crossroads: The American Steel Industry in the 1980s, American Iron and Steel Institute, January 1980.

[5]See Marian Krzyzowski, "Magnesium: A Competitor to Aluminum in Automotive Casting Applications," manuscript, Industrial Development Division, The University of Michigan, 1980.

[6]Richard B. Stein, "Magnesium vs. Aluminum Energy and Cost," Bechtel Power, March 1976.

[7]Robert W. Crandall, The U.S. Steel Industry in Recurrent Crisis, The Brookings Institution, Washington, D.C., 1981.

[8]Costs of iron ore, scrap, coal, oil, natural gas, electricity.

[9]For example, U.S. Steel put its Minntac plant (Mountain Iron, Minnesota) into operation in 1972 (production capacity of 12,000,000 tons per year) and Cleveland Cliffs put its Tilden Mine (Marquette, Michigan) into operation in 1971 (12,000,000 tons per year capacity). Reserves are defined as deposits which can be profitably mined under current economic conditions. Other resources are those deposits judged to have potential to be profitably mined under future demand and cost conditions.

[10]The component costs are given in Terry D. Monson, "Effects of Domestic and International Competition," pp. 169-200.

[11]O.E.C.D., Trade by Commodities (Series C): Market Summaries: Imports, Paris, 1979.

[12]American Iron and Steel Institute, Steel at the Crossroads: The American Steel Industry in the 1980s, Washington, D.C., 1980, p. 62. For a study which provides some evidence on the effect of geographic demand patterns on

the location of the steel industry, see John S. Hekman, "An Analysis of the Changing Location of Iron and Steel Production in the Twentieth Century," American Economic Review, March, 1978, pp. 123-33.

[13]I conjecture that a very large scale steel mill in the Upper Great Lakes would be cost effective. This is because of the shift toward western coal combined with ore processing in the Lake Superior Basin. The additional cost advantage is that only finished products rather than intermediate products would be shipped to manufacturing centers in the Lower Great Lakes. As a result, total material shipping costs would be reduced. Limestone could be shipped to the mill on return trips from the Lower Great Lakes.

[14]Ibid., p. 16.

[15]Based on the 1972 input-output table for the U.S.

[16]As of December 1980 the industrial rate in Japan was 20.3 yen per kwh and the residential rate was 27.8 yen per kwh.

[17]The Japanese plan to use coal from the western U.S. in transforming their energy supply.

[18]Reported in Michigan for Robotics, Office of Economic Development, Michigan Department of Commerce, Lansing, September 1980.

[19]The U.S. Auto Industry 1980, U.S. Department of Transportation, Washington, D.C., January 1981, p. 41.

[20]Reported by Haruo Shimada in The Japanese Employment System, the Japanese Institute of Labour, Tokyo, 1980. The original analysis is in Nankin Seido Kihon Koso Kondankai (Committee on Basic Ideas for Pension Reforms) Interim Report, 1977.

[21]MITI'S Vision for the 1980's, Ministry of International Trade and Industry.

[22]For example, Kent E. Calder, "Japan's 'Minimalist' Government," Wall Street Journal, Friday, February 13, 1981.

[23]In the U.S. it has been common practice to have two-tier pricing of energy with prices lower to consumers and higher to firms. In contrast consumers have paid a higher price while industry has paid a lower price in Japan. Also, the use of vehicle taxes based on approximate fuel consumption encourages less use of fuel in transportation and favors industrial use of fuel.

[24]Cited in Phyllis A Gunther, Japan's Industrial Policy; Effects on the Automobile Industry's Development, Transportation Systems Center, Cambridge, Massachusetts, April, 1981.

[25]For the 1970s the protection rate has been estimated as 5.1 percent for the U.S. In contrast, rates for the Common Market countries, England, and Sweden, were in the 30 to 40 percent range. Japan led the competition with a protection rate of 75.7 percent. See Bela Belassa, "Tariff Protection in Industrial Countries: An Evaluation," Journal of Political Economy, December 1965, pp. 573-94. Though the U.S. currently has a nominal tariff of 2.9 percent, effective protection rates are probably zero or even negative. In contrast, while Japan now has a zero tariff on auto imports, it has substantial rates of effective protection by virtue of selective commodity taxes on imports as well as nontariff barriers to distribution in Japan.

[26]Ryutaro Komiya, "Planning in Japan," in Economic Planning East and West, Morris Bornstein, Editor (Cambridge, Mass.: Ballinger, 1975).

[27]The commodity tax on a typical small car (1,600 cc engine) has been 15 percent in Japan until recently. It has recently been increased to 17.5 percent. In addition, there is a local sales tax of 5 percent and annual road taxes based on engine displacement and car dimensions. The high road taxes on larger cars presumably contributes to the previously mentioned share of total energy consumption by industry and the small share of energy consumption going to the household sector. For 1979 there was a biannual tax of $63 per half ton and the annual road tax was $110 for vehicles in the 1,001-1,500 cc engine range and $337 for vehicles in the 2,001-3,000 cc engine range.

[28]The commodity tax exemption is more than enough to offset shipping costs to the U.S. A Japanese car costs the buyer less in Detroit than in Tokyo for many current models.

[29]This development proves that the "holistic" planning process which Calder describes is not necessarily clairvoyant. Record auto production in Japan has coincided with record payments for their raw materials and slowed economic growth.

[30]A straightforward way to meet, or to improve on, emission standards is to burn low sulphur coal such as that shipped via Duluth from North Dakota or other western states. See William Ramsey, Unpaid Costs of Electrical Energy (Washington: Resources for the Future, 1979), p. 25.

[31]Adam Smith's Wealth of Nations was written to persuade us that policies designed to alter trade patterns by artificial means will diminish rather than increase a nation's real wealth. The logic of exempting exports from any significant tax is not obvious, particularly if taxes are used to finance essential public services. Most international trade models ignore the use to which tax revenues are put.

Chapter 8

Industrial Location: Causes and Consequences

by

Wilbur R. Thompson

Wayne State University

INTRODUCTION

From the long list of conditions that could possibly influence the location of economic activity, emphasis will be placed here on the two locational factors most often mentioned in surveys of businessmen and most often found to be statistically significant in econometric studies: market orientation and labor skills and costs.[1]

The first major challenge will be to identify, better than is usually the case, the many components of the vague term "market orientation." An automobile assembly plant may be drawn (oriented) toward a broad regional market (e.g., Southern California); an automobile parts manufacturer may locate within an hour's drive of that assembly plant; a retail store must find a site within minutes of the households of the employees of those plants; a specialty retailer will be drawn to this growing aggregation of population and income as soon as this market grows a little more; and construction activity must arise amid this growing market to deliver that growth. "Market orientation," as a survey response, blurs and confuses: intermediate products (sales to other businesses) with final products (sales to households), and area "exports" to other local labor markets that generate flows of new income from outside are not distinguished from derivative local sales that keep the money circulating internally.

Again, while the survey approach may seem to get close to the "real" location decision-making process, asking individual businessmen why they moved or stayed in place suffers from imposing a very narrow and short-range perspective on a highly interactive and extended process;

that is, focuses on a single link in a long chain reaction. The location and relocation of businesses and households unfolds over decades and should therefore be placed in a strong growth and development, often historical, setting. While the many studies of location have inquired into where industries locate and why they move, almost no attention has been paid to when these business decisions and actions take place.

This indifference to timing in business location and relocation studies stands in sharp contrast to household migration theory and surveys which emphasize the age and life-stage of the migrants. Individual businesses and whole industries also are born, boom, mature and die, and they change their locational priorities, often radically, during these successive life-stages. So, too, do the localities, into and from which these industries and households come and go, inexorably age and change. The strong and subtle linkages between businesses, households and localities in space and through time will become the central and recurring theme of this attempt to fuse location theory and practice with the nature of the local growth process.

Most econometric analyses of industrial location also rank market orientation (usually measured as the level of or change in local population or income) first, well ahead of second place labor orientation. But most of this work is based on manufacturing data of the early postwar period and is therefore biased by the special circumstances of that boom period. The East North Central states, and the Northeast region to a lesser extent, dominate these statistical studies because they accounted for about two-thirds of manufacturing employment and three-quarters of durable goods production. The huge postwar backlog demand for durables could be accommodated most easily, quickly and cheaply by expanding outputs of existing plants. Early postwar increases in manufacturing employment were therefore highly correlated with existing levels of manufacturing employment and population. Manufacturing activity was growing fastest in large places and therefore appeared to be <u>moving</u> toward its markets; that is, a cyclical boom was misread as a structural change.

The early Thompson-Mattila study (1959) found, for example, that product markets, as measured by changes in population and income, "explained" between one-half and three-quarters of manufacturing growth from 1947 to 1954.[2] The later Wheat study (1973) essentially replicated this finding by assigning about 60 percent of manufacturing growth to changes in product markets.[3] In general, market orientation is important but not that important. Accordingly, local labor markets will be given at least equal attention here, as seems especially appropriate in a Michigan study. A second, strong theme of this analysis will then emphasize the way in which product and labor markets interact in locational decisions and local growth processes.

MARKET ORIENTED LOCATION AND LOCAL GROWTH AS INTERACTING, CUMULATIVE PROCESSES

The State of Michigan is basically a political entity over-arching a large number of separate "local economies," which are in turn most often delineated in space as largely self-contained local labor markets. The location of economic activity and regional growth in Michigan can therefore be approached most readily by seeing the state as a collection of local economies and by tracing a typical sequence of business and household interactions through time and within a typical local economy. We begin then with business location, household migration and the local growth process.

<u>The "Local Multiplier" as Lock-step, Market Oriented Location</u>

Regional economists and planners typically begin their analyses of the local growth process by dividing all business activity into either "export" ("basic") industries, selling to customers located outside of the local economy, or "local service" industries, serving residents of that local labor market. In locational terms, local service industries are the most precisely "market-oriented" of all industry, wholly dependent on selling to households located less than an hour or so away. With the location of retail trade, local government, and most professional and personal services locked into the local economy, that is, with little to explain, location studies turn their attention to market-orientation in the more mobile export industries. (The grand opening of stores, schools, and pediatricians' offices may not even lag appreciably behind the initiation of operations in the new factory, given the ease and accuracy of forecasting the new market.)

Local service business would not therefore seem to be sensitive to the level of local taxes in that all competitors are similarly affected and simple observation reminds us that retail trade accounts for almost the same proportion of total activity everywhere. It would be trite to dwell on this form of market-oriented location, except for the fact that local service employment accounts for between one-half and three-quarters of all employment. Thus we are reminded that the locational cutting edge of local taxes, subsidies, services and regulation is very thin and public policy designed to influence location and growth should therefore be sharply focused on those businesses that are more "footloose." (Intraurban location of local services may be much more sensitive to local tax differentials.)

Intermediate-Product Market Orientation: "Industrial Agglomeration"

Market-oriented location is also common in the production of intermediate products, especially in sales and purchases between businesses occupying successive stages in the production process. Both location theorists and regional economists speak of "industrial agglomeration,"[4] and classic examples abound in the Michigan economy where metal-making, metal fabricating, machinery and motor vehicle production have clustered into tight industrial complexes. Clearly, high transportation cost, relative to the value of the product, induces this form of market orientation but other powerful forces are also acting to draw together in space firms that are functionally linked. To illustrate, we can reach back in industrial history to the complementary labor demands that drew female-employing textile and apparel operations into male-employing steel-making centers. We can observe closer to home the many research and testing laboratories, design studios and advertising agencies that gather near the automobile production lines to facilitate face-to-face contacts. The Detroit metropolitan area has, for example, drawn to it almost twice its pro rata share of employment in advertising agencies reflecting both its highly styled products and the strength of agglomerative forces.

We might note here that to the extent that industrial agglomeration proceeds vertically, that is, carries the local production process back toward parts and material manufacturing and/or forward toward the final user (consumer), local taxes and regulations become more important in the cost of production and final sales price of the product. Michigan-produced automobiles would therefore be more heavily impacted by the relative level of state and local taxes than would, say, airplanes made in Wichita be advantaged or disadvantaged by the relative level of Kansas taxes, simply because less of the airplane is made in Kansas.

Whether the local suppliers of parts and business services to the principal local export industries tend to be smaller or larger than their customer is not deductively obvious (compare small firms making sub-assemblies on one hand with large banks and utilities on the other hand), but it seems safe to infer that a substantial share of those "market-oriented" businesses are intermediate-product-market-oriented and subject to powerful forces of industrial agglomeration. Differentials in local taxes would have to exceed the very considerable transportation and face-to-face communication advantages of clustering in these industrial complexes before taxes could be counted as a major locational factor.

Industrial agglomerations form because they enhance productivity, but Michigan's power to share (tax) this surplus is limited by the cost of re-forming the industrial complex in some other less exacting jurisdiction. The state's power to export Michigan automobile production taxes is probably substantially less than Montana's power to export its new severance tax on coal.

Interlocking linkages between industrial firms act to reduce individual firm mobility and thereby add to local stability but only at considerable risk: the small probability that the exit of a key firm or industry could touch off a general exodus of independent suppliers and customers. Specifically, if major elements of the metals-machinery-automotive complex were to move to another region or overseas, then much (most?) of the industrial complex would move in lock-step. In this all-or-nothing game, again, the cutting edge of local public policy may be thin but sharp.

Locational Linkages in Migration

The many different local businesses not only make interlocking markets for each other, the jobs they create attract migrants who also interact to produce and attract additional population, amassing an even larger local market. Rapid growth in local output leads first to overtime and then to increased labor force participation rates, but continuing increases in output and labor input can only be met by increased in-migration. Young adults, eighteen to twenty-eight years of age, exhibit migration rates two to three times average and tend to account for about one-half of all moves between labor markets. Given then both the high mobility and high fertility of young adults, we would expect areas growing rapidly due to net in-migration to be reinforced in population growth by a relatively high rate of natural increase. In the early postwar period Michigan grew in population at about one and one-half times the national rate, growth fed not only by net immigration but also by birth rates that ran about 2 percentage points above the national rate, attaining a maximum difference of 27.1 to 24.6 births per thousand population in 1955. And the Michigan death rate ran about 0.5 to 1.0 percentage points lower throughout our fast-growth 1950s.

Migration acts in another way to add momentum to the local growth process, further enlarging the local market. Newcomers draw, in due course and in unending flow, relatives and friends by providing a cheap place to live and job leads, igniting a kind of human chain reaction. The "beaten path" phenomenon of migration probably accounts for about one-half of the population flow[5] and also promotes local growth through the local labor market by increasing the elasticity of the supply of labor.

Local Market Size and "Import Substitution" Growth

In what is perhaps one of the purest forms of market-oriented location, population growth to larger city size attracts wholly new local services, not just more of the same services as described by the local multiplier. The larger local market opens the way to produce profitably goods and services that have up to now been purchased from outside suppliers; general practitioners are joined by specialists in medicine, law, and finance. "Import substitution" growth may be either a catching-up operation that closes the lag of the local service sector behind the export sector (a delayed multiplier effect) or a very distinctive filling-in operation that broadens the range and variety of locally produced goods and services. If, for example, the national average is 4 hospital beds per thousand population and the minimum efficient hospital size is 200 beds, then a general hospital is indicated when the local economy amasses a market of 50,000 population.

Import substitution growth acts primarily, at least initially, to expand the local service sector. But a community that gains experience with new products and processes--that develops new skills--may progress past the point at which it supplies its own needs to where it begins serving export markets--expanding for example, that community hospital base into a major medical center. Progression from production for local use to export sales may even take place within a given firm. Japanese electronic firms have evolved from buying semi-conductors from U.S. firms to making them in-house and are beginning now to export them in competition with their former suppliers.

Note that, in this local growth scenario, market-oriented location has driven the local economy to the point of recycling, as new export activity has led to larger city size and greater industrial sophistication and around back again to the initiation of new export industries.

Asymmetry in Mobility and the Bias in Migration Toward Larger Cities

The growth of the local market may reach beyond creating new employment opportunities in local services and new skills in the export sector to the point of attracting households seeking a wider range of choice in consumer goods. A new wave of in-migrants adds a legitimate theatre to the universal movie house, making life easier for the next wave of newcomers, making the place a little more "civilized." The new library in town more than compensates for the more crowded beach or hiking trail, at least to those newcomers. As scale and choice mount, the growing place begins to look more and more attractive to corporate executives and their spouses, whoever makes the key locational decisions. In a 1971 U.S. Population Commission poll of preferred place of residence, the proportion of respondents who preferred "large urban places" was about twice as high among the highest income and education classes (22 and 21 percent, respectively) as among the lowest (12 and 10 percent, respectively). And if preferred (most advantageous) workplace had been incorporated, the gap would surely have been larger.

If the early townbuilders (the oldtimers) sense a net loss of well-being as "their" town grows larger, they are steadily losing the political power to slow growth. Another asymmetry is that those entering the growing place tend to be more mobile younger adults, while those wanting but hesitating to leave are older adults, ever more immobilized by advancing age, nearby friends and the ownership of homes and businesses. Few oldtimers suffer community growth in silence, but most tend to suffer it in place. The earlier inhabitants of fast-growing places do however tend to receive the soothing (if not healing) balm of capital gains in land and the quasi-rents of larger business profits (but only of course to the extent that they are property owners).

Almost a decade ago this author argued that towns and even small cities suffered the disadvantage that small local labor markets do not assemble an occupational mix of sufficient breadth and balance to ensure that both a college educated husband and his equally highly (and narrowly) trained wife can find appropriate, specialized professional and technical work. Moreover, this labor offered in "joint supply" requires two job openings in the same place and at almost the same point in time, again a matter of scale, with the probability of that joint event equal to the product of the two individual probabilities for that size place. The importance of the size of the local market (city size) becomes even more apparent when we add in the demand for graduate (continuing) education in specialized fields. And while higher education offerings have proliferated over the postwar period, we appear to have entered into a long period of consolidation in higher education. Spatial concentration in graduate education would then act as "growth poles," partially offsetting the many dispersive forces at work.

Nor would the rapidly rising divorce rate seem to weaken at all the attraction of moderate to large size population concentrations, even if divorce also breaks the bond of joint labor supply. Divorced persons, even more, need social scale. Not only is the divorced person out of place in a "good family town" but the search for a new mate[6] or just social diversity in general demands greater scale and wider choice than most small places can offer. Adding amenity-seeking to the migration equation of highly educated persons, we see today net movements from larger, older (high tax) places, but still might expect net flows of population into newer, middle-sized places, propelling them toward large size.

If market oriented location in business and linkages in migration interact so as to lead to larger city size and then back again to new growth, so inexorably, why then have so many large metropolitan areas slowed to near zero population change? In response, one could repeat the familiar litany of the pathology of great city size: high density and heavy spillovers (e.g., traffic delays, noise and pollution), loss of control over residential land use (e.g., massive ghettos and lengthy cross-commuting) and anonymity and street crime to name but a few. Given the complexity of these issues and the general familiarity with them, we turn here instead to the examination of a less appreciated brake on local growth, "industrial filtering," and reinterpret this key piece of the regional growth puzzle as "labor-oriented location."

LABOR-ORIENTED LOCATION AND RELOCATION AS STAGES OF GROWTH

The powerful and pervasive impact of labor as a locational factor is unintentionally demonstrated by the widely publicized Alexander Grant and Company index of "business climate" in the forty-eight contiguous states.[7] Working from rankings of the states in various measures of business costs and benefits, as weighted by the manufacturers themselves, their overall index for both 1979 and 1980 ranked Michigan dead last. But what seems to have been only dimly seen is that, while fully eighteen selected factors were used in that composite index, eight of them were drawn from assorted measures of labor power (level and rates of change in wages, unionism and labor laws), accounting for a combined weight of about 52 percent. Moreover, if we assume that advanced industrialization and labor power generate high income that leads to high quality public services and high business and personal taxes, we can add in another 29 percent of "indirect labor factors." Labor power, directly or indirectly, profoundly affects four-fifths of the base of that index and probably about as much of the interstate variation of it as well. The tendency for "business climate" to become a code word for labor power is also reflected in the widespread use of the presence or absence of a "right-to-work law" as a simple proxy for that elusive community characteristic.

Even though labor market orientation usually ranks second only to product market orientation in both surveys of businessmen and in econometric studies of industrial location, students of the subject seem to have become distracted from probing deeper into the way in which local labor supplies, skills and costs affect location at different stages of an industry's life cycle. And almost no attention has been given to the many and varied interactions between product markets and labor markets in the local growth process. We turn now to the complex and rising role of labor in location.

The Local Labor Market Hierarchy and "Industrial Filtering"

The theory of industrial filtering holds that industries age and descend through an urban hierarchy based on industrial sophistication. New industries, especially if challenged by the demands of a new process, germinate best in the larger, industrially mature centers, where technical skills, specialized facilities and risk capital are easiest to find. In locational terms, the central question is: where can this new work be done? But with time and experience, the production process becomes rationalized and routinized. As the maturing industry slides down its "learning curve," calling for lower skills, competition forces it to seek out cheaper labor markets. The central question has changed to: where can this familiar work be done most cheaply?

More often than not, the most inviting pools of low wage labor are the depressed trade and service centers of agricultural areas that have mechanized farming operations and released hundreds of former farm hands. Displaced farm workers with good work habits can easily rise to the very modest demands of the increasingly simple work routine. The high wage rates, traffic congestion and delays, expensive local public services and high taxes of big cities need no longer be borne as a necessary cost of production, not for such a routine production process.

Under industrial filtering theory, manufacturing plants settling in smaller places not only pay low wages but also are in older and therefore slower growing industries. Such places manage to achieve an average rate of growth (even higher for awhile) by acquiring a growing share of a slow growing industry. Constrained by simple skills, low wage rates and an average rate of growth, small places find that they must run to stand still. But the larger, more industrially sophisticated places must also run to stand still as they continue to give birth to new industries--by innovating if not inventing--and continue to spin-off maturing ones. Of course, by always having in hand the newest and therefore most highly skilled activities, these larger places do run for the highest stakes.

But industries differ markedly. In sharp contrast to the apparel and textile industries that filtered down rapidly from New England to the Carolina Piedmont, the automobile industry has resisted filtering. Extended internal economies of scale created very large automobile plants and substantial economies of agglomeration kept them clustered together. Most of all, early and strong unionization eliminated geographic wage differentials. But mounting international competition, the trend to multi-national operations among the very large surviving corporations, and the near impossibility of forming international unions has opened up huge wage differentials and caused a now world-wide motor vehicle industry to filter down from Michigan and other U.S. locations to a multitude of foreign assembly and parts plants, most paying much lower wage rates.

The relevance of this industrial-locational theory for our present purposes is that the larger, older metropolitan economies of the Frostbelt require a continuing transfusion of new growth-industries just to keep up with their continual loss of old industry (plus any natural increase in population and labor force). But the impression that prevails today is that invention and innovation are slowing, based in part on the fact that research and development spending is declining as a percent of gross national product. If so, we may then be feeding in fewer high technology jobs at the top of the urban-industrial hierarchy than the number needed to maintain even an average rate of growth in these larger, industrial centers.

But it does not automatically follow that a new surge in invention and innovation (more R&D) will necessarily re-establish an average rate of growth in employment and population in the largest urban areas. Times have changed and new technologies may adapt almost as well to middle-size places and employees' families may adapt better. Recent advances in transportation and communication technology may allow industries to escape congestion without suffering appreciable isolation. And our inability or unwillingness to master the governance of large, dense population clusters has probably also acted to shift the balance of comparative advantage away from larger places. But, in a paradox more apparent than real, we are both moving away from larger, older cities and simultaneously building a whole new set of large cities to host many of our newest industries, in Houston, San Jose, and Phoenix, to name a few.

To bring this fifteen-year-old theory of industrial filtering up to date, we need to know whether the flow of jobs in older, simpler manufacturing work is welling up or drying up, and whether it is filtering down farther through the city size hierarchy or not so far, and whether its rate of descent is speeding up or slowing down. Again, do services follow a path similar to manufacturing, especially with service jobs outnumbering those in manufacturing two to one, and growing faster? Finally, does the industrial filtering process change shape as it crosses national boundaries? Certainly, worldwide industrialization portends a worldwide system of industrial filtering, but probably significantly altered by national foreign trade policies (e.g., import quotas and "local content" laws).

As background studies for public policy, we would benefit from bringing together a number of inter-related factors and trends. Manufacturing seems to be filtering down farther and faster through the city size hierarchy. On the other hand, trade and service activities, seeking economies, and qualities, of scale in modern marketing, and capitalizing on the greater travel radius of nonmetropolitan households seem to be "filtering up" toward larger places. Enclosed (climate-controlled) regional shopping malls have come to dominate the obsolete, small downtowns of every place within twenty or thirty miles. Under such a pattern of industrial relocation, manufacturing would, more often than not, become the principal export base of small towns and export services would more often support the economies of small cities. This would be a major change from the factory cities and farm-service centers of yesteryear.

Industrial filtering would proceed most smoothly if the maturing firm's (industry's) local public service demands fell along with its falling skill requirements. A firm seeking lower wage labor must be willing to accept a lower income community and lower quality public services. That community will be less able, if not less inclined, to pay for educational services and accustomed to receiving less in return. Thus the lower tax rate of the smaller place would seem to match its place near the bottom of the labor market hierarchy.

The relocation of industries to smaller places would be encouraged by local public economics even if the progressive simplification of work skills led to the use of less labor, that is, induced greater mechanization of the production process. As the capital-to-labor ratio increases, that is as taxable property per worker (or dollar of value added) mounts, so does the incentive to locate in a small town where public spending and taxes are relatively low. Finally, it is worth noting at this point that the industrial filtering theory stands at odds with the conventional wisdom of area industrial development policy of assigning the highest priority to the retention of existing businesses. Paradoxically, it may not even be easiest to hold an existing (aging) industry, unless the area would find it easier to accept sharp cuts in wage and tax costs than to find replacement industry.

The Location of Entrepreneurship

Entrepreneurship has been defined in various ways: doing new things or old things in new ways (Schumpeter, 1934), risk-taking (Drucker, 1965), organization building (Harbison and Meyers, 1964), or simply exercising control over production (McClelland). However defined, almost everyplace would like to have more of it, either to stimulate raw growth or to move beyond that to achieve "economic development." And high-cost Frostbelt places may well depend on entrepreneurship in high technology industries to replace their mature industries.

How well is Michigan positioned in the rising competition to create new products and processes? Different observers have reached very different conclusions, ranging from the quick-draw pessimism of outsiders to the hearty optimism of insiders. A recent newspaper report[8] of a study of the economic outlook for the Midwest (conducted by Robert R. Nathan Associates for an unidentified private firm) concludes that a high technology rescue of this region is not likely. The Midwest is seen as lacking in research and at a disadvantage in attracting science and engineering graduates, relative to New England and California. A structural shift to service industries, such as health care and travel, is seen as more likely. (Why health care could not lead to a high-tech specialization is not clear.) Conversely, a staff paper for the State of Michigan Special House Committee on Job Development argues that appropriate public policy could build on the state's strong potential in high technology industry and produce a commanding headstart over our competition.

If invention, innovation and willingness to take risk do indeed flow more from small than large business, which seems to be the conventional wisdom, is not Michigan at a disadvantage in this regard? Apparently not. Establishments with less than twenty employees accounted for 65.6 percent of total manufacturing employment in Michigan in 1977, a little above the 63.6 percent for Massachusetts and a little below the 71.5 percent figure for California, reflecting the many small suppliers to the automotive giants. Moreover, if entrepreneurship must, more and more, break through into world markets, such that very large firms have an advantage, Michigan would be better positioned than either Massachusetts or California. That is, this state's "golden extremes" in firm size may bridge well the diverse demands of rapid technological progress and the speedy exploitation of changing world markets.

The current rash of corporate mergers seems also to be saying that corporate managers feel that larger size tends to insulate the firm (them?) from the heaviest risks of rapid change in products, processes and markets, perhaps by lengthening grace periods and adding options. Again, there may even be much to be said, in broad social terms, for an industrial-organization structure in which large firms acquire regularly the new products and processes of new small firms and thereby often prevent talented inventor-entrepreneurs from languishing as mediocre managers of increasingly routine operations, funding them to get back to full-time inventing.

One might argue instead, or in addition, that the existence of high technology firms gives birth to new entrepreneurs by spinning off gifted scientists and engineers,[9] and that these creative former employees tend to stay in the community to be near family and friends for psychological and financial support and/or near trusted colleagues for technical assistance. Different industry mixes generate very different occupational profiles and especially wide variations in "professional, technical and kindred workers." For example, in 1970 the motor vehicle industry engaged 9.6 percent of all workers in professional and technical activity, slightly below the all-manufacturing figure of 9.9 percent, but far below that recorded in aircraft (26.0 percent), chemicals (18.5), and electrical machinery (18.1). For full perspective, the motor vehicle industry substantially exceeds the steel industry with 6.2 percent engaged as professional and technical workers and is far above the apparel industry with only 1.9 percent so employed. Still, if entrepreneurship in manufacturing flows in important measure from some simple or subtle interrelationship between industry and occupational mixes, Michigan industry, which may have once stood very high in technology and skill levels, has matured into barely average standing. And one main source of the strong flow of invention and innovation in aircraft-and-computer-rich California becomes all too readily apparent.

One sees the technological surge and sag of the automobile industry and of the State of Michigan by tracing over the past half century the share of U.S. patents granted to Michigan residents. Beginning from a position of a little over a <u>pro rata</u> share of patents in 1900 (3.19 percent of the national population received 3.37 percent of the patents), the rise of the automobile industry lifted Michigan to one and one-half times its <u>pro rata</u> patent share by 1940 (with 3.99 and 6.05 percent of population and patents, respectively).[10] Note that the great technological growth-power of the automobile industry is reflected in both the dramatic increase in the state's patent share and in the equally impressive increase in its population base from a little over three to four percent of the national totals. Since that high water mark of 50 percent above average, the state's share of patents has ebbed steadily to 30 percent above parity in 1970 and down to 22 percent above average in 1976. (This may be compared to current patenting rates of 50 percent above average in Massachusetts and in the combined New York, New Jersey, and Connecticut areas.) All in all, on first and too-quick approximation, Michigan's present competitive position in high technology manufacturing is such that leadership here seems to be neither within as easy reach as local optimists suggest, nor nearly as far out of reach as outside pessimists argue.

Finally, not only are there different sources of entrepreneurship and different processes in its formation, invention and innovation can occur at very different stages in the life cycle of an industry. Michigan's industrial legacy may today open up more new opportunities in the later stages of industrial development, such as in new ways of managing long runs of not so new (consumer) products keyed to world markets. The most supportive state policy would then be quite different here then in, say, the Boston and San Jose areas.

But in general, taxes imposed on business assets and/or operations, whether profitable or not, tend to inhibit entrepreneurship. The Single Business Tax might have been a good choice for the vigorous Michigan economy of the early postwar period, given its tendency to encourage allocative efficiency by charging business for their use of and/or the availability of valuable (expensive) public services, regardless of profitability. But today with a shift in emphasis from economic efficiency to economic development, taxes that fall on early-life, almost inevitably unprofitable, operations place Michigan at a competitive disadvantage in the interstate contest for invention and innovation. And this burden is made heavier by the fact that research and development work is especially labor intensive, and labor costs are added into the tax base, as argued in detail in Chapter 22. (It is perhaps worth noting here that the federal Kemp-Garcia Bill establishing "enterprise zones" in depressed inner cities also misses the mark by emphasizing tax breaks that largely benefit well-established, profitable firms.)

Oligopoly and Union Power in the Long Run: Hurdle or Springboard?

In general, a local economy may generate high wage and labor income out of either skill or power. The Ann Arbor metropolitan area, for example, exhibited a 1978 per capita income of 117 percent of the national average, earned through higher educational and skill levels. High wage income may be won instead through the exercise of market power, as in the coupling of oligopoly and union price power. The Flint metropolitan area provides a classic example here with a 1978 per capita income of 112 percent, matched with below average levels of education. (In 1970 only 7.2 percent of persons 25 years old and over in the Flint metropolitan area had completed 4 or more years of college, compared to a U.S. average of 12.8 percent.) The short run benefits of market power are obvious.[11]

Turning to the likely long run effects of raising local income through the exercise of oligopoly and union power, we see again how "the past is prologue." Each stage of development, and even the very rate of growth itself, transforms the local economy by altering the local stock and/or cost of land, labor, capital and entrepreneurship, and predetermines in part the next stage of that process, as it unfolds over generations.

Clearly, localities can and do exploit market power, but to live off of wage rates that exceed relative physical productivity is to live well but dangerously on over-priced labor. As the beneficent industry matures, its national rate of job formation tends to slow, due perhaps to automation or the rise of substitute products or to the emergence of foreign competition that breaks the monopoly power of both the oligopoly and the union. The ever more automated production of an ever simpler "world car" in international competition could combine all three forces.

Further, the rate of _local_ job formation will fare even worse if locational decentralization accompanies the maturing of the industry. Even if the local oligopolist faces a nationwide union and can not cut wage rates by relocating into low wage areas as its operations become more routine, as argued under the filtering theory above, decentralization to reduce transportation costs is common, when only ubiquitous skills are needed. The locality comes then to face a rate of local job formation inadequate to absorb the natural increase in its labor force, and an anxious search for new industries begins, a search heavily burdened by overpriced labor.

Local power to exploit the rest of the country may, in the long run, backfire in another way. Strong unions are inclined to set rigid work standards and work rules that become more binding and more expensive as time passes and technology progresses. Historically, new processes that permitted a worker to tend more spindles at one time or drill more holes in a given time period, with no more effort than before, often could not be introduced in the original plants of the industry. But simpler, new processes _will_ be innovated, one place or another, leaving an unyielding local labor force with a sharply declining share of the work in what may still be a slowly growing industry, thereby subjecting that local economy to declining employment.

Thus the classic advantages of a head start--a pool of labor where "the skill is in the air" and receptive local bankers who have come to know the new industry and identify with it--all may be undone by obsolete work standards and too rigid work rules in a world of rapid technological change. In many ways, a local economy that tries to rest on its laurels (or merely its luck) can age into chronic unemployment and may need to go through a painful wage deflation before it can rebuild. In short, there may be a day of retribution.

Then, again, there may not. If the beneficent local oligopoly enjoys a long period of vigorous growth in output and employment and is slow to decentralize, due to sizable economies of scale and low transportation cost, this single, strong industrial base could enrich its host area for a full generation or more. This advantaged locality could come in time to acquire a general level of education and skill that truly warrants a relatively high wage rate. High wage rates, however acquired, provide the personal income and build the local tax base needed to finance the good schools, research libraries and museums that are so attractive to an even more sophisticated set of new industries and to their employees. By the time the honeymoon is over, the local labor force could have matured in education and skill to the point where it is no longer overpriced, and could even have become a scarce factor and major locational attraction to new industries.

Thus, in this latter case, the normal equilibrating forces never come to bear. Market power leads instead to a dominant set of disequilibrating forces: power leads to affluence which leads to education and skill which leads back to greater affluence. Clearly, whether equilibrating or disequilibrating forces come to prevail is in part a matter of timing: the longer and more fully a locality can exploit monopoly power, the more likely it is that there need not be a day of reckoning. Still, local leadership and community values weigh at least as heavily in the scales. The grace period counts for little if the time is not well used to raise local educational levels and to found strong research and development facilities. Michigan has produced leading universities but its sports stadiums are better than its museums, and while the state has conserved its natural environment reasonably well, its urban development certainly does not match its well-over-average income level. The case is hard to make that Michigan has grown (matured) into the high wage rates and personal income levels that it has won through market power.

In more prescriptive terms, limits of managerial time, talent and budget dictate that Michigan economic development policymakers and managers must trade-off the relative benefits and costs of promoting high-tech work against the higher unemployment rates and lower mobility of low skill workers. They can not retreat realistically into the bland and inconsistent position of "placing the highest priority on both goals." Appropriate strategies differ: business tax cuts usually count for more in low skill competitive industries and better schools surely are more effective in attracting outside or nurturing inside entrepreneurs of new products and processes. Moreover, priorities must be assigned in an environment in which low skill manufacturing work is becoming increasingly scarce and the competition for high-tech industries is becoming increasingly intense.

Dual Labor Markets and Labor Relations

Strong unions and slow local growth--job formation slower than the natural increase in the labor force--tend to leave another heavy legacy: the burden of "dual labor markets" and a bi-modal distribution of wage income. Throughout the postwar period, one of the principal blessings that came with specialization in manufacturing has been that of a relatively high income, relatively equally distributed.[12] Unpublished analysis of the 1970 census data indicated that manufacturing areas had slipped to about average income but had retained their characteristically egalitarian distribution of income. But the 1970 income pattern still reflected a high growth national economy, one running at near full employment and dominated by the vigorous manufacturing economies of the Midwest and Northeast.

Slowing growth in manufacturing coupled to strong unions could twist local income patterns throughout the Midwest into bi-modal distributions: compressed high wage rates in the unionized metals, machinery and motor vehicles industries, and similar low wage and transfer payment income received by the growing number in the "secondary" labor market. The assumption here is that high wage rates, rigidly held, inflate costs and product prices over competitive levels, and this reduces consumption, production and employment in the "primary" labor market. With more workers displaced into the "secondary" labor market, invidious comparisons and vocational frustrations seem certain to grow in that climate and induce greater alienation among the excluded class--paupers, many of whom had themselves once been princes. The bitter harvest of poor work habits, expressed in absenteeism, shoddy workmanship, and general uncooperativeness, would seem to lead inexorably to high and rising labor costs and a general business-labor climate that stunts local growth. The excess supply of labor that might have offered business the attraction of choice among workers turns into the liability of a high labor cost location, whether rooted in high wage rates of some or the low productivity of others.

Wage Rollout and the Local Cost of Living and Doing Business

If the principal local export industry enjoys not only substantial price-making power but also rapid growth in demand for its product, this community can exploit the nation. (Note that the demand for automobiles has been historically both price inelastic and income elastic, nicely filling this prescription for power.) Under rapid growth in the demand for labor, the inflated wage rate of the export sector more easily and fully "rolls-out" into the local service sector, raising the wages of teachers, bus drivers, and supermarket cashiers. The rollout effect is double-edged: the higher wage-income of export workers increases the demand for local goods and services (and service workers) at precisely the time that high wages in the growing export sector are attracting service workers and reducing the supply of labor to the expanding service sector.

And the high wage rates secured by union and oligopoly power in the export sector tend to rollout beyond the competitive local service sector into the local public sector. A local example is compelling. In a recent Bureau of Labor Statistics comparison of municipal pay levels in twenty-six very large cities, for the years 1978-79, the City of Detroit indexes (and rank orders) were as follows: clerical workers 153 percent of average (first rank), janitorial, 145 (first), skilled maintenance, 138 (second) public safety, 115 (fourth) and sanitation workers, 119 (seventh).[13] Recent labor arbitration awards have moreover raised the salaries of policemen and firemen to first rank, and roughly 24 percent above the average of sixteen very large cities.[14]

The strength of the wage rollout into the local public sector in Detroit is also attested to by municipal pay levels relative to the local private sector. Drawing from the same study, clerical workers in the city government received 133 percent of the private sector average, skilled maintenance workers, 116 percent, janitors, 116 percent, truck drivers, 102 percent and helpers, 93 percent of the private sector level.

All in all, the motor vehicle industry combined the highest level of market concentration of any major industry (with the four largest firms accounting for about 90 percent of sales, value added and employment) with the highest proportion of workers organized (72 percent in 1977) and, by dominating the Detroit area economy, has lifted municipal pay levels in the City of Detroit to first rank among large cities, and even appreciably above those in the local private sector.

Assuming that labor productivity in the local public sector is only average, the exercise of oligopoly and union price power may enrich the local population but it also acts to inflate municipal costs and taxes and redounds in the long run to inhibit local industrial diversification and/or industrial redevelopment. Further, to the extent that it is to the <u>export service</u> industries that many aging manufacturing centers must look for a new economic base (e.g. insurance, tourism, conventions), high wage rates in service occupations become a serious barrier.

Finally, in search for new basic industry, whether export manufacturing or export services, the prospective employer must not only pay higher wages to his (her) own workforce and higher business taxes, but in addition the real income of these employees must be deflated to correct for the high cost of living that follows from the wage rollout into consumer services and local government services to households. That is, these high money wage employees do not feel all that well paid.

Nor have national developments eased Michigan's uncomfortable position. In a demand-pull inflation, most labor markets tighten together and nonunion wages rise about as much as union wages (e.g., in the 1950s). But in a "stagflation" arising more from cost-push forces (the 1970s?), only union wages would tend to keep up with rising prices, activated by automatic cost-of-living adjustments in labor contracts. Wage rollout requires reasonably tight labor markets, such that unionized employers compete for nonunion labor, a condition not at all characteristic of the high chronic unemployment of the 1970s. Cost-push stagflation could then explain the finding in Chapter 4 that the Michigan manufacturing wage premium rose dramatically from 124 percent of national average in 1970 to 132 percent in 1978, during a troubled decade for the automobile industry. Thus, while the real income of Michigan workers was protected better through the inflation of the 1970s, the competitive position of Michigan employers apparently deteriorated. Wage freezes over the next few years, forced by mounting foreign competition, could reverse this trend by substituting a more competitive international labor market for the fully unionized national market of the past.

La Ronde

We come full circle in the thesis of this chapter when we reflect on the possible origins of the various pools of cheap labor that attract older and simpler operations.

Labor surpluses with low wage levels are found most often in small towns that grew up as trade and service centers for natural-resource-based regions, typically county seats in agricultural areas. In time, depletion of the principal natural resource or, more often, technological progress in the farming or mining operation displaces large numbers of low skilled workers and dumps them on the rural regional center. Ironically, the rise of the natural-resource-based activity first built that rural service center, then matured and depressed it and indirectly created its principal attraction for replacement industry, namely cheap labor.

Finally, in the course of closing the circle, we should take note of the rising importance of natural resources in promoting local economic growth. The extraction and processing of energy resources explains much of the recent growth of our fastest growing states and localities, rivaling high technology manufacturing in this regard. We have progressed over the course of the past century from one set of resource-based locations to a second set of places based on new resources, and the gathering places of workers displaced from the decline of the first set of resource-based industries. If we add in amenity-seeking as a natural resource oriented location decision, one is struck with the increasingly central role played by natural resources, directly and indirectly, in the location of economic activity and regional growth, especially in the very long run.

We have progressed in our locational and regional growth logic from the primary location of (labor intensive) extractive industries through the pull of market oriented location and the generation of invention and innovation to the high cost push of big cities all the way around and back to the low wage pull of trade centers serving capital-intensive (labor-saving) extractive industries and searching desperately for replacement work. Finally, this elaborate sequence of inter-locking location decisions--this (almost) inexorable local economic development process--may take a century to unfold. It did in Michigan.

NOTES, CHAPTER 8

[1]See, for example, T. E. McMillan, Jr., "Why Manufacturers Choose Plant Locations vs. Determinants of Plant Locations," Land Economics 41, no. 3 (August 1965), pp. 239-46.

[2]Wilbur R. Thompson and John M. Mattilla, An Econometric Model of Postwar State Industrial Development (Detroit: Wayne State University Press, 1959).

[3]Leonard J. Wheat, Regional Growth and Industrial Location: An Empirical Viewpoint (Lexington, Mass.: Lexington Books, 1973).

[4]See, for example, Joel Bergsman, Peter Greenston and Robert Healy, "The Agglomeration Process in Urban Growth," Urban Studies 7 (1972): 263-88.

[5]This estimate was made in the now almost twenty-five-year-old but still widely quoted study by John B. Lansing and Eva Mueller, The Geographic Mobility of Labor (Ann Arbor, Mich.: Institute of Social Research, 1967), and has not been substantially changed by more recent evidence.

[6]The divorce rate has more than doubled over the past two decades from around fifteen divorces per thousand married women in the 1950s to thirty-two per thousand during 1972-74. The remarriage rate has also risen significantly from around 130 remarriages per thousand widowed and divorced women in the 1950s to over 160 in recent years. Social Indicators, 1976 (Washington, D.C.: U.S. Department of Commerce, USGPO, 1977), 66.

[7]See the appendix to this chapter for more detail on the Alexander Grant and Company study and other studies of interstate differences in tax costs to corporations.

[8]James Worsham, "Grim Economy in '80s Predicted for Midwest," Chicago Tribune, July 28, 1981, section 1, p. 3.

[9]For example, Dennis W. Carlton found a statistically significant relationship between the number of engineers in a metropolitan area and the number of firm births in the three industries studied, and strongest in the most technically sophisticated one (SIC #3662, radio and television transmitting apparatus), reported in "Why Firms Locate Where They Do: An Econometric Model," in William

C. Wheaton, ed., Interregional Movements and Regional Growth (Washington, D.C.: The Urban Institute, 1979), pp. 28, 35-6.

[10]Derived from U.S. Department of Commerce, Patent and Trademark Office, Technological Assessment & Forecast, Seventh Report, March 1977, appendix A, tables A-1 and A-2, pp. 185-95.

[11]Lest one wonder whether Flint's blue collar affluence arises out of a relatively large amount of capital per worker in motor vehicle manufacturing, fixed assets per worker (in SIC #3711) in 1976 amounted to $20,900, or almost exactly the median value for 150-odd manufacturing industries examined by the author. Detroit Area Economic Opportunities Project, Greater Detroit Chamber of Commerce, April 1980, pp. 32-44.

[12]"Internal and External Factors in the Development of Urban Economies," and "Toward an Econometric Model of Urban Economic Development" (joint author with John M. Mattila), Issues in Urban Economics, Perloff and Wingo, eds. (Baltimore: The John Hopkins Press, 1968).

[13]U.S. Department of Labor, Bureau of Labor Statistics, Wage Differences Among Large City Governments and Comparisons with Industry and Federal Pay, 1978-79, Report #633, Washington, D.C., USGPO, March 1981.

[14]Newspaper report in the Detroit Free Press on the "City of Philadelphia Survey of Police and Fire Pay and Related Practices, 1981," April 6, 1981.

Appendix 8.1

Interstate Differences in Tax Costs to Corporations: A Look at Some Accounting Studies

by

James E. Wheeler

The University of Michigan

INTRODUCTION

This appendix has been developed largely as a by-product of work on another research project, Rehabilitation of Industrial Buildings (RIB).

Key tax and financial management personnel in two major nonautomotive corporations were interviewed as to their plant location, relocation or rehabilitation decisions. In addition, each of the nine largest certified public accounting firms was contacted to ascertain if they had prepared any rehabilitation studies for their clients and whether they had made any studies of state and local tax aspects of plant location or relocation. Several studies which focused on or included state tax systems were located. These are by (1) Alexander Grant Co., (2) Arthur Andersen Co., and (3) Price Waterhouse Co.

An immediate summary of these studies would conclude that they are meritorious efforts but are generally lacking rigor and scientific methodology. One study is based on a survey questionnaire and the other two are based on hypothetical state tax computations for a certain specified firm or firms.

STUDIES

The Alexander Grant Study

This 1980 study, essentially a repeat of their 1979 study, utilized a survey questionnaire methodology in attempting to gauge the relative "business climate" among the forty-eight contiguous states. The participants (thirty-six state manufacturing associations) were asked to allocate points among a wide spectrum of attributes (eighteen attributes which were considered to be relevant to the location decision) according to the perceived importance of each such attribute. The votes were then processed, relative weights were assigned to each attribute, and these weights were then applied to the ranking of each state for each attribute. From this processing methodology, a composite ranking was determined and the desirability of various state locations was ascertained. In each of the two years, Michigan ranked last, or forty-eighth.

The attributes dealing directly or indirectly with state taxes were:

(1) state and local taxes per capita, and

(2) percentage change in state and local taxes per capita. In addition there were attributes for labor union membership, average weekly manufacturing wage, workmen's compensation, unemployment benefits and unemployment trust fund size per covered worker.

Of the eighteen factors selected, state and local taxes per capita was rated the most significant (closely followed by labor union membership and average weekly manufacturing wage) and based on this attribute alone, Michigan was ranked thirty-ninth, in both years, out of the forty-eight states. However, the use of per capita figures can be quite misleading. Alaska, for example, while not in the survey, has the highest per capita tax of any state. The bulk of Alaska's tax receipts, however, consist of the yield of a severance tax on oil and gas, borne largely by nonresidents of the state. The same may be true for Texas and other oil-producing states. Nevada, which ranked forty-fourth in regard to the per capita tax (fifth highest tax per capita), has a tax on gambling as its principal source of revenue. This tax would be borne primarily by residents of other states. Thus ratings based in part on per capita figures can produce misleading results.

The low rating for desirability for Michigan was due more to the labor cost factors than to the tax factors. In the factors for labor union membership and average weekly manufacturing wage, Michigan ranked last and these were both heavily weighted factors.

This study, which is in its second year, does not claim to be, nor should it be construed to be, using scientific methodology in that a whole host of internal and external validity problems exist.

The lack of internal validity is a major problem. The participants were not randomly selected; they probably were not unbiased; and there was not proportional representation between the sample and the population of relevant decision makers. In addition there was no control for the decision-making process within the associations. The voting scheme and ranking mechanism did not reflect dollar differences (the distributions were collapsed when the rankings were made), nor were interactions among the variables considered. In addition, there is always an external validity problem when individuals (persons in manufacturing associations in this case) are asked what they believe instead of observing what they do.

This study has been conducted for only two years and the results obtained have been relatively stable between years. There has been no attempt to test the changes in the composite ratings with changes in state business activity over the same time periods.

The study could be improved by asking individual decision makers (randomly selected with appropriate controls for industry membership, firm size, etc.) to rank a set of hypothetical states by giving them the attributes for each state. By processing the rankings by state one could then ascertain the decision-making function which is used by the respondents (multiple regression).

While the Alexander Grant study has many validity problems, the fact that a significant group (manufacturing associations) ranked Michigan last, two years in a row, as a place to locate a business is not at all comforting.

The Arthur Andersen Study

This study was prepared for the Ohio Development Sales Council by Arthur Andersen Co. and was completed in April, 1977. Unlike the Alexander Grant study, this one concentrated on a comparison of certain state and local taxes among fourteen states (Illinois, Indiana, Kentucky, Maryland, Michigan, Missouri, New Jersey, New York, Ohio, Pennsylvania, Tennessee, Virginia, West Virginia, and Wisconsin).

To develop the comparisons the study used four hypothetical corporations (large manufacturer, large distributor, medium manufacturer, medium distributor), and examined their property and income taxes (including franchise taxes, gross and adjusted gross receipts taxes, and single business taxes as income taxes). The study also examined the tax burden of five individuals at different levels of income for each state.

In the study the effect of the Michigan single business tax seems to reflect itself in significantly lower taxes on distributors than on manufacturers. The following shows the Michigan taxes as a percentage of the comparable Ohio taxes by the four hypothetical corporations.

	Ohio	Michigan
Large manufacturer	100%	104%
Medium manufacturer	100%	73%
Large distributor	100%	18%
Medium Distributor	100%	23%

In each comparison for distributors the simulations showed that Michigan had the lowest tax burden of all fourteen states in the comparison.

The Andersen study uses a simulation-oriented methodology and is encouraging but not rigorous in that a well constructed model could generate hypotheses about location decisions of different industries, except that one must control for the other attributes of the location decision.

Taken together the Arthur Andersen and the Alexander Grant studies would seem to indicate that it is not the business tax system that is Michigan's major obstacle in attracting and retaining industrial plants, but this observation would be based on the assumption that the studies are reasonably valid.

<u>The Price Waterhouse Study</u>

This study was prepared for the Division of Commerce and Industrial Development of the State of Missouri by Price Waterhouse Co., and was completed in August, 1978. Like the Andersen study, it concentrated on a comparison of tax attributes, in this case for twenty-one states. In addition, more tax attributes were examined, six in this instance (income, sales and use, property, unemployment, workers' compensation, and franchise taxes).

In this study only the taxes of a single "typical" manufacturing concern were compared among the twenty-one states.[1] It is quite possible that size and industry change would affect these results. The results of this study showed Michigan to have the lowest tax at the end of the first year of operations and the fourth lowest at the end of the second year of operations, with Missouri being the lowest tax state at the end of two years of successful operations.

These results were significantly affected by the assumed income apportionment between states. The three-factor formula (based on payroll, property and sales) used in this simulation allocated 31 percent of the income to the target state while the single factor formula (based on sales) allocated only 16 percent of the income to the target state. Missouri is the only state of the twenty-one that allows either the three-factor formula or the single-factor formula, whichever produces the lowest allocation.

The results were also significantly affected by the assumption of a large federal income tax liability. Missouri is the only state in the group which allows a full deduction for the federal income tax.

While the Price Waterhouse study appears to be "loaded" in favor of Missouri (the state engaging the preparation of the study), it is interesting to note that Michigan, nevertheless, finished with the lowest tax rate of the twenty-one states at the end of the first year of operations.

The Price Waterhouse study seems to support the Andersen study in that the Michigan tax system appears quite favorable relative to that of the other states for the types of entities chosen for comparison. But these analyses are susceptible to significant change by changing circumstances. For example, in the Price Waterhouse study, if the "typical" manufacturing entity were labor intensive and had started out with losses (not an unusual result for a new enterprise) instead of profits, the Michigan single business tax, due to the add back of labor costs, might well have caused Michigan to be the highest or one of the highest rather than the lowest tax state at the end of the first year.

INTERVIEWS WITH MANAGEMENT PERSONNEL IN TWO MAJOR MANUFACTURING ENTITIES LOCATED OUTSIDE OF MICHIGAN

These interviews were initially established to obtain data on the rehabilitation of industrial buildings and more specifically on the tax aspects. During these interviews (in which the corporations desired to remain anonymous) questions concerning Michigan as a state for plant location were posed.

The harsh cash flow result of the single business tax on nonprofitable operations was expressed as a significant negative factor. The fact that one of these major corporations had recently closed down a six-year-old plant (located in an eastern state) due to unprofitable operations, may have influenced their opinions. In addition, there was an assumption that Chrysler was paying significant single business tax even in its worst years. There appeared to be an aversion to risking a significant investment in a state which taxes losing operations. If major corporations have such reluctance it must be magnified for small and medium size firms considering Michigan as a site of operations. In addition, the smaller the firm, the more labor-intensive it is apt to be, thus increasing the single business tax liability (but not to exceed the established tax rate (2.35 percent) times 50 percent of the gross receipts) for many levels of income. This problem is likely to be even greater for research and development (R&D) operations which are often highly labor-intensive and frequently operate at losses when R&D costs are typically expensed.

Another factor which was mentioned was the high cost of unionized labor, especially the United Auto Workers. There seemed to be an assumption that the wage rates in the automobile industry affect the level of labor costs for the entire State of Michigan. The package of labor-related expenses including workmen's compensation, perceived high wage rates, and the add back of labor in the single business tax were frequently mentioned as disincentives to locate in Michigan.

Another conclusion of the interviews is that there is an optimum level of taxation that does not equal zero. Government expenditures on behalf of a firm are frequently viewed as more important than tax abatements. These expenditures include job training and screening programs and improved transportation through upgraded highways. Job training and screening is viewed as particularly beneficial in that the corporation's goodwill in a new community is retained if the state turns down unacceptable potential employees from the local population. The expenditure route is often favored by local politicians in that the expenditures are often less visible to other taxpayers than tax abatements and provide jobs. Often this route is favored also by the corporation in that each dollar of expenditure by the state or local government is usually excluded from the corporation's taxable income, whereas a similar amount of property tax abatement may be offset in part by federal income tax increases. If the corporation expends funds to supply the desired item, the expenditure is often capitalized and recoverable over future periods.

NOTE, APPENDIX 8.1

[1]The states are Arkansas, California, Connecticut, Illinois, Indiana, Iowa, Kansas, Kentucky, Massachusetts, Michigan, Minnesota, Missouri, Nebraska, New Jersey, New York, Ohio, Oklahoma, Pennsylvania, Tennessee, Texas, Wisconsin.

Chapter 9

Developing High-Technology Industry

by

Marian Krzyzowski, B. Michael Conboy, and Jesse Hall

The University of Michigan

INTRODUCTION

Current interest in high-technology industry is intense in Michigan and many other states. Its growth potential and its record of generating quality jobs at good salaries stir this interest. A broad spectrum of development activities among the states reflects their commitment to high technology.

How Michigan should compete for this special growth industry is now a pressing question in both government and industry. Analysis of other states' high-technology programs, covering a period of twenty years, points to success in job creation. The details of these programs and their results provide clues to alternatives available to Michigan.

Accepted definitions of high-technology industry tend to be circular and elusive. For the purposes of this discussion, the typical process of company evolution is more revealing.

Growth Stages of High-Technology Firms

One scientific idea plus one entrepreneur to commercialize it are the basic ingredients for creation of a high-technology company. Three subsequent stages of development may follow:

Stage One--The entrepreneur draws on personal savings and credit to refine the idea. A small group (1 to 10) of scientists and technicians are employed. Operating losses are incurred.

Stage Two--Commercial potential of the applied idea is

recognized by venture capital investment organizations. The entrepreneur exchanges equity for working capital. Employment grows quickly (10 to 200) as manufacturing facilities are acquired or licensing agreements executed. Over time, rapidly increasing receipts from product sales are realized.

Stage Three--In an expanding market for the now commercialized idea, the entrepreneur further dilutes personal equity through the public sale of stock. Venture capital investors may also take profit at this stage of development. Control of the company passes from the entrepreneur to a board of directors representing diverse interests. Expanding production or sales require increased employment (200 to 2,000). The company becomes a nationally attractive investment prospect, vulnerable to merger or takeover.

THE MICHIGAN EXPERIENCE

Michigan has had a long history of high-technology industry, some of it stemming from the state's role as World War II's "arsenal of democracy." Although Michigan since has had limited success in fostering high technology growth, it has fallen far short of the accomplishments of several other states. The purpose of this section is to review Michigan's experience, focusing on those factors that have been instrumental in aiding high-technology growth in the state and others which have hindered it.

Federal Research and Development (R&D) Facilities in Michigan

The role of federal R&D facilities in stimulating high-technology industry development is an open question. Sirbu et al. (1976) suggest that government research laboratories in general do not appear to act as a catalyst, attracting private technology-oriented facilities, nor are they a major source of spin-offs.

Other studies indicate, however, that federal labs may have significant spin-off potential. Roberts in his analysis of Massachusetts' high-technology industry traced sixteen private enterprises back to ideas emanating from the Air Force Cambridge Research Laboratories. When linked with universities, government labs may nurture considerably more spin-off activity. In his study, Roberts documents at least fifty companies which grew out of technology under development at Massachusetts Institute of Technology's Lincoln Lab (Roberts 1968).

A similar evolution of spin-offs flowed from The University of Michigan's Willow Run Laboratories, set up in 1946 to conduct defense-related R&D. Approximately seventeen companies emerged from ideas originating in this federally-funded facility, making it the largest known source of spin-offs in Michigan (Evaldson 1970). In 1972, the Willow Run installation was severed from the University and renamed the Environmental Research Institute of Michigan. The quasi-public facility now specializes in remote sensing technology, conducting R&D under federal contract and for private application.

Although a number of federal R&D installations have been located in the state since World War II, including the E.P.A. Automotive Emissions Laboratory, efforts to attract many others have proven unsuccessful. During the past twenty years, Michigan was rated among the top contending states for the following major labs: the Nuclear Accelerator Laboratory, the National Electronics Laboratory, the National Transportation Laboratory, and the Solar Energy Laboratory. Ultimately, all were located elsewhere.

Michigan's unfruitful campaigns to attract these federal facilities have seemed to follow a predictable pattern. Early warning of the opportunity to host a new national laboratory came from a variety of sources; congressional representatives, university scientists, or industry executives. Invariably, an ad hoc group was formed, frequently employing the leadership of the governor, staffed by state administrative officials, and including representation by relevant technical business and labor interest groups (Ann Arbor MCCP 1963; Ann Arbor IDC 1966; "Atoms..." 1967).

In retrospect, this formal group approach proved unwieldy. Reaction time was slow. The facilities were located in states which responded through informal channels, quickly launching a creative dialogue between federal and local scientists.

Michigan's Research Parks

In the early 1960s, several Michigan communities established planned landsites, designated research parks. Locations were close to universities. Much interaction between industry researchers and their university counterparts was anticipated. In general, this attempt achieved limited success. Three examples will illustrate Michigan's research park experience.

The Greater Ann Arbor Research Park was created in 1960 following three years of planning and negotiations led by an economic development committee of the Chamber of Commerce (Ann Arbor EDC 1965; Lamont 1971). The park concept was patterned after other research areas near Boston, Massachusetts, and Palo Alto, California. It was alleged to be the first research park of its kind in the midwest, and promotion plans included the slogan "Ann Arbor, Research Center of the Midwest."

A first laboratory site was purchased in 1961. The balance of the research park filled up slowly, over a period of twenty years. Constraints to more rapid growth included small lot size and restrictions on the type of manufacturing or processing permitted in the park. It is generally conceded that the park did serve to attract technology-based firms into the Ann Arbor area, albeit slowly. Although the Greater Ann Arbor Research Park did not meet the expectations of its planners, it was by far the most successful experiment of its kind in Michigan and was the first such success in the midwest.

The Red Cedar Research Park, East Lansing, was

established in the mid-1960s by a private developer, encouraged by Michigan State University officials (Danilov 1971). Within a few years it hosted three R&D labs. One was operated by a major manufacturer. Another was established by a university professor.

Once the first three buildings were in place, a slow sales period followed. Development financing costs created pressure to sell the land. So, compromises were made in restrictive covenants, allowing professional offices and eventually wholesale and warehousing operations. Over time, the research park concept became obscured. As developed, the area is typical of any commercial-industrial urban land use.

Also during the mid-1960s, the Wayne State University Research Park was started, near interstate highways and adjacent to the campus. The first building constructed in the Wayne State Park was a chemical laboratory, founded by a professor. The company is still operating on the site, but it is still the only firm to locate in the area.

When 90 percent of the park had been cleared for development, negotiations with a small number of remaining homeowners stalled. This impediment and changing economic forces blunted industry interest in the development. During the 1970s a portion of the Wayne State University Research Park was rezoned for residential housing.

Michigan's R&D Concentrations

Michigan has a broad-based network of R&D facilities. A 1980 survey indicated there were nearly 400 such operations (Directory 1981). Most are located in the state's southeastern region, including Washtenaw (sixty-eight), Wayne (sixty-seven), and Oakland (sixty-one) counties. A western Michigan concentration of R facilities is present in Kent (twenty-three), Berrien (fourteen), Kalamazoo (twelve), and Ottawa (ten) counties.

During the past decade, the number of Michigan R&D facilities expanded by 20 percent. During this period, major growth has occurred in Oakland County with thirty new facilities, an increase of nearly 100 percent. Washtenaw County gained twenty facilities or 42 percent of the number it had in 1970, and Kent County hosts eight new facilities or 50 percent more than in 1970.

Michigan's R&D facilities are diverse. There are fifty which focus on chemicals and polymers, twenty on controls and machine tools, fifteen on computers, and fourteen on energy related devices. Roughly half of all R&D facilities in the state carry out projects for other companies or allow other firms to use their facilities.

Ann Arbor/Washtenaw County, Michigan

"Quality of life" in the Ann Arbor/Washtenaw County SMSA was rated "outstanding" overall by Liu (1976). Independent statistical indicators of economic, environmental, health and education, and social quality were combined to yield this overall rating. Among all medium size SMSA's nationally, Ann Arbor's health and education quality indicators ranked second (Liu 1976).

Ann Arbor is the nucleus of a high-technology complex in Michigan. This city of approximately 110,000 people has ten government laboratories and some sixty technology-based companies employing 8,000 people (Sirbu 1976). A strong impetus to the development of this industry has been the presence of The University of Michigan. Many area companies emerged as spin-offs, transferring technology from university labs to commercial application.

In a 1971 study by John Lamont, 126 spin-off firms of all kinds were identified in Michigan (1971). Seventy-four of these firms were located in the Ann Arbor area. Among the Ann Arbor spin-offs, twenty-five had The University of Michigan as their source. More than fifteen of these grew out of technology conceived at the university's Willow Run Laboratories.

Two important industrial sources of area spin-offs were Bendix and Lear Siegler. Bendix generated eight spin-offs.

Earlier, the Aerospace Systems Division of Bendix was founded by University of Michigan researchers.

The history of high-technology industry in Ann Arbor suggests that sporadic support from local institutions played a pivotal role in its growth. In recent years there has been increasing interest in development of high-technology industry within the university and the community. In 1981, this interest culminated in the formation of the Michigan Technology Council by industry executives, university officials, and community representatives.

Despite the activities of this forum for cooperation, one cyclical phenomenon continues to plague Ann Arbor high-technology development. The area has not succeeded in capturing the third stage of high-technology company growth and expansion, the ultimate payoff in terms of jobs and related economic rewards. Once a company has reached a level of about 1,000 to 1,500 employees, it has become hamstrung by several factors. Typically, the end result has been transfer of company operations elsewhere. Two striking examples of this pattern are Conductron and Sycor.

Conductron was a major spin-off of university research at Willow Run Laboratories. The company expanded its radar-based business rapidly in the 1960s, doubling gross sales each year until employment reached 2,000. At that stage, the Ann Arbor firm merged with McDonnell-Douglas of St. Louis, Missouri, while retaining its local management team. This management arrangement was not mutually satisfactory. A steady decline in Conductron's business occurred. Ultimately, the Ann Arbor operation was closed.

Sycor, a computer terminal producer, did not grow as rapidly as Conductron, but during the mid-1970s it also reached a level of 2,000 employees. At that point, the firm was sold to Northern Telecom Systems of Canada. A local management team agreement, somewhat similar to the Conductron arrangement, was forged. The Ann Arbor operation experienced a turnover rate of 30 percent in its labor force. Other production cost and competition problems soon led to major cutbacks in the Ann Arbor manufacturing operations. Research operations continue there.

Similarities between Conductron and Sycor are numerous. Each grew to become one of Ann Arbor's largest high-technology companies, then suffered setbacks. Effective public policy to preserve the third stage growth of such firms could have a dramatic impact on area employment totals over time. If Michigan can retain third stage growth companies, either in the Ann Arbor area or elsewhere in the state, other investments in high-technology entrepreneurship and second stage growth can be expected to double their job creation yield.

In August, 1981, a workshop was conducted with executives of Ann Arbor area high-technology companies to probe possible precursors of third stage departure. The following concerns were expressed by participants:

1) The area lacks specialized legal, accounting, and banking services appropriate to the needs of stage one and two high-technology companies.

2) Available land is often beyond the means of many smaller, stage one and two, high-technology companies and few large land areas are available for construction by stage three firms.

3) Michigan's Single Business Tax may represent an excessive burden on stage one and two companies which commonly record operating losses, but pay tax on the basis of "value added" or payroll.

4) Michigan "Blue Sky" laws restricting the public sale of stock may prevent high-technology companies from tapping local sources of capital.

5) Property tax abatement programs, offered at municipal discretion to manufacturing and commercial firms, under certain circumstances exclude full-time R&D facilities. (There are legislative initiatives pending which would remedy this problem.)

OTHER STATES' EXPERIENCES

During the post-World War II era, certain regions of the nation have successfully developed high-technology complexes, generating hundreds of thousands of jobs and providing an example for other regions to follow. To put Michigan's experience in perspective, it is useful to examine selected success stories, focusing on those factors which were instrumental in achieving high-technology development.

Sirbu et al. have divided high-technology development into four broad categories (1976). These four typologies were used as a guide in the selection of successful development examples:

1) Locally generated companies or spin-offs.

2) Research-oriented companies within a planned research park.

3) The attraction of manufacturing facilities of high-technology companies in an area.

4) Large expenditures of government funds on a developmental facility.

As previously noted, much of the existing high-technology industry in Michigan is a result of spin-offs from The University of Michigan or from local companies. Consequently, it falls under the first typology described by Sirbu.

Several nationally prominent high-technology "complexes" also fall under typology one. Perhaps the best known such development, "Silicon Valley," surrounds the Stanford University area of California. From typology two, the North Carolina Research Triangle Park provides an excellent example. Within the third typology is the Minneapolis/St. Paul area. Government labs, representative of typology four, were discussed earlier.

Stanford/Santa Clara County, California

Santa Clara County defines the San Jose SMSA and

includes the communities of Stanford and Palo Alto. "Quality of life" there was rated "outstanding" overall by Liu. Among all large SMSAs, San Jose's health and education quality indicators ranked first (Liu 1976).

The Bay Area of California enjoys a tradition of pioneering scientific and technological advances. The electronic age started in Palo Alto with the discovery of the vacuum tube. Through the work and encouragement of Frederick Terman, an electrical engineer at Stanford, several high-technology companies were organized. The most famous of these is Hewlett Packard, founded in 1937 (Bylinsky 1974; Dallas 1981).

Stanford University, struggling with financial limitations after World War II, began to negotiate federal defense contracts under the guidance of Terman, then Dean of Engineering. Concurrently, the university launched development of a tract of pasture land. Through the marketing abilities of Terman and David Packard, Stanford Industrial Park grew rapidly. By the mid-1970s, the park was occupied by fifty-five tenants, employing 17,000 people. During this period, Stanford University received $18 million in prepaid leases, producing $1 million in annual interest income (Bylinsky 1974).

Meanwhile, William Shockley, a co-discoverer of the transistor effect, brought together a group of electronics experts in Palo Alto. In 1957, several members of the group left Shockley to found Fairchild Semiconductor. Spin-offs from this single company eventually spawned forty others, turning Santa Clara County into "Silicon Valley."

The presence of high-growth companies in California's Bay Area has stimulated the growth of venture capital firms. Many new millionaires later became investment backers for start-up companies. This in turn has attracted the attention of national venture capitalists. In 1980, "Silicon Valley" companies received $700 million in the form of venture capital investment (Dallas 1981).

High-technology industry formation and expansion has led to unprecedented economic growth for the area. Between 1950 and 1975, employment in this industry sector soared from 3,000 to 150,000 (Bylinsky 1974).

Research Triangle, North Carolina

Research Triangle Park is surrounded by three university communities--Chapel Hill, Durham, and Raleigh. Only the small and medium SMSAs, Durham and Raleigh, respectively, were considered by Liu. Both were found to possess "good" overall "quality of life." Health and education indicators fell in the "excellent" range with neither ranking among the top ten for its population size class (Liu 1976).

Historically, the State of North Carolina has had a very limited industrial base. Tobacco processing was the leading industry. State officials became concerned about this dependency on a single industry during the early 1950s. Several interest groups began to discuss the possibility of a major initiative to attract new industry to North Carolina.

By 1954, a diversification plan took form. A "research triangle" was conceived, with vertices at Duke, North Carolina, and North Carolina State Universities. It was proposed that an area within this triangle be developed into an industrial research center. The governor of the state, Luther Hodges, adopted the concept and became its biggest promoter. He brought together leading university administrators and elicited their support (Hamilton 1966).

Through the forceful personality of Luther Hodges and the assistance of several North Carolina civic leaders, the research triangle concept was brought to fruition. In 1957, a nonprofit organization assembled 4,000 acres of undeveloped land. One year later, the Research Triangle Foundation was formed by a coalition of government leaders, industrial executives, and university officials.

The land development was named Research Triangle Park,

and the Research Triangle Institute was formed as a wholly-owned subsidiary of the three participating universities. Thereupon, the Research Institute took the lead in promotion and development of the park. In 1959, Chemstrand Corporation became its first major private tenant (Hamilton 1966).

Earlier construction of university, joint-research facilities set the architectural tone for subsequent development. Carefully planned, the park has become a campus-like extension of each of the nearby universities. Building requirements include ample open space and many trees.

Research Triangle Park's success was preserved by the state's ability to attract two major federal laboratories at financially critical times. In 1958, when a national recession threatened the entire project, the governor helped lure a U.S. Forest Service Lab to the park. Between 1960 and 1963, when park development reached a second plateau, Hodges, then U.S. Secretary of Commerce, again helped the park acquire the National Environmental Sciences Center. Together, these facilities made it possible to weather difficult times until success was finally secure (Hamilton 1966; "Planning..." 1965). In 1965, IBM announced plans to construct a development and manufacturing plant in the park, costing $15 million and employing 2,500 persons.

Today, there are about thirty research organizations in the park, employing 13,000 people. The surrounding three communities, with a total population of 500,000, have the highest number of Ph.D's per capita in the U.S. Many of the research specialists who work in the park also hold adjunct professorships at one of the three affiliated universities. Park administration is financially self-sufficient, deriving revenue from the sale or lease of land ("A Park..." 1977; Carter 1978; King 1977; RTI 1979).

<u>Minneapolis/St. Paul, Minnesota</u>

The "Twin Cities" of Minneapolis and St. Paul comprise

a single large SMSA, rated "outstanding" overall in "quality of life" by Liu. The two communities' health and education quality indicators ranked seventh among all large SMSAs (Liu 1976).

Minnesota's high-technology companies shipped $6.4 billion worth of products in 1977, or about 40 percent of the state's total manufacturing output. These companies accounted for about $290 million in tax revenues, or 10 percent of total state collections for the year. Minnesota's electronics and medical-related companies added about 100,000 jobs in the state between 1950 and 1980, twice the growth of general manufacturing.

In 1946, William Norris founded Engineering Research Associates (ERA), a technical contributor to the computer industry and a major source of Minnesota spin-off companies. In the late 1960s, Norris and his associates created a second company called Control Data, another prolific source of high-technology spin-offs ("Minnesota..." 1981).

The significance of Norris' ventures had impacts far beyond their own successes. His long-standing interest in the development of small computer-oriented businesses in Minnesota led to tremendous growth in new, high-technology companies. Control Data alone spawned seventeen other computer firms. Norris personal initiatives also led to the formation of three important development institutions: 1) the Microelectronics and Information Sciences Center at the University of Minnesota is a strong technical resource; 2) the Minnesota Cooperation Office provides management help to start-up companies; and 3) the Minnesota Seed Capital Corporation grants planning and development funds to entrepreneurs.

The state's technology-based industry growth is mostly home-grown. Remarkably, this growth has been achieved within a state business climate characterized by relatively high taxes and strict regulation of industry. Few outside high-technology companies have come into Minnesota. As a consequence of state loyalty, technological infrastructure, available seed money, and venture capital, there has been significant local expansion and new company formation (Brennan 1980; "Minnesota..." 1981).

Minneapolis/St. Paul has an extensive record of successful high-technology start-ups and spin-offs. Forty area companies trace their origin back to Norris' ERA. Companies such as Control Data, Cray, and Data Card now invest in high-technology start-ups. This readiness by existing companies to support new ones has led to the area being ranked among the top five nationally in venture capital availability. Only Boston, Palo Alto, Denver, and Dallas rank higher (Brennan 1980).

Through its own resources, the University of Minnesota has been hard pressed to continue the institutional growth required to support such technology expansion. Major research centers help it to attract grants, professors, and students. Privately, Control Data and Honeywell contributed $2 million each, and Univac gave $1 million toward development of the Center for Microelectronics and Information Sciences.

Elements of Success

Several key elements of success in high-technology development can be identified from the preceding discussion.

1) A climate of "economic necessity" prompted officials at Stanford and Research Triangle Park to take far-reaching, cohesive action.
2) Aggressive and visionary leadership:
    a) encouraged the start-up of new companies;
    b) successfully promoted and raised funds for land development and administration;
    c) attracted major federal installations and laboratories; and
    d) involved major universities in the process.

This leadership originated from a variety of sectors.

In California it came from a Stanford University faculty member, in North Carolina from the governor's office, and in Minnesota from an entrepreneur. Other success elements included:

3) Engineering and scientific orientation of a major university or universities and their willingness to interact with industry.

4) Availability of large tracts of land, both at Stanford and in North Carolina.

5) Accumulation of "home-grown" venture capital from successful local companies at Stanford and in Minnesota.

6) Outstanding "quality of life" indicators apparent at Minneapolis/St. Paul and Stanford prior to development take-off.

MICHIGAN'S POTENTIAL FOR HIGH-TECHNOLOGY DEVELOPMENT

Industrial R&D Activity

Federally-funded R&D activity has played an important role in helping launch several high-technology complexes, including "Silicon Valley." To a lesser extent, it has contributed to the development of a high-technology nucleus in Michigan's Ann Arbor area. Another powerful resource has not been fully exploited in Michigan--industrial R&D activity within major private companies.

Table 9.1 compares selected state industrial R&D volumes by source of funding. Michigan occupies a strong position in industrial R&D, relative to population and to surrounding states. Private sector R&D volume in Michigan accounted for more than 14 percent of the U.S. total in 1974. California and Massachusetts, which enjoy similar levels of total research activity, are much more reliant on the federal government. On the surface, this situation would appear to be quite advantageous for Michigan's high-technology potential, especially during a period of federal budget trimming.

TABLE 9.1
GEOGRAPHIC DISTRIBUTION OF FUNDS FOR
INDUSTRIAL RESEARCH AND DEVELOPMENT
BY SOURCE OF FUNDS

(Pecentages of Total U.S.)

State	1975 Population	1970 Percentage of U.S. Research and Development			1974 Percentage of U.S. Research and Development		
		Total	Federal	Company	Total	Federal	Company
Michigan	4.28	7.0	1.0	11.6	9.2	1.0	14.2
Illinois	5.26	4.0	0.3	6.7	4.4	n.a.	n.a.
Indiana	2.50	2.4	0.8	3.6	1.8	1.0	2.3
Ohio	5.03	5.1	2.6	7.0	5.0	3.2	6.0
Wisconsin	2.15	1.3	0.4	1.9	1.3	n.a.	n.a.
California	9.95	21.3	n.a.	n.a.	19.7	36.9	9.4
Massachusetts	2.73	5.5	6.8	4.5	5.1	8.0	3.4
North Carolina	2.55	1.0	n.a.	n.a.	1.0	0.2	1.4
Minnesota	1.84	1.6	1.0	22.1	1.8	1.4	2.1

Source: Research and Development in Industry, Survey of Science Resources, National Science Foundation, published bi-annually.

TABLE 9.2
RESEARCH AND DEVELOPMENT SPENDING
BY LEADING MICHIGAN-BASED MANUFACTURES[1]
(1979)

Company	Research and Development Spending (In Millions of Dollars)
General Motors	1949.8
Ford Motor Company	1719.7
Chrysler	358.4
Dow Chemical	268.8
Bendix	63.0
American Motors	59.8
Burroughs	169.3
Fruehauf	17.8
Whirlpool	33.4
Kellogg	11.4
Clark Equipment	26.3
Upjohn	129.3
Ex-Cell-O	13.6
Masco	10.2
Federal Mogul	6.0
Gerber Products	4.2
National Standard	3.2
Hayes-Albion	2.7
Herman Miller	3.8
	4,850.7[2]
Percent of total Private Research and Development Spending	20.4%

Notes: [1]List does not include all Michigan Fortune 1000 companies. Notable exceptions include Tecumseh Products, McLouth Steel, Hoover Universal, and Dow Corning.

[2]Only includes those firms covered.

Source: Business Week, July 7, 1980, McGraw Hill.

Table 9.2 presents annual volumes of industrial R&D spending by Michigan-based firms. (Admittedly, a firm headquartered in Michigan may not spend all of is R&D here, but a rough measure of relative levels of spending is provided by this comparison.) Approximately four-fifths of all state R&D activity is accounted for by the automobile companies. Upjohn, Burroughs, and Dow, together, account for about one-tenth of private spending and represent the major nonautomotive R&D sectors in the state.

Automotive

Unfortunately, innovation in a mature industry such as the automobile industry is as likely to decrease employment as to increase it. This is especially true of manufacturing process innovations, such as automation and robotics. However, the automotive industry does consume many high-technology products. Changing relationships between the vehicle-producing companies and suppliers of tooling and components now present a number of opportunities for development of new, small high-technology companies in the automotive supply sector.

Although the vehicle producers historically have emphasized internal R&D and vertical-integration, current capital constraints may influence major company executives to consider alternative approaches, including joint ventures, technological spin-offs, and other forms of supplier chain development. The challenge of Japanese competition also has led U.S. automakers to examine the "supplier circle" concept of nested development and manufacturing facilities. In Japan, each vehicle manufacturing facility is typically surrounded by many small supplier R&D facilities, promoting communication, cost-reduction, and quality enhancement.

An immediate role the automotive industry could play in fostering Michigan's high-technology potential would be to provide both technology and initial markets for products to be developed and manufactured by new, small companies. Later, these companies might expand into other markets.

Defense

Increased defense spending offers new opportunities for development of technology-oriented industry. Yet to avoid becoming tied to the defense spending cycle, the potential for commercial applications must guide the selection of technologies at an early stage.

One promising avenue for Michigan is defense-related manufacturing equipment. Another is the development of technology to produce technology, such as computer-aided design and manufacturing software. Both would build on current strengths in capital goods production. Michigan leads the nation in the development and manufacture of metalworking machinery, accounting for one-quarter of total domestic output.

As previously noted, defense research activity has provided an impetus for high-technology industry development in other states, and it may be responsible for a large share of the existing industry nucleus in Ann Arbor. However, it appears that to progress beyond such development, strategies to promote the growth of private spin-offs may be critically important.

Spin-Offs

Michigan already hosts many, diverse R&D facilities in both public and private sectors. Several concentrations of these installations are apparent in state communities. This base of high-technology industry can be expected to generate future spin-offs.

The spontaneous formation and expansion of high-technology companies in Michigan now occurs naturally. In many cases, development has proceeded through the third stage of growth. At this stage, under current business conditions, a number of disincentives to continued development appear to encourage company departure or dissolution.

Based on previous analysis, it appears that development of high-technology industry in Michigan could be accelerated in the early growth stages and retained in stage three through several initiatives. The unmet needs of smaller, newer companies may include specialized professional services, banking facilities, inexpensive real estate, public assistance in assembling land parcels, and sources of venture capital.

SUMMARY

The previous analysis suggests that many economic factors are linked with successful high-technology industry development. Nearly all of these factors are now present in Michigan, indicating strong potential. The following observations may guide action to capitalize on this opportunity.

Special-purpose organizations, created to promote high-technology development, have proven effective in several states. Such organizations can speak for industry on questions of taxation, financing, and other special concerns of technology-oriented firms. They also can develop and manage research parks, contribute to professional assistance programs for start-up companies, and administer low-cost incubator facilities.

Land development for research parks has played an important role in the success of other states. Attractive, substantial building sites are a basic requirement of third stage high-technology companies. In terms of job creation, the third stage is most important. This is also the growth stage in which high-technology firms are most vulnerable to mergers and takeovers, and most attractive to competing regions.

Financing for high-technology industry is often focused on during the second stage of growth when millions of dollars in venture capital is needed. Yet, experience indicates venture capital can do little to promote growth unless technical, economic, and living conditions are favorable to high-technology industry formation and expansion.

Promising target industries for high-technology growth in Michigan are numerous and varied. Thus a diversified development strategy is indicated. There are as many successful precedents for diversity as for specialization in the technological experience of other states.

To provide structure in the midst of such diversity, Michigan requires an integrated development program. Otherwise, each small, new company must solve its seemingly unique problems in relative isolation. This atmosphere could continue to inhibit technical entrepreneurship, and it could discourage the few who achieve major market success from remaining in the state during their third stage of development.

A climate of "economic necessity" now motivates Michigan high-technology development initiatives. Perhaps this is the clearest indication of strong potential. It creates an opportunity to put in place a comprehensive, sustained development program which will improve conditions for high-technology industry proliferation, job creation, and economic growth.

REFERENCES, CHAPTER 9

"A Park that Reversed a Brain Drain." Fortune, June, 1977.

"Amid Stagnation, High Technology Lights a Path." New York Times, August 20, 1980, p.1.

Ann Arbor, Michigan Chamber of Commerce Papers. A Location Proposal for the Electronics Research Center of the National Aeronautic and Space Administration. December, 1963. Michigan Historical Collection, Bentley Historical Library, The University of Michigan, Box 4, 10-E.

______. Economic Development Committee. Minutes. April 26, 1965. Michigan Historical Collection, Bentley Historical Library, The University of Michigan, Box 3, 10-D.

______. Industrial Development Committee. Minutes. June 10, 1966. Michigan Historical Collection, Bentley Historical Library, The University of Michigan, Box 3, 10-D.

"Atoms in Suburbia." Electronics News, March 20, 1967, p.1.

Bohne, Walt. "How the Weston Pact Was Won." Electronic News, January 2, 1967, p.6.

Brennan, Peter J. "Minnesota Technology Wellspring." Scientific American, October, 1980.

Brophy, David J. Finance Entrepreneurship, and Economic Development. Ann Arbor: Institute of Science and Technology, The University of Michigan, 1974.

"Budget Knives are Nicking NASA." Business Week, January 3, 1970, p. 21.

Bylinsky, Gene. "California's Great Breeding Ground for Industry." Fortune, June, 1974, p. 128.

Carter, Luther J. "Research Triangle Park Succeeds Beyond Its Promoters' Expectations." Science, June 30, 1978.

Charles River Associates, Inc. Innovation Competition and Government Policy in Semiconductor Industry. (1980: Boston, MA).

Dallas, Daniel B. "California Today--Where the Action Is." Manufacturing Engineering, March, 1981.

Danilov, Victor J. "The Research Park Shake-Out." Industrial Research, May, 1971.

Directory of Research, Development, and Testing Facilities in Michigan. Ann Arbor: Industrial Development Division, Institute of Science and Technology, The University of Michigan, 1981.

"Electronic Gift Horse." Economist, December 5, 1964, p. 1136.

Evaldson, Rune. "Willow Run Laboratories." Unpublished paper, March, 1970.

Haber, W., McKean, E.C., and Taylor, H.C. The Michigan Economy: Its Potentials and Its Problems. Kalamazoo: The W.E. Upjohn Institute for Employment Research, 1959.

Hanieski, John F. "Diversifying the Michigan Economy." The Michigan State Economic Record, February, 1981.

Hamilton, W.B. "The Research Triangle of North Carolina: A Study in Leadership for the Common Weal." The South Atlantic Quarterly, Spring 1966.

"Is Solar Lab Lost With Nomination?" Ann Arbor News. December 15, 1976, p. 14.

King, Wayne. "A Research Center Flourishes in North Carolina." New York Times, February 4, 1977.

Kleene, Tom. "Industry Given Research Tool." Detroit Free Press, February 26, 1961, p. 5C.

Knight, Michael. "Taxes Hurt Massachusetts Jobs." The New York Times, March 26, 1979.

Lamont, L.M. Technology Transfer, Innovation and Marketing in Science Oriented Spin-off Firms. Ann Arbor: Institute of Science and Technology, The University of Michigan, 1971.

Lamonte, Suzanne, ed. "Engineering College Research and Graduate Study." Engineering Education, March, 1981.

Liu, Ben-Chieh. Quality of Life Indicators in U.S. Metropolitan Areas. New York: Praeger Publishers, 1976.

"Michigan Loses Solar Energy Site." Detroit News, March 25, 1977, p. 3F.

"Michigan Solar Lab Bid Still Logical." Ann Arbor News, November 28, 1976, p. 10.

"Minnesota Spirit Nurtures Computer Companies." Minneapolis Star-Tribune, April 14, 1981.

National Science Foundation. Division of Science Resource Studies. Federal Funds for Research and Development: FY 1977, 1978, and 1979. Report No. 80-315. Washington, D.C., 1980.

______. National Patterns of R&D Resources: Funds and Manpower in the United States 1953-1979. Report No. 78-304. Washington D.C. 1978.

______. National Patterns of Science and Technology Resources: 1953-1980. Report No. 79-309. Washington, D.C., 1979.

______. National Patterns of Science and Technology Resources: 1980. Report No. 80-308. Washington, D.C., 1980.

______. Research and Development in Industry: 1976. Report No. 79-306. Washington D.C., 1978.

______. Research and Development in Industry: 1977. Report No. 79-325. Washington D.C., 1979.

______. Research and Development in Industry: 1978. Report No. 80-307. Washington D.C., 1980

______. Science Indicators: 1976. Report No. 75-1. Washington, D.C., 1978.

______. Science Indicators: 1976. Report No. 78-1. Washington, D.C., 1978.

______. Science Indicators: 1978. Report No. 80-1. Washington, D.C., 1980.

"New England Revival." Wall Street Journal, September 22, 1980.

"Planning Helped Triangle: Hodges." Chapel Hill Weekly, November 7, 1965.

"R&D Scoreboard: 1979." Business Week, July 7, 1980, pp. 47-70.

"R&D Scoreboard: 1980." Business Week, July 6, 1981, pp. 60-75.

Roberts, Edward B. "A Basic Study of Innovators: How to Keep and Capitalize on Their Talents." Research Management, July, 1968.

Roberts, E. B. and Peters, D. H. "Commercial Innovation From University Faculty." Research Policy, April, 1981, pp. 108-126.

Roberts, E. B. and Wainer, H. A. "New Enterprises on Route 128." Science Journal, December, 1968.

Romney, George. Volume I Gubernatorial Papers. Box 113, Michigan Historical Calling, Boards and Commissioners 1965. Economic Expansion, B.M. Conboy file through State Board of Education Agenda Meetings.

"RTI: 20th Year of Operation." Research Triangle, North Carolina: Research Triangle Institute, 1979.

Shepherd, Robert and Raia, Rod. "The Emphasis Is On Practicality." Industrial Development, August, 1963.

Sirbu, Jr., M. A., Tretel, R., Yorsz, W., and Roberts, E. B. The Formation of a Technology Oriented Complex: Lessons from North American and European experience. CPA Report 76-78. Cambridge, Massachusetts: Center for Policy Alternatives, Massachusetts Institute of Technology, 1976.

Taylor, Hal. "Awards by Cambridge Center Before Fiscal Year '71 Held Unlikely." Electronic News, March 30, 1970, p. 21.

Touhy, Therasa. "State Pushes Solar Test Site." Detroit News, February 28, 1977, p. 6A.

"Waiting for ERDA." Ann Arbor News, October 25, 1976, p. 14.

"Washington Ignores State Again." Detroit News, March 27, 1977, p. 8E.

Chapter 10

Tax Abatement as an Incentive to Industrial Location

by

Michael Wolkoff

The University of Rochester

INTRODUCTION: THE ROLE OF INDUSTRIAL INCENTIVES[1]

Industrial incentives have long been used as a mechanism to induce regional development. Until recently, most industrial subsidies were given in the South. However, as the Sun Belt became an increasingly more attractive location for industrial development, the manufacturing states of the North and East began to use fiscal incentives as a way of maintaining their industrial bases. The use of industrial subsidies throughout the nation is easily explained. First, the potential payoff to a locality that is able to attract a new industrial plant is large. Second, subsidy programs can be used to encourage investment at specific locations, making the programs attractive to economic development officials. The spread of these programs has been accelerated by the competition that subsidies induce between localities. Once one jurisdiction offers a fiscal incentive, neighboring jurisdictions are compelled to respond defensively to forestall the relocation of existing businesses. Adding to their popularity is the fact that certain subsidies can be provided at virtually no cost to the granting jurisdiction.[2] Michigan is no stranger to subsidy programs. Currently over one dozen programs are aimed at economic development in this state,[3] many of which offer fiscal incentives.

In this chapter I will focus upon the use of tax abatement policy in Michigan. First I discuss the theory of fiscal incentives and when they should be used. Then, I examine the two Michigan abatement laws (P.A. 198 and P.A. 255), estimate the size of the Michigan program, and evaluate its success. Finally, I present a summary of findings and conclusions.

The theory of fiscal incentives is straightforward. By reducing factor input prices to an investing firm, the subsidy increases the attractiveness of a specific location for investment. If the firm is indifferent in its choice of two sites, the subsidy can be instrumental in determining the firm's location decision.[4] The effectiveness of the subsidy depends upon two interacting factors: first, the value of the subsidy to the firm,[5] and second, alternative investment opportunities open to the firm. The most common form of incentives are tax reductions or borrowing cost subsidies. In this chapter I consider property tax abatements. Industrial revenue bonds are examined in Chapter 11.

PROPERTY TAX ABATEMENTS

Property tax abatements reduce the price of capital to investing firms by excluding a portion of new investment from taxation for a period of time. The size of this price reduction will depend upon the terms of the abatement, the time rate of preference for the firm, the importance of capital in the firm's production process, and the interaction between local property taxes and other tax obligations facing the firm.

The availability of tax abatement will have two effects on a firm. First, the lower factor price should increase the probability that a firm looking to expand or relocate will do so in the community offering the incentive. Second, if the investment occurs, the plant will be more capital intensive than it would have been at the old factor prices.

The decision of local governments to offer tax abatements depends upon the benefits they receive from the subsidy. It is difficult for local governments to make this evaluation. Care must be taken to account for changes in local service costs that accompany new industrial development. The valuation of the firm's benefit stream must also be made net of the cost of the subsidy. As part of this evaluation the locality should try to establish the importance of the subsidy to the firm's investment decision. When a subsidy merely rewards an action that would otherwise have been taken it is of no value to the community.

Property tax abatements, like other fiscal incentives, enable local officials to influence the path of economic development in their community. Local governments can use fiscal incentives to encourage a specific type of development at a specific location.[6] For instance, Ann Arbor might encourage high technology industry in an attempt to complement the existing economic base.

Ultimately, the extent of tax abatement activity in any community should depend upon its success in inducing economic development. Since the impact of the abatement will affect different firms differently, and will yield different benefit streams, localities should be able to vary the abatement award to different applicants.[7] Those firms which make large contributions to the local economic base and which are sensitive to the availability of tax incentives should receive larger awards than firms which is unaffected by an abatement program.

The decisions of local units to use fiscal incentives to induce economic development create a potential set of problems for the state because many local decisions involve significant externalities.[8] For instance, investment induced in one county of the state may create severe economic hardship in another county. Although the locality may be indifferent to its neighbor's plight, the state is not. State-wide evaluation of a tax abatement program must consider whether gains to one community are at the expense of losses to another. The State of Michigan's attempt to offer itself as an attractive alternative for investing firms considering the Great Lakes region must be tempered by the impact of such programs upon intrastate competition. The issue must be kept in mind during any discussion of fiscal incentive policy.

Another important issue that property tax abatements

raise involves the intergovernmental relationships among local units. The decision to offer property tax abatements by one governmental unit affects the revenue-raising capability of the other taxing units at that location. Any city, township or village which can offer tax abatement is able to do so without consultation with county or schoolboard officials whose tax base is also diminished. In Michigan, where local taxing jurisdictions, on average, levy only 20.4 percent of total millage,[9] the intergovernmental effects are potentially large.

Despite their attractiveness it is unlikely that tax abatements play a major role in determining the location of new industrial or commercial investment. They are simply too small a portion of the firm's cost function to compete with such factors as quality of labor force, output markets, and raw material availability.[10] On the other hand, tax abatements may enjoy particular success in encouraging the investment behavior of firms that are already present within a given community. When a firm need not take other location factors into account, the impact of tax reduction will be larger. The usefulness of subsidy strategies is further magnified when we recognize that they are among the few policy instruments within the local government's control.[11] In addition, local officials find tax abatements to be an attractive option because they appear to involve no visible budget costs. However, this assessment, although convenient politically, is wrong if the abatement is awarded to a project that would have invested without subsidy.

TAX ABATEMENT IN MICHIGAN

Cities, townships and villages in the State of Michigan are permitted to offer property tax abatements to industrial and commercial firms. By enabling local jurisdictions to make these awards, Michigan joins thirty other states which use the property tax concessions as a way of inducing economic development. In the following sections I discuss the legislative history and program content of the Michigan laws which permit property tax abatement. I then place the Michigan program in the context of tax abatement programs in states with which Michigan competes for new economic development.

Legislative History

Michigan currently offers two programs, P.A. 198 and P.A. 255, that may reduce the property tax burden faced by industrial and commercial firms that are either substantially rehabilitating their capital stock or making new investment.

P.A. 198, the Plant Rehabilitation and Industrial Development Districts Act, was signed into law on July 9, 1974 by Governor Milliken. Prior to enactment the bill had spent little time in the legislative corridors of Lansing, moving quickly through the required House Committees with only minor modification. The bill, in fact, passed through the House without a single dissenting vote. P.A. 198 was formulated to meet the needs of a specific development project in Detroit. In 1973, the Chrysler Corporation was planning to invest $50 million to rehabilitate substantially the Mack Street stamping plant which employed 5,000 workers. Chrysler indicated to city officials that it would have difficulty proceeding with the new investment without some form of governmental assistance. Faced with the prospect of losing an additional 5,000 jobs from an already declining economic base, local officials turned to the state to enact the necessary enabling legislation to permit Detroit to offer property tax relief to Chrysler; the state legislature then passed P.A. 198. It is ironic that the first project to receive a property tax abatement has already folded: Chrysler closed the Mack Street plant as part of an attempt to salvage the company during the spring of 1980. In this case, the combined effect of the economic cycle and Detroit's failure to produce fuel-efficient cars overwhelmed any advantage that the incentive provided.

Once P.A. 198 was in place for industrial firms, tax relief for commercial establishments would not be far behind. By 1978 over 600 industrial firms had received tax abatements under P.A. 198. State economic development officials pointed proudly to the success of this program in convincing firms to invest in Michigan. Naturally, business interests pushing for assistance in expediting commercial revitalization of the state's older cities viewed tax abatements as a potentially valuable tool. If tax abatements were successful in influencing industrial investment decisions, would they not do the same for commercial concerns? The result was the development of a tax abatement program for commercial investment, P.A. 255.

Although P.A. 255, the Commercial Redevelopment Districts Act, was signed into law nearly four years after its antecedent, its path through the legislature was not nearly as smooth. Fifteen months passed after its introduction before P.A. 255 reached the governor's desk. The bill met determined opposition in the legislature, in part because economic conditions in Michigan were far better in 1978 than they had been in 1974. Further, many believed that tax incentives were inappropriate in the case of commercial development since commercial ventures will gravitate to the location of consumer demand in any event. In addition, the objection was raised that the act would encourage ruinous competition between local units of government over commercial development and tend to be a zero-sum game for the state as a whole. Despite these arguments, the governor signed the bill into law on June 21, 1978.

Program Content

P.A. 198 and P.A. 255 are essentially identical laws aimed at industrial and commercial investment respectively. Under these laws the State of Michigan grants local communities the authority to award property tax abatements to firms investing in a new facility or substantially rehabilitating obsolete property.

The process requires two steps. First, a redevelopment district is established. P.A. 198 permits virtually any municipality or township to establish industrial development districts as long as the owners of 75 percent of the state equalized valuation for that district agree.[12] P.A. 255 limits commercial development districts to obsolete commercial areas.

Once a district is established, investing firms can apply for, and obtain, an exemption certificate. This certificate entitles the facility to be exempted from a portion of taxes on real and personal property.[13] A new firm need only pay half the total mills levied as _ad valorem_ taxes for that year by all taxing units within which the facility is located. In the case of a rehabilitation project, all accretion in value to the site as a consequence of the new investment is exempt from property taxes. In either case the exemption may be extended for up to twelve years.

The state's grant of autonomy to local governmental units mandates no rigid set of criteria for making abatement awards although two requirements are imposed. The law requires the locality to make a separate finding that the abatement does not impair the fiscal capacity of the taxing jurisdiction when five percent of the local SEV is exempt.[14] The locality is also asked to assure that there exists a reasonable likelihood that employment will be created or retained as the result of the abatement award. Without a more rigorous definition of the reasonable likelihood criterion it is difficult to imagine any project that could fail to meet this requirement. Thus the state leaves considerable discretion to the localities for deciding how property tax abatements should be awarded.

P.A. 198 and P.A. 255 differ in two significant aspects. First, although P.A. 255 was based on P.A. 198, it closes a loophole flaw in the original law. Under P.A. 198, abatements can be awarded even as late as one year after the project has been built.[15] A program that offers an incentive twelve months after the investment will have difficulty distinguishing between those investments that were conducted with the expectation of receiving the award and those that were not. This feature causes the program to function as a reward rather than an incentive. P.A. 255 does not contain this "grandfathering" clause.[16] Application for the abatement must precede work on the project. Although this requirement does not assure that all investment undertaken under this program was induced by the abatement award, it does prevent firms from receiving tax incentives, if they clearly did not need the abatement to motivate their investment decision.

The second important difference between the two acts is that P.A. 255 does not contain the antipirating provision found in P.A. 198. This provision was included to prevent intrastate jurisdictional competition over industrial location. Before an in-state firm can accept tax incentives at a new Michigan location it must receive approval from the local legislature at the original site. Without this approval the firm will not qualify for property tax abatement. Conceivably, the 'raided' community can negotiate with the firm for a portion of the tax savings as payment for the loss it incurs. It is difficult to understand exactly why the antipirating clause was excluded from P.A. 255. It may be that the law's framers believed that the targeting provision within the law was sufficient protection against the most ruinous form of competition for downtown development--the suburban mall.

The original legislative intent behind P.A. 198 and P.A. 255 was to promote economic development through use of property tax favors. Discretion was to be left to local jurisdictions to decide which projects were appropriate for assistance and to what extent any jurisdiction would use the program. It is unclear from Michigan's experience with these laws whether these objectives have been reached. It now appears that virtually no industrial development occurs in the state without P.A. 198.[17] Although some may read this as evidence of program success, a careful econometric examination shows that property tax abatements have become too accessible.[18] Many of the firms that were awarded abatements would have invested without them. A second observation is that while responsibility has been conveyed to the localities, this may not be as useful a concept as originally thought. Up to now jurisdictions have not shown themselves capable of implementing selective abatement policy. The flexibility and discretion that the law allows have for the most part gone unused. Abatement applications are virtually always approved for the maximum period permitted by law.

INTERSTATE COMPARISONS

In the past three decades property tax abatements have become an increasingly popular way for local governmental units to attract industrial and commercial investment. In 1950 only seventeen states permitted the use of this economic incentive. By 1980, thirty-one states enabled localities to offer abatements.

Most of the states in the midwest and northeast offer local governments the opportunity to abate property taxes. A band stretching across the industrial corridor, from Illinois to Massachusetts, includes ten states that make this incentive available. Despite considerable doubt over the importance of property tax differentials in firm location and investment decisions, this regional grouping of states has elected to use tax abatements. However, the decision to use tax abatements may reflect each state's attempt to defend against "pirating" rather than confidence in the efficacy of the program to induce development.

The form of Michigan's tax abatement program differs little from the programs offered by competing states. In general, a certain percent of new investment is exempt from property taxes for a fixed period of time. But interstate comparisons of program details are difficult because abatement of property taxes alters only one dimension of the complex of business tax factors that influence firm investment decisions. Thus, we find that while Michigan

TABLE 10.1
INTERSTATE COMPARISON OF TAX ABATEMENT PROGRAMS

STATE	LOCAL AUTONOMY	COVERED SECTION	ABATEMENT TERMS	RESTRICTIONS
Illinois	Cook County Only	Commercial Industrial	Property asessed at 1/2 legal assessment for 13 years	Can only be used in CETA district where unemployment rate > county average
Indiana	Local designation	All property holders	Abatement declines from 100% to 50% during 10 year period	Only locally designated urban development areas eligible
New York		Commercial Industrial		
1. JIBP	Local designation		Up to 100% for 16 years	Must generate one job for every $10,000 invested
2. BIEP	All localities eligible unless they opt out		Abatement starts at 50% and declines to 0% over 10 years	
3. ICIB	New York City only		Negotiated award	
Ohio	All localities	Commercial Industrial Residential	100% abatement up to 15 years	Local determination
Pennsylvania	All localities	---	Up to 100% abatement for 10 years	Local determination
Michigan	Virtually all localities with state approval	Commercial Industrial	50% abatement on new investment and 100% on rehabilitation for maximum of 12 years	Commercial abatements are restricted to designated areas. Industrial abatements must have a likelihood of retaining or creating jobs

Source: Program details obtained from state economic development offices of Illinois, New York, Ohio, and Michigan.

permits localities to abate taxes on real and personal industrial property for up to twelve years, Wisconsin offers no such program at all. However, Wisconsin levies no property tax on equipment and machinery used in production. Thus tax abatements can not ensure that the tax burden facing an investing firm will be lowest in the jurisdictions offering the abatement.

Table 10.1 summarizes tax abatement program provisions for five states with which Michigan's economic development efforts are frequently compared. Contained in this table are brief descriptions of property tax abatement terms and restrictions. In general, the programs differ in the level of reduction the abatement permits, although the general program structure is the same across states.

Michigan's program falls in the middle of this group of states in terms of award generosity. New York and Ohio permit localities to make more generous awards.[19] On the other hand Michigan imposes fewer requirements as to where the abated projects must be located. Unfortunately, it is not possible to make comparisons of the state-by-state level of program activity because Michigan is the only state in this sample to aggregate awards on a state-wide basis.

INDUSTRIAL TAX ABATEMENT AWARDS IN MICHIGAN

The use of property tax abatements to encourage industrial development increased rapidly from 1974-79 before subsiding in 1980.[20] By 1980, over $8.5 billion had been invested at 2,108 project sites under P.A. 198.[21] Investment in new facilities accounted for 84 percent of the dollars spent under this program. The remaining $1.3 billion was spent to substantially rehabilitate obsolete capital stock. Interestingly, in Detroit the predominant form of P.A. 198 participation was in rehabilitation investment.

Table 10.2 summarizes the extent of P.A. 198 awards. This table lists investment activity by year and includes estimated employment impacts of P.A. 198 projects. The

TABLE 10.2
MICHIGAN INDUSTRIAL TAX ABATEMENT AWARDS

YEAR	NUMBER OF AWARDS	RETAINED JOBS	NEW JOBS	DOLLARS INVESTED
1974	5	5,540	379	$65,755,000
1975	122	15,289	7,912	453,425,200
1976	195	10,479	12,599	435,842,500
1977	306	23,899	20,428	1,311,516,000
1978	455	23,342	21,643	2,173,250,400
1979	516	14,691	19,714	1,859,973,600
1980	434	14,964	18,573	2,277,545,200
TOTAL	2,108	108,587	105,596	8,686,646,400

Source: Michigan Department of Commerce, Office of Economic Development.

TABLE 10.3
LOCATION OF HEAVY ABATEMENT ACTIVITY, BY COUNTY (1974-1980)

COUNTY	NUMBER OF ABATEMENTS	DOLLARS INVESTED
Genessee	46	$580,106,000
Kent	259	480,030,600
Oakland	55	893,430,000
St. Joseph	45	452,295,000
Washtenaw	36	737,784,000
Wayne	190	1,848,054,000

Source: Michigan Department of Commerce, Office of Economic Development.

employment figures are based upon projections provided by applicant firms and are almost surely subject to significant upward bias.[22] Reported new and retained jobs total nearly 200,000, nearly 20 percent of Michigan's manufacturing workforce.[23] Not surprisingly, 86 percent of the new jobs are associated with new facilities. Almost all of the money spent for rehabilitation projects retained jobs rather than created new ones. Average project investment was over $4 million for the seven year period although in the last reported year average project investment was nearly $5.25 million. Whether this represents a move towards larger investments or simply reflects inflation cannot be discerned from the data.

The authority to offer tax abatement awards rests with Michigan's cities, villages and townships. Nearly 400 units throughout the state have taken advantage of the enabling legislation. Although awards are made at the local governmental level, we can get some sense of the geographic distribution of these awards by grouping them by county. Only twelve of Michigan's eighty-three counties have no abated industrial development within them. These dozen counties,[24] in the northern half of the state, make poor industrial locations because of their low population densities, remoteness from markets, and heavy forestation.

Most abatement activity has occurred in the counties that have served as the traditional source of Michigan's economic strength. Table 10.3 shows the six counties with the largest dollar total of investment under P.A. 198. Represented here are 30 percent of the total projects, accounting for 58 percent of the dollars invested. Five of these counties are typically thought of as the industrial heart of the state. Wayne County, the state's most populous, has had the largest volume of abatement activity within it. The appearance of the relatively rural St. Joseph County on this list is a surprise. This county faces competition from neighboring Indiana communities and is forced to use all available programs to retain its manufacturing base.

Commercial Tax Abatements

During the first three years of program experience over 300 commercial projects have been awarded tax abatements in over seventy different communities in Michigan. Investments eligible for abatement totalled nearly $300 million. With few exceptions, commercial abatements have been awarded for the full twelve-year time period allowable under P.A. 255.

The level of abated commercial investment is a sufficiently small portion of the investment activity conducted under Michigan's tax abatement laws that we focus solely upon the industrial investment program in the rest of this chapter. In the next section we evaluate the tax revenue costs of awarding tax abatements.

Program Costs

The use of tax abatements to encourage industrial development has imposed revenue losses upon both the state and units of local government. Local governments forego property tax revenue by offering tax abatement to development that would otherwise have occurred. If the abatement is responsible for the new development, then the abated tax revenue should not be regarded as a cost to the program because it would never have been received without the abatement. The revenue loss to the state due to P.A. 198 occurs because the school finance formula requires the state treasury to compensate school districts that qualify under the formula, for a portion of the property taxes foregone due to tax abatement. The school finance formula imposes this requirement whether the abatement was successful in inducing investment or not.[25] Under present law, the state will always assume part of the cost of the tax abatement program.

Determining whether tax abatements have been responsible for new industrial development or merely have rewarded firms for investment that would have occurred without the program is a difficult task. Undoubtedly, tax

TABLE 10.4

AGGREGATED TAX COST AND TAX SAVINGS OF ALL PA 198 PROJECTS
(cumulative totals in thousands of dollars)

YEAR	TAX SAVINGS[1]	LOCAL NON-SCHOOL COST[2]	SCHOOL DISTIRCT COST[3]	STATE COST[4]
1974	$2,473	$1,343	$ 103	$ 965
1975	15,180	6,616	1,438	6,727
1976	36,494	15,146	3,693	16,655
1977	82,700	33,331	8,642	38,366
1978	166,020	65,049	24,360	72,114
1979	275,794	105,000	44,707	118,828
1980	417,150	154,379	70,873	180,883

Notes: [1]Horizontal totals do not add because school debt millage applied under different formula rule and not needed here.

[2]Maximum foregone tax revenue by local non-school districts.

[3]Cost incurred by those districts levying over 30 mills and those districts not qualifying for school finance formula.

[4]Cost to state treasury of school finance formula provisions.

Source: Compiled from unpublished data; Michigan Department of Commerce.

abatements both award and reward, although there is evidence that the inducement effects are minor.[26] Therefore, in this section I present cost estimates that are based on the assumption that all investment would have proceeded without P.A. 198. These estimates are clearly an upper-bound of the cost to governmental units.

Table 10.4 presents estimates of P.A. 198 tax revenue costs to local school districts, local units of government and the state. In addition, it includes an estimate of the total property tax savings to investing firms. The estimates in Table 10.4 are calculated using all 2,108 projects active as of May, 1981. I assume all projects to have been completed and the amount of investment to equal the firm's estimates at the time of application.

In order to calculate the estimates in Table 10.4 it was necessary to make a number of simplifications. In doing so we lose some accuracy in the actual dollar figures although the relative size of the revenue effects should change little. The loss of precision results from using the local jurisdictions' 1979 millage rates in each year that revenue costs are calculated.[27] These millage rates are higher than preceding years and thus form an upper bound. This overestimate is reasonable because all of the projects awarded in previous years are also assessed in 1979 and are therefore subject to the 1979 millage level. Since program participation was considerably smaller in the earliest years of the program (1974-76) the mistakes we make using the 1979 rates for that time period are small. A second source of error in these estimates comes from using the 1979 school finance formula to calculate state costs in each year.[28] However, since the formula was, on the margin, essentially unchanged from 1977 to 1980, during which time over 75 percent of the investment conducted under P.A. 198 occurred, the errors are small.

The recipient of these revenue losses is, of course, the investing firm. Column 1 of Table 10.4 gives the property tax savings to firms receiving abatement. By 1980 over $417 million in property taxes had been saved by firms investing under P.A. 198. By the time each of the current 2,108 projects has received all of the benefits under the law, tax savings will reach $1.7 billion. At that point, all abated property will revert to the regular tax rolls to supplement local property tax collections.

The cost of awarding tax abatements is shared by the local governing unit, the county, the school district, special districts and the state. Column 2 gives the cumulative cost of tax abatements to noneducational local units. Although nonschool millage in Michigan averages only 18 mills, by 1980 these units had foregone over $154 million in property tax revenue. Local school districts also share in the cost of offering tax incentives but they do so to a lesser extent than local governments because of the school finance formula. Qualifying school districts only forego that portion of school millage beyond thirty mills when an abatement is offered.[29] Nonqualifying school districts bear the full cost. Column 3 indicates that tax abatements have cost local school districts nearly $71 million in property tax revenue.

Column 4 shows that it is the state treasury that bears the largest share of the cost of awarding tax abatements. By 1980 nearly $180 million had been paid under the school finance formula to school districts subject to tax abatement decisions of cities, townships and villages. Local jurisdictions are able to offer tax abatement with only minimal state supervision. Yet over 45 percent of the cost of tax abatements is assumed by the state, and over 35 percent by jurisdictions that have no voice in making abatement decisions.

Table 10.4 clarifies the financial obligations imposed by P.A. 198 upon school districts, local governments, and the state. These costs are passed on to investing firms as tax savings but their value to the firm is diminished by the interaction between the federal corporate income tax and local taxes. For every dollar abated under P.A. 198, approximately 46 cents is transferred to the federal treasury. Thus what Table 10.4 fails to show is the transfer of resources between levels of government due to P.A. 198.

Program Evaluation

An evaluation of the tax abatement programs in Michigan requires a comparison of the benefit stream net of public service costs generated by the tax incentive with the cost of providing the abatement. Although different communities will have different welfare functions, in general, the induced development would be expected to add to the local employment base and increase the community's fiscal capacity. Increased pollution accompanying the new development should be considered a program cost. The optimal abatement program would award abatements in such a way that community welfare (in this case defined in terms of employment, revenues and pollution) would be maximized.[30]

The difficulty in conducting this evaluation is a consequence of there being no definitive method for determining how much development the tax incentive has induced.[31] Benefits that would have resulted without the existence of the program should not be included as program gains. Similarly, only the portion of the abated tax base that would have been developed without the incentive should be considered a revenue loss.

More work remains to be done at the industry level to determine the impact of incentives on industrial development and the cost of providing public services to new development. In particular, a framework is needed to establish which investments would proceed without assistance. Presently, local officials are too often coerced into believing that the incentive is crucial to the firm's investment decision. In principle, local abatement officials should be familiar enough with local economic conditions that they can make at least some crude determination of how important the abatement is to subsequent firm behavior, and then base their abatement awards on this information.

In order for local officials to make distinctions between applicants when awarding tax abatements, they must have more flexibility than current state law allows. P.A. 198 sets the abatement rate for different types of investment and restricts the maximum abatement period to twelve years. Therefore, even if the local abatement board determined that the value of a project was sufficiently high to justify a large award, or that a larger abatement would significantly influence the firm's decision to invest, they are still constrained in the amount of abatement they can offer.

Oddly, what local discretion P.A. 198 does allow has gone virtually unused. Few of the 2,108 abatement awards have been for less than the maximum time allowed.[32] Clearly, local officials are not exercising the discretion they possess. Two factors might explain the generosity of abatement awards. First, local governments may simply lack the sophistication to differentiate between applicants when making decisions. Rather than run the risk of being charged with political favoritism, they choose to treat everyone the same, and award the maximum abatement allowed by law. The second possible explanation is that the allowable maximum is simply too low. Localities would offer even higher abatements if permitted, but the constraint results in all awards being made at the same rate.

It is unlikely that the maximum award is too low for all projects. Clearly, those firms that have already invested at the time they apply for the incentive need no encouragement. Rather, local units need assistance in determining how awards should be made.[33] One appropriate role for the state is to help local officials answer such important questions as: What are the likely costs associated with tax abatements, how important is any project for local economic growth, how dependent is the firm upon the proposed location, what is the impact of new development upon local public services, and can the local revenue structure be adapted so that the property tax revenues foregone from the abatement can quickly be recouped through other revenue sources? Answers to these questions would lend guidance in determining the level of abatement to be awarded.

Program Changes

It is unlikely that local governmental units will take a closer look at the pattern of abatement awards until they face the full price of their awards. Present law allows villages, townships and cities to abate property tax on not only the millage they levy but also the property millages of the school district, county and special taxing authorities. Allowing these jurisdictions to have a voice in determining whether or not portions of their SEV are to be given away might be a first step in imposing more local responsibility. However, even instituting a structural change in the decision process may not be sufficient to change decision outcomes. This is because those units that have potentially the most to lose, such as school districts, are in most cases insulated from the cost of abatement by the school finance formula. As may be seen in Table 10.4, 45 percent of the tax revenue cost of abatement is assumed by the state. This reduces the "price" of abatement and encourages granting jurisdictions to be less selective in determining awards. More sophisticated local decision making would be encouraged by allowing other local units to be involved in the decision to award abatements and at the same time changing state-wide formulas that insulate local units from the revenue effects of tax abatement.

Rather than encourage more local autonomy the state could provide more direct supervision. Two possible paths suggest themselves here. Abatement policy can be targeted at industries with high growth potential in regions chosen for more development. This strategy would keep most of the state's local property tax base intact but would have the advantage of providing some direction for future industrial growth in the state. Decisions about which industries should be encouraged could be reached by both local and statewide officials. The second option is for the state to take a more active role in determining the method by which abatement awards are calculated. Currently only capital investment is encouraged by the incentive. The formula could be adjusted to take account of the employment generated by the new investment. The result would be a lowering of the factor prices of both capital and labor. This is a logical step to take. Increased employment is one of the primary stated goals of the program. Further, sixteen cities within Michigan, and the state itself, levy income taxes. Encouraging employment through the abatement formula would generate tax revenues.

CONCLUSIONS

Property tax abatements have been used by virtually all recent major industrial projects in Michigan. Undoubtedly, they have influenced some firms to invest more than they would have otherwise. In these cases the abatements have been successful. However, the existing empirical evidence suggests that it is unlikely that even full property tax abatement has had a major impact upon the level of investment. The inframarginal investor whose investment decisions were unaffected by reduced property taxes receives a windfall from state taxpayers. Further, given that these transfers are only valued at as little as 54 percent of their amount because of the federal tax deduction, the question must be raised whether this is the best way for localities to induce economic development.

Future abatement policy must recognize the inherent limitations of tax abatement. Even full property tax abatement has too small an impact upon the user cost of capital to have a major influence on firm investment decisions. Limited results deserve more limited application. Future awards should be tied more closely to other economic development incentives and applied where they will do the most good. This will require closer examination of potential abatement awards by local decision makers. The state can encourage this change by providing greater technical assistance and by allowing fuller participation by local jurisdictions in making abatement awards.

NOTES, CHAPTER 10

[1]I would like to thank Carl Courant and Smothers Shaw for their conscientious research assistance. I would also like to thank the Michigan State Office of Economic Development for providing me with P.A. 198 project data.

[2]The cost of industrial revenue bonds is borne almost entirely by the federal treasury.

[3]These include tax abatements, industrial revenue bonds, tax increment financing, downtown development authorities, etc.

[4]Research on plant location decisions, however, has established that fiscal subsidies, especially tax abatements, are not crucial determinants of the location decision.

[5]For a model of the cost savings of different subsidies to the firm see Hellman, Wassall and Falk (1976).

[6]Dayton, Ohio revitalized its downtown using location directed tax abatements.

[7]Although this may seem to create an horizontal equity problem, any fixed formula will implicitly treat firms differently because of varying use of the subsidized factor.

[8]One common problem is that a series of local optimizations is unlikely to achieve a global optimum (Shoup, 1971).

[9]See Chapter 16 on the Michigan Property Tax in this volume.

[10]If we allow subsidies to be larger than full tax abatement they could have a greater influence in determining industrial investment decisions depending upon the sensitivity of the investment decision to the subsidy level.

[11]Other policy instruments under local control are site assembly or new building construction.

[12]Since there is no restriction on district size any industrial property owner that wishes to establish a district will easily meet this requirement.

[13]In fact the firm pays the industrial facilities tax, based upon the real and personal property invested, in lieu of the property tax.

[14]This requirement has not slowed the rush to award abatements. In 1978, over one-third of the 277 communities offering abatements exceeded the five percent requirement.

[15]Firms that submit applications after the project is built are eligible for only a maximum of eleven years of tax abatement.

[16]One unanticipated outcome of this provision of P.A. 255 was that firms that failed to qualify under the commercial law, because they filed too late, attempted to be reconsidered under the industrial program.

[17]Due to the newness of P.A. 255, it would be difficult to make the same claim.

[18]See Michael J. Wolkoff, "An Analysis of the Use of Property Tax Abatements to Spur Urban Economic Development," (Ph.D. diss., University of Michigan, 1981).

[19]I define generosity in terms of the abatement rate. The dollar value of the abatement to firms depends upon the local property tax rate.

[20]The decline in awards in 1980 was most likely due to cyclical economic factors which reduced the attractiveness of industrial investment.

[21]This figure differs slightly from the numbers used by the Michigan State Department of Commerce although the same work sheets were used.

[22]Firms are required to report project employment figures at the time they file P.A. 198 applications. These estimates are probably biased upward for two reasons: one, they probably represent full employment estimates, and two, higher estimates make the application appear more deserving.

[23]Peak manufacturing employment in Michigan in this time period was 1,179,000 jobs (1978). The trough was in 1980: 1,007,000 jobs.

[24]These counties are: Alcona, Alger, Antrim, Benzie, Cheboygan, Isabella, Lake, Marquette, Montmorency, Oscoda, Presque Isle and Roscommon.

[25]In fact, if one community pirates industry from another community the school finance formula pays the bill. Thus, intrastate competition over existing industries could lead to rising school finance costs without any new development.

[26]Wilbur Thompson indicates in Chapter 8 that local taxes are not important determinants of firm location decisions. I find that it is unlikely that tax abatements had much impact upon the amount of industrial investment in Detroit from 1974 to 1978 (Wolkoff, 1981, Ph.D. diss.).

[27]The decision to use 1979 millages was made for a number of reasons. With close to 400 jurisdictions offering tax abatements, the task of assigning individual school and general millages to each project for each year was simply too large. I chose to use the actual 1979 millage rather than the annual average county rate because the millage variance within counties in general exceeds the millage variance across years for a specific jurisdiction, and because the direction of bias with the 1979 millages is more certain.

[28]Here, too, I overestimate revenue cost because from 1974-76 the state compensated less than the thirty mills required in subsequent years.

[29]Interestingly, only 153 projects are in districts that don't qualify under the school finance formula. Only nine percent of the school population lives in those districts.

[30]For a discussion of how local decision makers should award abatements see my unpublished doctoral dissertation, "An Analysis of the Use of Property Tax Abatements to Spur Urban Economic Development," (1981).

[31]Morgan and Hackbart (1974), in their study of tax abatement programs, assume that a certain percent of development was noninduced. Wolkoff, Ibid., uses a more sophisticated probabilistic framework to reach his conclusions.

[32]This includes those firms who apply for the abatement after the project is built, and are awarded the eleven year maximum.

[33]Conversations with Department of Commerce personnel indicate that this is a frequent complaint made by local jurisdictions.

REFERENCES, CHAPTER 10

Due, J. F. "Studies of State-Local Tax Influences on Location of Industry." National Tax Journal, 1961, 14(2), pp. 163-173.

Hellman, D. A.; Wassall, G. H.; and Falk, L. H., State Financial Incentives to Industry. Lexington, Mass.: Lexington Books, 1976.

Michigan State Economic Record, 1979, 21(8).

Morgan, W. E. and Hackbert, M. H. "An Analysis of State and Local Industrial Tax Exemption Programs." Southern Economic Journal, 1974, 41(2), pp. 200-205.

Shoup, D. C. "Effects of Suboptimization of Urban Government Decision Making." Journal of Finance, 1971, 26(2), pp. 547-564.

Stober, W. J. and Falk, L. H. "Property Tax Exemptions: An Inefficient Subsidy to Industry." National Tax Journal, 1967, 20(4), pp. 386-394.

Wolkoff, M. J. "An Analysis of the Use of Tax Abatements to Spur Urban Economic Development," Ph.D. dissertation, University of Michigan, Ann Arbor, Michigan, 1981.

Chapter 11

Industrial Revenue Bonds

by

Ann R. Thomas

The University of Michigan

INTRODUCTION[1]

Proceeds of municipal industrial revenue bonds (IRBs) are used in Michigan and most other states to finance selected industrial and commercial development. These bonds carry below-market interest charges because the interest paid on them is exempt under federal and state income tax laws. The objective of the authorities issuing IRBs is to induce business firms to locate new plants or retain renovated or expanded existing ones within their jurisdictions.

In recent years the use of industrial revenue bonds has increased dramatically in Michigan as well as in other states, stimulating considerable debate about the effectiveness of the programs and the efficiency of the subsidy from the viewpoint of both the federal and the state governments.[2] The purpose of this chapter is to assess the bond programs as a public policy issue of the State of Michigan.

This study examines the use of industrial revenue bonds in Michigan for the years 1975-80, and discusses the costs and benefits that accrue to Michigan residents and taxpayers. The first section consists of background and empirical data; the second discusses the effects of the programs; the third discusses the program costs for Michigan taxpayers at both the national and state levels; the last section presents conclusions and recommendations.

INDUSTRIAL REVENUE BONDS IN THE U.S. AND MICHIGAN

Industrial revenue bonds are really corporate bonds

that are issued as municipal bonds so as to qualify for exemption under Section 103 of the Internal Revenue Service code. In Michigan the bonds are issued by a governmental unit and backed by a lease agreement between that unit and the firm receiving the funds. The lease payments are specifically structured to cover all the costs of servicing the municipal bonds. Thus purchasers of the bonds look to the credit-worthiness of the firm in evaluating the riskiness of the bond. The bonds do not carry the guarantee of the issuing state or local government. For the firm, the major appeal of the IRBs is the substantial cost saving, as IRB interest costs typically run 25 to 35 percent less than the interest on equivalent business debt.

National Origin and Limits of IRBs

The interest paid on bonds issued by state and local governments has been exempt from the federal income tax since its inception in 1913. Industrial revenue bonds are a specific type of municipal bond, the proceeds of which are used to finance private enterprises that create benefits considered to be in the public interest. So far the federal government has left the definition of public interest to state and local governments, even though the immediate benefits of the tax exemption flow to private firms. At this time federal law does not even require state or local issuers to report IRB sales to federal agencies.

Industrial revenue bonds were first used in 1936 by the State of Mississippi to encourage more diversification in the economic base of that state's rural areas. Use gradually increased, becoming especially prominent during the 1960s as Michigan and other northern states attempted to stem an outflow of industry towards the South. In 1968, alarmed at the amount of IRB financing being undertaken and the fact that some very large companies were financing some very large projects, Congress passed the Revenue Expenditure and Control Act. This legislation, which limited the project size and defined the structure of allowable tax-exempt interest, has governed the issuance of municipal IRBs since. Tax exemption is allowed on the interest of any sized bonds that finance air and water pollution control equipment, industrial parks, and a variety of private-public facilities such as docks and convention centers. The legislation also allows tax exemption for bonds with face values of up to $10 million, with the stipulation that for projects exceeding $1 million, the total capital expenditures on the borrowing firm's facilities within a given city or county will exceed $10 million for three-year periods preceding and succeeding the date of bond issue. The objective was to cut the flow of subsidies to large corporations.

Legislative History of IRBs In Michigan

Over the years the Michigan legislature has developed three programs that allow for the issuance of IRBs within the federal legislative constraints. The three programs differ somewhat in target and method of implementation, but all are directed towards the creation and retention of jobs.

The oldest program, the Industrial Development Revenue Bonds Act of 1963 (Public Act 62), enables local governmental units (county, city, incorporated village, township or port district) to issue revenue bonds to finance up to 100 percent of the cost of certain industrial projects. These include the acquisition, purchase, construction, reconstruction or remodeling of industrial buildings, the acquisition and improvement of sites, and the acquisition of industrial machinery and equipment, including pollution control equipment. Industrial Development Revenue (IDR) bonds are subject to approval by the Municipal Finance Commission, a division of the Michigan Department of Treasury, though no state or local guarantee of the bonds is implied.

In 1974 the Michigan Legislature passed the Economic Development Corporation Act (Public Act 338), which allows local units of government to establish public economic development corporations (EDCs) for the purpose of financing commercial and industrial facilities. This program expands the purposes for which IRBs can be used, and allows EDC bonds to be issued without MFC approval.

The Michigan Job Development Authority (JDA) was created in 1975 (Public Act 301) to provide additional financial incentives, especially for smaller business development. The objective was to gain scale efficiencies in the costs of issuing bonds by pooling several small projects and to use Small Business Administration loan guarantees for further interest cost reduction. JDA bonds finance only industrial projects. The program was slow in starting and has not worked the way it was intended. One reason is that a "moral obligation" clause which would have permitted (though not required) the legislature to act as a guarantor did not receive full Supreme Court support when an advisory opinion was issued. As a result the bonds that have such clauses are not salable.[3]

In addition, federal Internal Revenue Service authorities began requiring individual loan applications from all participants of pooled industrial revenue bonds. This requirement eliminates the expected economies of pooling. Thus far, JDA bonds have been issued on a pooled basis for small pollution control equipment projects where the IRS requirement does not apply, and individually for independent industrial projects that are of sufficient quality and size to attract bond purchasers without reserve or guarantee requirements. The JDA program now offers economic development financing that is similar to that offered by the other two programs. It is, however, administered at the state rather than local level.

In 1980 Public Act 501 amended the EDC Act, expanding the range of projects to include agricultural and forestry enterprises, but removing rental housing for the elderly from the list of allowable projects. Some procedural matters, including a new reporting requirement, were also changed. Perhaps the greatest impact of the amendments arises from a new requirement regarding prevailing wages and fringe benefits to be paid during project construction.

Objectives of IRB Programs

As would be expected of public officials in any state, Michigan legislators are concerned about economic development in Michigan and seek methods of promoting it. Of the various incentives available, IRB programs probably are the most attractive from the viewpoint of local government. The only direct costs are administrative, and IRBs seem to offer something for everyone: recipient firms, local citizens, state and local governments, and even the local banks that buy the bonds apparently derive benefits from using tax-exempt financing for industrial development. From the viewpoint of state officials, the benefits to be gained seem great, and the costs of implementing the program seem relatively small.

Stated objectives. The concern about economic development in the state is evident in the enabling legislation. All three bills speak to the "continuing need to alleviate and prevent conditions of unemployment" and the need to strengthen and revitalize the economy of the state through industrial and commercial development. Implementation of the bills is defined as public purpose.[4]

Implicit expectations. The objectives of the IRB programs in Michigan seem to be the location and retention of industry and the provision of commercial services. Underlying the general stated goals, however, is a set of more specific objectives. They are:

1) Expanded employment opportunities in new business facilities and secondarily in support services.

2) Reduced public expenditures on unemployment benefits and other social programs.

3) Broadened tax base which may lower tax the burden for existing residents.

4) Expanded markets and increased profits for existing firms.

5) Increased values of land.

6) Increased diversity of industrial base.

Of these objectives, the most important for this state are job creation and industrial diversification. The program assessment that follows takes into account both stated and implied objectives.

Estimated Volumes of IRBs Issued in Michigan

Measuring the total volume of IRBs issued in Michigan has been difficult up to now because information about EDC bond issues is not reported beyond the local level. With 277 EDCs in Michigan, the task of gathering complete information has been formidable. Some surveys have been used. The data for this study are based on a Michigan Department of Commerce survey of EDCs conducted in November 1980.

In contrast, information about the IDR and JDA bond programs is available in census form from the Municipal Finance Commission and the Job Development Authority files.[5]

Total volumes. The amounts of bonds issued by program and by year for the period 1975-80 are presented in Table 11.1. The data reflect the start-up and expansion of the EDC and JDA programs. Whereas the level of IDR bonds has fluctuated over the years, the volume of EDC bond issues has grown steadily since the inception of the program in 1976.[6] For the first nine months of 1980 EDC bonds totaled approximately $201.8 million, about 90 percent of the IRBs issued in Michigan.

The data for EDC bonds and total bonds are based on known bond issues. These figures underestimate the actual issues, but the degree of underestimation cannot be determined. Nevertheless, the rapid growth of the EDC program can be observed.

Regional patterns. As might be expected, IRB financed projects have been concentrated in certain areas of the state. Of the eighty-three counties in Michigan, forty-six report some IRB issues. Of those, however, only ten counties report more than $10 million total activity over the 1975-80 period. As can be seen in Table 11.2, those counties that report the most activity tend to be the more populated, economically active areas of the state. The two counties for which the highest volumes of bonds are reported, Wayne and Kent, also contain the two largest cities in Michigan.

Of the ten most active counties, four are among the ten Michigan counties most dependent on manufacturing as a source of employment and income. Six of the counties listed in Table 11.2 had 1978 unemployment rates that were higher than the national average. There were, however, seventy-two other counties in Michigan that also reported above average unemployment rates for 1978.[7] In general, IRB programs seem to be used in the most populated and economically active areas of the state. Regional unemployment, per se, appears not to be a determinant of IRB use.

Patterns of use. Types of businesses that are funded in Michigan depend somewhat on the program used. The IDR and JDA programs finance industrial projects where "industrial building" means a "building or structure suitable for and intended for or incidental to use as a factory, mill, shop, processing plant, assembly plant, fabricating plant, warehouse, or research and development facility, or engineering, architectural or design facility or tourist and resort facility."[8] Industrial machinery and equipment means "such machinery and equipment as shall be necessary, suitable, intended for, or incidental to the use of such a facility."[9] All of the IDR and JDA projects financed during the period of study fit within the "industrial" classification as defined by the legislation.

Projects financed with EDC bonds include a much more broadly defined set of enterprises. EDC projects can be "land and existing or planned improvements suitable for use by an industrial or commercial enterprise...and the machinery, furnishings and equipment necessary, suitable, intended for or incidental to a commercial or industrial

TABLE 11.1
VALUE OF IR BONDS ISSUED IN MICHIGAN
1975-1980

	1975	1976	1977	1978	1979	1980
Industrial Development Revenue Bonds						
Number of Projects	11	7	20	12	22	13
Value of Bonds (millions of dollars)	21.0	5.5	29.1	9.9	26.0	25.0[1]
Job Development Authority Bonds						
Number of Projects	0	0	0	0	6	7
Value of Bonds (millions of dollars)	0	0	0	0	12.0	8.9[1]
Economic Development Corporation Bonds[2]						
Number of Project	0	1	5	22	120	160
Value of Bonds (millions of dollars)	0	2.8	5.6	24.5	152.6	201.8[1]
Total Value of Bonds All Programs (millions of dollars)	21.0	8.3	34.6	34.5	190.6	235.7[1]

[1]Data for 1980 are for the first nine months only.
[2]EDC data include actual surveyed totals.

TABLE 11.2
CHARACTERISTICS OF COUNTIES WITH LARGEST INDUSTRIAL REVENUE BOND PROGRAMS

COUNTY	TOTAL VALUE OF BONDS (millions of dollars)	RANK IN POPULATION	RANK IN 1978 UNEMPLOYMENT RATE[1]
1. WAYNE	69.4	1	64
2. KENT	68.7	5	83
3. BERRIEN	51.5	10	41
4. OAKLAND	50.0	2	64
5. ST. CLAIR	50.0	15	64
6. GENESSEE	28.3	4	47
7. MUSKEGON	28.2	11	40
8. CALHOUN	25.8	14	60
9. MACOMB	20.0	3	64
10. WASHTENAW	15.9	7	82

[1]Ranked 1 to 83, from highest to lowest unemployment rate.

Source: Population and unemployment data from Michigan Statistical Abstract, 1980, pp. 29-32, 154-168.

use."[10] To the extent that identification of use was possible from the EDC surveys, all projects fit the legal definition of permissible use. About 10 percent of the EDC projects could not be identified. These involved privately owned firms for which no public records are available, and were probably commercial or retail development projects.

Table 11.3 shows the various classes of projects that were financed by the three programs. Clearly, the greatest amount of financing has gone for manufacturing facilities--about 60 percent. Wholesale and retail trade accounts for 18 percent and service facilities for another 10 percent.

Michigan in the National Scene

The rapid growth of IRB issues in Michigan exceeds growth estimates of IRB issues for the nation as a whole over the 1975-80 period. A recent study by the Congressional Budget Office estimates that annual U.S. IRB issues increased from $1.3 billion in 1976 to $8.4 billion in 1980, a six-fold increase.[11] Michigan bond issues increased from $21 million to about $313 million during this period, a fifteen-fold increase. As a share of the national yearly volume, these figures represented 1.6 percent in 1975 and 3.7 percent in 1980. On a per capita basis, however, dollar value bond issues in Michigan are below the average for the nation. A recent estimate shows that Michigan ranks thirtieth in per capita bond volume.

Some qualitative comparisons can also be made from information about the programs in Michigan and other states. Of the forty-seven states that allow IRBs to be issued, fifteen maintain some restrictions on the types of projects that can be financed. Most of the restrictions apply to commercial or retail businesses. Michigan has no such restrictions on EDC-funded projects. Michigan is also one of only five states that allow IRBs to be issued by the state and local governments and local development corporations, which suggests that a wide variety of IRB sources is available. EDCs do not have to receive state approval on funding and, until this year, they did not have

TABLE 11.3
IRB FINANCED PROJECTS, 1975-1980, BY INDUSTRY CLASS

STANDARD INDUSTRIAL CLASSIFICATION	DESCRIPTION	NUMBER OF PROJECTS	TOTAL AMOUNT FINANCED (millions of dollars)
1000-1999	Mining and Construction	8	6.0
2000-2999	Nondurable Goods Manufacturing	51	78.5
3000-3999	Durable Goods Manufacturing	137	191.6
4000-4999	Transportation	13	21.0
5000-5999	Wholesale/Retail Trade	62	84.3
6000-6999	Finance, Insurance, and Real Estate	26	25.0
7000-8900	Other Services	28	46.6
	Total Identified	325	453.0
	Other	88	71.7
	Total All Programs	413	524.7

to report their activities to the state. Similar local autonomy exists in only eight other states.[12] These factors could account for Michigan's relatively rapid growth in IRB volume during the past few years.

BENEFITS OF IRB PROGRAMS

An assessment of the benefits accruing to Michigan residents from IRB programs requires that those economic effects that result from the program incentives be distinguished from those that would have occurred with normal growth. In this section, we review previous studies that have attempted to measure the incremental effects of IRB programs, and discuss the benefits that may accrue to Michigan residents.

Previous Background and Research

IRBs may influence a firm's location decision, its investment decision, or both. Many studies have attempted to measure these effects. The research has included both survey-based and econometric analysis and has focused on industrial firms. No empirical studies of IRB impacts on commercial firms are available.

Location effects. Other things being equal, a firm may be expected to locate where its costs of capital are lowest. Several surveys have sought to determine the importance of IRBs in the location decision of manufacturing companies, the class of firms which usually has some latitude in choosing sites. Most studies have found that factors such as wage rates, labor supply, community amenities and market proximity are the most important determinants for such firms.[13] A few studies that explicitly ask about the importance of IRBs report that the availability of IRB financing influences some firms. A recent study of IRB-financed firms in Massachusetts found that three of the thirteen firms in the sample were influenced in their choice of location by the IRB incentive.[14] Another study of fifty-four firms that located in Alabama prior to 1970 reported that about one-third of the firms were influenced by the availability of IRB financing.[15] A study of fourteen industrial projects financed in Michigan prior to 1969 found that eight of the investment projects would have been carried through completely even if the aid had not been available, four would have been reduced in size and two would not have been built without the IRB subsidy.[16]

These studies present rather consistent findings that IRB incentives have effect on some location decisions. The Michigan study also indicates that IRB incentives may encourage greater investment than otherwise would have occurred.

Investment effects. Economic theory predicts that in addition to influencing the location decision, the lowering of interest costs for long-term capital increases the amount of business investment. Because availability of IRB financing reduces the cost of capital, IRB programs can affect the amount, timing or location of investment. The degree to which IRB subsidies lower the costs of capital and the degree to which reduced costs of capital increase investment will vary across firms and industries.[17] Firms for which interest costs are a large share of total costs are likely to take advantage of IRB programs. This suggests that the industry mix may shift as a result of IRB programs.

Regression estimates were used to test the effect of an IRB program on investment in Kentucky for the years 1951-72.[18] The findings indicate a positive effect of the IRB program on investment, but the results may be biased by the fact that a property tax exemption program was in effect at the same time. No empirical information about the specific effects of IRB programs on industry mix has been reported previously.

Employment effects. IRB programs implicitly assume that additions to the stock of business capital automatically create additional opportunities for employment. From the theoretical and practical viewpoints, however, the relationship between capital and labor, two inputs into the production process, is not that simple. Only when IRB financing is indispensable in the industrial firm's decision to locate, can one say that the IRB program creates jobs. When IRB financing does encourage greater investment, the impact of the decrease in the cost of capital on employment will depend upon relative costs and the degree to which capital and labor are substitutes in the production process. Theory suggests that the overall impact of IRB subsidies on employment via the investment effect is small.

The effects of IRB incentives on permanent employment also depend upon the type of industry that is aided. Industrial firms have latitude in their location decisions because they produce transportable products. Commercial firms, in contrast, usually must locate near the demand for their services. If local demand is adequate to support a commercial business, the project will proceed without subsidy. If a commercial project proceeds because of IRB incentives, but demand for the services is not adequate to support the additional output, market adjustment will occur. The subsidized firm may be able to attract business away from existing businesses because of its subsidized cost advantage. In time, however, the apparent IRB-induced new jobs in the new facility will be cancelled by employment losses in other firms. No net employment gains are expected to arise from subsidized commercial firms that service local areas.

In spite of the fact that job creation is a major objective of most IRB programs, surprisingly little research has been reported on the employment effects of these programs. A 1966 study designed to evaluate the effect of an IRB program in Pennsylvania found a positive correlation between volume of bonds issued and growth in employment at state and county levels. The author was unable to conclude, however, that the relationship was causal.[19] The study of IRB-financed firms in Massachusetts reported that only fifty jobs were created by the fourteen projects examined, and none of the projects were located in areas of the state with especially severe unemployment.[20]

Employment Effects in Michigan

Projections of the employment effects of IRB financing are required from firms during the application process.[21] Of the 18,755 jobs reported by IRB-financed projects in Michigan from 1975 to 1980, about two-thirds were reported in the industrial sector (mining, manufacturing, and transportation) and one-third in the commercial sector (trade and services).

The figures would provide clear evidence of the social and economic benefits of IRBs if it could be assumed that all of the employment was a direct result of IRB incentives. As discussed previously, however, that is not the case. Consequently, the reported employment figures cannot be used to develop quantitative measures of benefit. No employment gains in commercial projects would be expected to occur in any event. What portion of the IRB-financed industrial projects were truly induced by IRB programs and what employment gains resulted therefrom have not been ascertained. Probably some of the industrial projects would not have been built in Michigan during the period of study were it not for IRB incentives. Probably too, some of the projects have provided incremental employment opportunities for local residents. Most likely, the net gain has been small--perhaps on the order of 0.1 percent increase in total state employment.

Public Economic and Fiscal Benefits

The IRB subsidies can be viewed as a public investment that should generate benefits at least as large as the cost of the subsidies. The benefits to be realized include the social value of reduced unemployment, the generalized economic growth resulting from increased income and spending, and the fiscal effects in terms of increases in income, sales, property and single business tax revenues and decreases in expenditures on social services. A complete evaluation of benefits would include estimates of all these effects.

Diversification Benefits: Effects of IRBs on Industry Mix

A prominent objective of IRB programs in Michigan is to diversify the industry base so as to decrease the state's dependence on durable goods manufacturing. Information about the industries financed with IRBs gives some idea of how effective the programs are in this effort. Table 11.3 lists the number of projects and total amount of financing by sector. Clearly the largest amount of investment took place in durable goods manufacturing industries. This sector accounted for 33 percent of the projects and 36 percent of the financing of all reported IRB programs from 1975 to 1980. Table 11.4 contains nonagricultural, nongovernment employment data for Michigan, and reported IRB-related employment in the various sectors. The distribution of IRB-reported jobs is quite different than was the overall employment mix in 1978, the midpoint of the study period. A comparison of the figures suggests that IRB programs have not contributed to a decrease in the concentration of workers in manufacturing industries.

Further breakdown of the durable goods manufacturing data yields some additional information. As can be seen in Table 11.5, IRB-financed investment in the transportation equipment group (3700) has been minimal. The largest concentration of financing has occurred in the nonelectrical machinery group (3500). It would seem, therefore, that IRBs have contributed to diversification. It is not possible to conclude, however, that less economic cyclicality now exists as a result.

Other Benefits

Even if IRB-financed projects do not create jobs in the long run to the extent expected, some projects do provide additions to the local property tax base, at least temporarily. These benefits accrue to the taxpayers of the local communities to the extent that the increased revenues exceed the costs of public services to the projects.

The private advantages accruing to Michigan businesses

TABLE 11.4
TOTAL EMPLOYMENT AND
EMPLOYMENT IN IRB-FINANCED FACILITIES
IN MICHIGAN, BY SECTOR, 1978

SECTOR	1978 EMPLOYMENT		ESTIMATED EMPLOYMENT IN IRB-FINANCED FACILITIES	
	Number	Percent	Number	Percent
Mining and Construction	152,100	5.1	79	2.2
Nondurable Manufacturing	226,800	7.5	759	20.8
Durable Manufacturing	952,800	31.8	2,707	74.0
Transportation and Communications	155,900	4.9	115	3.1
Commercial Trade and Services	1,510,400	50.4	0	0.0
Total	2,998,000	100.0	3,657	100.0

Source: Employment data, Michigan Statistical Abstract, 1980, pp. 170-171.

TABLE 11.5
AMOUNT OF IRB-FINANCING
IN DURABLE GOODS MANUFACTURING GROUPS
1975-1980

SIC GROUP	DESCRIPTION	AMOUNT (millions of dollars)
3000	Rubber and Plastic Products	19.4
3100	Leather Goods	1.0
3200	Stone, Clay, Glass, and Concrete Products	21.3
3300	Primary Metals	9.5
3400	Fabricated Metal Products	22.5
3500	Machinery except Electrical	70.0
3600	Electrical and Electronic Machinery	15.6
3700	Transportation Equipment	15.0
3800	Instruments	5.1
3900	Miscellaneous Manufacturing	2.3

that use IRB financing are estimated to be about $10 million for 1981. This represents the difference between market interest rates and subsidized IRB rates for the IRB projects funded between 1975 and 1980. Some of that benefit may result in lower prices to consumers or additional business expansion in the state; some of it may increase individual wealth in or out of the state.

Investors who buy IRBs do so because the interest on the bonds is at least as great as the after-tax interest on alternative taxable bonds. To the extent that the tax-exempt return is greater than the after-tax return, the investor is better off. About 65 percent of all IRBs issued during the study period were sold to in-state purchasers. Therefore, most of the advantage accrued to Michigan investors, primarily banks.

COSTS OF IRB PROGRAMS

Other things being equal, the granting of tax advantages to one group of taxpayers requires that compensating tax increases be imposed on other taxpayers. For IRBs, this impact occurs on both the federal and state levels, although it is much greater at the federal level. The cost of providing the tax concession depends upon the volume of bonds issued, the prevailing interest rates, and the marginal tax rate for those who invest in tax-exempt bonds.

The total federal revenue loss due to the exemption of interest paid on all IRB bonds has been estimated by the CBO to be about $700 million for fiscal year 1980 and $1 billion for 1981.[22] If we can assume that Michigan taxpayers share in revenues forgone in the same proportion as they share in taxes paid, 4.6 percent of the $1 billion for 1981 was borne by Michigan taxpayers. That is, the IRB subsidies paid by Michigan taxpayers for IRB-financed projects throughout the country amounted to about $46 million in fiscal year 1981.

Michigan's share of total IRBs outstanding is not as great as is its tax burden. Of the $24.9 billion of IRBs outstanding, CBO estimates that $783.5 million, or 3.1 percent of all the bonds, including pollution bonds, were issued in Michigan. Therefore, the cost of Michigan IRB programs to the nation was about $31 million in 1981--$21 million for development subsidies and $10 million for pollution control subsidies.

From a state policy viewpoint, however, the cost to Michigan taxpayers is much less. The IRB system exists; the only part that can be controlled at the state level is the issuance of IRB bonds in Michigan. Therefore, Michigan's share of cost of its IRB program was only 4.6 percent of the $31 million, or $1.4 million. The rest of the cost was borne by taxpayers in other states, just as Michigan taxpayers paid for a share of all other states' programs.

A calculation of the state tax loss attributed to IRB programs requires accurate information about the substitutability of IRBs in the portfolios of commercial banks and individual investors. Of the $495 million of IRBs for which purchasers were identified, $315 million (65 percent) were sold in-state, all but $2.4 million to commercial banks. To calculate the true cost of IRB programs in terms of taxes forgone, one would have to know the composition of investor portfolios had IRBs not been available. Alternative investments include financial instruments that produce taxable interest such as commercial loans and ones that generate tax-exempt interest such as municipal bonds. Because tax-exempt bonds are purchased to shield profits from taxes, the alternative investment to IRBs would be primarily other tax-exempt bonds. Thus the true state tax loss attributed to IRBs is probably small. The existence of IRBs, however, may impose another cost for Michigan residents.

To induce investors to buy additional IRBs the interest rate must rise relative to the interest on other securities. As investors shift from buying other securities, the rates on those securities must also rise. The greater the relative volume of IRBs, the greater the effect on the costs of other municipal debt. A crowding out effect may be pronounced during periods of low profitability and in small communities that depend upon local banks to purchase their municipal bonds.

SUMMARY OF FINDINGS AND CONCLUSIONS

During the six year period 1975-80, Michigan governmental units issued $525 million worth of industrial revenue bonds that financed more than 400 projects. Most of the projects were built in southern Michigan which contains the more populous counties but not necessarily the areas with highest unemployment rates. About two-thirds of the projects were industrial facilities (mining, manufacturing, and transportation) and one-third were commercial facilities (trade and services). The volume of bonds issued per year grew from $21 million in 1975 to about $313 million in 1980. These amounts represent 1.6 percent of national IRB volumes in 1975 and 3.7 percent in 1980. In spite of this growth, Michigan's per capita share of IRB issues is less than the national average.

The IRB programs may have been directly responsible for the location and expansion of some industrial and commercial development. To the extent that firms located in Michigan rather than in other states, some employment gains can be attributed to the IRB programs. To the extent that more job-creating investment occurred than would have, had the IRB subsidies not been available, state employment increased. In addition to the direct employment effect, Michigan residents benefited from increases in income, expenditures, profits and tax revenues and decreases in social service expenditures.

IRB programs are also expected to help diversify the Michigan economy by encouraging the development of industries that offer more stable employment patterns than now exist. That has not happened. Of the industrial projects funded with IRBs, nearly two-thirds were in durable goods manufacturing which is generally quite cyclical. Of the durable goods projects, however, few were in the traditional automobile-related industries. Thus, IRB programs have marginally encouraged industrial diversification but have not contributed towards the reduction of cyclical employment patterns in the state.

The cost of IRB programs is borne by Michigan taxpayers at both the federal and state levels. The $525 million of IRBs issued from 1975 to 1980 represent about $1.4 million per year in federal revenue losses. Some state taxes are forgone also. On the state level, the estimated loss is likely to be less than the probable gain attributable to the program. Another cost to Michigan residents may arise through the impacts of IRBs on capital markets. Municipalities in Michigan that wish to borrow for traditional public purposes may face higher interest costs as they compete in-state with IRBs for a limited, interest sensitive supply of funds.

From a state policy perspective, IRB programs in Michigan probably yield net positive benefits to state taxpayers on a collective basis. Some new jobs are created by firms that wouldn't have located in Michigan if the incentive weren't available. The industrial mix in the state, though not made less cyclical, has been made somewhat more diverse.

As long as the IRB system exists as primarily a federally subsidized program, Michigan should take full advantage of it. The ability to offer tax-exempt financing to industrial firms is a competitive necessity these days since nearly all states offer locational incentives.

An assessment of IRB programs at the national level is quite different from that at the state level. From a national perspective, IRB programs really constitute a nation-wide system of investment subsidies. Michigan taxpayers can join in asking the question, What public purpose objectives are being served by federal subsidies for private industry? It may be in the interest of all taxpayers to hold back on further IRB issues. From the viewpoint of the individual state participants, however, it is in the interest of the state to issue bonds, the cost of which is mostly paid by other states. The paradox is that all may lose when all pursue their self interest, yet each state has no assurances that its restraint will be matched by the restraint of other states.

Whether viewed from either the national or state level, the broad subsidization of capital is inefficient in encouraging new employment and ineffectual in promoting economic stability. As the system now exists, use of the program has grown dramatically, but the firms that are likely to be attracted to it do not necessarily create permanent, steady employment opportunities. Since Michigan taxpayers share in financing the national program, they may want to encourage continued assessment at the national level. At the same time the Michigan legislature should consider tightening the focus of Michigan programs towards the objectives of more jobs and more diversity in the industrial base. The legislature should consider removing the IRB eligibility for commercial developments that serve local areas.

By limiting IRB financing to firms for which site location is discretionary, the resources of the IRB programs are more likely to achieve permanent employment gains. As for building a more diverse industrial base, there may be no reasonable way that state policy can use fiscal incentives to attract specific industries. Perhaps the best approach is to provide an overall attractive business climate and expect that a broad mix of industry will evolve naturally.

APPENDIX, SOURCES OF DATA

Data on the IDR and JDA bonds were obtained from public records in state agencies and are complete for all industrial development projects.

Data on EDC bonds were obtained from a Michigan Department of Commerce survey of the 277 EDCs in Michigan, mailed in November 1980. Follow-up phone calls were made to nonrespondents over the following six months. Of the 277 EDCs, 176 eventually returned questionnaires, and of those, 62 reported at least one completed project. It is my belief and that of the state officials who administered the survey that most, if not all, active EDCs returned their questionnaires. Many EDCs were still in the start-up stage at the time of the survey. For these reasons the reported total volume of bond issues may be less than the actual amount and the distribution of bond issues among the counties may be somewhat different than reported. These effects are thought to be small.

Many of the survey responses contained incomplete data. In cases where appropriate, percentages were applied to fill in for missing data. For instance, employment data were not reported for 26 of the 309 bond issues. Based on the jobs per dollar of financing that were reported, the employment data are adjusted to represent all projects.

Industry classification data were obtained from actual reports or from various business directories. Information on small, private firms that are not industrial producers was generally unavailable and is not included in the industry analysis.

NOTES, CHAPTER 11

[1]The research assistance of Michele Belfie and the cooperation of Linda Apsey and William Cochran of the Michigan Department of Commerce and Donald Fichter of the Michigan Department of Treasure are gratefully acknowledged.

[2]At the request of the chairman of the Oversight Subcommittee of the House Committee on Ways and Means, the Congressional Budget Office prepared a study entitled Small Issue Industrial Revenue Bonds, which was released in April 1981. The controversial issues are addressed there.

[3]The Michigan Constitution (Article 9, Section B) prohibits the use of state credit for private purposes. However, a similar clause is allowed for Michigan Housing Authority Bonds. Resolution of the issue awaits a court test.

[4]Sec. 2, Act No. 338 of 1974, The Economic Development Act.

[5]This study includes only bonds used to finance economic development; bonds that were issued to finance pollution control equipment are excluded. The reason for this decision is that during the early 1970s IDR bonds financed many projects that sought compliance with federal pollution control requirements rather than the objectives of development and job creation. Since 1975 pollution control financing has become increasingly less significant, and economic development and job creation objectives now account for most of the IRB issues.

[6]See Appendix for descriptions of the data base and methods used for estimations.

[7]The northern half of the Lower Peninsula and most of the Upper Peninsula report consistently high unemployment rates. These areas tend to be sparsely populated.

[8]Sec. 2(a), Act 62 of 1963.

[9]Sec. 2(d), Act 62 of 1963.

[10]Sec. 3(e), Act 338 of 1974.

[11]See CBO, Small Issue Industrial Revenue Bonds, p. 70.

[12]CBO, Small Issue Industrial Revenue Bonds, p. 31.

[13]See, for instance, Leonard Lund, "Factors in Corporate Location Decisions," Information Bulletin no. 66, The Conference Board, 1979; Roger Vaughn, State Taxation and Economic Development, (Washington, D.C.: Council of State Planning Agencies, 1979); and Patricia L. Braden and Susan R. Rideout, "Location Decision Making in Export-Oriented Business and Industry," working paper (Ann Arbor: The

University of Michigan Graduate School of Business Administration, 1978).

[14]Margaret Dewar, "The Usefulness of Industrial Revenue Bond Programs for State Economic Development: Some Evidence from Massachusetts," working paper, Joint Center for Urban Studies of MIT and Harvard, March 1980.

[15]Alabama Business Research Council, Industrial Development Bond Financing: Business and Community Experiences and Opinions (Alabama: University of Alabama Press, 1970).

[16]Vincent P. Apilato, "Corporate-Government Interplay: The Era of Industrial Aid Finance," Urban Affairs Quarterly, December 1971, pp. 219-41.

[17]W. J. Stober and L. H. Falk, "The Effects of Financial Inducements on the Location of Firms," Southern Economic Journal 36, July 1969, pp. 25-35; and M. K. Evans, Microeconomic Activity: Theory, Forecasting and Control (New York: Harper and Row, 1969), pp. 135-136.

[18]D. A. Hellman, G. H. Wassall, and L. H. Falk, Financial Incentives to Industry (Lexington, Mass.: Lexington Books, 1976), pp. 63-65.

[19]Ronald B. Gold, "Subsidies to Industries in Pennsylvania," National Tax Journal 19, September 1966, p. 296.

[20]Dewar, "The Usefulness of Industrial Revenue Bond Programs."

[21]These figures are subject to error since they are estimated prior to project initiation. Too, it may be in the interest of applicant firms to overestimate the job creation effects.

[22]CBO, Small Issue Industrial Revenue Bonds, p. 39.

REFERENCES, CHAPTER 11

Alabama Business Research Council. Industrial Development Bond Financing: Business and Community Experiences and Opinions. Alabama: University of Alabama Press, 1970.

Apilato, Vincent P. "Corporate Government Interplay: The Era of Industrial Aid Finance," Urban Affairs Quarterly December 1971, pp. 219-41.

Braden, Patricia L. and Rideout, Susan R. "Location Decision Making in Export Oriented Business and Industry." Working paper. Ann Arbor: The University of Michigan Graduate School of Business Administration, 1978.

Cornia, Gary C.; Testa, W. A.; and Stocker, F. D. "State-Local Fiscal Incentives and Economic Development." Columbus: Academy for Contemporary Problems, 1978.

Dewar, Margaret. "The Usefulness of Industrial Revenue Bond Programs for State Economic Development: Some Evidence from Massachusetts." Cambridge: Joint Center for Urban Studies of MIT and Harvard, 1980.

Evans, M. K. Macroeconomic Activity: Theory, Forecasting and Control. New York: Harper and Row, 1969.

Friedenberg, H. and Bretzfelder, R. "Sensitivity of Regional and State Nonfarm Wages and Salaries to National Business Cycles, 1948-79." Survey of Current Business, May 1980, pp. 15-27.

Galper, Harvey and Toder, Eric. "Modelling Revenue and Allocation Effects of the Use of Tax Exempt Bonds for Private Purposes." Washington: U.S. Treasure Office of Tax Analysis. Paper 44, 1980.

Gold, Ronald B. "Subsidies to Industries in Pennsylvania." National Tax Journal 19, September 1966, pp. 296-305.

Hellman, D. A.; Wassall, G. H.; and Falk, L. H. Financial Incentives to Industry. Lexington: Lexington Books, 1976.

Keischnick, Michael. Venture Capital and Urban Development. Washington, D.C.: Council on State Planning Agencies, 1979.

Lund, Leonard. "Factors in Corporate Location Decisions." Information Bulletin 66, The Conference Board, 1979.

Michigan, State of. Economic Development Corporation Act, Act No. 338, Public Acts of 1974; Act No. 501, Public Acts of 1980.

Michigan, State of. Job Development Authority Act, Act No. 301, Public Acts of 1975.

Michigan, State of. Industrial Development Revenue Bond Act, Act No. 62, Public Acts of 1963.

Stober, W. J. and Falk, L. H. "The Effects of Financial Inducements on the Location of Firms." Southern Economic Journal 36, July 1969, pp. 25-35.

U.S. Congress, Congressional Budget Office. Small Issue Industrial Revenue Bonds. Washington, D.C.: U.S. Government Printing Office, April 1981.

U.S. Department of Commerce, Bureau of Economic Analysis. " Regional Economic Information System," published in The Michigan State Economic Record 22, May 1980, pp. 2-3.

Vaughn, Roger J. State Taxation and Economic Development. Washington, D.C.: Council of State Planning Agencies, 1979.

Verway, David, ed. Michigan Statistical Abstracts. East Lansing: Michigan State University, 1980.

Chapter 12

Michigan State Expenditures and the Provision of Public Services

by

John G. Cross

(with Catherine E. Jensen, Michael J. Moore, Janet C. Wolfe)

The University of Michigan

OVERVIEW[1]

The State of Michigan is by no means unique among northern industrial states in facing unpleasant financial pressures. Most states have experienced dramatic increases in social service and medical needs, growing pressures upon the judicial and correctional systems, and ever-increasing demands for support from older, declining cities. In common with other states, too, is the growing concern with "tax revolts," and with the accompanying threat that rising demands for state services may be met with declines in the resources available to fund them. However, the dependence upon a single concentrated industry, one which itself is apparently losing its market position to competitors, exacerbates these trends to such an extent that the financial problems faced by the State of Michigan during fiscal years 1980 and 1981 neared crisis proportions.

It is often alleged that pressures upon the budget of the state are the consequence of an excessive expansion in spending during the decade of the 1970s. In fact, over this period, state spending has not grown at all relative to personal incomes in Michigan. It is true that real personal income in the state has not grown significantly, and this fact may have somehow exacerbated a belief that growth in the government sector must have been excessive, but, in fact, that spending has not grown significantly faster than the rate of inflation.

Since FY 1971, personal income net of transfers in Michigan has increased at an average rate of 9.47 percent per year, only a little higher than the average rate of increase of the Detroit-based consumer price index (8.5 percent per year over the same period). Since 1974, in fact, the CPI and Michigan personal income net of transfers have moved almost exactly in step at an average rate of 9 percent per year. If we include transfers (largely composed of Social Security payments), the rate of income increase is about 0.5 percent higher. On the other hand, since Michigan population increased slightly over the last ten years, the rate of per capita income increase is 0.4 percent lower. Finally, since labor force participation has been increasing over the decade (approximately 1 percent per year), it is clear that real employee incomes in Michigan have not been increasing, and indeed, over the last five years, they have declined.

Michigan state expenditures have been following a course roughly parallel with income. Thus, while total personal income rose at 9.91 percent per year over the last decade, Michigan state expenditures (excluding federal grants and user fees) have risen at a slightly lower rate of 9.74 percent per year. This growth has been supplemented by a great increase in federal spending through such programs as AFDC, Medicaid, CETA, special school programs, and transportation subsidies. Overall, federal aid to Michigan has increased at a rate of 17 percent per year over the last decade, and when this is combined with all of the state's own resources, gross spending in Michigan is found to have risen at just over 11 percent per year.

It is clear that the expansion in state and local government activity which characterized the 1960s came to an end during the 1970s. Certainly, our figures provide no support for a contention that state spending in Michigan has grown excessively, or that it is inappropriately high, at least by 1970-71 standards. On the other hand, spending patterns within this total have changed markedly, and it is evident that the financial pressures under which the state budget presently suffers are attributable in large part to changes in its composition.

Even a cursory review of social and economic trends in Michigan must engender a pessimistic view of the condition of the state. Using the 9.91 percent annual rate of growth of personal income in Michigan as a convenient benchmark, we note that over the last decade:

* The state share of spending on the Aid to Families with Dependent Children program has been increasing at over 13 percent per year.

* The state share of spending on Medicaid and related services has been increasing at over 14 percent per year.

* State spending on general assistance has been increasing at over 19 percent per year (this figure, however, is exaggerated by the fact that during the 1970s, the state assumed all responsibility for this program from the counties).

* The state share of spending on juvenile services has been increasing at over 20 percent per year.

* State spending on corrections has been increasing at 19 percent per year.

These financial trends are matched by equally discouraging demographic data:

* While unemployment naturally fluctuates in response to general economic conditions, there has been an unremitting underlying trend upward, adding about 0.4 percent each year to the unemployment rate about which cyclic fluctuations are centered.

* Caseloads in the Aid to Families with Dependent Children program have increased at an average rate of 7.8 percent per year--7.4 percentage points higher than the rate of population growth in Michigan.

* General assistance caseloads have increased over the decade at an average rate of 8.6 percent per year--8.2 percentage points higher than the rate of population growth.

* Prison inmate population has grown at an average rate of 4.8 percent per year, and evidence suggests that this rate would be substantially higher were it not for the overcrowding of all available prison facilities.

In the case of social services such as AFDC and GA,

these high rates of growth are not entirely due to changes in the economic and social climate. During the late 1960s and early in the 1970s, social policies were deliberately directed toward expanding eligibility for social services, locating eligible individuals who were not receiving benefits, and enhancing the benefits themselves. As a consequence, caseloads and expenditures increased dramatically during this earlier period, and the growth rates listed above reflect in part the consequences of an intentional policy of increasing the delivery of social services.

Nevertheless, even after this administratively determined expansion in services came to an end, social service caseloads continued to expand at a very high rate. By 1981, the underlying rate of growth of AFDC caseloads has apparently fallen to 2.5 percent per year, but this rate is still far higher than the 0.4 percent rate of population growth, and it is being maintained in the face of a slight decline in the real value of AFDC benefits. The rate of caseload growth in the general assistance program has actually increased, and this too in spite of the declining real value of assistance payments.

As a consequence of these trends, the role of the Department of Social Services expanded greatly over the decade of the seventies, as did that of the smaller, but equally rapidly growing Department of Corrections. Moreover, since the activities of these departments are determined largely by social forces outside of immediate legislative control, it has proven to be very difficult to curtail their growth, even in the face of revenue declines. This has led to a concentration of any budgetary pressures which do arise upon other programs elsewhere in the state expenditure system.

Naturally, in an expenditure budget which has remained relatively constant in real terms, the expansion in social services and corrections has forced a displacement of funds away from other spending categories. Thus while social services was increasing its share of the state budget (excluding federal contributions) from 18.2 percent in FY 1971 to 27.6 percent in FY 1981, state expenditures on school aid (K-12) fell from 40.4 percent to 29.2 percent of the total. While state expenditure on corrections was increasing from 1.4 percent to 3.1 percent over the same period, the share of the state budget going to the Department of Natural Resources was halved from 1.1 percent to 0.51 percent, and expenditures on higher education fell from 14.4 percent to 12.5 percent. Even the Department of Transportation has lost ground somewhat in this respect (from 10.2 percent to 9.2 percent), although this is largely a reflection of the rate of growth of gasoline tax revenues which are constitutionally earmarked for transportation.

These trends reflect an important change in the general character of Michigan government spending. Social services and corrections are "targeted" programs whose expenditures are concentrated upon a relatively small minority of Michigan citizens, while the programs which have been displaced were serving a much broader cross-section of the population. In part, this shift in the composition of spending reflects the increased concern for income redistribution which characterized the 1960s, and this growth in interest in one function of government naturally led to real declines in the more traditional public sector services. However, public opinion polls (see Courant, Gramlich, and Rubinfeld, 1980) suggest that this shift in composition is extremely unpopular. "Welfare spending" is the single category in which an overwhelming majority of voters would support reduction.

A consequence of this displacement from general public services to targeted programs is the fact that most taxpayers become aware of a greatly reduced return on their tax dollars. Services which were formerly freely available are reduced (such as school music and arts programs or highway patrols) or are accompanied by sharply increased user fees (ranging from park entrance fees and fishing and hunting license fees to high tuition rates in the community and four-year colleges and an increased reliance upon local property taxes to support local schools). A popular impression of decreasing efficiency in state government is inevitable. This tendency is compounded by two other developments which have taken place over the last decade. First is the growth in state to local revenue sharing and related grants, transfers, and other forms of direct subsidy for local governments. Cash transfers to local jurisdictions have increased from approximately 2.5 percent of state spending in FY 1971 to over 11.5 percent in FY 1981. Politically speaking, the "credit" for the resulting programs naturally goes to local government and, to an equivalent extent, the state is seen to be taking in revenues but to be delivering no comparable product. Second, overhead and administrative costs in state government have in fact grown more rapidly than have actual services. Compared to the gross spending increase for the entire state of 11.2 percent per year, general government spending has been increasing at 15.6 percent, and the Department of Management and Budget at about 22 percent (after taking account of the large number of office and function transfers which have taken place over the decade). Quantitatively, expenditures on central administration, executive, and overhead do not constitute a large share of state operations, and elimination of such "fat" as may have accumulated would provide only trivial savings in terms of the overall budget. Nevertheless, these increases do tend to reinforce any impressions of inefficiency which may have been obtained from other sources.

ACCOUNTING PROCEDURES AND BUDGET ANALYSIS

Budget Concepts

It is not always the case that accounting procedures which are consistent and which meet traditional definitional standards are equally effective for the analysis of the actual operations of an organization. A prime example of this dilemma is provided by the so-called General Purpose component of the Michigan General Fund. Most observers treat the General Purpose fund as the pool of resources over which the executive and legislature have discretionary authority, and therefore as the fund in which incremental revenues are placed and from which incremental spending programs must be funded. Unfortunately, this is far from the truth. The General Purpose fund includes some revenues which are best described as "user fees" and which therefore could not reasonably be diverted from the programs which generate them. On the other hand, it excludes a number of expenditures which are clearly incurred at the discretion of the state, but which have been "earmarked" by legislative action, action which can be reversed whenever the desire to do so arises. Since the inclusion and exclusion of resources in the General Purpose fund varies significantly from year to year, annual comparisons of spending patterns are impossible, and the fund itself provides no guide as to the resources available to the state, or to the burdens placed on the state by various spending programs.

The total state budget is an equally unreliable guide for analysis in that it includes resources which are clearly not fungible from program to program. The bulk of the federal money spent in the state--which constitutes some 28 percent of the entire state budget in FY 1981--is specifically earmarked for certain programs and could not be diverted elsewhere. Similarly, the total budget includes innumerable user fees which would certainly be reduced or cease to be collected altogether if the associated spending programs were reduced or terminated.

It is impossible to perform any reasonably accurate analysis of Michigan state operations with such erratic and even arbitrary budget data. Our review therefore began with a tentative reconstruction of the Michigan State Budget with the objective of determining the extent to which expenditures are genuinely discretionary. In our definition, a "discretionary" expenditure is one which is

(1) subject to control by the executive or legislature, and (2) free of offsetting variations in revenues ("user fees") which would arise as a natural consequence of expenditure changes. Such a criterion must be applied with a fairly long time horizon in mind. If the Department of Natural Resources were to abandon the maintenance of parks and waterways, park fees and fishing license fees might not fall off immediately. Eventually, however, such fees would decline, and hence reductions in these expenditures would lead to offsetting revenue losses. On the other hand, hunting and fishing license fee revenue is also used to support financial transfers to counties "in lieu of taxes" on state-owned land. Since elimination of these transfers would not have any significant effect on license revenues, such expenditures were deemed to be discretionary. A more difficult question arises in the case of federal grants in that most of these funds require state matching funds; in a typical instance (such as AFDC or Medicaid) a $2 reduction in total expenditure would lead to a $1 loss in federal income. In these cases, it was deemed to be most appropriate to consider the entire state share to be discretionary and to treat the federal grant as a device for reducing the cost to the state of any given unit of service. Moreover, there are floors below which certain expenditures cannot legally go. The Michigan constitution requires that 50 percent of the sales tax be earmarked for "education" (not specifically K-12 education, however), and the state could not reduce Medicaid coverage or AFDC benefit levels below certain standards without losing all federal approval for these programs. In each of these cases, however, actual Michigan expenditures greatly exceed the minima, and as they stand, they are subject to discretionary control over a very wide range. We therefore included all expenditures in these areas in the discretionary category. Finally, since gasoline tax revenue is constitutionally earmarked for transportation purposes, these funds are treated as user fees and are not included with discretionary resources.

Gross state expenditures in FY 1981 amount to $9,875

million. The "discretionary" component of this is found to be $6,068 million. The difference between these two figures is accounted for by $2,655 million in federal spending and about $903 million in user fees.

Our purpose in developing such a budgetary classification is to clarify the potential consequences of general revenue increases or decreases. A tax cut program, for example (such as a reduction in local property taxes to be reimbursed in whole or in part from state revenues), would have to be financed out of discretionary funds. The impact of such a cut cannot be appraised by reference to the (higher) gross expenditure budget or the (lower) General Purpose fund. It is a common practice for such summary statistics to be used in debate over taxes, and confusion often results from a failure to use appropriate budget measures. For example, the 1980 "Tisch II" tax cutting referendum was generally believed to propose a $2 billion cost to the state. Supporters of the measure chose to describe this as a 20 percent budget cut (using gross expenditures as a base), while opponents characterized it as a 45 percent cut (using the General Purpose fund as a base). In fact, the cut would have amounted to about one third of state discretionary spending.

Revenue Control by Generating Agencies

Unfortunately, available data do not permit us to include all forms of user fees in our budget analysis. County mental health units, for example, receive a number of fees for services which are not treated as revenue to the state. It is therefore very difficult to ascertain the extent to which gross revenue to these units is dependent upon state expenditure policies. Community colleges and four-year colleges and universities are treated as fully autonomous units, and only their state subsidy is included in the budget, although it is clear that their ability to attract tuition revenue is strongly influenced by the extent of their state support. In fact, there is very little consistency in the budgetary treatment of revenue-generating units of state government. Colleges and universities are regarded as independent units which are granted state subsidies. Even though these subsidies are ostensibly determined by formulas which reflect specific aspects of their operations, there is very little direct control exerted over management operations, tuition levels, curriculum, or admissions policies. At the other extreme is the Department of Licensing and Regulation, which receives none of the revenue generated by its licensing operations but is funded instead through the General Fund, while the General Fund receives all license fee revenues. The inappropriateness of this arrangement for both budgeting and operations is obvious when one considers that a reduction in activities of this department would inevitably produce a corresponding reduction in revenue generation.

Quite apart from the difficulty in determining actual levels of discretionary spending is the question of whether the accounting system may actually interfere with the efficient delivery of services. It is a principle of organizations in any setting that the greater the managerial separation between income generation and expenditure, the less efficient the operation is likely to be. If those who deliver the services and charge the fees are not funded by the revenues, they will naturally lose interest in the efficiency and effectiveness of their activities, and the quality of the product will decline. There are a number of areas in Michigan state government in which this principle applies. Until FY 1981, third-party (insurance) fees paid by patients in state mental hospitals were transferred to the general fund, and this naturally reduced the incentive of the Department of Mental Health to obtain such fees. The same problem arises at the level of the County Mental Health Board, which is expected to "share" patient fees with the state. Inevitably, this reduces (and sometimes eliminates) the incentive to collect the fees. Ultimately, it degrades service, increases the tax burden of mental health programs, or both.

Efficiency in state government would be greatly enhanced were steps taken to increase the budgetary autonomy of direct-service delivering units. A good model for such a development is provided by the recent experiment with "contract boards" in the Department of Mental Health. These are county boards which have been granted both more autonomy and more responsibility for the care of patients from their districts. Such a board, for example, would no longer simply transfer a patient into the state system should hospitalization be required, but would instead retain responsibility (including financial), for the patient no matter what setting is chosen. Naturally, the budget of the local board must be increased in compensation for this change (although the increased spending is initially only an accounting transfer of state spending on hospitals); however, it can be expected that this program will greatly improve the efficiency and quality of community mental health care delivery. On the one hand, it will no longer be possible for a county to dispose of a difficult case simply by transferring it to the state system, and on the other, a larger share of patient fees will be retained by the board, increasing the incentive to take advantage of available resources.

This procedure of establishing relatively independent units with more comprehensive program responsibility could be applied effectively to a variety of state services. Licensing, pollution surveillance, bank examination, and insurance regulation all could be organized into comprehensive and self-funding operations. Even some aspects of corrections and social services might be provided on the model of the Contract Mental Health Board, reducing both costs of providing services and the political dissatisfaction that these statewide operations seem to produce.

The Headlee Amendment

In 1978, the voters of Michigan approved the so-called Headlee Amendment to the Michigan constitution. This amendment was designed to restrict growth in state revenues to the rate of growth in Michigan personal income, to limit the introduction of new local taxes or new bonding issues without a popular vote, and to ensure that the share of Michigan expenditures redistributed to local units of government remains at the level established during fiscal year 1978 (this fraction was then 41.6 percent). The first of these restrictions has had no effect, because state revenues have not been increasing as rapidly as Michigan personal income in any case, and the second, for similar reasons, has had only minor consequences. The third, however, removed what was an important source of flexibility in state budgetmaking. Before this amendment was passed, cyclical fluctuations in revenues and expenditure demands upon the state were passed on in part to local units of government. An economic downturn that increased the Michigan unemployment rate by 1 percent would lead roughly to a 1.6 percent decrease in gross state expenditures, and a 2.1 percent decrease in state discretionary expenditures. (The difference between the 1.6 and 2.1 is due to the fact that federal aid to Michigan is insensitive to variations in employment.) However, since the same one-point increase in the Michigan unemployment rate is generally followed by an increase in expenditures by the Department of Social Services, other departments are forced to sacrifice more than their proportional share of the 2.1 percent decline in discretionary spending. Before 1978, grants and transfers accounted for a large part of these offsetting declines, being reduced by about 5.3 percent for every one point increase in unemployment. The Headlee Amendment requirement that all state payments to local governments (including grants and transfers) remain at (or above) 41.6 percent of gross expenditures has eliminated this flexibility. In recent years this has placed great pressure upon the state budget as other programs which use discretionary funds have been required to sacrifice much more than proportional shares of the overall cuts. While local units of government are now protected to some extent from economic fluctuations in the state, other state programs, primarily in the areas of mental health and higher education, have been forced to make up the difference.

The Headlee Amendment also affects the role of social service programs in Michigan. Most federal money which comes to the state is paid through the Department of Social Services. Since most welfare programs are matched by federal funds, a $1.00 reduction in state spending on one of these programs also reduces federal spending through the state by $1.00. This in turn reduces the requirement to spend at the local level by 41.6 cents. In effect, state-level spending on other programs can be increased by $1.42 for every dollar taken out of social services.

Finally, this same Headlee Amendment has changed the meaning of any proposed budget cut at the state level. Since the 41.6 percent applies to gross state expenditures rather than discretionary spending, and since almost all federal and user fee income is spent at the state level, virtually all of the money which is spent at the local level (and which meets the Headlee requirement) comes from the fund of discretionary resources. That is, the amendment requires that much more than 41.6 percent of state discretionary money be spent at the local level (the 1981 ratio is about 69 percent). If the supply of discretionary revenue were reduced by some amount, then the consequences of that reduction would be divided between the state and local units of government, the latter absorbing 41.6 percent of the reduction. However, a number of recent proposals have suggested cuts at the local level which would then be reimbursed by the state in addition to the existing 41.6 percent requirement. This would focus any spending cuts upon the 31 percent of state discretionary money which is not already spent locally. To give an extreme example, a $2 billion reduction in property taxes which was to be reimbursed by the state might reduce gross state spending by 21 percent and discretionary spending by 33 percent, but would reduce state-level discretionary spending by 48 percent. Since it is these discretionary resources which fund higher education, mental health, and social services, the effect of such a cut on public services would be considerable. The state would probably be forced to respond to this situation by giving up federal subsidies--that is, by focusing its cuts upon the Department of Social Services.

THE FEDERAL SHARE OF MICHIGAN STATE EXPENDITURES

Contributions by the federal government have risen from 16.7 percent of gross expenditures in FY 1971 to 27.6 percent in FY 1981. In general, these federal dollars have had strings attached. Apart from relatively small amounts of revenue sharing and CETA funds, most of this money is designated for particular programs. Over 60 percent of federal aid in Michigan is directed through the Department of Social Services, and if we include certain education programs and transportation, we will have accounted for over 81 percent of all federal contributions to the Michigan state budget. It is furthermore the case that the bulk of these federal grants require matching funds from the state. The growth of federal aid in Michigan has thus required equivalent expansion in state contributions to certain program areas from its own discretionary funds. Generally speaking, in order to obtain the $1.6 billion in social service support from the federal government, the state has had to put in $1.6 billion of its own.

It is likely that the increased share of the state budget which is spent on targeted sub-groups of the population is in part a consequence of the increased role of (deliberately) highly targeted federal aid in Michigan and its tendency to draw state discretionary expenditures along with it. Federal subsidy programs actually have two general effects. First, they reduce the local tax cost of providing certain services. The direct cost to Michigan residents of each dollar in medical service to low income recipients is only $0.50, the direct cost of $1.00 of AFDC benefits is $0.50, and the cost of certain special education and school lunch programs is reduced to little more than administrative overhead. Inevitably, a system which thus reduces the cost of certain services will stimulate the willingness to provide these services in preference to alternative programs for which the state must provide full cost. Second, it makes possible the substitution of federal dollars for state discretionary funds in ongoing programs. Thus, whereas federal subsidy programs can usually be expected to lead to expansion of targeted state programs, it does not follow that the state programs will expand in proportion to the subsidy, and to that extent the federal program will make state money available for other purposes.

Since state discretionary spending over the last decade has not increased more rapidly than personal income, it is clear that the great increase in federal spending in the state has not led to an overall increase in state spending, but has primarily had the effect of displacing resources away from unsubsidized programs. Table 12.1 describes department-by-department gross expenditures in FY 1981, the fraction of gross spending accounted for by the federal government, and annual growth over the preceding decade of gross expenditures, expenditures from state discretionary funds, and federal funds. The data are obtained from the FY 1971 and FY 1981 appropriations bills (including supplements). It is noteworthy that many of the departments with the highest rate of growth of gross expenditure (social services, public health, and labor) also enjoy a substantial proportion of federal subsidy, while those departments which receive negligible federal assistance (the Departments of State, Treasury, Higher Education, and the School Aid Fund), have been expanding at substantially less than the average rate for the state government as a whole. It is also easy to see from Table 12.1 that some departments have tended to replace existing state spending with federal dollars. The Department of Education, for example, has expanded its operations relatively rapidly over the last decade (12.8 percent per year compared to the 11.2 percent for the state government as a whole), but it has done so entirely at the

TABLE 12.1
SPENDING GROWTH RATES

(*** applies to departments with zero federal aid in 1971)

DEPARTMENT	FY 1981 GROSS EXPENDITURE ($ millions)	PERCENT FEDERAL FUNDS	GROWTH RATES IN:		
			Gross Expenditure	Discretionary Expenditure	Federal Funds
Governor	2.222	0	10.05	10.05	***
Legislature	43.294	0.16	11.37	11.14	***
Judiciary	35.347	1.1	12.72	16.47	2.3
Att'y General	20.653	17.1	17.86	16.2	***
State	38.162	4.7	8.85	4.92	26.4
Man. & Budget	101.877	35.6	20.83	15.7	29.26
Treasury	38.689	3.2	7.84	7.55	***
Civil Service	9.771	86.3	13.64	-8.27	***
Civil Rights	9.082	20.4	9.49	7.08	***
Education	407.006	90.4	12.8	-0.28	15.11
School Aid	1,800.820	1.7	6.68	6.49	***
Higher Ed.	757.773	0.44	8.24	8.42	***
Public Health	202.305	54.1	12.3	13.33	11.37
Mental Health	569.346	12.4	10.85	10.18	31.58
Social Services	3,270.044	47.1	14.93	14.5	15.27
Corrections	193.737	1.66	19.01	18.97	20.33
Mil. Affairs	10.616	7.47	4.54	14.08	---
State Police	145.420	12.9	13.38	12.44	18.86
Commerce	84.986	8.8	12.24	5.91	24.01
Labor	211.621	86	39.32	12.81	90.97
Lic. & Regul.	9.761	0	11.36	***	***
Nat. Resources	128.896	24.2	11.94	1.91	38.02
Agriculture	25.172	9.6	6.57	7.27	5.07
Grants & T.	722.452	2.9	25.55	27.82	4.59
Transportation	956.819	18.0	10.09	***	30.84
Cap. Outlay	76.161	41.7	-7.82	-17.62	16.83
Total	9,626.385	27.6	11.16	9.93	17.03

expense of the federal government. In fact, nominal spending from state discretionary funds in this department has actually fallen slightly (-0.3 percent per year). Converting to constant dollars, this amounts to an annual decrease in funding at a rate of 8.8 percent per year The same tendency appears in several other departments: military affairs, civil rights, and natural resources.

During fiscal years 1980 and 1981, the state budget was put under severe strain as a consequence of the economic downturn in the automobile industry together with the continuing demand for social services and the Headlee Amendment requirement that transfers to and expenditures for local services be maintained. The ensuing budget cuts were often extremely painful if not actually disruptive to the provision of all state services. During this period, it was frequently suggested that the presence of federal matching programs had an influence over the distribution of the cuts: if one dollar were cut from such a program, the state would only save about fifty cents, whereas in areas not matched with federal funds, the state would save the entire amount of the cutback. A number of news reports contributed to the impressions that general assistance benefits (which are not subsidized by the federal government) were being cut more than AFDC benefits (which are), and that hospitals for the developmentally disabled (which receive support from the Medicaid program) were being partially exempted from cuts which did apply to hospitals for the mentally ill (which do not receive such support). In fact, there is no evidence that such differential economizing took place during this period: hospitals for the developmentally disabled were actually reduced disproportionately more than the others, and substantial changes were made in AFDC eligibility rules and benefit rates as well as in general assistance.

Such results as these are actually to be expected. The presence of federal subsidies certainly influences the amount of services to be delivered--federal support for AFDC, for example, induces an AFDC program more generous than would otherwise have existed--but it does not follow that such programs are either immune from cuts or more vulnerable to them. The very expansion in a program which is induced by a federal subsidy brings about a condition in which we see ourselves to be less in need of the service and we are to that extent less likely to resist cutbacks. Whether these programs are cut more or less than others is more likely to depend upon the conditions under which the necessity for cutbacks arises. The Department of Corrections, for example, was relatively immune from budget cuts during FY 1980 and FY 1981, not because of any significant federal support, but because of a legislative reluctance to make cuts in an area of such obviously growing need, while the cuts in the Department of Mental Health were facilitated by a conviction on the part of its administration that (less expensive) community residential facilities are more suitable for patients in any case.

There is considerable debate at the federal level as to the appropriateness of current program levels, especially in areas of social services. If these programs were reduced, we would expect a reversal of the trends which we observed over the last decade--certain welfare benefits and eligibility standards would be reduced, and state money would be returned to those programs (e.g., in the Department of Education) from which they have been released. Quite different consequences might be expected were the federal government to abandon its attempts to focus federal support upon targeted low-income groups, replacing existing entitlement programs with a system of "block grants" which were defined broadly enough to include program areas which do not presently receive federal support. If it became possible to use low income assistance subsidies for general assistance as well as AFDC, for example, there would certainly be a tendency to make substitutions in this direction. More broadly defined educational grants would probably lead to less emphasis upon special and remedial educational programs in deference to adult education and experimental teaching formats for normal or even "gifted" children. In short, just as the existing configuration of federal subsidies has tended to focus state programs upon targeted elements of the population, movement toward block grants would enable the state to redirect its expenditures toward a broader cross-section of its citizens.

ADMINISTRATION AND OVERHEAD

A persistent complaint directed at state government alleges that the bureaucracy itself is consuming an ever-increasing share of state resources, leaving less and less for the delivery of actual public services. There are generally four dimensions to this claim: (1) civil service and administrative salary rates are too high, (2) salary rates have been rising faster than is justified by economic conditions, (3) staff sizes are increasing more rapidly than is necessary to deliver the services, (4) managerial incompetence extending even to corruption and fraud is draining resources. Unfortunately, it is easy to find specific instances in support of each of these charges. State legislators are the third highest paid in the nation (behind California and Illinois), while the governor's salary is seventh highest in the U.S. The Civil Service Commission routinely seems to grant cost of living increases in an economy few of whose citizens have been keeping up with inflation. Staff sizes in mental institutions have grown dramatically relative to patient loads. Cases of managerial ineptitude, improper contract relationships, and even outright theft are described periodically in the news media. That such circumstances should engender distrust and even hostility from the general public is understandable. The pragmatic issues, however, are whether they can legitimately be generalized to apply to the entire state government, and, even if they can, whether they account for substantial financial losses.

There is no doubt that executive and bureaucratic overhead components of state operations have expanded more rapidly than the average. Compared to the 9.9 percent annual growth rate in state discretionary funds, departmental executive costs have expanded at 22.0 percent. Similarly, the nine departments constituting general government (governor, legislature, judiciary, attorney general, state, management and budget, treasury, civil service, and civil rights) have consumed discretionary funds at a rate which grew at 12.6 percent over the last decade. This is a slight overstatement of actual expansion because a few activities have been transferred into these departments over the period. Nevertheless, the rate of growth is much larger than the 9.9 percent rate of growth of government as a whole. On the other hand, the amount of money involved is only moderate. If executive components of government had grown at the average rate of 9.9 percent instead of the 22.0 percent, the consumption of discretionary funds in 1981 would have been reduced by $118.4 million (about 2 percent of the total). If all the nine departments responsible for general government had grown at the 9.9 percent rate, their use of General Fund money in FY 1981 would have been reduced by $40.8 million (about 0.6 percent of the total). These numbers are moderate simply because the categories themselves are small. General government (at $183 million) only absorbs about 3 percent of state discretionary resources, and all executive offices together only absorb about $181 million.

The most rapidly expanding branch of general government is the Department of Management and Budget, whose claim on discretionary resources grew at an annual rate of 16.9 percent per year over the last decade. Much of this, however, is accounted for by increases in services rather than in overhead. The Michigan Council for the Arts, human resource programs and the Michigan Women's Commission are all operated within the Department of Management and Budget, and the sum of their claims upon discretionary resources has grown at an annual rate of 28.5 percent per year. The residual grew at 12.3 percent per year, about the same rate as the other departments comprising general government.

It is worth noting that just as overhead categories were the most prone to expansion during 1971-81, they were also the most vulnerable to cuts when the state revenue condition worsened. The state discretionary resources used by the Department of Management and Budget declined 15.6 percent from FY 1980 to FY 1981, and the governor's office and legislative branch declined by over 7 percent and 12 percent respectively. These reductions are much larger than the reductions experienced by the entire fund of discretionary resources (-0.5 percent), and this fact lends some support to the proposition that some "fat" has accumulated in these areas (or at least that they provide less essential services than do operations elsewhere).

If we turn to the entire civil service in Michigan, we find a similar pattern of growth slightly higher than would seem to be justified by general circumstances, but not by enough to make a dramatic difference to overall expenditure levels. Between FY 1971 and FY 1981 the average classified civil service salary has increased from $9,061 to $19,935, a rate of increase of 8.2 percent per year. Since this matches the increase in the CPI almost exactly, the impression that the Civil Service Commission routinely grants cost of living increases (after taking into account ordinary career advancements) is strongly reinforced. Compared to other wages and salaries in Michigan, this rate of increase is high, but only by about 0.15 percent per year. Over the decade, this suggests that civil service salaries have increased relative to other wage rates in Michigan by 1.5 percent in total. If we were to eliminate this differential, reducing these salaries to the relative level they occupied in 1971, the FY 1981 saving in discretionary funds would be trivial.

Quite a different pattern emerges if we compare the level of civil service salaries in Michigan to those in neighboring states and in the nation as a whole. Nationally, average salaries of noneducation state employees in October 1979 were $1,193 per month compared to $1,475 in

Michigan. Average salaries of noneducation employees in the Great Lakes states excluding Michigan (Illinois, Indiana, Ohio, and Wisconsin) were $1,228 at the same time. Thus Michigan state salary rates were typically 23.6 percent higher than the national average and 20 percent higher than those in the neighboring states. In 1979, Michigan state government salaries were the third highest in the nation behind Alaska ($1,758) and California ($1,523). If Michigan were to pay salaries comparable to those in the other Great Lakes states, there would be a substantial saving in expenditures, amounting to about $217 million.

It would be inappropriate to compare civil service salaries to those in neighboring states without considering them in the context of the wage and salary structure in Michigan itself. In fact, wages in Michigan are high generally, especially wages in the unionized sectors of the economy. Average 1979 incomes for production workers in Michigan, for example, were 16.5 percent higher than average production incomes in the other Great Lakes states, and 41 percent higher than production wages averaged across all 50 states. If we were to use local production wages as a benchmark, civil service salaries in Michigan would not appear to be seriously out of line. Other wage and income statistics do not put Michigan so far above the other states (although even the most pessimistic has Michigan incomes 6.5 percent above the other Great Lakes states), but this is because they are less heavily weighted by wages in the unionized sector of the economy. Michigan civil service salaries are apparently high because they have come to be established with reference to production wages rather than with Michigan incomes generally or civil service incomes elsewhere.

Michigan also has more state employees per capita than do the neighboring states. Whereas the Great Lakes states excluding Michigan averaged about sixty-four state government employees per 10,000 in population in 1979, Michigan had almost eighty state employees per 10,000 population. This employee level is not in itself evidence of inefficiency. It may simply reflect a higher level of services or a different distribution of service responsibilities between state and local governments, and Michigan is below the national average in this respect: nationally, there are 92.1 state government employees per 10,000 population.

SOCIAL SERVICES

We have already remarked upon the rapid growth of spending on social services which has taken place over the last decade. Not only have benefits per caseload been rising, but caseloads themselves have increased sharply. Since 1971, for example, AFDC caseloads have been expanding at 8.8 percent per year while GA caseloads have been growing at 7.3 percent per year. Although these figures provide a good overall indication of the rise in the number of adults in Michigan who are found in a state of dependency upon the social service system, they obscure two important details. First, the expansion in AFDC cases took place most noticeably during the first third of the decade. This expansion was a continuation of the rapid increase which began in the latter half of the 1960s and which continued into FY 1973. This rapid expansion is usually attributed to three factors: (1) a deliberate attempt, both nationally and in Michigan to expand the coverage of welfare programs, (2) the activities of the National Welfare Rights Organization, and (3) various court decisions which struck down local restrictions upon welfare eligibility (see Brinker and Kloss 1976). There has been a steady decline in the number of welfare recipients per caseload: AFDC recipients per case declined from 3.9 in 1970 to 3.1 in 1980 while general assistance recipients per case declined from 2.9 to 1.2 over the same period. As a consequence of these two offsetting trends, the number of total welfare recipients has grown (albeit erratically) at less than 2 percent per year since 1975 despite the continuing growth in caseloads. This recent stability has been maintained in the face of the slightly declining real value of benefits. AFDC benefits per recipient have grown at about 8.5 percent per year since 1975, about a 0.6 percent annual reduction compared to the Detroit CPI, but very close to the rate of increase of other income sources in Michigan. General assistance benefits have fared worse: although benefits per case have been rising, benefits per recipient have grown at only 4.2 percent per year since 1975. This amounts to a considerable decline in real benefits. Real GA benefits per recipient did not change significantly from 1974 to 1978. The more recent decline may reflect in part program changes initiated in 1979.

Wayne County welfare (AFDC and GA) cases account for approximately half of state totals. Between 1970 and 1980, the Wayne County AFDC caseload grew at 12.0 percent per year while the non-Wayne County caseload grew at 13.2 percent per year. However, during this period, the population of Wayne County has declined while the state as a whole has grown slightly. Hence, the per capita growth rate in AFDC caseloads has been higher in Wayne County, 13.5 percent per year compared to 11.9 percent per year for the remainder of the state.

Provision of social services has also expanded during the decade. Appropriations for children and youth services (including youth institutional services) have grown at 20.6 percent per year over the 1971-81 decade. Appropriations for the operation, administration and field services for adult and family services and income maintenance, taken together, have grown at 14.5 percent per year. Radical changes in the organization of the department make distinguishing the growth rates for field services for income maintenance from those for provision of social services difficult.

Most observers draw a close parallel between unemployment rates and welfare caseloads, and it is not uncommon to encounter a reference to purely cyclical fluctuations in unemployment rates as explanations for changes (usually increases) in the caseload level. This is stimulated partly by the fact that a large portion of new applicants for welfare benefits cite "unemployment" as the basis for their need, and partly by the observation that unemployment rates and welfare caseloads have a strong positive association in state-by-state comparisons. Figure 12.1 depicts the relation between unemployment and AFDC caseloads per capita for all states excluding the South in 1978. The "M" represents Michigan.

Statistical analysis of these data suggest that a state with an unemployment rate one point above average will have an AFDC caseload per capita approximately 15 percent above the average. It is not true, however, that short-run fluctuations in unemployment have an important influence over welfare caseloads. The relation described by Figure 12.1 is much more structural than it is cyclic, and it is quite unresponsive to temporary changes in unemployment levels. Reviewing the data which has accumulated since 1973 (the year in which the rapid expansion in eligibility standards seems to have come to an end), a one point increase in the Michigan unemployment rate adds only 1.8 percent to the total number of recipients. The dependence of general assistance caseloads upon short run changes in unemployment is more definite, and a one point increase in unemployment may produce as much as a 8.7 percent increase in GA caseloads and a 7.6 percent increase in GA recipients per capita. Presumably this result is a reflection of the character of welfare itself. Most studies of AFDC families indicate that as many as 70-80 percent of current AFDC recipients will stay in the program for longer than two years (although there is considerable turnover in the remaining 20-30 percent, see Coe 1981). In effect, these are people who are mainly outside of the labor force and who are therefore relatively unaffected by fluctuations in labor market conditions. On the other side of the coin, those who become unemployed in Michigan are to a great extent protected by relatively generous unemployment benefits provided by the state unemployment compensation program, by

FIGURE 12.1
AFDC CASELOADS PER CAPITA BY STATE VS. UNEMPLOYMENT RATE
(Unemployment lagged two years; excludes Southern states)

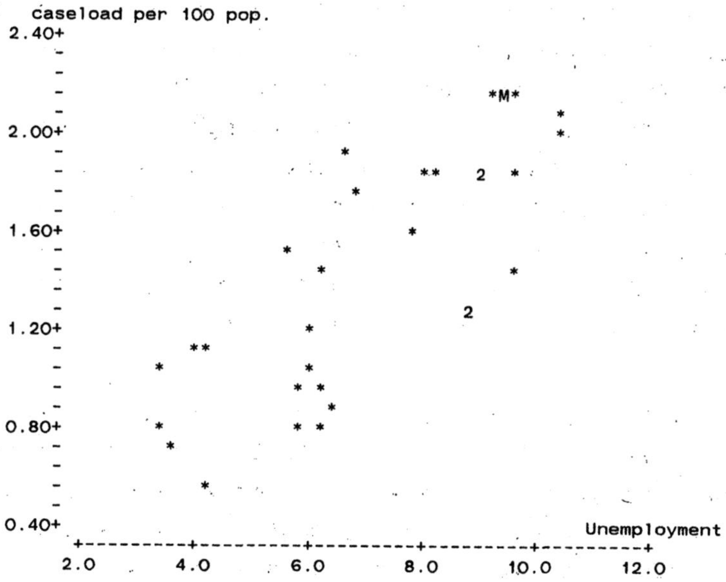

union-negotiated supplemental benefits, and by the federal unemployment and trade adjustment programs. These programs extend over long enough periods to prevent a strong direct short run influence of unemployment on welfare caseloads. There is some suggestion of an influence of short term fluctuations in the unemployment rate over benefit levels, and this might be expected as high unemployment would make it more difficult for welfare recipients to obtain supplemental earnings on their own. This effect is small, however, probably because increases in unemployment also put the state budget under pressure, making it necessary to tighten eligibility rules and limit benefits at the same time.

Michigan is one of the most generous states with respect to welfare benefits. In 1979, an AFDC family of four was eligible for benefits which were third highest in the nation behind Hawaii and Vermont. These benefit levels were 52 percent above the national average, 42 percent above the average for the other Great Lakes states, and 29 percent above the national average if the traditionally lower-paying southern states are excluded. Actual payments per recipient are similarly high; in calendar year 1978, Michigan payments per recipient were 27 percent above the national average excluding the South, and by this measure, Michigan ranked sixth in the nation. This was not always the case; during the mid 1960s, Michigan benefits were only slightly above the national average in actual payments per recipient.

Since the AFDC program in Michigan consumed $449 million of state discretionary dollars in FY 1981, this generosity incurs a substantial cost. Reducing benefits from 1978 levels to those of the other Great Lakes states would reduce costs by $133 million. A reduction to the national average excluding southern states would save $110 million. A recent legislative proposal to reduce AFDC benefits to a level no more than 10 percent above those in neighboring states would reduce costs by about $96 million below those implied by the relative 1978 position of

Michigan benefits. Some of these potential savings have probably already been realized, however. During FY 1981, AFDC benefit standards were reduced, and these cuts, together with inflation, have amounted to a 21 percent real reduction in standards compared to 1978. (This reduction has not been reflected by as large a reduction in actual expenditures, because the needs for assistance have increased at the same time.) Since the inflation has affected all state programs similarly, it is unlikely that Michigan benefits have been reduced so far as to eliminate the benefit differential, but some reduction in this differential may have taken place.

One might go farther than this, suggesting that the generous benefits in Michigan actually induce potential welfare recipients to move into the state (or discourage them from leaving) and at the same time make it easy for some individuals to forego the unpleasantness of an honest day's work, collecting welfare payments instead. In effect, it might be the case that generous welfare programs exacerbate the problem by making a lifestyle of dependency both easy and (relatively) comfortable. This point of view is reinforced by the observation that, for many recipients, total welfare benefits exceed what would be earned for full time work at the minimum wage. According to a Department of Social Services study, in 1975 approximately 50 percent of Michigan AFDC recipients received benefits in excess of the BLS lower consumption budget once all forms of income supplement were taken into account.

It is certainly plausible to expect some relationship to exist between the generosity of a state welfare program and its welfare caseload. In fact, however, no important relationship can be found from available evidence. This is not to say that the dependence does not exist at all, but only that is is not powerful enough to be detectable with the data and statistical methods at hand. It does imply, however, that the dependency-creating potential of high state benefit levels is not large enough to justify any change in our estimates of the savings attributable to a reduction in benefit levels.

It should be borne in mind that welfare benefit levels in Michigan are only a part of the overall wage/income distribution in the state, and that all income levels are relatively high. We have already observed that production workers' incomes in Michigan are 41 percent above the national average, and that civil service salaries are 24 percent above the average as well. This generally high level of wages is a much more significant inducement to migration than welfare benefits alone (or any other single income measure, for that matter), and indeed, Michigan experienced a steady population in-migration throughout the 1950s and 1960s. Under ordinary circumstances, even the influence of extensive union membership in Michigan would have been unable to prevent wage rates from drifting toward the national average in the face of this influx of potential workers. However, until the late 1970s, the state was insulated from traditional competitive economic pressures by the unique features of the automobile industry which dominates the economy. The establishment of competition in this industry is extraordinarily difficult, requiring massive amounts of capital investment, extensive distribution and service systems, and the development of favorable reputations among consumers. For many years, the higher-than-average production wage rates in Michigan were sustainable because the higher automobile costs which they engendered did not induce rapid entry of lower-priced competition. Even the increase in energy prices in 1973 and the consequent shift in preferences away from traditional American automobile models required several years to take effect. By the late 1970s, of course, the competition was in place and Michigan was facing the high unemployment levels which economists would ordinarily have expected to have arisen years earlier. This, however, is simply the culmination of a trend which was in process throughout the decade: the above-average wage/income structure was maintaining the presence of a large potential workforce (either through in-migration or the discouragement of out-migration) without providing the employment opportunities which customarily accompany high wages. The result was a steadily expanding structural unemployment level (growing at about 0.4 percent per year) and a concomitant expansion in welfare caseloads. In effect, it is not high welfare benefit levels which have induced high caseload levels, it is the high wage structure which has produced both the unemployment and the welfare caseloads.

One often encounters statements in the news media questioning the efficiency (and sometimes even the honesty) of the administration of the welfare programs in the Department of Social Services. Unfortunately, there are no data available which are adequate to evaluate this aspect of the department. Existing estimates of the staff which would be necessary to reduce fraudulent welfare claims suggest that the cost would be far greater than the savings to be realized, although these savings themselves may be much smaller than those which would result from the deterrent effect of more intensive review of applications. It is equally difficult to identify the efficiency of welfare case administration. We have determined that in 1981 it cost about twelve cents to distribute one dollar in welfare benefits, but the data are inadequate to afford any meaningful comparisons with earlier years.

EDUCATION

Public School Aid

In simple dollar terms, the most conspicuous losers in the competition for state resources during the last decade have been educational programs. The School Aid Fund which is used to aid local districts in K-12 education has grown at an average rate between 6 and 6.5 percent per year over the last decade--almost 3.5 percent below the rate of personal income growth and 2 percent per year below the inflation rate as measured by the CPI. Over the entire period, this growth differential has cumulated to a substantial sum: if the School Aid Fund were given the same share of discretionary expenditures in 1981 as it received in 1971, the fund would receive $2,449 million--$680 million more than actually budgeted. Higher education has suffered a similar, although less dramatic decline relative to other dimensions of state operations. The average growth in higher education spending has been about 8.5 percent per year over the decade, about equal to the inflation rate as measured by the CPI, but about 1 to 1.5 percent per year lower than the rate of growth of Michigan personal income. If this program were to receive the same share of state expenditures in 1981 as it did in 1971, the budget would be $873 million--$115 million more than actually appropriated.

The relative decline in these expenditure categories is usually justified by making reference to the declining population in school and college age groups. This applies particularly to the case of K-12 education. Enrollments in public schools have been declining over the last half of the decade, and this rate of decline has now reached about -2.5 percent per year. Over the entire decade, the average decline has been about -1.7 percent per year, and as a fraction of total Michigan population, the decline has been -2.1 percent per year. If we take the declining school-age population into account, then a School Aid Fund in FY 1981 which compared in expenditure to its FY 1971 counterpart would receive $2,010 million--$240 million more than was actually appropriated. In order to maintain a stable share of Michigan income on a per-student basis, the School Aid Fund would have had to grow at about 7.8 percent per year instead of the 6 to 6.5 percent which actually occurred. In fact, local support for schools has been growing at almost exactly the indicated rate of 7.8 percent per year, but, together with the state School Aid Fund, this means that school spending has not been maintaining 1971 levels, rising at just under 7 percent per year. It is furthermore the case that the local share of school funding has risen from 54 percent in FY 1970 to 60 percent in FY 1982.

We remarked in the first section on the tendency for state expenditures to become increasingly "targeted" over the decade. That tendency is apparent in the distribution of the School Aid Fund. In the interests of more equitable school financing, the state has employed school aid formulas (the "Bursley" plan) designed to reduce the impact of variations in property tax base per pupil across the state. The effect of this has been to focus the School Aid Fund more narrowly upon districts with lower tax bases (and upon Detroit/Wayne County schools). In fact, these targeted districts have received school aid support per pupil which has kept up with the consumer price index. The "wealthier" districts have absorbed all of the decline in real per capita school aid. Figure 12.2 contains a superposition of two histograms describing the distribution of values of school aid per pupil across the state, one for FY 1972 and the other for FY 1980. Both histograms are presented in 1980 dollars. It is apparent from the figure that most of the reduction in real school aid has been concentrated on relatively few districts.

Higher Education

Although a decline in college age population is anticipated in the future, this reduction has not yet occurred, and over the last decade the pool of potential college students has increased. Estimates of college-age population vary too widely to be reliable, but actual enrollment statistics reflect a growth in student enrollment demand. Over the decade, the total number of full-time equated students enrolled in community colleges and the four-year institutions was rising at 1.7 percent per year, although the underlying rate of increase has been declining slightly in recent years. In this case it would be quite misleading to calculate a 1981 equivalent to 1971 expenditures because the character of higher education in Michigan has changed substantially over the decade. In particular, the increase in college enrollment is concentrated in nonresidential "commuter" situations and in

FIGURE 12.2
HISTOGRAM OF SCHOOL AID PER PUPIL IN MICHIGAN DISTRICTS: 1972 AND 1980
(1980 dollars)

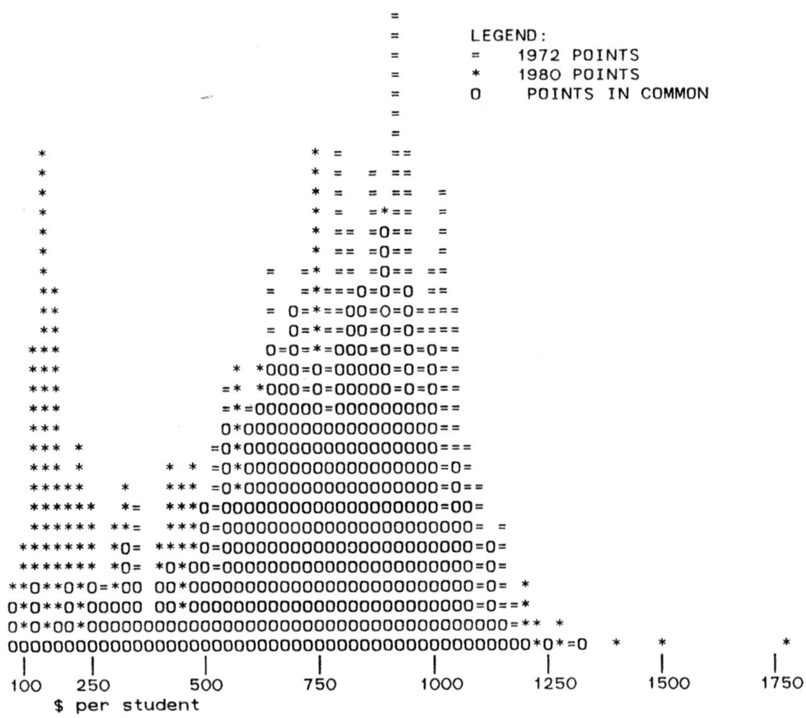

part-time student programs rather than in the more traditional full-time four-year college settings. This is reflected in a 4.3 percent annual growth in community college (full-time equated) enrollments compared to 0.5 percent growth in enrollments in four-year colleges and universities. In both types of institution, moreover, "head counts" have expanded much more rapidly than full-time equivalent enrollments, indicating an expanding role for part-time training.

If we were to take these enrollment changes into account, funding of four-year colleges and universities at the FY 1971 level would require $700 million in FY 1981 compared to the actual appropriation of $590 million. This real reduction in state support per student has been accompanied by a reallocation of resources along the lines already indicated. The increased importance of commuting compared to residential students has been reflected by a redistribution of higher education funds toward smaller regional colleges and away from the large residential centers of education. Those colleges which are more accommodating to part-time enrollments have similarly enjoyed generous appropriations compared to others. Thus the small regional branch campuses of The University of Michigan at Dearborn and Flint, both of which have large part-time student populations, have been receiving fund increases at rates of 14.4 percent and 16.1 percent respectively compared to Ann Arbor campus growth of only 6.7 percent per year. Similarly, Grand Valley State College and Saginaw Valley College have large part-time student enrollments, and have enjoyed funding increases of 13.2 percent and 11.6 percent over the last decade (compared to the average four-year college growth of 8.1 percent). Naturally, overall enrollment statistics parallel these funding changes to some extent, but the relationship is not a particularly close one. The total student load at Grand Valley State College has increased by 32 percent over the decade compared to 51 percent at Saginaw, despite the substantially higher rate of funding increase for Grand

Valley. Funding at Michigan State University has increased at a rate of 7.9 percent per year compared to 6.7 percent at the Ann Arbor campus of The University of Michigan, despite identical enrollment experiences over the decade. Three universities--Wayne State, Eastern, and Western Michigan--have lost enrollment over the decade, but two of these three have nevertheless received appropriations increases at rates exceeding that of The University of Michigan at Ann Arbor, whose enrollment has grown.

The community college system has fared better than the four-year institutions in terms of gross funding. Appropriations have increased at over 10 percent per year over the last decade, making this the only educational category which has kept pace with inflation. However, over this same period, enrollments have been rising at almost 4.4 percent per year, and thus the per-student level of support has actually been growing at just under 6 percent per year. Taking enrollments into account thus transforms the community college system from the best financed part of the system to the worst.

We have already mentioned that fluctuations in the Michigan state economy lead to pressures upon both revenues on the one hand, and the Department of Social Services on the other, and that these pressures are often focused upon particular departments in the state. Higher education is noticeably vulnerable in this respect--typically, a one point increase in the Michigan unemployment rate is translated into a 5 percent lower level of four-year college funding, a 2.5 percent reduction in community college funding, and a 3.7 percent cut in the general School Aid Fund. Ironically, unemployment is also accompanied by an increase in enrollments in institutions of higher learning--about 1.2 percent in the case of four-year colleges, and perhaps 3 percent in the case of community colleges. It is in the nature of educational services that existing facilities and staff can accommodate temporary overloads, but it is not likely that the system can withstand the protracted unemployment over the period 1979-81, together with funding declines, without suffering some long-term damage.

MENTAL HEALTH

At first glance, expansion in the Department of Mental Health over the last decade appears to have been modest compared to the other health and social service units of state government. After accounting for patient fees and federal support, discretionary funds allocated to this department have grown at an average rate of 10.2 percent per year, well below the rates set by other human service departments. Such figures take no account of the substantial decline in mental health caseloads, however, and when these are considered, the impression of moderation in growth is quickly dissipated.

Most striking is the extraordinary decline in patient population in state hospitals which has occurred over the last fifteen to twenty years. Patients in hospitals for the "developmentally disabled" have declined from a high of 12,516 in FY 1965 to an anticipated 3,065 in FY 1982--a decline of about 8 percent per year--while patients in state psychiatric hospitals have declined from a high of 19,059 in FY 1960 to an anticipated 3,787 in FY 1982--a decline of over 7 percent per year. Three facts are usually given prominence in explanations for these declines: First, new drug treatments have been introduced which have reduced the necessity for hospitalization of the mentally ill. Second, the expansion of federal and state programs for medical care for the aged and for the indigent made it possible for elderly patients in state institutions to be transferred to nursing homes supported, at least in part, by the Department of Social Services. Some of the expansion in the latter department during the early 1970s therefore was actually a transfer of responsibility from the Department of Mental Health. Third, at least since 1973, the department, in common with its counterparts in many other states, has espoused a policy of "de-institutionalization": removing patients from hospitals in order to place them in community-based residential settings. Indeed, the decline in patient population has been accompanied by a very large expansion in support for residential programs (about 22.5 percent per year), and these have grown from 12.3 percent of the total mental health program in FY 1971 to 33.8 percent in FY 1981.

In spite of these very substantial declines in inpatient loads, staff levels in the hospitals have shown no inclination to follow suit: indeed, until the budget crisis of FY 1980, there were 74 percent more employees in centers for the developmentally disabled than there were in 1965, even though the patient load had fallen by 59 percent over the period. In 1979, staff levels in psychiatric hospitals were 40 percent above their 1960 level even though patient loads were reduced by almost three-quarters. Some increase in staff/patient ratios was to be expected. The patients who are discharged are naturally the easiest ones to care for, and after such a large decline in patient loads, only those requiring great amounts of attention have remained. Moreover, the now-discharged patients may have provided some domestic service to institutions and to other patients, and these now must be provided by paid staff. Finally, there may have been some improvement in the quality of service over this fifteen to twenty year period. Nevertheless, it is unlikely that these facts can account for staff/patient ratios of 1.6 to 1.7 in 1979 when they were only 0.3 to 0.35 in 1960. This fact was not lost on the state when the budget pressures of 1981 arose, and contraction in state spending fell heavily in this area. So far, the department has laid off over 3,500 employees, most of whom were state hospital employees, and projections for 1982 suggest the elimination of at least 2,000 more. A total hospital employee force of 16,378 in 1978 is projected at only 8,808 in 1982--a reduction of 46 percent.

The dollar implications of these staff/patient ratios are substantial. If the intermediate FY 1971 ratios (of

0.58 in hospitals for the developmentally disabled and 0.7 for the mentally ill) had been in effect in FY 1981, the total mental health budget would have been $172 million smaller--nearly 31 percent of the entire department budget for that year. Even if all of the proposed layoffs are put into effect, a restoration of FY 1971 staffing ratios would reduce the proposed FY 1982 budget by an additional 24 percent.

One naturally is led to wonder how it was that such an apparent surplus of employees could have been permitted to accumulate in the first place. In part, this is probably a consequence of a natural resistance to contraction in one branch of a department when it is other branches (in this case, community mental health services) which are taking on increased responsibility. Moreover, staffing has been strongly influenced by the California-based "Staff Needs Assessment Program"--a set of "needs" definitions which are noticeably sensitive neither to costs nor to any objective measure of treatment effectiveness. However, it is also possible that the organization of this department is not structured in a way which would be conducive to the rigorous treatment of questions of cost-effectiveness in service delivery. It has not been possible in this study to engage in an extensive analysis of the administration of any department, but in the case of mental health, there are several indications that such an analysis might be in order. Besides the hospital staffing questions, we note that:

* Per patient operating costs at various regional state hospitals are extremely variable. In the case of psychiatric hospitals, they range from a low of $27,414 per patient-year at Ypsilanti Regional Psychiatric Hospital to a high of $61,057 per patient-year at the Detroit Psychiatric Institute, staff/patient ratios ranged from a low of 1.06 to a high of 1.86. Centers for the developmentally disabled display similar variability, with staff/patient ratios ranging from 0.98 to 1.33. (The variation was reduced from FY 1980 when the ratios ranged from 1.09 to 1.78.) Since units in unique circumstances or with special functions such as research or day-treatment as well as children's facilities (which are considerably more expensive) were excluded from these comparisons, we have been able to

uncover no adequate explanation for the extreme variability in patient costs which is observed.

* Administrative and executive overhead in the Department of Mental Health has grown at a rate of 36.3 percent per year over the last decade, far higher than that of any other department. Administrative costs increased from less than 1 percent of the department budget in FY 1971 to more than 7.4 percent in FY 1981. This expansion persisted even in the face of the budget pressures of FY 1980 and FY 1981. While the mental health service units were laying off 3,700 employees, the executive branch added 695. This executive expansion was probably associated with the residential service programs which were being expanded as alternatives to the hospitals, but it is unreasonable that the 54 percent increase in employees which took place in these programs should necessitate a 76 percent increase at the executive level.

* The Department of Mental Health seems to have been the target of more than an average amount of unfavorable publicity. Charges of nepotism, lawsuits directed at state institutions, neighborhood confrontations over residential facilities, and charges of fraud and corruption in the leasing of residential facilities have been common during the early 1980s. Many of these problems may be inherent in any mental health care delivery system, but not all of them are, and there may be a need to tighten the system to prevent these difficulties from getting out of hand.

We have noted that the decline in patients in state hospitals is due largely to a policy of de-institutionalization which has been in place for several years. This policy has costs which should be given more attention, not only in their own right, but because they point to a type of problem which may arise in the case of any contraction of public services at the state level. The problem is that state cutbacks of any sort are usually translated into increased costs at the local level. When mental patients are removed from hospitals and placed in residential facilities, some degree of control is lost, and the patients may become an irritant to the community--by frightening some, by offending others, or occasionally even by endangering local residents. Moreover, patients in some "halfway" facilities may simply walk out--placing the burden of their care upon family or acquaintances. No data are available concerning the status of the thousands of patients who by the standards of 1960 would be in hospitals, but by the standards of 1980 are not. They are certainly not all in residential mental health facilities or even in nursing homes, and while many of those not accounted for may in fact not be ill at all (subject perhaps to regular drug treatments), others may be imposing the responsibility for their care upon friends and relatives, whereas formerly that would have been the responsibility of the state.

State cutbacks in this form also impose financial burdens upon certain unlucky individuals. One of the attractions of residential settings is that they are believed to be much cheaper (although in fact the data are not sufficient to determine whether this is really the case). On the other hand, the acquisition of such "halfway-houses" for the developmentally disabled or the mentally ill frequently encounters virulent opposition from potential neighbors who fear inconvenience, unpleasantness, and most of all a loss of property values. Usually, these objections are not taken especially seriously by department officials who see the facilities as "good" for the patients, and who regard the opposition as the manifestation of prejudice and antagonism toward people with mental health problems. The loss of property value may nevertheless be real, and a direct financial loss has thereby been imposed on the neighbors. In a fairly subtle way, the state has saved money by imposing other costs upon certain of its citizens.

Savings calculated solely on the basis of cuts in mental health services will overestimate the benefits of any de-institutionalization program. This is the case partly because of the impacts upon local communities, but also because many services offered by the Department of Social Services (particularly juvenile services) are indistinguishable from those offered in the Department of Mental Health, and a cut in one area only increases the demand for services (and funding needs) in the other. Although the data are too sketchy to enable us to make good estimates of the magnitude, there is some evidence of a linkage between the Departments of Mental Health and Corrections as well.

The 1974 Michigan Mental Health Code enables the formation of a new form of mental health organization called the "contract" community mental health board. Existing community boards can be reorganized to provide care for all patients from their areas, using state facilities when necessary, but always at their own expense. Increased funding is provided to match the expenses of community patients currently residing in the state hospital system. It is anticipated that such boards will make less use of state hospitals because it will no longer be possible to shift the burden of care of certain patients on to the state by placing them "for free" in the state system. At the same time, the smaller, more community-oriented organizations might provide more efficient service. From the community point of view, they would certainly be able to handle the "halfway house" problems more effectively than the state has been able to. A further incidental advantage is that these boards exploit a loophole in the Headlee Amendment. By transferring the funds for state hospitals to local boards, the state increases the local expenditure which qualifies for the 41.6 percent requirement. Of course, the local boards could eventually come to spend the money elsewhere (indeed, it is hoped that they will), but so long as the hospitals do realize the savings from further decreases in patient loads by reducing staff and overhead, such a redirection amounts only to an improvement in service.

So far, five of these boards have been established on an experimental basis, and it is still too early for any review of their effectiveness. From the standpoint of economic efficiency, it is clear that the contract board provides a very promising model for future development. There are still problems to be faced, however. First, it is by no means certain that all of the existing community boards have managerial staff capable of handling increased decision-making responsibility, and it may prove to be necessary to acquire professional managers if the program is to be expanded any further. Second, the state is in effect giving up control in exchange for efficiency, and contract boards may adopt policies which are contrary to the preferences of the Department of Mental Health at the state level. There already are proposals to constrain the behavior of local contract boards to conform to a menu of state "mandates," and to the extent that such proposals are adopted, the effectiveness of the contract board may be destroyed. Third, so long as local units are required to turn over to the state a portion of third party payments and other user fees, incentives for revenue generation will remain weak. Finally, decentralization as embodied in the contract system is unlikely to afford similar treatment to similar patients in different districts. Thus a certain measure of equity may be sacrificed as the state moves in this direction.

CORRECTIONS

As a fraction of total Michigan state expenditures, the Department of Corrections is not particularly prominent. The FY 1981 budget for corrections is $190 million, and this represents only 3.1 percent of total state discretionary funds. The rate of growth of this department is the highest of any in the state, however, and the problems faced in this area are often considered to be symptomatic of the problems in the state as a whole.

Most states in the nation have experienced an increased pressure on correctional facilities over the last decade, but the experience in Michigan has been exceptional. In 1968 there were 7,548 male prisoners in the Michigan correctional system. By 1978, that figure had nearly doubled to 14,273. This represents a growth rate of about 6.5 percent per year, over 6 percent above what would be expected from population growth alone. Total state expenditures on correctional facilities have grown at about 13.5 percent per year. (Nationally, expenditures on correctional facilities have grown at 11.5 percent, and in the other Great Lakes states, expenditures have grown at only 8.2 percent.) New (male) commitments in Michigan have expanded similarly, from 3,194 in 1968 to 6,230 in 1978, an average growth of 6.9 percent per year. Michigan also has a greater than average number of prisoners. In 1978, the total population in both federal and state systems together was 162 per 100,000 population compared to a national average of 141 prisoners per 100,000 (although this is one area in which the southern states, with 186 prisoners per 100,000, clearly surpass the North).

These inmate population growth rates actually understate the severity of the problem because they do not reflect the change in composition of the prison population. In 1974, 5.6 percent of new commitments represented individuals with sentences longer than eleven years, but by 1979, 7.1 percent of new sentences were for more than eleven years. Average minimum sentence length (excluding life sentences) has risen from 3.13 years in 1974 to 3.46 years in 1978, and the fraction of life sentences has risen from 2.78 percent to 3.18 percent. A doubling of new commitments in conjunction with an increase in average sentence length implies the need for more than a doubling of capacity--the figures listed above suggest that a doubling of commitments would require a steady-state increase in capacity by a factor of 2.2. In fact, sentence lengths stand to increase even more than this: in 1978, the voters of Michigan approved a constitutional amendment eliminating "time off" for good behavior for certain crimes, and it is estimated that this will increase the effective sentence length of 66 percent of the inmates now entering the system.

It is possible that the increasing burden of the prison population is a reflection of some tendency on the part of the judiciary to impose longer sentences, but it is equally plausible that the pressures on the correctional system have been inducing judges to be more moderate in their sentencing behavior because there is so little room for the increased number of inmates that harsher procedures would entail. Moreover, there is a great deal of supporting evidence that the crime rate in Michigan has grown as fast as the inmate population. The judicial system in Michigan has been growing as fast as the Department of Corrections, suggesting that there are many more individuals being brought before courts. Employment levels in "criminal justice activity" (police protection, legal services, public defense, etc.) have been growing at 7.6 percent annually in Michigan compared to the national average of 6 percent (and 4.4 percent in the other Great Lakes states), while dollar expenditures on payroll, by far the largest cost component of total expenditures have been expanding at 14.1 percent in Michigan. Even more disturbing is the increased demand for youth services in the Department of Social Services. The growing need for foster care, services for abused children, and care and control of delinquent children has produced an expansion of 21 percent per year in these offices of the Department of Social Services since 1971. This fact suggests further that the problem of corrections in Michigan is not a temporary one, and that the pressures on prison facilities will continue when today's children become adults.

The cost of operating Michigan correctional facilities has been growing at about 17.5 percent per year since 1971. This growth is accounted for by three factors: (1) the annual increase in prisoners, (2) the (civil service) salary increments of correctional employees, and (3) an increase in the number of employees per inmate in the system. While the prison population was growing at 6.5 percent per year, the number of (full time equivalent) employees in prisons was growing at 7.9 percent per year, and the administrative overhead was growing at 21.1 percent per year. This disproportionate increase may be due in part to increasing difficulty of administrating a system with increasingly violent inmates, but the primary cause seems to be the increasing emphasis being placed upon smaller facilities. Attempts have been made throughout the decade to place the prison population away from the large institutions at Jackson and Ionia. It is believed that the smaller facilities are more manageable, can be more readily tailored to the characteristics of different types of prisoners, and are more effective in achieving rehabilitation. Unfortunately, they are also more expensive. Review of facilities suggests that for every 10 percent increase in capacity, the ratio of employees to inmates declines by 2.5 percent: Marquette prison, for example, with 1,000 inmates has .37 FTE employees per rated inmate capacity compared to .23 at Jackson, with a population of about 5,200, while the Dunes facility with a population of only 328 has an FTE/ inmate ratio of .52. Costs per inmate reflect this variation, ranging from a low of $7,184 at Jackson to a high of $15,088 at the Dunes facility. Naturally, a move to smaller prisons such as the proposed "regional" plan (Public Act 485) could lead to a substantial increase in per inmate operating costs over and above the sizeable capital outlays needed in the first place.

Wages paid by the Michigan Department of Corrections reflect the general level of civil service salaries in the state. In 1977, the monthly payroll in Michigan was $1,550 per FTE corrections employee, whereas it was $1,120 in the United States as a whole and $1,185 in the other Great Lakes states. As in many other departments, administrative overhead has grown disproportionately rapidly. The (very small) executive office has expanded from .09 to .25 percent of its share of discretionary funds over the FY 1971-FY 1981 period. As was the case in many other departments as well, the budget contraction of the last two years produced a relatively large contraction in administrative overhead (almost -15 percent per year), while the rest of the department continued to expand.

BUDGET CHANGES AND FORECASTS

It would be extremely foolish to imagine that the trends outlined above will continue for the next decade.

There are already many indications that economic priorities within the state are changing. The political support for social services is showing signs of eroding, and expansions along the lines of the last decade are therefore unlikely. The patient populations of state mental hospitals have been reduced to only the most seriously ill. The department may persist in its de-institutionalization policy, but the social costs of this program are increasing, and it is likely that local communities will eventually force the policy to come to an end. Perhaps most important, economic conditions within the state are changing. The unemployment and industrial problems which are presently so painful may have the effect finally of bringing the incomes structure in Michigan more in line with that in the rest of the country. In the long run, this is the best solution to the welfare problem on the one hand, and the high civil service costs on the other.

There are a few aspects of Michigan state operations which are difficult to review. These are expenditures of questionable merit from a cost-effectiveness point of view, but which are regarded as politically very sensitive. Examples are the (trivial) subsidy for the Pontiac Silverdome, the (less trivial) state support for the Department of Military Affairs (whose annual reports reveal no accomplishments whatsoever), and the $25 million subsidy for private colleges and universities (which takes the form of a tuition credit and simply duplicates existing state support for higher education). These expenditures (some $32 million of state discretionary dollars) have survived despite the lack of any objective justification, and it is unlikely that budget cuts at the state level would have a significant impact upon them, however desirable that may be.

The futures of corrections and higher education are more problematic. The juvenile caseloads now faced by the Department of Social Services can only engender a gloomy forecast of the future for the Department of Corrections, and the population pressures on correctional facilities are showing no signs of subsiding. The future funding of higher education will depend simply upon the preferences of the state as a whole. Student enrollment pressures may continue, but they will not do so for much longer unless there is an expansion in the desire of Michigan citizens to acquire additional education. In fact, some such expansion is likely. The growing awareness that neither the state nor its citizens can rely upon the automobile industry for income or employment is stimulating a general search for alternatives. Educational institutions (particularly the four-year institutions) are central to such a search, and there are already indications that state priorities are moving back in this direction.

Throughout our discussion, we have noted dollar savings which might plausibly accrue were Michigan to imitate the operations of some other states. The question naturally arises as to whether these particular reductions would occur were the state to be subjected to further budget cuts. The experience of FY 1980 and FY 1981 provides some evidence on this matter. We note that during this period:

* Both AFDC and general assistance benefit levels were reduced somewhat.

* Staff levels in the state hospitals were reduced dramatically.

* Executive branches of state government were cut proportionately more than were the operating branches.

* Civil service salaries were reduced through the imposition of "unpaid holidays," and unclassified employees absorbed small salary cuts.

All of these events suggest that expenditure reductions might take place along the lines noted in earlier sections. On the other hand:

* Higher education appropriations were also cut, putting some higher education institutions under severe pressure.

* Other departments, such as natural resources, state police, public health, and education (at all levels) were severely cut, despite the absence of any

indication of surplus in their operations.

* User fees were increased sharply--many such fees were given their first serious review in years--indicating that one consequence of further budget cuts would be an increase in such fees.

* The reductions in civil service salaries were only temporary, and there was no indication of even a slight long-term reduction.

These facts suggest that state revenue contraction might not entirely take the directions which we have indicated but would spread as well over state departments which have already lost a substantial relative share of government resources over the decade. Of course, these were only short-run responses, and over a longer term, the actual budget might not follow these lines at all. Nevertheless, it is clear that there is a tendency to accommodate budget reductions by cutting across the board, and that further reductions would lead (at least initially) to cutbacks in all services, and not in any particularly targeted programs.

NOTE, CHAPTER 12

[1]This chapter excludes the detailed statistical material upon which the conclusions are based. The entire report, including statistical appendix, may be obtained from John G. Cross, Department of Economics, University of Michigan, Ann Arbor, MI 48109.

REFERENCES, CHAPTER 12

Brinker, Paul A. and Klos, Joseph J. _Poverty, Manpower, and Social Security_. Austin Press, 1976.

Citizens Research Council of Michigan. _Council Comments_. Nos. 899, 900, 901, 902, 905, 917, 918, 919, 922.

Coe, Richard D. "A Preliminary Empirical Examination of the Dynamics of Welfare Use." In vol. 9 of _Five Thousand American Families_. Ann Arbor: Institute for Social Research, University of Michigan, 1981.

Coe, Richard. "Dependency and Poverty in the Short and Long Run." In vol. 4 of Five Thousand American Families. Ann Arbor: Institute for Social Research, University of Michigan, 1981.

Cohen, Wilbur J. Health, Education, and Welfare: Accomplishments 1963-1968, Problems and Challenges, and Look to the Future. A report to Lyndon B. Johnson. Department of Health, Education, and Welfare.

Courant, Paul N.; Gramlich, Edward M.; and Rubinfeld, Daniel L. "Why Voters Support Tax Limitation Amendments: The Michigan Case." National Tax Journal, March 1980.

Gongwar News Service, Inc. Gongwar Michigan Report, January 1, 1980 through May 19, 1981.

Johnson, George. Effective Wage Index by States.

Matthews, Lois. "What Happens to Human Services During a Recession? A Case Study of Michigan." New England Journal of Human Services, October 1980.

Michigan Efficiency Task Force. Summary Findings and Recommendations of the Michigan Efficiency Task Force - 1976.

Michigan Efficiency Task Force Implementation Progress Report: A Second and Final Summary of Accomplishments - April 1979.

Michigan State University, Graduate School of Business Administration. Michigan Statistical Abstract, 1979.

Michigan Welfare Study Commission. Report of the Michigan Welfare Study Commission. February 1971.

O'Donnell, Peter S. Social Services: Three Years After Title XX. Washington, D.C.: National Governors' Association Center for Policy Research, 1978.

Platky, Leon D. "Aid to Families with Dependent Children. An Overview, October 1977." Social Security Bulletin, vol. 40, no. 10, October 1977.

Social Security Bulletin. July 1978, vol. 41, no. 7 through June 1979, vol. 42, no. 6.

Social Security Bulletin, Annual Statistical Supplement, 1977-79.

State of Michigan. Budget Message of the Governor, FY 1971, FY 1972, FY 1973, FY 1974, FY 1975, FY 1976, FY 1977, FY 1978, FY 1979, FY 1980, FY 1981, FY 1982.

State of Michigan. Constitution of 1963.

State of Michigan. Detail of Current Operations of the Executive Budget, FY 1972.

State of Michigan. Detail of State Operations and Local Benefit Budget, FY 1966, FY 1967, FY 1968, FY 1969, FY 1970.

State of Michigan. Detail of the Executive Budget, FY 1973.

State of Michigan. Economic Report of the Governor, FY 1971, FY 1972, FY 1974, FY 1975, FY 1979, FY 1980.

State of Michigan. Executive Budget, FY 1974, FY 1975, FY 1976, FY 1977, FY 1978, FY 1979, FY 1980, FY 1981, FY 1982.

State of Michigan. Public Acts, sessions 1970-1981

State of Michigan, Department of Commerce. General Fund: Estimate of Revenue and Expenditure to 1975. Technical Report no. 11, March 1967.

State of Michigan, Department of Corrections. 1978 Statistical Presentation.

State of Michigan, Department of Education. 1979-80 Fact Book on Higher Education in Michigan.

State of Michigan, Department of Education. Ranking of Michigan Public High School Districts by Selected Financial Data, Bulletin 1012. FY 1972, FY 1980.

State of Michigan, Department of Management and Budget. Michigan Manual, 1980.

State of Michigan, Department of Management and Budget, Bureau of the Budget, Planning and Policy Analysis Division. Population Projections of the Counties of Michigan. Revised October 1974.

State of Michigan, Department of Mental Health. Fiscal Year Update 1980-81 to the 1976 Michigan State Plan for Comprehensive Mental Health Services.

State of Michigan, Department of Social Services. Monthly Trend Report of Key DSS Statistics, March 1981.

State of Michigan, Department of Social Services. Profile of Michigan ADC Caseload. Research paper no. 1, October 1969.

State of Michigan, Department of Social Services. Public Assistance Statistics Monthly, July 1969-June 1971, October 1979-September 1980.

State of Michigan, Department of Social Services. Seventeenth Biennial Report, Fiscal Years 1971-1972.

State of Michigan, Department of Social Services. Sixteenth Biennial Report, Fiscal Years 1973-1974. Financial Report, FY 1978, FY 1979.

State of Michigan, Department of Treasury. Annual Report, FY 1973, FY 1979.

State of Michigan, Office of the Governor. Into the 80's: 80 Recommendations. "The Final Report of the Governor's Committee on the Unification of the Public Mental Health System."

State of Michigan, Senate Fiscal Agency. "An Analysis of Proposal A." Prepared by Theodore A. Ferris, April 29, 1981.

State of Michigan, Senate Fiscal Agency. Statistical Report, 1971, 1971, 1974, 1975, 1978, 1980.

U.S., Department of Commerce, Bureau of Economic Analysis. Newsletter, table 3: Total Personal Income by States and Regions; table 4: Population by States and Regions, selected years 1969-1979.

U.S., Department of Commerce, Bureau of the Census. Census of Population and Housing Advance Reports, PHC80-V-24.

U.S., Department of Commerce, Bureau of the Census. Estimates of Population of Countries and Metropolitan Areas, July 1, 1976 and 1977, series P-25, no. 810; July 1, 1977 and 1978, series P-25, no. 873.

U.S., Department of Commerce, Bureau of the Census. General Population Characteristics, Michigan, PC(1)B24, 1970.

U.S., Department of Commerce, Bureau of the Census. Public Employment in 1979. Series GE79, no. 1.

U.S., Department of Commerce, Bureau of the Census. Statistical Abstract of the United States, 1979-1980.

U.S., Department of Health, Education and Welfare. Public Assistance Programs: Standards for Basic Needs, July 1973. DHEW publication no. (SRS) 74-03200; July 1974. DHEW publication no. (SRS) 75-03200.

U.S., Department of Health, Education and Welfare. State Data and State Rankings in Health, Education, Welfare, Part 2 of Health, Education and Welfare Trends, 1964 and 1965 Editions.

U.S., Department of Justice. Bureau of Justice Statistics. _Sourcebook of Criminal Justice Statistics - 1980_. Washington, D.C.: U.S. Printing Office.

U.S., Department of Justice. _Trends in Expenditure and Employment Data for the Criminal Justice System - 1978_. Law Enforcement Assistance Administration and U.S. Bureau of the Census.

University of Michigan. _An Analysis of Salaries Paid to the Instructional Staff_, 1980-1981.

University of Michigan RSQE Forecasting Service. "March Update of the 1981-81 Forecast Supplement: The State of Michigan; Economy," April 6, 1981.

Westendorp, Floyd and Brink, Kirk L. "A Comparison of Six Adolescent Treatment Settings." College of Human Medicine, Michigan State University, 1980.

Chapter 13

State-Local Fiscal Relations: Counties, Cities, Villages, and Townships

by

Gary L. Wolfram

The University of Michigan - Dearborn

This chapter[1] describes and analyzes Michigan's program of aid to counties, cities, villages, and townships. The first section provides a general discussion of the theory of intergovernmental grants. The second section describes the state's system of aid, with special attention to revenue sharing. The third section traces some historical trends in intergovernmental transfers and comments briefly on the success of Michigan's program in achieving its objectives. A summary comprises the fourth section.

THEORY OF INTERGOVERNMENTAL GRANTS

One can identify four general purposes for state aid. First, the state may wish to stimulate activities in which there is state-wide or regional interest. Second, it may wish to equalize the fiscal capacity of units of government throughout the state. Third, there may be some economies of scale in the collection of certain taxes which make it cheaper and more efficient for the state to collect the funds and return them to local jurisdictions. Fourth, many states wish to reduce reliance on the property tax.[2]

Benefit Spillovers

Grants from the state to local units of government may be justified when the activities of one locality affect another and no compensation between the local units occurs. When the residents of one jurisdiction benefit from the program of another we have what are known as "benefit spillovers." For example, the City of Livonia might build a park and find it difficult or impossible to prevent residents of Westland from using it free of charge. In such a case, economic inefficiencies and inequities arise. The residents of the jurisdiction which provides the program will not take into account the additional benefits provided to citizens who live outside its boundaries. Not enough resources will go into activities which provide these spillovers. At the same time, people living in the second jurisdiction benefit from services for which they do not pay.

The state may attempt to stimulate those activities which produce benefit spillovers in either of two ways. It may stimulate expenditures indirectly by altering jurisdictional boundaries so that everyone who benefits from locally provided services is included in the decisionmaking and tax-paying group; or it may act more directly by providing a share of the revenue used to fund the service. The former technique would, theoretically, require a structure of government in which the jurisdiction that determined the level of provision of each public good included exactly the set of individuals who consumed the good. Although regional park, sewer, and water pollution districts are representative of this technique, in most cases this method is administratively and politically costly or impossible. Thus, intergovernmental grants are frequently used to induce local units to spend more on those activities which provide benefit spillovers.

Grants for this purpose should be designed so that the grantor's share of the total cost of providing the service is set equal to the outsider's share of the program benefits. The result will be as if the providing jurisdiction received payments from the outside individuals who benefit from the program, and the activity will be expanded until the extra benefits to all persons exactly equals the cost of the expansion.

Intergovernmental grants which are designed to correct for benefit spillovers should be open-ended; there should be no arbitrary limit at which the grantor government cuts off funds to the grantee government. As long as additional units of the service provide benefits to nonresidents, state aid should be forthcoming. Obviously, open-ended grants render the grantor government's budget not fully controllable. For this reason, few grant programs in the U.S. are of this type.[3]

Another problem lies in estimating the volume and value of benefit spillovers. Determination of this value is quite difficult, as problems arise in pricing and measuring output for local services. Thus, the matching rate actually used by the state is more likely to be determined through the political process than through some explicit estimation of the value of benefit spillovers. It is, therefore, not surprising that matching grants of any kind by state governments, except in the field of education, are rare.

<u>Other Justifications for Grants</u>

A second justification for grants from higher to lower levels of government is to equalize the fiscal capacity of various units of local government. It seems unfair to many people that some local governments are able to provide a high level of public service with a relatively low tax effort, while other local governments are only able to supply low levels of these services, even with high tax effort. But one may ask if there is any difference between the ability of individuals in one community to provide themselves with fire protection and the ability of poor individuals to provide themselves with food. Why should revenues be transferred to the governments where the poor live, in the former case, and directly to the individuals in the latter? One may argue that a federal income redistribution program combined with an emphasis on local tax collections on a benefit-received basis would be a better policy.

In the absence of fiscal-capacity equalizing grants a market reaction to fiscal disparities among local communities will occur. Those communities that have high quality services and low tax rates will attract new residents who will bid up land and housing prices. Communities with low levels of services or relatively high tax rates will lose residents, and land and housing prices will decline. Attempts by higher levels of government to equalize fiscal capacity upsets this market mechanism and encourages inefficient provision of local government services. In such a situation, grants encourage resources, including labor, to remain in areas where they are less productively employed than they could be elsewhere, and also attract resources to areas where they are less efficiently used.

These arguments rely crucially on the assumption that resources, especially labor, are highly mobile. In fact, certain subgroups of the population find themselves unable to move. Low income families, for example, are typically perceived as being less mobile than others. In addition, zoning laws and other market imperfections prevent real estate markets from fully capitalizing all differences in tax/service bundles of local governments. Thus, an argument may still be made for intergovernmental transfers to those areas which have a high concentration of low income and relatively immobile persons, and which are surrounded by exclusive communities with relatively high-income populations. However, the transfers would provide benefits to all members of the receiving community and not just to the low income persons in the community.

Despite these reservations, the state may wish to reduce disparities in the fiscal capacity of its local units, on the ground that this is the most practical way to reduce inequalities in the consumption of public goods. This may be accomplished by a grant program wherein transfers to the local units are based on some combination of measures of fiscal capacity, tax-effort, and need. There have been a number of suggestions as to how one might arrive at these measures. Problems arise from the necessity of distinguishing between communities which truly have low fiscal capacity and high needs, and those which merely appear to have these characteristics, due to poor local government performance. For example, a community may pay its public employees unnecessarily high wages and salaries or be very inefficient in providing services. An aid program which rewards communities for high tax effort or high expenditure levels may encourage such inefficient behavior.

A third justification for intergovernmental transfers is based on the proposition that while there are economies of scale in the collection of taxes,[4] expenditure decisions are best made at lower levels of government, where the consuming groups are more homogeneous and better able to convey their preferences to the decisionmakers. This justification gives rise to revenue sharing programs. But this form of state-local transfer may be thought to conflict with the second goal of state aid, equalization of fiscal capacity. If shared taxes, such as sales or income taxes, are returned to the district of origin, the richer districts will receive more of the transferred revenue than the poorer districts. This need not, of course, be the case; distribution formulae may be so devised as to be either neutral towards or to favor poor districts.

The fourth goal of state aid is to reduce reliance on the property tax. Any number of grant programs can reduce reliance on the property tax by increasing the revenue of local units. Another alternative is to expand the range of taxes available to local units. Evidence of this strategy in Michigan is the Uniform City Income Tax of 1964 and the recent legislation which raised the limits on Detroit's income tax on both residents and commuters.

Having briefly outlined some of the primary theoretical justifications for the use of intergovernmental grants, and some of the problems involved in putting the theory into practice, we now examine the current system of intergovernmental transfers in Michigan.

MICHIGAN'S SYSTEM OF STATE AID TO COUNTIES, CITIES, VILLAGES, AND TOWNSHIPS

The dependence of local units on the state for revenue is a function, among other things, of the taxing authority granted these units by the State of Michigan. Michigan has long had a strong tradition of local autonomy. This tradition was officially recognized in the Michigan Constitution of 1908, which gave a mandate to the legislature to pass a law which would give cities and villages considerable power over their own affairs. At the same time, however, the constitution sought to impose reasonable limits on the taxing power of municipalities. The legislature fulfilled both of these requirements with passage of the Home Rule City Act of 1909.[5] Today there are nine taxes available to local governments but only the general property, city income, city utility use, and industrial facility use taxes yield a significant amount of revenue. Use of all these taxes is limited in one way or another by state law, usually through maximum rate provisions which can be lifted by approval of the legislature and/or the local electorate. Against the background of this brief summary of the revenue raising powers of municipalities, townships, and counties we now turn to the state's aid programs.

<u>Categorical Grants</u>

The major categorical grants to local units are for education,[6] highways, and mental health. Of immediate interest here is the fact that of the balance in the Michigan Transportation Fund (MTF) after the costs of administration and special grants are met, 34.3 percent is allocated to county road commissions and 19.0 percent to cities and villages. These local units will receive $402.8 million for transportation expenditures through this program in fiscal year 1981.

The mental health program is financed through the General Fund of the state. The state finances fifty-five community health boards serving eighty-two of the state's eighty-three counties on a matching grant basis. Ninety cents of every dollar of expenditure of the health boards is provided by the state. Appropriations for this part of the program for fiscal year 1981 are $113.1 million. An additional $171.4 million has been appropriated to finance the shift of inpatient care and alternative programs from the state to the counties, as called for by Section 116 of the Mental Health Code, Public Act 258 of 1974. These funds are also allocated on a 90:10 matching basis.

Additional transfers to counties for mental health care include $27.8 million to finance community placement services, and $7.5 million for pilot contract mental health boards. The addition of smaller programs make total transfers from the Department of Mental Health to local units $324.4 million in fiscal year 1981.

Appropriations for miscellaneous grants falling in the "Grants and Debt Service" budgetary category in fiscal year 1981 range from $400 to the City of Detroit for a soldiers' monument to $35.6 million for a Grants to Cities program. The latter is actually a set of grants primarily to the City of Detroit. The large items are $10.5 million for the Art Institute, $9.2 million for Detroit's Department of Transportation, $7.0 million for the Detroit Public Library, and $6.9 million of state aid to counties, cities, and townships for library services. The latter grant is for head librarians' salaries and per capita grants to units raising required local revenue. Each of these grants is program specific, generally nonmatching, and must be reviewed each year.

Several departments within the state government administer categorical grants to local units. For example, the Department of Management and Budget will provide $6.4 million to counties in fiscal year 1981 for secondary road patrol, the judiciary will transfer $3.5 million to counties as a partial reimbursement for judges' salaries, and the Department of Commerce will distribute $5.0 million to municipalities and townships for liquor law enforcement based on a percentage of license revenue collected in their jurisdiction. Many of the grants from the departments finance locally administered services which would otherwise have to have been provided by the state. Except for 50 percent state funding of the Child Care Fund through the Department of Social Services, they are generally nonmatching and are program specific.

In fiscal year 1981, $1.477 billion was appropriated for state payments to nonschool-district local units. Of this appropriation, about $315 million could be classified as matching categorical grants, and about $573 million as nonmatching categorical grants. The rest, $589 million, is either revenue sharing or grants to local units in lieu of tax revenues lost because of state legislative action.

A distinguishing feature of the categorical grant program is its general failure to fit the criteria set out in the first section of this chapter. Categorical grants are justified on the basis of benefit spillovers. But, for example, it seems unlikely that 90 percent of benefits provided by a community's mental health program accrue to persons outside its jurisdiction.

Nearly all other grants to counties, municipalities, and townships have no matching provision; in theory, this implies that there is a large statewide benefit for a specified local program and no benefits to any enlargement of it beyond the amount of the grant. The system of categorical grants could be improved by determining what the state is trying to accomplish with these grants and determining if each funded program actually provides benefits to residents outside the grantee jurisdiction and the approximate distribution of these benefits. If the grants are really designed to aid the local unit in providing benefits to its own citizens, then a simple block grant with no strings attached would seem most appropriate.

Revenue Sharing

The centerpiece of the state's attempt to provide for

the general support of its counties, municipalities, and townships, is the General Revenue Sharing program. The motivation for such a program can be traced back at least to 1944, when a Legislative Tax Study Commission recommended that the state reduce its sales tax rate and allow local excise taxes, the argument being that the state was pre-empting taxes which might be used by local governments.[7] Instead, in 1946 a sales tax sharing amendment to the 1908 constitution was passed. It earmarked one-sixth of the net revenue of the sales tax to cities, townships, and villages on a per capita basis. Article 9 of the 1963 constitution provided for continued sharing of the sales tax, with one-eighth of the tax to go to cities, villages, and townships, on a per capita basis, and 50 percent to the School Aid Fund. The 1974 amendment to article 9 raised the shares to 15 percent for cities, villages, and townships, and 60 percent for the School Aid Fund as compensation to local units for the revenue lost when food and prescription drugs were removed from the sales tax base.

Three taxes are shared between the state and local units under the Revenue Sharing Act as amended:[8] the sales tax, the personal income tax, and the intangibles tax. Fifteen percent of sales tax revenue is returned to cities, villages, and townships on a per capita basis. The first $9.5 million of the intangibles tax is also distributed to cities, villages, and townships on a per capita basis.

The sharing of the personal income tax is more complicated. The income tax is shared with counties as well as cities, villages, and townships. The total amount returned to these local units is 12.1 percent of that portion of the gross receipts (before credits) of the personal income tax which would have been collected had the tax rate been 2.6 percent. Counties receive 39 percent of the local units' share on a per capita basis. The remainder goes to the cities, villages, and townships on a per capita basis weighted by local relative tax effort.

The relative tax effort for a municipality or township

(RTE_i) is defined as follows: the ratio of total tax collections in jurisdiction i to SEV in jurisdiction i divided by the ratio of total local tax collections in the state to total SEV in the state. (SEV is state equalized value of property.) Thus the RTE for a particular city, village, or township is the ratio of that unit's tax rate to the average tax rate of all local units in the state.

In order to determine a local jurisdiction's share of the personal income tax, its population is first multiplied by its RTE. For each local unit the ratio of that product to the sum of all the cities', villages', and townships' RTE times population is calculated. This ratio is then multiplied by the total amount of income tax funds available for revenue sharing to obtain the local share. Thus, the formula for the local unit's share is:

$$Share_i = RTE_i \times POP_i / \Sigma_i RTE_i \times POP_i$$

There are also some minor addenda to the formula which are primarily minimum payment provisions and the option of using an alternative relative tax burden formula which takes into account taxation by overlapping jurisdictions, rather than the relative tax effort formula.[9]

During fiscal year 1981, the General Revenue Sharing program is expected to yield to local units $178.1 million from the personal income tax and $236.1 million from the sales tax, while payment of the $9.5 million of the intangibles tax has been suspended until July 1, 1982.[10]

The Single Business Tax (SBT) is shared with counties, cities, villages, and townships to compensate them for the revenue losses imposed when enactment of the Single Business Tax in 1975 was accompanied by exemption of inventories from the local property tax. Each year cities, villages, townships, and counties receive an amount equal to their reported tax rate for that year times the 1975 SEV of inventories subject to tax in their jurisdiction in 1975. An additional amount is distributed to cities, villages, and townships on the RTE basis and is to account for growth in the tax base. The total amount distributed to the local units from the SBT in fiscal year 1981 will be $161.4 million.

The use of a relative tax effort formula to allocate funds was rather innovative when the General Revenue Sharing Act was passed in 1971. In fact, the Advisory Commission on Intergovernmental Relations in a report issued in January 1972 stated "there is no history of modifying grant payments as a reward for fiscal effort."[11] It is not clear, however, that it is a desirable innovation. Allocation by tax effort under the current formula discourages the use of user charges which, in certain instances, are the most efficient way to finance public services. The formula is biased in favor of those municipalities whose residents happen to have a preference for public goods relative to private goods. And Fisher has recently shown that revenue sharing by tax effort formula has an expenditure effect due to the interjurisdictional competition for funds.[12] This effect will result in an increase in general local government expenditures beyond the pure income effects of the grant. Revenue sharing based on tax effort can thus lead to an excessive amount of resources being directed to the public sector.

Furthermore, assuming that tax effort is to be used in allocating state aid, it is not clear that the present formula is the best one. The ACIR suggests that a more broadly based measure which takes into account nontax local revenue will give rankings of cities different from the more narrow tax revenue rankings. And given the fact that cities have the right to impose income taxes as well as property taxes, SEV should not be the sole weighting factor in the RTE formula.

The revenue sharing program, like the categorical grant system, appears to suffer from the absence of a clearly articulated set of objectives. If the justification for revenue sharing relies on the argument that there are economies of scale in the collection of taxes and greater efficiency if expenditures are managed by the local units, then the tax sharing should be based on origin rather than population or relative tax effort.

If the state is using revenue sharing in order to equalize fiscal capacity, that concept must first be carefully defined. Governor Milliken's suggestion that state aid be allocated to distressed cities on the basis of a weighted average of several factors, including tax base growth, percent elderly, percentage of families below the poverty line, and declining population, as well as tax effort, seems to reflect a broader and more accurate conception of what one might think of as the ability of a local unit to raise revenue relative to its need. Yet care must be taken in using this type of formula as well. Faith has developed a model of intergovernmental grants that demonstrates that grants to "distressed" cities are likely to encourage the behavior which led these cities into fiscal crisis.[13]

The constitutional requirement that 15 percent of sales tax receipts be distributed to the municipalities and townships on a per capita basis precludes efficient use of the huge sums involved. Clearly some jurisdictions receive more than either their needs or their tax effort could justify while others are in dire fiscal straits. A constitutional amendment placing the 15 percent of the sales tax earmarked to local units in a revenue sharing fund is worthy of serious consideration.

<u>State Aid by Type of Jurisdiction</u>

More than one-half of Michigan's state aid to local units, 54.5 percent, goes to school districts. Counties receive 19 percent of the state's intergovernmental expenditure, municipalities 17.7 percent, and townships less than 3 percent. This distribution among jurisdictions is not far different from the U.S. averages of 48.8 percent for school districts, 21.8 percent for counties, 16.5 percent for municipalities, and 1.2 percent for townships. However, a look at the data for seven comparison states shows that the U.S. average masks considerable variation in the aid programs of the individual states. This is, no doubt, due to legal restrictions placed on the own-revenue generating capacity of local governments and the different divisions of functional and fiscal responsibilities between the state government and local units. For example, California, in 1979, transferred $3.6 billion to its counties for public welfare, a figure which included $2.17 billion in AFDC money. Michigan counties, on the other hand, do not receive state aid for public welfare because the state has assumed complete functional and fiscal responsibility for the welfare system. Thus, although the distribution of intergovernmental expenditure across units of local government in Michigan is about average for the fifty states, there is no "typical" distribution against which to make comparisons.

Table 13.1 provides a summary of the relation of state aid to taxes and to total revenue for counties, municipalities, and townships in Michigan. One gets a different impression of the importance of state aid to the the various types of jurisdiction depending on the nature of the comparisons that are drawn.

A broad measure of where state aid is going may be seen by looking at figures on state aid per capita. In this case cities appear to be the most favored, receiving $97.08, while townships are the least favored, receiving only $23.03. Counties and villages lie between cities and townships with $75.34 and $60.28 respectively.

It is also useful to know to what extent state aid goes to units that make large fiscal efforts. Although townships receive far less aid per capita, they are not called on to provide many of the services that cities are expected to deliver. This disparity in service provision and fiscal effort is indicated by the variation in per capita tax figures. When one looks at the amount of state aid which each type of unit receives relative to each local tax dollar it raises, one gets a somewhat different picture. Cities

TABLE 13.1
STATE AID AND TAXES PER CAPITA, BY JURISDICTION
FISCAL YEAR 1979

	Counties[1]	Cities	Villages	Townships
Taxes Per Capita	$44.20	$155.32	$74.52	$27.61
State Aid Per Capita	$75.34	$97.08	$60.28	$23.03
State Aid/Taxes	1.70	0.63	0.81	0.83
State Aid/Total Revenue	33.4%	18%	20%	23%

Note: [1]County data taken from Governmental Finances in 1978-79, U. S. Department of Commerce, Bureau of the Census. This was due to data limitations of the LUCI file as outlined in note 14 in the text.

Source: LUCI computer file of the State of Michigan, Department of Treasury. Data are only as accurate as the accounting measures of the local units. See notes 14 and 15 of the text. Non-reporting units for FY 1979 were, cities: Holland, Midland, Benton Harbor, Lansing, Burton, Ionia, Brown City, Milan, Northville, Ypsilanti, Ecorse, Gross Pointe Farms, Romulus, and Taylor; counties: Bay, Washtenaw, and Wexford. Eighteen villages and sixty-four townships also failed to respond.

TABLE 13.2
STATE AID PER CAPITA, BY SIZE OF RECEIVING UNIT,
FISCAL YEAR 1979
(in dollars)

CITIES			
Size	Mean	Minimum	Maximum
>100,000	86.46	44.36	181.82
50,000-100,000	77.72	52.68	118.62
10,000-50,000	78.16	35.82	153.94
2,000-10,000	70.81	26.35	130.25
<2,000	78.56	30.48	155.60

COUNTIES			
Size	Mean	Minimum	Maximum
>100,000	46.71	6.47	89.06
50,000-100,000	51.09	7.47	74.04
10,000-50,000	57.01	7.67	103.57
<10,000	144.50	96.02	299.95

Source: LUCI computer file of the State of Michigan, Department of Treasury.

are now the least favored type of jurisdiction, receiving only sixty-three cents in state aid for every dollar of local taxes. Counties are the most favored, receiving more in state aid than they raise in taxes. Townships and villages fall in between with about eighty cents of state aid for every tax dollar raised locally.

Finally, one may wish to look at state aid relative to all revenue sources available to local units, which would include federal aid, fees, and other nontax revenues. This would be an appropriate measure if one believes federal grants are relatively fungible in actual use despite the fact that they are usually earmarked to particular programs. Again, one gets a different impression from this comparison. State aid makes up about one-fifth of the total revenue for cities, villages, and townships. Counties rely most heavily on state aid, with 33 percent of their revenue coming from this source. Cities rely the least heavily, with 18 percent of their total revenue coming from state aid.

State Aid by Size of Jurisdiction

As may be seen in Table 13.2, the mean per capita state aid for the eight cities with over 100,000 population was $86.46 for fiscal year 1979. This was the highest of the five size classes, while the fifty-four cities with under 2,000 population had the second highest mean per capita state aid of $78.56. The 124 cities in the 2,000-10,000 population group had the lowest mean of $70.81.

But the striking feature of state aid when analyzed by size of jurisdiction is the tremendous variation within each population size class, for both cities and counties, when compared to the variation across size classes.

Within each size class for cities, the maximum per capita aid is at least 2.25 times the minimum. For the largest cities, the maximum figure is four times the minimum. For the smallest cities, the maximum figure is more than five times the minimum.

For counties there is a decline in the mean per capita

state aid as population size increases.[14] Counties of less than 10,000 receive an average of $144.50 per capita, while the counties over 100,000 have an average of $46.71 per capita. For counties, the variation within size class is even greater than for cities. Within the 10,000 to 50,000 size class, the maximum state aid per capita is 13.5 times the minimum. The smallest counties have a minimum per capita aid which is greater than the maximum for both counties over 100,000 in population and for those between 50,000 and 100,000.

Thus, small counties, both individually and as a group, seem to be doing very well in terms of receiving state aid relative to other counties, while within each size class the most-favored cities and counties do very well relative to the least-favored cities and counties.

The variation in state aid within size class is due almost solely to categorical grant programs in the case of counties. Using the Local Fiscal Unit Report[15] we found that for 1979, revenue sharing per capita had a mean of $6.11 and a standard deviation of $2.20. The mean for other state grants per capita was $68.99 with a standard deviation of $54.91. Thus the categorical grants comprise most of the variation in total grants to counties.

For cities, on the other hand, revenue sharing and categorical grants contribute more equally to the total variation in state aid. Per capita revenue sharing receipts for the ninety reporting cities and villages with population over 10,000 was $44.76 in 1979, with a standard deviation of $20.69. The mean per capita amount of other state grants was $28.26, with a standard deviation of $16.53. It appears that both types of state grants are contributing to the large variation in per capita state aid within size classes for cities.

<u>State Aid by Region</u>

If one divides the state into three general regions -- the Detroit Metropolitan area, outstate Lower Peninsula

(LP), and Upper Peninsula (UP)--one does find some variation by region in state aid per capita. Table 13.3 shows that the Detroit Metro Area receives the highest state aid per capita at $148.35, the UP has the second highest figure, $121.23, and the outstate LP receives only $96.00 per capita. However, as we did when looking at state aid by jurisdiction, one can make comparisons of state aid in a number of ways. The UP receives more in state aid than it raises in local taxes, while the Detroit Metro Area, which is the highest taxed region, receives only seventy-seven cents in state aid for every local dollar. Although the outstate LP receives the smallest amount of state aid per capita, state aid is a slightly higher percentage of total revenue, 20.37 percent for this region, than for either the Detroit Metro area, 9.10 percent, or for the UP, 18.30 percent. It appears that none of the three broad regions is strongly favored by the current state aid system.

Detroit

Detroit, as the largest city in the state, is the center of much of its economic activity and receives the lion's share of the state's revenue sharing and categorical grants. In 1979, Detroit's state revenue sharing grant amounted to $113.5 million. Grand Rapids received the second highest amount of revenue sharing funds with $10.3 million. Other state grants to Detroit amounted to $111.9 million, while Flint's total of $5.9 million was the second highest.

Detroit's revenue sharing per capita of slightly more than $86 is almost twice the state average for cities of over 10,000 population. Other state grants to Detroit are a little more than $85 per capita, compared to a state average of $28.

Detroit also raises far more in taxes than any other municipality. Its property tax revenue in 1979 was nearly $121 million, compared to $21.9 million for Dearborn, with the next highest total. This was $92 per capita for Detroit and $231.75 for Dearborn. But Dearborn has no city income

TABLE 13.3
STATE AID AND LOCAL TAXES BY SUMMARY REGION
FISCAL YEAR 1978

	Detroit Metropolitan Area[1]	Outstate Lower Peninsula	Upper Peninsula
Taxes Per Capita	$193.32	$97.68	$95.13
Property Taxes Per Capita	$157.87	$89.65	$95.13
State Aid Per Capita	$148.35	$96.00	$121.23
Aid as a Percentage of Revenue	19.10%	20.37%	18.30%
Ratio of Aid to Taxes	0.77	0.99	1.29

Note: [1]Includes Livingston, Macomb, Monroe, Oakland, Washtenaw, and Wayne counties.

Source: LUCI computer file of the State of Michigan, Department of Treasury.

TABLE 13.4
PROPERTY TAXES AND STATE INTERGOVERNMENTAL EXPENDITURE
AS A PERCENTAGE OF TOTAL LOCAL REVENUE BY TYPE OF JURISDICTION
SELECTED YEARS, 1957-1977

State Intergovernmental Expenditure			
	UNIT		
Year	Counties	Municipalities	Townships
1957	36.2	16.2	47.4
1962	38.6	16.0	39.1
1967	42.0	13.9	35.4
1972	39.2	14.7	27.3
1977	37.4	18.6	28.4

Property Taxes			
	UNIT		
Year	Counties	Municipalities	Townships
1957	45.4	38.0	21.2
1962	46.5	39.0	30.0
1967	38.7	30.6	28.5
1972	28.3	27.1	37.7
1977	22.2	21.1	32.5

Source: Census of Governments, Compendium of State Finances, various years.

tax while Detroit realized income tax revenues of $141.7 million. Flint had the second highest income tax revenues of less than $20 million. This was $107.85 per capita for Detroit and $115.28 for Flint. Detroit's per capita total tax figure of $201 ranked it eighth among the forty-two Michigan cities with a total revenue of more than $10 million. This, combined with the nearly $142 million in federal grants to the city, results in Detroit's relying on state aid for only 15.3 percent of its total revenue, less than the state's average for cities. From this perspective, Detroit does not appear to be overly reliant on state aid.

Of all the local jurisdictions in the state, Detroit (along with Wayne County) can make the strongest case that it provides significant benefit spillovers to nonresidents through its local public services. Due to its very size, its being surrounded by suburbs, and its place as an economic and cultural center, many of the local public goods provided by Detroit are used by residents of other cities, thus providing justification for major aid through categorical grants. The Art Institute, for example, benefits thousands of non-Detroit residents, and the city will receive $10.5 million in fiscal year 1981 for its operation. But this grant is neither matching nor open-ended, and may not reflect even roughly the value to nonresidents of its services. Nonetheless, the grant itself and many others to Detroit could be justified on the basis of benefit spillovers.

Although Detroit receives a major share of the state's grants to municipalities, and a larger than average amount per capita, it is not unusually reliant on state aid in terms of its total revenue. While the precise form of the categorical and revenue sharing grants to Detroit are not clearly consistent with the economic theory discussed above, the city can make a good case that its claim to state aid can be justified by the benefit spillovers the city provides and by its high fiscal effort.

Tax Sharing and Earmarking of Taxes

A primary feature of state aid in Michigan is its reliance on shared and earmarked taxes. State taxes are shared either through constitutional requirement or legislative mandate. The three major tax sharing programs are the School Aid Fund, through which the sales, cigarette, and liquor taxes are shared with the school districts; the Michigan Transportation Fund, whereby the gasoline, diesel fuel, liquified petroleum gas, and motor vehicle weight taxes are shared with counties and municipalities; and General Revenue Sharing of the personal income, sales, and intangibles taxes. The SBT and the commercial forest tax are shared with local units to replace property tax revenues lost due to state legislative action, and the horse race wagering tax is shared with cities in which racetracks are located. Of the $6.126 billion in taxes raised by the state in fiscal year 1980, about 30 percent was shared with the local units, while an additional 8 percent was earmarked for specific programs.[16]

There is some support in the economics literature for certain kinds of earmarking of taxes. Public finance texts will point out that to the extent that highway taxes approximate user charges, they increase the efficiency of the tax system. Buchanan has argued that earmarking gives the individual a better chance to relate the benefits to the costs of a particular program.[17] But he also notes that earmarking may merely be a way to generate support for an expansion of certain taxes by assigning them to expenditure purposes which are popular; his example is the earmarking of the sales tax to finance education. There is no question that earmarking reduces the budget flexibility of the legislature. This problem assumes critical importance in the long run as demand for a particular government service changes in ways not consistent with changes in revenue from the earmarked tax. One may also find that entrenched government agencies may desire a dependable source of revenue free from the vagaries of political change in the legislature, and thus they will favor earmarked taxes.

The recent decline in revenue from the motor vehicle and fuel taxes has led to a suggestion that the rates on these taxes be raised rather than allow a reduction in expenditures on highways and streets. With respect to those tax receipts earmarked to the School Aid Fund, the issue of the virtues of earmarking does not arise as the legislative appropriation for school aid always exceeds the receipts of the School Aid Fund from earmarked taxes. Thus, although there is the potential for excessive restriction of the state legislature through constitutional earmarking, there does not currently appear to be a major problem in this area. The real restriction is due to section 6 of the Headlee Amendment, which mandates that the ratio of state payments to local units to total state spending from own revenue sources remain equal to at least 41.16 percent.[18] In any case, the passage of this amendment indicates a reluctance of the electorate to increase the discretion of the legislature in allocating funds.

HISTORICAL TRENDS AND ACCOMPLISHMENTS

Trends in Importance of Aid

Michigan has long been one of the leading states in intergovernmental transfers. Since 1942 it has been among the top five states in total intergovernmental expenditure, usually ranking behind only New York and California. On a per capita basis, in Census of Government years since 1942, Michigan has ranked from fifth to twelfth in intergovernmental expenditure, with its highest ranking occurring in the mid 1950s. As a percentage of total general expenditure, intergovernmental expenditures have declined slightly from 40.6 in 1957 to 36.5 in 1977. The provisions of the Headlee Amendment ensure that, unless there is a large increase in federal aid to Michigan, a downward trend in the ratio of state intergovernmental expenditure to total state expenditure is unlikely.[19]

Table 13.4 gives the historical trend of the importance

of state aid to local units in Michigan from 1957 to 1977. State aid as a percentage of total revenue rose for counties in Michigan from 1957 to 1967. Since then there has been a slight, but steady decline. The takeover of the general assistance program from the counties by the state has been a factor in this decline during the late 1970s.

There was a significant downward trend in the proportion of total municipal revenues coming from state aid between 1957 and 1967. However, there has been some turnaround since then, with state aid as a percentage of total revenue rising from 13.9 to over 18 percent by 1977. The institution of General Revenue Sharing in 1971 produced this upward trend.

State aid to townships since 1957 has become a much less important source of revenue. In 1957, nearly one-half of township revenue was provided by the state; today, only about one-quarter of township revenue comes from this source. This trend is consistent with the recommendation of the 1958 Tax Study[20] that townships be asked to provide more of their revenue from their own sources.

<u>Changes in Form of Aid</u>

There have been a number of changes in the form of the state's intergovernmental aid program since it was reviewed in the 1958 Tax Study. Among these are the merger of the Primary School Interest Fund with the School Aid Fund, the drastic decline in tuberculosis care programs, the elimination of the Veteran's Homestead Exemption reimbursement, the institution of General Revenue Sharing, the takeover of the counties' general assistance program, and the recent rapid expansion of mental health grants. Yet one basic aspect of state aid, its reliance on shared taxes, remains the same. The 1958 Tax Study calculated that, in 1957, 94.1 percent of total state aid to local units was supplied through shared taxes. Although there has been a decline in this percentage, today nearly three-quarters of state payments to local units still come from some form of shared taxes.

Accomplishments

One may reasonably ask whether Michigan's aid to local units has accomplished or is accomplishing the goals set out for it. As we noted in our discussion of categorical grants, it does not appear to have been a clear goal of the state to use its aid program either to correct for benefit spillovers or as a means of taking advantage of economies of scale in tax collection. Our primary concern, then, is to evaluate the state's intergovernmental aid program in terms of the other two objectives discussed above: 1) reducing fiscal disparities among local units and 2) reducing reliance on the property tax.

Fiscal equalization. Defining fiscal capacity, fiscal need, or any measure of fiscal equality among local units is fraught with difficulties. Rather than become embroiled in methodological controversy, we look at one very straightforward and simple concept of fiscal equality for cities and counties.

One obvious way to see if state aid has reduced the variance of cities' revenues is to compare the coefficient of variation of the total revenue of local units net of state grants with the coefficient of variation[21] of total revenue including state grants. If the latter is smaller then the state grants do act to reduce the dispersion of revenue across localities.

We used data from the 1979 Local Fiscal Unit Reports to calculate coefficients of variation for the eighty-one reporting counties and the ninety reporting municipalities with populations of over 10,000. There were two ways to view federal grants in the calculations. If federal grants are considered fairly program specific and are for programs the local unit would not undertake in the absence of the federal grant, then the relevant figures, for our purpose, would exclude such federal aid. On the other hand, if one argues that federal categorical grants are in fact highly fungible, then the revenue figures should include all federal grants. It is beyond the scope of this chapter to resolve the issue. We thus calculated the coefficients of variation both with and without federal nonrevenue-sharing grants.

For municipalities the coefficient of variation for total revenue per capita including federal grants but minus state aid was 0.603. When state grants were included the coefficient of variation was reduced to 0.518, a 14 percent reduction. By this measure, then, state aid was somewhat equalizing for cities.

The coefficient of variation of per capita total revenue without state grants but including federal funds was 0.509 for counties. When state grants were included, the coefficient of variation in revenue per capita was 0.454, about a 10 percent reduction. Thus we find that, according to this simple measure, state grants to counties are also slightly equalizing.

When one excludes the federal categorical grants from the revenue figures for cities, the picture does not change much. The coefficient of variation for per capita total revenue, excluding state grants, was 0.639. The addition of state grants reduced this figure by about 16 percent to 0.536.

The exclusion of federal nonrevenue-sharing aid from the county data improves the equalization figures somewhat for state aid, although the total effect is still a reduction in variation of less than one-fifth, from 0.575 without state aid to 0.474 with state aid.

Although our simple measure of fiscal equalization presents some methodological difficulties, it suggests that state aid has at best been modestly equalizing. This is not surprising, since the major categorical grants are not designed to be equalizing and revenue sharing is dispersed largely on a per capita basis,[22] weighted for municipalities and townships by a formula which rewards preferences for publicly provided goods and only crudely accounts for fiscal need.

Reliance on the property tax. State aid seems to have helped reduce the reliance of municipalities on the property tax. Returning to Table 13.4, one may observe a trend of both increasing importance of state aid and decreasing importance of property taxes for municipalities, at least since 1967. Townships have increased their reliance on the property tax since 1957. This, however, is a consequence largely of their urbanization in the more heavily populated areas of the state. Counties have reduced their reliance on the property tax to less than one-half of the 1957 figure. However, they have not increased their dependence on state aid. Federal aid appears to have been a more important contributor to the falling relative dependence of the counties on property tax receipts.

SUMMARY

It is likely that state aid to local units will continue to be a large portion of total state expenditure and that it will continue to consist mainly of shared taxes. Improvements could be made in the categorical grants programs by moving toward a system under which these grants would actually compensate local units for benefit spillovers. Revenue sharing could be more effective in meeting fiscal needs of local units if a formula based more on need, assuming that acceptable means of measuring it can be developed, and less on population and preferences for public goods, were substituted for the present one. With the state constitution requiring a large intergovernmental expenditure program, and state funds being in short supply, it seems incumbent now on the legislature to examine closely its goals with respect to aid to local governments.

NOTES, CHAPTER 13

[1]I am indebted to William Donnelly and especially Gary Wyckoff for their valuable research assistance. We thank

all individuals who helped us obtain data from the LUCI computer file, especially Ralph Nichols of the University of Michigan's State Relations section, Tom Hickner of the Senate Fiscal Agency, State of Michigan, and Tom Martin, Office of Intergovernmental Relations, Department of Commerce, State of Michigan. I also thank the editor for his invaluable comments and assistance.

[2]For a discussion of the theory of intergovernmental grants see George F. Break, Financing Government in a Federal System (The Brookings Institution, 1980).

[3]The notable exceptions are federal grants for AFDC and Medicaid. Michigan's Community Mental Health Board program is a closed-ended matching grant.

[4]See Richard Netzer, "State-Local Finance" in Robert Havenman and Julius Margolis, eds., Public Expenditure and Policy Analysis (Rand McNally, 1970).

[5]Public Act 279 of 1909, MCL 117.1 - 117.38.

[6]See Chapter 14.

[7]Michigan Tax Study Advisory Committee, Michigan Finance Commission, preliminary report (Lansing: January, 1945), pg. 21.

[8]M. S. A. 5.3194(401) - 5.3194(406); 5.3194(411) - 5.3194(419).

[9]The minimum payment to a city, village, or township must be at least $17 per capita. If a local unit imposes a property tax, there is a minimum payment scale based on the property tax millage, with this minimum payment rising by $1 each July 1. The difference between the computed share and the minimum payment is to be paid out of the state's General Fund. County governments also receive additional aid whenever local units within their jurisdiction receive payments above what they would have received under the RTE formula. Each municipality and township may choose to receive its revenue sharing funds under a relative tax burden formula (RTB) if it will increase its share of revenue sharing funds. The RTB formula is the ratio of total taxes in the jurisdiction plus one-quarter of overlapping taxes and special assessments divided by SEV in the jurisdiction to total taxes in the state plus one-half of overlapping taxes and special assessments of all units in the state divided by SEV in the state. The total amount of funds distributed under these provisions is small.

[10]See Executive Order 1980-3; 80PA375; 80PA394.

[11]U.S. Advisory Commission on Intergovernmental Relations, Measuring the Fiscal Capacity and Effort of State and Local Areas (U.S. Government Printing Office, 1972), Report M-58.

[12]Ronald Fisher, "A Theoretical View of Revenue Sharing Grants," _National Tax Journal_, vol. 32 (June 1979), pp. 317-32.

[13]Roger Faith, "Local Fiscal Crises and Intergovernmental Grants: A Suggested Hypothesis," _Public Choice_ (1979), 34: 317-32.

[14]In preparing the data base for the LUCI system state aid to local units is identified only for the revenue funds commonly used by Michigan municipalities. As county governments tend to have special revenue funds not common to municipalities, the LUCI data will underestimate state aid to these units. To the extent that small counties have fewer special funds, it will appear that they receive relatively more in state aid than the larger city governments.

[15]The _Local Fiscal Unit Report_ is issued by the Michigan Department of Treasury. It is a digest of financial data on each of the 81 counties, 1,228 townships, and 520 cities and villages that completed and returned the local fiscal unit report forms to the Michigan Department of Treasury. The information contained in the reports serves as the data base of the Local Unit Computer Information System (LUCI).

[16] This data was calculated by the author using the State of Michigan Executive Budget for fiscal year 1981, pages 97 and 98. It was estimated that the following amounts, in thousands of dollars, of state taxes were shared: sales tax, 1,127,978; personal income tax, 171,603; SBT, 162,177; cigarette tax, 25,674; liquor excise tax, 18,584; horse wagery tax, 12,487; motor vehicle weight tax, 125,921; gasoline tax, 238,886; diesel fuel tax, 13,621; all other taxes, 469. Additional taxes, such as those for the Motor Vehicle Fund, are earmarked for specific purposes although not shared with the local units.

[17]James Buchanan, "The Economics of Earmarked Taxes," _Journal of Political Economy_, vol. 71 (Oct. 1963).

[18]See Governor Milliken's _Budget Message of the Governor_, Fiscal Year 1981.

[19]Public Act 258 of 1980 states that if the state assumes financing and administration of functions after December 22, 1978, which were previously performed by a unit of local government, state payments directly attributable to the state's assumption of these functions will be counted as state spending on local units of government.

[20]_Michigan Tax Study Staff Papers_ (Lansing, 1958).

[21]The coefficient of variation is the standard deviation divided by the mean.

[22]Per capita sharing of revenues collected through a progressive tax can be equalizing. However, neither of the two main revenue sharing taxes, sales and income, are significantly progressive.

Chapter 14

Elementary and Secondary School Financing

by

Harvey E. Brazer, Deborah S. Laren, and Frank Yu-Hsieh Sung

The University of Michigan

INTRODUCTION

The financing of elementary and secondary education in the United States is now a joint venture of federal, state, and local governments. For the year 1978-79 the federal government, as the junior partner, provided directly or through the states, $8.1 billion, 8.8 percent of all public school revenues. State aid contributed $39.4 billion, 42.7 percent of the total, and local school districts raised 47.1 percent, $43.5 billion, on their own; other local governments[1] raised $1.2 billion, 1.3 percent, to bring the total to $92.2 billion. In the same year total general revenues of Michigan's school districts amounted to $4.4 billion. Its distribution among sources was substantially different from that for schools in the nation as a whole. In contrast with the national average of 9 percent for federal aid, it was 6.4 percent in Michigan, and the state's share here was only 33.9 percent while that of the local jurisdictions was 59.7 percent.[2] For all of the states the proportion of school revenues raised locally declined steadily between 1962 and 1979; and in Michigan, while the proportion dropped from about 64 percent in 1962 to 54 percent in 1967, since 1972 it has hovered between 57 and 60 percent.[3]

Our concern in this chapter is with the role of the State of Michigan in the financing of the public schools. The state constitution stipulates that "The legislature shall maintain a system of free public elementary and secondary schools as defined by law."[4] But local school districts in Michigan have always enjoyed a large degree of autonomy in the actual operation of schools. The state has acted and continues to act in a supervisory and regulatory capacity, and it has provided financial assistance since the beginning of statehood in 1837. State aid for elementary and secondary education has evolved from an initial distribution based on the proceeds of the sale of federal lands under the terms of the Northwest Ordinance of 1787, through the "foundation" program of the second and third quarters of this century, to the present modified "equal yield" system. We shall here examine, first, the general principles of school aid, looking to its purposes or objectives and then to the alternative instruments available for their attainment. We shall then go on to develop the historical background of state aid for schools in Michigan, with emphasis on the period since 1973 when the Bursley Act was passed. The third section of the chapter provides an analysis of the fiscal impact of that act and its amendments to date. Following this we turn to so-called "categorical" assistance, interstate comparisons of the role of state aid, and, finally, to discussion of alternative directions for future policy and a summary of findings and conclusions.

GENERAL PRINCIPLES OF SCHOOL AID

This section of the chapter deals with the objectives of state aid for schools and with the instruments that may be employed in the pursuit of those objectives.

Objectives

As we have seen, the state legislature is responsible for the provision of the system of free public schools. In fact, however, like the legislatures of all of the states except Hawaii, the Michigan legislature has delegated this responsibility in very large measure to local school districts. But, in the matter of financing the operation of the schools, the state has always recognized some obligation to participate. The objectives sought in this participation have not, generally, been clearly articulated or, if articulated, not pursued in a manner or in a degree adequate to the attainment of the declared legislative intent.

Nevertheless, some objectives that command widespread support in practice and among contributors to the debate in this arena can be discerned.

The objective that probably enjoys more currency than any other is that of assuring that every child in the state attends a school that commands sufficient resources to provide its pupils an "adequate educational opportunity." The rub, of course, comes in defining adequacy in this context. However it may be defined, this objective of state aid may be said to be attained if all school districts in the state are able, with state aid and local fiscal resources and reasonable effort, to spend that amount considered by the legislature to be adequate. So defined, this objective of state aid would appear to be a minimum requirement where, as is typically the case, the state, charged with the responsibility for establishing and maintaining the public schools, delegates this responsibility to local school districts. This delegation may properly be seen as dereliction unless it carries with it the fiscal means to sustain it throughout the state.

A second frequently acknowledged objective of state aid is to ease the burden of carrying school financing that is generally allotted to the local property tax. Through state aid the whole range of state taxes and other revenue sources is tapped for support of local schools. In fact, constitutional or statutory earmarking of sales, cigarette, and liquor tax receipts and lottery earnings does not restrict state aid to these sources. Appropriations for local schools always exceed the earmarked revenues and, in addition, "money mingles," so that specific revenue sources cannot, in general, be tagged for specific uses. The substitution in part of state revenue sources for the local property tax clearly is unlikely to ease the total tax burden, but it will change its distribution among income groups and between in-state and out-state taxpayers; it will also change the relative size of the initial tax impact on businesses as opposed to individuals, and among kinds of business activity. Whether or not these changes constitute improvements depends on one's criteria for evaluation of tax policy and the nature of the state's tax system. Given contemporary views on tax incidence, it is not clear that state aid in Michigan can be justified on this ground.

Another consequence of this substitution is the shifting of the onus of levying part of the tax bill for schools from local to state politicians. This implies some loss of local control and weakening of the ties between local preferences and the political decision-making process in taxing and spending.

For some observers the most important justification for state aid is based on the view that the quality of a child's education, at least to the extent that that quality is a function of the dollars spent to provide it, ought not depend on the income, wealth, or even adult preferences of the residents of the local school district in which the child lives. In this view, given its constitutional responsibility for education, the state is obliged to ensure equal educational opportunity; this may be interpreted to mean equal dollars spent or equal real resources for pupils everywhere in the state. State aid, then, should be designed to equalize revenues per pupil or to equalize local capacity to raise revenue, or it and the local property tax should be supplemented by a system of full-state funding of elementary and secondary education.

Full state funding may be seen as an extreme version of per pupil revenue and expenditure equalization in which local preferences with respect to the level of school spending are given no rein at all. At the other extreme, perhaps the weakest version of equalization is that under which the role of the state is to equalize local capacity to raise revenue irrespective of variance in the local tax base, while local preferences are given full political expression in the determination of the amount to be raised and spent.

Finally, by itself or in combination with other

objectives, stimulation of local tax effort for schools may be among the goals of state aid. This objective clearly finds justification if it is believed that local school districts tend to under-tax and under-spend on education because current local taxpayers lack the vision to take the interests of future generations adequately into account or because benefit spillovers to the rest of the state tend to be ignored. As has been observed in detail in Chapter 13, the existence of spillovers or externalities associated with local educational programs is in itself a rational justification for state aid. For some observers this is the most fundamental of all reasons for state aid for education. The basic validity of this position is not disputed here. We note only that while we can point readily enough to the "black box" marked "educational spillovers," we cannot adequately define its contents and we certainly cannot measure them in a way that is adequate to the task of guiding state policy in this area.

Instruments

The state's participation in the financing of elementary and secondary education does take a wide variety of forms. These include the distribution of equal amounts per pupil to all local districts, either for general support or in "categorical grants," grants in aid of specified activities such as transportation of pupils, special programs for the handicapped, vocational education, and so forth. A refinement of the equal per pupil grant may be found in variable grants designed to reflect differences in "need," particularly in categorical aid.

The early "foundation" programs, and those still found in many states, combine several objectives of state aid, including assurance of a minimum amount of revenue per pupil in all districts and some degree of equalization of revenue raising capacity. This policy instrument typically involves a calculation of state aid per pupil as a "basic grant" less the tax base per pupil multiplied by an arbitrarily established "deductible millage." To qualify for aid a school district would be required to levy a specified minimum millage.

A more recent development that seeks to achieve a larger element of equalization of revenue-raising capacity and to stimulate local tax effort is found in "power equalization" or "equal yield" formulas for state aid. They involve the selection of a support level in terms of tax base per pupil that affords all districts either a minimum or precisely the same yield per mill in their tax rates. Pure power equalization requires that districts with per pupil taxable property in excess of the support level receive negative aid, while in its less rigorous application those fortunate districts simply move "out-of-formula" and receive no general support aid.

Full state funding is an alternative instrument under which little or no revenue raising responsibility is left to local school districts. It makes state aid, in effect, redundant.

In examining objectives of state aid we focused on specific immediate goals. But if we are to evaluate objectives and instruments employed in their pursuit, we need to recognize the role of broader goals as well. These are, in general, definable in terms of equity and efficiency. Equity is, of course, a highly subjective concept. For our purposes, and without normative bias, we define it to mean equality. Thus, one outcome is more equitable than another if it yields a more equal distribution of per pupil revenues or expenditures among school districts. Efficiency connotes not absence of waste in administration, important as that may be, but the degree to which local budgets reflect the preferences of the residents of the community.

These definitions imply that in this area of public policy, as in so many others, equity and efficiency goals are likely to be often in conflict. And resolution of that conflict remains essentially a political decision through processes that draw little help from economists or other social scientists.

HISTORICAL BACKGROUND AND STRUCTURE OF GENERAL AID

Pre-1974

Prior to fiscal year 1973-74, the state distributed aid for general assistance to elementary and secondary schools through a "foundation" program. The amount of aid per pupil (often called "membership" or "formula" aid) was determined by a formula of the form: Aid per pupil = gross allowance per pupil - state equalized value per pupil (SEV) x the deductible millage. Aid was constrained to be nonnegative and school districts were required to levy a minimum number of mills for operating purposes in order to qualify for full membership aid. The values of the gross allowance and the deductible millage were set each year by the legislature.

Aid received under the foundation program was a lump sum amount, invariant with the district's tax effort, provided at least the mandated millage was levied. In economists' terms, foundation aid had only an "income effect" and no "price effect."[5] The gain to a district from raising its tax rate, unaffected as it was by the foundation grant, was directly proportional to the district's SEV.[6]

For fiscal year 1972-73, the last year in which the foundation formula was in effect, the legislature set the gross allowance at $644 and the deductible millage at 16 for districts with SEV greater than or equal to $17,750. For districts with SEV less than $17,750, they set the gross allowance at $715 and the deductible millage at 20. A district at this time had to levy at least 10 mills to be eligible for full membership aid; those levying less received a prorated amount.

The design of the foundation aid program was not without some logic. The program did equalize the ability of every district to finance the state-determined gross allowance. More accurately, and specifically for 1972-73, all districts with SEV greater than $17,750 could finance the gross allowance of $644 with a tax effort of 16 mills. All districts with SEV less than $17,750 could finance the gross allowance of $715 with a millage of 20. Odd inequities, however, came into play as districts chose levels of per pupil expenditure different than the gross allowance and (simultaneously) tax rates other than the deductible millage.[7]

There were several efforts over the years prior to 1974 to reform Michigan's system of aid to education. In the late 1960s, the state commissioned a comprehensive study of school finance in Michigan. The study, known as the "Thomas Report," identified several alternatives for reform, among them, that the state "reimpose its right to tax property" and levy a state-wide property tax, distributing the proceeds equally among pupils.[8] The report itself entitled this alternative "a radical proposal." Another less "radical" proposal set forward was a variant of the "equal yield" concept under which each district would be guaranteed the same amount of revenue per pupil for each mill levied. A third proposal called for the use of the "classroom unit" as the basis for funding. A specific number of students would be deemed as constituting a unit, with that number varying depending on the grade level or type of student. The report suggested additional adjustments to allow for the variation in teacher salaries among districts. Under this third alternative, the state would guarantee that each "classroom unit" was funded at the same level.

In 1969, Governor Milliken appointed a Commission on Educational Reform. In September of that year, following the commission's report, the governor proposed the imposition of a statewide property tax, the proceeds of which would go to the schools. The governor also recommended that many of the features of the "classroom unit" concept or the "Equal Quality Plan," be incorporated into the funding system. Meanwhile, the State Board of Education was developing its own recommendations for reform based on the equal yield concept.[9]

Despite these many efforts, no major changes were made in the method of distributing membership aid in 1969 or 1970. In 1970, the legislature did adopt a two-year plan which featured in the second year a variant of the equal yield concept, but this was repealed.

In 1971, the governor and various members of the legislature developed proposals for constitutional amendments, but the support needed to get these amendments on the ballot did not materialize. The Michigan Education Association, however, also developed a proposal and ran a successful petition drive, obtaining the necessary number of voter signatures. Governor Milliken threw his support behind the M.E.A. The amendment, placed on the ballot in November 1972, would have cut the number of mills allowed by the constitution from fifty to twenty-six. Up to six mills could be voted for "educational enrichment" and four-and-a-half mills were to be allocated for vocational, compensatory, and intermediate school district purposes. But the basic operating expenses of the schools were to be financed by an increase in the income tax. The amendment was defeated. With its defeat went that of advocates of state "full funding." Attention once again began to focus on the equal yield concept.

<u>The Bursley Act, 1973-74, and Subsequent Legislation to 1981</u>

Public Act 101, the "Gilbert E. Bursley School District Equalization Act," was signed into law by the governor in August of 1973. Under this act, the state "reformed" its system of membership aid, moving from the foundation grant system to a "district power equalizing" or equal yield scheme. Governor Milliken, at the signing of the bill, stated, "This act will virtually eliminate property tax base wealth as a factor in school finance among districts."[10] In December of 1972, the Michigan Supreme Court had declared the foundation grant program of 1970-71 to be unconstitutional. A few months after the signing of the Bursley Act, however, this opinion was vacated.

Under the power equalization scheme, aid per pupil is determined by a formula of the form: Aid per pupil = (SEV* - SEV) x operating millage. SEV* is the "support level" of state equalized value per pupil; its value is set by the legislature.

Unlike a foundation program which provides lump sum grants invariant with local tax effort, a power equalization plan introduces price effects. Under such a plan, the marginal prices to districts of an additional dollar of revenue vary with their tax bases. For example, with SEV* set at $40,000, the district with $10,000 of SEV would gain an additional dollar of revenue per pupil by raising an additional 25 cents per pupil in local taxes. The district with $35,000 in SEV would have to raise 87.5 cents per pupil in local taxes to gain an additional dollar. The marginal price facing a district can be expressed as SEV/SEV*.

In altering the price structure so that the price of an additional dollar of revenue varies directly with SEV, a power equalization formula equalizes the revenue-raising abilities of districts. Under the formula, the same tax effort nets each district, regardless of its taxable wealth, the same amount per pupil in combined revenues (local taxes plus membership aid). The amount of revenue raised then depends simply on the district's choice of tax rate.

In equalizing the revenue-raising abilities of all districts, a power equalization scheme can also be expected to equalize combined revenues per pupil. This is so not simply because, as under the foundation program, greater amounts of aid per pupil go to districts with lower wealth, but also because of the change in the price structure. Districts with lower wealth, in response to the "bargain" price set by the state for an additional dollar of revenue per pupil, can be expected to raise their tax rates, and therefore, their revenues.

In practice, Michigan's post-1973 program for the distribution of membership aid has not followed a pure power equalization scheme. Because the formula has been subject to a zero limit, the revenue-raising abilities of the out-of-formula districts remain greater than those of the in-formula districts.[11] Only if provisions for recapture were made would the out-of-formula districts not have an advantage.[12]

Not only absence of recapture provisions in past years, but a maximum placed on the number of mills eligible for matching, have rendered Michigan's power equalization plan less than pure. There is no price effect for districts levying mills in excess of the eligible maximum. In fact, for such districts, a power equalization plan is equivalent to a foundation grant.[13] The number of mills eligible for equalization continued to be limited through fiscal year 1979-80, although the limit, or maximum, was raised several times. In 1980-81, the maximum was completely eliminated.

The legislature changed the power equalization aid formula in each of the four years following the enactment of Bursley. In 1977-78 the power equalization principle was partially abandoned when the legislature added a flat per pupil amount to the aid formula. The formula took on the form: Aid per pupil = flat amount per pupil + (SEV* - SEV) x millage. A district with SEV less than SEV* received the flat amount per pupil regardless of its tax effort. The amount received by such districts in addition, however, was still dependent on tax effort and the marginal price faced was still SEV/SEV*. For districts with SEV less than SEV*, aid increased with tax effort, up to the point where tax rates were greater than the limit eligible for matching.

A district now went out-of-formula when (SEV* - SEV) x millage was negative <u>and</u> greater than or equal to (in absolute value) the flat amount. The point at which this occurred was, of course, at a level of SEV considerably greater than SEV*. But how much higher than SEV* a district's SEV could be before membership aid dropped to zero now depended on its tax effort. For those districts with SEV greater than SEV*, the amount of aid they received varied <u>inversely</u> with tax rates up to the point where they went out of formula. Under this formulation it is actually to the advantage of any district with SEV greater than SEV* for a limit to be placed on the mills matched.

This change in the character of the formula increased the state's ability to "target" membership aid. By raising the flat amount per pupil, rather than the support level of SEV, the state channels relatively more aid to districts with low millages; by the opposite, it channels more aid to districts with high millages. The addition of the flat amount introduced some progressivity, with respect to millage rates, into the system. The change may also reflect the state's desire at this time to discourage higher property taxes.

THE FISCAL IMPACT OF BURSLEY

The Formula Since 1973-74

In this section we examine in detail the provisions of Michigan's equal yield plan in each year since the enactment of Bursley. Because Michigan's plan has fallen short of pure power equalization, price effects have been inoperative for some districts. It is, therefore, important to look closely at the formula for each year in order to gauge the effects it might reasonably be expected to have on the budget decisions of school districts.

In fiscal year 1973-74, aid per pupil was set equal to ($38,000 - SEV) multiplied by the number of operating mills, up to 22. No provision was made for matching mills over 22. Districts with SEV equal to or greater than $38,000 received no membership aid. In this year, only 186 of the 531 K-12 districts, or 35 percent, were both still in formula and levying less than 22 mills.[14] Only 186 districts then were subject to a price effect. But only 7 percent of K-12 districts were receiving no formula aid at all. In this first year of the plan, provisions were made to assure that low tax effort districts would not initially suffer an excessively large drop in the amount of aid received, and that certain districts would be protected from an absolute loss, relative to the previous year, in the amount received.

In 1974-75, the SEV support level was increased to $39,000 and the number of mills subject to matching to 25. In this year, the percentage of districts subject to a price effect increased to 52 percent; 10 percent of districts were out-of-formula.

In 1975-76, in an effort to reconcile the conflict between high and low SEV and high and low millage districts, the "two-tier" system was adopted. Aid per pupil was set equal to: ($42,400 - SEV) x mills, up to 20, plus ($38,250 - SEV) x mills over 20, up to 27.[15] In this year aid functioned as a lump sum grant (i.e., was invariant with tax effort) for all districts levying over 27 mills and for those districts with SEV greater than $38,250 and levying between 20 and 27 mills; 347 of the 530 districts both received aid and levied less than 27 mills. But 13 of these 347 had SEV greater than $38,250 and levied over 20 mills. Thus, only 334 districts, 63 percent, were actually subject to a price effect. The percentage of districts which were out-of-formula increased slightly to 11 percent.

The state continued to employ the two-tier formula in 1976-77, with slight upward adjustments in the support levels of SEV and the "cap" rate. Aid per pupil was set equal to ($43,900 - SEV) x mills, up to 20, plus ($39,600 - SEV) x mills over 20, up to 28. Price effects were operative for 321 of the 530 districts. The percentage of districts which received no formula aid held this year at about 11 percent.

In 1977-78, the legislature again altered the character of the formula with the addition of a flat amount per pupil. Aid per pupil in this year was set equal to $164 + ($40,000 - SEV) x mills. All districts with SEV less than $40,000 received the flat amount of $164 per pupil regardless of their tax effort. Additional amounts received continued to depend on tax rates. A district was out-of-formula only if ($40,000 - SEV) x mills was less than or equal to -$164. For those districts with SEV greater than

TABLE 14.1
FISCAL VARIABLES, 1971-72 TO 1979-80

Year	Mean	Median	Minimun	Maximun
STATE EQUALIZED VALUE				
71-72	$17,449	$14,958	$2,080	$66,844
72-73	$19,128	$15,971	$2,732	$83,288
73-74	$21,163	$17,618	$3,317	$126,340
74-75	$23,934	$19,858	$4,386	$172,723
75-76	$26,715	$22,782	$4,939	$216,926
76-77	$28,163	$23,649	$6,188	$286,282
77-78	$31,703	$26,346	$9,671	$301,074
78-79	$36,308	$30,231	$11,980	$366,224
79-80	$42,315	$35,114	$12,834	$461,566
OPERATING MILLAGE				
71-72	22.64	22.40	9.00	37.90
72-73	22.79	22.46	10.00	36.90
73-74	23.28	22.66	11.38	37.65
74-75	24.42	23.91	8.38	37.65
75-76	25.10	24.77	8.38	37.80
76-77	25.84	25.43	8.29	39.69
77-78	26.68	26.23	8.29	41.30
78-79	26.90	26.55	6.86	41.40
79-80	26.91	26.47	6.21	40.76
LOCAL OPERATING TAXES PER PUPIL				
71-72	$394	$338	$25	$1,397
72-73	$436	$370	$27	$1,488
73-74	$491	$418	$50	$1,649
74-75	$574	$496	$88	$1,754
75-76	$657	$576	$101	$1,990
76-77	$711	$659	$126	$2,399
77-78	$819	$714	$213	$2,496
78-79	$943	$812	$263	$2,616
79-80	$1,097	$943	$327	$2,866
LOCAL REVENUE PER PUPIL				
71-72	$452	$399	$75	$1,443
72-73	$530	$439	$95	$1,590
73-74	$571	$498	$133	$1,810
74-75	$667	$577	$159	$1,972
75-76	$753	$659	$204	$2,386
76-77	$741	$652	$179	$2,474
77-78	$858	$747	$240	$2,603
78-79	$993	$852	$297	$2,693
79-80	$1,166	$1,000	$385	$3,124

MEMBERSHIP AID PER PUPIL				
71-72	$326	$351	$0	$618
72-73	$358	$396	$0	$660
73-74	$381	$433	$0	$667
74-75	$391	$439	$0	$772
75-76	$415	$467	$0	$823
76-77	$435	$491	$0	$864
77-78	$456	$525	$0	$1,007
78-79	$474	$541	$0	$1,136
79-80	$472	$532	$0	$1,240
TOTAL STATE AID PER PUPIL				
71-72	$383	$401	$22	$660
72-73	$410	$443	$0	$708
73-74	$451	$505	$14	$780
74-75	$467	$514	$23	$888
75-76	$476	$525	$5	$968
76-77	$530	$568	$18	$1,129
77-78	$569	$617	$0	$1,388
78-79	$600	$656	$38	$1,605
79-80	$623	$675	$49	$1,771
EXPENDITURES PER PUPIL				
71-72	$795	$761	$554	$1,510
72-73	$866	$832	$497	$1,608
73-74	$959	$926	$667	$1,859
74-75	$1,093	$1,058	$745	$2,077
75-76	$1,201	$1,157	$730	$2,280
76-77	$1,295	$1,251	$632	$2,399
77-78	$1,455	$1,394	$1,049	$2,662
78-79	$1,636	$1,571	$1,190	$3,092
79-80	$1,842	$1,754	$1,290	$3,535

Note: Our unit of observation for these calculations is the district; the means and medians shown are the average and middle values of the 500-odd K-12 districts; see note 20 in the text.

Source: Michigan Department of Education, SADIE tapes, and Bulletin 1012, various years.

$40,000, an increase in the tax rate meant a decrease in aid, up to the point where aid went to zero. In this year, 64 percent of districts had SEV less than $40,000 and levied less than the matching limit of 30 mills and were, therefore, subject to a positive price effect. Sixteen districts, those with SEV greater than $40,000 and levying less than 30 mills, were receiving aid and were subject to a negative price effect, an incentive to cut operating millage. The percentage of out-of-formula districts increased to 15 percent.

The flat amount per pupil has continued to be an element in the aid formula through 1981-82. In 1978-79, this amount was raised to $274; there was no increase in this year in the support level of SEV. Millage eligible for equalization continued at 30. In this year, 300 of the 529 districts were subject to a positive price effect while 37 districts were subject to a negative one. Once again, the percentage of out-of-formula districts climbed, this year to 16.5 percent. There was some limited provision for matching for millages in excess of 30, designed to encourage rollbacks among high rate districts.[16]

In 1979-80, both the flat amount and the support level were raised, to $325 and $43,000, respectively. In this year, 53 percent of districts were subject to a positive price effect and about 10 percent to a negative one. Nineteen percent of K-12 districts were out-of-formula. There was again some provision for matching of rates above 30 mills, designed to phase out the previous year's provision for millage rollbacks and phase in full matching of operating levies.[17]

In 1980-81, the flat amount was raised to $357 and the support level of SEV to $46,240. For the first time, all operating mills were eligible for full matching. In addition, limited recapture of up to one-half the categorical aid of out-of-formula districts began.[18] In 1981-82, the flat amount per pupil was raised minutely to $360, while the support level of SEV was raised to $50,550.

In 1980-81 the percentage of districts which were out-of-formula leaped to 29 percent, and in 1981-82 increased still again to about 32 percent.[19]

Fiscal Variables

Table 14.1 presents some basic information on the values of SEV, operating millages, and local taxes and revenue, membership aid, total state aid, and current operating expenditures per pupil. Although our focus is on the post-Bursley Act period, data for the two years preceding the act are included for the purposes of comparison.

Over the period 1971-72 to 1979-80, the interdistrict average SEV grew at an average rate of 11.7 percent a year, while millage rates increased at an average rate of 2.2 percent. The growth in local revenues averaged 12.6 percent a year. Membership aid grew at the significantly slower average rate of 4.7 percent, while total state aid per pupil grew at an average rate of 6.3 percent. Operating expenditures per pupil went up at the rate of 11.1 percent per year.

In order to isolate the effects on the growth in membership aid of the changes in the terms of the formula alone, we calculated yearly values of membership aid per pupil for three hypothetical districts. We assigned the first district a low value of SEV (about one standard deviation below the 1971-72 mean), the second district a mid-range value, and the third a high value (about one standard deviation above the 1971-72 mean). We made the calculations first assuming a 1971-72 millage of 18, and then 26, assuming in both cases that SEV grew at 10 percent a year and the millage rate at 2 percent.

These calculations demonstrated that changes in the terms of the formula had quite different impacts on districts in different circumstances. For the district with low SEV initially levying 18 mills, aid increased in every year but 1973-74. For the low SEV district initially levying 26 mills, increases occurred in every year. But the increases varied widely from year to year. For the district with the mid-range value of SEV, aid increased in some years and decreased in others, but, in general, did rise. The district with high SEV experienced more decreases than increases and aid generally fell over time. The point we gleaned from our calculations is that, even had a district experienced constant growth in SEV and millage rates, a great deal of volatility existed in the amounts of per pupil aid received. And even for the low SEV district, growth in membership aid did not keep pace with growth in SEV. Growth in membership aid for the district with the mid-range value lagged even further behind, and for the high SEV district, growth was negative.

Impact on Wealth Neutrality

A pure equalization plan would result in complete neutrality with respect to SEV, "wealth neutrality." Such a plan would have to employ full recapture, have no limit on the millage rate matched, and not make use of the additional lump sum amount. Differences among districts in the revenue raised would then be completely independent of differences in SEV and simply a function of differences in tax effort.

The degree of wealth neutrality can be determined directly from the provisions of the power equalization formula. Michigan's system has fallen far short of equalizing the revenue raising abilities of districts. High SEV districts have retained an advantage because of the absence of recapture. Further, until 1980-81, limits on the number of mills matched have meant that, among districts levying millages above the limit, high wealth districts again have held an advantage. The "two tier" support level formula and the formula using the lump sum amount have given a relative advantage to low tax effort districts, as they were designed to do.

Table 14.2 presents the interdistrict[20] simple correlation coefficients measuring the relationship among SEV and millage rates, local revenues, "combined revenues"

TABLE 14.2
CORRELATIONS, 1971-72 TO 1979-80

Year	Correlation between SEV and:			
	Millage	Local Operating Taxes Per Pupil	Combined Revenue (Local Taxes plus Membership Aid) Per Pupil	Operating Expenditure Per Pupil
71-72	-.02	.88	.55	.58
72-73	.00	.90	.63	.50
73-74	-.04	.89	.60	.48
74-75	-.19	.85	.54	.47
75-76	-.22	.84	.55	.48
76-77	-.25	.81	.56	.41
77-78	-.30	.79	.50	.39
78-79	-.32	.76	.54	.40
79-80	-.31	.73	.54	.42

Note: The correlations are computed using the district as the unit of observation; see note 20 in the text.

Source: See Table 14.1.

TABLE 14.3
VARIANCE OF FISCAL VARIABLES, 1971-72 TO 1979-80

Measure of Variance = Standard Deviation/Mean*100					
Year	Operating Millage	SEV	Local Operating Taxes Per Pupil	Local Taxes plus Membership Aid Per Pupil	Operating Expenditure Per Pupil
71-72	21.3	51.6	52.1	14.9	15.7
72-73	20.8	54.3	54.4	15.5	16.1
73-74	18.3	56.3	52.9	15.2	15.8
74-75	15.8	60.1	50.0	14.9	15.6
75-76	14.9	60.3	49.0	15.2	15.7
76-77	17.4	65.1	46.8	15.0	15.7
77-78	16.5	62.3	45.2	15.2	16.0
78-79	16.6	64.9	45.4	16.2	16.4
79-80	18.2	65.8	44.8	17.8	17.2

Note: Variances are computed using the district as the unit of observation; see note 20 in the text.

Source: See Table 14.1.

(local operating taxes plus membership aid), and expenditures over the period 1971-72 through 1979-80.

The correlation coefficients suggest that lower SEV districts have responded over time to the price incentives contained in the school aid formula. The correlation between SEV and millage rates has become more negative since the enactment of Bursley.[21] However, the response has not been strong enough to do much toward reducing the correlation between combined revenues and SEV. The correlation between operating expenditures and SEV does exhibit a downward trend. Other factors such as state categorical and federal aid which may help explain this latter trend will be examined below.

Impact on Variance

In this section we examine the change over time in the variance of the fiscal variables. The central question here is the extent to which membership aid has reduced the variance in revenues over time. Our measure of variance is simply the standard deviation as a percentage of the mean.[22]

As might be expected from the information provided by the correlation coefficients, power equalization does appear to have led to some reduction in the variance of tax rates, as shown in Table 14.3. The variance of local taxes also shows a downward trend, although disparities in SEV have actually increased.

Membership aid clearly plays an enormous role in decreasing, in any given year, the variance in revenue per pupil that would otherwise exist. This can be seen by comparing the measures of the variance of local operating taxes with those for combined revenues. For example, in 1979-80, about two-thirds of all districts had values of local taxes per pupil within plus or minus 44.8 percent of the mean. But two-thirds of all districts had values of combined revenue per pupil within only plus or minus 17.8 percent of the mean.

Our primary interest, however, is in whether membership

aid has played an increasingly larger role over time in the reduction of variance in combined revenues. The answer appears to be that it has not done so, as the variance of combined revenues does not, in fact, show any reduction over time.

CATEGORICAL ASSISTANCE

Description of Major State Categorical Programs

State categorical assistance encompasses a wide variety of purposes, ranging from reimbursement of transportation costs to alternative education programs for "pregnant persons" (sic). In this section we focus on those several categorical programs which have received the largest allocations of state funds.

Under provisions for aid for transportation, districts receive reimbursement for up to 75 percent of the actual costs incurred in the transport of pupils living one-and-a-half or more miles from their schools.[23] If the total amount allocated for transportation aid is not sufficient to reimburse all qualifying districts for 75 percent of their costs, districts receive prorated amounts. A portion of transportation aid funds is reserved for reimbursement of the cost of the transport of students attending special education programs. Reimbursement is also provided for up to 75 percent of the costs of alternative tutoring programs set up for children whose residence in remote areas makes transport "impossible or prohibitively expensive" during a portion of the year. The legislation for transportation aid gives the state the authority to review and order changes made in districts' transportation systems. The state may refuse reimbursement if it disapproves a district's bus route. Aid for transportation has been distributed generally in this same manner over the entire period of our analysis. In 1979-80, the total state allocation for transportation aid was about $103 million; it 1980-81 it dropped to $72 million.[24]

Under the legislation for aid for special education,

TABLE 14.4
DISTRIBUTION OF CATEGORICAL AID, 1972-73 TO 1979-80

Year	Mean ($/pupil)	Median ($/pupil)	Maximum ($/pupil)	Variance (SD/Mean*100)	Percentage of Districts Receiving Aid
			Transportation		
72-73	26	28	92	53	99.4
73-74	32	34	81	51	99.8
74-75	38	40	91	47	99.4
75-76	41	43	99	46	99.4
76-77	42	44	121	45	99.6
77-78	51	52	131	45	99.6
78-79	58	59	154	43	99.8
79-80	65	67	227	43	99.8
			Special Education		
72-73	13	11	97	82	91.5
73-74	17	14	125	81	91.9
74-75	21	18	144	75	94.2
75-76	18	14	261	105	94.7
76-77	18	13	422	129	91.9
77-78	20	13	794	190	92.5
78-79	22	15	1111	233	93.6
79-80	25	18	1303	234	93.2
			Vocational Education		
72-73	NA	NA	NA	NA	NA
73-74	6	4	39	123	72.1
74-75	7	4	85	126	76.8
75-76	7	4	51	116	78.1
76-77	6	4	49	119	77.2
77-78	7	5	46	117	76.6
78-79	8	5	176	149	70.5
79-80	10	7	195	141	75.8
			Compensatory Education		
72-73	3	0	48	274	12.6
73-74	3	0	41	275	12.6
74-75	3	0	43	276	12.6
75-76	4	0	51	234	17.9
76-77	4	0	59	238	16.2
77-78	6	0	67	208	20.9
78-79	8	0	68	163	29.7
79-80	9	0	80	158	32.7

All Other Categorical					
72-73	4	3	84	179	86.8
73-74	6	4	89	158	87.0
74-75	6	4	93	144	87.7
75-76	21	11	159	113	92.3
76-77	31	21	326	134	99.1
77-78	30	18	379	141	94.7
78-79	35	27	418	113	93.6
79-80	40	33	403	89	90.4
Total Categorical					
72-73	47	43	158	40	99.8
73-74	63	60	163	34	100.0
74-75	75	71	187	32	99.8
75-76	91	86	294	38	99.8
76-77	102	92	452	48	99.8
77-78	113	104	840	51	99.8
78-79	130	120	1,202	52	100.0
79-80	149	136	1,395	52	100.0

Notes: NA = not available.

The district is again the unit of observation; means, medians, and variances were calculated for the 500-odd K-12 districts.

Source: Michigan Department of Education, SADIE tapes.

districts may receive reimbursement for up to 75 percent of the "added costs" of operating special education programs and services for physically handicapped students and those with learning disabilities. "Added costs" are determined by subtracting from the total state-approved cost of a district's program the district's membership aid "gross allowance" multiplied by the number of special education pupils. The "gross allowance" is essentially that amount per pupil under the membership aid formula that a district would receive if its SEV were zero.[25] Again, if the total allocation is insufficient to fund 75 percent of the added costs of all the districts, districts receive prorated amounts.[26] Federal funds received by the state for the education of the handicapped are also redistributed under this legislation for aid for special education. In 1979-80, the state-only allocation for special education was $110 million; in 1980-81 it dropped to $77 million.

Under the legislation for aid for compensatory education, qualifying districts are granted a flat amount for each elementary school pupil determined to be "in need of substantial improvement in the basic cognitive skills."[27] The flat amount has varied from year to year; in 1980-81 it was $175, down from the 1979-80 value of $250. Funding is currently for grades kindergarten through eighth; in some years it has been for grades through the sixth, and in others for grades through the seventh. The results of reading and mathematics tests (administered state-wide to certain grades) are used to estimate the number of students in the district in need of compensatory education. A district is then eligible for funds only if a specified minimum percentage of its students have been found to be in need of compensatory education. This minimum percentage has varied from year to year.[28] Where the total allocation for compensatory education is insufficient to fully fund all qualifying districts, the amounts disbursed are not prorated but rather disbursed to districts following the order of the highest concentration of pupils in need, until the allocation is exhausted. In 1979-80 the allocation for compensatory education was $33 million; in 1980-81 it was $23 million.

Districts operating vocational education programs may receive reimbursement of up to 75 percent of the "added costs" of the programs. One hundred percent of the added costs of programs run after regular hours or during the summer may be reimbursed. The added costs of vocational education programs are determined by the state based on information submitted by the districts on the type and length of programs and the number of pupils. To be eligible for reimbursement, programs must conform to the state's definitions of vocational education. Prorated amounts of aid are disbursed in the event that the allocation is insufficient.[29] In 1979-80 the allocation for vocational education was $29 million; it also dropped in 1980-81 to $20 million.

Quantitative Importance of Categorical Aid

In this section we examine in detail the distribution of per pupil categorical aid. Table 14.4 presents the interdistrict mean and median per pupil amounts for K-12 districts, as well as the maximum amounts, for the years 1972-73 to 1979-80. The quantitative importance of categorical aid falls far below that of membership aid. The mean amount of categorical aid received under all programs was only $149 in 1979-80. But, as can be seen from the values of the maximums in Table 14.4, categorical aid is very important to some districts.

To measure the variance in categorical assistance received we again use the standard deviation as a percentage of the mean. In general, aid distributed under the transportation program has the least variance. About two-thirds of all districts received a per pupil amount within plus or minus 43 percent of the interdistrict mean in 1979-80. The variance of the distribution of aid for special education is much larger, having increased considerably over the years. The variance in funds received for compensatory education has decreased over time but is still large. The variance in funds received for vocational education is somewhat less than that of compensatory education.

The mean and median values for transportation are fairly close, indicating that about the same number of districts receive amounts less than the mean as receive amounts greater than the mean. The medians of the other three programs are generally below the mean telling us that a greater number of districts receive amounts less than the mean than amounts above the mean.

Table 14.4 also shows the percentages of districts which received any aid at all under each of the four programs. Virtually all districts received some aid for transportation. The percentage of districts which received aid for special education is also high, ranging between 91 and 95 percent over the years; for vocational education, it ranged between 72 and 79 percent. Not surprisingly, given the method by which aid for compensatory education is distributed, the percentage of districts has increased from only 12.6 to 32.7 percent for compensatory education since 1972-73.

Equalizing Effects

In this section we look at the effect of categorical aid on the variance in per pupil revenues. The objective here is to help develop a clear picture of the impacts of the entire state aid system on school finance. Given the nature of categorical assistance, however, we do not specify equalization as one of its objectives.

The addition to revenues of categorical aid did decrease the interdistrict variance of revenues in every year, 1972-73 to 1979-80, but only by a very small amount. The addition of categorical aid also resulted in an again very slight decrease in the correlation between revenues and SEV.

Municipal Overburden Assistance and Issues

In this section we examine the state's program for

TABLE 14.5
DISTRIBUTION OF FEDERAL AID,
1972-73 TO 1979-80

Year	Mean ($/pupil)	Median ($/pupil)	Maximum ($/pupil)	Variance (SD/Mean*100)	Percentage of Districts Receiving Aid
72-73	$37	$26	$330	103	98.7
73-74	39	27	493	116	98.5
74-75	50	34	585	112	99.3
75-76	61	47	714	99	99.6
76-77	60	46	576	95	99.4
77-78	82	60	1,529	116	99.3
78-79	92	69	1,001	91	99.8
79-80	95	72	871	90	100.0

Note: The district is the unit of observation.

Source: Michigan Department of Education, Bulletin 1012, various years.

"municipal overburden" assistance. This program is designed to aid districts whose residents pay high nonschool property taxes. The nonschool operating property tax rate in each district is compared with the state average nonschool rate. Each district's membership aid gross allowance is then increased by the percentage, if any, by which its tax rate exceeds 125 percent of the state average rate. The district is then entitled to the difference between the amount of membership aid it would receive had the higher gross allowance been used in computing membership aid and the actual amount of membership aid received.[30] For example, a district in 1979-80 with a nonschool property tax rate equal to 130 percent of the state average, would recalculate membership aid per pupil as: 1.05 x [$325 + ($43,000 - SEV) x millage]. It would receive in municipal overburden assistance the difference between this amount and the actual membership aid received.[31] Where the total allocation for municipal overburden assistance is not sufficient to fully fund all entitlements, districts receive prorated amounts.

In 1980-81, municipal overburden assistance amounted to $25 million for all districts. While less than 10 percent of districts receive such assistance, more than a quarter of all pupils live in those districts. Aid from this program has the most consistently high variance of aid from any categorical program yet examined.

Taking a closer look at those districts receiving municipal overburden assistance, we find that in every year, 1972-73 through 1979-80, the Detroit school district received either the highest or second highest amount per pupil and between 70 and 90 percent of the total distribution. In 1979-80, Highland Park received $121 and Detroit, $112. All other districts in this year received less than $75 per pupil.

Even given that residents of some school districts do indeed face higher nonschool property tax rates than residents of others, it is unclear why one might wish to compensate them for this. These higher rates may very well be accompanied by better or more services. But even if it is thought desirable to compensate residents of urban areas who are subject to high municipal service costs, it makes little sense for such compensation to be made by providing additional aid for schools rather than for nonschool services.

A second more plausible and pragmatic reason for increasing aid to districts whose residents face high nonschool tax rates is that it is difficult to get voter approval of higher school millages in areas where residents are already "overburdened" by other taxes. However, the average level of school operating millages among districts receiving municipal overburden assistance is higher than it is among all districts. The average school operating millage for districts receiving assistance over the period 1972-73 through 1979-80 ranged from 16 to 26 percent higher than the average school millage for all districts.

In fact, the "municipal overburden" argument for school aid would appear to be mainly a politically acceptable justification for supplementing the revenues of Detroit and a few other communities.

Federal Aid

To complete our picture of the distribution of aid among Michigan school districts, we examine federal aid. Table 14.5 presents the basic information on the distribution of federal aid over the years 1972-73 through 1979-80. The amounts shown include both aid received by local districts directly from the federal government and federal aid redistributed by the state.

Since 1972-73, the interdistrict average value of federal aid per pupil has increased from $37 to $95. The median district received only $72 per pupil in 1979-80, whereas the district at the top of the range received more than twelve times as much, $871 per pupil. All K-12 districts received some federal assistance in 1979-80.

The addition to revenues of federal aid, in every year

1972-73 through 1979-80, decreased the correlation among districts' SEV and per pupil revenue. In 1979-80, for example, the correlation between SEV and revenue per pupil from all sources save federal aid was 0.493. Adding federal aid decreased the correlation to 0.468. The addition of federal aid tended generally to increase slightly the variance of per pupil revenues, but not consistently in every year.

INTERSTATE COMPARISONS

In this section we look briefly at the relative importance among states of state and federal aid to the financing of public school systems. Table 14.6 shows the percentage distribution of public school general revenues among all sources in 1978-79 for the U.S. as a whole, Michigan, and seven other states.

Michigan school districts obtained 6.4 percent of their general revenues in the form of federal aid, compared with 8.8 percent for the the U.S. as a whole, 9.6 percent for California, and, lowest among the eight states, 4.9 percent for Wisconsin.

In 1976-77, the earliest year for which census data are available on state aid excluding federal funds, Michigan ranked second to last among the eight states in the percentage of revenues supplied by the state. By 1978-79 it ranked a poor last. The position of Michigan schools in terms of revenues supplied by the state has clearly worsened over the years, relative to the other select states. But the percentage of Michigan school revenues supplied by the state (inclusive of redistributed federal aid) has not changed much over the years. In 1961-62 it was 35.6; by 1966-67 it had jumped to 44.9. Ten years later, by 1976-77, the proportion of school revenues accounted for by state aid had dropped to 39.2 percent and by 1978-79, it had fallen further to 38.3 percent (33.9 percent exclusive of federal funds).[32] On the other hand, each of the other states save New York experienced a large increase over the years in the

TABLE 14.6
PERCENTAGE DISTRIBUTION OF GENERAL REVENUES
OF PUBLIC SCHOOL SYSTEMS IN 1978-79,
SELECTED STATES

STATE	PERCENTAGE FROM:				
	Federal Aid	State Aid	Other Local Gov'ts	Local District Own Sources	Local District Own Taxes[1]
U.S.	8.8	42.7	1.3	47.1	30.7
CALIFORNIA	9.6	57.9	0.7	31.8	24.9
ILLINOIS	7.2	37.4	0.2	55.2	47.3
INDIANA	5.9	48.6	0.9	44.5	38.0
MICHIGAN	6.4	33.9	2.0	57.7	49.3
NEW YORK	7.5	40.4	0.0	52.1	30.4
OHIO	8.6	40.3	0.1	51.1	44.3
PENNSYLVANIA	7.7	38.2	0.1	53.9	45.9
WISCONSIN	4.9	41.7	0.3	53.1	32.0

Note: [1]"Own Taxes" is a subset of "Own Sources."
Source: U. S. Bureau of the Census, _Finances of Public School Systems, 1978-79_.

percentage of revenues supplied by the state.

CONCLUSIONS

In recent years Michigan has fallen behind other states, both in its own region and nationally, in the extent to which the state shares in the costs of providing elementary and secondary education in the public schools. An increasing number of school districts receive no general assistance from the state at all. Increases in the basic level of support have fallen far behind the rate of inflation, thus shifting an increasing load for school financing from state tax and other revenue sources to the local property tax.

The legislature that has moved the system of state aid from the pre-1973 foundation grant program toward an equal yield system has traveled only part of the way in halting and not always consistent steps. The current general aid formula is a hybrid, containing as it does a major equal yield element and a flat per pupil grant for in-formula districts as well.

We observe that state aid for schools in Michigan appears to pursue these principal goals: to ensure that all districts are fiscally able to offer an acceptably adequate quality of educational opportunity; to equalize per pupil revenues among districts; and to provide special assistance targeted to the City of Detroit's schools and other troubled central city or inner suburban districts. But none of these goals can be said to be even approximately achieved.

The system is not without its merits and some gains have been realized in the past decade. There is far less variance in total revenue per pupil, including state aid, than there is in revenue from local sources alone. Full equity, defined as equality among districts in per pupil revenues, has not been achieved, but the system is efficient in the sense that local districts do enjoy in very large measure effective freedom to reflect the preferences of their residents in school programs.

Perhaps what is now most needed in a reexamination of state aid to elementary and secondary education is a clear-cut delineation of objectives, together with the matching of appropriate selected instruments to separate specified objectives. At present the general school aid formula is designed with a view to achieving at least three distinct objectives and it is extremely unlikely that the one instrument can ever be so designed as to enable it to carry that load. A productive first step would recognize that financing schools in Detroit may require an approach that cannot be fitted into a system that is adequate to the needs of the rest of the state.

NOTES, CHAPTER 14

[1]The contribution to school revenues of other local governments is important only in a few states.

[2]U.S. Bureau of the Census, Finances of Public School Systems, 1978-79 (Washington D.C., 1980).

[3]U.S. Bureau of the Census, Census of Governments, vol. 4, no. 1, 1962, 1967, 1972, and 1977.

[4]Constitution of the State of Michigan (1963), Article VIII, Sec. 2.

[5]See the glossary of this volume for an explanation of price and income effects.

[6]For example, a district with $35,000 of SEV would gain $35 per pupil from a one mill increase, while a district with $10,000 of SEV would gain but $10.

[7]Under Michigan's foundation program, combined revenues from local taxes and membership aid increased with SEV for districts levying more than the deductible millage, but decreased with SEV for districts levying less. Actually, however, very few districts levied less than the deductible millage. Of course, among out-of-formula districts, those receiving no membership aid, revenues increased with SEV regardless of the relationship between the actual and deductible millages.

[8]J. Alan Thomas, School Finance and Educational Opportunity in Michigan (Michigan Department of Education, Lansing, 1968).

[9]See Gene Caesar, Robert McKerr, and James Phelps, New Equity in School Finance, the Story of the Bursley Act (the Senate Committee on Education, Lansing, 1974), p. 9.

[10]Caesar, McKerr, and Phelps, New Equity, p. 26.

[11]From the formula above, one can see that a district goes out of formula at the point where SEV becomes greater than SEV*.

[12]Recapture would be unnecessary if SEV* were set equal to the highest existing value of SEV. The state's budget constraint obviously precludes this.

Beginning in 1980-81, a limited form of recapture was in fact incorporated into the aid system. Where the application of the formula results in a negative amount, the lesser of this amount or half the categorical aid that the district would have otherwise received is subtracted from categorical aid. Recapture of up to 66 percent of categorical aid is in effect in 1981-82. Even with recapture of up to 100 percent of categorical aid, however, some out-of-formula districts would continue to hold an advantage.

[13]The aid received, if the district levies mills above the limit, is: Aid=(SEV* - SEV) x limit = SEV* x limit - SEV x limit. But SEV* x limit is a constant analogous to the gross allowance of the foundation aid program and the "cap" millage, or limit, in the second addend is analogous to the deductible millage.

[14]The analysis in this section, and in the next on categorical aid, generally is confined to K-12 districts. Over 99 percent of the public school population is served by K-12 districts.

The data for this section and the next is from the Michigan Department of Education's SADIE tapes, supplemented by published data from the department's annual Bulletin 1012. We would like to extend our sincere thanks to Mr. Robert Witte of Department Services, Michigan Department of Education, for the gracious assistance he provided in helping us to access the SADIE tapes.

[15]Both halves of the formula were subject to a zero limit. SEV greater than $38,250 and mills over 22 did not decrease the amount due the district on the first 22 mills.

[16]Reimbursement of mills over 30 was limited to districts with SEV less than $40,000 and for which the following condition held: actual mills over 30 levied < authorized mills over 30 x SEV/$40,000.

[17]The number of mills over 30 reimbursed was equal to one-half of the authorized number over 30, subject to the condition that the total number of mills reimbursed not exceed the actual levy. So, for example, a district levying

34 mills with an authorization also of 34 would be reimbursed for 32 mills. A district levying 34 with an authorization of 36 would be reimbursed for 33. A district levying 34 with an authorization of 38 mills or more would receive reimbursement for 34.

[18]See note 12 above.

[19]Information on the number of K-12 districts out-of-formula in 1980-81 and 1981-82 was supplied by staff members of the Department of Education.

[20]Throughout the analysis that follows, we use "interdistrict" calculations which use the district as the unit of observation. For example, an interdistrict mean is the simple average of the 500-odd district values. Although not published here, we also made corresponding "interpupil" calculations, weighting district values by the number of pupils in the district. Weighting by number by number of pupils did not alter the character of any of our results.

[21]The demonstrated decrease over time in the correlation between SEV and millage rates may be due to one or both of two factors: low SEV districts raising their tax rates or high SEV districts lowering their rates. It is important to our analysis of the effectiveness of the power-equalization price incentives to separate these two factors.

In fact, increases in tax rates among low SEV districts <u>have</u> been the predominant factor in the change of the correlation coefficient. Among K-12 districts with low SEV, millage increases outweighed millage decreases in each year 1973-74 through 1978-79. This did not hold true in 1979-80, possibly due to rollbacks mandated by Headlee. On the other hand, among K-12 districts with high SEV, millage decreases did <u>not</u> outweigh increases in any year, 1973-74 through 1978-79, although did do so in 1979-80.

[22]The value of this measure tells one that about two-thirds of all observations fall within plus or minus this percent of the mean.

We also calculated a second measure of variance, the semi-interquartile range, for all the fiscal variables. The magnitude of the semi-interquartile range is unaffected by extreme values. We found the same trends in the variance of the fiscal variables using this second measure.

[23]See Public Act 320 of 1980, section 71.

The costs of the transport of handicapped and certain pregnant students living less than a mile and a half away may also be reimbursed.

[24]This is the allocation for all districts, not just K-12, as are the allocations cited below for special, compensatory, and vocational education.

Information on allocations for categorical aid is taken from Public Acts 94 of 1979 and 320 of 1980, various sections.

[25]Prior to 1975-76, reimbursement was based on the actual salary costs incurred for special education.

[26]See Public Act 94 of 1979, section 52, and Public Act 320 of 1980, sections 51 and 53.

The legislation also provides for reimbursement of up to 100 percent of the added costs of special education programs for community placed or institutionalized children; the amounts disbursed may again be prorated. A power equalizing formula is also employed for the partial reimbursement of intermediate school district special education millages. We do not deal with this here as our analysis is confined to K-12 districts. However, the intermediate school district may redistribute monies received under this provision to its constituent districts.

[27]See Public Act 320 of 1980, sections 33 and 34.

[28]In 1980-81, the percentage was fourteen, with the added proviso that the absolute number of students in need be at least thirty.

[29]See Public Act 320 of 1980, section 61.

Legislation also provides a power equalization formula for the partial reimbursement of vocational education millages levied by intermediate school districts.

[30]See Public Act 320 of 1980, section 25.

[31]As an alternative, districts may receive the difference between the amount of membership aid actually received and the amount they would have received had their SEV been reduced by the excess percentage.

[32]Data for interstate comparisons are from U.S. Bureau of the Census, _Finances of Public School Systems_, 1978-79, and _Census of Governments_, vol. 4, no. 1, 1962, 1967, 1972, and 1977.

Chapter 15

The Role of Tax Limitation Referenda in State Fiscal Policy

by

Edward M. Gramlich and Gary C. Woodard

The University of Michigan

INTRODUCTION

In the last five years Michigan voters have been asked to vote on nine separate fiscal referenda. Only one of these nine passed, and that gained only 52 percent of the total vote. Hence one way to read the experience is that the voters do not want tax limitation measures and will consistently reject them. But there have been nine referenda and there will no doubt be more. An alternative reading is that voters are trying to tell state and local legislators that they desire a more direct voice in state-local fiscal matters, and that one way or another they will get it.

The uncertainty in reading these results reflects a basic quandary faced now by all state and local governments. There are many reasons why representative democracies might not yield the fiscal outcomes preferred by voters, and why voters should have a more direct way to determine their tax and expenditure levels. But it turns out to be extremely difficult to design proposals that arrange for this in a sensible way. There are at least two basic problems. One is that the standard approach, adopted now by sixteen states (including Michigan), features a tax or expenditure limit that is permanent, fairly inflexible, and can only be overridden with difficulty. As time passes, this limit is likely to become more or less stringent in ways that cannot possibly be foreseen at the time the limitation measure is first passed. Some mechanism is needed either to relax those limits becoming too stringent or tighten those becoming less stringent. The second problem is that these limitation measures are increasingly taking on the character of actual legislation--that is, they are getting more and more complicated. The results are that voters may pass unwise measures, they may not pass wise measures because they simply do not understand them, and highly detailed and numerical provisions best left to legislation are creeping into state constitutions. Hence while there may be valid reasons for passing tax limitation amendments, there are also intrinsic difficulties with them, and it is by no means obvious that limits inevitably or even usually lead to improved fiscal outcomes.[1]

In this paper we discuss these issues, paying particular attention to Michigan's recent history. We also advance our own proposal for allowing voters to determine their tax and expenditure levels. This proposal tries to present budget issues to voters in a way that gives them a clearer idea of what they are voting on, is flexible and does not build detailed fiscal restrictions permanently into the state constitution, and can readily be tailored to deal with a host of fiscal and legal complexities that arise in the actual implementation of tax limitation measures.

The paper begins with an examination of the rationale for tax limitation measures in general--just what is wrong with unconstrained fiscal systems and why do limitations have the potential for making improvements? It goes on to discuss the limitations now in effect in sixteen states and their main drawbacks. We then introduce our proposal and discuss its relative benefits and costs. Finally, we show how it could be tailored to deal with several technical problems of implementation.

THE RATIONALE FOR TAX LIMITATION

The classical literature in public finance does not recognize the rationale for tax or expenditure limitation because of what is known as the median voter theory. (See Hotelling 1929, Bowen 1943, and Downs 1957.) Under this theory, politicians desiring to stay in office will be led to represent the wishes of the median voter. If they did

FIGURE 15.1
THE MEDIAN VOTER IN A REPRESENTATIVE DEMOCRACY

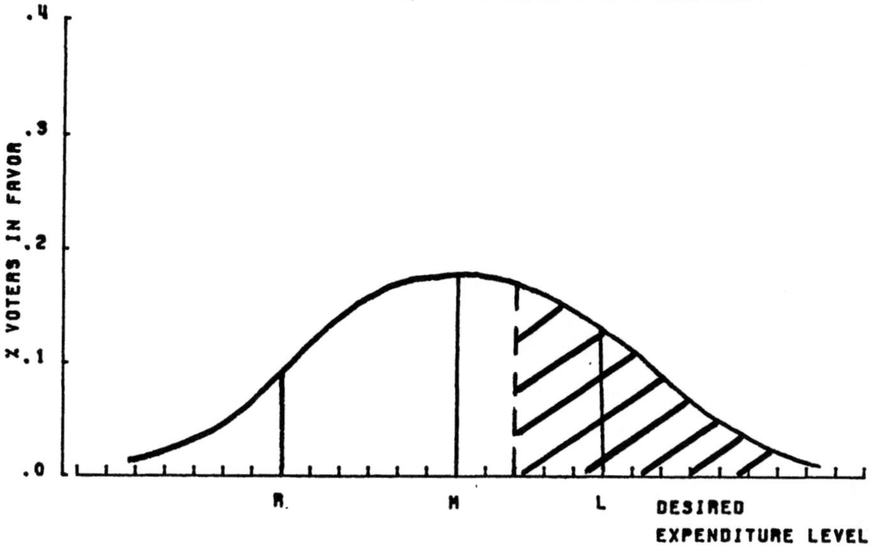

not, some other politicians would be able to capture the middle and get more votes. To see how this works, say the distribution of voter tastes by desired tax and expenditure level is as shown in Figure 15.1. M designates the level of spending favored by the median voter (with half the distribution on either side), and B designates the level favored by some "big-spending" legislator. It can be seen from the graph that any politician proposing M will capture more than half the total vote and, other things equal, win the election. Moreover, there will be competition among politicians to "capture the middle," a well-known phenomenon often observed in politics that here means favoring that spending desired by the median voter. Tax limitations in such a scheme are quite unnecessary because the law of political competition already brings about median voter outcomes, the best that a democracy can do.[2]

Giving this argument in its simplest form indicates the many problems there are with it. For one thing, political candidates often do not know what they will do once in office; and even if they do, the voters may not. For another, any campaign features a number of issues and forces voters to vote for politicians for a composite set of reasons, hence not insuring that the winning politician accurately reflects median voter tastes on any one particular issue such as budgeting. Then there is the so-called "iron triangle" of lobbyists, bureaucrats, and sympathetic legislators who may be able to push tax and spending levels past M and get away with it. Sometimes public employees are able to become strategic voting blocks and make compromises with political candidates that trade political support for higher wages or expanded employment. When it comes to fiscal referenda on actual outcomes, public employees sometimes may be able to set the agenda--for example, to pose to voters the choice between the high spending level B and some budget reversion level L. In such a case B will defeat L even though it would lose to M if voters were allowed to make that choice.

TABLE 15.1
SUMMARY INFORMATION ON RECENTLY ENACTED
TAX LIMITATION MEASURES

STATE	YEAR	STATUTORY OR CONSTITUTIONAL	STATE OR LOCAL	EXPENDITURES OR TAXES	ITEM BEING LIMITED	INI-TIAL CUT	GROWTH LIMIT	OVERRIDE PROVISION
New Jersey	76	Statutory	Both	Expenditures	Total	no	Income(State) 5%(Local)	Majority Referendum
Colorado	77	Statutory	State	Expenditures	Total	no	7%	Majority of Legislature
Rhode Island	77	Statutory	State	Expenditures	Total	no	8%	Non-Binding
Tennesse	78	Constitutional	State	Taxes	Total	no	Income	Majority of Legislature
Arizona	78	Constitutional	State	Expenditures	Total	no	Income	2/3 of Legislature
Hawaii	78	Constitutional	State	Expenditures	Total	no	Income	2/3 of Legislature
Michigan	78	Constitutional	Both	Taxes	Total(State) Property Tax (Local)	no	Income(State) Price Level (Local)	2/3 of Legislature(State) Majority Referendum(Local)
Texas	78	Constitutional	State	Taxes	Total	no	Income	Majority of Legislature
California	78	Constitutional	Both	Taxes	Total(State) Property Tax (Local)	yes	2%(Local)	2/3 of Legislature(State) 2/3 Registered Voters(Local)
Idaho	78	Statutory	State	Taxes	Property Tax	yes	2%	Majority of Legislature
Alabama	78	Constitutional	Local	Taxes	Property Tax	yes	Property Value	Majority of Legislature & Majority Referendum
North Dakota	78	Statutory	State	Taxes	Income Tax	yes	Income	Majority of Legislature
Arkansas	80	Constitutional	Local	Taxes	Property Tax	no	10%	?
Massachusetts	80	Statutory	Local	Taxes	Property Tax	yes	Property Value	2/3 Referendum
Missouri	80	Constitutional	Both	Taxes	Total(State) Property Tax (Local)	no	Income(State) Price Level (Local)	Majority Referendum
Montana	80	Statutory	State	Taxes	Income Tax	no	Income	Majority of Legislature

Source: ACIR Reports.

All of these problems, now being analyzed and reanalyzed in a new conservative tradition among public finance economists, suggest that there could be a role for tax limitation amendments to try to keep actual fiscal outcomes closer to M. But simply asserting that the potential benefits of tax limitation measures are positive does not mean either that these benefits outweigh the costs or that benefits are inevitably positive. To gain some idea of whether they are, we make a closer examination of the actual limitation measures that have been passed now in sixteen states.

PRESENT-DAY TAX LIMITATION AMENDMENTS

Before 1976 no state had a statutory or constitutional limitation on aggregate tax or expenditure levels. In that year New Jersey passed the first one, a statutory limitation on total expenditures. In 1977 Colorado passed another statutory limitation and Rhode Island passed one that was nonbinding. In 1978 the first of the constitutional limitations was passed, by Michigan (the Headlee Amendment) and six other states. Two statutory limits were also enacted in that year. There was a brief respite in 1979, when no new limits were passed, but another four passed in 1980 (out of nine on the ballot). As of now sixteen states have passed tax limits by popular referendum, and nine of these limits are constitutional. Summary information on these limitation measures is given in Table 15.1.

While the intent of all of these measures is similar, their impact can vary widely depending on the type of limit and the initial condition of the states' finances. To give some illustration of the types of differences that can arise, both California and Massachusetts passed amendments requiring a large cutback in property taxes. But California's measure passed when the state government had a huge surplus that could be used to aid local governments and forestall service cutbacks, while Massachusetts did not have this initial surplus (though the Massachusetts measure is to be phased in gradually). In nine states the limit is on taxes or expenditures at the state level, in three it is on local taxes, and in four it is on both state and local taxes or expenditures. It also matters whether the limit is on expenditures or taxes, unless expenditures financed by federal grants are explicitly exempted from the limitation. All limits have some feature for limiting the growth of taxes or expenditures--sometimes as an explicit nominal percentage change regardless of price or income growth in the state, sometimes based on price, income, or property value growth. All measures contain override provisions, but these too vary widely--sometimes the limits can be overriden by two-thirds of the legislature, sometimes by a popular referendum, and in the case of California by two-thirds of the registered voters, whether they actually vote or not.

While there are any number of potential technical flaws with the amendments, many of these appear to be particular to the specific state or type of measure. But there are at least two general types of difficulties with tax limitation proposals, one involving their permanence and one involving their complexity. As it happens, both sets of difficulties can be nicely illustrated by two examples from the Michigan experience, the Headlee Amendment that passed in 1978 and Proposal A that was defeated in 1981.

The Headlee Amendment illustrates the problem of permanence. When it first passed, the amendment was viewed as a conservative measure, generally favored by those wanting to limit the growth in government. Now, just two years after its enactment, it is widely viewed as a failure. Its sponsor, Richard Headlee, is quoted in the press as saying he is "disappointed" with the amendment, and the Detroit Free Press has gone so far as to call the amendment "fraudulent" (May 21, 1981).

The reasons for this disappointment are not hard to divine, though they are hard to correct. The amendment contains a state component, a local component, and what might be called an evasion provision. The state component limits taxes to the preexisting share of state personal income (10.0 percent) unless the governor declares an emergency and two-thirds of the legislature concurs. The local component automatically rolls back local property tax rates so that tax revenues (excluding those on new construction) increase at the rate of increase in consumer prices unless a majority of the electorate approves an override. The evasion provision prohibits the state from reducing the portion of state spending paid to local governments below the preexisting share (41.6 percent), thereby shifting the burden of the limit onto local governments. The two limitation provisions seemed likely to constrain government growth at the time the measure was passed, and the evasion provision was barely even discussed. Now with the wisdom of hindsight, all judgments differ.

As for the state component, a long list of empirical studies have indicated that rich areas, states, and communities, spend a lower proportion of their income on public services than do poor areas, after controlling for demographic variables, federal grants, prices, and so forth.[3] If these cross-sectional spending propensities can be used to make time series predictions and if federal grants grow at the same rate as income, over time there would be a natural tendency for state revenues as a share of income to decline, and for the state component of the Headlee Amendment gradually to become less binding. Cross-section parameters cannot be too mechanically extrapolated to time series contexts because of changing ideas about the scope of the public sector, new programs, and so forth. But Brazer (this volume, Chapter 2) does show that between 1972 and 1979, the years before the Headlee Amendment was officially adopted, the ratio of state taxes to income (T/Y) had not risen at all, indicating the cross-sectional parameters may not be too far off. This judgment is supported by more careful time series econometric examinations of the Michigan budget reported by Cline (1981). It therefore should not come as an enormous surprise that this state component of the limit has not been binding on the state legislature, even in the first few years.[4]

The reasoning is different for the local component but the result is the same. As shown by Courant (this volume, Chapter 16), established commercial-industrial property, comprising about one-third of the overall tax base, typically rises in value at rates a good deal less than the rate of consumer price inflation because of physical depreciation. Even if residential property values rise at rates nearly 50 percent more than the general rate of inflation, an extremely unlikely result for a state suffering an economic recession, the local rollback provision in Headlee will not take effect.[5]

But the evasion provision, almost unnoticed at the time of passage, has become a severe constraint. As discussed in the chapter by Cross (Chapter 12), this provision is now limiting the degree to which the state government can spend on state functions (mental health, prisons, higher education), even as the demands for spending on state grant supported functions (local education) decline.

Hence the limitation features of the Headlee Amendment are now viewed as being insufficiently constraining on state and local governments, only coming into effect in sporadic instances. But if the measure had been made much more stringent, as for example those in California and Idaho are (allowing only a 2 percent growth in assessed values per year), we might now be hearing complaints that the amendment was too strict. The fact of the matter is that it is difficult, if not impossible, to have a one-time vote on any tax limit amendment and not have it grow either too lenient or too strict over time. To do this, voters must make projections of long term economic, social, demographic, and policy changes in their jurisdiction, projections that are simply impossible to make and write into limitation measures.

The second important difficulty with present-day tax limitation amendments is their sheer complexity. Every one necessarily comes equipped with stipulations about what is to be limited, how, by how much, how the limit will change over time, the circumstances under which deviations are allowed, and a host of provisions needed to assure that the intent of the amendment is being followed. But recent amendments have gone beyond that minimum necessary complexity, and have begun to look like legislative "Christmas Tree" bills themselves. Perhaps the high-water mark in amendment complexity was achieved by Michigan's 1981 Proposal A, which received only 27 percent of the popular vote despite the fact that almost all major politicians in the state were campaigning for it, and that it was supported by many newspapers, civic groups, business groups, and labor unions. The proposal directly mandated general property tax cuts, special cuts for farmers and the elderly, an alteration in the circuit-breaker provision, a sales tax rate increase, and state general fund spending reductions. It raised the probability of local income tax increases and more state support for the City of Detroit. It either raised or lowered the probability of yet further property tax cuts in the future--arguments on this question could be found on both sides. Dozens of reasons were given in the press and by voters for favoring or opposing the proposal, and the post-election analysis of the results has never been vaguer or more confused. One person who does allege that he understands the voters' message is a well-known county drain commissioner, but apart from him the main lesson being drawn is that whether these proposals are good or bad, they have certainly grown too complex. Voters are not legislators; there is a limit to the degree to which they will assume what should be the legislative function of working out the complex details of fiscal proposals, and there is also a limit to the degree that complex and detailed legislation with uncertain effects should be added to the state constitution.

AN ALTERNATIVE PROPOSAL

With these lessons from the Michigan experience in

mind, we now try to sketch out a different sort of procedure for voting on fiscal matters. At the outset, we make no claims that such a procedure is clearly better than having none at all, because such a claim would be hard to defend at this stage. There are reasons why elected representatives may tend to overspend and overtax the private sector, but there are also some costs to any form of tax or expenditure limit and the ultimate evaluation just cannot yet be made.

We have tried to design our proposal to deal with the major weaknesses we see in the present-day limitation proposals of Michigan and other states. Specifically, we have tried to develop a procedure that allows for alterations in budgets over time as conditions change, and that allows voters to have a clearer idea of what they are voting on. For obvious reasons, we have also tried to tailor this proposal so it can be easily adapted to existing legal precedent and fiscal institutions.

The basic idea would be to have voters vote on a "real resources" budget.[6] Instead of having to convert complex limitation formulae or millage rates into an effect on public services, voters would simply vote on the level of services they desire. As one illustration, voters might be asked to select the percentage amount by which they would favor adjusting real levels of both government spending and taxes:

-4%

-2%

No change

+2%

+4%

The limits should be kept fairly narrow to prevent voters from opting for extreme and unrealistic changes. These elections could be held by any autonomous taxing and spending jurisdiction--that is, the school board could hold them, the regular local general government could hold them, the state government could hold them, and special districts could hold them. Since large capital expenditures are already voted on by referenda, the votes should apply only to the general operating fund budgets of the state and its local governments.

To give an idea of how the system might work, say the results of three elections (A, B, and C) were as shown in Table 15.2. For each election the winning outcome would be that favored by the median voter (in the 50th percentile), the bracketed number in the table. An election like this must use medians instead of means because if the mean were used, there would be an invitation for what is known as strategic voting: voters might actually favor a one percent reduction, but vote for a larger one if they felt the rest of the electorate would favor no change. Hence there would be a tendency for votes to pile up on the extremes, a tendency that is absent if the median is used to designate the winning outcome.

For legislative reasons it is necessary to refine the proposal further. Article II, section 9 of the state constitution says:

> Referendum, approval. No laws as to which the power of referendum properly has been invoked shall be effective thereafter unless approved by a majority of the electors voting thereon at the next general election.

It is unclear whether this language applies only to referenda as defined by Article II or whether it would also pertain to our proposal. However, even if it is determined not to be pertinent, there is no known precedent for declaring the median voter choice, as opposed to the mode, or most popular choice, the winner in a proposal. (The median and mode are not necessarily the same, as Table 15.2, outcome B, illustrates.) So some way must be found to convert the median voter outcome into a majority rule in the sense of Article II.

There are several possibilities. One is that the preference vote could be made nonbinding on the legislature,

TABLE 15.2
ILLUSTRATIVE OUTCOMES: DESIRED SPENDING AND TAX CHANGES

CHOICE(% CHANGE)	PERCENT OF VOTERS FAVORING		
	A	B	C
-4	25	-	5
-2	[40]	40	15
No Change	25	[30]	20
+2	10	20	[30]
+4	-	10	30
Total	100	100	100

TABLE 15.3
PREFERENCES FOR STATE AND LOCAL SPENDING AND TAX CHANGES
2001 MICHIGAN HOUSEHOLD RESPONDENTS, 1978

	PERCENT OF RESPONDENTS FAVORING	
CHOICE(% CHANGE)	STATE LEVEL	LOCAL LEVEL
-10 or more	11.3	6.3
-1 to -10	20.1	8.7
No Change	[51.4]	[59.5]
1 to 10	8.4	18.4
10 or more	1.0	2.6
No Response	7.9	4.6
Total	100.0	100.0

as in the Rhode Island statute. A second is that the choices could be converted to "less than or equal to" form, and be tested sequentially. If, for example, voters were asked to select the percentage change in government spending or taxes that would serve as an upper limit to actual spending, the test could first be made on the highest ceiling of all, +4%. Should this option not receive a majority, it could be eliminated, those favoring the highest ceiling of +4% could be assumed to favor the next highest ceiling of +2%, and the test could be repeated. Proceeding sequentially, the winning outcome will be at the same time the median voter outcome and the majority rule outcome in the sense of Article II.[7]

A third possibility entails higher costs, but also has some advantages. The wording could be left as is, but there could be a second runoff election between the winning outcome in Table 15.2 and the "no change" option, if none of the options captures a majority in the first election. If some option does capture a majority, it is automatically both the majority and median voter outcome and no runoff election is necessary. If "no change" wins the first election, as in column B in Table 15.2, no second election would be necessary. But if some other outcome wins with less than a majority, there would need to be a runoff election. As in other runoff elections there would be the additional advantages that voters would have an incentive not to make their first choice too extreme for fear of losing out to "no change" in the runoff; and that voters could "think about" what they had done in the first preference vote.

Details on the proper timing of the votes are quite flexible, but the most sensible procedure appears to be to administer the preference vote (the illustration of which is described in Table 15.2) every November in the biennial election. Two years seems about the right interval for voting--it is a long enough time from the previous election that conditions and political preferences might have changed meaningfully, but a short enough time that voters need not fear they are locking their government into a long term straightjacket (as is now the case). While the range of possible outcomes shown in Table 15.2 is intentionally set up to be rather narrow to avoid disruptive changes, having a sequence of biennial elections would allow for quite significant changes in government spending over time, should the voters desire them. And administering the preference vote in November permits the runoff election to be dropped if one choice wins a majority or if the "no change" option wins. Whenever a runoff is necessary, there are explicit costs in simply holding the election. For the 1981 Proposition A vote, these came to $3.5 million, $1.75 per voter. (Two million people voted on Proposition A, 35 percent of the registered electorate.) There is no way to avoid incurring some of these costs, but there are ways of reducing them. One possibility is by mailing out punch card ballots, as was recently done by the City of San Diego. For a recent referendum, they were able to raise turnout rates to 60 percent and cut costs to just $1.35 per voter, $0.36 in mailing costs.[8]

It would be rash to try to predict what would happen were some such preference voting procedure in effect, but there is at least some evidence at hand. In late 1978 Courant, Gramlich, and Rubinfeld (1980) administered a question sequence very similar to that listed above to a random sample of 2,001 Michigan households just after the Headlee vote. Other information from the survey (vote on tax limitation amendments, turnout rates, income, employment patterns, etc.) agreed very well with information from other sources on Michigan; hence there is at least some indication that the survey results are reliable.

Table 15.3 shows the results obtained for state and local government spending and taxes on the question sequence. In each case there is an enormous concentration of voters on "no change," leading to the feeling that the extent of voter dissatisfaction with prevailing levels of taxes and expenditures is highly overrated.[9] This feeling is at least partly confirmed by the consistent defeats of limitation measures aimed at changing tax and expenditure levels by significant amounts. Were these to be the results obtained in a real-world preference election, the runoff votes would not have been necessary. A final encouraging sign is that the "no response" vote is very low--evidence that respondents (only about half of whom actually voted) do seem to be able to answer questions of this sort.

IMPLEMENTATION ISSUES

With any limitation measure there are a host of fiscal, institutional and legal details involving the actual implementation of the measure that must be settled. In this section we discuss a few of the important points. We do this mainly with reference to our own proposal, but many of the comments refer to existing tax limitation measures as well.

A first issue is whether the limitation measure should set a ceiling, a floor, or an actual fiscal result. Since the problem that occasions these limitation measures in the first place is the fear that tax and spending levels will become excessive, all present day limitations are ceilings, allowing taxes or expenditures to be at or less than a designated level. We see no reason to deviate from this tradition in our proposal, even though (unlike others) ours does contain a mechanism to correct undertaxing and spending. But such cases are probably not as often encountered in practice, and it would add unnecessary complexity to the measure to include provisions forcing jurisdictions to raise tax and spending levels.

A second issue involves the timing of the desired changes. By November or December of year t, voters should have completed the voting process and have settled on a desired spending and tax change. This is in time for the constraint to be incorporated in the budget proposal for the appropriate governmental unit for the fiscal year starting six or nine months hence. As an illustration, if we let T_t refer to the level of taxes in year t, I_t to state money income in t, N_t to the number of school district pupils in t, P_t to the price level in t, T_{t+1}, N_{t+1} and P_{t+1} to the appropriate variables in year t+1, and x to the percentage change winning the election, the limit for fiscal year t+1 can be written either as

$$T_{t+1} \leq T_t \frac{(100+x)}{100} \left(\frac{P_t}{P_{t-1}}\right) \qquad \text{A), or}$$

$$T_{t+1} \leq T_t \frac{(100+x)}{100} \left(\frac{I_t}{I_{t-1}}\right) \qquad \text{B), or}$$

$$T_{t+1} \leq T_t \frac{(100+x)}{100} \left(\frac{P_t}{P_{t-1}}\right) \left(\frac{N_t}{N_{t-1}}\right) \qquad \text{C).}$$

In each case we attach an adjustment to account for rising prices, and in each case this adjustment must necessarily be based on a comparison of magnitudes for t and t-1, because t+1 variables would not yet be known. The question of whether the adjustment factor should be based on prices (A), prices times number of pupils (C), or income (B) is difficult to determine. For school districts the combined measure C) seems to be clearly superior, to cover cases where either the number of pupils or prices might change from one year to the next. For other types of expenditures, money incomes (I) will normally grow more rapidly than prices and variant B) would be less constraining. But in a recession real incomes fall, money incomes grow less rapidly than prices, and variant B) becomes more constraining. Some other possibilities might be to lag the adjustment factor if it is based on income to eliminate this cyclical problem, as the Headlee Amendment now does, or to choose whichever adjustment factor is the highest (since we are setting ceiling levels of taxes). Whatever is done, the amendment could be written like the Headlee Amendment to add slight excesses of taxes over the limit to governmental asset stocks, and to rebate large excesses of taxes over the limit.

Since voters are voting over a two year cycle, it is

then necessary to write the constraint for the next year. Following the logic used before, this can be done as either

$$T_{t+2} \leq T_t \left(\frac{100+x}{100}\right) \left(\frac{P_t}{P_{t-1}}\right) \left(\frac{P_{t+1}}{P_t}\right) \qquad \text{A), or}$$

$$T_{t+2} \leq T_t \left(\frac{100+x}{100}\right) \left(\frac{I_t}{I_{t-1}}\right) \left(\frac{I_{t+1}}{I_t}\right) \qquad \text{B), or}$$

$$T_{t+2} \leq T_t \left(\frac{100+x}{100}\right) \left(\frac{P_t}{P_{t-1}}\right) \left(\frac{P_{t+1}}{P_t}\right) \left(\frac{N_t}{N_{t-1}}\right) \left(\frac{N_{t+1}}{N_t}\right) \qquad \text{C),}$$

depending upon the scaling device used in year one. Note that we have now used growth rates in t+1, because by that time the information would be available. Note also that the year 2 limits are set independently of whether taxes are actually at the ceiling in year t+1--that is, they are based entirely on taxes in year t and the two year adjustment factors.

Another issue involves the treatment of federal categorical grants. During the sixties and seventies these grew at high rates, implying that limits written in terms of taxes would have been less confining than those in terms of expenditures. Federal grants could finance additional governmental expenditures over and above the limited level of taxes. Had the measures been written instead in terms of expenditures, and grant-financed expenditures not exempted, states would have been forced to respond to federal grants by cutting their own taxes. Now with President Reagan's sharp budget cutbacks, all that is turned around. For the next few years it seems likely that categorical federal grants will decline, and if taxes are limited, lower levels of government will not be able to pick up these programs on their own.

The proper treatment here depends on whether federal grant-supported programs are viewed as federal programs or state programs. When categorical grants are growing, they are supporting programs the state was not conducting in their absence, and there is little doubt that the state should at least be allowed to add these expenditures on top of own-financed expenditures. In such a situation, the limit should either be written in terms of taxes, or on expenditures with grant-financed expenditures exempted. But if long-standing federal grants are cut back, the programs might by that time have been incorporated into the state's menu of public services even if initially financed by grants. In such a case the state should at least have the option of picking up the program. Probably the best way to do this is to add some measure of lost grant funds onto T_t in the above limit formula. Alternatively, exemptions to the limit could be allowed whenever real federal grants were cut a certain amount (say one percent or more). Both of these provisions would permit taxing and spending to rise to levels above those indicated by voters in the short run, but the dangers seem minimal because soon there would be another limitation election. This does recall one advantage of our procedure: since elections are held periodically, essentially arbitrary choices become less significant and less damaging--if they in fact are not what voters want, voters can change them.

A related issue involves the internal allocation of these constrained budgets. Should the limit be on overall expenditures and taxes of the relevant governmental unit, or on functional subtotals? The question only arises for the state budget and local general funds--to the extent that the limits apply to school boards or some other special district, functional spending is already limited. But for general funds (including intergovernmental transfers), there appears to be no alternative to imposing the limit on overall spending, and allowing the elected representatives to allocate within these totals. The one experience with trying to tie the hands of the legislature in this regard, the evasion provision in the Headlee Amendment, certainly appears to be working very badly, and there is no evidence that any other provision would work any better.

A final issue involves nontax revenues such as user charges, license fees, lottery revenues, and so forth. These nontax revenues could be included in T for voting and limitation purposes, hence allowing state or local governments the flexibility to allocate tax and nontax revenues in the way they wish within overall budget totals. Or these items could be left out, with the limit defined solely in terms of taxes. Were this to be done, there might be a shift toward nontax revenues over time, as legislators tried to escape the provisions of the limit. We do not think such a shift poses major problems, because there is a natural limit to the degree to which governments can be financed by user fees, after a certain point, the population will simply not pay these fees. Moreover, even if nontax revenues do grow sharply, two years later the electorate gets another chance to vote on whether the tax part of the limit should be tightened.

SUMMARY

While there are valid grounds for trying to limit state and local taxing and spending levels, all present-day limitation measures have two important problems:

1) They build rigid standards in for long periods of time, standards which probably should be revised fairly often.

2) They are complex and poorly understood.

We here propose a procedure to deal with both problems. The inflexibility of permanent standards can be dealt with by having a procedure whereby voters vote at regular biennial intervals on fiscal matters. The complexity issue is dealt with by framing the electoral choice in terms voters can more easily understand--do you want public spending and taxes to go up or down, and if so, how much? Under such a scheme voters would no longer have to figure out the real impact of millage rate changes and the even more undecipherable results of complicated tax packages. Over time voters should be able to relate their vote to actual fiscal changes, to make more informed choices, and perhaps even to develop a sense of participating in the fiscal process.

At the same time, we hasten to add that this procedure is advanced mainly as a way to get around serious problems with present-day limitation measures. As with other measures now in effect, our proposal does entail costs and complexities--some of which we see no way to get around with any limitation procedure. These costs and complexities must be weighed against the benefits of tax limitations, and we ourselves have no idea how the tally will come out. We think our procedure compares favorably with existing measures, but not necessarily with a world of no tax limitations at all.

NOTES, CHAPTER 15

[1]A theoretical analysis arguing this point is given by Courant-Rubinfeld (1981).

[2]In fact, the theory of public goods does not say that the median voter outcome is optimal. If voters have varying tastes for public goods, aggregate social welfare can sometimes be increased by a nonmedian voter outcome. For the purposes of this paper, however, we will assume away this philosophical possibility and content ourselves with the usual democratic assumption.

[3]Illustrations of these studies, with their income elasticity of demand for public goods, are given below. When this income elasticity is less than unity, the statement in the text is true. Some studies are: Barlow (1970) 0.64; Bergstrom-Goodman (1973) 0.88; Borcherding-Deacon (1972) 0.83; Feldstein (1975) 0.48; Inman (1978) 0.72; Lovell (1978) 0.32.

[4]Cline finds the relevant income elasticity of demand for public goods in Michigan over the 1948-74 period to be 0.72. But he also shows that because the limit is based on lagged income, it might be constraining in the expansion phase of the business cycle.

[5]Say that one-third of total assessed values consist of commercial-industrial property depreciating at the rate of d and two-thirds consist of residential property that does not depreciate at all. Excluding new construction, the rise in nominal value of commercial-industrial property is (c-d), where c is the rate of consumer price inflation, assumed to be the same as the rate of inflation for the capital goods used to sell or produce consumer goods. If v is the rate of inflation of residential values, the Headlee

local limit becomes binding only when $(2/3)v + (1/3)(c-d) \geq c$, or $v - d/2 \geq c$. The parameter d is about .08 per year, so v must exceed c by .04 for the limit to become binding. Recently c has been about .1, so v must be .14--well above what it actually is for most communities.

[6]Both the name and idea for this proposal came from our colleague, Frank Stafford. See his unsigned memo proposing what he called a Targeted Real Resource Tax, fall 1980.

[7]The only case where it matters whether we start with the lowest or the highest number in this sequential process is when the preferences are not single-peaked--that is when those favoring a ceiling of +4% would _not_ be next happy with a ceiling of +2%. But while this case of nonsingle-peaked preferences has received a good deal of attention in the theoretical literature on voting, it does not seem to be very likely in the case of not-terribly-well-informed voters voting on overall operating expenditure levels.

[8]This information was obtained by telephone from Dean Klampe, the San Diego City Clerk.

[9]There is a modestly higher degree of satisfaction with local government fiscal outcomes than with state outcomes, a fact that agrees with other polls on the topic. See, for example, The Advisory Commission on Intergovernmental Relations (1979).

REFERENCES, CHAPTER 15

Advisory Commission on Intergovernmental Relations. _Changing Public Attitudes on Government and Taxes_. Washington, 1979.

Barlow, R. "Efficiency Aspects of Local School Expenditures." _Journal of Political Economy_, Sept., 1970.

Bergstrom, T. C. and Goodman, R. P. "Private Demand for Public Goods." _American Economic Review_, June, 1973.

Borcherding, T. E. and Deacon, R. T. "The Demand for the Services of Nonfederal Government." _American Economic Review_, Dec., 1972.

Bowen, H. "The Interpretation of Voting in the Allocation of Economic Resources." _Quarterly Journal of Economics_, 1943.

Cline, R. J. "The Economic Impact of Tax Limitation Proposals: The Michigan Experience." Mimeograph. 1981.

Courant, P. N.; Gramlich, E. M.; and Rubinfeld, D. L. "Why People Vote for Tax Limitation: The Michigan Case." National Tax Journal, March, 1980.

Courant, P. N. and Rubinfeld, D. L. "On the Welfare Effects of Tax Limitation." Journal of Public Economics, in press, 1981.

Downs, A. An Economic Theory of Democracy. New York: Harper and Row, 1957.

Feldstein, M. S. "Wealth Neutrality and Local Choice in Public Education." American Economic Review, Sept., 1975.

Hotelling, H. "Stability in Competition." Economic Journal, March, 1929.

Inman, R. P., "Testing Political Economy's 'As If' Proposition: Is the Median Voter Really Decisive?" Public Choice, 1978.

Lovell, M. C., "Spending for Education: The Exercise of Public Choice." The Review of Economics and Statistics, Nov., 1978.

Chapter 16

The Property Tax

by

Paul N. Courant

The University of Michigan

INTRODUCTION[1]

Local property taxes[2] generate more revenue and more controversy than any other fiscal institution in the state. In 1980, over $4.4 billion in property taxes were collected; between 1978 and 1981, five ballot proposals that would have directly reduced local property taxes by amending the state constitution were rejected by Michigan voters.

Property tax revenues are roughly twice those of their nearest competitor, the state income tax, and property taxes are by far the most important source of revenue to local governments, accounting for roughly two-thirds of all locally raised revenue[3] and slightly over one-third of revenue from all sources.[4]

Looking at the property tax in the aggregate can be seriously misleading, however. The set of fiscal institutions usually referred to as "the" property tax is in fact made up of taxes levied by 264 cities, approximately 270 villages, over 1,200 townships, 83 counties, and about 600 school districts. Each of these units of government taxes five classes of personal property and six classes of real property, and in 1980 the average tax rates paid in Michigan's 83 counties (to all units of government within the counties) varied by a factor of more than 2.5, from 27.57 mills (taxes per thousand dollars of state equalized value)[5] in Leelanau County, to 67.60 mills in Washtenaw County.

In addition to intrastate variation in tax rates, there is also significant variation in the composition of the tax base. In the southern part of the state, residential,

TABLE 16.1
GENERAL PROPERTY TAXES BY LOCAL UNIT OF GOVERNMENT IN MICHIGAN, SELECTED YEARS, 1958-1980
(all dollar amounts in millions of dollars)

YEAR	SCHOOL		CITY		COUNTY		TOWNSHIP		VILLAGE		TOTAL
	Dollars	Percent	Dollars	Percent	Dollars	Percent	Dollars	Percent	Dollars	Percent	
1958	354	47.7	234	31.6	135	18.2	10	1.4	8	1.1	741
1970	1,167	62.3	418	22.3	240	12.8	39	2.1	10	0.5	1,874
1974	1,725	65.1	526	19.8	320	12.1	63	2.4	16	0.6	2,650
1975	1,900	65.4	565	19.4	347	12.0	75	2.6	18	0.6	2,904
1976	1,952	65.9	571	19.3	342	11.5	79	2.7	18	0.6	2,961
1977	2,141	66.8	587	18.3	370	11.5	90	2.8	19	0.6	3,207
1978	2,342	67.2	621	17.8	400	11.5	101	2.9	21	0.6	3,485
1979	2,623	67.4	677	17.4	447	11.5	119	3.1	23	0.6	3,889
1980	3,009	68.2	736	16.7	504	11.4	134	3.0	26	0.7	4,411

Note: Details may not add to totals due to rounding.

Source: Michigan State Tax Commission.

commercial, and industrial property account for almost all of the tax base. The farther north one goes, (on average) the less important are industrial and residential property, and the more important are agricultural and timber/cutover lands. Thus, the property tax is not one tax, but thousands of taxes, and its economic effects are different in different parts of the state both because of differences in tax rates and because of significant differences in the types of economic activity that are taxed.

Equally important, the tax base has changed over time. In 1972, residential property accounted for 49.2 percent of total state equalized value (SEV). In 1980, residential property accounted for 56.5 percent of SEV, while commercial and industrial property fell from a share of 39.7 percent to 31.0 percent over the same period. Indeed, it is possible that this shift has contributed to political pressures directed at statewide property tax reduction. For this reason, a major focus of the following discussion will be the description and evaluation of the increasing extent to which the property tax has become a tax on housing.

Uses of the Property Tax

While the property tax is the main source of locally raised revenue for all types of units of local government in Michigan, its importance to different types of units exhibits considerable variation. Property taxes account for about half of all school district revenue in the state, while they support less than 25 percent of county and municipal functions.[6] Furthermore, in 1980, 68.2 percent of all property taxes went to school districts, while 16.7 percent was levied by cities, 11.4 percent was levied by counties, and 3.7 percent supported the budgets of townships and villages.[7] These numbers have also changed over time. The share of property taxes going to school districts has been rising steadily for over two decades, while the share received by cities and counties has been falling over the same period (see Table 16.1).

The "Burden" of the Property Tax

While Table 16.1 documents recent trends in the use of property taxes in Michigan, care must be taken in interpreting the meaning of the dollar figures. The figures accurately measure governmental receipts of property taxes, but they do not measure the burden of the property tax on Michigan residents. There are four important reasons for this, all of which will be developed in some detail later in this chapter: (1) The Michigan Homestead Property tax credit (circuit breaker) provides a refundable income tax credit to households that pay more than 3.5 percent of their household income in property taxes. In recent years, the credit has amounted to between 9 and 10 percent of total property tax levies, and this amount should be deducted from total levies when calculating the net cost of property taxes to Michigan taxpayers.[8] (2) Property taxes, like all other taxes, are not always borne by the immediate payer; they may be shifted to other economic actors. To the extent that Michigan's property taxes are shifted to consumers and holders of claims on Michigan's capital and land who reside in other states, the tax will be exported, and exported taxes should also be subtracted from total Michigan levies. Such exporting accounts for about 16 percent of total Michigan property taxes and this amount should be subtracted when calculating the net cost of property taxation to Michigan residents.[9] (3) Property taxes are deductible from income subject to federal tax, both for individuals and for corporations. Deductibility of the property tax means that for many Michigan taxpayers (especially residents of owner-occupied housing) the cost of a dollar's property tax levy is shared with taxpayers across the U.S., with the latter group picking up m percent of the tab, where m is the Michigan taxpayer's marginal federal tax rate. Federal deductibility of local property taxes reduced the burden on Michigan residents by about 11-12 percent of total property taxes levied in the state. (4) While the three points made immediately above are conceptually quite straightforward, and each calls for simple subtraction of an estimate of taxes borne by non-Michigan residents from the total Michigan levy, the fourth source of divergence between the magnitude of the tax levy and its burden on Michigan residents is far more complicated. Property taxes (like all other taxes) affect the level, composition, and location of economic activity. In general these effects lead to reductions in economic efficiency that are termed the "excess burden" or deadweight loss of the tax. Measurement of the excess burden of property taxation in Michigan is well beyond the scope of the study, but the issue is an important one, and will receive some attention in the discussion that follows.

Property Taxation in Michigan and the Nation

Nationwide, the property tax has steadily declined as a share of total state and local tax collections since 1962. The latest available figures show that in 1978 property taxes nationwide accounted for 34.3 percent of state and local taxes, as compared with 45.9 percent in 1962. The decline has been somewhat steeper in Michigan, where gross property tax collections (including the state property tax on real utility property) were 36.5 percent of total state and local taxes in 1978, down from 49.3 percent in 1962.[10] Table 16.2 displays data on this statistic for the United states as a whole, the Great Lakes states, California, Pennsylvania and New York. All of the states shown have experienced a substantial reduction in dependence on the property tax.[11]

The comparisons in Table 16.2 do not account for circuit breaker laws. When adjustments are made for the impact of these laws, the falling trends are steeper in all of the states shown, and Michigan's measured dependence on the property tax relative to other states falls as well. For accounting reasons, state income tax credits against property taxes paid (circuit breakers) are treated as reductions in income taxes, although behaviorally they are clearly equivalent to reductions in residential property taxes. The only year for which comparative data on circuit

TABLE 16.2
PROPERTY TAXES AS A PERCENTAGE OF TOTAL STATE-LOCAL TAXES, SELECTED STATES, SELECTED YEARS, 1962-1978

STATE	1962	1967	1972	1977	1978
California	50.2	51.4	47.7	42.0	40.2
Michigan	49.3	43.8	40.0	37.8	36.5
New York	44.4	39.4	36.6	35.8	36.0
Illinois	53.4	48.9	41.6	37.0	35.5
Ohio	51.7	51.7	43.7	38.9	35.2
Indiana	56.2	48.4	51.2	37.2	34.6
Wisconsin	55.6	41.7	44.7	34.3	33.6
Pennsylvania	34.7	33.6	27.3	26.1	25.8
United States	45.9	42.7	39.1	35.6	34.3

Source: Advisory Commission on Intergovernmental Relations (ACIR), Significant Features of Fiscal Federalism, 1979-1980, p. 87.

TABLE 16.3
THE EFFECT OF CIRCUIT BREAKERS ON PROPERTY TAXES AS A PERCENT OF TOTAL STATE AND LOCAL TAXES, SELECTED STATES, 1977

STATE	EXCLUDING CIRCUIT BREAKER	INCLUDING CIRCUIT BREAKER
California	42.0	41.7
Ohio	38.9	38.2
Indiana	37.2	37.2
Illinois	37.0	36.0
Michigan	37.8	34.4
Wisconsin	34.3	33.1
Pennsylvania	26.1	25.5
New York	38.8	na

Source: See text.

breakers is available is 1977.[12] If circuit breaker payments made in 1977 are deducted from total property tax payments in each of the states shown in Table 16.2, the results are as shown in Table 16.3. Of the seven states for which data are available, the effect of circuit breakers is to change Michigan's rank from third to fifth. Michigan's circuit breaker reduces total property taxes by over nine percent and reduces residential property taxes by about 16 percent.

On a per capita basis, Michigan's circuit breaker is the third most generous in the nation, with only Oregon and Minnesota ranking higher in 1977.[13] Because of this, other interstate comparisons of the importance of the property tax are qualitatively similar to the measures presented above. Not counting circuit breakers, Michigan is at or slightly above the national average; when the circuit breaker is taken into account, Michigan comes out at or slightly below the national average in its dependence of the property tax. It is also true that the broad trend, both nationwide and in Michigan, in any measure of the importance of the property tax, has been downward for the past decade.[14] As a fraction of personal income, gross property tax collections in 1972 averaged 5 percent nationwide, while the figure for Michigan was 5.3 percent. In 1978, the national average was down to 4.4 percent, while Michigan had fallen to 4.6 percent;[15] adjusting for the circuit breaker, the Michigan figure would be about 4.2 percent.[16]

Every year the Advisory Commission on Intergovernmental Relations ranks states in terms of the dependency on property taxes, which is defined to be property tax revenues (state and local) as a fraction of total state and local general revenue from all sources. In 1977, Michigan ranked twentieth on this list with 23 percent of all state and local general revenue deriving from property taxes.[17] Adjusting for circuit breakers in all states that have them moves Michigan to twenty-fifth on the list, at 20.9 percent--exactly at the national median and lower than any other state in the Great Lakes Region. Unfortunately, the data necessary to make a similar adjustment for the other states are not readily available for 1978, a year in which Michigan ranked sixteenth on the ACIR list. While it is certain that Michigan's rank would fall if the adjustment were made, it is impossible to predict exactly how much.

Summary

There are three major conclusions of this introductory material. (1) In the aggregate, the level of property taxation in Michigan is roughly in line with the U.S. as a whole. When gross property tax collections are compared, most conventional measures indicate that Michigan's reliance on property taxes is at or slightly above the national average; when circuit breakers are taken into account, Michigan is at or slightly below average in the share of income going to property taxes and in the reliance of its governments on property taxes as a means of support. (2) Although the importance of property taxes has been falling for at least a decade, both nationally and in Michigan, it remains true that property taxes in the aggregate are by far the largest source of revenue to Michigan governments. (3) Aggregate analysis of property taxes can be quite misleading, as the tax is levied by close to 2,400 different jurisdictions and falls, with differing effect, on eleven different types of property. Both the uses of the property tax and the composition of the tax base have been changing in recent years, with an increasing share of tax revenues going to schools and an increasing share of the tax base accounted for by housing.

THE INSTITUTIONAL SETTING AND ITS MAJOR CONSEQUENCES

Authority for local taxation of real and personal property derives from the state constitution, from numerous legislative acts, and from charters adopted by local units of government, which are in turn subject to state-level restrictions.[18] The relevant constitutional and legislative provisions set limits on the taxing power of various types of local jurisdictions, require uniformity of the tax base across jurisdictions, and provide for county and state level administrative mechanisms designed to assure that uniformity is, in fact, achieved.

Taxing Authority and Limits to Taxing Authority[19]

Property taxes may be levied by cities, townships, counties, school districts, intermediate school districts, community college districts, and various kinds of special purpose districts. The rates of tax applicable to taxable property are subject to a number of limits, some more binding than others. Article IX, Sec. 6 of the Constitution places a limit of fifteen mills (which can be raised to eighteen mills by majority vote in a county) on the sum of school district, township and county tax rates. This limit may be exceeded by majority vote, provided that the total tax levy, including voted millage above the fifteen or eighteen mill limit not exceed fifty mills. Furthermore, both the fifteen (or eighteen) mill and fifty mill limits apply only to operating revenue. Repayment of principal and interest on debt are excluded from the limitations.

The fifteen (or eighteen) and fifty mill limits do not apply to cities, villages, or charter townships. These units of government (as well as a number of other charter units) are limited instead by their own charters, which in turn must conform to state-level limitations on the amount of millage levied. Cities, for example, may not levy more than twenty mills for general operating purposes. Thus, although a city's charter limit may be raised to twenty mills by majority vote, the state does not permit the residents of the city to levy more than twenty mills. Currently, about 40 percent of Michigan's cities are at, or near, their charter limits.[20]

Because of the exemption of cities and other local units, as well as the exemption of millage levied to repay debt, it is somewhat misleading to refer to the fifteen (or eighteen) and fifty mill limits as limits. Indeed, the average statewide millage rate levied for all purposes has exceeded fifty mills in every year from 1973 to the present. In some cases the provisions of Article IX, Section 6, may lead to the substitution of debt-finance for operating millage, but because either route generally requires voter approval, the effect of the millage limitations has been more to require that voters approve increases in property taxes than to prevent such increases.

The millage limitations provided for in Article IX, Section 31 (part of the "Headlee Amendment," which was approved by a statewide referendum in November of 1978) operate in quite a different manner from the limitations discussed above. Section 31 and associated implementing legislation require that if the tax base in a given jurisdiction should increase in value more rapidly than the Consumer Price Index (CPI) then millage rates must be reduced such that the annual percentage increase in the amount of tax levied on existing property (i.e., excluding new improvements, annexations, etc.) does not exceed the previous year's percentage increase in the CPI. The limitation applies only to the aggregate of existing property in a jurisdiction, not to individual parcels, and, as with the other limitations, taxes levied to repay indebtedness are exempt from the limit. Furthermore, voters may choose to exceed the Section 31 limit by majority vote. Thus, the Section 31 limit is not designed to operate on the absolute level of millage rates, but to prevent the property tax revenues of local governments from growing more rapidly than the inflation rate unless voters explicitly endorse such growth. It is estimated that in 1979 about two-thirds of all local jurisdictions in the state were affected by Section 31, and that the volume of tax rollbacks required by this provision amounted to about $50 million, or somewhat over one percent of total property tax collections.[21]

The Tax Base

The constitution (Article IX, Sec. 3) states that "The legislature shall provide for the uniform general *ad valorem* taxation of real and tangible personal property not exempt by law. The legislature shall provide for the determination of true cash value at which such property shall be uniformly assessed, which shall not...exceed 50 percent; and for a system of equalization of assessments." The legislative provisions that implement this part of the Constitution determine the tax base upon which property taxes are levied by local jurisdictions. It should be noted that the constitution does not require that all taxable property be assessed at 50 percent of "true cash value." It only requires that the assessment ratio be uniform throughout the state and that 50 percent be the maximum. The legislation that implements this part of the constitution (MCL 211.27) provides that ratio of assessed value be equal to the maximum permissible rate of 50 percent. Thus, one mechanism for reducing (but not increasing) property taxes statewide without constitutional amendment would be legislation that reduced the uniform assessment ratio. Such legislation could lead to problems for local governments that are at or near their millage limits--the voters in the affected jurisdictions might be willing to finance the existing level of services, but the combination of existing rate limitations and a state-imposed reduction in the tax base could prevent them from doing so.

Potentially, the tax base is 50 percent of the true cash value of all real and personal property in the state. In fact, many types of property are exempt from the tax and thus are not part of the tax base. Exemptions are of two broad types: (1) Much property is exempt because it is owned by institutions, such as the federal government and many types of charitable and religious organizations, that are exempt from taxation under state law; (2) Certain types of property are exempt from property taxation no matter who owns them. Notable examples of this type of exemption are agricultural personal property, household personal property, and business inventories. Over time, the tax base has become more and more circumscribed, as there has been frequent legislation that exempts either types of property owners or types of property, and little legislation that adds new classes of property to the tax base. The net effect of new exemptions in recent years has been to increase the importance of real property in the overall tax base and also to increase the share of the tax base accounted for by residential property relative to commercial, industrial, and agricultural property. The major recent exemptions that have led to this outcome have been the virtual elimination of agricultural personal property from the tax base (in 1966), the elimination of special tools and dies, primarily used in the automobile industry (in 1964), and the elimination of business inventories (in 1975).[22] Another exemption that has tended to increase the share of residential housing in the tax base is that for industrial and commercial facilities that are granted tax abatements under P.A. 198 and P.A. 255, respectively. These facilities are exempt from the general property tax and instead pay a special tax of 50 percent of the usual rate (for new facilities) or 0 (for rehabilitation that exceeds the value of the original facility).[23]

In most of the cases discussed above, there are no current estimates of the assessed value of the exempt property, so it is impossible to provide a precise measure of the effect of these exemptions on the tax base. By making a few simplifying assumptions, however, we can provide somewhat less precise estimates.

In 1965, the last year in which agricultural personalty was fully taxable, the SEV of such property was 8.5 percent of the SEV of real agricultural property. Assuming that this proportion still holds, the 1980 SEV would be $534 million, about 0.7 percent of the tax base. The State Tax Commission estimated that the exemption of tools and dies cost $13 million in 1973.[24] If this property were taxed at the statewide average tax rate of 50.84 mills in that year, the implied SEV in 1973 was $255.7 million. Inflating the last figure by the growth of real industrial property between 1973 and 1980 yields an estimate of $398 million (about 0.5 percent) as the reduction in the 1980 base due to this exemption. The assessed value of inventories in 1975 was $4.67 billion.[25] Had the value of inventories grown at the same rate as commercial and industrial real property, the SEV of inventories in 1980 would have been $6.72 billion, or 8.1 percent of the tax base. The Department of Management and Budget estimates that industrial facilities exemptions cost $100 million in 1980.[26] At the statewide average tax rate, this implies an SEV for the exempt property of $1.87 billion, or 2.39 percent of the tax base. In sum, exempt property in these four categories amounted to $9.5 billion in 1980, about 11.5 percent of the tax base. Had none of these exemptions been in effect, real residential property would have accounted for only about 50.7 percent of the tax base in 1980, as compared with the actual figure of 56.5 percent. In 1965, real residential property accounted for 45.6 percent of the property tax base. Somewhat over half of the increase can be accounted for by these four exemptions alone.

It should be emphasized that local jurisdictions are at least partially compensated for the two largest reductions in the tax base discussed above. In both cases, school districts that are beneficiaries of the school aid formula are compensated through the formula. Counties and municipalities are compensated for the loss of inventories by an earmarked portion of the single business tax. However, the real value of compensation falls over time, because it is based on the 1975 SEV of inventories, and growth in the value of inventories that has occurred since then is not reflected in the compensation formula. Additionally, the industrial facilities tax levied under P.A. 198 replaces up to half of the property tax revenues that counties and municipalities would have received from property exempted under P.A. 198 (see Chapter 10 for details). Thus, if somewhat more than half of the investments exempted under P.A. 198 would not have taken place without the inducements, local jurisdictions are net fiscal gainers. In short, the fact that some revenues are replaced in both of these cases means that the effect of the exemptions on the property tax base overstates their effect on the fiscal position of the affected governments. One doubts that this is widely understood by homeowners, however, who see an increasing share of total property taxes (even if not such a rapidly increasing share of total local government revenues) being derived from their property.

The preceding discussion should not be taken to imply that any or all of the four exemptions discussed do not have benefits that outweigh their costs. All four of the exemptions were enacted with the express purpose of stimulating business or agriculture in the state and to the extent that they have been successful the net effect on the state's economic and fiscal well-being may have been positive. However, their effect on the measured property tax base has almost certainly contributed to the political problems faced by the property tax, and it is worth noting that many of the fiscal benefits of induced economic activity would appear at the state level, not the local level.

A complete discussion of tax-exempt property is beyond the scope of the current treatment, and the fact that there is no formal assessment of much exempt property (and no reason for such assessment) makes it impossible even to estimate the magnitude of the difference between the potential and actual tax bases. As a general matter, it should be recognized that tax exemptions provide subsidies to the activities that receive the exemptions, and thus the exempt user will use more real resources (and increase the tax burden on all other classes of property) than if there were no exemption.[27] While some exemptions, such as those for federal and state government property, are firmly grounded in the Constitution and the traditions of fiscal federalism, many exemptions do not have such a natural justification; they should be evaluated the same way a direct subsidy program is evaluated. Does there exist a public purpose that warrants the degree of subsidy implicit in the exemption? In the case of exempt property such an evaluation is complicated by the fact that if property of a given type or owned by a given class of user is exempt, it will be exempt statewide, while the costs of exemption will be borne largely by localities.

Equalization. The constitution requires that there should be a system of "equalization of assessments" in order to assure uniformity of the tax base across jurisdictions. Property owners in Michigan pay taxes that are equal to the product of the relevant millage rate and the state equalized value (SEV) of the property that they own. The tax base, then, is SEV, and this is generated in three stages: (1) Each township, village, and city in the state assesses the value of all taxable property within it, resulting in an assessed value (AV) for all taxable property; (2) at the county level, studies are undertaken to determine whether the AV of the units of government within the county corresponds to the state requirement of 50 percent of true cash value. If, for example, it is found that property in township X is assessed, on average, at 40 percent of true cash value, the county will equalize the assessments by multiplying AV in township X by a factor of 1.25, yielding 50 percent of true cash value; (3) the state performs essentially the same function across the counties that the county equalization process performs across localities; if property in County X is found to be assessed, on average, at less than 50 percent of true cash value, the state will multiply all the assessments of property in county X by the appropriate factor. An individual's tax bill will then be the product of his state equalized value (AV times the county equalization factor times the state equalization factor) and the relevant millage rate.

If there were no equalization at the county and state levels, local assessors could reduce local tax burdens by deliberately underassessing property in their jurisdictions. Such practices would increase state aid to local schools (see Chapter 14) and would also reduce county taxes for residents of municipalities where property was

THE COMPOSITION OF THE PROPERTY TAX BASE, SELECTED YEARS, 1965-1981
(dollar amounts in millions)

		CLASS													
		AGRICULTURAL		COMMERCIAL		INDUSTRIAL		RESIDENTIAL		TIMBER CUTOVER		UTILITY		TOTAL	
YEAR	TYPE	$	%	$	%	$	%	$	%	$	%	$	%	$	%
1965	Real	1,782	6.6	3,208	11.9	3,367	12.4	12,346	45.6	121	0.4	0	0.0	20,823	76.9
	Personal	151	0.6	1,280	4.7	3,618	13.4	28	0.1	0	0.0	1,161	4.3	6,238	23.1
	Total	1,933	7.1	4,488	16.6	6,985	25.8	12,374	45.7	121	0.4	1,161	4.3	27,061	100.0
1970	Real	2,430	6.3	4,483	11.6	4,358	11.3	18,426	47.7	152	0.4	0	0.0	29,849	77.3
	Personal	*	**	1,962	5.1	5,010	13.0	26	0.1	0	0.0	1,759	4.6	8,758	22.7
	Total	2,430	6.3	6,445	16.7	9,368	24.3	18,452	47.8	152	0.4	1,759	4.6	38,606	100.0
1974	Real	3,254	6.3	6,749	13.0	5,614	10.8	25,186	48.5	260	0.5	0	0.0	41,062	79.1
	Personal	*	**	2,591	5.0	5,812	11.2	36	0.1	0	0.0	2,380	4.6	10,820	20.9
	Total	3,254	6.3	9,340	18.0	11,426	22.0	25,222	48.6	260	0.5	2,380	4.6	51,882	100.0
1975	Real	3,681	6.5	7,252	12.8	5,825	10.3	27,680	48.7	290	0.5	0	0.0	44,727	78.7
	Personal	*	**	2,845	5.0	6,551	11.5	39	0.1	0	0.0	2,652	4.7	12,088	21.3
	Total	3,681	6.5	10,096	17.8	12,376	21.8	27,719	48.8	290	0.5	2,652	4.7	56,815	100.0
1976	Real	3,931	7.1	7,644	13.8	6,357	11.5	29,652	53.5	339	0.6	0	0.0	47,923	86.4
	Personal	*	**	1,525	2.7	3,569	6.4	42	0.1	0	0.0	2,403	4.3	7,539	13.6
	Total	3,932	7.1	9,168	16.5	9,926	17.9	29,694	53.5	339	0.6	2,403	4.3	55,462	100.0
1977	Real	4,410	7.4	8,078	13.6	6,585	11.1	32,151	54.0	382	0.6	0	0.0	51,606	86.7
	Personal	*	**	1,622	2.7	3,703	6.2	44	0.1	0	0.0	2,529	4.3	7,898	13.3
	Total	4,411	7.4	9,699	16.3	10,288	17.3	32,195	54.1	382	0.6	2,529	4.3	59,503	100.0
1978	Real	5,050	7.8	8,651	13.3	6,936	10.7	35,257	54.3	423	0.7	0	0.0	56,316	86.8
	Personal	*	**	1,782	2.7	4,029	6.2	53	0.1	0	0.0	2,691	4.1	8,555	13.2
	Total	5,050	7.8	10,433	16.1	10,965	16.9	35,309	54.4	423	0.7	2,691	4.1	64,871	100.0
1979	Real	5,766	8.0	9,581	13.2	7,502	10.3	39,954	55.1	467	0.6	0	0.0	63,271	87.2
	Personal	*	**	1,972	2.7	4,304	5.9	54	0.1	0	0.0	2,927	4.0	9,257	12.8
	Total	5,767	8.0	11,553	15.9	11,807	16.3	40,008	55.2	467	0.6	2,927	4.0	72,528	100.0
1980[1]	Real	6,328	7.7	10,633	12.9	8,182	9.9	46,669	56.5	688	0.8	0	0.0	72,500	87.7
	Personal	*	**	2,214	2.7	4,667	5.6	63	0.1	0	0.0	3,201	3.9	10,146	12.3
	Total	6,328	7.7	12,847	15.5	12,849	15.5	46,733	56.5	688	0.8	3,201	3.9	82,646	100.0
1981[1]	Real	6,851	7.4	11,556	12.6	9,124	9.9	53,018	57.6	529	0.6	0	0.0	81,492	88.5
	Personal	na	na	na	na	na	na	na	na	0	0.0	na	na	10,567	11.5
	Total	na	na	na	na	na	na	na	na	na	na	na	na	92,059	100.0

Notes: Values through 1970 are 50% of true cash value; 1971-81 values are SEV. Details may not add to totals due to rounding; na = not available; *less than $500,000; **less than 0.05%; [1]A new class, developmental property, was added in 1980. SEV in this class, which contains only real property, was $183 million in 1980 and $413 million in 1981. These amounts are included in the totals for both years.

Source: Michigan State Tax Commission.

underassessed. Both county and state equalization are designed to assure that residents of all jurisdictions are treated equitably (on average).

Until 1981, equalization was done separately for aggregate real and aggregate personal property. A new system, "equalization by class," was begun in 1981. Under this system equalization is done separately for each class of real property (agricultural, commercial, industrial, residential, timber/cutover, and developmental) and is still performed on personal property in the aggregate. Disaggregation of the classes of real property is designed to prevent local assessors from systematically underassessing one class of property and overassessing others. It is still true, however, that equalization can only correct interjurisdictional errors in assessments within a class, and not intrajurisdictional errors. For example, if the assessor in township X assesses half of the residential properties in the township at 30 percent of true cash value, and the other half at 70 percent, there will be no adjustment made at the county or state level as long as the average assessment ratio in the class is 50 percent.[28]

Table 16.4 shows the evolution of the property tax base and its components between 1965 and 1981. Between 1965 and 1980, the aggregate tax base grew by 305 percent, at an average annual rate of 7.7 percent. By comparison personal income in the state grew by 359 percent, or at an average annual rate of 8.9 percent. Most of the divergence between the two growth rates can be accounted for by the four major types of property (discussed above) that were exempted from the tax base during the period. The most striking thing about Table 16.4, however, is the change in the composition of the tax base. In 1965, commercial and industrial property accounted for 42 percent of the tax base; in 1980, they accounted for only 31 percent of the tax base.

WHO PAYS THE PROPERTY TAX?

This section will provide detailed analyses of the

behavior of property taxes in the years 1974-80. Special emphasis will be placed on analyzing changes in the geographical and sectoral composition of tax payments. The relationships among property taxes and three sectors of the state's economy--housing, industry, and commerce--will be discussed at some length.[29] Earlier in this chapter it was pointed out that the nominal payer of a tax is not necessarily the same as the ultimate bearer of the burden of that tax. This distinction is an important one, and an understanding of the theory of property tax incidence (to the extent that it can be understood) will be necessary in interpreting the detailed analyses of Michigan's property taxes that follow.

The Incidence of the Property Tax - Theoretical Considerations

The incidence of the property tax has been a subject of continuing controversy in the academic literature. Two quite different analyses of the problem have emerged in the past twenty years, and they have come to be referred to as the "new view" and the "old view" of the property tax. In 1977, McLure[30] showed that the two "views" of the property tax are not necessarily inconsistent with each other, because the differences between them are largely due to differences in what is being analyzed rather than methods of analysis. Most importantly McLure showed that when analyzing the effects of property taxes levied by jurisdictions that are small relative to the total size of the economy in question, the general equilibrium effects that are at the heart of the "new view" are unimportant for practical purposes, and the "old" partial equilibrium analysis is essentially correct.[31] Michigan is about four percent of the U.S. economy, and all taxing jurisdictions within the state are, of course, much smaller than the state as a whole, implying that general equilibrium effects of property taxes within the state can be safely ignored in the discussion that follows.

Property taxes are levied on the value of land and

capital. Because the supply of land is essentially fixed, the tax on land is borne by the owner of the land. The incidence of the tax on capital depends largely on the competitiveness of the industry and the geographical extent of the market. If a good is produced competitively for local consumption (e.g., housing), then the property tax will directly raise the cost of using capital in the relevant jurisdiction, and this increase in cost will be shifted to consumers.[32] If a good is produced for national consumption, the incidence of the tax will depend on whether producers in the locality in which it is levied have monopoly power in the production of the good. If they do not, the tax must be borne by profits, as producers in the locality cannot affect the retail price of the good.[33] If there is some monopoly power, the tax will be borne in part by profits and in part by consumers nationwide, depending on the elasticity of demand for the good.

Implications

The standard partial equilibrium view of incidence used in this study implies that taxes on owner-occupied housing are borne by the owner-occupants; taxes on rental housing and commercial enterprises are borne by tenants and consumers, respectively, except to the extent that the taxes are on the value of land, in which case they are borne by landlords; taxes on industrial property are borne by shareholders if Michigan possesses no monopoly power in the industry, and are divided between shareholders and consumers nationwide when Michigan does possess monopoly power; taxes on agriculture are shared between farmers (land owners) and consumers of agricultural products.[34]

The Distribution of Tax Liabilities, 1974-80

There is no official tabulation of tax liabilities by class of property, so the estimates made in this section were developed from available data on assessed values, state equalized values, and tax liabilities for each of Michigan's 83 counties. The counties themselves were also divided into two groups: those counties that contain the central cities

TABLE 16.5

PROPERTY TAX COLLECTIONS
1974-1980
(dollar amounts in millions)

		CLASS													
		AGRICULTURAL		COMMERCIAL		INDUSTRIAL		RESIDENTIAL		TIMBER CUTOVER		UTILITY		TOTAL	
YEAR	TYPE	$	%	$	%	$	%	$	%	$	%	$	%	$	%
1974	Real	110.8	4.2	371.5	14.0	307.3	11.6	1,287.3	48.6	8.0	0.3	0.0	0.0	2,084.9	78.7
	Personal	*	**	137.3	5.2	309.1	11.7	1.5	0.1	0.0	0.0	117.3	4.4	565.2	21.3
	Total	110.8	4.2	508.8	19.2	616.4	23.3	1,288.8	48.6	8.0	0.3	117.3	4.4	2,650.1	100.0
1975	Real	124.6	4.3	403.3	13.9	324.1	11.2	1409.8	48.6	9.1	0.3	0.0	0.0	2,270.9	78.2
	Personal	*	**	151.6	5.2	350.5	12.1	1.7	0.1	0.0	0.0	129.9	4.5	633.6	21.8
	Total	124.6	4.3	554.9	19.1	674.6	23.2	1,411.5	48.6	9.1	0.3	129.9	4.5	2,903.7	100.0
1976	Real	136.0	4.6	446.1	15.1	370.4	12.5	1,578.4	53.4	10.5	0.4	0.0	0.0	2,541.4	86.0
	Personal	*	**	86.5	2.9	202.1	6.8	1.8	0.1	0.0	0.0	124.0	4.2	414.4	14.0
	Total	136.0	4.6	532.6	18.0	572.5	19.4	1,580.2	53.5	10.5	0.4	124.0	4.2	2,956.6	100.0
1977	Real	155.2	4.8	479.4	15.0	386.9	12.1	1,732.6	54.0	12.1	0.4	0.0	0.0	2,766.1	86.3
	Personal	*	**	93.0	2.9	211.8	6.6	1.9	0.1	0.0	0.0	132.4	4.1	439.2	13.7
	Total	155.2	4.8	572.4	17.9	598.7	18.7	1,734.5	54.1	12.1	0.4	132.4	4.1	3,206.4	100.0
1978	Real	175.0	5.0	512.6	14.7	411.0	11.8	1,896.4	54.4	13.2	0.4	0.0	0.0	3,008.2	86.3
	Personal	*	**	102.0	2.9	232.0	6.7	2.2	0.1	0.0	0.0	140.0	4.0	476.2	13.7
	Total	175.0	5.0	614.6	17.6	643.0	18.5	1,898.6	54.5	13.2	0.4	140.0	4.0	3,484.9	100.0
1979	Real	197.8	5.1	563.8	14.5	442.1	11.4	2,156.6	55.5	14.7	0.4	0.0	0.0	3,374.9	86.8
	Personal	*	**	113.2	2.9	248.0	6.4	2.2	0.1	0.0	0.0	151.1	3.9	514.5	13.2
	Total	197.8	5.1	677.0	17.4	690.1	17.8	2,158.8	55.5	14.7	0.4	151.1	3.9	3,889.6	100.0
1980[1]	Real	222.1	5.0	620.5	14.1	486.1	11.0	2,497.6	56.6	16.4	0.4	0.0	0.0	3,850.9	87.2
	Personal	*	**	126.2	2.9	269.3	6.1	2.6	0.1	0.0	0.0	164.8	3.7	563.0	12.8
	Total	222.1	5.0	746.7	16.9	755.4	17.1	2,500.2	56.6	16.4	0.4	164.8	3.7	4,415.2	100.0

Notes: *less than $500,000; **less than 0.05%; details may not add to totals due to rounding; [1]A new class, developmental property, was added in 1980. Property tax collections in this class, which contains only real property, were $8.2 million (or 0.2% of the total for 1980) and are shown in the total for 1980.

Source: See text.

of the five largest Standard Metropolitan Statistical Areas (SMSAs)[35] and the other seventy-eight counties were treated differently in developing the estimates of tax liabilities by class. For the seventy-eight counties, tax liabilities were estimated as follows: For each of real and personal property, SEV was divided by AV to obtain the final equalization factor used to determine the value of property upon which taxes are levied. This factor was then multiplied by the assessed value of each class of property within the county, yielding an estimate of "synthetic" SEV by class of property. Finally, the synthetic SEVs were multiplied by the average tax rate in the county (total collections divided by total SEV in the county) to obtain an estimate of tax payments by class.[36] Up to the last step, this procedure mirrors the outcome of the state equalization process. In practice, of course, there can be substantial variation in tax rates within a county, and the procedure for estimating tax payments that was used here fails to capture such variation. As a final step in estimating tax payments by class, an adjustment was made in the state aggregates to account for the fact that there is essentially no agriculture or timber/cutover property in cities anywhere in the state.[37] The results of these efforts are shown in Table 16.5, which displays estimated tax payments by class of property in each of the years 1974 through 1980.

Comparison of Table 16.5 and Table 16.4 shows that most of the changes in the composition of tax payments by class can be explained by changes in the composition of the tax base. From 1976 (the first year in which inventories were exempt from property taxes) on, the relationship between the share of SEV accounted for by each class and the share of tax payments levied on each class is quite stable. Agriculture, which tends to be located in relatively low-tax jurisdictions, consistently accounts for about 2.7 percentage points less of total tax payments that it does for the total tax base. Commercial and industrial property, on the other hand, tends to be in higher-tax jurisdictions, and each consistently accounts for between

TABLE 16.6

PERCENTAGE COMPOSITION OF THE TAX BASE,
TAX LEVIES, AND MILLAGE RATES,
SELECTED COUNTIES, 1979

	Percent of Tax Base							Avg. Tax Rate	
County	Agri-cultural	Commer-cial	Indus-trial	Resi-dential	Timber Cutover	Utility	Levy (millions)	Rank	Mills
Washtenaw	8.4	25.2	12.4	50.3	-	3.6	139.9	1	67.62
Muskegon	3.7	16.7	17.6	59.6	0.1	2.9	4.8	10	51.62
Kent	2.3	21.3	13.5	60.1	-	2.8	141.6	20	46.74
Chippewa	9.9	18.4	6.2	52.6	7.9	4.9	8.9	30	44.97
Gladwin	12.6	6.4	2.1	71.6	3.7	3.6	7.3	40	42.77
Grand Traverse	6.1	24.9	4.8	59.0	0.6	5.7	22.7	50	40.50
Emmet	8.2	20.1	4.4	60.5	2.0	4.8	11.3	60	38.42
Sanilac	51.5	5.7	3.7	36.0	0.5	2.5	14.6	70	35.20
Montmorency	8.1	4.5	2.3	72.8	9.9	2.4	3.2	80	30.51
Leelanau	14.2	9.2	0.9	70.0	4.1	1.6	6.5	83	25.96
STATE TOTAL	8.0	15.9	16.3	55.2	0.6	4.0	3,889.4	-	53.64

Note: Details may not add to totals due to rounding.
Source: Michigan State Tax Commission.

1.4 and 1.6 percentage points more in tax payments than tax base. The share of tax payments accounted for by residential property tends to be slightly higher (0 to 0.3 percentage points) than the residential share of the tax base, while both timber/cutover and utility personal property account for a slightly lower share of tax payments than they do of the total tax base. The stability of the relationship between shares of tax payments and the tax base, class by class, implies that the problem of explaining the rather marked change in the composition of tax payments since 1975 can be reduced to explaining the equally marked change in the composition of the tax base. This issue will be considered both later in this section and in the fourth section, under the topic of property tax assessments.

Tax Rates

The average property tax rate, defined as total tax collections divided by total SEV, has exhibited an upward trend since the 1950s. Since 1976, however, after a rather large jump of 2.25 mills, the average tax rate has stayed roughly constant, moving from 53.37 mills in 1976 to 53.89 mills in 1977, and then declining slowly back to 53.38 mills in 1980.[38] Intrastate variation in millage rates is far greater than recent time series variation. In 1979, tax rates ranged from 67.6 mills in Washtenaw County to 26.0 mills in Leelanau County. Table 16.6 shows the average tax rates in ten Michigan counties, ranked, 1, 10, 20, to 80, and 83 by tax rate. The table also shows the percentage composition of the tax base in each of the counties, and is consistent with the statewide finding that the share of the tax base accounted for by commercial and industrial property (agriculture and timber/cutover) tends to rise (fall) with the tax rate.

Property tax levies and personal income. As was noted in the second section of this chapter, total property tax collections as a fraction of personal income in the state have fallen considerably since 1972. The downward trend in this statistic was reversed in 1980, however, largely

TABLE 16.7
PROPERTY TAXES AND PERSONAL INCOME,
MICHIGAN COUNTIES, 1979

COUNTY (highest to lowest)	TOTAL PAYMENTS ($ millions)	TOTAL PERSONAL INCOME ($ millions)	RATIO, TAXES TO INCOME (%)	COUNTY (highest to lowest)	TOTAL PAYMENTS ($ millions)	TOTAL PERSONAL INCOME ($ millions)	RATIO, TAXES TO INCOME (%)
1 Lake	3.9	41.1	9.4	43 Livingston	39.4	796.3	5.0
2 Crawford	4.9	53.4	9.2	44 Macomb	344.8	7,192.5	4.8
3 Kalkaska	5.8	63.8	9.0	45 Delta	12.6	263.3	4.8
4 Oscoda	2.8	31.7	8.8	46 Lenawee	35.4	743.5	4.8
5 Alcona	4.7	54.1	8.6	47 Oceana	6.5	137.1	4.7
6 Roscommon	8.0	96.5	8.3	48 Oakland	576.8	12,301.0	4.7
7 Mason	13.6	170.7	7.9	49 Isabella	14.9	324.2	4.6
8 Charlevoix	11.2	143.8	7.8	50 Berrien	63.2	1,378.6	4.6
9 Ogemaw	7.1	91.1	7.8	51 Van Buren	21.2	468.6	4.5
10 Antrim	8.5	113.6	7.4	52 Kalamazoo	87.6	1,946.8	4.5
11 Presque Isle	6.4	88.7	7.2	53 Gogebic	5.8	130.2	4.5
12 Mackinac	4.8	67.6	7.1	54 Iosco	8.3	186.5	4.5
13 Montmorency	3.2	46.9	6.9	55 St. Joseph	18.8	431.1	4.4
14 Ontonagon	4.0	58.2	6.9	56 Allegan	24.3	564.8	4.3
15 Osceola	6.9	10.4	6.7	57 Eaton	31.6	734.2	4.3
16 Cheboygan	8.9	133.8	6.7	58 Marquette	23.9	557.9	4.3
17 Clare	9.4	141.9	6.6	59 Wayne	1,013.2	23,911.0	4.2
18 Emmet	11.3	172.0	6.6	60 Ingham	110.3	2,607.9	4.2
19 Benzie	4.9	75.9	6.5	61 Gratiot	13.1	312.2	4.2
20 Missaukee	3.5	54.3	6.5	62 Tuscola	18.7	444.5	4.2
21 Leelanau	6.5	100.5	6.4	63 Saginaw	87.8	2,096.0	4.2
22 Schoolcraft	3.6	57.0	6.4	64 Jackson	53.0	1,272.6	4.2
23 Gladwin	7.3	115.3	6.4	65 Cass	15.5	371.6	4.2
24 Otsego	7.0	110.7	6.3	66 Baraga	2.3	54.6	4.1
25 Alger	3.4	53.7	6.3	67 Clinton	19.1	464.4	4.1
26 Manistee	9.3	156.2	6.0	68 Branch	13.3	324.9	4.1
27 Midland	39.6	679.3	5.8	69 Barry	12.6	307.8	4.1
28 St.Clair	60.3	1,042.7	5.8	70 Genessee	180.3	4,417.8	4.1
29 Huron	16.1	282.9	5.7	71 Hillsdale	12.4	307.2	4.0
30 Monroe	63.1	1,129.1	5.6	72 Lapeer	21.9	544.5	4.0
31 Iron	5.2	94.6	5.6	73 Ottawa	55.1	1,321.8	4.0
32 Wexford	9.1	164.0	5.5	74 Dickinson	8.7	217.1	4.0
33 Alpena	13.1	239.9	5.5	75 Menominee	7.1	178.1	4.0
34 Washtenaw	139.9	2,609.2	5.4	76 Muskegon	48.5	1,225.9	3.9
35 Chippewa	8.9	169.7	5.2	77 Calhoun	49.8	1,277.8	3.9
36 Arenac	4.7	90.4	5.2	78 Montcalm	12.2	323.2	3.8
37 Keweenaw	0.7	13.6	5.1	79 Kent	141.6	3,979.3	3.6
38 Newaygo	10.8	210.3	5.1	80 Shiawassee	19.9	600.2	3.3
39 Sanilac	14.6	285.0	5.1	81 Houghton	7.3	223.6	3.3
40 Grand Traverse	22.7	445.1	5.1	82 Ionia	11.0	346.2	3.2
41 Bay	51.2	1,009.0	5.1	83 Luce	1.5	52.6	2.8
42 Mecosta	9.1	180.5	5.0	STATE	3,889.7	86,369.0	4.5

Sources: Michigan State Tax Commission.
U.S. Bureau of the Census.

because of the depth of the recession in Michigan and the fact that property tax assessments lag current economic trends. Compared with 1979, property tax collections in 1980 rose by 13.4 percent while personal income rose by only 5.4 percent.[39] As a result, total property tax collections per dollar of state personal income rose from 4.5 cents in 1979 to 4.8 cents in 1980. It is reasonable to expect that the downward trend will resume with economic recovery in the state. Indeed in 1981, the property tax base grew by 11.4 percent, and millage rates are likely to fall slightly, implying that the rate of growth or tax collections will be considerably lower than in 1980, while personal income can be expected to rise more rapidly in 1981 than it did in 1980.

Property tax collections as a fraction of personal income exhibit substantial variation across Michigan's eighty-three counties. Table 16.7 displays 1979 tax collections, personal income, and the ratio of the former to the latter for all of the counties in the state.[40] It should be emphasized that tax collections as a fraction of income are a very imperfect measure of the burden of the tax, partly because the circuit breaker is not taken into account, and also because a substantial and varying fraction of taxes paid by property located in a county may be ultimately borne outside of the county. It is striking, however, that counties of all sizes and types are spread quite widely on this statistic.

Thus far, the analysis in this section has been confined to a discussion of gross property tax liabilities, and has not accounted for tax shifting, tax exporting, or property tax credits that are claimed against state income tax liabilities. The remainder of this section will be devoted to providing estimates of net property tax liabilities with a view to estimating not only who pays the property tax, but how much property taxes cost residents of Michigan. The discussion will be divided by economic sector, dealing first with housing, then with industrial and commercial property, and finally (briefly) with agriculture, timber/cutover, and utility personal property.[41] The discussion will conclude with a revised version of Table 16.5 estimating net property tax liabilities by type of taxpayer.

The Property Tax and Housing

There are a number of important sources of divergence between taxes levied on housing and taxes ultimately paid by consumers of housing. These differ somewhat between owner-occupied and rental housing. For owner-occupied housing, there are two major deductions that must be made from taxes paid in arriving at an estimate of the burden of the tax on homeowners: (1) the circuit breaker directly reduces the gross property tax liabilities of homeowners by exactly the amount of circuit breaker tax credits received; (2) the deductibility of property taxes from federal taxable income reduces the homeowner's net tax liability attributable to property taxes by the taxpayer's federal marginal tax rate multiplied by property taxes paid net of the circuit breaker.[42] For rental housing, the circuit breaker must be apportioned between the tenant and the landlord in the same proportion that the property tax itself is apportioned. In a competitive rental housing market, the proportion of property taxes that is levied on structures will be shifted forward onto tenants, and the same fraction of the circuit breaker will be retained by tenants. The part of property taxes that is on the land will be borne by landlords, and the same part of the circuit breaker (by increasing the demand for land) will raise the incomes of landlords. After apportioning the tax net of circuit breaker between landlords and tenants, estimation of the tax on rental housing borne by Michigan residents requires that taxes borne by landlords who reside out of state be subtracted from total property taxes paid, and that a federal tax offset be calculated and subtracted from the estimates of taxes borne by resident landlords.

Derivation of estimates along the lines discussed above

is complicated by the fact that data on property tax collections is not organized by tenure of residence. The residential class of property contains both owner-occupied and small-scale rental housing while larger apartment buildings are assessed as commercial property. The most careful adjustment for this in the available literature is that made by Roberts (1975). Application of Roberts' estimates to the estimated tax liabilities by class shown in Table 16.5 yields the estimates of gross property tax payments by rental and owner-occupied housing, respectively, shown in Table 16.8.

The circuit breaker. The property tax liabilities shown in Table 16.8 are overestimates of the "burden" of the tax because of the Homestead Property Tax Credit, or circuit breaker. In calculating net tax payments for homeowners and renters, total circuit breaker payments are deducted from the numbers shown in Table 16.8 and divided between renters and owner-occupants under the assumption that renters received 6.24 percent of circuit breaker revenues in 1979, 6.7 percent in 1978, 6.6 percent in 1977 and each of the preceding years.[43]

Net payments by rental housing. After deducting circuit breaker credits received by renters, all that remains in estimating the effects of the tax on rental housing is to apportion the tax payments between Michigan residents and residents of other states. A standard assumption in analysis of property taxes is that 25 percent of the value of rental housing is land value, and therefore 25 percent of the tax is borne by landlords.[44] A very careful study of property taxation in California, which relies on detailed data from the Survey of Income and Education and the Statistics of Income, finds that in California 41 percent of landlord income accrues to landlords living outside the state, and that the mean marginal federal income tax rate of resident landlords in California is 0.37 (Chernik and Reschovsky, 1980). Lacking any better data, we assume that these figures will hold in Michigan and thus net property

TABLE 16.8
ESTIMATED GROSS PROPERTY TAX PAYMENTS BY HOUSING TENURE, 1974-1980
(millions of dollars)

	1974	1975	1976	1977	1978	1979	1980
Owner Occupied	1,178.7	1,291.0	1,445.3	1,586.4	1,736.5	1,974.4	2,286.7
Rental	212.2	232.0	241.9	263.1	285.6	320.3	363.5

Note: Gross payments by owner-occupied housing are equal to 91.46 percent of gross payments by property classified as residential. Gross payments by rental housing comprise the remaining 8.54 percent of residential property plus 20.08 percent of commercial property, the fraction of commercial property estimated by Roberts (1975) to be apartment buildings. See Roberts (1975) for details.

Source: Table 16.5.

TABLE 16.9
PROPERTY TAXES AND RENTAL HOUSING 1974-1980
(millions of dollars)

	1974	1975	1976	1977	1978	1979	1980
Gross Payments	212.2	232.0	241.9	263.1	285.6	320.3	363.5
Payments Net Of Circuit Breaker	199.4	216.7	223.7	243.1	264.0	296.6	333.4
Borne by Tenants	149.5	162.5	167.8	182.3	198.0	222.4	250.0
Borne by Landlords	49.8	54.2	55.9	60.8	66.0	74.1	83.3
Non-Resident	20.4	22.2	22.9	24.9	27.1	30.4	34.2
Resident	29.4	32.0	33.0	35.9	38.9	43.7	49.2
Resident Net of Federal Tax Offset	18.5	20.1	20.8	22.6	24.5	27.5	31.0
Payments borne by all Michigan Residents	168.0	182.6	188.6	204.9	222.5	249.9	281.0

Note: Details may not add to totals due to rounding.

Source: See text; Circuit Breaker Data from State of Michigan Fiscal Year 1982 Budget (1980 is an estimate in the budget).

taxes on rental housing paid by Michigan residents are derived as shown in Table 16.9. About 77 to 80 percent of gross tax payments attributable to rental housing over the period 1974 to 1980 were ultimately borne as property taxes on Michigan residents.[45]

Net payments by owner-occupants. Net property tax payments by owner-occupants are calculated by starting with Table 16.8, deducting circuit breaker payments to owner-occupants, and then deducting federal income tax offsets accruing to owner-occupants. This last step requires an estimate (for each year) of the mean federal marginal tax rate facing taxpayers who itemize deductions. For 1978, this number is assumed to be 34 percent, which was the number found by Chernik and Reschovsky in their study of property taxes in California.[46] The 34 percent estimate is also used for 1979 and 1980, under the assumptions that the 1979 income tax cut and bracket creep about cancelled out in 1979 (for higher-income filers) and that bracket creep and the recession about cancelled out in 1980. For each of the years preceding 1978, the estimate of the mean marginal tax rate is arbitrarily reduced by one percentage point per year, reflecting the effect of bracket creep.

Given assumptions of the applicable mean marginal federal tax rate, this rate must be applied to the dollar amount of property taxes claimed as deductions on returns filed by Michigan residents. Actual data on this amount are only available for 1975 and 1977. For 1978 through 1980, the 1977 ratio of residential property taxes deducted to gross residential property taxes paid (66.0 percent) was used to estimate deductions. For 1974 and 1976, the 1975 ratio of 66.7 percent was used. Derivation of net property tax payments by owner-occupants in Michigan is shown in Table 16.10.

The striking difference between Table 16.10 and Table 16.9 is that net property tax payments on the part of Michigan residents are a substantially lower fraction of gross payments in owner-occupied housing than in rental

TABLE 16.10
PROPERTY TAXES AND OWNER-OCCUPIED HOUSING, 1974-1980

	1974	1975	1976	1977	1978	1979	1980
Gross Payments	1,178.7	1,291.0	1,445.3	1,586.4	1,736.5	1,974.4	2,286.7
Payments net of Circuit Breaker	998.7	1,074.9	1,188.4	1,302.7	1,435.7	1,617.6	1,833.7
Federal Tax Offset	200.7	222.3	253.7	283.7	322.2	363.0	411.5
Net Payments	798.0	852.6	934.7	1,019.0	1,113.5	1,254.6	1,422.2

Sources: Table 16.8; State of Michigan Fiscal Year 1982 Budget; Text.

TABLE 16.11
PROPERTY TAXES ON COMMERCIAL ENTERPRISES
(millions of dollars)

	1974	1975	1976	1977	1978	1979	1980
Gross Payments	406.6	443.5	425.7	457.5	491.2	541.1	596.8
Payments borne by Consumers	305.0	332.6	319.3	343.1	368.4	405.8	447.6
by Michigan Residents	295.9	322.6	309.7	332.8	357.3	393.6	434.2
by Non-resident Tourists	9.2	10.0	9.6	10.3	11.1	12.2	13.4
Payments borne by Owners							
by Michigan Residents (net of federal tax offset)	48.1	51.8	49.0	51.9	54.9	60.5	66.7
by Non-residents	32.8	35.8	34.4	37.0	40.0	43.7	48.2
Net Payments borne by Michigan Residents	344.0	374.4	358.7	384.7	412.2	454.1	500.9

Notes: Gross payments are equal to the figures shown in Table 16.5 less the 20.08 percent of commercial property taxes that are derived from rental housing. See Tables 16.8 and 16.9.

Details may not add to totals due to rounding.

Source: See text.

housing. The main reasons for this are that the circuit breaker reduces gross payments by a much larger fraction for owner-occupants than it does for renters and that property taxes may be deducted for federal income for purposes for homeowners but not for renters. It is also worth noting that net property tax payments by owner-occupants have been almost constant as a fraction of personal income over the period--about 1.5 percent. In other words, once the circuit breaker and federal deductibility are taken into account, the part of the property tax that most observers credit with being responsible for the recent "tax revolt" has not grown as a fraction of the most widely used measure of ability to pay.

The Property Tax and Commerce and Industry

As noted above, gross property tax payments attributable to commercial and industrial property have been falling as a share of total tax collections throughout the period of this study (1974-80). Ever since 1976, the first year that inventories were exempt from property taxes, the growth in tax collections over has barely matched inflation as measured by the GNP deflator and has fallen well short of inflation as measured by the consumer price index. Furthermore, taxes on industrial property fell from 2.2 percent of state value added in manufacturing in 1974 to 1.5 percent in 1977, the last year for which value added data are available.[47]

There is considerable intrastate variation in the share of tax collections attributable to industrial and commercial property. Industrial tax payments are particularly concentrated, with the four counties of Wayne, Washtenaw, Kent, and Genessee accounting for 48.1 percent of industrial payments in 1979, while they accounted for only 37.9 percent of total property tax payments. The degree of concentration was even greater in earlier years. For example, in 1974, the four counties accounted for 52.0 percent of industrial property taxes, as compared to 41.9 percent of all property taxes.

The incidence of the property tax on commercial and industrial property is very different. To a first approximation, taxes on commercial property will be borne by Michigan residents, because most of the tax is shifted onto consumers directly (commercial output is elastically supplied) and the bulk of ownership and consumption of commercial property is local, implying that most of the tax that is not shifted is also borne locally. Payments of taxes by industrial property, on the other hand, are largely exported, because both consumers of the products and owners of the property itself are generally distributed nationally. It is here that some of the conceptual difficulties in determining tax incidence become most serious. For industrial firms that reside in Michigan, produce for national markets, and are nationally owned, it is clear that almost all of taxes paid will be borne outside of the state, by consumers and stockholders in some combination depending on the monopoly power of the firms and the elasticity of demand for the product. On the other hand, this approach to incidence, which has been taken throughout this study, ignores the indirect effects that changes in property tax rates could have on wages in Michigan. Presumably, capital is mobile in the long run, so that firms that cannot shift the bulk of their property taxes onto consumers will tend to move capital out of the state in response to the tax, to the point where the net rate of return to capital after tax is equal in all states. The reduced capital stock in Michigan implies that wages and land rents will be lower than would otherwise be the case. If labor is relatively immobile, this means that much of the long run burden of the property tax on such firms is borne by Michigan labor. If labor is mobile, and net wages also equalize nationwide, then population will leave the state and the equilibrium with the tax will be one with both less capital and less labor than would obtain without a tax. The incidence of these population shifts is undefined; the effect on landowners in the state unambiguously negative. In either case, the fact that this study (like its predecessors) only considers the allocation of the dollar volume of taxes actually paid in estimating "incidence" means that the allocation of the major part of industrial property taxes to nonresidents overstates the extent to which Michigan can levy such taxes without negative effects on the incomes of landowners and some combination of negative effects on the incomes of labor and the size of the state's population.

Property taxes on commerce. Seventy-five percent of property taxes levied on commercial property are assumed to be borne by consumers, three percent of whom are assumed to be tourists. Of the remaining 25 percent of the tax levy, Roberts' careful (if somewhat dated) study found that 74.6 percent was borne by corporations, the ownership of which was distributed 56.7 percent to Michigan residents and 43.3 percent out of state. The share of taxes attributable to unincorporated enterprises is assumed to be entirely locally borne, except for the federal tax offset, which is arbitrarily assumed to be at the same rate as that for all itemizers in Michigan (see the discussion of owner-occupied housing, above). Because locally-owned corporations do not generally have enough income to be taxed at the maximum federal corporate rate, taxes borne by local corporations are also (and even more arbitrarily) assumed to be offset at the same rate as for all itemizers in Michigan.[48] The tax burden on commercial enterprises (net of rental housing) is allocated as shown in Table 16.11.

Property taxes on manufacturing (industry). Previous studies of taxes in Michigan have carefully separated automobile manufacture from the rest of the state's industrial sector.[49] This separation turns out to make very little difference to the estimate of the share of taxes on industry that are exported. In earlier work, the key difference between automobiles and the rest of the manufacturing sector was that automobile manufacture is assumed to have considerable monopoly power--permitting taxes to be shifted onto consumers nationwide through higher product prices. It is by now commonplace that Michigan's monopoly power in automotive manufacture for the U.S. market has suffered considerable erosion in recent years. Even if this were not the case, however, the reason that almost all property taxes on industry are exported is independent of market power. If the industry is monopolistic, taxes are exported through higher product prices, and Michigan residents bear the tax in proportion to their own consumption of the manufactured good. If the industry is competitive (or nearly so) taxes are borne by shareholders and Michigan residents bear the tax in proportion to their ownership of stock in relevant firms (less a federal income tax offset). In either case, the proportion of the tax borne by Michigan residents will be very low (Michigan residents receive about four percent of dividends paid nationwide, and their share of national consumption of manufactured products is roughly the same).

A number of factors tend to indicate that the very high estimates of exporting implicit in the previous paragraph should be lowered somewhat. It is very likely that the share of stock in Michigan's industrial plant owned within the state is somewhat higher than the state's share of stock in corporate enterprises nationwide. It is also likely that some property classified as manufacturing produces almost entirely for local markets, and thus can shift taxes onto consumers in the same manner that commercial enterprises do. Lacking the detailed data and analysis that would permit discrimination, it is arbitrarily (and conservatively) assumed that 90 percent of the property tax is exported, with the 10 percent borne by residents of Michigan allocated 3 percent (net of federal tax offsets) to stockholders and 7 percent to consumers. These assumptions are reflected in Table 16.12.

Agriculture, Utilities, Timber/Cutover and Development

There are only three potentially important reasons why net taxes in any of the remaining four classes of property would be substantially less than the estimates of gross tax payments shown in Table 16.5: (1) as noted above, some utility property is classified as industrial real property.

TABLE 16.12
PROPERTY TAXES ON INDUSTRIAL PROPERTY
(millions of dollars)

	1974	1975	1976	1977	1978	1979	1980
Gross Tax Payments	590.8	646.3	545.4	569.8	612.5	657.1	719.4
Borne by Michigan residents	59.1	64.6	54.5	56.9	61.3	65.7	71.9
by Consumers	41.4	45.2	38.2	39.8	42.9	46.0	50.3
by Stockholders	17.7	19.4	16.4	17.1	18.4	19.7	21.6

Notes: Details may not add to totals due to rounding.

Gross payments equal industrial payments as shown in Table 16.5, less estimated payments by utility property classified as industrial. The latter are estimated as 21.82 percent of total personal property taxes on utilities following the procedure used in Roberts (1975).

Source: See text.

TABLE 16.13
PROPERTY TAXES ON AGRICULTURE, UTILITIES, TIMBER/CUTOVER AND DEVELOPMENT
(millions of dollars)

	1974	1975	1976	1977	1978	1979	1980
Gross Taxes	261.7	291.9	297.6	328.6	358.7	396.3	447.5
Gross Taxes less Farmland Credit	261.7	291.6	296.6	327.1	352.0	380.7	426.1
Taxes Borne by Consumers	172.6	191.6	187.5	202.8	215.7	233.6	255.1
Gross Taxes Borne by Property Owners	89.1	100.0	109.1	124.3	136.3	147.4	171.0
Net Taxes Borne by Property Owners	71.3	80.0	87.3	99.4	109.0	117.9	135.7
Net Taxes Borne by Michigan Residents	243.9	271.6	274.8	302.2	324.7	351.2	390.8

Notes: Developmental amounts to 8.2 million dollars (gross) in 1980, the year in which it was classified.

Details may not add to totals due to rounding.

Gross taxes are the sum of the four categories shown in Table 16.5 plus estimated taxes paid by utilities on behalf of property classified as industrial. See notes to Table 16.12.

Source: See text.

Taxes paid on behalf of such property must be added to the utility total given in Table 16.5; (2) there is a special state income tax credit for property taxes paid on farmland under certain circumstances (See Chapter 29); (3) for agricultural, timber/cutover, and developmental land, taxes paid are deductible on federal income tax returns.[50] The special income tax credit for farmland is directly obtainable from the state budget; estimates of the value of deductibility of taxes require determination of both the fraction of the tax borne by the property owner and the mean federal marginal tax rate of property owners in each class.

Because developmental, agricultural, and timber/cutover property account for such a small fraction of total property tax revenues in the state, the admittedly arbitrary assumptions that are used in estimating the fractions of these payments borne by Michigan residents will make little difference in the estimates of the share of property taxes statewide that is borne externally. For agricultural and timber/cutover property, it is assumed that 25 percent of the tax is borne by Michigan consumers and the remaining 75 percent is borne by property owners, all of whom are assumed to be Michigan residents.[51] The mean marginal federal income tax rate of farm owners and owners of timber/cutover land is assumed to be 20 percent[52] while the mean marginal tax rate for owners of developmental property is assumed to be 34 percent, the same as for households itemizing deductions. Under these assumptions, the relationship between gross property taxes levied on the four classes of property and net taxes borne by Michigan residents is derived in Table 16.13.

<u>Summary: The Net Incidence of Property Taxes in Michigan</u>

Table 16.14 provides a recapitulation of the main results in this section. While there is some year-to-year variation, roughly 60 percent of Michigan's gross property tax levies stay in the state as property taxes. (The circuit breaker stays in the state, but is deducted from property taxes.) As a fraction of state personal income,

TABLE 16.14
THE INCIDENCE OF MICHIGAN PROPERTY TAXES
(millions of dollars)

	1974	1975	1976	1977	1978	1979	1980[1]
Gross Tax Collections	2,650.1	2,903.7	2,956.6	3,206.4	3,484.9	3,889.6	4,415.2
Net Property Taxes Borne by Michigan Residents	1,613.0	1,745.8	1,811.7	1,966.8	2,133.3	2,374.5	2,665.8
by Consumers	509.9	559.4	535.7	574.5	615.0	671.9	738.6
by Tenants	149.5	162.5	167.8	182.3	198.0	222.4	250.0
by Homeowners	798.0	852.6	934.7	1,019.0	1,113.5	1,254.6	1,422.2
by Other Property Owners	155.6	171.3	173.5	191.0	206.8	225.6	255.0
Net Taxes/Gross Taxes	0.609	0.601	0.613	0.613	0.612	0.611	0.604
Net Taxes/Personal Income	0.031	0.032	0.029	0.028	0.027	0.027	0.029

Notes: [1]1980 gross collections are not consistent with Table 16.1 due to inconsistencies in Michigan State Tax Commission data.

1980 personal income estimated by Michigan Department of Management and Budget.

Details may not add to totals due to rounding. of

Sources: Tables 16.5, 16.8, 16.9, 16.10, 16.11, 16.12, and 16.13.

net property tax levies fell steadily from 1975 until the recession year of 1980, when property tax levies continued to rise but the rise in personal income is estimated to have slowed sharply. Even so, the 1980 percentage is fully two-tenths of one percent below the figure for 1974. In sum, although the burden placed on state residents by the general property tax has declined slightly since 1974, it has declined; the trend is such that if it were not for the recession, the decline would probably have continued apace. In any event, there seems to be little substance to claims that property tax burdens on the state's residents have been increasing in recent years.

Equity

Notably absent from this study, especially when comparison is made with its predecessors, is an estimate of the incidence of the property tax by income class. Because federal offsets are so important to the difference between gross tax levies and net tax burdens, the property tax is undoubtedly regressive, as is any other deductible state or local tax that is not more progressive than the federal income tax. The circuit breaker, as is pointed out in Chapter 2, attenuates this effect somewhat, but the fact remains--deductibility of the property tax assures its regressivity. There is no reason to believe that the pattern of incidence of the property tax has changed much since the work of Roberts (1975) or even that of Musgrave and Daicoff (1958). Those seeking a discussion of the incidence of the property tax with respect to current incomes are well-advised to read those studies.

The incidence of the property tax, especially the residential property tax, with respect to permanent incomes is another matter. A number of economists have argued that measures of the effect of taxes on the income distribution should not be based on a single year's income. The biases inherent in using just one year's income are especially serious in the case of owner-occupied housing, because people do not sell their homes because they are having a bad year in the labor (or stock) market, nor do they rush out and buy mansions because they had a good year. Housing purchases are based on an expectation of income over a relatively long period of time, and consequently, the burden of taxes on housing should probably be evaluated with respect to income averaged over a period of years.[53]

If property tax rates were the same everywhere, the progressivity of the residential property tax would depend only on the (permanent) elasticity of demand for housing. The tax would be progressive if the elasticity exceeded unity, and regressive if the elasticity were less than unity. Based upon this reasoning Aaron (1975) concluded that the residential property tax must be progressive, as he found the income elasticity of demand for housing to be 1.13, consistent with previous work of Muth (1959), Reid (1962), and de Leeuw (1971), all of whom find the elasticity to be in the neighborhood of unity or higher. More recent work by Polinsky (1977) and Polinsky and Ellwood (1979) implies that the income elasticity of housing demand is somewhat lower than unity--in the neighborhood of 0.7 to 0.9. Taken by itself, this finding suggests that the residential property tax is slightly regressive. However, Ihlanfeldt (1979) has pointed out that property tax rates are not uniform, and presents evidence that tax rates are positively correlated with house value for a sample of households nationwide. The net effect of an income-elasticity of housing demand that is less than unity (0.79 in Ihlanfeldt's study) and a positive relationship between housing value and tax rates is that the tax is mildly progressive nationwide. For the North Central region, which includes Michigan, Ihlanfeldt found the tax to be slightly regressive, but, of course, no adjustment was made for circuit breakers or federal deductibility. The former would make the incidence of tax payments more progressive; the latter, because of the progressivity of the federal income tax, assures that the incidence of net tax burdens is regressive.

ASSESSMENT PRACTICES AND THE COMPOSITION OF THE TAX BASE

The preceding sections have shown that the burden of property taxes in Michigan is considerably less than one would infer from examination of statistics on aggregate tax collections. It remains true, however, that the composition of net tax payments has been shifting toward owner-occupied housing, which accounted for 49.5 percent of the net property tax burdens in 1974, 51.6 percent in 1976 (the first year that inventories were exempt from tax) and 53.4 percent in 1980. There is every reason to believe that the share will be higher yet in 1981, because the share of the gross tax base rose by 1.2 percentage points between 1980 and 1981. Moreover, while the total net property tax burden has been falling as a fraction of state personal income over the period, net property taxes on owner-occupied housing as a fraction of personal income have been roughly constant. There has been widespread public outcry concerning the fact that owner-occupied housing has been bearing an increasing fraction of the tax burden, and a major purpose of this section is to analyze and discuss the causes of the increase in the share of the burden on home-owners. Of particular interest is the relationship between this phenomenon and assessment practices. The shifting composition of the tax burden arises from a similar shift in the composition of the tax base, and the tax base is determined by assessments and equalization. The question is whether these shifts are due to some sort of quirks in assessment practices, or whether they arise from other factors, including tax abatement programs for industry and genuine changes in the relative value of owner-occupied housing and industrial and commercial property. The following discussion will attempt to provide some answers to this question in the context of a more general evaluation of assessment and equalization as practiced in Michigan.

Overall Assessment Quality

The essential processes of assessment and equalization have been discussed earlier in this chapter (see the second section) and need not be repeated here. Rather, this discussion will emphasize evaluation of the quality of the assessment and equalization processes. The quality of assessments is extremely important for the equity and legitimacy of property taxes. Intrajurisdictional variation in assessment ratios (the ratio of assessed value to market value) cannot be corrected by equalization if the variation is within a class of property. Put simply, if my house is assessed at a higher percentage of market value than is your house, the equalization process is designed to assure that on average we will be at 50 percent of market value, but it will not correct the inequity between us. I will pay a higher effective tax rate than you will.

The best available measures of assessment quality in Michigan are found in the studies done every five years by the U.S. Bureau of the Census, in connection with the Census of Governments. These studies compare assessed value with market sales prices in SMSAs in the state. For single family housing, the studies measure both intrajurisdictional variation in assessment ratios and interjurisdictional variation. The former is of most interest here, because the latter can be corrected by equalization. A straightforward measure of assessment quality is the "coefficient of intra-area dispersion," defined as the average percentage difference between the assessment ratio for all parcels studied and the median of the assessment ratio in the jurisdiction. If the coefficient is equal to ten, for example, this means that on average the assessment ratio is ten percent above or below the median assessment ratio. If, for example, the median assessment ratio is 41 percent, a coefficient of intra-area dispersion of 10 would imply that the average parcel sold during the study would be within 4.1 percentage points of 41 percent--10 percent of the median. Obviously, the lower the statistic the better is the quality of local assessment.

Compared to the nation as a whole, Michigan scores very well in assessment quality. In 1977, the median coefficient of intra-area variation for all jurisdictions studied in the U.S. was 22; in Michigan the median jurisdiction had a coefficient of 15.7, the third best in the nation. Moreover, Michigan improved between 1972 and 1977. The state median in 1972 was 18.4 or tenth best. Over the same period assessment quality in the country as a whole has deteriorated; the national median in 1972 was 20.2. Michigan's improvement between 1972 and 1977 may be questioned in light of the fact that the average of the coefficients in the state weighted by total property value deteriorated somewhat between 1972 and 1977 from (14.6 to 16.6). Still, the state's rank on the weighted average improved from third in the country to second over the same period. In short, at least for single-family houses, city and township assessors in Michigan SMSAs are among the best in the nation at assuring that the tax burden is shared equitably. Unfortunately, similar data are not available for non-SMSA parts of the state, where the problem is likely to be more serious due to the general absence of professional appraisers involved in the assessment process.

Even within SMSAs, there is considerable variation in assessment quality. Coefficients of intra-area dispersion measured over all sales of property (not just single-family housing, as above) show that in 1977 Dearborn was the worst locality in the state, at 29.3, while Farmington Hills was the best, at 6.8. In addition to Dearborn, Lansing, Saginaw and Detroit had coefficients that exceeded 20 percent, while Sterling Heights and Ann Arbor were the only other jurisdictions below 10 percent. Again, the above comparisons were made only for jurisdictions within SMSAs, and many jurisdictions in SMSAs did not have sufficient sales for the statistic to be computed.[54]

Assessment Practices

State law requires that all taxable property in the state be equalized at 50 percent of true cash value. The best method of assessing property at a given percentage of its market value is simply to observe enough market transactions in similar types of property so that the market value of properties that do not change hands can be readily estimated. This method, which is by far the most reliable method available, is generally practical only in the case of single-family residential housing. Here, the assessor can observe many transactions in the market, and the task of assessing property values so that they follow the market is relatively straightforward. Thus, part of the cause of the increased share of property taxes borne by residential housing is easy to understand--the price of owner-occupied housing has been rising rapidly in recent years, and the assessors have been doing their job in tracking the increase. Homeowners may not enjoy paying higher tax bills, and may perceive that it is unfair to be taxed on unrealized capital gains on their housing. But the base on which property taxes are levied is property value, and there is no reason to believe that assessors in general have been inflating assessments at a faster rate than the true appreciation of residential property over the last seven years.

There is, however, one quirk in assessment and equalization practice that has led to assessments continuing to rise (for the 1981 tax year) even though the appreciation of residential property values clearly slowed down during 1980. Basically, when property values appreciate the equalization procedures used in the state permit the assessor to spread the effects of inflation out over a three year period. Thus, for example, if inflation were to increase from five percent to fifteen percent (as it did, during the 1970s, in single-family housing prices), equalization rules in Michigan would permit assessments to rise by only about eight percent in the first year after the higher inflation rate took hold, about eleven percent in the second year, and then fifteen percent in the third year and all subsequent years. Moreover, as long as the inflation in owner-occupied housing stayed at 15 percent, assessed values would be about 43 percent of true market, instead of the mandated 50 percent. If inflation should suddenly attenuate, however, and go back to its original level of five percent per year, assessed values would then "catch up" to market values over the succeeding three years. This is what is happening in 1981, and it results in assessed values rising faster than market values, to the considerable displeasure of homeowners. No one remembers that at the beginning of the inflationary episode market values rose faster than assessed values.[55]

Aside from the problems arising from the phased adjustment to changes in inflation, owner-occupied housing assessments follow market values quite closely. Thus, if changes in the composition of the tax base are due to faulty assessment practices, the fault must lie in the assessment of commercial and industrial property. Assessment of commercial and industrial property is much more difficult to evaluate (and to practice) than is the case for residential housing, because as a general matter there will not be enough market transactions in any jurisdiction to permit assessors to use sales data in determining market value. In most cases, assessors use what is called the "cost" method in determining the value of commercial and industrial property. Briefly, this involves calculating what it would cost to replace structures, and then deducting for physical depreciation, obsolescence (functional depreciation), and finally adjusting for market conditions generally (economic depreciation or appreciation). Estimates of functional and economic depreciation are inherently far more subjective than observation of sales prices or calculation of building costs.

Both the calculation of replacement cost and physical depreciation are relatively straightforward. A number of national organizations, as well as the State Tax Commission, publish manuals that can be used to determine replacement cost, and these are updated to account for increases in costs on a regular basis.[56] Physical depreciation is calculated based on the expected remaining economic life of the structure in question. As long as building costs keep pace with inflation generally, inflation should not introduce any bias into the assessment process. If a building has a 30 year life remaining and construction costs rise by 10 percent, assessed value would rise by about 7 percent. In addition to considering costs and physical depreciation, the assessor may deduct from value because a building has become functionally obsolescent. For example, modern technology permits warehouses to hold more material per square foot (due to larger forklifts) than was once the case. Thus, an old warehouse may lose value because it cannot accommodate new equipment optimally.

Finally, market conditions are weak in an area, the value of a structure may fall, over and above any reduction due to obsolescence or physical depreciation. If market conditions strengthen, values will rise by more than construction costs do. Determination of these factors is very difficult and intrinsically somewhat subjective. But there is no reason to believe that they should lead to a bias on average, and there is good reason to believe that market conditions facing much commercial and industrial property in Michigan have tended to be relatively weak in recent years as the state has undergone a severe economic recession. This would (quite properly) lead to a lower rate of increase in the assessed value of existing commercial and industrial property than for residential, where the market has, for the state as a whole, been much stronger.

Summary evaluation. Nationwide, the last half of the 1970's has been a period in which owner-occupied housing has been increasing in value at a much more rapid rate than has the value of industrial plant and equipment. The reasons for this are not entirely understood, but one important reason is that federal tax law reduces the net cost of owning housing capital during inflation, while it increases the net cost of holding business capital.[57] Assessed values imply Michigan has been part of the national trend, with the state's recent economic difficulties contributing to sluggish growth in the value of business property. In short, it is perfectly plausible that the rapid rates of increase in the assessed value of existing owner-occupied housing relative to existing commercial and industrial property accurately reflect actual changes in the relative values of the assets in question. Plausibility, of course, is not the same thing as proof, and the behavior of assessed values of business property during inflationary times is an area that deserves serious academic and practical study. Absent such study, however, general trends in the state do not indicate that assessors are erring in their measurement of the tax base. Rather, the tax base itself is changing, in part due to economic conditions, and in part due to the exemption of much new industrial property from the tax base under P.A. 198.

Other Issues in Property Tax Administration

While the focus of the discussion in this section has been on the relationship between assessment practices and the changing composition of the tax base, there are a number of other issues in property tax administration that bear on the fairness of the tax. Foremost among these is the quality of assessment in less urbanized parts of the state. Under state law, the township supervisor, an elected official, is the assessing officer in each of the state's 1260-plus townships. Obviously, training in property appraisal is not a requirement for political success (in Michigan or elsewhere) and although since 1969 supervisors have been required to complete a training course in assessment procedures before assuming their duties as assessing officers, the quality of local assessment in townships is still uneven. The problem is potentially serious, because, as was pointed out above, equalization cannot correct intrajurisdictional errors in assessments within a class. Every study of property tax administration in the state that this writer has seen has pointed to assessment quality in the smaller jurisdictions as a serious problem.[58] The requirements that assessors be certified has probably led to some improvement, but a professionally trained staff, perhaps charged with assessments over a fairly large geographical area, could improve matters still more. In short, the state requirement of uniformity is hard to meet when there are over 1500 assessing officers statewide, and the burden placed on the equalization process by the heterogeneity of primary assessment practices is potentially enormous.

The 1981 requirement that equalization be done separately for each class of real property should add greatly to the workload both of county equalization departments and the State Tax Commission. Equalization by class has only been in effect for one tax year, and it is thus too soon to tell if it will make much difference in practice. The aggregate data for the state show a continuation of the trends of the last five years, with no dramatic changes in the composition of the tax base statewide. The effect may have been more noticeable in individual counties and smaller units, especially those (such as Dearborn) where local assessors engaged in the practice of deliberately underassessing certain classes of property relative to others, and underassessing property in general, allowing the blame for increasing tax bills to be placed on the equalization process rather than on local political officials.

One important thing that could be accomplished by equalization by class is evaluation of whether or not industrial and commercial property has been systematically underassessed relative to residential property in recent years. The first year's data do not indicate that there has been such a bias. If equalization by class is to be successful, however, both county and state equalization staffs must (in principle) accomplish many times more work than they have in the past. Data on the response of counties to the new requirements are not available. However, the state proposes to accommodate a potential sextupling of the Tax Commission's workload by increasing the size of State Tax Commission staff from eighty-eight full time equivalents to ninety FTEs.[59] This hardly seems adequate to the task, especially in light of the state Auditor-General's finding that equalization by class "should necessitate a considerable increase in field staff equalization studies." Moreover, this finding was in the context of a report alleging that equalization studies had been inadequate in scope even before equalization by class was promulgated.[60]

CONCLUSIONS

The emphasis in this study has been on recent changes in property taxation in Michigan, primarily because it was hoped that recent changes could provide some insight into the sources of the "tax revolt" of the past few years. The results are mixed. Depending on one's prior views on property taxes, one could choose to emphasize any of the following four findings from this study: (1) as a fraction of both personal income and total tax collections in the state, property taxes are lower now than they were in 1974; (2) as a fraction of personal income in the state, property taxes paid by homeowners are higher now than they were in 1974; (3) as a fraction of personal income, property taxes net of the circuit breaker and federal tax offsets have been about constant at 1.5 percent since 1974; (4) the share of total property taxes paid by homeowners has been rising steadily since 1974, and in 1980 it was 8.0 percentage points higher than in 1974 as a share of gross collections (at 56.6 percent) and was 3.9 percentage points higher net of relevant offsets (at 53.4 percent).

The Changing Tax Base

Taken together, these four findings are part of a fairly consistent story of what has happened in the last seven years, but they also leave out an important part of the story. The most striking regularity in the data since 1974 is that the fraction of the property tax base (and of property tax collection) accounted for by commercial and industrial property has been falling steadily. Much of the decline, however, can be attributed to two explicit statewide policies, and, moreover, both of the relevant policies compensate local units of government for a substantial portion of the lost property taxes. Thus, while property tax collections from business have fallen as a share of total property tax collections, revenues accruing to local governments and school districts from business sources have fallen by considerably less than would be indicated by looking at property taxes alone. The two policies are the exemption of inventories from the property tax base and the exemption of industrial facilities under P.A. 198. In both cases, most school districts are compensated for the loss in tax base through the School Aid Fund. Municipalities and counties are partially compensated for the loss of inventories through an earmarked portion of the Single Business Tax that reimburses local units by applying their current millage rate to the 1975 SEV of inventories. Obviously, the value of this reimbursement declines with inflation, but slightly over $100 million are given to local units every year. Local governments are reimbursed for the exemption of industrial facilities at rates that depend on whether the facility is new or rehabilitated. For new facilities, the localities receive half of what they would if the facility were not exempt from property taxes. In both cases, although local units would receive more revenue if the relevant property were not exempt (provided it were extant at all), just looking at aggregate property tax data overstates the burden of the exemptions.

The two exemptions of business property account for more than half of the increase in the share of the tax base accounted for by residential property (again assuming the P.A. 198 property would have been built without the exemption). The rest of the increase is due to the fact that assessments of residential property have been rising faster than assessments of business property. This is hardly surprising in light of national trends in housing prices and the prices of business assets as well as the difficulties experienced by the Michigan economy in recent years. A number of factors, including recently legislated changes in federal tax treatment of business depreciation, and the demise of the fixed rate long term mortgage, lead one to predict that the days of rapid increases in housing value are about over--but at least until 1980 it is perfectly plausible that the fact that assessed values of housing rose faster than assessed values of business property can be explained by the fact that market values were behaving in exactly the same way.

Administrative Problems

Unfortunately, a reduction in the inflation of owner-occupied housing prices will only reduce the rate of growth of assessed values over a period of two years. The reason for this is that the state's formula for calculating equalization factors permits assessment ratios that are farther below the mandated 50 percent the higher is the inflation rate. Thus, as inflation attenuates, actual assessment ratios will rise for two years (with assessments rising at a faster rate than housing prices) after which assessments and housing prices will move together, but at a higher effective assessment ratio. This feature of the way in which property taxes are administered can be expected to lead to continuing taxpayer dissatisfaction through the 1982 assessments. To have one's property tax bill rise in proportion to a capital gain is annoying--to have it rise without the capital gain is infuriating. And the fact that one got a "break" when housing price inflation was accelerating (and indeed when it was at a higher level) is unlikely to be of much comfort when assessments rise faster than house prices in any given year.

A second source of dissatisfaction stems from the quality of assessments themselves. Because market values of property are not directly observable unless there has been a recent sale, even careful assessors will make errors within a jurisdiction, some properties will be assessed at a higher fraction of market value than will others. This problem can never be entirely corrected, but devoting more resources to the assessment process, especially in the smaller townships, could at least help. In SMSAs, the only areas for which there are good, recent studies, the quality of assessments in Michigan has been found to be among the best in the nation. Even so, in the median jurisdiction sampled in the state the average error in assessment ratios within the jurisdiction is about 15 percent. This means that one is likely to find two taxpayers whose effective tax rates differ by 30 percent of the median assessment ratio. The taxpayer on the high end of the difference is likely to feel that the tax is unjust, and with good reason. The only way to correct problems of this kind is to devote more resources to property tax administration, especially at the local level. There is little direct reward to localities for devoting resources to the task, as their revenues will depend on average assessments, not intraclass variations in assessment ratios. Yet the political viability of the tax, as well as its equity, depends on the minimization of intrajurisdictional variations, and there is certainly room for improvement.

Concluding Remarks

From the perspective of the homeowner, the last half decade looks as if it were designed to accentuate dissatisfaction with property taxes. Two important policies designed to attract industry to the state have led to a sharp increase in the share of property taxes paid by homeowners. One sees the increase, but not the direct benefits of the policies. A booming housing market has increased property taxes in proportion to the boom, and the taxes have continued to go up even as the boom has attenuated. Michigan's circuit breaker law, among the most generous in the nation, is so far removed from property tax payments themselves that people see only the gross burden of the tax, which has been rising as a share of personal income.

In spite of all this, the property tax remains central to local government finance, especially to school districts. Moreover, in June of 1981, about 97 percent of millage renewals on the ballot statewide were approved by the voters, indicating that at least at the local level the tax is still politically viable, if not exactly loved. Whether it is a good tax or not depends on one's subjective evaluation of the alternatives. If the homeowner can clear away the emphasis on aggregate data and gross tax payments, however, he or she should find that it is no worse a tax than it was in 1974.

NOTES, CHAPTER 16

[1]This paper could not have been written without the tireless and able research assistance provided by Edith Brashares, Cynthia Browning, and Karen Goldstone. I am grateful to George Kostishak, chairman of the Michigan State Assessor's Board, Wayne Johnson, assessor for the City of Ann Arbor, and Roland Anderson and Harold Seifert of the State Tax Commission staff for the time and energy they devoted to helping me obtain the data and institutional background necessary for preparation of this study. Robin Barlow, Raleigh Barlowe, Harvey Brazer, and Edward Gramlich provided valuable comments on an earlier draft. Deborah Swift's manifold talents more than compensated for my own inability to organize any research project that requires more than pencil and paper. My gratitude for all of the help that I have received requires that I absolve all of the people mentioned above from any responsibility for errors, which are mine alone.

[2]The discussion of property taxation in this chapter will be confined to the general local property tax as levied by cities, villages, counties, townships and school districts. The statewide property tax on real utility property is discussed in Chapter 24, "Other Taxes." State taxation of intangible personal property is the subject of Chapter 20, "The Intangibles Tax." Property taxes levied on industrial and commercial facilities that qualify for reduced tax rates under P.A. 198 or P.A. 255 are discussed in Chapter 10, "Tax Abatement as an Incentive to Industrial Location."

[3]_U.S. Census of Governments_, 1977.

[4]Advisory Commission on Intergovernmental Relations (ACIR) (1980), p. 78.

[5]State equalized value (SEV) is the value to which millage rates are applied, and is nominally equal to 50 percent of actual value. The procedures used to determine SEV for individual properties are described at length below.

[6]ACIR (1980).

[7]Michigan Department of the Treasury, State Tax Commission.

[8]Of course, other state taxes are used to pay for the homestead credit. The credit reduces net property tax liabilities, not total tax liabilities of state residents.

[9]Of course, some property taxes levied in other states will be paid by Michigan residents due to the same mechanisms that permit exporting some Michigan property taxes. In this study, imported property taxes, because they are beyond the control of state policy, will be ignored.

[10]ACIR (1980), p. 87.

[11]It should be noted that the 1978 figures shown in Table 16.2 predate the full impact of Proposition 13 on California's property tax collection.

[12]Data on circuit breakers is taken from ACIR (1979), p. 63.

[13]Ibid.

[14]The obvious exception to this generalization is property tax payments per capita, which have been rising nationwide, largely because of inflation. In 1977, the national average was $289, with Michigan at $322 gross and $302 net of the circuit breaker (ACIR (1980), p. 90). Michigan exceeds the national average on this statistic, while being below it (net of circuit breaker) for property tax payments as a fraction of personal income because Michigan's per capita personal income exceeds the national average. ACIR (1980), p. 90.

[15]ACIR, (1980), p. 89.

[16]Assumes Michigan circuit breaker to be 9 percent of Michigan property tax collections.

[17]ACIR, (1979), p. 60.

[18]Article IX, Sections 3, 4, 5, 6, 25, 31, and 33 of the constitution are the major relevant parts of that document; Act 206 of 1893 (as amended many times) is referred to as the "General Property Tax Act" and is the basic legislative authority for local property taxation. The amended act runs some 112 pages in *The Assessor's Training Manual*.

[19]Much of this discussion is taken from the Assessor's Training Manual, Michigan State Assessor's Board, Chapter 1, pp. 3-6. See also Taylor (1978), and Verberg (1978) for more extended discussions.

[20]Michigan Municipal League.

[21]Economic Report of the Governor (1980), pp. 88-89.

[22]For a complete list of exempt property, see "The Governor's Advisory Task Force on Property Tax Revision," Interim Report, app. 3.

[23]The formula is more complicated than this. See the chapter by Wolkoff in this volume.

[24]"Governor's Advisory Task Force," Interim Report, pt. 2, p.91.

[25]State Tax Commission.

[26]Executive Budget, State of Michigan FY 1982, Tax Expenditure Appendix, p. 38. Note that these exemptions are granted by local governments.

[27]Some possible ramifications of this point are spelled out in some detail in "The Governor's Advisory Task Force on Property Tax Reduction," Interim Report, pt. 5, pp. 45-56.

[28]Before 1981, the same problem could occur among classes of real or personal property within a locality. For example, if residential property were assessed at 40 percent of value and commercial property were assessed at 60 percent, there would be no equalizaton adjustment as long as real property on average was assessed at 50 percent.

Property owners who are overassessed may appeal their assessments first to the locality in question and then to the state tax tribunal. Thus, intrajurisdictional inequities of the magnitude of the example in the text would not be sustained if the right to appeal is exercised.

[29]The effect of property taxation on agriculture and forests is a major topic of discussion in Chapter 29, "Taxation of Agriculture and Forestry in Michigan," so these topics will be given only limited attention here.

[30]See C. McLure, "The New View of the Property Tax: A Caveat," National Tax Journal, March 1977.

[31]This chapter is not the place to reproduce doctrinal squabbles among economists. Briefly, the idea behind the new view (see Mieszkowski, 1972; Aaron, 1975; and Courant, 1977) is that from a national perspective property taxes as a whole must be borne by owners of property, rather than by users of goods produced with property. If all jurisdictions in the country taxed property at the same rate, then the

effects would appear in a reduced rate of return (after tax) to capital and land, rather than in higher prices for goods using capital and land. To the extent that some jurisdictions tax property at higher rates than other jurisdictions, the system of property taxes will have "excise effects," leading consumers of goods produced in the lower tax jurisdictions to pay lower prices than consumers of goods produced where taxes are higher. On average, however, the excise effects will cancel out, leaving the burden of the tax on capital and land nationwide. While this analysis is very important for an understanding of the effect of property taxation on the national income distribution, (it leads to the conclusions that property taxes in the aggregate are quite progressive, as they fall on wealthholders, who tend to occupy the upper reaches of the income distribution) it is essentially irrelevant when considering the effect of property taxes in a state the size of Michigan. For example, if Michigan were to abolish all property taxes, the effect on the nationwide return to capital (the new view effect) would be about one-tenth of one percentage point. If any jurisdiction within the state were to lower property taxes significantly, the nationwide effect would be essentially unmeasurable.

[32]This assumes that the prices paid for other factors of production remain constant. In practice, if the property tax increases in a town, it will affect all local production, and it may be that some of the tax can be shifted backward onto lower wages. If labor is perfectly mobile, however, the analysis in the text will hold.

[33]This must be true in the short run. In the long run, the producer can restore his profit by moving to a location with lower taxes, provided that all other factors of production can be purchased at the prices available in the original location. The fact that producer location does not appear to be very responsive to taxes indicates that in many cases producers earn location-specific economic rents (which are essentially indistinguishable from profits), and that property taxes are borne by these rents. Absent such rents, it is hard to see how competitive suppliers to national markets could absorb <u>any</u> increases in property taxes without going out of business.

[34]It should be emphasized that the analysis based on the discussion in the text only applies to allocation of the tax burden arising from tax payments made by economic actors that operate in the state. The analysis is thus seriously incomplete, in that if tax rates change, the location of economic activity will also change. A complete study of the incidence of the tax would take these locational changes, and their impacts on the prices and quantities of goods and services, into account. Ideally, one would compare the current system of property taxes in the state with some other system that raised the same revenue, and one could then define the incidence of Michigan's property taxes with

respect to the alternative system. Even then, there would be important conceptual difficulties in evaluating the incidence of the property tax system on Michigan residents. The distribution of population would change as the tax system changed, and some people who would be Michiganders under one tax system would not be Michiganders under an alternative system. In calculating the burden of property taxes in Michigan, it is not at all obvious how one should deal with people who leave or enter the state in response to a tax change. This issue is not trivial, in that it is easy to imagine a change in Michigan's taxes that would make the national economy better off while making those who remain in Michigan worse off, or vice versa. Because we are implicitly ignoring the rest of the country in the analysis here, we are restricted to allocating taxes paid in Michigan to their ultimate payers (in Michigan and elsewhere). The notion of economic efficiency within a state is simply not well defined, and the effect of the tax system on economic efficiency nationwide (i.e., the excess burden of the tax and its incidence) is not considered.

[35]Genesee, Ingham, Kent, Washtenaw and Wayne.

[36]In each of the five counties containing the central cities of the state's largest SMSA's, the above procedure was done separately for the central city and the rest of the county.

[37]The adjustment involved reducing the estimate of agricultural and timber/cutover payments by the fraction of property tax revenues used by cities (see Table 16.1) and assigning the revenue to all other classes of property in proportion to their estimated payments.

[38]It is worth noting that the decline started in 1978, before the Headlee Amendment took effect.

[39]1980 income estimated by the Department of Management and Budget. See <u>Economic Report of the Governor</u> (1981), p. 118.

[40]1979 is the most recent year for which county-level data are available.

[41]Utility real property, it will be recalled, is taxed only at the state level.

[42]Because the circuit breaker reduces state income tax liabilities, and state income taxes are also deductible from federal income for tax purposes, one must subtract the circuit breaker from property tax liabilities before subtracting the federal offset due to deductibility of property taxes.

[43]The figures for 1977-79 are from the Department of the Treasury. The 1979 figure is assumed to hold in 1980, while the 1977 figure is assumed to hold for the prior years.

[44]This assumption is made in Musgrave and Daicoff (1958) and Roberts (1975) for example.

[45]Two assumptions implicit in the above procedure are worth noting: (1) It is assumed that all tenants are Michigan residents; (2) It is assumed that federal income tax offsets against renters' circuit breaker credits are zero. Both assumptions are strong, but their effects are offsetting, as the first tends to overstate the burden of the tax on Michigan residents, while the second tends to understate the burden.

[46]Per capita income in California is higher than it is in Michigan, implying that the California estimate may be too high for Michigan. Countering this, the 1978 statistics of income show that average adjusted gross income is higher in Michigan ($28,726 compared to $27,340 in California); Average deductions per itemized return were higher in California by about $1,500; the fraction of filers in California with incomes over $20,000 was lower than in Michigan (26.8 percent vs. 31.5 percent). All of these factors indicate that the mean marginal tax rate facing itemizers in Michigan may be higher than in California.

[47]The industrial property tax payments are calculated as payments attributable to all property classified as industrial (Table 16.5) less payments made by utilities that are classified as industrial. See notes to Table 16.12.

[48]This is a conservative estimate of the amount of offsets.

[49]See Musgrave and Daicoff(1958) and Roberts (1975), for example.

[50]Taxes on utilities are deductible, as well, but utilities are regulated and it is assumed here that they are permitted some fixed rate of return after all taxes. Thus, if property taxes rise (or fall) gross incomes will rise (or fall) by the same amount in order to restore initial net revenues.

[51]This assumption reflects the fact that land represents much of the value of agricultural property.

[52]This is a conservative estimate, especially because much timber is owned by large, national corporations. However, taxes on timber land amounts to less than one-half of one percent of total property tax collections in the state, so even a large error here will have negligible effects on the totals shown in Tables 16.13 and 16.14.

[53]Note that this argument suggests that the upward "blip" in tax collections as a fraction of personal income in 1980 should not be taken too seriously.

[54]Data for the preceding discussion are taken from Taxable Property Values and Assessment/Sales Price Ratios, U.S. Census, Census of Governments, 1972 and 1977.

[55]The assessment ratio consistent with an inflation rate of 5 percent per year is 0.48. In general, the state method of calculating equalization factors permits assessed value to be 0.5/(1+P) where P is a constant inflation rate.

[56]The entire manual is not updated. Rather, multiplicative factors that can be used to update costs are published regularly.

[57]See Hendershott and Hu (1980), Poterba (1980), and deLeeuw and Ozanne (1981) for documentation of this fact and much of the argument that follows.

[58]Barlowe, et al. (1958); Verberg (1978); Taylor (1978); Governor's Advisory Task Force (1975).

[59]Executive Budget, FY 82, p. G14.

[60]Annual Report, Office of the Auditor General, State of Michigan, 1979-80.

REFERENCES, CHAPTER 16

Aaron, Henry. Who Pays the Property Tax? The Brookings Institution, 1975.

Advisory Commission on Intergovernmental Relations. Significant Features of Fiscal Federalism, 1978-1979.

Advisory Commission on Intergovernmental Relations. Significant Features of Fiscal Federalism, 1979-1980.

Chernick, Howard and Reschovsky, Andrew. "Tax Policies for Managing Urban Decline: A Microsimulation Approach." Manuscript, 1980.

Courant, Paul. "A General Equilibrium Model of Heterogeneous Local Property Taxes." Journal of Public Economics, December 1977.

deLeeuw, Frank and Ozanne, Larry. "Housing." in Aaron and Pechman, eds., How Taxes Affect Economic Behavior. The Brookings Institution, 1981.

Hendershott, Patrick, and Hu, S. "Government-Induced Biases in the Allocation of the Stock of Fixed Capital in the United States." in von Furstenberg, ed., Capital, Efficiency, and Growth. Ballinger, 1980.

Ihlanfeldt, Keith. "The Incidence of the Property Tax on Homeowners: Evidence from the Panel Study of Income Dynamics." National Tax Journal, December 1979.

McLure, Charles. "The New View of The Property Tax: A Caveat." National Tax Journal, March 1977.

Michigan Statistical Abstract. 15th ed. Graduate School of Business Administration, Michigan State University, 1980.

Mieszkowski, Peter. "The Property Tax: An Excise Tax or a Property Tax?" Journal of Public Economics, 1972.

Muth, Richard. "The Demand for Non-Farm Housing." in A.C. Harberger, ed. The Demand for Durable Goods. University of Chicago, 1959.

Polinsky, A. Mitchell. "The Demand for Housing: A Study in Specification and Grouping." Econometrica, March 1977.

Polinsky, A. Mitchell and Ellwood, D. "An Empirical Reconciliation of Micro and Grouped Estimates of the Demand for Housing." Review of Economics and Statistics. 1979.

Poterby, James. "Inflation, Income Taxes, and Owner-Occupied Housing." NBER working paper no. 553. Cambridge, Massachusetts, 1980.

Reid, Margaret. Housing and Income. University of Chicago, 1962.

Roberts, Douglas. "Incidence of State and Local Taxes in Michigan." Ph.D. dissertation. Michigan State University, 1975.

State of Michigan, Department of the Treasury, State Tax Commission. "State Equalized Valuations and Average Tax Rate Data: City Tax Levy, Village Tax Levy, Township Tax Levy." 1974-1980.

State of Michigan, Department of the Treasury, State Tax Commission. "Factors, Assessed Valuation and Units Portion of State Equalized Valuation." 1974-1980.

State of Michigan, Economic Report of the Governor. 1981.

State of Michigan, Executive Budget. Fiscal Year 1972.

State of Michigan, Governor's Advisory Task Force on Property Tax Revision. Interim Report. Lansing, 1976.

State of Michigan, State Assessor's Board. Assessor's Training Manual. n.d.

Taylor, Milton. _Michigan's Tax System: Equity or Ripoff?_ Institute for Community Development. Michigan State University, 1978.

United States Bureau of the Census. _Census Governments: Taxable Property Values and Assessment - Sales Price Ratios, 1972-1977._

U.S. Department of the Treasury, Internal Revenue Service. _Statistics of Income: Individual Income Tax Returns, 1975-1978._

Chapter 17

Property Tax Reduction in Michigan

by

Daniel L. Rubinfeld and Robert W. Vishny

The University of Michigan

INTRODUCTION

In the past few years, there have been numerous attempts to limit state and local government spending and taxes. The most famous of these, Proposition 13 in California, passed by an almost two-to-one margin and reduced property taxes about $7 billion. At the present time, limitations of one sort or another are in effect in sixteen states, seven of which apply specifically to property taxes.

It is perhaps no coincidence that the most successful attempts to limit taxes have focused on the property tax. Widely recognized in opinion polls as the most unpopular tax in the land, the property tax fell into even greater disfavor in the 1970s. With residential property values increasing at a rate higher than the rate of inflation, property value assessment increases have become a matter of grave concern for many taxpayers. While these increases may have acted as catalysts for the proliferation of property tax relief plans in the 1970s, the public's dissatisfaction with the property tax may run deeper.

Is the public's apparent desire for property tax relief related solely to the tax itself? Current evidence suggests an alternative point of view. The property tax serves as a useful outlet for individuals' frustrations arising from a number of factors unrelated to the tax itself--declining real incomes, unemployment and so on. Why focus on the property tax? First, the tax is the primary source of revenue for local expenditures which provide services such as fire, police and education--services which directly affect individuals on a regular basis. Frustration about the quality of public services may be directed against the revenue source which finances those services--the property tax. Second, the tax is authorized through a series of referenda. In many communities these property tax-service referenda provide the only direct outlet through which individuals can express their preferences. Third, the tax is often paid up-front, in a few large payments, rather than being withheld from individual pay checks. Even the use of bank escrow accounts does not fully eliminate the effect caused by relatively direct payment of the tax.

Is there anything special about Michigan that suggests it ought to be the focus of a tax-relief program? Unlike California, the Michigan state government has not used increases in assessed values to obtain higher taxes and a large government surplus. Increases in assessments have been slow relative to the recent California changes. And while property tax levies roughly doubled during the 1972 to 1979 period, the amount of state and local property taxes per $1,000 of state personal income steadily declined from $53 to $44, a 17 percent decrease. Examination of some national figures does not provide the answer to our question. A 1980 ACIR study reveals that in 1978 the amount of state and local property taxes paid per $1,000 of state personal income in Michigan was only 5 percent above the national average. Also, in Michigan in 1978, the property tax comprised 36.5 percent of all state and local taxes, while the national average was only slightly lower at 34.3 percent. Michigan taxes are higher than average, but not unusual in their magnitude. In fact, these figures are misleading, since they exclude the benefits from Michigan's property tax relief, or circuit-breaker program, one of the most extensive programs of its kind in the country. In 1979 for example, benefits of the circuit-breaker in Michigan equalled 9.5 percent of all property tax collections (ACIR 1980).

All of this evidence suggests that Michigan's property tax system is not very different from that of other states.

Why the apparent desire for tax reduction? Perhaps one answer lies in the residential portion of the property tax. Between 1971 and 1980 taxes on residential properties measured in current dollars rose about 2.5 times. And residential taxes per capita rose at a faster rate (150 percent) than average per capita personal income (133 percent). While these trends were moderated by the circuit-breaker system, the increase in two-earner households and in younger workers may cause our income per capita measure to overstate the growth of average homeowner income.

Whatever the reason however, there is a clear sentiment among many citizens that property tax reductions would be desirable. For some this sentiment is based on the belief that cuts in government expenditures can be made with little or no loss in real output. For others, however, real cuts in expenditures are expected and are desirable. Our objective here is not to answer the questions of why or whether cuts are desired and whether they really make sense at this time. Rather, we will take as given that property tax reductions are to be made, and we will ask, what are the advantages and disadvantages of making cuts in a number of different ways.

Before proceeding with the detailed analysis of alternative tax cut plans, some additional information will prove useful. In the next section we briefly review and characterize tax relief plans that have been in effect in other states, as well as the Michigan circuit-breaker. We will see that tax relief is not a new idea. Following this, in the third section, we begin the analytical portion of the chapter by discussing the set of criteria that one might use to evaluate property tax relief plans. Our focus will be on the distributional consequences of various plans, but other criteria are worthy of serious consideration as well. In the fourth section, we utilize data from a sample of 2,000 Michigan individuals in 1978 to analyze a set of reasonable tax reform plans.[1] The fifth section describes the problem of program participation and how it can be improved, while the last section contains some concluding comments.

TAX RELIEF PROGRAMS IN MICHIGAN AND OTHER STATES

Property Tax Relief in Other States

Homestead exemptions and credits are the most prevalent form of property tax relief. In 1979, homestead credits or exemptions were administered in thirty-seven states and the District of Columbia (Gold 1979). In eight of those states and the District of Columbia, benefits are not related to age. Approximately half of the remaining states only distribute benefits to senior citizens, while in the other half, nonelderly person households receive exemptions which are less than those received by senior-citizen households.

Most homestead credits are given either for the tax on a certain number of dollars of assessed valuation or a certain number of dollars of tax. However, several states have enacted credits which pay a certain percentage of property tax liability, sometimes up to a maximum amount.

Another widespread form of property tax relief is the circuit-breaker. As of mid-1979, twenty-eight states and the District of Columbia had circuit-breaker programs (Gold 1979). Most programs are only for elderly households, although nine cover nonsenior-citizen households. In addition, benefits from existing programs are skewed in favor of households with relatively low income. The four largest circuit-breakers in the country are in Minnesota, Oregon, Michigan, and Wisconsin. In 1979, these programs had per capita expenditures of $47.22, $36.32, $35.79 and $19.77 respectively (Gold 1981).

Deferral programs represent another type of relief. These programs enable homeowners to postpone all or part of their tax liability until they sell their home or die. At least eight states and the District of Columbia have deferral programs. Benefits in these programs are limited to the elderly.

One more important type of property tax relief involves

limits on the annual increase of assessed values. By now, such limitations are in effect in seven states. The original intent as well as the design of these limitations vary greatly from state to state.

The Michigan Circuit-Breaker (Homestead Property Tax Credit)

The Michigan circuit-breaker provides an income tax credit to all property taxpayers who qualify regardless of their age, income or homeownership status. Program benefits are determined using a threshold approach which defines an acceptable tax burden as being 3.5 percent of household income for most taxpayers. Sixty percent of property tax payments beyond this level are refunded by the state to the taxpayer, up to a maximum of $1,200. For people aged sixty-five and over, 100 percent of the taxes paid over the threshold percentage of income are rebated up to a $1,200 maximum. Those elderly households with incomes less that $6,000 are assigned threshold percentages of 0, 1, 2, 3, depending on whether they have incomes in the $0-$3,000, $3,000-$3,999, $4,000-$4,999, or $5,000-$5,999 range.[2] The handicapped and blind, some veterans and farm owners face different formulas. The state assumes that 17 percent of rent paid is the portion that goes to property taxes, so that renters substitute 17 percent of rent for taxes when calculating their credit.[3]

Taxpayers must file a separate form with their Michigan state income tax returns in order to receive the circuit-breaker refund. Despite the need to file a separate form, over 1,330,000 Michigan residents received a total of over $380,000,000 in program benefits in 1979. Moreover, the average benefit to those who receive credits in Michigan is the third highest in the country. From 1975 to 1979, the average benefit to the general taxpayer successfully filing for a credit increased from $144.02 to $232.27. In the senior-citizen category, average benefits increased from $274.08 to $420.53 over the same period.

CRITERIA FOR EVALUATION OF TAX RELIEF PROGRAMS

In this section, we list and discuss a set of criteria for use in evaluating the various property tax relief plans. First, the tax relief program should be structured and administered so that it facilitates public understanding and maximum participation. Second, we must consider the fiscal implications of the various proposals. Assuming that a plan is meant to obtain relief for a targeted group in the population, the costs of the various plans in terms of foregone tax revenue will be very important. Comparing two programs which yield the same targeted benefits, the one with the smaller budgetary cost is preferred. In addition, the administrative cost associated with a given plan will be relevant to the decision maker. Plans which are difficult to administer may be dominated by "more expensive" plans that are administratively more manageable.

Third, we will want to judge the effects of the plans on equity, both horizontal and vertical. While horizontal equity with respect to income cannot be achieved with a tax on housing, it is still meaningful to ask whether identical properties are assessed equally. Such a measure of "horizontal equity" might also involve equal "effective tax payments" by renters in similar situations. Vertical equity entails consideration of income distributional effects.

We will see that for many tax reduction plans the goals of horizontal and vertical equity may conflict. For example, a plan which gives a lower assessment to an elderly low income individual will be horizontally inequitable, but progressive in terms of vertical equity. To the extent that there is a choice, we consider vertical equity to be the more important of the two. Thus, we will analyze plans to ascertain whether they have progressive, proportional, or regressive effects on the tax system as a whole. Because individuals often differ about the desirable distributional consequences of a tax system, we will avoid any normative judgments about distribution. We should point out that equity judgments are difficult here because for certain taxpayers income and net worth may not be closely related. Thus, an individual with a low income but owning an expensive house will be viewed as paying a high percentage of current annual income in property taxes, whereas the ratio of property taxes to wealth will be substantially lower. Because of data limitations we will concern ourselves solely with equity as measured in relation to current income. In addition, there may be a limit to the amount of redistribution that can be accomplished at the state and local levels, given the incentives to households to move into low-taxing areas and out of high-taxing areas.

A fourth criterion is whether the program does benefit targeted groups such as the poor and the elderly. Finally, the effects of the plans on various classes of property (residential, commercial, industrial, farm, etc.) can be important. Unless otherwise indicated, a property tax structure which is balanced in terms of its treatment of different classes of property is desirable. For example, one benefit of a plan might be its ability to avoid a shift of the property tax burden from business onto homeowners.

ANALYSIS OF TAX-REDUCTION PLANS

Coverage of the Study

In our analysis we consider the current Michigan homestead property tax credit (circuit-breaker) along with a series of alternative tax reduction plans. In each of the cases under consideration it is possible and often desirable to target some of the benefits of the plan to special groups, such as renters and the elderly. The current homestead credit does both. However, in the interests of making our points clear and concise, we have chosen to focus our detailed analysis on the benefits that accrue to homeowners. We find further justification for not giving separate consideration to renters in our simulation analysis in the fact that renters do not receive a significant part of current benefits. According to Robert Kleine, Director of the Office of Revenue and Tax Analysis in the Michigan

Department of Management and Budget, renters receive somewhere between 6.2 and 6.6 percent of current benefits.

While we have no benchmark figure for determining the share of benefits which they deserve, renters seem to be shortchanged by the operation of the current system. Much of this problem may be a result of lower participation rates among renters. Data from our survey suggest that there may be a large discrepancy between homeowner and renter participation rates. Of those renters in our sample who were eligible for property tax credits of $1 or more, only 13.8 percent said they filed for their credit, while 59.4 percent of homeowners eligible for credits of $1 or more reported filing (Rubinfeld and Wolkoff 1980). Thus, a successful restructuring of the present program might do much to increase the renters' share of circuit-breaker benefits. Benefits to renters might also be enhanced by raising the proportion of rent which renters can claim to pay in property taxes. In fact, early in 1981, Governor Milliken was backing a similar proposal which included a provision for raising the amount of rent which could be claimed as property tax from 17 percent to 25 percent.

We consider the adequacy of renter subsidies to be important both on efficiency and on equity grounds. The efficiency issue is important because the current program (with little in the way of renter benefits) is likely to bias individual housing decisions away from renting and towards owning a home. The equity issue is also important, since renters tend to have lower incomes and are thus often ill-equipped to handle the burden of the property tax shifted onto them by landlords. Clearly, the distributional impact, and the progressivity in particular, of each of the plans to be discussed can be improved substantially with special targeting plans, and as we see it, there is little difference among these programs in the administrative problems that might arise were such targeting to be pursued.

Participation in the Michigan Circuit-Breaker

Our analysis of the Michigan property tax circuit-breaker and various other tax relief alternatives uses survey data collected in November and December of 1978. The principal advantage of using these survey data rather than Treasury Department data in order to simulate the effects of various tax relief plans is that they enable us to study those households not receiving benefits which are nevertheless eligible to receive them. State data are taken from individual tax returns, so that those who did not file for the property tax credit are excluded from the sample. While suitable for the purpose of describing those that take part in the program, it provides no information about those not reached by the program.

Based on a sample of homeowners,[4] we have estimated that while 59.4 percent of households eligible for property tax credits file for those credits, only 45.7 percent of eligible households with incomes less that $8,000 filed. (The corresponding number in the highest income group was 66.2 percent.) Hence, we have reason to believe that because of incomplete filing, the circuit-breaker program, which might have had a substantial redistributive effort down the income ladder, may even operate in the opposite direction. At the very least, the redistribution which actually takes place is less than that which would have taken place if all eligible households had participated in the program.

Theory

The plans that we wish to consider include the following basic options:

a. The homestead tax credit as currently used in Michigan.

b. The elimination of the homestead credit.

c. An equal dollar tax credit to all homesteads.

d. An equal assessment exemption to all homesteads.

e. An equal percentage tax cut to all households paying the property tax.

The number of plans to be considered is not limited to five, however. One reason is that any of plans c, d, or e can be implemented with the current homestead tax credit in place, or with the homestead credit removed. We will see that this choice can have substantial impact on the final distributional effects of the tax reduction scheme. A second reason is that the current homestead credit can be substantially improved in its distributional impact if the participation rate is improved. We will pursue this point in more detail later; for the moment, we will analyze all plans under the assumption that full participation occurs. This assumption most likely overstates the degree of progressivity resulting from any plan, but the bias is likely to be greatest for the current system in which participation is a serious problem.

The five types of plans listed appear to be quite distinct in their focus and presumably in their impact. However, their similarities should not be underestimated. A somewhat technical but useful way to see their similarities is to view each plan as a special case of a general plan which gives tax credits to individuals according to the following formula:

$$\text{CREDIT} = \text{Minimum}\ (a(tAV - bY),\ L)$$

where,

t = nominal millage rate on property (including all property tax sources),

AV = state equalized assessment on individual homestead,

tAV = property taxes paid (rate times base),

Y = household income,

a = credit rate, measuring the percentage of the excess of tax liabilities over income to be given as a credit, b = income exemption rate, determining the percentage of income to be exempt from the credit allowance,

L = limit, the maximum tax credit allowable.

Thus, a, b and L are the parameters of the tax-credit formula that can be varied legislatively to select among alternative plans. Each of these three policy parameters may be chosen to be constant, or may vary with age, income, housing tenure, or other characteristics of households or houses.

How does such a relatively simple formula cover all of the possible tax reduction plans? Consider the five choices outlined above.

Plan a, the homestead tax credit is chosen by setting a = 0.6, b = 0.35, and L = $1,200, for the nonrenter, nonelderly population. Plan b, the elimination of the homestead credit, is simply chosen by setting a = 0.

Plan c, an equal dollar credit to all households, is chosen by setting a = 1, b = 0, and L = the dollar value of the credit to be given. In this case, the actual credit will be L or the tax liability, whichever is lower. The equal assessment exemption is somewhat different from the equal dollar credit, because tax rates vary among jurisdictions. The equal assessment exemption is achieved by setting a = 1, b = 0, and L = exemption x t. Finally, the equal percentage tax cut is achieved by setting b = 0 and a = the desired tax cut percentage. This plan may or may not involve an effective limit, L.

To reiterate, all tax reductions involve choices among three parameters, and all are within the legislature's power to control. Our simulation analysis of alternative plans will consider changes in each of the three policy parameters, much as our analysis here has done.

Analysis

Having established a general formula for viewing various types of property tax relief plans, we proceed to our analysis of several important special cases of that formula. In order to analyze the advantages and disadvantages of these plans relative to our criteria, we first need to discuss reasonable summary measures of their effects.

First, we need a means by which to gauge the vertical equity (income-distributional consequences) of the various plans. To focus on the income regressivity of the property tax, we calculate the income elasticity of the ratio of property taxes paid net of rebates/credits provided for in the relief plan. Specifically, the elasticity, θ, is defined as follows:[5]

$$\theta = \frac{d\{(T-R)/Y\}}{dY} \times \frac{\overline{Y}}{\{\overline{(T-R)/Y}\}}$$

where T represents reported property taxes paid (annually), Y is household income, and R is our calculated estimate of relief that would be provided if the individual were to participate in the given plan. θ is calculated from a multiple regression using cross-sectional data from our survey. A multiple regression calculation is necessary because we have information about the relationship between tax payments and income for over 1,000 individuals. Since the relationship is not an exact linear one for all individuals, we calculate θ by fitting the best line which relates the percentage of income paid in property taxes to income itself. The summary measure turns out to be equal to -0.366 in Michigan if we do not take into account circuit-breaker benefits.

By construction, θ has the property of being equal to zero when property taxes paid (after tax relief) are proportional to income, greater than zero when the system is progressive, and less than zero when the system is regressive. Thus, using current income as our income measure,[6] we determine that the current tax system is regressive. However, the program becomes less regressive when we incorporate the effects of the circuit-breaker. Any tax credits given under the circuit-breaker are deducted from current property tax liabilities before a new summary measure is calculated. With a circuit-breaker and full participation, the new measure of -0.168 is less negative than before, and shows, therefore, that the tax system is less regressive.

As a measure of the cost of the various programs in terms of foregone tax revenue, we calculate the average benefit provided by each plan. These average benefit figures are each related to the cost of the current circuit-breaker program (assuming full participation) by means of a cost index set equal to 1.00 for the current formula. In doing our analysis, we group the relief plans based on cost and compare alternatives which involve approximately equal revenue losses.

Besides vertical equity and program cost, benefits to targeted groups are an important consideration. Accordingly, in our table of summary statistics we report the average benefit to the elderly from the various relief plans. In addition, we report the average absolute benefit and relative share of total benefits by income group.

Now we are in a position to discuss the effects of various property tax relief alternatives, each of which is briefly described in Table 17.1. We note first that the current circuit-breaker formula also provides for substantial benefits to the elderly. While we calculate the average benefit to all homeowners to be $152.92, based on data from the 1978 survey, the average benefit to those sixty-five and older is more than twice that, $345.65. Those in the lowest income group ($Y < \$8,000$) also do very well under the current circuit-breaker formula. While they comprise only 11.5 percent of our sample of homeowners, they receive over 21 percent of the benefits. Thus, the current circuit-breaker program, if fully taken advantage of, would significantly reduce the regressivity of the property tax and accrue substantial benefits to the poor and the elderly.

As we explained above, however, these figures can be

SIMULATION OF PROPERTY TAX RELIEF PLANS[1]

TAX RELIEF PROGRAM	θ	AVERAGE BENEFIT	COST INDEX	AVERAGE BENEFIT TO THE ELDERLY
PLAN 1 Status quo circuit-breaker: 60% rebate of taxes paid over 0.035Y up to $1,200	-0.168	$152.92	1.00	$345.65
PLAN 2 Circuit-Breaker Modification: 100% Rebate of Taxes paid over 0.035Y up to $1,200	-0.091	$217.53	1.42	$345.65
PLAN 3 Circuit-Breaker Modification: 60% Rebate of Taxes paid over 0.025Y up to $1,200	-0.177	$221.54	1.45	$345.65
PLAN 4 25% Homestead Credit: $1,400 max, eliminate circuit-breaker	-0.366	$213.48	1.40	$167.22
PLAN 5 $225 Homestead Credit: eliminate circuit-breaker	-0.280	$216.44	1.42	$209.46
PLAN 6 $5,500 SEV exemption: eliminate circuit-breaker	-0.272	$218.54	1.43	$227.75
PLAN 7 Circuit-Breaker Modification: 100% Rebate of Taxes paid over 0.025Y up to $1,200	-0.090	$326.07	2.13	$345.65
PLAN 8 25% Homestead Credit: $1,400 max, retain circuit-breaker	-0.186	$289.40	1.89	$378.72
PLAN 9 $225 Homestead Credit: retain circuit-breaker	-0.109	$303.47	1.98	$406.59
PLAN 10 $5,500 SEV exemption: retain circuit-breaker	-0.093	$294.44	1.93	$413.95

[1]Our simulation assumes 100% participation in the circuit-breaker program.

misleading because they assume full participation in the program. Unfortunately, a big drawback to the current program is that participation is well below its maximum.[7] Thus, the actual reduction in income regressivity under the present system might be much less than that under a system in which rebates were more or less automatic. Later in the chapter we discuss alternative plans for making rebates easier to obtain than they are presently.

First, we compare several plans which cost 40-50 percent more than the current system would if there were full participation, i.e., plans whose cost indexes are in the range of 1.40 to 1.45. These plans include modifications in the circuit-breaker formula, a 25 percent cut in operating millage coupled with elimination of the circuit-breaker, a $225 homestead credit combined with elimination of the circuit-breaker, and a $5,500 SEV exemption without any circuit-breaker benefits. Specifically, plan 2 involves changing the current circuit-breaker formula so that 100 percent instead of 60 percent of property taxes paid over 3.5 percent of income is rebated. The $1,200 maximum is maintained. Plan 3 lowers the threshold percentage of income paid in property taxes from 0.035 to 0.025. Thus, under plan 3, 60 percent of property taxes paid over 0.025 Y are refunded, up to a $1,200 maximum. Plan 4 provides for a homestead credit equal to 25 percent of property taxes paid with a maximum of $1,400. The circuit-breaker program is eliminated under this plan. Plan 5 involves reducing the property taxes of each household by $225 or the amount of taxes paid, whichever is less. In addition, the circuit-breaker is eliminated. Under plan 6, the circuit-breaker is eliminated and an exemption from $5,500 of state equalized assessed valuation is implemented in its place.

The effects of these plans on our measure of the income regressivity of the property tax vary widely. (See Table 17.1.) Under plan 2, we calculate θ to be -0.091, about half of the value for the status quo and at least 50 percent lower (in absolute value) than any of the other plans in its cost range. Thus, raising the rebate proportion from 0.6 to 1.0 substantially reduces the income regressivity of the property tax. This occurs because more lower than higher income households are eligible for credits when a 0.035 Y threshold level is established. Decreasing taxes for this "eligible" group by increasing the rebate proportion thus decreases the income regressivity of the property tax system as a whole.

While increasing the rebate proportion to 1.0 has desirable distributional effects, such a plan should be regarded with caution. The problem arises because stipulating that no property taxes beyond 3.5 percent of household income be levied amounts to giving a substantial portion of Michigan taxpayers a zero marginal tax rate. This zero marginal tax rate would remain in effect up to the point at which property taxes paid are equal to $1,200 more than 3.5 percent of the taxpayer's income. At that level, the $1,200 limit on circuit-breaker benefits would become effective.

Faced with such a situation, many taxpayers will demand at least as much in additional public services as would give them a property tax bill $1,200 above 3.5 percent of their incomes. This could create a substantial divergence between the value of public services and the cost of providing them. Whether the efficiency problem becomes worse over time as the increase in public services demanded triggers further increases in taxes depends upon whether fewer or more households are in the zero marginal tax rate range.

In addition to the efficiency problem, there is a fiscal problem of how to finance the increased public services demanded by an increasing number of taxpayers who are not required to pay for them. Thus, the cost of plans which raise the rebate proportion to 1.0 may be substantially understated by a simulation analysis which does not incorporate expenditure effects. It is worth noting that the current senior-citizen circuit-breaker formula also provides for a rebate proportion of 1.0. Thus, raising the rebate proportion to 1.0 in the general circuit-breaker formula would not introduce a completely new phenomenon in Michigan property tax relief.

Lowering the threshold proportion from 0.035 to 0.025 increases the regressivity of the tax slightly. Lower income individuals are not as prevalent in the group of those paying between 0.025 Y and 0.035 Y in property taxes. In fact, what seems to be happening is that the greater benefits being paid to those already eligible (disproportionately lower income households) serve to offset the disproportionate increase in higher income households receiving credits due to expanded eligibility, making plan 3 only slightly more regressive than the status quo.

Plans 4, 5, and 6 all involve the substitution of homestead credits or exemptions for the current circuit-breaker program. Under each of these plans, our measure of the income regressivity of the property tax is higher in absolute value than under the present tax system (including the circuit-breaker). This probably reflects the fact that benefits under these plans are at best unrelated to income (and probably positively related to income in the case of plan 4) while benefits seem to be inversely related to income under the circuit-breaker.

The least regressive of plans 4 to 6 are the $225 homestead credit with $\theta = -0.280$ and the $5,500 SEV exemption with $\theta = -0.272$. While our results show no appreciable difference between the effects of these two plans on the income regressivity of the property tax as a whole, in theory, there is reason to believe that the two plans will have differential impacts. The $5,500 SEV exemption, while providing approximately the same overall average benefit as the $225 credit, distributes higher benefits to those with higher tax rates. To the extent that tax rates are positively (negatively) correlated with income, plan 6, the SEV exemption, should be more regressive (progressive) than plan 5, the homestead credit. In our sample the proxy individual property tax rate was essentially uncorrelated with income and showed no effect.

The percentage homestead credit, plan 4, is easily the most regressive of the 5 plans simulated in the 1.40 - 1.45 range. This is understandable, as under plan 4 benefits are roughly proportional to taxes paid (except for the effect of the $1,400 maximum) and taxes paid are positively correlated with income. Under plans 5 and 6 (especially 5), benefits are more or less equal between households paying different amounts of property tax.

Since the present circuit-breaker formula is especially generous to the elderly, one might also expect plans 4 to 6 to substantially worsen the position of senior citizens. This is indeed the case. While the average benefit to the elderly is $345.65 under the current formula, it is only $227.75 under plan 6, $209.46 under plan 5 and $167.22 under plan 4. These large declines in absolute benefit levels combined with cost indexes of 1.4 make for even larger reductions in the elderly's share of program benefits. For example, the elderly receive 23.7 percent of program benefits under the current program, whereas they receive only 8.2 percent of the benefits under plan 4. As plans 2 and 3, the circuit-breaker modifications, do not involve any changes in the circuit-breaker formula for seniors, the absolute level of benefits for that group is the same under those plans as under the status quo formula. However, since the total amount of benefits distributed rises, the elderly's share drops to 16.7 percent under both plans.

For much the same reason as for the elderly, plans 4 to 6 significantly reduce even the absolute level of benefits to the lowest income group from the status quo level and lag far behind the circuit-breaker reforms with similar costs. The average benefit to those with incomes less than $8,000 under the $225 credit for example, is only $204.32 as compared with $348.55 and $295.42 for plans 2 and 3 respectively. The share of total benefits enjoyed by this income group is 10.9 percent under plan 5 as compared with

TABLE 17.2
PERCENTAGE DISTRIBUTION OF DOLLAR CREDITS BY INCOME CLASS

	\$0-\$7,999	\$8,000-\$13,999	\$14,000-\$19,999	\$20,000-\$25,999	≥\$26,000
PLAN 1	21.2	16.9	18.4	23.3	20.2
PLAN 2	18.6	16.3	19.4	24.4	21.4
PLAN 3	15.5	14.1	18.6	25.2	26.7
PLAN 4	7.0	10.4	17.9	26.4	38.3
PLAN 5	10.9	15.3	21.3	24.7	27.8
PLAN 6	11.8	14.1	21.1	25.1	27.8
PLAN 7	13.3	13.5	19.5	26.1	27.6
PLAN 8	12.6	12.5	17.7	24.9	32.2
PLAN 9	13.6	15.2	20.2	24.7	26.2
PLAN 10	14.6	14.4	19.2	24.7	27.1

TABLE 17.3
PERCENTAGE DISTRIBUTION OF HOMEOWNERS BY INCOME CLASS

	\$0-\$7,999	\$8,000-\$13,999	\$14,000-\$19,999	\$20,000-\$25,999	≥\$26,000
ENTIRE SAMPLE (N=1,277)	11.6	16.1	21.1	24.4	26.9

In order to simulate the \$5,500 SEV exemption we needed a proxy for each homeowner's property tax rate. We used the ratio of reported property taxes paid to half of reported market value. Those households (56) for which ratios of reported taxes paid to half of reported market value were less than 0.005 or greater than 0.1 were not included in the simulation of the SEV exemption plans.

18.6 percent and 15.5 percent under the circuit-breaker reforms. The discrepancies are even larger for plan 4. Those with incomes less than $8,000 fare the best under plan 2 as there is no expansion of program eligibility involved. Thus, the increased benefits are distributed only to those eligible for the current circuit-breaker program and those households tend to have lower incomes.

As may be seen in Table 17.2, the middle income groups ($14,000 - $19,999 and $20,000 - $25,999) receive approximately the same share of the benefits under all of the plans simulated in the 1.40 - 1.45 cost range, although they do slightly better under plans 5 and 6. The distributional difference between the plans simulated lie in their impact on the upper and lower income groups. For example, while those in the highest income group receive 38.3 percent of the benefits under plan 4, they receive only 21.4 percent of the benefits under plan 2. Conversely, the lowest income group receives 18.6 percent of the benefits under plan 2 while receiving only 7.0 percent under plan 4.

We now move on to our analysis of four more expensive property tax relief plans. Plan 7 is another modification of the circuit-breaker formula. It provides for a 100 percent rebate of property taxes paid above 2.5 percent of income. Plan 8 cuts property taxes by 25 percent up to a $1,400 maximum and retains the current circuit-breaker program and formula. Circuit-breaker benefit calculations are based on the property tax owed after deducting the 25 percent credit. Under plan 9, each homestead is given a $225 property tax credit. In addition, circuit-breaker benefits are distributed based on the current formula using the property tax owed after the credit in the benefit calculations. Finally, plan 10 provides for a $5,500 SEV exemption and retains the current circuit-breaker formula, calculating benefits using property tax paid on the new, lower assessment figure. Thus, plans 8 to 10 correspond to plans 4 to 6 respectively, but differ in that they retain the circuit-breaker.

Assuming full participation, plans 8, 9, and 10 each cost about twice as much as the current circuit-breaker program. The reduction in property taxes attributable to the credits or exemption produces a decline in circuit-breaker costs which keeps the total cost of these plans to only twice that of the current program, compared with a cost index of at least 1.4 for plans 4 to 6 which eliminate the circuit-breaker.

Despite the reduction in circuit-breaker benefits under plans 8 to 10, retaining the circuit-breaker substantially reduces income regressivity relative to the corresponding plans analyzed above. While θ is calculated to be -0.366 under plan 4, it is only -0.186 under plan 8. Thus, retaining the circuit-breaker makes reducing property taxes 25 percent only slightly more regressive than the status quo. Under plans 5 and 6, θ is calculated to by -0.280 and -0.272 respectively, but under plans 9 and 10 it drops well below even the status quo value of θ (-0.109 and -0.093 respectively versus -0.168 for the status quo).

The elderly and the lower income groups are also much better off when the circuit-breaker is retained. For example, while the cost of plan 8 is only 1.4 times the cost of plan 4, benefits to the lowest income group under plan 8 are over 2.4 times the benefits received under plan 4. Similarly, under plan 8 benefits received by the elderly are over twice as great as benefits received under plan 4. While the differences between benefits received by the poor and the elderly are less prominent in the cases of plan 5 compared with 9 and 6 with 10, they still substantial. Moreover, a large part of the added share of benefits received by low income groups when the circuit-breaker is retained is shifted away from the highest income group rather than the middle income groups.

Now consider a comparison of plans 7 to 10. Just as before, the effects of the various plans on the income regressivity of the property tax system differ substantially. Under plan 7, we calculate θ to be -0.090, about half the value of θ that we obtain for plan 8. Slightly more regressive than plan 2 are plans 9 and 10 in which benefits before adding in the circuit-breaker are more or less independent of income. Overall, three of the four plans in this cost range substantially reduce the status quo level of income regressivity.

In relative terms, the elderly do not fare as well under any of the four plans as under the present system. While the elderly obtain over 23 percent of the benefits under the circuit-breaker formula, they only get 11.1 percent of the benefits under plan 7. Senior citizens command their highest share of benefits under plan 10 with 14.5 percent, still well below the status quo level. Under plans 8 and 9, senior citizens also receive approximately 14 percent of the total benefits.

In relative terms, the two lower income groups ($Y \leq$ \$8,000 and \$8,000 $< Y \leq$ \$13,999) fare best under plans 9 and 10 with respective combined shares of 28.8 percent and 29.0 percent. As expected, these groups did worst under plan 8 with a combined share of 25.1 percent. The combined share of the two middle income groups (\$14,000 - \$19,999 and \$20,000 - \$25,999) is approximately equal under plans 7 - 10.

The Classified Property Tax

One type of tax relief which is frequently discussed provides for varying amounts of relief to different classes or property. This is usually accomplished by establishing different assessment ratios for different property classes, the so-called "classified property tax." Presumably, if such a tax relief program were implemented in Michigan, residential and agricultural property would receive the biggest assessment ratio reductions.

It is important to recognize that the purpose of adopting such a plan may go beyond providing tax relief. As a result, an evaluation of classification relief plans may not fit well into the analytical framework that we employed in looking at plans 1 to 10. However, we can employ that approach to evaluate classification as a means of providing relief to homeowners (and renters), presumably the primary goal of any of the plans currently under consideration in the legislature.

Considered as a means of providing relief to homeowners, classification is essentially equivalent to a program which reduces property tax liabilities proportionately. We see only three differences between lowering the assessment ratio on residential property under a classification tax relief plan on the one hand, and proposals like plans 4 and 8 on the other. First, for a given amount of tax relief to residential property, the classification plan is more costly because it provides benefits to other property classes as well. Second, plans 4 and 8 have a maximum tax credit which saves the state money and improves the progressivity of the plans. Third, with constitutionally mandated tax rate limits currently in effect in Michigan, a program of assessment ratio reduction could arbitrarily limit the spending of some jurisdictions while leaving others completely unaffected. On net, a tax liability reduction seems preferable to a lowering of the assessment ratio under a classification tax relief plan.

In addition to being dominated by proposals like plans 4 and 8, classification tax relief plans suffer from another important disadvantage. Like plans 4 and 9, assessment ratio reductions provide benefits which are roughly proportional to property taxes paid. Hence, those with higher incomes tend to receive higher benefits, making such plans much more regressive than any of the plans simulated other than 4 and 8.

Overall, classification appears to be an inferior means of providing tax relief to homeowners. However, there may be other reasons for considering a classified property tax system. First, such a system may be more efficient than one in which effective tax rates are the same for different property classes. Grieson (1974) argues that maximum efficiency is achieved when those property classes which are most immobile are taxed most highly. This is true because the "deadweight loss" (as a result of reduced output) caused by the imposition of a tax is minimized when those who are least responsive to the impact of a tax are taxed at a higher rate.

This not only makes intuitive sense, but may very well be the operable effect of current assessment practice. For example, the structure of effective tax rates in Massachusetts seems fully consistent with the view that more mobile structures are afforded tax breaks by assessors. Holland and Oldman (1977) found effective tax rates on new commercial property to be substantially lower (3.7 percent) than on old commercial property (10.6 percent). Residential properties faced an average effective tax rate of 5.5 percent, somewhat less than the state average.

A classified property tax system in which commercial property is assessed at a higher rate than residential property might therefore be justified on efficiency grounds, as commercial property (other than new commercial property) is more immobile than residential property. Industrial property, perhaps the most mobile property class, currently receives large property tax breaks in Michigan as a result of generous abatement programs (such as P.A. 198). Thus, in a sense Michigan does have a classified property tax system. (Note also P.A. 116 for farmers.) Expanding the degree of classification in the system by constitutionally mandating specific assessment ratios for the various classes of property may not be the best way to achieve efficiency, however. The problem is that the conditions which dictate what the various property class burdens and assessment ratios should be (mobility, relative market values of property classes, etc.) may change. A rigid standard for assessment ratios may be inefficient.

In addition to improving efficiency, a classification system might be used to shift part of the burden of the property tax from one property class to another. For example, it might be thought that homeowners bear too large a share of the property tax burden. Then, by making the assessment ratio on residential property lower than the assessment ratio for other classes of property, part of the homeowners' share of the property tax burden could be shifted onto other property classes.

It should be noted that the credits and exemptions which we simulated also have the effect of reducing the homeowners' share of the property tax burden. The principal advantage of classification is that frequent adjustments need not be made a result of inflation and rising property values, whereas many of the plans we simulated would require such adjustments. On the other hand, unchanging assessment ratios do not make for constancy of the homeowners' share of the property tax burden. The operation of the same factors that created the need for a shift of the tax burden away from homeowners may produce further problems that necessitate frequent adjustment of assessment ratios. Thus, a constitutionally mandated assessment ratio schedule seems less capable of preventing undesired shifts in the relative property tax burdens than plans which provide for more frequent adjustments.

In sum, classification seems to be an inferior means of providing property tax relief to homeowners. However, such a system may be desirable on efficiency grounds or for the purposes of altering the relative tax burdens of different classes of property. If either of these latter goals is to be pursued, constitutionally mandated assessment ratios are probably too inflexible to provide for either maximum efficiency or the desired balance of property tax burdens.

THE PROBLEM OF INCOMPLETE PARTICIPATION: MODIFYING THE CIRCUIT-BREAKER

We have shown that a number of different property tax reduction plans can be designed by setting three parameters in our tax credit formula. If the participation rate can be increased in the current tax relief program, progressivity of the tax will be increased, as will the public's perception of the tax reductions that are available. We are not in a position to provide all of the details of a program to increase participation, but we do believe that there are several prospects, not necessarily mutually exclusive, that ought to be given serious consideration. Their costs are low compared to the cost of introducing a major new tax reduction program and their benefits may be substantial.

A Program to Educate the Public about the Circuit-breaker

Current participation rates are highest among the elderly; in part because they receive substantial benefits, but also because the program has been advertised as treating the elderly in a special way. On the other hand, those with low incomes and renters are likely to have the lowest participation rates. An informational advertising campaign directed at renters and lower income households could improve participation substantially. This campaign might be achieved in a number of ways, but one relatively simple approach would be to require all property tax bills sent to homeowners to include detailed information about the circuit-breaker and its workings. Renters could be reached if all landlords were required to provide equivalent information when a rental agreement is signed and when a guideline of renters' rights is given to the renter.

Front-loading the Circuit-breaker

Low participation results because individuals file separate forms to receive the circuit-breaker credit, and because the credit is given as a credit on the state personal income tax and not on the property tax directly. Two possible plans to front-load and make the tax credit more visible might be considered. The first moves the credit from the income tax to the property tax, but requires a separate form, while the second involves no additional forms to be filled out (at least regularly) by individuals.

Making the credit a property tax credit. Once or twice each year, local governments issue property tax bills. At these times, the billing notice could include a form to be filed for application for the property tax credit. (Equivalently, landlords could be required to send such forms to their tenants.) The applicant would be given information about taxes that would be due based on current millage rates as applied to the current equalized assessed value of the property. The homeowner would need to supply his or her past year's household income, selected from the appropriate line on the past year's state income tax form.[8] Those not filing income tax returns would be given additional instructions on how to estimate the prior year's income. The individual would also have to certify that the homestead is eligible for the credit and whether the individual is a senior citizen and eligible for special status. The individual could be given enough information to calculate the credit, but ideally this would be done by the local assessor's office. The tax credit can then be deducted directly from the individual's tax liability when the next tax bill is sent, or conceivably mailed as a separate check.

There are a number of technical administrative complications involved in making such a program operable, but we do not see them as being insurmountable. It would be important for the state to administer the program in a consistent and fair manner, and for details about the timing of bills and credits to be worked out. In addition, some computer-based method would be needed to check, at least on a random basis, on the reporting of last year's taxable income.

Eliminating the tax credit form. The preceding plan suffers from one risk - that a substantial number of individuals will not complete the tax credit forms, making increased participation somewhat problematic.[9] A better scheme in terms of participation would be to have the city assessor and the state determine all credits directly. To complete such a scheme, individuals would be required on state income tax forms to fill in sufficient information to make the credit calculation possible. (This would not help those who do not file.) Age is already given, but rental-owner status and rent paid would be needed, as would additional information about income not included in taxable state income that would be included in the circuit-breaker determination under existing rules. The most important item is social security benefits, but unemployment insurance and other cash transfers are now also included. The city (or state) would then use computerized preceding-year's information to calculate the household's tax credit. The credit would then appear on the individual's property tax bill if a homeowner, and would be sent as a check from the local assessor if a renter. There are added costs here in terms of state-local confidentiality problems and computer costs, but the outcome is likely to be a more progressive tax relief program.

CONCLUSIONS

The property tax in Michigan, relative to the tax in other states, does not appear to be unusually burdensome, especially in light of the current homestead property tax credit program. Thus, the question of whether property taxes ought to be reduced is still an open one. However, if reductions are to take place, we have seen that there are a substantial number of reduction plans available which can be achieved legislatively. If a more progressive property tax system is the goal, the most obvious policy and the cheapest is to improve the administration of the current tax credit program, through a front-loading system. The front-load increases participation as well. The net effect is a better public awareness of the program's benefits, and a more progressive property tax.

If more substantial reductions are to take place, a number of alternative plans are worth treating. Once again, all can be viewed as variations on a state income tax credit plan, and thus not inherently different in structure from the present system. Of these alternative plans, the most progressive plan is one which increases the circuit-breaker rebate from 60 percent to 100 percent while lowering the threshold from 3.5 to 2.5 percent. However, such a plan may involve serious problems associated with the incentive effects produced by zero marginal tax rates. Among the remaining plans, a 25 percent reduction in tax liabilities is less progressive than a fixed $225 homestead credit or a $5,500 SEV exemption, the difference arising primarily because the latter two plans yield essentially equal credits for all, while the 25 percent reduction gives greater benefits to those with larger houses and, other things equal, higher incomes. Among the latter two plans, a $225 credit and a $5,500 SEV exemption, our simulation shows little difference.

NOTES, CHAPTER 17

[1]The survey followed the 1978 election and included questions about house value, family income, property tax payments and filing for the circuit-breaker credit. There were 338 households that did not answer the question concerning household income. We were able to assign predicted income values for all but fifty-three of these households by using a multiple regression model to arrive at predicted income values. The model was estimated from the rest of the sample and used the following predictors of income: race, age, education, occupation, sex of head, hours employed by head and wife. No assignment was given to those who failed to answer any questions used to create the predictor variables. For more on the survey design and its purpose, see Courant, Gramlich and Rubinfeld (1979).

[2]There may be a problem with the simple step function approach employed in the current senior-citizen formula, since it is possible that an individual could make himself better off by deliberately earning less income. Specifically, an individual could increase the sum of his income and his property tax credit by earning less. This feature of the senior-citizen formula is a consequence of assigning threshold percentages by means of a step function; a very small increase in income can result in a large "jump" in the threshold percentage. For example, suppose Mr. A has

an income of \$3,999 and Mr. B has an income of \$4,001. Under the current senior-citizen formula, Mr. A receives a rebate for any property taxes paid over 0.01 x \$3,999 =\$40, while Mr. B's rebate is only for the property taxes paid over 0.02 x\$4,001 = \$80. Thus, by earning \$2 less income Mr. B can receive \$40 more in property tax credits.

[3]As far as we can tell, the 17 percent attempts to account for the shifting of the tax onto renters and is based on Netzer (1966, p. 28). The data which follow were taken from the State of Michigan, Office of Revenue and Tax Analysis: Property Tax Fact Sheets.

[4]We were not able to calculate rebates for 228 of the 2,000 households because of nonresponse on such key variables as house value, income or homeownership status. After eliminating renters as well, our sample size fell to 1,277.

[5]We have chosen to specify a linear form with the elasticity calculated at the point of means to avoid distortions which arise (for low income individuals) when a constant elasticity formulation is used.

[6]The term regressive is used here only to measure the direct relationship between taxes and current income. We wish to make no further presumption about the true "incidence" of the property tax. Whatever that incidence may be, our empirical results suggest the relationship between various tax relief plans and that incidence.

[7]In a personal conversation, Gary Olsen, of the staff of the Taxation Committee of the Michigan House of Representatives, said that the concensus opinion in Lansing was that the participation rate among those eligible for credits was in the 60-70 percent range for nonelderly households.

[8]The measure of household income required for the circuit-breaker does not currently appear as a line on the state income tax return. Thus, a slight change in the state income tax return may be needed. Conversely, the measure of household income required for the circuit-breaker could be changed in order to correspond to a line on the income tax form.

[9]One could make failure to file a credit form a form of tax delinquency, but even if enforceable for homeowners, this procedure would not help much with renters.

REFERENCES, CHAPTER 17

Boskin, M. J. "Some Neglected Economic Factors Behind Recent Tax and Spending Limitation Movements." National Tax Journal. June 1979, 38: 37-42.

Courant, P. N.; Gramlich, E. M.; and Rubinfeld, D. L. "Tax Limitation and the Demand for Public Service in Michigan." National Tax Journal. June 1979, 32: 147-57.

Gold, S. D. "The Changing Shape of Property Tax Relief in the 1970s." Presented at the annual conference of the Committee on Taxation, Resources, and Economic Development in Cambridge, Massachusetts, September 14, 1979.

Gold, S. D. "Property Tax Relief Trends in the Midwest: Where it All (or much of it) Began." Presented January 16, 1981 at a conference on Financing State and Local Governments in the 1980s held in Chicago, Illinois.

Grieson, R. E. "The Economics of Property Taxes and Land Values: The Elasticity of Supply of Structures." Journal of Urban Economics. October 1974, 1(4): 367-81.

Holland, D. M. and Oldman, O. "Estimating the Impact of Full Value Assessment on Taxes and Values of Real Estate in Boston." In Metropolitan Financing Principals and Practice. Edited by Break, G. F., Madison: University of Wisconsin Press, 1977.

Michigan, State of. "Property Tax Fact Sheets." Lansing, Michigan: Office of Revenue and Tax Analysis, Department of Management and Budget.

Netzer, D. Economics of the Property Tax. Washington, D.C.: Brookings, 1966.

Rubinfeld, D. L. and Wolkoff, M. J. "The Distributional Impact of Statewide Property Tax Relief: The Michigan Case." Institute of Public Policy Studies Discussion Paper no. 148, The University of Michigan, May 1980.

Sonstelie, J. "The Incidence of a Classified Property Tax." Journal of Public Economics. August 1979, 13(1): 75-85.

U.S. Advisory Commission on Intergovernmental Relations. Significant Features of Fiscal Federalism 1979-1980. Washington, D.C., October 1980.

Chapter 18

The Personal Income Tax

by

Robert J. Cline

Hope College

INTRODUCTION[1]

The Michigan personal income tax was adopted in 1967 following an unprecedented level of deficit spending of almost $156 million during the fiscal year. In addition to the fiscal pressures, partly attributable to a "slump" in the automobile industry, there was widespread political support for major tax reform centered around the adoption of income taxes. The personal income tax was expected to provide a productive and elastic source of revenue. The income tax was also seen as the cornerstone of a more equitable system of state taxation.

The purpose of this chapter is to analyze the performance of the Michigan personal income tax in terms of equity in the distribution of tax burdens, revenue productivity and response, and economic efficiency. This study will focus on the distorting effects of continuing inflation on the vertical and horizontal distribution of tax burdens. Attention will also be paid to a developing trend, possibly as a reaction to inflationary tax increases, toward increased erosion in the personal income tax base. The interaction between state and federal personal income taxes will be examined in this context. Where appropriate, the Michigan tax is compared to income taxes in the following states: Illinois, Indiana, Ohio, Wisconsin, New York, Pennsylvania and California.

OVERVIEW OF THE INCOME TAX

The Michigan personal income tax is a flat-rate tax on the income of Michigan residents and the income earned within the state by nonresidents. The tax base is federal adjusted gross income (AGI) modified by a limited number of additions and subtractions. Michigan does not permit the subtraction of either itemized or standard deductions in deriving taxable income. Personal exemptions of $1,500 per taxpayer, spouse and dependent are allowed. The use of federal AGI in defining the state tax base simplifies the filing process for individuals. It also reduces the administrative and compliance costs involved in collecting taxes. On the other hand, any changes in the federal definition of AGI automatically affect the state tax base.

The Michigan income tax rate has risen from 2.6 percent in 1967 to the current level of 4.6 percent. The state constitution prohibits the use of any income tax "graduated as to rate or base." Since 1967 voters have defeated three separate amendments authorizing graduated rates. However, the combination of a flat rate and a large personal exemption results in a progressive effective tax rate structure. A number of refundable and nonrefundable credits are allowed in determining net tax liabilities.

Three states used for a comparison in this study--Indiana, Illinois, and Pennsylvania--have proportional statutory tax rates, while New York, Wisconsin and California have fairly steep progressive rate schedules. In a recent study of the distribution of state and local taxes, Phares (1980) provides estimates of effective state income tax rates by income classes using a uniform, comprehensive definition of household income. A comparison of the author's estimates suggests that Michigan occupies a mid-range position in terms of overall personal income tax burdens.[2] Wisconsin, California and New York have effective tax rate distributions which exceed Michigan's for incomes greater than $15,000 to $20,000. The effective tax rates for Michigan and Indiana coincide up to $10,000 of income with Michigan's becoming one-third higher for incomes above $10,000. Ohio's effective rates are significantly below Michigan's at all income levels; the difference is approximately 50 percent for incomes above $20,000.

However, the income tax in Ohio accounts for only 18 percent of total state revenue; the figure for Michigan in 1979 was over 31 percent. The average proportion for all income tax states was 26 percent in 1979.[3]

The absolute growth in revenues and the increasing relative importance of the income tax in the Michigan tax structure are illustrated in Table 18.1. Since fiscal year 1968, the personal income tax has grown from 14.3 to 31.3 percent of total state government tax revenues and from 10.9 to 20 percent of all state government revenues. With increased tax rates and rising incomes, partly offset by one increase in the exemption level, the ratio of taxes to state personal income has increased from 1.2 percent in 1969 to 2.2 percent in 1980. However, this ratio has recently declined from a high of 2.9 percent in 1976. In 1980 net personal income tax revenues exceeded sales tax revenues, the next largest category, by 27 percent.

The income elasticity of Michigan income tax revenues provides a quantitative measure of the response of tax revenues to changes in state income. Estimates of the income elasticity of personal income tax revenues were derived from a set of regression equations used to forecast state income tax revenues.[4] According to these estimates, the income elasticity of Michigan income tax revenues was approximately 1.21 in 1978-79. This implies that a 10 percent increase in state personal income leads to a 12.1 percent increase in income tax revenues. Income tax revenues grow more than in proportion to the growth in income because of the fixed dollar value of the exemptions. This source of responsiveness in the income tax "wears off" over time as income rises relative to the value of exemptions.

Table 18.2 provides a general overview of Michigan personal income tax returns for the 1979 tax year. The information is based on a stratified, random sample of individual tax returns. The table provides information on the distribution of AGI, taxable income, taxes and the

TABLE 18.1

MICHIGAN PERSONAL INCOME TAX REVENUES, 1968 TO 1980

Fiscal Year	Net Revenue: Amount (millions of dollars)	Net Revenue: Percent of Total Tax Revenues	Net Revenue: Percent of Total Revenues	Net Revenue: Percent of State Personal Income[1]	Tax Rate (percent)	Exemption (dollars)
1980	1912.1	31.3	19.8	2.2	4.6	1500
1979	1943.5	32.3	21.3	2.5	4.6	1500
1978	1712.3	31.8	21.0	2.5	4.6	1500
1977	1465.5	30.7	20.4	2.4	4.6	1500
1976	1566.7	30.9	19.9	2.9	4.6	1500
1975	962.8	26.4	17.2	1.9	4.6	1500
1974	965.7	26.6	18.0	2.0	3.9	1500
1973	917.3	26.4	18.3	2.1	3.9	1200
1972	726.9	24.3	17.5	1.9	3.9	1200
1971	476.0	19.2	13.8	1.3	2.6	1200
1970	409.1	17.9	13.3	1.1	2.6	1200
1969	388.0	17.6	13.5	1.2	2.6	1200
1968	263.4	14.3	10.9	0.1	2.6	1200

Source: State of Michigan, _Economic Report of the Governor and Executive Budget_, various years.

Note: Net revenue equals total tax collections minus refunds due to overwithholding and credits.

[1] Fiscal year revenues divided by personal income for the prior calendar year.

TABLE 18.2

1979 MICHIGAN PERSONAL INCOME TAX RETURNS

Adjusted Gross Income ($ thousands)	Number of Returns (thousands)	Adjusted Gross Income ($ millions)	Taxable Income ($ millions)	Tax After Nonrefundable Credits ($ millions)[1]
Under 3	478.3	738.2	154.0	6.9
3-5	284.6	1129.3	491.7	22.2
5-7	257.4	1540.2	759.0	34.2
7-10	346.8	2936.1	1676.1	75.6
10-15	494.1	6122.0	4050.2	182.8
15-20	468.2	8198.6	5972.8	270.1
20-25	405.3	9070.3	6873.5	311.5
25-35	520.7	15334.0	12199.4	553.8
35-50	265.9	10782.4	9038.8	410.7
50-100	78.2	4926.9	4209.8	191.8
Over 100	16.1	2913.2	2351.8	107.3
Total	3615.6	63691.2	47777.2	2166.9
		Percentage Distribution		
Under 3	13.2	1.2	0.3	0.3
3-5	7.9	1.8	1.0	1.0
5-7	7.1	2.4	1.6	1.6
7-10	9.6	4.6	3.5	3.4
10-15	13.7	9.6	8.5	8.4
15-20	12.9	12.9	12.5	12.5
20-25	11.2	14.2	14.4	14.4
25-35	14.4	24.1	25.5	25.6
35-50	7.4	16.9	18.9	19.0
50-100	2.2	7.7	8.8	8.9
Over 100	0.4	4.6	4.9	5.0

Source: Michigan Department of Treasury, T-A12-020 series 9 statistics, January 1981.

Note: Details may not sum to totals due to rounding.

[1]Nonrefundable credits include credits for city income taxes, higher education contributions and income taxes paid to another state.

number of returns by AGI class. Percentage distributions appear in the lower half of the table. The 1979 data shows the concentration of taxes paid in the AGI range of $15,000 to $50,000; over 70 percent.

THE INCOME TAX BASE

The ability-to-pay principle of tax equity requires taxpayers to pay taxes in line with their economic capacity or ability to pay. Traditionally, economists have favored the use of income, broadly defined, as the best measure of ability to pay. The tax base under a comprehensive personal income tax would include income from all sources net of the costs of earning income. More technically, a taxpayer's annual income can be defined as the sum of consumption and the change in net worth during the year. This accretion definition of income, often referred to as Haig-Simons income, implies that income from all sources should be viewed as equivalent in defining the tax base. In the following sections the accretion definition provides a framework for evaluating the actual tax base under the Michigan income tax.

Tax Expenditures

The Michigan personal income tax base falls far short of the comprehensive base suggested by the Haig-Simons definition. Certain components of the tax base, such as unrealized capital gains and the rental value of owner-occupied housing, are excluded due to problems of measurement. Additional measurable income flows are excluded in deriving federal AGI. State tax provisions allow further exclusions from the tax base and provide credits to offset tax liabilities.

The foregone income tax revenues resulting from federal and state exclusions and state credits are often referred to as "tax expenditures." The most recent estimates of tax expenditures for the Michigan personal income tax are summarized in Table 18.3. The total reduction in state income tax liabilities of $1,053 billion is 36 percent of

TABLE 18.3

ESTIMATED INDIVIDUAL INCOME TAX EXPENDITURES
(millions of dollars)

Federal provisions	
Accelerated depreciation	7.2
Capital gains	
long-term gains or assets	27.7
sale of residence	12.3
Employer contributions to health and life insurance	23.6
Income maintenance benefits	73.1
Interest on life insurance savings	25.5
Social security benefits	209.2
Unemployment insurance benefits	41.6
Veterans' benefits	34.2
Individual retirement contributions	7.3
Other	15.4
Total federal	477.1
State provisions	
City income tax credit	23.0
Farmland development credit	21.4
Higher education tax credit	4.9
Home heating assistance credit	2.0
Property tax credit	380.5
Lottery winnings	11.1
Pension income	25.0
Military income	25.0
Other subtractions	104.4
Total state	576.3
Total federal and state	1053.4

Source: State of Michigan, Executive Budget, Tax Expenditure Appendix, Fiscal Year 1982.

Note: Estimates of federal tax expenditures are based upon calendar year 1979 data; state estimates are for different calendar and fiscal years including 1979, 1980 and 1981.

the gross income tax yield, including tax expenditures, for fiscal 1980. Note that an estimated 45 percent of total tax expenditures represent foregone taxes on income excluded from federal AGI. At the state level, 67 percent of tax expenditures generated by state provisions are due to the property tax credit.

In addition to requiring a higher tax rate to raise any given level of revenues, these exclusions from the tax base violate the horizontal equity concept of equal treatment of taxpayers with the same ability to pay. This occurs when income from specific sources is taxed at preferential rates or not at all. For example, the exclusion of transfer payments and unemployment benefits may create horizontal inequities at lower income levels. The preferential treatment of capital gains may lead to similar distortions among high income taxpayers with the same total income but different income sources.

Vertical inequities arise from the fact that tax expenditures are not a constant proportion of AGI for every income class. As a result, tax expenditures reduce average tax rates more in some income brackets than in others. Table 18.4 provides information on the distribution of selected sources of income subject to preferential treatment under the Michigan or federal income tax. The data is from the Internal Revenue Service 1978 State Tax Model File for Michigan residents filing federal tax returns. The table shows that excluded net long-term capital gains are heavily concentrated in higher AGI brackets. Taxpayers with adjusted gross incomes of $50,000 or higher accounted for 41 percent of excluded capital gains but received only 11 percent of AGI. In contrast, the distribution of pension and annuity income, which is partially or completely excluded from the Michigan tax base depending upon the source, is relatively more concentrated in the $3,000 to $15,000 income range.

It is clear from Table 18.4 that the preferential treatment of specific income sources alters the distribution

TABLE 18.4

PERCENTAGE DISTRIBUTION OF ADJUSTED GROSS INCOME AND SELECTED ITEMS, FEDERAL TAX RETURNS FOR MICHIGAN RESIDENTS, 1978

Adjusted Gross Income Class (thousand of dollars)	Adjusted Gross Income (AGI)	Excluded Long-Term Capital Cains[1]	Tax preferences Excluded from AGI[2]	Pension and Annuity Income[3]
Under 3	1.0	3.2	3.6	2.8
3-5	2.2	2.3	2.3	7.5
5-7	3.5	1.8	2.0	15.7
7-10	4.4	3.9	3.8	15.1
10-15	10.7	6.6	6.2	22.3
15-20	14.7	11.0	10.1	14.6
20-25	17.0	5.9	6.1	7.5
25-35	20.7	5.7	6.7	7.0
35-50	14.7	19.0	18.9	5.1
50-100	6.9	15.2	14.5	1.8
Over 100	4.3	25.5	25.8	0.6
Amount (millions of dollars)	59980.0	601.5	712.8	1251.4

Source: Internal Revenue Service, 1978 State Tax Model File for Michigan.

[1]Fifty percent of net long-term capital gain in excess of any short-term capital loss.

[2]Includes excluded dividend income, excluded net long-term capital gains and preference item on Form 4625, except for excess itemized deductions.

[3]Fully taxable pensions and annuities reported on Form 1040 plus taxable portion reported on Schedule E. Although subject to federal taxation, a portion of this source of income is excluded from the Michigan income tax base.

of tax burdens which would exist under a more comprehensive definition of the tax base. The potential horizontal and vertical inequities generated by the structure of tax expenditures in the Michigan income tax justify a reexamination of the rationale for a number of these tax provisions. The impact of recent changes in federal tax laws on the definition of AGI for state tax purposes should also be considered in a comprehensive evaluation of the Michigan tax base. A number of the major exclusions from the Michigan personal income tax base are discussed below.

Excluded Capital Gains

One of the most significant, and controversial, exclusions from the tax base results from the preferential treatment of capital gains income. Federal law exempts 60 percent of realized net long-term capital gains (in excess of net short-term capital losses) from AGI. The 1978 increase from 50 to 60 percent in the federal capital gains exclusion rate automatically reduced the Michigan tax base. Based on the data in Table 18.4, a 10 percentage point increase in the capital gains exclusion rate would result in roughly a $120 million increase in excluded capital gains for Michigan residents. Table 18.4 shows that the tax savings from this reduction in the base were highly concentrated among taxpayers with incomes above $35,000.

The preferential treatment of capital gains income is often defended as a practical, although imperfect, method of adjusting capital gains for inflation. Under the accretion definition of income, only the change in the real value of assets would be included in the tax base. This implies that full taxation of capital gains as ordinary income is only justified if inflation-related gains are removed from the tax base. Therefore, the exclusion provisions may be viewed as one method of offsetting increases in the real effective tax rate on capital gains caused by inflation. Proponents of the current exclusion provisions also argue that this preferential treatment provides an additional incentive for capital investments and encourages the realization of accrued capital gains.

The Michigan income tax base could be expanded by including a greater proportion of realized capital gains in taxable income. Several states do tax realized capital gains more heavily than the federal government. Pennsylvania currently taxes net capital gains as ordinary income regardless of the holding period. New York includes one-fifth of excluded gains from federal AGI as ordinary income and taxes the remainder as preference income. In Wisconsin, long-term capital gains are fully taxable with the exception of gains on the sale of a home. Illinois taxes capital gains as regular income with limited exemptions.

The taxation of a greater proportion of realized capital gains could improve the vertical and horizontal equity aspects of the state income tax. However, any resulting loss in economic incentives would also have to be considered. In evaluating such a proposal, careful attention should be given to the problem of adjusting nominal capital gains for inflation. Indexing the basis for determining capital gains is a complex problem which has not been solved at either the federal or state level.[5]

State Exclusions

The Michigan personal income tax does allow several additional exclusions from the tax base not found in the federal definition of AGI. State lottery winnings and income from military service, including retirement benefits, are two examples of tax expenditures provided only at the state level. Although the state may benefit by being able to raise a given level of revenue with a lower pay-out rate, exempting lottery winnings does create horizontal inequities in the distribution of tax burdens among individual taxpayers. The inclusion of lottery winnings in the Michigan tax base would be consistent with the federal tax code. Pennsylvania and New York also include state lottery winnings in the income tax base.

The preferential treatment of military income may no longer be justified in light of the voluntary nature of present military service. Current levels of compensation more closely reflect the opportunity costs of being in the armed services. As an alternative to full exclusion, Michigan might provide a fixed dollar amount of exemption for military income (e.g., $1,000); income in excess of the exemption would be fully taxable. Wisconsin, Minnesota and California use this alternative approach in the taxation of military pay.

The Michigan income tax treatment of pension or retirement income differs substantially from the provisions in the federal income tax. Under federal law pension benefits received from private or state and local government retirement plans are taxable to the extent that benefits exceed employee contributions to the plan. A tax credit for the elderly is available to reduce the horizontal inequity arising from the tax-free treatment of social security benefits in contrast to the taxation of other pension income.

In contrast to the federal treatment, pension benefits received from Michigan public retirement systems are excluded from the Michigan income tax base. Pension benefits from all other plans are excluded up to a maximum of $7,500 for a single return and $10,000 for a joint return. Public Act 517 of 1980 extended the full exclusion of public retirement system benefits to income received from other states permitting similar exemptions or providing reciprocal treatment for Michigan public retirement systems.

The estimated current loss in Michigan income tax revenue from the preferential treatment of pensions is $25 million annually. One rationale for this exclusion is that it provides tax relief to elderly taxpayers who have a limited ability to pay income taxes. However, there is no means test associated with this exclusion and tax savings accrue to the elderly at all levels of income, as can be seen in the last column of Table 18.4. Approximately 37 percent of federally taxable Michigan pension and annuity income was received by taxpayers with adjusted gross incomes in excess of $15,000 in 1978. The pension provisions appear to be a very insufficient method of providing tax relief to those with limited economic resources.

Alternatively, the exclusion of all or a portion of pension income could be justified as necessary to correct the horizontal inequity between those who receive tax-free social security benefits and those who have taxable pension income. Even if this rationale is accepted, there appears to be no defensible reason to treat Michigan state and local public pension income any differently than other pension income under the personal income tax. Taxpayers receiving public pensions from Michigan governments enjoy a tax-free return of employer contributions and interest earned on all contributions. Other taxpayers only receive this preferential treatment on pension income below the ceiling amounts.

Under the accretion definition of income, pension benefits in excess of employee contributions would be fully taxable regardless of the source. A more limited alternative would be the uniform taxation of all private and state and local public pension benefits under the Michigan income tax. In addition, the excluded amount of pension income could be inversely related to the taxpayers' total money income.[6] For example, the taxable portion of pension benefits to be included in AGI could equal 50 percent of the amount by which AGI from all other sources plus pension income exceeds $10,000 for a joint return or $7,500 for a single taxpayer.[7] This proposal is similar to the federal taxation of unemployment compensation. At the state level, Minnesota excludes a maximum of $11,000 of private or public pensions, but reduces this amount dollar-for-dollar for social security and railroad retirement benefits plus federal AGI exceeding $17,000.

Interest Deductions

The accretion definition of income, consumption plus

the change in net worth, is a net income concept. Expenditures representing the costs of producing income are properly subtracted in deriving taxable income. However, the federal income tax provides a somewhat limited opportunity to subtract such expenses for employees and the self-employed, although most business expenses are fully deductible. In particular, the federal tax divides deductible business and nonbusiness expenses into two categories, those subtracted in deriving AGI and those subtracted from AGI as itemized deductions. Most employee business expenses and nonbusiness investment expenses must be claimed as itemized deductions, rather than as subtractions in arriving at AGI. Since Michigan does not allow itemized deductions, these expenses are not recognized in defining taxable income. This is inconsistent with the accretion definition of net income, and results, for example, in unequal effective tax rates on income from different sources.[8]

Interest which is incurred to finance consumption, such as credit card and automobile loan interest, would not be subtracted from gross income under the accretion definition of income. Although it is deductible under federal law as an itemized deduction, interest on consumer debt is properly not deductible from the Michigan tax base. Interest costs related to investment income or business operations should be deducted if the gross investment income is taxable. Business interest related to earning rent or royalty income is, however, excluded from federal AGI and thus Michigan taxable income. But individuals who borrow money to finance income yielding assets (e.g., stocks and bonds) are not allowed to subtract this investment-related interest expense in determining taxable income.

If nonbusiness interest on borrowing to purchase or hold investment property were allowed as a subtraction from Michigan gross income, horizontal inequities inherent in the present treatment would be reduced. On the other hand, the state tax would be more complex due to the difficulties involved in determining the true purpose of taxpayers' borrowing. The 1978 Federal State Tax Model File provides a rough estimate of the potential size of this deduction. Investment interest was estimated to be $307.2 million for Michigan residents in 1978.[9] At a tax rate of 4.6 percent, Michigan taxpayers would have saved a maximum of $14 million for the year, assuming that interest payments would only be deductible up to the full amount of taxable investment income.

The above discussion has examined selected revisions in the Michigan personal income tax designed to reduce the level of tax expenditures or to measure net income more accurately. The primary benefit derived from a more comprehensive definition of taxable income is improved horizontal and vertical equity compared to the current base. The revenue-generating potential of the suggested changes is of secondary importance.

EXEMPTIONS

The Michigan income tax base defines the amount of income subject to tax; exemptions, tax rates and tax credits determine actual tax liabilities. In place of a complex system of exemptions, itemized deductions and a standard deduction, Michigan greatly simplifies the tax structure by allowing only the subtraction of a $1,500 personal exemption for each exemption claimed on federal returns in deriving taxable income. An extra exemption is available for a taxpayer or spouse with certain physical disabilities.

There were 8.76 million exemptions claimed on Michigan tax returns in 1979.[10] Of this number the equivalent of 8.47 million full exemptions were used to offset positive tax liabilities. The remaining exemptions were "unused." Approximately 25 percent of the total exemptions were claimed by taxpayers with adjusted gross incomes less than $10,000. The total reduction in taxes due to personal exemptions was $584 million in 1979.

Exemptions can be viewed as a necessary deduction in

defining a taxpayer's net income or taxpaying capacity. They are designed to improve the measure of ability to pay by recognizing a minimum level of subsistence income which should be sheltered from the income tax. In this capacity exemptions also allow for differences in taxpaying ability due to differences in family size.

In addition to defining a tax-free minimum standard of living, Michigan's exemption structure provides a mechanism for creating progression in effective tax rates over the lower- and middle-income ranges, even though the statutory tax rate is proportional. This follows from the fact that, for families of equal size, fixed dollar exemptions decrease as a proportion of AGI as incomes increase. As a result, a lower percentage of income is sheltered from tax and, conversely, a higher percentage of income is subject to the proportional tax rate. The effective tax rate begins at zero and approaches the statutory rate as income increases.

In terms of providing a tax-free minimum level of income, the dollar amount of the Michigan exemption can be compared to the U.S. Social Security Administration's poverty index for individuals and families. Table 18.5 presents ratios of total value of exemptions to the poverty income level for different Michigan taxpayers over time.

Two important conclusions follow from this comparison. First, inflation has significantly reduced the real value of the exemption over time. Due to the fact that the poverty threshold measure is adjusted each year for inflation, it represents the current cost of maintaining a real standard of living. Compared to this standard, the relative value of the exemption for a married couple has fallen from 1.06 to 0.63 since 1968. The real value of the $1,500 exemption in 1980 was $617 in 1968 dollars using the Detroit Consumer Price Index as the deflator.

The data in Table 18.5 can also be used to evaluate the degree to which exemptions provide the proper adjustment for differences in ability to pay by size of family. Although the total amount of exemptions has fallen short of the

MICHIGAN PERSONAL INCOME TAX EXEMPTIONS, RELATIVE TO POVERTY INCOME LEVELS, 1968 TO 1979

Year	Exemption (in dollars)	Ratio of Exemptions to Poverty Level		
		Single	Married	Married 2 Dependents
1968	1200	0.69	1.06	1.35
1973	1200	0.53	0.83	1.06
1974	1500	0.60	0.93	1.19
1977	1500	0.49	0.76	0.97
1979	1500	0.41	0.63	0.81

Source: Poverty level of income from Social Security Bulletin, Annual Statistical Supplement, 1977-79, p. 59.

TABLE 18.6

1979 MICHIGAN PERSONAL INCOME TAX CREDITS, PERCENTAGE DISTRIBUTION

Adjusted Gross Income (thousands of dollars)	Income Tax Paid to Cities		Contributions to Higher Education		Income Tax Paid to Other States		Total Nonrefundable Credits		Home Heating Credits	
	Percent of Tax Before Credits	Total Amount	Percent of Tax Before Credits	Total Amount	Percent of Tax Before Credits	Total Amount	Percent of Tax Before Credits	Total Amount	Percent of Tax Before Credits	Total Amount
Under 3	2.8	0.9	0.10	0.1	0.33	0.6	3.3	0.7	380.6	85.3
3-5	1.9	1.8	0.07	0.3	0.23	1.4	2.2	1.5	10.5	7.5
5-7	1.8	2.7	0.06	0.4	0.16	1.5	2.0	2.2	3.7	4.1
7-10	1.7	5.8	0.08	1.3	0.14	2.8	2.0	4.8	0.8	1.9
10-15	1.6	13.3	0.12	4.8	0.11	5.7	1.9	11.1	0.1	0.4
15-20	1.5	17.3	0.13	7.5	0.12	9.2	1.7	14.9	0.0	0.2
20-25	1.2	16.4	0.14	8.8	0.16	13.6	1.5	14.9	0.0	0.1
25-35	1.0	23.1	0.17	19.8	0.19	28.9	1.3	23.3	0.0	0.1
35-50	0.8	14.0	0.26	22.2	0.20	22.3	1.2	16.2	0.0	0.1
50-100	0.4	3.6	0.58	23.1	0.17	8.7	1.2	7.2	0.0	0.1
Over 100	0.2	1.0	0.52	11.5	0.17	5.1	0.9	3.1	0.0	0.1
Total (thousands of dollars)		23015.6		4880.2		3705.2		31601.0		31621.1

Source: Michigan Department of Treasury, T-A12-020 series 9 statistics, January 1981.

poverty income level for all three types of filers since 1976, large families are relatively better off than individuals or smaller families. In 1979, the proportion of poverty income covered by exemptions was twice as high for a four person family as for a single taxpayer. For the federal income tax, the use of a fixed dollar standard deduction (zero bracket amount) partially offsets the relatively generous treatment of larger families. Under the present Michigan tax structure, increases in the level of the exemption to compensate for inflation would not alter the favorable treatment afforded larger families.

One possible revision in the Michigan personal income tax exemption would be to replace the current full exemption for dependents with an exemption equal to a fraction of the taxpayer's personal exemption. None of the states included for comparison in this study have a lower exemption for dependents; however, California's credit for a dependent is one-third of the single taxpayer's credit. Although a two-tier exemption would provide a more equitable measure of ability to pay by family size, this adjustment would not solve the problem of inflation-induced vertical inequities in taxes paid by families of the same size at different income levels. An alternative proposal for adjusting the exemption level which recognizes this distorting effect of inflation will be discussed below.

TAX CREDITS

Michigan taxable income equals federal AGI, after additional state adjustments, minus the value of exemptions. The proportional tax rate of 4.6 percent is applied to the adjusted base to determine the gross tax liablility. A number of income tax credits may be claimed against this tax liability. Credits are allowed for residential and farm property taxes, city income taxes, home heating assistance, college contributions, income taxes paid to another state, and solar energy expenditures.

Total credits have grown by 488 percent since fiscal

year 1969; Michigan personal income grew by 185 percent over the same period. The homestead property tax credit is by far the largest, accounting for 83 percent of total credits of $460 million in fiscal year 1980. The property tax credit, which is properly viewed as a reduction in property rather than income tax liabilities, is analyzed in detail in Chapter 17 of this volume. Therefore, the following discussion is limited to credits other than the property tax credit.

The city income tax credit provides a partial credit for income taxes paid to Michigan cities. The sliding-scale credit is equal to 20 percent of the first $100 of local income taxes paid and declines to 5 percent of taxes paid in excess of $200. The total credit is limited to $10,000. The college contribution credit equals 50 percent of contributions to institutions of higher education and public libraries. The credit is limited to the lesser of 20 percent of the tax liability or $100 ($200 for joint returns). Michigan residents may also claim a credit for income taxes paid to states and cities outside Michigan or to a Canadian province. The credit is limited to personal compensation earned and taxed outside the state. The above income tax credits are nonrefundable (i.e., the credits cannot exceed the actual tax liability before credits).

The home heating and solar energy credits are refundable if they exceed the tax liability after subtracting nonrefundable credits. The home heating credit, introduced in 1978, is a sliding-scale credit which varies with both income and the number of exemptions. The credit is equal to the difference between a standard allowance, which varies with the number of exemptions, and 3.5 percent of household income. In 1980, the standard allowance varied from $226 for a single person to $417 for households with more than five exemptions. The corresponding income ceilings for eligibility ranged from $6,457 for one exemption to $11,914 for households with more than five exemptions. AFDC and General Assistance recipients, as well as full-time dependent students, are not eligible for the home heating credit.

The percentage distribution of the individual credits by AGI class is presented in Table 18.6. The overall distribution of tax savings from the nonrefundable credits is moderately progressive. This result follows from the combination of a strongly regressive higher education contribution credit, a steeply progressive city income tax credit and a credit for income taxes paid to another state which is proportional over most income classes. The net effect is that nonrefundable credits result in a slightly more progressive pattern of effective income tax rates.

The city income tax credit achieves a progressive tax savings through the combined effects of the diminishing rate of deductibility and the $10,000 ceiling. On equity grounds the credit for city income taxes can be defended as a necessary adjustment in defining ability to pay state taxes. The city income tax credit may also serve as a means of encouraging local governments to adopt an income tax.[11]

The regressive nature of the higher education contribution credit reflects the substantial amount of educational contributions concentrated in middle- and upper-income brackets. Table 18.6 shows that 77 percent of educational credits were claimed by taxpayers with $25,000 or more in AGI. The effect of the credit is to provide all state taxpayers a matching grant at the rate of 50 percent of the value of donations up to the ceiling amounts. In other words, the state lowers the cost of contributing a dollar to a Michigan college to fifty cents. Taxpayers who itemize deductions on their federal tax returns, as well as nonitemizers beginning in 1982, face even lower effective costs due to the federal offset.

Recent empirical studies of the price elasticity of demand for giving suggest that higher education contributions have a price elasticity of demand significantly greater than one in absolute value.[12] This implies that the incentive effect inherent in the credit may be significant; colleges and universities will receive more in additional donations than the state loses in revenues due to the credit. Thus the higher education credit may be an efficient instrument for stimulating private donations and a justifiable tax expenditure. This credit has recently been expanded to include contributions to municipal art galleries and public broadcasting stations.

The home heating credit program cost the state almost $32 million in fiscal year 1980, more than the total amount of all nonrefundable credits. Table 18.6 indicates that the benefits were heavily concentrated in the lower income brackets due to the sliding scale aspects of the credit. Because the credit is not directly related to actual energy expenditures, the home heating credit could also be described as a modest negative income tax program. It contains a basic allowance which increases with family size but at a decreasing rate. The marginal tax rate of 3.5 percent results in fairly high break-even levels of income under the program; for example, a family of four would receive a positive credit up to a household income level of $10,000.

Viewed as a low-income allowance, the home heating credit has a number of shortcomings. A major problem with the credit is the fairly detailed filing requirements needed to claim the credit. Taxpayers must fill out a separate credit form which involves calculating the household income concept used for the property tax credit. A significant portion of eligible lower income taxpayers probably fail to file for the credit.[13]

A second problem with continuing the home heating credit is that the low marginal tax rate, which extends benefits from the credit into relatively high income brackets, makes it very expensive to adjust the basic allowance for inflation or to expand the credit into a more comprehensive low-income allowance. For a given level of tax credits, a greater percentage of the tax savings or refunds could be concentrated in the lower income brackets by using a credit which is reduced as income increases. If continued, the home heating credit should probably be reevaluated in terms of income redistribution objectives and compared to alternatives for achieving the objectives.

EFFECTIVE TAX RATES

The distributional pattern of personal income tax burdens can be analyzed by comparing average tax rates at different levels of adjusted gross income. Table 18.7 presents estimates for Michigan effective income tax rates before and after state credits for 1975 and 1979. The credits referred to in the table are the nonrefundable credits which exclude property tax and home heating credits. Estimates are also provided for the impact of federal deductibility of state income taxes on the distribution of effective rates. The effective tax rates are calculated as the ratio of Michigan income taxes paid to reported AGI. The pattern of before-credit effective tax rates in 1979 clearly illustrates the role of the $1,500 exemption in generating a progressive effective rate structure. The before-credit effective tax rate increases continually up to the $100,000 AGI level and falls thereafter.

Effective tax rates increase with income due to a decrease in the ratio of the dollar value of exemptions to AGI as income increases. The decrease in the over $100,000 class reflects the fact that net adjustments which reduce AGI, such as interest income from U.S. government securities, are a significantly larger proportion of AGI for high income taxpayers.[14] A comparison of the 1979 tax rate distributions before and after nonrefundable credits indicates that nonrefundable tax credits have little impact on the vertical distribution of tax burdens.

The deductibility of state income taxes on federal returns allows a portion of the state tax to be exported or "offset" through a reduction in federal tax liabilities. Referring to the last two columns of Table 18.7, it is clear that the federal offset significantly reduces the

TABLE 18.7

EFFECTIVE TAX RATES, MICHIGAN PERSONAL INCOME TAX
(Percent)

Adjusted Gross Income (thousands of dollars)	Rate Before Credits		Rate After Nonrefundable Credits		Rate After Nonrefundable Credits and Federal Offset	
	1979	1975	1979	1975	1979	1975
Under 3	1.0	0.7	0.9	0.7	0.9	0.7
3-5	2.0	1.6	2.0	1.6	2.0	1.5
5-7	2.3	1.9	2.2	1.8	2.2	1.8
7-10	2.6	2.3	2.6	2.2	2.6	2.1
10-15	3.0	2.6	3.0	2.5	2.9	2.4
15-20	3.4	2.9	3.3	2.8	3.0	2.6
20-25	3.5	3.1	3.4	3.1	2.9	2.7
25-35	3.7	n.a.	3.6	n.a.	2.7	n.a.
35-50	3.9	3.4[1]	3.8	3.3	2.5	2.8
50-100	3.9	3.6	3.9	3.6	2.0	2.6
Over 100	3.7	3.3	3.7	3.2	1.7	1.8

Sources: 1979 data are from Michigan Department of Treasury, T-A12-020 series 9 statistics January 1981. 1975 data are from Department of Management and Budget, A Study of the Michigan Tax Structure, Tables 19 and 20.

[1] The effective tax rates for the 35-50 AGI class in 1975 are actually for the combined income class of 25-50.

progressivity in effective after-credit tax rates. In fact, the inclusion of the federal offset turns the income tax into a regressive tax for incomes above $20,000 in 1979. There are two reasons for the regressive impact of the federal offset on state tax burdens. First, taxpayers must itemize deductions to gain the offset, and higher income taxpayers are more likely to itemize. The second reason is that the federal offset provides a relatively greater tax saving to higher income taxpayers due to the progressive federal rate structure. As a result of federal deductibility, the effective state tax rate is inversely related to the federal marginal tax rate.[15]

A comparison of the distribution of effective tax rates before credits for the years 1975 and 1979 shows that effective rates increased in each AGI class. Continuing inflation over this period contributed substantially to the increase in tax burdens.[16] For individual taxpayers an increase in money income, whether from inflation or real growth, increases the effective tax rate due to the fixed dollar personal exemption. The interaction between inflation and the tax structure also alters the vertical distribution of individual tax burdens through greater relative increases in average tax rates at the lower end of the income distribution.

The increase over time in effective income tax rates illustrated in Table 18.7 represents the net effect of a number of factors including inflation, real income growth, shifts in the overall distribution and composition of income and changes in the tax structure. The average increase in effective before-credit tax rates was approximately 20 percent between 1975 and 1979. Rates increased by 43 percent in the lowest bracket, 25 percent in the next bracket and 21 percent in the $5,000 to $7,000 bracket. The increase was between 13 and 15 percent for AGI income classes above $7,000.

When the impact of the federal offset is included in the comparison of effective tax rates for 1975 and 1979, the state income tax becomes regressive at income levels above $20,000 in 1979 as compared to a $50,000 income level in 1975. The data in Table 18.7 show that effective rates rose from 1975 to 1979 for taxpayers with AGI below approximately $35,000, while the rate for taxpayers over $35,000 actually decreased during the period.

INFLATION AND TAX REFORM

The rather arbitrary and unintended cumulative effects of continuing inflation on the distribution of state income tax burdens are now significant enough to justify a careful consideration of personal income tax revisions to deal with the problem. As two possible policy approaches, the state legislature could periodically revise the personal income tax structure to offset inflation's impact or adopt a system of indexing which automatically adjusts for inflation. At the federal level, discretionary tax changes between 1970 and 1979 reduced the overall average effective tax rate sufficiently to offset the average increase due to inflation. In addition, the Economic Recovery Tax Act of 1981 provides for formula indexing of the major tax components. In Michigan, however, there has been no increase in the exemption level since 1974 and the nominal tax rate has increased from 2.6 to 4.6 percent since 1967.

Full adjustment for the effect of inflation on the Michigan income tax would involve adjustments in the measurement of the tax base as well as changes in the tax structure. As noted earlier in the discussion of capital gains taxation, adjusting the tax base for inflationary distortions is a complex problem which has not been addressed in existing state or federal index provisions. The revisions to be discussed below will deal with inflation adjustments in the tax structure rather than in the tax base.

A fully-indexed tax structure could be achieved in Michigan through annual adjustments in the level of all fixed dollar amounts to compensate for previous rates of inflation. For example, all dollar values for the 1981 tax year could be adjusted for the average annual percentage change in the Detroit consumer price index (CPI) for the twelve months ending in July 1980 and July 1981. Examples of fixed dollar components include the exemption level, the ceiling on higher education contribution credits and the dollar brackets in the sliding-scale city income tax credit. Nine states, including California and Wisconsin, currently provide full or partial indexing of income tax components.[17]

The importance of Michigan's personal exemption in providing a tax-free minimum level of income and in creating progressive rates suggests that any inflation adjustments should begin with the level of the exemption. The first consideration in adjusting for inflation is whether the exemption should be increased now to offset inflation that has occurred since 1974 when it was raised to $1,500. In 1980 an exemption of approximately $2,500 would be necessary to equal the real value of $1,500 in 1974. The second question to be addressed is the degree to which the tax system should be automatically indexed for future increases in prices.

Past rates of inflation have increased effective tax rates, before credits and federal offsets, in all real income classes. This inflation surcharge becomes a permanent component of the distribution of tax burdens even if future rates of inflation are reduced to zero. Therefore, a "one-shot" adjustment would be necessary to remove the influence of recent inflation on the overall level and relative distribution of tax liabilities. It is assumed that the tax effects attributable to rising real incomes do not require an offsetting adjustment in the tax structure.

Increases in the personal exemption of the magnitude necessary to restore real purchasing power would involve a substantial reduction in total tax collections and a significant change in the distribution of tax burdens. The distinction between used and unused exemptions and the interaction between taxable income and the value of allowable credits greatly complicate the evaluation of proposed changes in the exemption level. To handle these complexities, a micro data file containing a one percent sample of 1978 Michigan individual income tax returns was used to simulate the impact of alternative proposals on total revenues and the distribution of tax burdens.[18] The results for three alternative proposals, described below, are presented in Table 18.8. The actual level and distribution of taxes under the 1978 income tax are also provided for comparison. In all cases the tax amounts represent liabilities after nonrefundable credits but before subtracting the refundable credits.

Proposal A

The first simulation estimates the impact of increasing the exemption from $1,500 to $2,000 with the tax rate remaining at 4.6 percent. Given inflation of 34 percent from 1973 to 1977, an exemption of $2,000 would restore the real value of the exemption to the 1974 level. As reported in Table 18.8, the resulting net loss in revenue is approximately $165 million, a reduction of over 8 percent compared to actual 1978 revenues.

The increase in the exemption reduces all effective tax rates, but the distribution of tax burdens becomes more progressive due to the fact that tax liabilities are reduced by a greater percentage for lower income taxpayers. Over 70 percent of the tax savings would accrue to taxpayers in the $10,000 to $35,000 income range who paid 64 percent of the actual taxes in 1978; 15 percent of the reduction occurs in AGI classes below $10,000 which accounted for 6.7 percent of 1978 taxes. This tax revision proposal illustrates the significant effect which a higher exemption has on progressivity in effective income tax rates.

Proposal B

An increase in the proportional tax rate from 4.6 to 5.0 percent, combined with a $2,000 personal exemption, will

TABLE 18.8

ESTIMATED DISTRIBUTION OF TAX SAVING FOR PERSONAL INCOME TAX CHANGES[1]

Adjusted Gross Income (thousands of dollars)	1978 Taxes		Proposal A			Proposal B			Proposal C		
			Tax Savings			Tax Savings			Tax Savings		
	Percent of Total Taxes	Effective Tax Rate	Percent of Total Change	Percent of 1978 Taxes	Effective Tax Rate	Percent of Total Change	Percent of 1978 Taxes	Effective Tax Rate	Percent of Total Change	Percent of 1978 Taxes	Effective Tax Rate
Under 2	0.1	0.3	0.5	64.5	0.1	2.1	61.4	0.2	0.6	88.8	0.0
2-4	0.8	1.8	3.3	37.1	1.1	12.5	31.5	1.2	6.2	82.6	0.3
4-6	1.3	2.1	3.2	20.8	1.7	9.4	13.7	1.8	6.4	49.1	1.1
6-8	1.9	2.4	3.6	15.7	2.1	8.3	8.2	2.2	6.2	32.1	1.7
8-10	2.6	2.7	4.4	14.4	2.3	9.3	6.8	2.5	6.5	25.0	2.0
10-14	7.1	3.0	10.9	13.0	2.6	19.7	5.3	2.8	11.5	16.2	2.5
14-18	10.1	3.2	13.8	11.4	2.9	19.0	3.5	3.1	11.9	11.7	2.9
18-22	12.4	3.4	14.9	10.1	3.1	14.0	2.1	3.3	12.6	10.2	3.1
22-26	12.4	3.5	13.1	8.9	3.2	5.6	0.9	3.5	11.1	9.0	3.2
26-35	22.2	3.7	19.0	7.2	3.4	-13.9	-1.0	3.7	16.0	7.2	3.4
35-50	15.4	3.9	9.6	5.3	3.7	-30.2	-3.1	4.0	8.1	5.3	3.7
Over 50	13.9	4.2	3.6	2.2	4.1	-56.0	-6.4	4.4	3.1	2.2	4.1
Net Change in Revenue: millions of dollars (percentage)			-165.13 (-8.4%)			-6.1 (-.03%)			-225.7 (-11.3%)		

Note: Estimate derived from the Michigan State Income Tax Simulation Model applied to a one percent sample of 1978 Michigan tax returns.

[1]Tax Parameters

Alternatives	Rate	Exemption
Actual, 1978	4.6%	$1500
Proposal A	4.6%	$2000
Proposal B	5.0%	$2000
Proposal C	4.6%	$2000 (plus low-income credit)

produce roughly offsetting tax changes as illustrated under Proposal B.[19] The net effect is a significant "tilt" in the vertical equity of the personal income tax. Note that effective rates fall, relative to actual 1978 rates, for all taxpayers with less than $26,000 of AGI; tax burdens increase for those in higher brackets. The percentage changes apply separately to taxpayers with increased and decreased taxes. In dollar terms, high-income taxpayers would pay $32.1 million in additional taxes under this proposal.

Proposal C

An increase in the exemption helps to insulate families with low incomes from positive tax liabilities on income considered necessary to maintain a minimum standard of living. However, it does not provide aid to taxpayers who have no tax liability or substantial unused exemptions. A second problem with increasing the exemption to offset inflation's effect on tax burdens is the interaction of inflation with the federal offset. Higher federal marginal tax rates due to inflation actually lower the effective state tax rate, and the benefits are skewed toward taxpayers with AGI in excess of $20,000. An increase in the personal exemption for all taxpayers, regardless of income, is a relatively expensive way to correct for this distortion.

In order to concentrate additional tax relief on low-income taxpayers, a dual adjustment could be made to the exemption and credit structure of the income tax. The personal exemption could be increased for all taxpayers as a partial adjustment for inflation. In addition, a diminishing per person credit which declines with income could be adopted to provide further tax relief for low to moderate income taxpayers. The third simulation examines the impact of this type of two-tier adjustment. Under Proposal C, the personal exemption is increased from $1,500 to $2,000 for all taxpayers. A vanishing low-income tax credit is incorporated into the tax structure as a nonrefundable credit for each allowable exemption. In this example, the credit is a maximum of $50 if AGI is less than $3,000 and falls to zero at $12,000 of AGI. Expressed as an equivalent vanishing exemption, the maximum value per person is $1,087 at the lowest income level and approximately $217 for taxpayers in the $10,000 to $12,000 AGI class.[20]

Table 18.8 indicates that the dual adjustment proposal would result in significantly greater tax savings, compared to Proposal A, for taxpayers with incomes below $22,000. By focusing the additional tax relief on this group of taxpayers, the progressivity of the income tax is increased substantially. The incremental cost in lost revenues, relative to Proposal A, is $60 million. A tax rate of approximately 5.13 percent would be needed to leave total revenue unchanged under this plan. The cost of the vanishing credit program alone would be an estimated $70 million, using the 1978 data. The loss in revenue would be significantly higher if the credit is made refundable.

SUMMARY OF FINDINGS AND CONCLUSIONS

The Michigan income tax has proven to be an elastic source of state revenues and currently accounts for over 30 percent of total state tax receipts. Its yield has responded more than proportionately to changes in real and nominal state income. Income tax burdens in Michigan appear to be comparable to those in other major industrial states.

The state income tax also plays a central role in determining the overall equity of the state tax system. Through the use of personal exemptions and a number of specific credits, tax liabilities can be adjusted to reflect both taxpaying ability and personal circumstances. The large exemption and flat statutory tax rate combine to produce a mildly progressive effective tax. The absence of itemized and standard deductions also simplifies the tax system and reduces potential tax-base erosion.

The Michigan tax base could be broadened by reducing the preferential treatment of lottery winnings, military pay and state-local pension income. A greater proportion of realized capital gains could be included in the base, but any improvements in tax equity would have to be weighed against any resulting disincentive effects. The problem of distinguishing between real and nominal capital gains would also have to be addressed.

Continued inflation has had a significant impact on the distribution of state tax burdens. The interaction of inflation and the federal offset is reducing the overall progressivity of the income tax. Indexing the exemption level would help to offset the unintended, inflation-induced changes in real tax burdens. An additional low-income credit could also be used to provide further tax relief for low and moderate income taxpayers.

NOTES, CHAPTER 18

[1]The author would like to thank Jeannette Eberhard for her excellent research assistance, and Robin Barlow, Harvey Brazer and Edward Gramlich for their extensive comments and suggestions.

[2]Phares (1980), Table A-26, p. 205.

[3]Advisory Commission of Intergovernmental Relations (1980), p. 92.

[4]The estimating equations are from the econometric model of the State of Michigan developed by the Research Seminar in Quantitative Economics, University of Michigan. The income elasticity concept is defined as the percentage change in state personal income taxes divided by the percentage change in state adjusted personal income. Adjusted personal income excludes transfer payments and includes employees contribution to social insurance.

[5]The Economic Recovery Tax Act of 1981 contains provisions for indexing federal income tax brackets, the personal exemption and the zero bracket amount. Although the maximum tax rate on long-term capital gains was lowered to 20 percent by the act, indexing was not extended to the measurement of capital gains.

[6]The Michigan Office of Revenue and Tax Analysis recommended the uniform treatment of pension income and a means test for determining exempted income in 1978. See Lawrence Leuzzi (1978), pp. 15-16.

[7]The Office of Revenue and Tax Analysis suggested a dollar-for-dollar reduction in the exemption ceiling with increases in nonpension income. Any proposal containing a diminishing exclusion or exemption will create a disincentive effect due to the higher marginal tax rate on nonpension income. The 50 percent rate of reduction would have a smaller disincentive effect.

[8]The division of expenses incurred to earn income between itemized deductions and deductions from AGI also creates problems in Michigan in the treatment of certain expenses such as education expenditures, membership dues and tools. These work-related expenses are not deductible under the Michigan income tax.

[9]Investment interest equals the itemized interest deduction (excluding home mortgage interest) but is limited to the amount of investment income. This derived number reflects the federal limits of the deductibility of investment interest. The total Michigan itemized interest deduction was $2,629.7 million in 1978.

[10]The data for 1979 individual income tax returns was provided by the Michigan Department of Treasury and is based upon a stratified, random sample of approximately 3.6 million tax returns.

[11]The city income tax credit does create one form of horizontal inequity relative to city income taxpayers. The city income tax rate for nonresidents is one-half the rate for residents; therefore, a nonresident with the same income as a resident would pay 50 percent less in city income taxes. Because the city income tax credit is a lower percentage of higher tax liabilities, the nonresident receives a relatively greater tax break. See Neenan (1972), Chapter 11.

[12]For an in-depth review of the empirical literature on charitable giving, see Clotfelter and Steurle (1981). Fisher (1977) found a price elasticity of demand for contributions to Michigan colleges and universities greater than two in absolute value.

[13]Information on the degree of participation of low-income taxpayers in the property tax credit program suggests that only 13 percent of taxpayers with AGI less than $2,000 claimed a property tax credit in 1977; the participation rate was 48 percent for taxpayers in the $2,000-$6,000 interval. See Fisher and Rasche (1980).

[14]The 1978 Michigan Individual Tax Model data shows that taxpayers with AGI over $100,000 received 40 percent of their income from sources other than wages and salaries; for all other taxpayers the average was 11 percent. Information is not available on the distribution of adjustments to AGI by income bracket for the state income tax.

[15]The value of the federal offset was based on the estimated marginal tax rate for a hypothetical couple filing jointly with the average taxable income and number of exemptions for each AGI bracket. The data is from the 1978 Michigan Individual Tax Model. The marginal tax rates were weighted by the percentage of taxpayers in the class who itemized deductions. For 1978 returns of Michigan residents, less that 23 percent of taxpayers with AGI between $10,000 and $15,000 itemized deductions; the percentage was 43 percent in the $15,000-$20,000 bracket. For taxpayers with AGI in excess of $35,000, the percentage who itemized exceeded 90 percent.

[16]From 1975 to 1979 current-dollar Michigan adjusted personal income, a measure of the aggregate income tax base, increased by 64 percent. However, real income only increased 20 percent. Assuming that the income elasticity of tax revenues is the same for both real and nominal increases in income, these figures suggest that approximately two-thirds of the increase in the effective state income tax rate between 1975 and 1979 resulted from inflation.

[17]For an extensive discussion of conceptual and practical problems in specifying the indexing formula for state personal income taxes, see State of California, Legislative Analyst (1980).

[18]The Michigan State Income Tax Simulation Model was developed by Robert Rasche and Ron Fisher, Department of Economics, Michigan State University. The authors' generous assistance made it possible to include the simulations in this study. Data for 1978 was the most recent available in the tax file.

[19]One insight gained from this simulation is that the elasticity of tax revenues with respect to changes in the tax rate is 1.02, rather that 1.0. The elasticity exceeds one because of the presence of nonrefundable credits.

[20]The vanishing credit per exemption claimed was specified as follows:

Credit (dollars)	AGI range (thousands of dollars)
50	0- 3
40	3- 6
30	6- 8
20	8-10
10	10-12
0	greater than 12

This credit is similar in structure to the state income tax credit for sales taxes paid on food which was only available in 1974.

REFERENCES, CHAPTER 18

Advisory Commission on Intergovernmental Relations. Significant Features of Fiscal Federalism, 1979-80. Washington, D.C. 1980.

California. Legislative Analyst. The Fiscal Implications of Income Tax Indexing in California. Sacramento, California. 1980.

Clotfelter, C. T. and Steuerle, C. E. "Charitable Contributions," in H. J. Aaron and J. A. Pechman, eds. How Taxes Affect Economic Behavior. Washington, Brookings Institution, 1981.

Fisher, R. "The Combined State and Federal Income Tax Treatment of Charitable Contributions." in NTA-TIA Proceedings, 1977.

Fisher, R. C. and Rasche, R. H. "The Incidence and Incentive Effects of Property Tax Credits: Evidence from Michigan." East Lansing: Department of Economics, Michigan State University, 1980.

Goode, R. The Individual Income Tax. Revised edition. Washington: Brookings Institution, 1976.

Leuzzi, L. Analysis of Michigan Tax Expenditures. Lansing: Office of Revenue and Tax Analysis, Department of Management and Budget, 1978.

State of Michigan. Department of Management and Budget. Office of Revenue and Tax Analysis. "A Study of the Michigan Tax Structure." Lansing, Michigan. 1978.

State of Michigan. Executive Budget and Economic Report of the Governor. Lansing, various years.

Neenan, W. B. Political Economy of Urban Areas. Chicago: Markham Publishing Co., 1972.

Phares, D. Who Pays State and Local Taxes. Cambridge, Massachusetts: Oelgeschlager, Gunn and Hain, 1980.

U.S. Internal Revenue Service. Statistics Division. 1978 State Tax Model File. Washington, D.C. 1980.

Chapter 19

The Sales and Use Taxes

by

Lawrence E. Blume

The University of Michigan

INTRODUCTION

The general sales tax is a single stage tax that is levied on retail sales of tangible goods. The use tax is levied on the storage, use, and consumption of most tangible goods (except when they have been subject to the sales tax) and on some services. These taxes are very important revenue sources for state governments. In 1980, general retail sales and use taxation provided 31.5 percent of all state tax revenues--more than any other tax. In Michigan the sales and use taxes provided 28.7 percent of all tax revenues, and were second in importance only to the individual income tax (32.2 percent).[1] General retail sales and use taxes are currently levied in forty-five states and the District of Columbia. In thirty-three of these states they are the largest source of tax revenue. They are highly regarded for their high revenue potential, economic efficiency, and ease of administration.

The plan of this chapter is as follows: The general retail sales and use taxes are put into historical perspective in the United States and Michigan. Then Michigan's tax base is described and compared with the tax bases of other states. Tax rates and revenue productivity are discussed, and consumer expenditures are studied in order to determine who actually pays the tax. A discussion of changes in the tax base follows, along with some proposals for sales tax reform.

GENERAL SALES TAXES IN THE U.S.[2]

The general sales tax is the youngest of the major state and local taxes. It evolved from a variety of business occupation taxes based on sales, purchases, and receipts. These were imposed in the nineteenth century in an attempt to tax merchants' stocks. The first state sales tax was introduced by Mississippi in 1932. Michigan was among the nine states that adopted the sales tax in 1933, and by the beginning of World War II the sales tax was a revenue source for twenty-two states.

The prosperity and materials shortages of the war years gave states little incentive to seek new revenue sources, and so it was not until 1947 that the trend toward adoption of the sales tax was renewed. By 1960, thirty-four states and the District of Columbia imposed sales taxes, and currently only Alaska, Delaware, Montana, New Hampshire and Oregon have no sales and use taxes.[3]

GENERAL SALES TAXATION IN MICHIGAN: LEGISLATIVE HISTORY

The Sales Tax Act of 1933 (P.A. 167) established a three percent tax on retail sales of tangible personal property. In 1937, the Use Tax Act (P.A. 94) levied a three percent tax on the storage, use, or consumption of tangible personal property.

The 1933 General Sales Tax Act exempted only sales for resale, sales to federal and state governments, and transactions not made in the ordinary course of business. Since 1933 the list of taxable transactions has shrunk. In 1935, sales of tangible personal property for direct use in industrial processing and agricultural production and sales to various nonprofit organizations were made exempt. Act 313 of 1939 and subsequent legislation in 1941, 1943, and 1945 exempted transactions pertaining to commercial vessels. Various other transactions were exempted in 1950 (newspapers and periodicals), 1952 (sales to operators of commercial radio or television stations), 1955 (artificial limbs and eyes, and new motor vehicles subject to special legislation and water purchased in bulk), and 1958 (used vehicles subject to special legislation). In 1974, prescription drugs and food purchased for home consumption were exempted from the general sales and use taxes (P.A. 310). In 1978 exemptions were added for component parts of air or water pollution control facilities (P.A. 457 and 490).

The Use Tax Act of 1937 exempted property subject to sales tax, property exempt from tax under state or federal law, property subject to another state's use tax or temporarily brought into the state by a nonresident, property sold for consumption or use in industrial processing and agricultural production, and property sold to various nonprofit organizations. The history of items subject to the use tax parallels that of the general sales tax with several important exceptions. P.A. 263 of 1959 imposed the use tax on the rental charge for hotel and motel rooms. P.A. 272 of 1959 imposed the use tax on intrastate telephone, telegraph, leased wire, and similar communications. Also included were purchases by contractors engaged in construction contracts with the State of Michigan.

The maximum sales tax rate is fixed by the Michigan Constitution. From its inception until 1960, the sales tax rate was three percent. A constitutional amendment adopted in 1960 authorized a four percent tax rate and P.A. 1 and P.A. 2 (Second Special Session, 1960) implemented the four percent rate for both the sales and the use taxes, effective January 1, 1961.

The use tax rate is not fixed by the constitution. However, the Michigan Supreme Court held in 1959 (Lockwell vs. Nims 98 N.W. 20753) that, when the use tax rate exceeds the sales tax rate, the difference cannot be applied to articles subject to the sales tax.

Although the use tax is a complement and extension of the general sales tax, a key difference between them was created in 1946 with the passage of the Sales Tax Diversion Amendment. This constitutional amendment established a formula for allocating sales tax revenues among local governments, school districts, and the state's General Fund.

This formula has been changed twice in the intervening years --most recently in 1975. Currently 15 percent of all general sales tax revenues are allocated to local governments, 60 percent to the School Aid Fund, and 25 percent to the General Fund. This formula applies only to the sales tax; all use tax revenues go to the General Fund.

THE TAX BASE

Michigan's general sales tax is levied on all persons engaged in retail sales, while the use tax is levied on all persons engaged in the storage, use, or consumption of certain tangible goods and services. The distinction between the two taxes with respect to tangible goods is that the sales tax applies to purchases within the state, while the use tax is levied on purchases outside the state for use within the state by residents and businesses.

Many transactions are exempt from taxation. These transactions can be divided into two broad categories: those involving certain goods and services and those involving certain consumers or purposes. The major tangible goods exempt from taxation are food for home consumption and prescription drugs (MSA 7.525(7)). All services are exempt from taxation except for those upon which the use tax is specifically levied (MSA 7.555 (3a)): intrastate telephone, telegraph, leased wire and other similar communications; and lodging furnished by hotelkeepers, motel operators and other persons providing accommodations available to the public except for lodging rented continuously for more than one month.

Transactions involving the State of Michigan, the federal government, and various nonprofit organizations are tax exempt. However, the most important classes of exempted transactions are the sale of goods to farmers for direct use in agricultural production and to firms for direct use in industrial processing (MSA 7.525 Sec. 4a (f) and (g), 7.555(4) Sec. 4 (f) and (g)).

Michigan's tax base is not unusual when compared to the

sales and use tax bases of other states.[4] Currently forty states exempt prescription drugs and twenty-five states exempt food for home consumption. Illinois taxes both food and drugs at three-quarters of the basic sales and use tax rate. On the other hand, New York, Pennsylvania, and Wisconsin exempt nonprescription as well as prescription drugs. Pennsylvania, in addition, is one of the few states to exempt clothes.

Eighteen states tax services to some substantial degree. Among neighboring states, Indiana, like Michigan, taxes hotel and motel rooms, although its taxes are imposed and collected by counties rather than by the state. Illinois extends its use tax to all services and Chicago has recently levied a professional service tax that applies to the services of lawyers, accountants, and the like. New York taxes all services, while Pennsylvania taxes only cleaning and car washing. Wisconsin taxes lodging, intrastate communications, laundry services, photo services, parking, docking of boats, cable television, and labor services involved in the repair, installation and painting of all personal property unless the property is exempt from the Wisconsin general property tax.

Significant tax exemption is granted to both farmers and businesses in most states. Two kinds of exemptions for manufacturing and processing firms exist. A few states, such as Illinois, exempt from taxation only those commodities that are or become physical ingredients of the commodity being produced. Most states, including Michigan, exempt all commodities used directly in the manufacturing process. Under this rule, machines used in the manufacturing process are exempt from taxation. They are not tax exempt in states such as Illinois which use the "physical ingredient" rule. A few states are more generous than Michigan. For example, Ohio uses the "direct use" rule, but also exempts all transportation equipment except cars, buses, and trucks. Thus, corporate aircraft would be taxed in Michigan but exempt in Ohio. No state currently

TABLE 19.1
GENERAL SALES AND USE TAX RATES[1]

STATE	TAX RATES (percent)	STATE	TAX RATES (percent)	STATE	TAX RATES (percent)
Alabama	4	Louisiana	3	Ohio	4
Arizona	4	Maine	5	Oklahoma	2
Arkansas	3	Maryland	5	Pennsylvania	6
California	4 3/4	Massachusetts	5	Rhode Island	6
Colordado	3	Michigan	4	South Carolina	4
Connecticutt	7 1/2	Minnesota	4	South Dakota	4
District of Columbia	6	Mississippi	5	Tennessee	3
Florida	4	Missouri	3 1/8	Texas	4
Georgia	3	Nebraska	3	Utah	4
Hawaii	4	Nevada[3]	5 3/4	Vermont	3
Idaho	3	New Jersey	5	Virginia	3
Illinois[2]	4	New Mexico	3 1/2	Washington	4 1/2
Indiana	4	New York	4	West Virginia	3
Iowa	3	North Carolina	3	Wisconsin	4
Kansas	3	North Dakota	3	Wyoming	3
Kentucky	5				

Notes: [1] CCH State Tax Guide 5-81 effective July 1,1981.

[2] 2% on food and drugs.

[3] Includes 3.75% required county sales and use tax.

levying sales and use taxes exempts all business transactions.

TAX RATES AND REVENUE PRODUCTIVITY

The general sales tax rate is currently four percent, and can be increased only by constitutional amendment. No such limitation exists for the use tax rate, but it too is currently four percent. Eighteen states tax at a rate less than four percent, thirteen states at a higher rate, and fifteen states tax at a rate of four percent (Table 19.1).

In over half of the states with sales and use taxes, local governments employ the tax as well. For example, California has a state rate of 4.75 percent, but California counties can levy a 1.75 percent tax and cities can levy a 1 percent tax. Indiana counties can levy a 1 percent food and beverage tax and a tax on lodging of up to 5 percent. In New York, counties can levy general sales taxes of up to 3 percent. In Ohio, counties are allowed to tax up to 0.5 percent, and transit authorities may impose a general sales and use tax of up to 1.5 percent, although currently no transportation authority taxes at a rate exceeding one percent. When these local taxes are taken into account, it becomes clear that Michigan residents pay sales and use taxes at a rate well below that paid by residents of many other states.

A history of Michigan's general sales and use tax revenues is given in Table 19.2. The yields of general sales and use taxes per capita and per dollar of personal income for Michigan and seven other states are given in Table 19.3. Michigan's performance in these two categories is about average. However, the comparisons provided in Table 19.3 must be viewed with caution since the tax bases vary widely across the states.

Two important issues are the responsiveness of tax revenues to changes in personal income and to changes in the tax base. The first is treated here, and the second is considered in a separate section.

TABLE 19.2
GENERAL SALES AND USE TAX REVENUES

YEAR	SALES TAX REVENUE (millions of dollars)	USE TAX REVENUE (millions of dollars)
1954	274.7	13.8
1955	285.5	15.7
1956	308.0	18.5
1957	308.5	20.3
1958	297.7	19.7
1959	300.8	19.7
1960	322.9	40.1
1961	353.3	36.8
1962	426.3	34.2
1963	454.7	45.2
1964	486.6	50.9
1965	536.4	57.6
1966	588.9	68.6
1967	608.7	71.6
1968	651.6	75.9
1969	713.3	81.5
1970	738.8	88.6
1971	783.1	95.0
1972	880.3	107.5
1973	972.7	124.6
1974	1,055.6	131.6
1975	1,111.7	153.5
1976	1,318.9	193.3
1977	1,223.7	183.3
1978	1,376.4	210.5
1979	1,506.3	232.9
1980	1,504.0*	232.3*

Notes: *preliminary.

Source: Budget Message of the Governor, various years.

TABLE 19.3
STATE GOVERNMENT GENERAL SALES AND USE TAX
COLLECTIONS, 1979

STATE	TAX RATE	GROSS REVENUES (millions of dollars)	REVENUES PER CAPITA (dollars)	REVENUES PER DOLLAR OF PERSONAL INCOME
All States with General Sales Tax		39,505.5	184.39	
Michigan	4	1,702.7	184.93	.0197
California	4 3/4	5,659.3	249.38	.0248
Illinois	4 *	2,195.5	195.52	.0200
Indiana	4	1,310.3	242.65	.0283
New York	4	2,588.7	146.67	.0160
Ohio	4	1,427.0	132.98	.0153
Pennsylvania	6	1,895.5	161.58	.0189
Wisconsin	4	819.7	173.66	.0205

Notes: *2% on food for home consumption and prescription drugs.

Sources: Tables 7 and 9, State Government Tax Collections In 1980, U.S. Department of Commerce, Bureau of the Census.

The Michigan Office of Revenue and Tax Analysis reports an income elasticity of 0.885 for Michigan's sales tax and 1.304 for the use tax.[5] This is to say that a 1 percent increase in state personal disposable income leads to an increase of 0.885 percent in state sales tax revenues and a 1.304 percent increase in state use tax revenues.

These estimates, however, are very inexact. A one percent increase in personal disposable income will have different implications for tax revenues depending upon who receives the income gain. If the increase in income is distributed mostly to high income households who spend (at the margin) only a small fraction of their income on taxable commodities (see Table 19.4), then the effect on revenues will be small. If the increase in income is distributed mostly to poor households with a high propensity to consume taxable items, then the revenue effects will be large. Unfortunately, these income distribution effects are not accounted for in the estimates of the income elasticities, and so they only roughly approximate the revenue response to changes in income.

INCIDENCE OF THE GENERAL RETAIL SALES AND USE TAXES

When a sales tax is levied on goods and services, a substantial portion of the tax is passed on to consumers. The exact share of the tax borne by consumers depends on the nature of consumers' demand schedules and firms' supply schedules, but it is generally thought to be near 100 percent. This burden is not shared equally (in percentage terms) by all consumers. Were the tax uniform on all goods and services (including savings), then the tax would be proportional. Since this is not the case, however, different consumers will bear a higher or lower share of the overall sales and use tax burdens depending upon whether they spend a higher or lower proportion of their income on taxable items. Thus the fairness of the tax base may be judged by seeing whether there is a systematic relationship between socioeconomic class and the percentage of consumer income spent on taxable commodities.

Fortunately, there are sufficient data available to study the incidence of the Michigan sales and use taxes on various socioeconomic groups. In 1972 and 1973 the U.S. Bureau of Labor Statistics undertook an extensive study of the consumption patterns of 10,000 American households chosen to give a representative picture of the whole population. Consumer expenditures are disaggregated sufficiently to make possible a reasonably accurate estimate of expenditures on taxable and nontaxable commodities.

Column 1 of Table 19.4 demonstrates the regressivity of the sales and use taxes taken together. The percentage of reported gross income spent on taxable commodities declines from 65 percent for families earning less than $3,000 in 1973 to 22 percent for families earning more than $25,000. A different view of the distribution of the tax burden is shown in column 2 of Table 19.4, which reports the fraction of consumption expenditures devoted to taxable commodities. With the exception of those families earning less than $3,000, the percentage of expenditures spent on taxable commodities increases with income, from 40 percent for families earning from $3,000 to $4,000 in 1973, to 51 percent for families earning $25,000 and over in 1973. Not only is the sales tax progressive when viewed in this manner, but the degree of variation in the percentages spent on taxable commodities is much less.

The two views of the distribution of the tax burden provided by columns 1 and 2 of Table 19.4 are not contradictory. The difference between income and consumption expenditures is savings, and the percentage of income devoted to savings is known to increase with household income. The sales and use taxes are not levied on savings, which is the major source of the regressivity observed in column 1.

The data in column 1 of Table 19.4 overstate the regressivity of the sales and use taxes at the lower end of the income distribution for two reasons. First, it is known

TABLE 19.4
PERCENTAGE OF INCOME AND CONSUMPTION EXPENDITURES SPENT ON TAXABLE COMMODITIES

INCOME CLASS	ALL FAMILIES		FAMILIES OF FIVE OR MORE INDIVIDUALS	
	INCOME (1)	CONS. EXP. (2)	INCOME (3)	CONS. EXP. (4)
< 3,000	64.96	50.55	187.12	51.78
3,000-4,000	44.23	39.97	47.15	35.40
4,000-5,000	40.65	42.28	41.67	36.59
5,000-6,000	39.06	43.12	45.18	40.57
6,000-7,000	36.49	44.33	45.23	41.97
7,000-8,000	35.24	44.46	38.95	41.23
8,000-10,000	35.07	47.15	39.63	43.34
10,000-12,000	33.95	49.01	36.33	45.19
12,000-15,000	31.38	48.76	33.41	45.87
15,000-20,000	29.81	49.08	30.64	49.10
20,000-25,000	28.16	49.56	39.40	47.03
> 25,000	21.90	50.58	23.41	46.13

Source: Consumer Expenditure Survey: Interview Survey 1972-3, Bulletin No. 1977 Vol. 1, U.S. Department of Commerce, Bureau of Labor Statistics, 1978.

TABLE 19.5
PERCENTAGE OF INCOME SPENT ON VARIOUS GOODS , 1979

AGE GROUP	TAXABLE COMMODITIES (1)	FOOD (2)	SELECTED SERVICES* (3)
UNDER 25	45.36	7.92	3.41
25-34	35.34	9.85	3.66
35-44	34.21	13.61	3.38
45-54	31.23	11.64	3.36
54-64	30.64	11.32	2.82
65 AND OVER	15.31	31.62	4.88

Notes: *Excludes medical and housing services.

Source: Consumer Expenditure Survey: Interview Survey 1972-3, Bulletin No. 1977 Vol 1, U.S. Department of Commerce, Bureau of Labor Statistics, 1978.

TABLE 19.6
PERCENTAGE OF INCOME AND CONSUMPTION EXPENDITURES SPENT ON SELECTED SERVICES

INCOME CLASS	ALL FAMILIES		FAMILIES OF FIVE OR MORE INDIVIDUALS	
	INCOME (1)	CONS. EXP. (2)	INCOME (3)	CONS. EXP. (4)
< 3,000	11.07	8.61	24.74	6.84
3,000-4,000	6.76	6.11	5.72	4.29
4,000-5,000	4.14	4.31	5.52	4.85
5,000-6,000	5.13	5.66	5.18	4.65
6,000-7,000	4.44	5.39	5.64	5.23
7,000-8,000	4.79	6.04	4.82	5.10
8,000-10,000	3.69	4.93	4.35	4.76
10,000-12,000	3.21	4.63	3.85	4.79
12,000-15,000	3.22	5.00	3.08	4.23
15,000-20,000	3.04	5.11	3.62	5.38
20,000-25,000	3.31	5.83	3.86	6.18
> 25,000	2.51	5.80	4.46	8.79

Source: <u>Consumer Expenditure Survey: Interview Survey 1972-3</u>, Bulletin No. 1977 Vol. 1, U.S. Department of Commerce, Bureau of Lanor Statistics, 1978.

TABLE 19.7
PERCENTAGE OF INCOME AND CONSUMPTION EXPENDITURES SPENT ON FOOD

INCOME CLASS	ALL FAMILIES		FAMILIES OF FIVE OR MORE INDIVIDUALS	
	INCOME (1)	CONS. EXP. (2)	INCOME (3)	CONS. EXP. (4)
< 3,000	32.01	24.9	148.47	41.09
3,000-4,000	22.27	20.12	47.89	35.95
4,000-5,000	17.73	18.44	34.61	30.59
5,000-6,000	17.30	19.10	36.76	33.01
6,000-7,000	14.91	18.11	30.36	28.17
7,000-8,000	14.02	17.69	26.88	28.46
8,000-10,000	12.35	16.50	22.45	24.55
10,000-12,000	11.60	16.75	18.70	23.26
12,000-15,000	11.11	17.26	16.15	22.17
15,000-20,000	10.11	16.99	14.13	21.01
20,000-25,000	9.19	16.17	11.90	19.04
> 25,000	5.72	13.21	8.01	15.78

Source: <u>Consumer Expenditure Survey: Interview Survey 1972-3</u>, Bulletin No. 1977 Vol 1, U.S. Department of Commerce, Bureau of Labor Statistics, 1978.

that transfer payments such as AFDC, Unemployment Insurance, and Food Stamps, which are included in household income, are under-reported. Thus, some households in the lowest income classes should be moved up a class, which would even out the proportions. Second, many families may be only temporarily earning low income, and thus spending more than their current income would otherwise permit. However, the overall impression conveyed by the data is correct.

Some economists view the data in column 2 as evidence that the distribution of the sales tax burden with respect to lifetime income is not regressive. This interpretation is based on a model of consumer behavior, the permanent income hypothesis, which suggests that consumption expenditures in any given year are a good proxy for lifetime income. Money saved today is spent in the future and taxed then, and so the regressivity indicated in column 1 is illusory when the entire lifetime of a consumer is taken into account. This view is not entirely correct, for a variety of technical reasons. Nonetheless, it seems clear that the lifetime regressivity of the sales tax is less than column 1 indicates.

Evidence on the horizontal equity of the sales and use taxes is provided by Table 19.4 for family size and Table 19.5 for age. A comparison of columns 1 and 3 of Table 19.4 shows that, regardless of income level, households with five or more individuals spend a larger proportion of their income on taxable commodities than does the average household. However, columns 2 and 4 show that households with five or more individuals devote a larger portion of their consumption expenditures to nontaxed items than does the average household. The bigger tax share of large families is due to their smaller savings. Columns 2 and 4 of Table 19.7 show that households of five or more individuals spend considerably more than average on food. In fact, 85 percent of all nontaxed consumption expenditures of the poorest households with five or more individuals are on food while the average for all households earning less than $3,000 is 50 percent. Thus although larger families bear a greater portion of the sales and use tax burden, the removal of food from the tax base in 1974 reduced this disparity, especially among lower income families.

Column 1 of Table 19.5 presents another source of horizontal inequity: younger households spend a larger share of their incomes on taxable items than do older households. Part of this is due to the larger size of younger households, and part perhaps to the fact that younger households are acquiring taxable consumer durables, such as washing machines and refrigerators already owned by older households. Columns 2 and 3 show that older households spend an increasing share of their income on nontaxed food and services.

In summary, the sales and use taxes are moderately regressive. Furthermore, a larger than average share of the tax is paid for by larger and younger households. However, this disparity has decreased due to the exemption from taxation of food for home consumption.

Another important incidence issue, apart from the relative sales and use tax shares of state residents, is the degree to which the taxes are exported to other states. Data on tourism have suggested that three percent of the sales and use tax revenues is collected from tourists.[6] Of course, this understates total tax exportation because Michigan manufacturers who pay taxes on purchases not exempt under the "direct use" rule may pass these taxes on to customers outside the state in the form of higher prices.

CHANGES IN THE TAX BASE

In this section we consider three possible changes in the tax base: the exclusion of all sales to business and the additions of services and food for home consumption.

Taxation of Business Purchases

The inclusion in the tax base of sales of intermediate goods to businesses produces different effective tax rates for different consumption goods. When a consumer good is sold by the manufacturer to the retailer, sales taxes that the manufacturer paid on intermediate goods are, in varying degrees, included in the wholesale price and passed along to the retailer. This in turn is included in the retail price to which the tax is again applied. Thus the intermediate good is effectively taxed twice, and the sales tax on the final product includes a tax on the tax paid for intermediate goods. This tax cumulation or pyramiding differs across consumer goods according to differences in technologies of production and distribution. Thus tax cumulation affects relative prices among commodities, thereby altering the allocation of resources.

Cumulation results from the fact that Michigan's businesses pay sales and use taxes on some of their purchases. Recall the "direct use" rule which exempts from taxation those purchases of goods which are used directly in the production process, such as raw materials and machines. Not exempt from taxation under this rule are any purchases of goods used for corporate administration such as computers used for keeping track of payrolls and accounts receivable (as opposed to computers used to run an assembly line) and telecommunications equipment for managerial offices (as opposed to telecommunications equipment used in the factory or warehouse). For large firms these taxable expenditures can be significant, resulting in substantial tax cumulation.

It is clear that exempting from taxation all transactions involving intermediate products would lead to an efficiency gain. But how much revenue would be lost? A rough answer to this question can be calculated from data in Tables 19.3 and 19.4. In 1980 Michigan's per capita income was $9,403. In 1973 dollars this is slightly over $5,000. Interpolating from Table 19.5, the average Michigan consumer spends roughly 40 percent of his income on taxable items, which gives a total sales and use tax bill of $150.45 (in 1980 dollars). But per capita tax revenues were $184.93 (see Table 19.3). Of the residual $34.48 per person, 3 percent is paid by tourists from other states. If we assume that the remainder is paid by businesses, then estimated tax collections on intermediate goods and service transactions were about $308 million in 1980, which is roughly 18 percent of all 1980 general sales and use tax revenues.

This estimation technique is open to criticism on several points, but it does indicate the order of magnitude of revenue losses. Since consumers pay a use tax mainly on lodging, telephone service, and motor vehicles, it is safe to assume that eliminating the taxation of all intermediate goods and services would have a severe impact on Use Tax revenues and a less significant impact on General Retail Sales Tax revenues. This distribution of the decrease in tax revenues could reduce the flexibility that the state has in setting expenditures because only 25 percent of general retail sales tax revenues, but all use tax revenues, go to the state's General Fund.

The revenue loss calculation assumes that resource allocation would be unaffected by the change in the tax base. However, two important resource allocation effects cannot be neglected. First, to the extent that removing intermediate goods from the tax base would actually improve the efficiency of resource allocation, some of this efficiency gain might be captured in the form of higher tax revenues. Second, reducing the tax burden of doing business in Michigan relative to other states would provide additional incentives for businesses to locate in Michigan, resulting in more jobs, income and tax revenues.

Taxation of Services

The first general retail sales taxes applied only to tangible commodities and not to services. One expert has argued that this is an historical artifact. Retail sales taxes evolved from manufacturers' and retailers' occupation and inventory taxes of the late nineteenth and early twentieth centuries, when the service sector was a small part of the economy.[7] Since World War II, however, services have constituted the fastest growing sector of the

American economy. An important revenue source is now lost when services are not taxed. Michigan currently taxes a few services--transient rentals of hotel and motel rooms, and telephone, telegraph, and other intrastate communications. The list of items currently untaxed includes amusements such as athletic events, concerts, and movies; barber shops, beauticians, cable television, country clubs and yacht clubs, delivery services, dry cleaning and laundry services, health centers, labor costs of vehicle and property repair, and professional services such as accounting, investment and legal services.

From the standpoint of economic efficiency there is no reason not to tax services. The demand for services is not sufficiently sensitive to price changes that increasing their price by four percent would cause a large change in the quantity of services consumed, and thus a significant shift in the allocation of resources. It is unlikely that the efficiency loss would be very large.

On the other hand, there is significant potential for revenue gain. A rough estimate of the increased revenue that would result from taxing all services other than housing and medical services can be calculated by multiplying the fraction of income spent on these services in the Consumer Expenditure Survey by Michigan personal income to estimate total expenditures on these services in Michigan. This product would then be multiplied by the tax rate. These calculations predict an increase in tax revenues of ten percent. This estimate may be too low because it ignores the purchase of services by businesses.

Columns 1 and 2 of Table 19.6 indicate that a tax on those services not in the tax base other than medical and housing services would be proportional except at the very bottom of the income distribution. In fact, with the exception of the very poorest households, the percentage of consumption expenditures devoted to services exhibits no simple systematic relationship to income. Thus, adding services to the tax base would not significantly add to the regressivity of the sales and use taxes.

A comparison of columns 1 and 3, and 2 and 4, of Table 19.7 shows that larger households spend a slightly higher percentage of their income, but a smaller percentage of their consumption expenditures, on services other than medical and housing services. Adding these services to the tax base would not significantly affect horizontal equity in this dimension. Column 3 of Table 19.5 illustrates the one conceivable adverse implication of taxing services. Families over the retirement age spend a significantly larger proportion of their current income on services than do other families. However, as column 1 indicates, households whose head is sixty-five or over spend a much smaller proportion of their income on taxable commodities than do other families, and the taxation of services will not alter this relationship.

In summary, the taxation of services would not significantly decrease the efficiency of the general retail sales and use taxes. Taxing services would not increase the regressivity of these taxes, and the only adverse effect on horizontal equity is to families whose head is past retirement age. Finally, the taxation of services has a large potential for increasing revenues.

Taxation of Food

Food for home consumption and prescription drugs were exempted from general retail sales and use taxation by constitutional amendment in 1974. The argument for exempting food from sales taxation is that an excise tax on food is extremely regressive. This argument is amply supported by columns 1 and 2 of Table 19.7. Food for home consumption is seen to be a large part of the family budget, 32 percent of gross income, for families earning less than $3,000 in 1973, while for families earning $25,000 and over in 1973, food for home consumption is only six percent. Furthermore, most of the regressivity is not concentrated at the ends of the income distribution as is the case for all taxable commodities (as seen in column 1 of Table 19.4).

Even in the middle of the income distribution the decrement to percentage of income spent on food is substantial. This picture of regressivity is confirmed by column 2 of Table 19.7, which shows that the food share of consumption expenditures declines as income rises, although not so dramatically as does the food share of income.

The taxation of food is also a source of horizontal inequity. A comparison of columns 1 and 3 or columns 2 and 4 of Table 19.7 shows that a larger share of income and of expenditures is devoted to food in families with five or more individuals than in the average family. It can be seen from column 2 of Table 19.5 that the percentage of income spent on food for home consumption increases dramatically with the age of the household, although most of the variation in the food share of income occurs in the youngest families and in post-retirement families.

There are arguments in favor of taxing food for home consumption. Expenditures on food for home consumption constituted, on average, 14 percent of gross income and 21 percent of all consumption expenditures for families from north-central states participating in the 1972-73 Bureau of Labor Statistics Consumer Expenditure Survey, and is thus a potentially large source of revenue. Further, some economists have argued that extending the tax base in this manner would lead to a more socially efficient sales and use tax system. The first argument is obviously correct. The second argument is correct only if the welfare of the poor is sufficiently discounted, or if some kind of compensation scheme is created to recompense the poor for their otherwise extraordinary tax burden.

One such compensation scheme is the sales tax credit. This is a state income tax credit that works much like the property tax circuit-breaker. Every individual (or family) filing a state individual income tax form is given a credit towards his total income tax bill. In the event that the amount of the credit exceeds the individual's income tax bill, the difference is refunded to the individual. In effect, the credit is a tax-free grant from the state to the individual taxpayer.

In theory, sales tax credits can be designed to mitigate the horizontal and vertical inequities present in the sales and use taxes. The credit due to any taxpayer can be made to depend upon the taxpayer's taxable income, family size, age, and whatever other characteristics are relevant. Thus, were food for home consumption added to the tax base, a schedule of tax credits could be designed to give large grants to large, poor and old families, and give small grants to small, rich and young families. The credit can be designed to recompense entirely families in lower income groups for their taxes paid on food, and still leave wealthy families with a residual food sales tax bill.

The difficulties with sales tax credits are not in their design but in their implementation. First, the tax credits can be effective only if they are claimed by most taxpayers, or at least those taxpayers bearing an above-average tax burden. This is unlikely. For example, in Michigan, only about 60 percent of all taxpayers who are eligible for the property tax circuit breaker credit actually claim it. Furthermore, there is less participation by lower income households.[8] Second, if all eligible taxpayers were to file for their credits, the costs of processing and administration could be large.

Sales tax credits are not popular among those states levying sales taxes. Several states have experimented with sales tax credits in the past, but only Hawaii, Nebraska, Vermont, and New Mexico currently allow a food sales tax credit.[9] The New Mexico food tax credit allows a $45 credit for each income tax exemption domiciled in the state. Average food consumption per household in the United States in 1973 was about $1,300. Correcting for inflation and multiplying by the New Mexico sales tax rate of 3.5 percent gives an average food tax bill per household of about $84. Since many households claim more than one exemption, the tax credit would return directly to residents a substantial portion of the revenue raised by taxing food if all eligible households filed for the credit.

Nebraska's food sales tax credit works much like New Mexico's but the credit per exemption is only $28. Vermont's food sales tax credit is tied both to the taxpayer's number of exemptions and taxable income. A taxpayer with less than $1,000 of taxable income and ten exemptions can receive a $91 credit. Any taxpayer earning more than $8,000 with less than four exemptions or earning more than $9,000 receives no credit.

Hawaii's tax credit, which is represented as a general excise tax credit, works much like Vermont's tax credit. The schedule allows $48 per exemption for families earning less than $5,000 and descends to $8 per exemption for families earning between $14,000 and $20,000.

Michigan had a food tax credit for a short period in 1974. Public Act 125 of 1974 provided a $10 credit for all families earning less than or equal to $5,000, $9 for all families earning between $5,000 and $7,000, and so on down to $6 for families earning between $11,000 and $15,000. Families earning more than $15,000 did not receive a credit. This act was effective for less than one year since, as was noted earlier, a constitutional amendment passed later that year exempting food for home consumption from the tax base. The language of section 4 of Public Act 125 provided that if the proposed amendment was adopted, the sales tax credit would lapse.

SUMMARY

The Michigan general retail sales and use taxes are broadly based excise taxes that, taken together, are second only to the individual income tax in revenue productivity. The sales and use taxes are somewhat regressive, and a disproportionately large share of the taxes are paid by large households and young households.

The sales and use taxes can be improved in two

dimensions. First, expanding the set of intermediate goods and services exempt from taxation would not only increase the efficiency of the taxes but also, by giving Michigan businesses a cost advantage over businesses in states with fewer exemptions, would provide an incentive to locate in Michigan. Second, the taxation of services would provide substantial new revenue without seriously affecting either the efficiency of the tax or substantially altering the distribution of the tax burden.

A very few states (Hawaii, Nebraska, New Mexico, and Vermont) tax food for home consumption and provide a sales tax credit in an attempt to offset the resulting horizontal and vertical inequities. Although the taxation of food is a tempting source of additional revenue, experience with the Michigan property tax circuit-breaker suggests that the benefits of these tax credit programs may not reach the groups to which they are targeted. The tax base is probably best not expanded in this direction.

NOTES, CHAPTER 19

[1]Table 6, State Government Tax Collections in 1980, U.S. Department of Commerce, Bureau of the Census.

[2]Most of this material is drawn from John F. Due, Sales Taxation (Urbana: University of Illinois Press, 1957), chap. 14.

[3]In Alaska, sales taxation is an important revenue source for local governments.

[4]The source for this discussion is the CCH State Tax Guide; All States, table 26.

[5]A Study of the Michigan Tax Structure, Office of Revenue and Tax Analysis, Department of Management and Budget, State of Michigan, 1978.

[6]Don Peppard and Douglas Roberts, Net Fiscal Incidence in Michigan (Michigan State University, East Lansing, 1977).

[7]See Due, Sales Taxation.

[8]See Chapter 17.

'Indiana and Iowa, among others, allow a sales tax credit for motor vehicle fuel taxes paid for commercial, nonhighway vehicles, and New York offers a sales tax credit for taxes paid on caustics and bleaching agents used in processing goods for resale. These are clearly minor. California, Illinois, Ohio, Pennsylvania, and Wisconsin have no sales tax credits of any kind.

Chapter 20

The Intangibles Tax

by

Paul L. Menchik

Michigan State University

INTRODUCTION

The intangibles tax is a tax on the owners of intangible (as opposed to real) property, with the tax based upon the income from or the value of the property. The historical justification for the taxation of intangible property was the view that all property regardless of its form should be taxed uniformly. Consequently, it is argued that taxation of intangible as well as real property is necessary in order to prevent (1) inequities in tax treatment among those holding assets of equal value but different composition and (2) distortion of asset composition in favor of intangible property. Although this neutrality argument for a supplementary intangibles tax may at first seem a compelling one, it does not stand up well under closer scrutiny and will be critically examined in a subsequent section of this chapter. There may be, however, some other justification for the intangibles tax. First, I will trace its historical development.

ORIGINS AND HISTORICAL DEVELOPMENT OF THE MICHIGAN INTANGIBLES TAX

The present tax on intangible property is a descendant of the intangibles tax of 1939. Before that time there was an effort (largely ineffective) to tax intangibles at the local level. It is argued that the tax was largely evaded and that few local assessors even attempted enforcement.[1] The Michigan intangibles tax, established by Public Act 301 of 1939, was instituted, in part, on the recommendation of the Special Tax Commission of 1939. The intangibles tax is imposed annually on the income from or the value of stocks, bonds, notes, money, and other intangible property. The Act also exempted such property from taxation at the local level. Although no longer a local tax, one aspect of the intangibles tax retains its local flavor: a portion of the revenue (currently $9.5 million) is returned to cities, villages, and townships with the remainder going into the state's General Fund.[2]

The first major amendment of the tax was in 1941. Deposits in savings and loans up to $3,000, pensions, royalties, and insurance policies were all exempted from the tax. In 1945 the tax rate on property income was reduced from 6 percent to 3 percent. The $3,000 exemption for savings deposits was repealed and provisions allowing banks to pay a tax for their depositors were added. In addition, mortgages on the land held by religious and charitable institutions were exempted from taxation.

In 1952 the tax rate on income-producing intangibles was raised from 3 to 3.5 percent and a special excise tax (repealed in 1967) of 4 mills per $1.00 of book value was imposed on banks and trust companies. In 1953 this tax rate was raised to 5.5 mills and based upon a bank's capital account. In 1959 the tax rate on cash on hand was raised from 40 cents to 50 cents per $1,000. This was lowered back to 40 cents in 1973, and lowered again in 1976 to 20 cents, the present level. In 1959 no par stock was declared to have a taxable value of $1 per share.

In 1967 the statutory deduction (actually a nonrefundable tax credit) was increased from $20 for a single person and $40 for a married couple filing jointly to $100 and $200 respectively, and the tax on shares of stock in banks and trust companies was abolished. In addition, the statutory credit was increased to the present level of $175 for single individuals and $350 for married couples. In 1974 the list of exempt property was expanded to include the property of bank holding companies and savings and loan holding companies that do business in Michigan.

A major change in the intangibles tax law occurred in

1975 when property subject to the new single business tax was exempted from the intangibles tax. Banks and savings and loans however, were to be treated somewhat differently. Before Public Act 229 of 1975, the intangibles tax was levied on the depositor but the bank or savings association was required to pay the tax and either assume the tax itself or collect the tax from the depositor. Under the 1975 Act, banks themselves were intangibles taxpayers, at a rate of 20 cents per $1,000 on their deposits, and those receiving interest from deposits at banks and savings and loans were not subject to intangibles taxation on this interest income. (I will discuss the question of tax incidence implications of this provision in a subsequent section.)

THE PRESENT MICHIGAN INTANGIBLES TAX LAW

Exempt Property

Much property has been declared exempt for tax purposes, including bonds issued by the United States, the State of Michigan and its political subdivisions, old age and retirement pensions provided by public or private employers, cash surrender values and loan value of insurance policies, and shares of stock in banks, trust companies, and national banking associations. Deposits in banks and savings and loan institutions (but not credit unions) are treated differently than other nonexempt intangibles. The depositor pays no tax on the interest income received, but the bank must pay a tax of twenty cents per thousand dollars, or 0.02 percent on the value of deposits.

The Tax Rates

The rate of tax on intangible property is 3.5 percent of the income or one-tenth of one percent of the face or par value of the asset, whichever is greater. Cash on hand is taxed at 0.02 percent. Under current law the statutory deduction on the total tax due is $175 for individuals and $350 for married couples filing jointly. Using the income basis, these deduction levels imply no tax due for those individuals and couples with less than $5,000 or $10,000, respectively, of taxable property income. Consequently this tax is largely confined to the wealthiest residents of the state. The tax situs is taken to be the state of domicile of the taxpayer.

Placing property in trust does not shield property from the intangibles tax. Trusts and estates (fiduciaries) are subject to the tax and must pay under the rules that apply to people. If the ownership of some property is divided such that one person receives the current income and another will receive the property or income in the future, the current owner or income recipient is responsible for paying the tax.

Enforcement

Under the current law the Michigan Estate Tax Division of the Department of Treasury audits estate tax returns that are up to four years old and cross checks these returns with the intangibles tax returns for evidence of missing assets. If there is evidence that intangibles tax returns should have been filed but were not, or that property that should have been included was omitted from a return, the state demands tax payments from the estate (with interest at three-quarters of one percent per month back to 1945). In addition to interest charges, the failure of a living person to file a tax return or to pay the tax invites penalties that accumulate over time, and, if the violation is judged to be "willful," a $1,000 fine and a one-year prison term.

RATIONALE FOR THE INTANGIBLES TAX

The historical justification for the intangibles tax is the neutrality argument mentioned in the introduction: all property regardless of its form should be taxed uniformly. The deleterious effects of taxing only real and not intangible property are two-fold. First, there would be a misallocation of investment resources and, second, if the tax is not fully capitalized into asset prices (which would be the case since the tax is not uniform across the country) unequal and inequitable treatment of those holding property of equal value but different composition results.

Although the neutrality argument for an intangibles tax at first may seem persuasive, it does not stand up well under closer scrutiny. First, real and intangible property taxes are *gross wealth*, not *net wealth* taxes. This means that mortgaged physical assets are subject to a higher rate of taxation than nonmortgaged physical assets. This can be seen by invoking the example used by Milton Taylor in the Michigan Tax Study of 1958:[3]

> Assume that two farms have the same capacity to produce net income and each is assessed at $10,000, but farm A has no mortgage and farm B has a mortgage of $5,000. If both the mortgage and the realty are taxed at the uniform rate, farm B will be taxed at a rate 50 percent higher than farm A.

This tax treatment tends to discourage separation between the use of an asset and its ownership, a disincentive effect that is hard to justify on economic grounds.[4]

The second problem with the neutrality argument revolves around current total tax treatment of real property. Current federal, state, and local income tax policy subsidizes home ownership by excluding the imputed rental (or in-kind) income of home owners from taxation.[5] The intangibles tax would exacerbate this misallocation of resources away from financial and toward real assets.

Other Arguments Supporting an Intangibles Tax

There are several possible reasons for retaining the tax, mainly on the grounds of "equity" (although an efficiency case can be made). The intangibles tax may even be seen as either a tax on capital income or a tax on wealth. The equivalence of these two types of taxes can be stated as: $t_v V = t_y rV$, where V is the market value of an asset, t_v the wealth tax rate, r the full yield (including all dividends, interest, and capital gains) earned by the asset, and t_y the income tax rate. An income tax rate of t_y is equivalent to a wealth tax rate of rt_y, which implies that if t is 0.035 and the yield is 10 percent, the equivalent rate of tax on wealth would be 0.0035.

If we think of the intangibles tax as an income tax, one justification for its continuance is that it may add to the degree of tax progressivity[6] in Michigan's linear (or nongraduated) state income tax.[7] Of the forty-one states that have broad-based income taxes, all but five states (Michigan, Illinois, Indiana, Pennsylvania, and Massachusetts) have graduated rate structures.[8] The principal source of progressivity in Michigan's income tax results from the exemption of $1,500 of income per dependent.[9] In fact, when taken as a whole, the Michigan tax system, like most state tax systems, is regressive.[10]

Second, if we view the intangibles tax as a wealth tax it serves the purpose of diminishing the concentration of wealth. There is ample evidence that wealth is distributed much more unequally than are labor earnings. Although it may be argued that distributional concerns and objectives should best be dealt with at the federal, not state, level, the fact that there are wide variations across states in the incidence of both their tax and expenditure programs suggests that subnational groups have differing tastes for income redistribution.

Another possible reason for wealth taxation is that suggested by Alfred Marshall: individuals derive benefits, e.g., power, security, and status, from the stock of wealth itself.[11] If this motive for holding wealth is valid, wealth taxation in the presence of consumption taxes is required on efficiency grounds.

Arguments Against Intangibles Taxation

Arguments can be made against intangibles taxation on the grounds that it leads to resource misallocation and diminished factor supply. In addition, the existing Michigan intangibles tax creates certain inequities. First, the taxation of intangible property fosters nonneutrality in asset composition since real property is favored by other tax provisions. Second, under an intangibles tax, mortgaged property is subject to multiple taxation, hence borrowing is penalized for no valid reason. Third, if the supply of savings schedule is not perfectly inelastic with respect to the net-of-tax interest rate, taxing property income results in a welfare loss. Fourth, even if savings are completely insensitive to the after-tax rate of return, the tax is likely to reduce savings if either high income people or people with significant amounts of property income have higher savings propensities than others. Fifth, people might locate in states other than Michigan because of the tax. Sixth, the tax is easy to evade so honest people are unfairly treated vis a vis dishonest people. Finally, there are specific features of the Michigan intangibles tax that are capricious and horizontally inequitable (a factor which does not condemn the principle of intangibles taxation).

In my view the first two criticisms are entirely valid, as I stressed earlier. The efficiency issue embodied in the third criticism requires elaboration. In order to make judgements about the efficiency of the intangibles tax compared, say, to an income or sales tax, we need to know the values of a host of behavioral parameters from a well-specified model (including, for example, the interest elasticity of labor supply). At this time, however, the values of most of these parameters remain unknown. If, as the evidence seems to suggest,[12] the lifetime propensity to save increases with income and the incidence of the intangibles tax falls heavily upon the rich, it follows that savings will be reduced more by this tax than by other taxes.[13] But, while the supply of capital is probably diminished because of the tax, abolishing it, coupled with an equivalent increase in the tax rate on, say labor earnings, would likely reduce labor supply and it is by no means clear that such a shift in factor supplies would constitute an improvement.

Whether or not people locate in states other than Michigan because of the intangibles tax depends upon two factors: (1) the "price" or relative fiscal benefits of living somewhere other than in Michigan, and (2) the sensitivity or elasticity of moving with respect to differences in the price. There is little evidence as to the size of this elasticity. The price effect can be measured by comparing total tax rates in Michigan to those elsewhere. According to the evidence presented by the Advisory Commission on Intergovernmental Relations,[14] higher income people subject to the intangibles tax face lower income tax rates in Michigan than in most other states. The price effect, then, should be quite minor.

The question of tax evasion. A tax that is evaded on a large scale creates morale problems among the population. People feel worse about paying a tax that others evade than a tax that applies to all. In the summer of 1980, the Michigan Department of Treasury embarked on a compliance study. The approach was to audit federal tax return data provided by the U.S. Internal Revenue Service, and compare this with information on file with the Intangibles Tax Division. This made it possible to determine the identities of those who should have been paying the tax but were failing to do so.

The outcome of this study was never published, but F.M. Gould, the Administrator of the Intangibles Division, provided me with an account of the study. An initial selection rule for determining who might be an intangibles tax payer was determined. The initial rule for a married couple filing jointly was $6,000 in dividend and $5,000 in interest income. Applying this rule through the IRS tape yielded 76,000 potential filers. It was determined that 35,000 of these potential filers were actually filing, while 41,000 were not. Since most (about 90 percent) interest is not taxed by the intangibles tax at the individual level, a new, more stringent criterion requiring $10,000 of dividend income was adopted. Of those 41,000 potential filers, only about 7,300 were now determined to be likely filers and letters inviting those people to file were sent. The Intangibles Tax Division estimates that as a consequence of this procedure an additional \$3.5 million has been collected. Since the selection criterion in the study changed over its course it is difficult to determine the percentage of income recipients who should legally file but do not. Comparing the 7,300 who were invited to file with the number who in the first run were potential <u>and</u> actual filers (35,000), the nonfiler/filer ratio is about 20 percent. This finding, that for every five people who file the intangibles tax return there exists one person who illegally fails to file, is an <u>optimistic</u> projection based upon the premise that none of the people in the earlier group of 41,000 people and absent from the final group of 7,300 <u>should</u> have been filers. If we use the opposite polar extreme, assuming that all potential filers (76,000) should, in fact, be filers, the noncompliance/compliance rate is 41,000/35,000 or 117 percent. If an audit study is repeated, the noncompliance will, of course, be lower since many people will have been "picked up" by the 1980 audit.

<u>Inequitable provisions of the current intangibles tax.</u> Although dividends are taxed by the intangibles tax, most interest income (with the exceptions of corporate bond interest and the yield of credit unions) is exempt. Under current law, banks and savings and loans pay a charge of twenty cents per \$1,000 of deposits. Whether such treatment creates horizontal inequities rests in part on the question of whether the incidence of this charge is shifted to depositors. However, even if the tax is fully passed forward to the depositors, the rate on wealth of 0.0002 would be equivalent to a rate on interest income of 0.035 <u>only</u> if the interest rate were about one-half of one percent. At interest rates exceeding that level, interest recipients would be treated preferentially to dividend recipients.

In fact, however, the incidence of the tax on savings deposits is not borne by the depositors; it is borne solely by the banks. This is because the interest rate on savings deposits is subject to a ceiling rate of interest lower than the market clearing interest rate (Regulation Q). The effect of a tax in a market in which the ceiling rate is below the equilibrium rate is solely to reduce the banks' excess demand for funds at the maximum legal rate. Hence, depositors continue to receive the ceiling interest rate on their savings and the incidence of the tax on bank deposits falls upon the banks.

The fact that a dollar of interest income is tax free while a dollar of dividend income is taxable is grossly inequitable. It also creates inefficiencies, as investment decisions are affected not only by the real economic merits of projects but by this differential tax treatment. Hence, on both equity and efficiency criteria, dividend and interest income should be treated equally by the intangibles tax.

The alternative, or value, basis of the tax creates rather curious equity and efficiency effects when applied to shares of stock. The idea that a nonyielding asset should, like an asset with a yield, be subject to tax may have merit, especially in a world where capital gains are treated preferentially and gains are forgiven at death. In principle this approach can assure equal taxation of equal potential income and avoid a tax bias against assets with current yield as opposed to those that offer only appreciation. However, the practice of the intangibles tax is deficient in several respects. First, the use of par values for stock (or one dollar for no-par stock) instead of market value as a basis of taxation is ludicrous to say the least. There is little systematic relation between par value and market value of stock.[15] Bonds are treated more harshly than stocks under the value basis, since face values of bonds are closer to their market values.

A second problem with the value basis is that the taxes on the two bases are equivalent only at unrealistic yields, e.g., a tax of 0.001 on value is equivalent to a 0.035 tax on income only if the rate of return is 2.857 percent. At market rates above this level nonyielding assets are treated preferentially. Hence tax neutrality, which would yield both more efficient and more equitable outcomes, requires either higher tax rates on values or lower rates on yields.

There are no readily available statistics on the amount of revenue raised under the alternative value formula. The administrator of the intangibles tax says this amount is "negligible," perhaps a comforting prospect given its problems. The alternative basis as it exists is capricious and should either be abolished or rationalized. One way of rationalizing this feature is to rely solely on market values as an alternative basis. For stocks one could use published market value on the standard assessment date. The value of nontraded stock would be determined by capitalization of the firm's income stream, just as it is for inheritance tax purposes.

REVENUES

The revenue yielded by the intangibles tax, and the number of tax payers, is presented in Table 20.1. It should be evident that the revenue yield of the intangibles tax is currently quite modest, at $42 million, less than one percent of total state revenue. The significant reduction in the number of taxpayers between fiscal years 1969 and 1970 is explained by the fivefold increase in the statutory deduction. Similarly, when the deduction level was again raised in 1973, the number of filers fell once more. The rather substantial reduction in revenue between 1976 and 1977 is explained by the change in the law, effective January 1, 1977, exempting property subject to the single business tax.

Of the total amount of revenue collected by the intangibles tax in the fiscal years 1978, 1979, and 1980, the amount of tax paid by the (approximately 450) banks and savings and loans was $8.2 million, $8.8 million, and $9.5 million respectively. Hence the share of the intangibles tax paid by commercial institutions has ranged from 22 to 26 percent of the total yield in recent years. The next topic

TABLE 20.1
INTANGIBLES TAX REVENUE AND NUMBER OF TAXPAYERS,
Selected Fiscal Years, 1950-1980

Fiscal Year	Net Receipts (in thousands of dollars)	Number of Taxpayers
1950	11,286	36,417
1955	18,786	56,710
1960	27,102	87,286
1965	37,269	115,640
1966	44,291	128,001
1967	46,950	145,895
1968	47,372	142,101
1969	33,804	129,261
1970	36,383	59,448
1971	40,269	55,760
1972	40,009	45,301
1973	44,609	41,236
1974	43,554	32,256
1975	47,625	31,909
1976	50,050	41,504[1]
1977	27,811	41,005
1978	30,579	47,682
1979	38,142	49,402
1980	41,698	55,086

Note: [1]Fiscal years ended June 30 through 1975. Fiscal year 1976 included a transition quarter, with the fiscal year ending as they do now, on September 30.

[2]Starting in fiscal year 1976, only the number of tax registrants, not actual taxpayers, was published. Trusts are subject to taxation and must file a tax return whether or not any tax is due. In fiscal years 1974 and 1975, there were 47,037 and 45,738 registrants, respectively. These numbers exceed the number of taxpayers by 14,781 and 13,824, respectively.

Source: Michigan Department of Revenue, Annual Report, various years.

discussed is the modeling of the household component of the intangibles tax.

MODELING THE INTANGIBLES TAX

In order to answer a basic question such as "Who pays the intangibles tax?" it is necessary to provide a model of the tax. An ideal approach would be to use actual micro data linking Michigan income tax schedules with intangibles tax returns. With such a data set one could analyze the incidence of the tax by income class. Unfortunately no such data exist. As a second best procedure, I have used national survey data containing both household income and detailed asset information in order to model the tax.

Although Michigan household income exceeds the national average, for purposes of tax incidence analysis the critical assumption used here is that the relationship between income and wealth is the same for Michiganians as it is for all Americans. If this assumption is satisfied we can not only present the incidence of the tax by income class, but demonstrate the incidence and approximate revenue effects of various plausible changes in the tax. The data set used is the 1977 consumer credit survey of the Board of Governors of the Federal Reserve System, a survey of 2,563 households. This micro data set provides the most detailed information on asset holding ever collected by survey. It provides the amount held of the following assets: deposits in credit unions, savings and loans, mutual savings banks, and commercial banks, U.S. government savings bonds, other U.S. government bonds, corporate stocks and bonds, mutual funds, investment clubs, certificates of deposit, and the value of real estate, whether principal residence, secondary residence, or investment property.

The approach followed in modeling the intangibles tax was to (1) assume that the income basis of the tax was used, and (2) assign a set of rates of return to the different classes of assets in order to impute property incomes to each household.[16] Next these households were "taxed" in

TABLE 20.2
DISTRIBUTIONS OF HOUSEHOLD INCOME, PROPERTY INCOME, AND TAXABLE PROPERTY INCOME

	Household Income			Property Income			Taxable Property Income		
POPULATION QUINTILES	Dollar Limits	Share of Total	Cumulative Share	Quintile Limits	Share of Total	Cumulative Share	Quintile Limits	Share of Total	Cumulative Share
1	<5,900	0.0401	0.040	0	0	0	0	0	0
2	5,900-11,000	0.0968	0.137	0-19	0.0020	0.0020	0	0	0
3	11,000-16,300	0.1524	0.289	20-154	0.0192	0.0212	0	0	0
4	16,300-23,750	0.2227	0.512	154-783	0.0951	0.1183	0-143	0.0208	0.0208
5	>23,750	0.4875	1.000	>783	0.8852	1.0000	>143	0.9792	1.0000
10th DECILE	>31,764	0.3340	1.000	>2033	0.7278	1.0000	>772	0.8875	1.0000
MEAN	17,620			849			434		
STANDARD DEVIATION	10,884			2,656			1,913		
COEFFICIENT OF VARIATION	0.617			3.12			4.40		
NUMBER OF RESPONDENTS	2,225			2,035			2,096		

TABLE 20.3
PROPERTY INCOME AND TAXABLE PROPERTY INCOME, BY HOUSEHOLD INCOME CLASS

	Property Income[1]					Taxable Property Income[2]				
HOUSEHOLD INCOME QUINTILES	Share of Household Income	Cumulative Share of Household Income	Mean Property Income	Share of Property Income	Cumulative Share of Property Income	Share of Household Income	Cumulative Share of Household Income	Mean Taxable Property Income	Share of Taxable Property Income	Cumulative Share of Taxable Property Income
1	0.0411	0.0411	$167	0.0378	0.0378	0.0405	0.0405	$46	0.0210	0.0210
2	0.0987	0.1398	$407	0.1172	0.1550	0.0982	0.1387	$151	0.0665	0.0875
3	0.1557	0.2955	$575	0.1299	0.2849	0.1550	0.2937	$207	0.0910	0.1785
4	0.2278	0.5233	$769	0.1732	0.4581	0.2265	0.5202	$334	0.1460	0.3245
5	0.4767	1.0000	$2943	0.5419	1.0000	0.4798	1.0000	$1543	0.6755	1.0000
10th Decile	0.3213	1.0000	$3719	0.4197	1.0000	0.3258	1.0000	$2521	0.5519	1.0000

Notes: [1]The number of respondents is 1,879.

accordance with existing intangibles tax law and the tax incidence across and within income classes was ascertained.[17]

<u>The Distribution of Intangible Property Income</u>

The evidence from the data set reveals that the distribution of financial wealth and property income is very concentrated, a finding in agreement with those of other studies. In Table 20.2 the distribution of property income for those who responded to the relevant questions is presented and contrasted with the income distribution. The 80 percent of the respondent households with the lowest income receive about 49 percent of total income. However, the 80 percent of respondents with the smallest amount of property income receive only about 9.5 percent of total property income. One measure of inequity is the coefficient of variation, the standard deviation divided by the mean. The coefficient of variation of property income is 3.12, over five times its value for household income.

Although property income is highly concentrated, there are important differences in the concentration of asset-holding by type. Most people have money in a bank or savings and loan association, but only 1 percent own state or local bonds, 2 percent own corporate bonds, 5 percent own shares in mutual funds, and 17.5 percent own common or preferred stock (excluding interest in private pension funds). As noted above, some forms of property income, interest from banks, government bonds, certificates of deposits, are not taxed. It appears (panel three, Table 20.2) that on net the property income that is taxable is distributed more unequally than property income taken as a whole. The amount of taxable property income is $434 per household, about one-half of mean property income. However, the data reveal that, while 23.5 percent of the households report no property income, 62.2 percent have no taxable property income. Even if there were no statutory credit, any proportional tax on property or taxable property income would reduce wealth concentration since a significant share of the population hold no wealth. The effect of a credit, of course, is to reduce both the base and the yield, and to increase the progressivity of a tax (reduce the concentration of wealth).

Aside from attenuating wealth inequality the other distributional justification for an intangibles tax is that it might augment the progressivity of the Michigan income tax. Based upon Table 20.2 alone, we can not necessarily conclude that a wealth or property income tax achieves this effect. The taxation of something that is unequally distributed does not guarantee that income will be made more equal as a consequence. In order for wealth taxation to be income equalizing the two must be sufficiently positively correlated. In Table 20.3, property income and taxable property income by household income class are displayed. Note that those in the top decile or quintile hold a greater share of both total and taxable property income than they do of household income. Hence a proportional property income tax would exact a greater tax share from the top income groups than would a proportional income tax. However, it does not necessarily follow that such a tax is progressive. As pointed out by Suits (1977), a tax can be progressive over one range and regressive over another. This would appear to be the case under a tax on all property income with no credit or exemption. It appears that the lowest 40 percent have a somewhat larger proportion of total property income than of total household income (14 percent of total household income and 15.5 percent of total property income). Since the next two quintiles hold a greater share of total household than total property income (38.35 percent and 30.3 percent, respectively) a comprehensive property income tax with no personal exemption would be regressive over the bottom four quintiles and progressive over the top quintile. Hence it is the exemption of low levels of property income that would make a comprehensive property income tax unambiguously progressive.

A slightly different picture arises when we look at

property income declared taxable by Michigan. The net effect of eliminating certain asset types is to increase the correlation between property income and household income. The ratio of taxable property income to family income is about the same for the lowest 40 and the next 40 percent, but rises rapidly in the top quintile. Hence a proportional tax with no exemption levied on the Michigan intangible tax base would be proportional for the bottom 80 percent and progressive over the top quintile.

Horizontal inequity. According to my simulations the Michigan intangibles tax law treats only 51 percent of total property income as taxable.[18] Hence, individuals with similar amounts of property income are subject to very different amounts of tax and (according to my simulations) nearly half of the households with property income above the exemption level do not pay the intangibles tax because of the asset types held. If all property income were taxed, intangibles tax payments from households would nearly double since both present taxpayers would pay more and more households would be taxpayers.

If the appropriate tax base is total income rather than wealth or property income, and no credit or exemption is allowed, the horizontal equity problems of the intangibles tax are even more severe. In Table 20.4 the joint distribution of household and property income is presented. If a proportional total property tax were in place, perfect horizontal equity would require all the cases (376 in each quintile) to lie on the center diagonal (all the members of the ith income quintile would be in the ith property income quintile). Although positions in the two distributions are positively related, this is far from the case. Most people in the top quintile (or decile) are not in the top household income quintile (or decile). Therefore, if "equals" refers to people with equal household income, equals are being taxed quite unequally under a property income tax. The situation is only very marginally better when only taxable property income is used (Table 20.5), with the difference a

TABLE 20.4
JOINT DISTRIBUTION OF HOUSEHOLDS
BY HOUSEHOLD INCOME AND PROPERTY INCOME
(N = 1,879)

Quintiles of Household Income	Quintiles of Property Income (number of cases and row proportions in each cell) 1	2	3	4	5	Addendum[1] 10th Decile of Property Income
1	193 0.513	75 0.199	52 0.138	38 0.100	19 0.050	6 0.016
2	101 0.268	92 0.247	78 0.207	53 0.141	51 0.136	22 0.059
3	53 0.141	104 0.277	91 0:242	65 0.173	63 0.168	31 0.082
4	27 0.072	72 0.192	101 0.269	111 0.296	64 0.171	37 0.098
5	3 0.008	32 0.085	54 0.144	108 0.287	179 0.476	92 0.245
Addendum[2] 10th Decile of Household Income	0 0	12 0.064	19 0.101	52 0.277	105 0.559	67 0.356[3]

Notes: [1]Proportion is share of quintile in top decile.

[2]Proportion is share of decile in a given quintile.

[3]Proportion is share of top deciles of both distributions.

TABLE 20.5
JOINT DISTRIBUTION OF HOUSEHOLDS
BY HOUSEHOLD INCOME AND TAXABLE PROPERTY INCOME
(N =1,932)

Quintiles of Household Income	Quintiles of Taxable Property Income (number of cases and row proportions in each cell)			10th Decile of Taxable Property Income
	1-3	4	5	
1	350 0.907	25 0.064	11 0.029	6 0.016
2	286 0.739	50 0.129	39 0.101	21 0.054
3	239 0.618	86 0.222	62 0.160	26 0.067
4	183 0.474	120 0.310	83 0.215	37 0.096
5	102 0.264	93 0.240	191 0.495	103 0.267
10th Decile of Household Income	32 0.166	42 0.218	119 0.617	71 0.368

consequence of the higher correlation between taxable property income and household income.

Incidence and Horizontal Equity of the Current Michigan Intangibles Tax

Under the provisions of the Michigan intangibles tax, only the wealthiest one percent of the population pay the tax because of the very high statutory credit. Given the high degree of correlation between wealth and income at the top of the wealth distribution, there is no doubt that the incidence of the intangibles tax mainly falls on top income recipients. Consequently the intangibles tax adds to the progressivity of the Michigan income tax. Using the demographic information on the Federal Reserve Board's survey tape to determine the credit level, I was able to simulate the incidence of the intangibles tax. Out of the 1,932 cases in which the respondents answered all the relevant questions only 21 owed taxes. Of those twenty-one cases one was in the third and one in the fourth income decile (they owed $75.84 and $55.32 in tax respectively). Aside from those anomolous cases, the remaining taxpayers had relatively high incomes. One taxpayer was in the eighth decile, two in the ninth, and the remaining sixteen cases were in the highest income decile. In Table 20.6 the accumulated household income and intangibles tax burden by income deciles are presented. The share of intangibles tax paid rises much faster than the share of total income earned by each decile. The bottom seventy percentiles earn about 40 percent of household income but pay only 2.33 percent of the tax. At the other extreme, the top income decile earns about 32.5 percent of household income but pays over 82 percent of the intangibles tax.

The progressivity of the intangibles tax can be measured by a single statistic and can be compared with the progressivity of other taxes. In a recent paper Suits (1977) derives an index of tax progressivity (see Chapter 27). The "Suits" index ranges from a low of -1 (perfect regressivity, the poorest household pays all) to +1 (perfect progressivity, the richest pays the entire tax).

In my simulations I have computed the exact value (using this data set) of the Suits index for the Michigan intangibles tax. The calculated index is 0.6152.[19] In spite of this high degree of progressivity, however, the intangibles tax does not alter the incidence of the Michigan tax system very much. The tax is paid by so few people and raises so little revenue that its effect on the total progressivity of the system may be negligible.

In order to get a sense of the impact of the intangibles tax on a broader view of state income tax progressivity, I hypothetically "integrated" the intangibles tax into the existing Michigan income tax. First, I constructed an accurate estimate of income tax paid by household. The Suits index for the Michigan income tax is a mildly progressive 0.1135. Using the relative yields of the two taxes, I computed that the integrated income tax would have a Suits index of 0.1212, which is about 0.0027 (or slightly less than 7 percent) more progressive than the income tax taken by itself. Whether this addition to tax progressivity is "negligible" or not, and whether such an increase in tax progressivity justifies the existence of the intangibles tax is beyond the scope of my analysis.

<u>The Effects of the Statutory Credit</u>

One of the features of the intangibles tax that makes it so progressive is the very high level of statutory credit, $175 for singles and $350 for a married couple, equivalent to exemptions of $5,000 and $10,000. In order to determine both the revenue and incidence effects of the deduction, I simulated what the intangibles tax would look like in its absence. First, elimination of the credit would increase revenues fivefold. This increase is partially due to the increased tax liabilities of those already paying the tax, but more importantly, to the enormous increase in the number of taxpayers. The percentage of households that would owe tax increases from 1 percent to about 38 percent of the population. The distribution of the tax burden of an

TABLE 20.6
ACCUMULATED INTANGIBLES TAX
BY INCOME CLASS
(N = 1,932)

Population Deciles	Accumulated Percentage of Household Income	Accumulated Percentage of Intangibles Tax Payments
1	0.0130	0.0000
2	0.0404	0.0000
3	0.0827	0.0135
4	0.1386	0.0233
5	0.2092	0.0233
6	0.2937	0.0233
7	0.3955	0.0233
8	0.5202	0.1110
9	0.6742	0.1760
10	1.0000	1.0000

TABLE 20.7
EFFECTIVE TAX RATES, SHARE OF TAX PAID,
AND ACCUMULATED SHARE OF TAX PAID
BY HOUSEHOLD INCOME CLASS
(under the assumption of no credit)

Household Income Quintile	Effective Tax Rate[1]	Share of Total Tax Paid	Accumulated Share of Total Tax Paid
1	0.000486	0.0210	0.0210
2	0.000632	0.0665	0.0875
3	0.000548	0.0909	0.1784
4	0.000603	0.1460	0.3244
5	0.001310	0.6755	1.0000
10th Decile	0.001580	0.5519	1.0000

Note: [1]Effective tax rate is tax paid divided by income.

intangibles tax without credits mirrors the distribution of taxable property income presented in Table 20.3. The top income decile would pay 55 percent of the tax, the top quintile, 67.5 percent of the tax, and so forth. Effective tax rates and burdens by income class are presented in Table 20.7. Elimination of the credits would lower the Suits index of progressivity of the intangibles tax to 0.2686. If the intangibles tax without credits were integrated with the Michigan income tax, the Suits index for the combined tax would be 0.1257, which is 0.01218 (or about 10.7 percent) higher than the Suits index for the Michigan income tax (0.1135). While eliminating the credit makes the intangibles tax far less progressive than it is now, it makes the integrated income tax more progressive. The reason why a less progressive tax adds more to income tax progressivity than a more progressive tax is the much higher yield of the former than of the latter tax.

The Effect of Taxing Forms of Property Income Now Considered Exempt

The present intangibles tax excludes approximately one-half of property income and, as argued above, this treatment creates inequities among people with similar property incomes. In order to examine the revenue and incidence effects of eliminating this inequity, I simulated intangibles tax payments under the assumption that previously exempt asset classes are taxable. I found that tax revenues from households would rise by 94 percent. The number of households paying the tax would increase by about 86 percent, so that about 2 percent of all households would be subject to the tax. This, of course, implies that tax rates could be lowered to provide the same yield as before, but in more equitable fashion. The progressivity of the intangibles tax would be reduced somewhat since currently taxable property income is more concentrated among top income recipients than total property income. The Suits index of tax progressivity would be lower, 0.4307, if no property income was exempt. If this version of the intangibles tax were integrated with the existing income tax, the Suits index for the combined tax would be 0.1216, which is only slightly larger than the combined Suits index for the income and the existing intangibles tax.

An intangibles tax in which excluded forms of property income were taxed would have about the same effect on income tax progressivity (and double the yield) of the current intangibles tax and also treat those with equal amounts of property income equally. Over 98 percent of the population would continue to pay no tax, so that most of those having similar incomes would pay the same (zero) tax.

The Effects of a Comprehensive Intangibles Tax Without Credits

In my final simulation I examine what the intangibles tax would look if all sources of property income were taxed and the statutory credit were eliminated. The effect on revenue yield is dramatic; revenue under this variant is over ten times higher than it is under the existing intangibles tax. Nearly 80 percent of the population would owe some tax. The changes in the incidence and horizontal equity of the tax are also dramatic over the first four quintiles. I have computed the effective tax rates (tax paid divided by income) and shares of the total tax paid, by income class under this variant of the intangibles tax. The mean effective tax rate among the lowest four quintiles is 0.00170, which is below that for the top quintile. However, among the bottom four quintiles the lowest 40 percent are taxed at a higher effective rate than the second 40 percent. The Suits index for this tax is 0.0899, which implies progressivity but less progressivity than the Michigan income tax. Hence integration with the income tax would reduce the Suits index to 0.1101 (although it would probably increase the progressivity of Michigan's tax system taken as a whole).

A comprehensive intangibles tax without credits might create severe problems of horizontal inequity. If income is taken to be the appropriate tax base, tax burdens within income class would mirror the joint distribution of household and property income (see Table 20.4). Given the wide disparities in property income within income classes, such a tax would score very poorly on grounds of horizontal equity. If, on the other hand, the tax is viewed as a wealth tax, it would score very well on horizontal equity grounds since (almost) all property income regardless of the source would be taxed at the same rate. As a wealth tax, however, this variant would have only a small effect on diminishing relative concentration since the tax rate is constant and only the lowest 23 percent of the wealth distribution have no property income and would owe no tax.

CONCLUSIONS

The main historical argument for the existence of the Michigan intangibles tax, tax neutrality between real and intangible property, is not particularly well founded. However, the continued existence of the tax, aside from the general issue of revenue need, rests on distributional grounds. The tax does make our linear income tax more progressive than it otherwise would be and the tax very modestly reduces wealth concentration.

Efficiency arguments against or in favor of the tax are not at all decisive. We simply do not know if other taxes distort behavior more or less than does the intangibles tax.

It is possible that a large degree of tax evasion has existed, but the 1980 audit study may have ameliorated much of the problem.

The intangibles tax has two capricious and inequitable features that should be changed. The alternative (or value) basis of the tax should either be eliminated or rationalized in ways suggested in this chapter. The use of the par value, or one dollar for no par stock, of stock as a basis of taxation seems the epitome of capricious practice.

Horizontal inequities could be greatly diminished by taxing property income that is now exempt. The levy on banks might also be dropped, with the banks, like other businesses, subject to the single business tax.

NOTES, CHAPTER 20

[1]See Taylor (1959), p. 394.

[2]See Office of Revenue and Tax Analysis (1975), p. 39.

[3]See Taylor (1959), p. 393.

[4]This disincentive effect, of course, would not result if the property taxes were levied upon the net as opposed to the gross value of the asset.

[5]See Rosen and Rosen (1980).

[6]A progressive tax is a tax in which the ratio of tax paid to tax base (income) rises as the tax base (income) increases.

[7]This hypothesis will be tested in a subsequent section modeling the intangibles tax.

[8]There are three other states that only tax property income.

[9]Michigan also allows a property tax circuit breaker and home heating credit.

[10]Phares 1980, pp. 142-143. The distributional effects of the intangibles tax may diminish this regressivity.

[11]"There are indeed some who find an intense pleasure in seeing their hoards of wealth grow up under their hands with scarcely any thought for happiness that may be got from its use by themselves or others. They are prompted partly by the instincts of the chase, by the desire to outstrip their rivals, by the ambition to have shown ability to acquire power and social position by its possession. And sometimes the force of habit, started when they were really in need of money, has given them, (as a) sort of reflex action, an artificial and unreasoning pleasure in amassing wealth for its own sake." Marshall (1949).

[12]See Menchik and David (1980).

[13]Note that it is an income effect, not any assumed price effect of the tax that yields this outcome. Note also that this effect is not an efficiency effect; whether reduced savings is good or bad depends upon our answer to the public choice question of how much capital should be available to the next generation.

[14]1980, p. 234.

[15]This aberration was convincingly demonstrated by Milton C. Taylor, in his paper on the intangibles tax over twenty years ago (see Taylor (1959)).

[16] The interest rates on savings accounts at credit unions, savings and loans, mutual savings banks and commercial banks were 5.25 percent for the first three and 5 percent for the last. These were the maximum legal rates in 1976, the year preceding the survey year. The rate of return on U.S. government savings bonds was 5.21 percent, the average rate in 1976. For other U.S. Government bonds I used 6.94 percent, the corporate rate on bonds and notes of three to five years. (Federal Reserve Bulletin, Table 1.36, December 1979). The rate of return on state and local government bonds is 6.64 percent, a composite rate reported in the FRB cited above. The rates of return on certificates of deposit, and corporate bonds (both from the FRB) were 5.27 and 9.01 percent respectively. For the return on stocks (a dividend/price ratio) I used the weighted average of dividend/price ratios on common and preferred stock, with the weights the relative values of common and preferred stock outstanding. The dividend/price ratios (taken from the FRB) were 0.0377 for common and 0.0797 for preferred, with 76 percent weight for common stock and 24 percent weight for preferred stock (see Block and Hirt 1981, pp. 341-342) for a weighted sum of 4.778 percent. This rate of return was also applied to assets in mutual funds and investment clubs. Since mortgages are taxed by the intangibles tax, I applied a (now) modest six percent interest rate on investment real estate.

[17] It should be pointed out that the results obtained in this section are approximations and should be interpreted with some degree of caution.

[18] Actually the taxable percentage is less than 51 percent because pension and insurance yields are also not taxed, but are not in the data set.

[19] Donald Phares (1980, pp. 142-143) has presented the Suits indices for a number of state and local taxes for all fifty states. Of the nearly 400 indices presented, not one is as great as the Suits index for the Michigan intangibles tax.

REFERENCES, CHAPTER 20

Advisory Commission on Intergovernmental Relations. Significant Features of Fiscal Federalism, 1979-1980. Washington, D.C.: U.S. Government Printing Office, 1980.

Block, Stanley B. and Hirt, Geoffrey A. Foundations of Financial Management. Richard D. Irwin. 1981.

Board of Governors of the Federal Reserve System. Federal Reserve Bulletin, December 1979. Publications Services, Board of Governors of the Federal Reserve System: Washington, D.C. 1979.

Board of Governors of the Federal Reserve System. *1977 Consumer Credit Survey*, Publications Services, Board of Governors of the Federal Reserve System: Washington, D.C. 1978.

Marshall, Alfred. *Principles of Economics* (8th edition). New York: MacMillan. 1949.

Michigan Department of Treasury. *Annual Report*. State of Michigan, Lansing, Michigan. Various years.

Menchik, Paul and David, Martin. "The Effect of Income Distribution and Redistribution on Lifetime Saving and Bequests." NBER Conference Paper Series, #58. 1980.

Phares, Donald. *Who Pays State and Local Taxes*. Cambridge, Massachusetts: Oelgeschlager, Gunn and Hain. 1980.

Rosen, Harvey S. and Rosen, Kenneth, T. "Federal Taxes and Homeownership: Evidence from Time Series." *Journal of Political Economy* 88 (1980): 59-75.

Suits, Daniel B. "The Measurement of Tax Progressivity." *American Economic Review* 67 (1977): 747-752.

Taylor, Milton C. *Michigan Tax Study Staff Papers* (Chapter 15). Lansing, 1958.

Chapter 21

The Inheritance Tax

by

John P. Laitner

with the assistance of Juha Kahkonen

The University of Michigan

INTRODUCTION

Michigan's inheritance and estate taxes are the subject of this chapter. After briefly discussing the philosophy of death duties in general, we examine Michigan's law in detail, compare it with corresponding taxes in other states, and investigate the revenues it has produced in the recent past. We close with some summary conclusions.

Before beginning our analysis however, we should clarify the definitions of "estate," "inheritance," "gift," and "pickup" taxes. Note that all such taxes apply to wealth "transfers," as opposed to payments made for goods or services rendered.

First, consider wealth transfers from decedents to beneficiaries. Such transfers may be taxed in two ways: an "estate tax" is a tax levied on the decedent's total estate, regardless of its division among heirs; an "inheritance tax" is a tax levied separately on each beneficiary's share. As an example, consider an estate of $10,000 which two heirs will divide equally. In one instance let there be an estate tax with an exemption of $1,000 and a proportional rate of 10 percent. Then the total tax liability will be $900. In a second instance let there be an inheritance tax with the same exemption and rate schedule. Then the total tax liability will be $800, $400 on each share. We sometimes use the term "death taxes" to refer to both estate and inheritance taxes.

A "gift tax" applies to wealth transfers from living donors to donees. Such a tax can be applied yearly to the aggregate sum of a donor's gifts, or separately to the sum of the gifts made to each donee by a given donor.

Twelve of the fourteen states which have gift taxes,[1] and the federal government, impose their gift taxes on cumulative inter vivos transfers. Thus, California, for example, has a tax rate schedule which must be applied once to cumulative transfers from a given donor to a given donee in the current and all previous years, and also to transfers from the same donor to the same donee during all previous years. The tax currently due is the difference between the two computed figures.[2] On the other hand, the federal gift tax applies to the cumulative aggregate inter vivos transfers of each donor, with the nature of the distribution of gifts in excess of the annual per donee exclusion among donees not being considered.[3]

Gift and death taxes can be "unified." In California the state gift and inheritance taxes are unified: a decedent's cumulative lifetime gifts to a given donee are summed with his or her bequest to the same person. Then an inheritance tax figure is computed. Gift taxes already paid (on transfers to the given donee) are deducted from the inheritance tax figure, giving the net tax due.[4] The U.S. Revenue Act of 1976 unified federal estate and gift taxes in an analogous manner.[5]

A "pickup tax" is a special kind of estate tax based on an important link between federal and state death taxes in the U.S. As an illustration, consider the federal estate tax liability of a citizen dying in 1981. We can use the unified estate and gift tax rate table of the federal government to compute a tentative tax liability on the estate. This must then be reduced by a "unified credit." In 1981, the unified credit for the estate that we are considering would equal the lesser of the tax liability computed above and $47,000.[6] Next, we compute a maximum federal credit for state death taxes. The calculation applies rates corresponding to 80 percent of the 1926 federal total estate tax liability to the entire taxable estate less an exemption of $40,000.[7] The actual credit allowed for state death taxes is then the smallest of the maximum credit, the amount by which federal taxes exceed the unified credit, and the amount of state death taxes actually due.[8]

If the lesser of the first two items in the preceding line exceeds state taxes due, the decedent's state could raise its death duties without actually adding to the given estate's total tax burden. A "pickup tax" is the device states use to ensure that no burden-free revenues are lost in such circumstances. For the example we have been considering, the pickup tax would be set equal to the difference between the sum of all other state death taxes due and the minimum of $Z and $X less the uniform credit. Every state except Nevada employs a pickup tax.

EQUITY AND EFFICIENCY

Death duties are highly controversial taxes. Although the energy expended on debates about them sometimes seems out of proportion to the amount of revenue involved in practice, the relevant issues are very interesting from a theoretical standpoint. The following is a summary of pro and con arguments organized under five headings.[9]

Horizontal Equity

One generally accepted principle is that taxes should manifest horizontal equity. Now every person can receive two types of inheritance from his or her parents: one type, which we label "financial," includes bequests and *inter vivos* gifts of intangible, tangible personal, and real property; the other type, which we call "nonfinancial," includes the abilities, talents, attitudes, and other traits which pass down genetically and socially within families. "Nonfinancial" inheritances play a substantial role in determining each individual's lifetime earning capacity. Hence, such inheritances are taxed indirectly through federal, state, and local income taxes. Equity, in the sense of consistency, requires, therefore, that "financial" inheritances should be taxed too, and that the progressivity of the structure of death and gift duties should be analogous to that of the income tax system.[10]

Equality

A second, more controversial, principle is that a tax system should serve to increase the equality of economic status among individuals, at least to the extent of preventing extreme (and, especially, permanent) wealth concentrations. Even opponents of death and gift taxes seldom dispute that such taxes can reduce wealth inequality.

Nevertheless, a contrasting viewpoint on this subject could be developed as follows. Egalitarians, it might be argued, should be concerned with the equality of the overall distribution of consumption spending, rather than of wealth holdings, since the former represents the distribution of actual claims on society's scarce resources. Private-sector bequest behavior, however, may well augment the equality of the consumption distribution. Because bequests tend to be a luxury good, wealthy families leave disproportionately large estates, making their lifetime consumption spending small relative to their wealth status. According to this line of reasoning, death duties might actually reduce equality by tampering with a natural, private-sector equalization mechanism.[11]

Efficiency

A lump-sum tax will not interfere with economic efficiency. Other taxes are less than perfect in this respect. Death duties, nevertheless, are often thought to have relatively favorable qualities in this regard.

A conventional argument would be as follows. We can think of individuals as budgeting their time to produce lifetime consumption, bequests (and gifts), and leisure. An income tax raises the "cost" of the first two products relative to the third, possibly leading to an overproduction of leisure. A tax on bequests does not change the price of lifetime consumption vis-a-vis leisure; it raises the "cost" of bequests relative to both. In other words, while an income tax tampers with all alternatives to leisure, a death duty interferes with only one.

The preceding line of reasoning suggests that gift and death duties might have a less deleterious effect on a benefactor's work incentives than income taxes do.[12] In fact, however, the argument is far from conclusive. Merely comparing numbers of tax-induced "cost" distortions does not constitute an analysis of their actual relative magnitudes in specific circumstances.

In the case of beneficiaries, on the other hand, death and gift taxes undoubtedly do increase work effort (via what economists call an "income effect" on leisure).

Saving

Death and gift taxes are sometimes said to discourage private-sector saving (although this argument, as in the case of beneficiaries and work effort above, is usually somewhat divorced from static efficiency considerations). The theoretical justification for this point of view again is unclear, however. A gift or death duty may, in actuality, cause the saving of potential benefactors to increase, as they seek to keep their net-of-tax transfers from falling below target levels. The savings of beneficiaries may also rise, as the beneficiaries attempt to substitute their own savings for net-of-tax transfer receipts.

Family Unity

Death and gift duties are sometimes also criticized as attacks upon family unity. The idea is that bequest (and gift) transfers provide one reason for family ties and, hence, help to strengthen them. The care of the elderly by their offspring may be encouraged by the anticipation of bequests.

Types of Wealth Transfer Taxes

On balance, the arguments in favor of gift and death

duties seem compelling. This is especially true in the case of horizontal equity and equality considerations. In light of our discussion above, we can see that one very good tax program for promoting both of the latter qualities would be an "accessions tax" imposed on the cumulative gifts and inheritances (from all sources) received by each individual.[13] A second-best alternative would be a unified gift and inheritance tax (such as California's system) or a unified gift and estate tax (such as the federal government's system).

MICHIGAN'S INHERITANCE AND ESTATE TAX LAWS

Michigan's first successful inheritance tax was passed in 1899 (a prior version of the law having been declared unconstitutional by the State Supreme Court). The law, patterned after a similar one enacted by New York in 1892, was up-to-date for its time. Direct as well as collateral heirs were taxed at 5 percent, with exemptions of $5,000 and $500, respectively. In 1919 a progressive rate system was instituted. In 1929 the legislature added a pickup tax to take advantage of the newly offered federal estate tax credit for state death taxes paid. Subsequent revisions of rates, exemptions, and other details have left the law's basic framework unchanged. Several very recent modifications are slight rate increases coupled with a doubling (to $10,000) of the exemption for close relatives,[14] an increase (from $30,000 to $65,000) of the exemption for spouses,[15] a new exemption (see below) for "qualified" farm property,[16] and a new exemption (see below) for artists.[17] Michigan has no gift tax.

The next section begins a detailed analysis of the chief elements of Michigan's current inheritance tax statute.

The Tax Base

Michigan's inheritance tax recognizes three types of taxable property: the real or personal property of any resident decedent (regardless of the place of death); the real or tangible personal property located within Michigan for nonresident decedents; and the intangible property located within Michigan of nonresident decedents from states not having reciprocal exemption statutes. The tax applies to all transfers at death and to transfers made "in contemplation of death." Transfers made in the two years prior to death are assumed to fall into the latter category, except in situations in which the opposite can be proven. (In practice, courts have been receptive to arguments in individual cases).[18]

For intangible property, taxing authority generally depends on the determination of a single legal residence, or "domicile," for each decedent. Because a person may own real or tangible property in several states, a decedent's domicile must be established judgmentally from his or her voting place, principal business and social center, references to "home," percentage time allocation, location of principal possessions, and local taxes paid indicative of residence. In practice, this is not a simple problem.[19]

Non-Taxable Transfers and Deductions

The intangible property of nonresident decedents from states having reciprocity exemption rules is not taxable. For resident decedents, transfers within the following categories are nontaxable: (1) all joint property and tenancies by entirety (this was established by court cases in 1953);[20] (2) insurance paid directly to a beneficiary, rather than the decedent's estate (this holds provided the donor has not retained both the right to change the beneficiary and the right to the policy's cash surrender value); (3) property given to charitable, religious, educational, or public institutions; and, (4) a spouse's share of a retirement plan or annuity. Similarly, all *inter vivos* gifts transferred two or more years before the donor's death are nontaxable. Debts, administrative expenses, executor's commissions, attorney fees, and funeral charges are deductible from an estate. Likewise, a widow's

TABLE 21.1
MICHIGAN'S 1981 INHERITANCE TAX

VALUE OF BENEFICIARY'S SHARE (dollars)	COLUMN I Rate 1[1] (percent)	COLUMN II Rate 2[2] (percent)
0 - 10,000	0.0	12.0
10,000 - 50,000	2.0	12.0
50,000 - 250,000	4.0	14.0
250,000 - 500,000	7.0	14.0
500,000 - 750,000	8.0	17.0
750,000 -	10.0	17.0

Notes: [1]Applies if the beneficiary is a spouse, parent, grandparent, child, grandchild, brother or sister, or son-in-law or daughter-in-law.

[2]Applies for all beneficiaries not listed above.

Source: Michigan Compiled Laws, 1981-1982, s. 205.202.

allowance for one year or less can be deducted if the widow has no other income accruing. Federal estate taxes are not deductible.

Preferential Exemptions and Deferrals

The Michigan Legislature has afforded special exemptions or deferrals to three classes of individuals: the estates of certain disabled veterans receive a homestead exemption; after January 1981, the estates of artists can defer inheritance tax payments (with no interest due) for up to ten years; and "qualified" farm real property left to "qualified" heirs is 50 percent exempt (after January, 1979), and the balance of the tax can be deferred, with no interest due, for up to 10 years. [21]

Tax Rates

The current rate schedule for the Michigan inheritance tax is given in Table 21.1. The rates indicated apply separately to three groups of taxable transfers:

1) A spouse is allowed a $65,000 exemption. A widow receives a $5,000 additional exemption for each minor child to whom property is not transferred. The remainder of the share is taxed using column I rates.

2) Parents, grandparents, children, grandchildren, brothers and sisters, sons-in-law, or daughters-in-law are taxed using column I rates.

3) All others are taxed using column II rates. However, transfers under $100 are exempt.

Other Death Taxes

Along with all other states except Nevada, Michigan imposes a "pickup" tax designed to exhaust the appropriate federal estate-tax credit. In addition, a one-half percent tax is levied on all death duties collected. The returns are awarded to the general fund of the county in which the decedent's domicile was located.

TABLE 21.2
STATE ESTATE TAX RATES AND EXEMPTIONS, 1980

STATE[1]	RATES	MAXIMUM RATE APPLIES ABOVE	EXEMPTION
Alabama	80% of 1926 federal rates	$10,040,000	$100,000
Alaska	80% of 1926 federal rates	10,040,000	100,000
Arizona	80% of 1926 federal rates	10,040,000	100,000
Arkansas	80% of 1926 federal rates	10,040,000	100,000
Colorado	80% of 1926 federal rates	10,040,000	100,000
Florida	80% of 1926 federal rates	10,040,000	100,000
Georgia	80% of 1926 federal rates	10,040,000	100,000
Massachussetts	5-16%	4,000,000	30,000[2]
Minnesota	7-12%	1,000,000	200,000
Mississippi	1-16%	10,000,000	167,333
North Dakota	80% of 1926 federal rates	10,040,000	100,000
New Mexico	80% of 1926 federal rates	10,040,000	100,000
New York	2-21%	10,100,000	--[3]
Ohio	2-7%	500,000	5,000[4]
Oklahoma	1-15%	10,000,000	60,000[5]
Rhode Island	2-9%	1,000,000	25,000[6]
South Carolina	5-7%	100,000	120,000[7]
Utah	80% of 1926 federal rates	10,040,000	100,000
Vermont	80% of 1926 federal rates	10,040,000	100,000
Virginia	80% of 1926 federal rates	10,040,000	100,000

Notes: [1]Excludes states with "pickup" and inheritance taxes. All states listed here do have pickup taxes in addition to the rates indicated.
[2]If the net estate is $60,000 or less, the exemption is equal to the net estate.

[3]There is a marital deduction of $250,000 or one half of the adjusted gross estate. $50,000 transferred to specified close relatives is exempt. The federal provisions for orphans apply. A credit is allowed as follows: for an estate tax under $2,750, the credit equals the tax; for a tax over $5,000, the credit is $500; and, for an estate tax in between, the credit is the amount by which $5,500 exceeds the tax.
[4]An additional $20,000 for spouse, $7,000 for a minor child, and $3,000 for an adult child.

[5]This exemption applies to specified close relatives. Tax rates are higher for others. Transfers to spouses are exempt.
[6]A $200,000 marital deduction is allowed.
[7]The marital deduction is $250,000 or one-half of the adjusted gross estate.

Source: Advisory Commission on Intergovenmental Relations, Significant Features of Fiscal Federalism, 1979-80, Washington, D.C. 1980.

A COMPARISON OF STATE LAWS

A useful way to evaluate Michigan's inheritance statute is by comparing it with the laws of other states and with the federal estate tax.

State Tax Rates

Tables 21.2 and 21.3 present basic information. By July, 1980, twelve states had only pickup taxes, eight had estate taxes (plus pickup taxes), and twenty-nine had inheritance taxes (plus pickup taxes). Nevada has no death duty of any type. As noted earlier, fourteen states also have gift taxes. In the cases of California, Vermont, and the federal government, gift and death duties are unified.

Table 21.4 attempts to summarize death-duty information in a more convenient form. The first six columns present "effective" tax rates for various states and the federal government. The rates were derived taking account of varying rate structures, exemptions, credits, marital deductions, rules for deducting federal estate tax liabilities, and treatments of joint (and community) property among the states.[22] In each case we allowed deductions for debts, charitable expenses, and administrative expenses, and for all states we subtracted (for the first six columns) the federal estate tax credit. We assumed that one-half of all estates in every class were passed to two adult children, and that one-half was divided between a surviving spouse and two such children.[23] We constructed tax rates by dividing the tax due (net of federal credit) by the corresponding gross estate less debts, and charitable contributions, and administrative expenses. The first six columns show weighted-average rate figures for the estates falling within each bracket.[24] The mean for all states of the "effective" tax rate (net of the federal credit) for estates between $0 and $60,000 is 0.10 percent, for those between $60,000 and $120,000 it is 0.73 percent, for those between $120,000 and $300,000 it is 1.24 percent, for those between $300,000 and $1,200,000 it is 1.40 percent, and for those between $1,200,000 and

TABLE 21.3
STATE INHERITANCE TAX RATES AND EXEMPTIONS, 1980

STATE[1]	EXEMPTIONS				RATES			
	Spouse	Adult Child	Brother or Sister	Non Relative	Spouse	Adult Child	Brother or Sister	Non Relative
California	$60,000	$ 5,000	$ 2,000	$ 300	6 -14%	3 -14%	6 -20%	10 -24%
Connecticut[2]	100,000	20,000	6,000	1,000	3 -8	2 -8	8 -14	8 -14
Delaware	70,000	3,000	1,000	none	2 -4	1 -6	5 -10	10 -16
Hawaii	100,000	50,000	5,000	5,000	2 -7	3 -8	3 -10	3 -10
Idaho[3]	50,000	30,000	10,000	10,000	2 -15	2 -15	4 -20	8 -30
Illinois	20,000[4]	20,000[4]	10,000	100	2 -14	2 -14	2 -14	10 -30
Indiana	---[5]	5,000	500	100	-[5]	1 -10	7 -15	10 -20
Iowa[6]	80,000	30,000	none	none	1 -8	1 -8	5 -10	10 -15
Kansas	250,000	30,000	5,000	none	.5 -2.5	.5 -2.5	3 -12.5	10 -15
Kentucky	50,000	5,000	1,000	500	2 -10	2 -10	4 -16	6 -16
Louisiana	5,000	5,000	1,000	500	2 -3	2 -3	5 -7	5 -10
Maine	50,000	25,000	1,000	1,000	5 -10	5 -10	8 -14	14 -18
Maryland[7]	none	none	none	none	1	1	10	10
Michigan	75,000	10,000	10,000	none	2 -10	2 -10	2 -10	12 -17
Missouri	20,000[8]	5,000	500	100	1 -6	1 -6	3 -18	5 -30
Montana	---[5]	7,000	1,000	none	2 -8	2 -8	4 -16	8 -32
Nebraska	10,000	10,000	10,000	500	1	1	1	6 -18
New Hampshire	---[5]	---[5]	none	none	---[5]	---[5]	15	15
New Jersey	15,000	15,000	---[9]	---[9]	2 -16	2 -16	11 -16	15 -16
North Carolina	100,000	---[10]	none	none	1 -12	1 -12	4 -16	8 -17
Oregon	---[11]	---[11]	---[11]	---[11]	12	12	12	12
Pennsylvania	none[12]	none[12]	none	none	6	6	15	16
South Dakota	---[5]	30,000	500	100	1.5 - 7.5	1.5 - 7.5	4 -20	6 -30
Tennessee	120,000[13] [14]	120,000[13]	120,000[13]	10,000[13]	5.5 -9.5	5.5 -9.5	5.5 -9.5	6.5 -16
Texas	200,000[13] [15]	200,000	10,000	500	1 -6	1 -6	3 -10	5 -20
Washington	100,000	10,000	-[16]	none	1 -10	1 -10	3 -20	10 -25
West Virginia	30,000	10,000	10,000	none[17]	3 -13	3 -13	4 -18	10 -30
Wisconsin	250,000	10,000	1,000	500	1.25 -6.25	2.5 -12.5	5 -25	10 -30
Wyoming	200,000	33,300	33,300	none	2	2	2	6

Notes: [1]All states listed also levy "pickup" taxes.
[2]An additional 30% surtax is also imposed. The exemptions shown must be shared by all beneficiaries in each class.
[3]All community property transferred to a spouse is exempt.
[4]In addition, the lesser of a $20,000 deduction or $1,200 credit is allowed.
[5]Totally exempt.
[6]Estates under $1,000 totally exempt.
[7]Estates under $7,500 totally exempt.
[8]In addition, one-half of the decedent's estate is exempt, or one-third if there are surviving lineal descendants.
[9]Shares under $500 are exempt; otherwise there is no exemption.
[10]Depends on unused part of spouse's exemption.
[11]An aggregate exemption of $70,000 is allowed. Spouses receive an additional credit of $51,600.
[12]A $2,000 family exemption is allowed.
[13]Exemption applies to an entire class.
[14]A spouse is allowed a deduction of $250,000 or one half of the estate.
[15]Only one-half of community property is taxable.
[16]$10,000 if no exemption for closer relatives claimed.

TABLE 21.4
STATE AND FEDERAL "EFFECTIVE" DEATH-TAX RATES, 1979

JURISDICTION	TAXES LESS FEDERAL CREDIT DIVIDED BY NET ESTATE[1] FOR GROSS ESTATE CLASSES[2]						AVERAGE TOTAL TAXES (GROSS OF FEDERAL CREDIT) OVER AVERAGE NET ESTATE (percent)	GINI COEFFICIENT FOR PROGRESSIVITY
	0-30,000,000 (percent)	0-60,000 (percent)	60,000-120,000 (percent)	120,000-300,000 (percent)	300,000-1,200,000 (percent)	1,200,000-30,000,000 (percent)		
U.S. Estate Tax	0.89	0.00	0.00	3.94	22.83	40.79	15.81	0.70
Federal Credit	0.04	0.00	0.00	0.19	1.10	4.11	0.95	0.75
California	0.77	0.37	2.31	2.99	3.74	5.55	3.94	0.37
Illinois	0.04	0.00	0.05	0.42	0.34	0.25	1.18	0.66
Indiana	0.34	0.21	0.92	1.24	0.86	0.11	1.76	0.38
Michigan	0.30	0.09	1.14	1.60	1.46	1.14	2.09	0.41
New York	0.07	0.00	0.00	0.68	1.38	1.52	1.67	0.64
Ohio	0.54	0.27	1.63	2.06	2.30	1.64	2.64	0.34
Pennsylvania	2.26	1.79	4.92	4.59	3.53	1.08	4.75	0.04
Wisconsin	0.61	0.21	2.10	3.21	3.15	1.44	3.18	0.30
Mean, All States	0.25	0.10	0.73	1.24	1.40	1.07	1.92	0.54

Notes: [1]Net estate here means gross estate less debts, administrative expenses, and charitable deductions.

[2]Based on raw data from Commerce Clearing House, Inheritance, Estate, and Gift Tax Reporter: States, Chicago, 1980.

$30,000,000 it is 1.07 percent. The corresponding federal rates are 0.00 percent, 0.00 percent, 3.94 percent, 27.83 percent, and 40.79 percent.

Table 21.4 shows that "effective" state death tax rates tend to be higher than federal rates for small estates, and that the reverse is true for large estates. In fact, the state rates are almost uniformly small. The seventh column shows the weighted average total death tax revenue (gross of federal credit) divided by the average estate size (net of debts, charity, and administrative expenses) in each case. Only for two states is the ratio higher than 4 percent.

In each column Michigan's entry is close to the mean value for all states. Michigan's numbers tend to be about 25 to 50 percent smaller than Minnesota's corresponding figures, substantially larger than Illinois', 25 percent or more smaller than Ohio's, 50 percent smaller than Wisconsin's, and roughly the same as Indiana's.

The Gini coefficients in the table's last column measure the progressivity of various death tax systems (gross of the federal credit).[25] A Gini of zero indicates a proportional tax; a higher Gini indicates that large estates pay higher taxes relative to their values than small estates. The figures confirm what the first six columns hinted: since state taxes tend to be relatively high for small estates, state rates tend to be less progressive than federal ones. Pennsylvania virtually has a proportional tax (although joint property is exempt for spouses), so its Gini is very low. Vermont's tax is 30 percent of the federal liability times a correction which approaches 1 for large estates and 0 for small estates, so its Gini is 0.74, which exceeds the federal figure. The federal credit is more progressive than the 1979 federal estate tax. The Gini for Michigan is equal to the average among the states.

Non-Taxable Property and Exemptions

Michigan is generous in its treatment of joint property, lifetime gifts, farm property, the estates of artists, and life insurance. We now examine each of these items individually.

The last section noted that joint property is not included in the tax base for Michigan's inheritance tax. With the possible exception of Wyoming, no other state is as generous in this regard. The federal estate tax law does not exempt joint property.[26]

Presumably the Michigan legislature's intent in allowing joint property to remain exempt is to aid the spouses of decedents. Otherwise horizontal equity would require the levying of death duties on any share of joint property which could be shown to have originated from a decedent. A more direct way of protecting surviving spouses, however, would be to tax a decedent's share of joint property fully, but to provide a substantial marital deduction (perhaps 100 percent). The federal estate tax, for example, allows a marital deduction equal to the greater of $250,000 or one half of the estate.[27] Over half of all states offer large marital deductions or generous treatment for joint (or community) property which is held only by a husband and wife.

Michigan is one of thirty-six states having no gift tax. Thus, any citizen can escape the state's inheritance tax by using <u>inter vivos</u> transfers two or more years before death. Again a problem of horizontal equity exists: if transfers of wealth via an estate are taxable, why should transfers two years before death to the same persons not be taxed?

Michigan allows a 50 percent exemption for "qualified" farm real property and a ten-year, interest-free tax deferral for the balance due. Such treatment is designed to make the perpetuation of the family farm possible. In fact it may impede free market forces that would otherwise tend to move land into its most profitable, and, hence, according to simple microeconomic theory, its most efficient, uses. At the very least, horizontal equity seems to require similar preferential treatment for other small businesses.

Furthermore, Michigan's exemption seems out of line with those of other states and the federal government. The federal estate tax, for example, allows "qualified" farm property to be assigned a value according to its use rather than according to the market (provided the difference falls short of $500,000). Taxes on the value-in-use can be deferred for five years, and then paid in ten annual installments. Interest must be paid over the entire period, although part of the estate is charged only four percent.[28]. The federal law grants symmetric concessions to closely held businesses as well. Among the states surrounding Michigan, Minnesota and Illinois allow farms to be valued as in the federal law, with no special exemption; and Indiana, Ohio and Wisconsin make no special provisions at all.

Michigan's inheritance tax now allows "artists" a ten-year, interest-free deferral. We can easily imagine the severe financial losses which might accrue to heirs who are forced to sell a large number of the paintings of a deceased artist on short notice to meet tax obligations. However, why should this special consideration be given only to artists? The federal estate tax law seems much more equitable in this regard: any estate can apply for up to ten one-year tax deferrals.[29] "Reasonable cause" must be demonstrated, and interest does accrue.

Michigan's inheritance tax exempts life insurance not left to the decedent's estate, provided the decedent had not retained both the right to change the beneficiary and the right to the policy's cash surrender value. This treatment is consistent with the absence of a gift tax. If a gift tax were instituted, the surrender of the incidents of ownership on an insurance policy could be taxed as an _inter vivos_ transfer.

DEATH TAX REVENUES

Although the figures of Table 21.4 would lead one to expect a rather average revenue performance for Michigan's inheritance and estate taxes, the actual outcome has been somewhat below the mean for other states. We now present a detailed interstate comparison of death-duty receipts. Then we examine time series data and the role (in terms of revenues) of the federal credit for state death taxes.

Comparisons of the States

Table 21.5 lists 1979 death and gift tax yields for various states. We can see that Michigan's death tax yield per capita was only $5.45. The mean for all states was $7.46, over 37 percent higher. Among neighboring states, Illinois, Minnesota, and Wisconsin enjoyed substantially higher per capita yields than Michigan; Indiana did moderately better; and, Ohio did worse. The average for the surrounding states was $9.00, about 65 percent above Michigan's figure. The latter percentage translates into a revenue loss for Michigan of about $32 million (for fiscal 1979).

Regression analysis. In order to analyze the connection between states' "effective" death-tax rates and revenues, we will now set up a simple regression model.

A state's death-tax revenues depend on the product of its average "effective" death-tax rate and the size of its death-tax base. The size of the base should depend on the state's population and average per capita income level. It might also depend on various other noneconomic and economic factors. The former might include the state's climate and crime rates; undoubtedly some retirees, for example, decide to abandon Michigan for Florida in order to escape harsh winters. Economic factors may also play a role. High state death taxes and high general state taxes may serve to encourage elderly people who are no longer employed to move elsewhere. On the other hand, low gift taxes may lower a state's death-tax base by making it advantageous for the elderly who do stay to distribute their wealth prior to death.

In our regression analysis of death and gift-tax revenues we tried violent and property crime rates, average

TABLE 21.5
STATE RECEIPTS FROM DEATH AND GIFT TAXES, 1979

STATE	DEATH TAX REVENUES ($1000)	GIFT TAX REVENUES ($1000)	DEATH AND GIFT TAXES PER CAPITA (dollars)	DEATH AND GIFT TAXES ($1000) PER $1000 OF PERSONAL INCOME (percent)	DEATH AND GIFT TAXES ($1000) PER $1000 OF TOTAL STATE TAX REVENUE (percent)
California	395,189	14,289	18.37	0.18	2.50
Illinois	136,809	--	12.16	0.12	2.16
Indiana	36,802	--	6.85	0.08	1.38
Michigan	50,079	--	5.45	0.06	0.83
New York	154,936[1]	--[1]	8.73	0.10	1.32
Ohio	42,850	--	3.97	0.04	0.93
Pennsylvania	172,827	--	14.71	0.17	2.55
Wisconsin	55,196	--[1]	11.79	0.14	1.69
Average all states	39,736	2,376[2]	7.46	0.09	1.36

Notes: [1]Gift and death tax revenues not shown separately.

[2]Average for all states having a gift tax and a gift-tax revenue figure available.

Source: U.S. Department of Commerce, Bureau of the Census, State Government Tax Collections in 1979, Washington, D.C. 1980.

yearly temperatures and temperature ranges, the percentage of sunny days per year, and tourist revenues per capita as explanatory variables. None proved to be statistically significant. Economic variables, on the other hand, did turn out to be very important. We estimated the following equation:

$$REV_i = \underset{(-2.6634)}{-9.3094} + \underset{(4.8522)}{2.2824} \times INC_i$$

$$\underset{(-3.9391)}{-0.0080983} \times OTAX_i + \underset{(4.0312)}{4.8450} \times DTAX_i$$

$$\underset{(3.2041)}{+125.24} \times GTAX_i, \qquad R^2 = 0.61$$

where i is the index of states, REV_i gives death and gift tax revenues per capita (in $1 units) for 1979, INC_i gives personal incomes per capita (in $1,000 units) in 1979, $OTAX_i$ gives 1979 state revenues per capita (in $1 units) for taxes other than gift and death taxes, $DTAX_i$ gives "effective" death tax rates as computed for the first column of Table 21.4, and $GTAX_i$ gives "effective" gift-tax rates calculated in an analogous fashion.[30] A t-statistic is given under each estimated coefficient.[31] The analysis used data for all states except Nevada. Letting $DREV_i$ give death-tax revenues per capita (in $1 units), and excluding states which in our data set do not report death and gift-tax receipts separately--New York, Oregon, South Carolina, Vermont, and Wisconsin--we have a second equation

$$DREV_i = \underset{(-2.1573)}{-8.3562} + \underset{(4.1593)}{2.1599} \times INC_i$$

$$\underset{(3.6702)}{-0.0079853} \times OTAX_i + \underset{(3.7066)}{4.7367} \times DTAX_i$$

$$\underset{(2.5965)}{+113.35} \times GTAX_i, \qquad R^2=0.58$$

For every explanatory variable except the "effective" gift-tax rate the two regression equations are virtually identical.

We would expect states with high per capita incomes to have large death-tax bases and, hence, high death and gift tax revenues. Our regression equations bear this out. We would also expect a high value of $OTAX_i$ to make a state unattractive to retirees--thus lowering its tax base. Again, this is borne out. A high "effective" death-tax rate should lead to high death-tax revenues for a given tax base. However, high death-tax rates should also discourage retirees from using the state as their "domicile," thereby lowering the tax base. Both equations show that the first of these effects predominates. Both imply that a one percent increase in Michigan's "effective" death-tax rate would increase the state's death-duty revenues by about 0.17 percent.

In the first equation, Michigan's residual, measuring the unexplained portion of the tax-revenue variable, is 54 percent as large as its REV_i figure, and the residual is negative. For the second equation, the residual is also negative, and it is 51 percent as large as $DREV_i$. Thus, variables we were not able to measure successfully, variables registering climate and crime, for example, might account for Michigan's below-average death-tax revenue performance.

On the other hand, the equations indicate that Michigan's generous treatment of joint property and <u>inter vivos</u> gifts also provide a possible partial explanation for its revenue results.[32] To see this, suppose we were to modify Michigan's laws in the following way: wealth transfers to spouses are made free of all taxes,[33] a decedents's joint property with people other than a spouse is made taxable in proportion to the decedent's original contribution to the joint interest, and a gift tax is imposed with an "effective" rate of 2.06 percent, the mean value of $GTAX_i$ among the sixteen states having gift taxes. (Notice that if joint property continued to be given a tax-free status, a gift tax could always be circumvented. Conversely, a change in the tax status of joint property could be circumvented with lifetime gifts under present laws. Then our second regression equation predicts a rise in Michigan's death-tax revenues of 28 percent. The first equation predicts that gift-tax revenues would contribute another three percent. The first (and larger) increase would be due to the expansion of the state's death-tax base as the current advantage to lifetime gifts and joint property disappeared. In 1979 the value of a 31 percent increase in wealth-transfer tax receipts would have been $15.5 million.

Revenue Histories

Table 21.6 presents time series evidence. During the interval 1957-79, total tax revenues in Michigan and in other states tended to grow faster than personal incomes. Death and gift tax revenues have not kept pace. This is not surprising since the overall trend among states has clearly been in the direction of lighter death and gift tax burdens. For example, in 1956 six states collected only pickup taxes, but by 1981 the number had risen to thirteen.[34] On the other hand, the death-tax revenue growth rate for Michigan (7.1 percent) is statistically significantly smaller than the rate for all states combined (8.2 percent). Had the growth rate in Michigan been 8.2 percent, death-tax revenues would have been about $12.5 million higher in 1979.

Federal gift and estate-tax revenues have also grown relatively slowly. The federal laws, however, underwent major revisions at the end of 1976. Among other changes, spouses received a 100 percent deduction for transfers under $250,000 and a "unified credit" (worth $38,000 in 1979) replaced the previous statutory exemption of $60,000. For the fiscal years 1957-77, the growth rate in federal gift and estate tax revenues was 8.0 percent.

The Federal Estate Tax Credit

As explained in the introduction of this chapter, the federal estate tax allows a credit for state death duties paid. It cannot exceed federal taxes due after the federal uniform credit has been exhausted. In the calculations for the seventh column of Table 21.4, the federal credit offsets

TABLE 21.6
TIME SERIES GROWTH RATES,
1957-1979

JURISDICTION	VARIABLE	GROWTH RATE
U.S.	Personal Income[1]	7.8%
U.S.	Total Tax Revenues[2]	6.8
U.S.	Death and Gift Tax Revenues[2]	7.3
All States	Total Tax Revenues[3]	10.3
All States	Death and Gift Tax Revenues[3]	8.2
Michigan	Personal Income[3]	7.8
Michigan	Total Tax Revenues[3]	9.7
Michigan	Death Tax Revenues[3]	7.1

Notes: [1]U.S. Department of Commerce, Statistical Abstract of the United States, Washington, D.C., various issues.

[2]U.S. Department of Commerce, Governmental Finances, Wahington, D.C., various issues

[3]U.S. Department of Commerce, State Government Finances, Washington, D.C., various issues.

about 46 percent of Michigan's inheritance tax. The state's pickup tax yields a modest 0.7 percent of the computed revenues.

Changes in gift and estate-tax laws now under consideration in the U.S. Congress would lower federal death taxes net of the uniform credit for most estates. Thus, the maximum credit allowed for state death duties paid would fall on average. This would tend to make the "effective" tax rates of the first six columns of Table 21.4 rise, except in states that have only pickup taxes. As a result, states in the latter category, such as Florida and Arizona, would become even more attractive as domiciles than at present. Michigan would presumably then experience some erosion in its death-tax base.

CONCLUSIONS

The following conclusions complete this chapter:

(1) In terms of promoting horizontal equity and equality, a unified gift and inheritance tax (or gift and estate tax) would be preferable to Michigan's current inheritance tax.

(2) The current favorable treatment of joint property is also inequitable, and it should be dropped. A marital deduction could serve as a partial replacement.

(3) The treatment of farm property in Michigan's inheritance tax law seems too generous in comparison to other states and the federal government. In the interests of horizontal equity, small businesses should be offered tax benefits analogous to those that farms receive. Similarly, in the interests of equity, the tax deferral available to artists should be extended more generally.

(4) Michigan's death-tax revenues are below average among the states. Our regression equations imply that instituting a gift tax might help significantly (assuming the present tax-free status of joint property

is changed). Michigan's current inheritance-tax rates are average.

(5) Reductions in the federal estate tax currently being considered, and the long-term trend of reductions in state death duties, may tend to erode Michigan's death tax base in the future. In the recent past Michigan's death-tax revenues have not grown as fast as the state's general tax receipts.

NOTES, CHAPTER 21

[1]The states taxing cumulative gift transfers are California, Colorado, Delaware, Louisiana, New York, North Carolina, Oklahoma, Oregon, Rhode Island, South Carolina, Vermont, and Washington. Tennessee and Wisconsin tax each year's gift transfers in a noncumulative fashion. See the Commercial Clearing House, Inheritance, Estate and Gift Tax Reporter: States (Chicago, Ill., 1980).

[2]State of California, Revenue and Taxation Code, Ch. 658, L. 1943, s. 15204; and, Ch. 403, L. 1957; s. 5.

[3]U.S. IRC, s. 2503(a). Exclusions of $3,000 per donee per year ($6,000 for married donors), however, are granted.

[4]State of California, Revenue and Taxation Code. Ch. 658, L. 1943, s. 13402; Ch. 1079, L. 1978, s. 3; and, Ch. 1388, L. 1978, s. 2.

[5]U.S. IRC, s. 2001 (b).

[6]U.S. IRC, s. 2010 (b) and (d).

[7]U.S. IRC, s. 2011 (b). The rates rise from 0.8 percent to 16 percent (for estates exceeding $10,040,000).

[8]U.S. IRC, s. 2011 (f).

[9]See also C.S. Shoup, Federal Estate and Gift Taxes (Washington, D.C., 1966); R.E. Wagner, Inheritance and the State (Washington, D.C., 1977); and J.E. Meade, Efficiency, Equality, and the Ownership of Property (Cambridge, Mass., 1965).

[10]Of course, any income originating from an inheritance or gift tax is subject to income taxes, although the principal is not.

[11]See J. Laitner, "Household Bequests, Perfect Expectations, and the National Distribution of Wealth," Econometrica (September 1978), pp. 1175-94.

[12]See, for example, page 186 of J.A. Pechman, Federal Tax Policy (New York, N.Y., 1971).

[13]Ibid., p. 208.

[14]State of Michigan P.A. 628, L. 1978, s. 1. (Note that this exemption is incorporated into the rate structure given in Table 21.1 below.)

[15]State of Michigan P.A. 628, L. 1978, s. 1.

[16]State of Michigan P.A. 628, L. 1978, s. 1.

[17]State of Michigan P.A. 474, L. 1980, s. 1.

[18]See Est. of H.L. Renz (1953), 338 Mich. 347, 61 N.W. 2d 148; Est. of James Hamilton (March 13, 1956), Circuit Court of Menominee County, Mich.; and, Leete v. Dept. of Rev. (Est. of C. B. Potter) (1958), 351 Mich. 356, 88 N.W. 2d 452.

[19]See the provisions for arbitration in the State of Michigan P.A. 173, L. 1956, s. 601-7. See also Schmoll v. Schenck (1907), 40 Ind. App. 581, 82 N.E. 805 and Est. of McCarthy (1963), 242 N.Y.S. 2d 82.

[20]See Est. of H.L. Renz (1953), 61 N.W. 2d 148 and Est. of S.A. DeWaters (1953), 61 N.W. 2d 779.

[21]See notes 12-14. "Qualified" farm property essentially means family-managed property which has been devoted to agriculture in five of the last eight years.

[22]For Michigan, we assumed that all property transferred to a spouse was joint property, but that all property passed to other beneficiaries was not joint.

[23]The latter division used fractions from Table 11 of U.S. Department of the Treasury, Statistics of Income 1976: Estate Tax Returns (Washington, D.C., 1979). In all cases we adjust dollar amounts for years other than 1979 by a factor reflecting changes in the nominal gross national product.

[24]The weights were derived from the distributions of large gross estates given in Table 1 of the Statistics of Income 1976: Estate Tax Returns, and of small estates given in Table III.9 of R.P. Strauss, Report of the Task Force on Personal Taxes to the Pennsylvania Tax Commission (Carnegie-Mellon University, 1980).

[25]The Gini coefficient was constructed as follows. Consider a diagram with percentage of average "adjusted" gross estate (i.e., gross estate less debts and administrative expenses and charity) accounted for by gross estates less than x arranged on the abscissa for increasing

values of x. On the ordinate, plot the percentage of average total state death duties paid by gross estates smaller than x. Find the area between the graph and a 45-degree line. Multiply the area by two (to express it as a proportion of the total possible area).

[26]See U.S. IRC, s. 2040 (a). Generally, all joint property is taxable other than such shares as can be proven to have been originally contributed by current beneficiaries. An exception is made for joint property held by a husband and wife, and created by a (taxable) gift--see U.S. IRC, s. 2040 (b).

[27]U.S. IRC, s. 2056 (a) - (d). Under the 1981 Revenue Act, the federal marital deduction will reach 100 percent over a number of years.

[28]U.S. IRC, s. 2032A (a) - (b), 6601 (j), and 6166 (a).

[29]U.S. IRC, s. 6161 (a).

[30]The calculations use Table 9 of U.S. Department of the Treasury, Statistics of Income 1965: Fiduciary, Gift and Estate Tax Returns (Washington, D.C., 1967), which gives information on donors' current and cumulative past *inter vivos* gifts (for donors who make positive transfers). The calculations also use information on individual state's laws from the Commerce Clearing House, *Inheritance, Estate and Gift Tax Reporter: States*, Chicago, 1980.

[31]A T-statistic gives an estimate of how significantly different from zero a coefficient is. See, for example, J. Johnston, *Econometric Methods* (New York, N.Y., 1960).

[32]Life insurance and farm property exemptions affect only relatively small parts of the death-tax base--see P. Courant's chapter on property taxes in this study and Table 18 of U.S. Department of the Treasury, *Statistics of Income 1976: Estate Tax Returns* (Washington, D.C., 1979).

[33]This is already implicit in our derivation of TAX_i--see note 22.

[34]During the 1970s, twenty-three states lowered their death duties, eighteen made no changes, and nine (including Michigan) made ambiguous changes--see Commerce Clearing House, *Inheritance, Estate and Gift Tax Reporter: States* (Chicago, 1980).

Chapter 22

The Single Business Tax

by

Robin Barlow and Jack S. Connell, Jr.

The University of Michigan

INTRODUCTION[1]

Along with the income tax and the sales tax, Michigan's single business tax (SBT) is one of the three main sources of tax revenue for the state. In FY 1982, SBT receipts are expected to reach about $1.1 billion, or about 15 percent of total state tax revenue.

The SBT is a type of value-added tax (VAT), the principle of which is that each firm is taxed on the value that it adds to the inputs purchased from other firms. Hence the base of the ideal VAT (before certain modifications that might be added) consists of the payments made by the firm to the factors which it employs--wages paid to labor, and profits, interest, and rent paid to the owners of capital (plus depreciation to reflect the using up of capital in the process of production, and also any direct taxes levied on the factor payments). These factor payments plus depreciation and taxes will be identically equal to the difference between the firm's sales receipts and its purchases from other firms. If the administration of a VAT calls for the summing of factor payments, the tax is said to be based on the "addition method"; if its administration calls for subtracting certain purchases from sales receipts, the "subtraction method" is being used. Michigan has tried both approaches.

The VAT is widely employed in the world today, currently being levied by the national governments of thirty-one countries, including all nine members of the European Economic Community. During the past fifteen years or so, there has been an active debate in the United States on whether the tax should be adopted by the federal government. The only American experience, however, in the actual administration of a VAT is that provided by Michigan. The present Michigan tax, it might be noted, has an ostensible purpose which is different from that behind most of the foreign VATs. Overseas, the VAT is normally seen as a broad-based tax on household consumption, and hence as an alternative to a sales tax. Michigan's SBT, as its name suggests, is viewed by its defenders as a charge levied on businesses for government services rendered, and hence as an alternative to other taxes levied on businesses as such, like the corporate income tax or the corporate net worth tax. For that reason Michigan is one of only six states which does not levy a corporate income tax.[2]

The history of value-added taxation in Michigan is outlined in the next section of this chapter. The structural details of the SBT are then described in a section which becomes mostly an account of special provisions representing departures from the ideal VAT mentioned above. We present estimates of the revenue costs of these provisions, which permit various exclusions, deductions and credits. It is also noted how the special provisions have led to major differences in effective tax rates between economic sectors, and how revenues have grown in relation to the Michigan economy as a whole. The VAT is then evaluated in comparison with the corporate income tax, which historically and in current political discussion is the main rival of the VAT in the Michigan setting. The criteria used for evaluating the two taxes are those of economic efficiency, equity in the distribution of personal income, economic growth, revenue stability and administrative costs. These same criteria are also used in evaluating the special provisions just noted. We then note how the SBT and certain other taxes in Michigan impose heavier burdens on business than those borne in some neighboring states, but lighter burdens than those borne in others. Some of the major differences between Michigan's VAT and the foreign versions of the tax are indicated. A final section offers a summary of findings and some suggestions for reform.

HISTORY OF VALUE-ADDED TAXATION IN MICHIGAN

Michigan has experimented with two separate versions of the VAT. The SBT, enacted in 1975, represents a return to the value-added concept, which had earlier been embodied in the business activities tax (BAT). The BAT was in force from 1953 to 1967. Indeed, for the last thirty years, business taxation policy in Michigan has been dominated by a contest between the VAT and the corporate income tax, with first one concept and then the other gaining ascendancy.

The enactment of the two VATs, in 1953 and 1975, was associated with fiscal crisis. In both years, the state budget had experienced recent major deficits, and the VAT was seen as a partial solution to the revenue shortage. In 1953 the major solution proposed by the Democratic administration, led by Governor G. Mennen Williams, called for the enactment of a personal income tax. The administration also felt that, for reasons of fairness, a tax on individual income should be accompanied by a tax on corporate income. This position was strongly supported by the labor movement in Michigan, which indeed over the years has taken a fairly consistent stand on matters of business taxation. It has favored the corporate income tax, in the belief that this tax is paid out of profits and does not burden the worker or consumer; it has often been critical of the VAT, arguing that the VAT is essentially a payroll tax (because most of value added typically consists of payroll), or that the VAT is shifted to consumers and hence is regressive.

But in the Michigan of 1953, the time was not ripe for income taxation, personal or corporate. Some of the major high-profit corporations in the state, recognizing that a new tax on business was inevitable, but wishing for obvious reasons that the new tax not be based on profits, proposed a tax with a different base altogether. Their proposal was accepted by the legislature, and was enacted as the BAT.

In principle, the BAT was an income-type VAT employing the subtraction method. (The base of an income-type VAT equals the sum of income payments paid to factors of production, and is to be distinguished from the base of a consumption-type VAT, which allows the subtraction of investment expenditures from the factor payments.[3]) The rate of taxation was initially 0.4 percent (0.1 percent for public utilities), and by the time of repeal in 1967 had risen to 0.75 percent (0.2 percent for public utilities). As a result of various exclusions, deductions, and credits, the BAT was far from being a pure version of the VAT. Anomalously, depreciation on real property was deductible from the tax base but depreciation on movable property was not. Hence the tax interfered in an unneutral fashion in a firm's choice between the two types of asset. A "gross receipts deduction" gave an advantage to firms, like those supplying professional services, with a high ratio of value added to gross receipts. A "labor intensity deduction" favored firms with a high ratio of payroll to gross receipts. Financial institutions and insurance companies were entirely exempt. Finally, the BAT was partially transformed into a profits tax through the introduction of a "net income credit," which gave relief to firms with a low ratio of profit to value added.[4]

By 1967 the pendulum had swung completely in favor of the profits tax. The administration in Lansing, this time headed by a Republican governor, George Romney, once again proposed the adoption of personal and corporate income taxes, mostly for reasons of equity. The proposal was adopted, and the BAT was repealed.

There was swift disillusionment, however, with the corporate income tax. Its revenues proved to be highly unstable, and in some years the state government incurred large deficits. In particular, the recession of 1970-71 in Michigan caused a catastrophic decline in corporate income tax receipts from $312 million in FY 1970 to $176 million in FY 1971. There was renewed interest in the VAT concept, which at least guaranteed some stability of revenue from one year to the next. To the concern for revenue stability was added the concern for stimulating the long-run expansion of the state's economy. The existing structure of business taxation was increasingly viewed as a deterrent to business expansion. First, the system included several highly complex taxes, which created heavy costs of administration and compliance. Second, the system imposed disproportionate burdens on capital and the return to capital, including as it did taxes on profits, net worth, and property, and therefore might have discouraged new investment in the state.

These concerns eventually led to a thorough overhaul of the system. In 1975 several business taxes were repealed, notably the corporate income tax, the corporate franchise tax (based on net worth), and local property taxes on business inventories. They were replaced by a new VAT, employing the addition method and labeled the SBT.[5] In order to stimulate investment the new VAT was of the consumption type, allowing businesses to reduce their tax base if they had undertaken new capital expenditures in Michigan. The rate of the SBT was set at 2.35 percent, with the object of achieving roughly the same aggregate revenue as had been yielded by the repealed taxes.

Although the replacement of the repealed taxes by the new VAT was not supposed to increase the burden of business taxation in the aggregate, it was clear that for many individual firms, the burden would increase substantially. In general there were two groups of firms which stood to pay higher taxes than before: unincorporated businesses (because the SBT applied both to them and to corporations, whereas the great bulk of the repealed taxes had been collected from corporations alone) and firms with a high ratio of value added to profits (or of payroll to profits, the two ratios being highly correlated). During the formulation of the 1975 legislation, firms in these threatened positions were able to secure the adoption of various special provisions which would reduce their tax liabilities. Thus unincorporated businesses, most of which were small, benefited from the adoption of a "statutory exemption," which materially reduced the tax base for small firms while leaving it essentially unchanged for large firms. The unincorporated businesses also managed to secure the insertion of an "unincorporated credit," which further reduced their tax liability by as much as 20 percent. Low-profit firms benefited from the sliding scales that were built into the statutory exemption and the unincorporated credit, and also from a "labor intensity reduction" similar to that allowed under the BAT. The labor intensity provision gave relief to firms with a high ratio of payroll to value added (or to profits).

Other concessions were tailored to the special characteristics of interest groups with significant political power. Professional firms and insurance companies won permanent concessions of this type, while temporary abatements (scheduled to expire in 1977) were given to companies in the fields of construction, transportation, rental housing, private security, building maintenance, and food retailing. The numerous concessions made to special interests were perhaps necessary for the assembly of the winning coalition which passed the 1975 legislation. This coalition cut across partisan lines to a remarkable degree. In the final vote on the SBT in the Michigan House of Representatives, thirty-seven Democrats supported the measure, but twenty-six were opposed. The Republicans were evenly divided, twenty-two for and twenty-two against.

As the SBT went into effect in 1976, firms that saw their business tax liabilities increased by the changeover continued to press for further concessions. Several of their demands were met by a series of amendments adopted in 1977. Small businesses won a liberalization of the statutory exemption; low-profit businesses won a liberalization of the labor intensity reduction; both groups benefited from the introduction of a new "small business/low profit credit"; agriculture was entirely exempted from taxation; and the sectors like construction which had been able to obtain temporary relief in the original legislation were given time extensions of their favored status.

Hence the SBT incorporates many departures from the ideal consumption-type VAT, mostly in the direction of providing relief to low-profit firms. Those interests which believe that business taxation should be based on the ability-to-pay principle continue to press for more relief of that sort. Like the BAT before it, the SBT has come to represent a compromise between the rival concepts of value-added taxation and profits taxation, and through successive amendments is likely to resemble a corporate profits tax more and more in the future.

STRUCTURAL DETAILS OF THE SBT

An ideal consumption-type VAT would require all organizations engaged in production to be taxed on their value added (minus capital expenditures). An account of the SBT's structural details is mainly an account of departures from this simple principle.

In the first place, some types of organizations are specifically exempted. These include federal, state, and local government agencies, nonprofit organizations, and farms. Next, companies need not file a return if their gross receipts are less than $40,000. This feature seems unobjectionable, since for companies of that small size, the costs of tax collection and compliance would typically outweigh the revenue yielded by a 2.35 percent VAT.

Taxable firms file a return which is shown in a simplified version in Table 22.1. As the table indicates, the process of determining tax liability starts (1) by specifying the various income payments which are components of value added (as measured by the addition method); then (2) companies operating in other states besides Michigan use an apportionment formula to determine what fraction of their total value added is subject to the SBT; then (3) several

TABLE 22.1
SIMPLIFIED TAX FORM FOR SINGLE BUSINESS TAX, 1981

	Compensation (Wages, salaries, fringe benefits)
	+Profits (before federal income taxes)
	+Interest Paid (less interest received)
	+Depreciation
equals	TAX BASE
	multiplied by Apportionment Percentage[1]
equals	APPORTIONED TAX BASE
minus	ADJUSTMENTS
	Capital Acquisition Deduction[2]
	Statutory Exemption[3]
	Adjustment for Transportation Companies[4]
equals	ADJUSTED TAX BASE
minus	REDUCTIONS[5]
	Compensation (or Labor Intensity) Reduction[6]
	Gross Receipts Reduction[7]
	Reductions for retail food stores, security guards, building maintenance firms, and rental investments[8]
multiplied by tax rate (2.35%)	
equals	TAX BEFORE CREDITS
minus	CREDITS
	Small Business/Low Profit Credit[9]
	Educational Contributions Credit[10]
	Public Utility Property Tax Credit[11]
	Unincorporated Credit[12]
equals	TAX[13]

[1] In most cases, a three-factor formula: the mean of (a) the percentage of the firm's property located in Michigan, (b) the percentage of its payroll located in Michigan, and (c) the percentage of its sales with Michigan destinations.

[2] Expenditures for the acquisition of depreciable real property located in Michigan plus apportioned expenditures for the acquisition of depreciable personal property minus adjusted receipts from property sales. The apportionment formula contains two factors (property and payroll).

[3] A disappearing exemption equal to (a) $40,000 plus (b) $12,000 for each partner or Subchapter S corporation shareholder (with a maximum of $48,000) minus (c) twice the amount by which net income (plus salaries paid to partners and owners) exceeds the sum of (a) and (b). Subchapter S corporations are small, closely held corporations electing to be taxed by the federal government as partnerships.

[4] Thirty percent of the Apportioned Tax Base. The adjustment is scheduled to decline to 20 percent in 1982 and to zero in 1983.

[5] No more than one of the listed reductions may be claimed on a tax return.

[6] A percentage of the Adjusted Tax Base equal to (a) compensation as a percentage of Tax Base before apportionment minus (b) 63 percent. The Compensation Reduction cannot exceed 37 percent of the Adjusted Tax Base, nor be less than zero.

[7] The amount by which the Adjusted Tax Base exceeds 50 percent of apportioned gross receipts. In most cases, a firm's gross receipts are apportioned by the three-factor formula (property, payroll, and sales).

[8] For retail food stores, (b) in footnote (6) is 50 percent; for security guards and building maintenance firms, it is 55 percent. For rental investments, the reduction equals the amount by which the Adjusted Tax Base exceeds 47 percent of apportioned gross receipts. The special relief for firms in these four categories is scheduled to expire by 1984.

[9] A disappearing credit for firms with net income under $60,000. For such firms with gross receipts under $2 million, the fraction of the tax which may be claimed as a credit is equal to 1-((BI)/(.45)(TB)), where BI is business income and TB is the Tax Base before apportionment. The credited fraction cannot exceed 0.5. As gross receipts rise from $2 million to $3 million, the credited fraction falls to zero in linear fashion.

[10] For contributions to Michigan colleges, universities, and public libraries, corporations may claim a credit equal to the smallest of (a) half of the contribution, (b) 5 percent of SBT liability after deduction of the Small Business/Low Profit Credit, and (c) $5,000.

[11] Certain public utilities may credit 5 percent of their property taxes against their SBT liability.

[12] Unincorporated businesses (and Subchapter S corporations) may claim a credit of 20 percent of their SBT liability (after deduction of all other credits) if net income is under $20,000, a credit of 15 percent if net income is between $20,000 and $40,000, and a credit of 10 percent if net income is over $40,000.

[13] The tax is paid in quarterly estimated installments, plus a final payment after the close of the firm's fiscal year.

adjustments and reductions are allowed against the apportioned tax base; and finally, (4) the tax calculated as 2.35 percent of the adjusted and reduced base is diminished by various credits. These four steps are now discussed in turn.

Components of the Tax Base

Value added as reported on the SBT return differs from the base of an ideal VAT (all payments to labor and capital, plus depreciation and direct taxes) in two main respects:

1) Rent paid does not have to be reported, even though such payments for the use of capital are clearly a part of value added. The correct treatment of rent under an income-type VAT would require the inclusion of rent paid (as a component of value added) and the subtraction of rent received (which contributes to the profit figure already reported on the return but which does not represent value added by the firm in question).[6] The treatment of rent paid and received would then be the same as the actual treatment of interest paid and received under the SBT.[7] The SBT's treatment of rent apparently arises in part from a desire to treat equally those firms which prefer to lease their physical capital and those which prefer to purchase it outright. A firm purchasing some equipment would qualify for a capital acquisition deduction under the VAT, and to that extent would reduce its tax liability. But a firm leasing equipment would not enjoy a tax reduction if the lease payments had to be included in the SBT base. The reduction in its profits (due to its extra rental cost) would be offset by the inclusion of the lease payments. Hence the treatment of rent under the SBT could be viewed as a necessary feature of a consumption-type VAT, which is designed to encourage the use of physical capital.

2) Insurance companies headquartered in Michigan can

TABLE 22.2
COMPONENTS OF SINGLE BUSINESS TAX BASE, 1977-78

	PERCENTAGE OF SBT BASE	
	FIRMS WITH MICHIGAN ACTIVITIES ONLY	FIRMS WITH MULTI-STATE ACTIVITIES
COMPENSATION		
Wages and salaries	57.7	59.2
Payroll taxes	4.0	3.8
Employee insurance contributions	3.6	4.1
Pensions and profit-sharing contributions	2.6	4.4
Other (net)	(0.1)	0.1
NET INCOME (before federal income taxes)	14.3	17.5
Plus state and local income taxes	1.4	1.1
INTEREST PAID	6.2	4.7
Less interest and dividends received	(1.6)	(6.5)
DEPRECIATION	9.2	10.0
OTHER ADDITIONS & SUBTRACTIONS (net)	2.7	1.6
Total	100.0	100.0
In millions of dollars		
Total tax base	$24,582	$331,108
Tax base apportioned to Michigan	24,582	29,665

Source: Michigan Department of Treasury, "SBT Annual Return Analysis" (January, 1981 Printout).

exclude part of their labor compensation payments from the base of the SBT (commissions on sales of insurance policies plus salaries of employees concerned with the adjustment of claims).[8] This provision continues the favored status which these companies had enjoyed under BAT.

Two other exclusions permitted in the early years of the SBT have since been terminated. These provided partial subtraction of depreciation on assets acquired before January 1, 1976, and of wages paid under construction contracts bid before September 1, 1975. All told, the tax base now reported by taxable firms is a fairly complete accounting of their value added. The relative importance of the different components of the base is shown in Table 22.2. About 70 percent of the tax base consists of outlays for the use of labor while about 30 percent consists of outlays for the use of capital.

The Apportionment Formula

Firms doing business in other states as well as Michigan multiply their total value added by an apportionment factor to determine what fraction of their value added will be subject to the SBT. Following the practice used for earlier business taxes in Michigan, including the BAT, the corporate income tax and the corporate net worth tax, the apportionment factor is derived from a standard three-factor formula based on the location of payroll, property and sales. The rationale of the three-factor formula is discussed below in a later section. As Table 22.2 indicates, its effect in 1977-78 was to treat 9.0 percent of the total value added of multi-state firms as taxable under the SBT.

Adjustments and Reductions

The apportioned tax base can then be decreased by claiming certain adjustments and reductions. Four of these are of particular importance in the aggregate, and three of them were inherited from the BAT:

1) The capital acquisition deduction is the one important innovation since the BAT. A firm may deduct all of its expenditures for the acquisition of depreciable real property located in Michigan; it may also deduct a fraction of its expenditures for depreciable personal property, the fraction being determined by the percentages of the firm's payroll and property that are located in Michigan. The capital acquisition deduction essentially converts the SBT from an income-type VAT to a consumption-type VAT, with the purpose of stimulating business investment in Michigan.

2) The statutory exemption provides a basic maximum deduction of $40,000, which starts to diminish as net income passes $40,000, and reaches zero as net income passes $60,000. (More complete details about this and other provisions are given in the notes to Table 22.1.) Hence only small or relatively unprofitable firms gain any benefit from this feature of the SBT.

3) The labor intensity reduction allows a firm to deduct what is called "excess compensation," defined roughly as labor costs in excess of 63 percent of value added. The provision obviously benefits labor-intensive firms, and also has the effect of aiding relatively unprofitable firms. (The lower are profits, the higher are labor costs in relation to value added.)

4) The gross receipts reduction in effect limits the SBT base to 50 percent of gross receipts. The provision is of major benefit to firms with a high ratio of value added to gross receipts, like those providing legal, medical, dental, accounting, and other professional services.

An economic evaluation of these four important deductions is provided in a later section. In addition, the SBT allows several other adjustments and reductions, all of which,

TABLE 22.3
EROSION OF THE SINGLE BUSINESS TAX BASE, 1977-78
(IN MILLION OF DOLLARS)

	Personal income in Michigan		$75,758[1]
times	U.S. ratio between gross national product at factor cost and personal income		1.130[1]
equals	Estimate of base of income-type value added tax in Michigan		85,630
minus	Estimate of capital expenditure in Michigan		13,696[2]
equals	BASE OF CONSUMPTION-TYPE VALUE ADDED IN MICHIGAN		71,934
minus	EXCLUSIONS		22,562
	Compensation paid by government agencies	8,116[3]	
	Compensation paid by nonprofit organizations	2,234[3]	
	Agricultural earnings	675[1]	
	Part of compensation paid by domestic insurers	506[3]	
	Part of compensation paid by contruction cos.	426[3] [4]	
	Other	10,605[5]	
equals	VALUE ADDED REPORTED ON SBT RETURNS (AFTER CAPITAL ACQUISITION DEDUCTION)		49,372
minus	DEDUCTIONS[3]		9,670
	Statutory Exemptions	2,932[6]	
	Labor Intensity Reduction	4,813	
	Gross Receipts Reduction	1,280	
	Reduction for retail food stores	350[4]	
	Reduction for rental housing	84[4]	
	Reduction for security guards and building maintenance	83[4]	
	Adjustment for transportation companies	128[4]	
equals	TAXABLE VALUE ADDED		39,702
multiplied by tax rate (2.35%)			
equals	TAX BEFORE CREDITS		933
minus	CREDITS[3]		34
	Small Business/Low Profit Credit	23	
	Unincorporated Credit	6	
	Public Utility Property Tax Credit	4	
	Educational Contributions Credit	1	
equals	SINGLE BUSINESS TAX REVENUE		899

[1]Source: U.S. Department of Commerce, Survey of Current Business.

[2]Capital Acquisition Deductions reported on SBT returns totalled $9.4 billion (State of Michigan, 1982 Executive Budget: Tax Expenditure Appendix), or 19.04 percent of value added reported on SBT returns (after Capital Acquisition Deductions). The same ratio is assumed to apply between total capital expenditures in Michigan and the base of a consumption-type VAT in Michigan.

[3]Source: ibid.

[4]Temporary tax relief scheduled for termination in or before 1983.

[5]A residual comprising value added of firms with gross receipts under $40,000 (not required to file), rent payments, interest paid by financial organizations, apportionment formula deficiencies, and evasion.

[6]Excluding unused Statutory Exemptions (excess of Statutory Exemption over Apportioned Tax Base after Capital Acquisition Deductions).

however, are scheduled to expire at the end of 1983 or earlier, and are in any case of less quantitative significance in the aggregate. They give special relief to firms in the fields of transportation, food retailing, private security, building maintenance and rental housing.

Credits

After subtracting adjustments and reductions from the tax base, the taxpayer makes an initial calculation of tax liability by applying the tax rate of 2.35 percent. Against this liability, certain credits are then allowed. Typically the largest is the small business/low profit credit, which is calculated according to a complex formula providing relief (inversely related to net income) to firms with gross receipts under $3,000,000 and net income under $60,000. Unincorporated firms are given an additional credit also inversely related to net income. A provision carried over from the repealed corporate income tax allows small credits for contributions to educational institutions in Michigan. Certain public utilities can credit against the SBT part of the property taxes that they pay to the state.

REVENUES

Revenue Cost of Tax Base Erosion

As a result of the exclusions, deductions and credits, the base of the SBT has been eroded to a size much less than the base of a pure VAT. The erosion implies that much revenue is being lost, or alternatively that the same revenue could be obtained by applying a rate significantly under 2.35 percent to an uneroded base. As shown in Table 22.3, the base of a pure consumption-type VAT in Michigan in 1977-78 would have been about $72 billion. Exclusions and deductions allowed under the SBT reduced this base by 45 percent, to a level of $40 billion. The tax liability computed as 2.35 percent of this reduced base was further lowered by the four types of tax credit permitted. As a result, the net revenue yielded by the SBT ($899 million) was only 53 percent of the revenue that would have been yielded by a 2.35 percent pure consumption-type VAT with no exclusions, deductions, or credits. Alternatively, the revenue actually yielded by the SBT could also have been generated by a pure VAT levied at a rate of only 1.25 percent.

Variations in Effective Tax Rate

The erosion of the tax base also implies that there are major differences between sectors in the effective rate of taxation (the net SBT liability divided by the base of a pure consumption-type VAT). For one reason or another, some sectors are able to claim much larger exclusions, deductions and credits (in relation to their value added) than is the case for other sectors. Differences in effective tax rates mean that the state is in essence encouraging resources to move into the favored low-tax sectors, and this reallocation of resources many not always necessarily be in the social interest. The differences in effective rates may also have undesirable effects on the distribution of personal income.

As noted earlier, the governmental, nonprofit, and agricultural sectors are entirely exempted from the SBT, and have an effective tax rate of zero. The taxable sectors were subjected in 1977-78 to the varying effective tax rates shown in Table 22.4. The effective rates ranged all the way from 0.39 percent in the case of other transportation to 3.34 percent in the case of real estate, etc.[9]

Table 22.4 also provides most of the explanation for the differences in effective tax rates by showing the relative importance of the major deductions and credits in each sector. The statutory exemption and the small business/low profit credit materially reduced effective tax rates in sectors containing large numbers of small firms: forestry and fisheries, local transportation, eating and drinking places, real estate, etc., hotels and other lodging, personal services and repair services. The labor intensity reduction was of major benefit to the sectors of construction, ordinance manufacturing, manufacturing of furniture and fixtures, instruments manufacturing, general

TABLE 22.4
EFFECTIVE RATE OF THE SBT BY SECTOR, 1977-78

	Effective tax rate[1] (percent)	As percent of consumption-type value added			Small Business/ Low Profit Credit as percent of SBT before credits
		Statutory Exemption[2]	Gross Receipts Reduction	Labor Intensity Reduction	
ALL TAXABLE SECTORS	1.93	5.30	2.83	8.68	2.50
FORESTRY & FISHERIES	1.43	30.38	7.74	5.26	10.08
MINING					
Metal & Coal	-1.01	-0.47	0.00	-6.41	0.98
Crude Petroleum & Natural Gas	2.50	3.93	7.59	1.77	2.07
Nonmetallic Minerals	1.53	5.94	2.17	7.56	9.19
CONSTRUCTION	1.49	13.44	3.97	16.74	8.97
MANUFACTURING					
Ordinance	1.55	6.04	4.24	20.58	3.54
Food & Kindred Products	2 24	0.58	0.11	6.93	3.98
Tobacco	2.32	0.00	0.00	0.45	0.00
Textile Mill Products & Apparel	1.87	3.51	3.67	13.51	4.37
Lumber & Wood Products	1.84	5.60	1.35	9.46	4.48
Furniture & Fixtures	1.71	1.88	0.37	22.71	3.37
Paper & Allied Products	2.17	0.57	0.16	12.69	0.84
Printing, Publishing, Allied Industries	1.89	4.32	6.53	9.65	6.44
Chemicals & Allied Products	2.23	0.38	4.15	6.71	0.33
Petroleum Refining & Related Industries	2.31	0.32	0.44	2.32	0.27
Rubber & Misc. Plastic Products	1.58	0.68	0.19	11.03	1.82
Leather & Leather Products	1.90	0.51	0.00	18.09	0.62
Stone, Clay & Glass Products	2.05	10.05	1.04	8.31	1.60
Primary Metal Industries	1.94	0.34	0.61	14.75	0.81
Fabricated Metal Products	1.92	1.35	1.88	13.20	2.65
Machinery, except Electrical	2.06	1.00	3.11	----	0.99
Electrical Machinery, Equipment, Supplies	2.30	0.57	7.09	7.72	0.74
Transportation Equipment	2.11	0.06	0.07	10.23	0.04
Instruments	1.82	0.97	4.90	15.40	1.01
Miscellaneous	1.96	2.08	2.92	12.35	2.86

TRANSPORTATION					
Railroad	0.89	0.15	2.66	0.12	0.10
Local	0.94	16.46	1.43	4.47	16.12
Motor Freight & Warehousing	0.88	2.07	1.58	2.02	9.32
Other	0.39	1.22	0.80	0.96	2.44
COMMUNICATIONS	----	----	----	----	0.36
OTHER UTILITIES	2.68	0.82	0.04	1.35	0.39
WHOLESALING	1.94	3.46	0.47	10.15	2.12
RETAILING					
Building Materials, Hardware, Farm Equipment	1.82	7.15	1.11	12.48	5.08
General Merchandise	1.33	3.32	1.87	31.22	1.83
Food	1.37	8.44	0.08	6.18	2.86
Auto Dealers & Gas Stations	1.64	12.13	0.60	12.83	4.59
Apparel & Accessories	1.84	9.74	0.99	12.48	3.59
Furniture & Home Equipment	1.65	13.82	0.58	13.77	6.82
Eating & Drinking Places	1.57	22.14	0.41	12.52	11.81
Miscellaneous	1.76	10.51	3.41	10.14	4.49
FINANCE, INSURANCE & REAL ESTATE					
Banking & Credit	2.20	0.54	0.54	3.71	0.47
Insurance Carriers	2.05	12.82	13.30	16.72	1.09
Real Estate, Insurance, Loans, & Investment Offices	3.34	59.05	24.84	10.05	10.25
SERVICES					
Hotels & Other Lodging	2.21	25.62	4.25	12.59	13.93
Personal	1.47	25.04	4.01	11.60	12.05
Business	1.76	10.22	10.21	9.23	4.78
Repair	1.62	27.66	4.24	10.95	11.42
Motion Pictures, Amusement, Recreation	1.89	15.66	4.66	8.16	9.68
Professional	1.64	9.46	18.38	9.39	3.50

[1]SBT liability after credits divided by base of consumption-type VAT (aggregate Apportioned Tax Base minus aggregate Capital Acquisition Deductions).

[2]Including unused Statutory Exemptions (excess of Statutory Exemption over Apportioned Tax Base after Capital Acquisition Deductions).

Sources: Michigan Department of Treasury, "SBT Annual Return Analysis" (January 1981 Printout).

FIGURE 22.1

SECTORAL SBT RATES AND AVERAGE FIRM SIZE, 1977-78

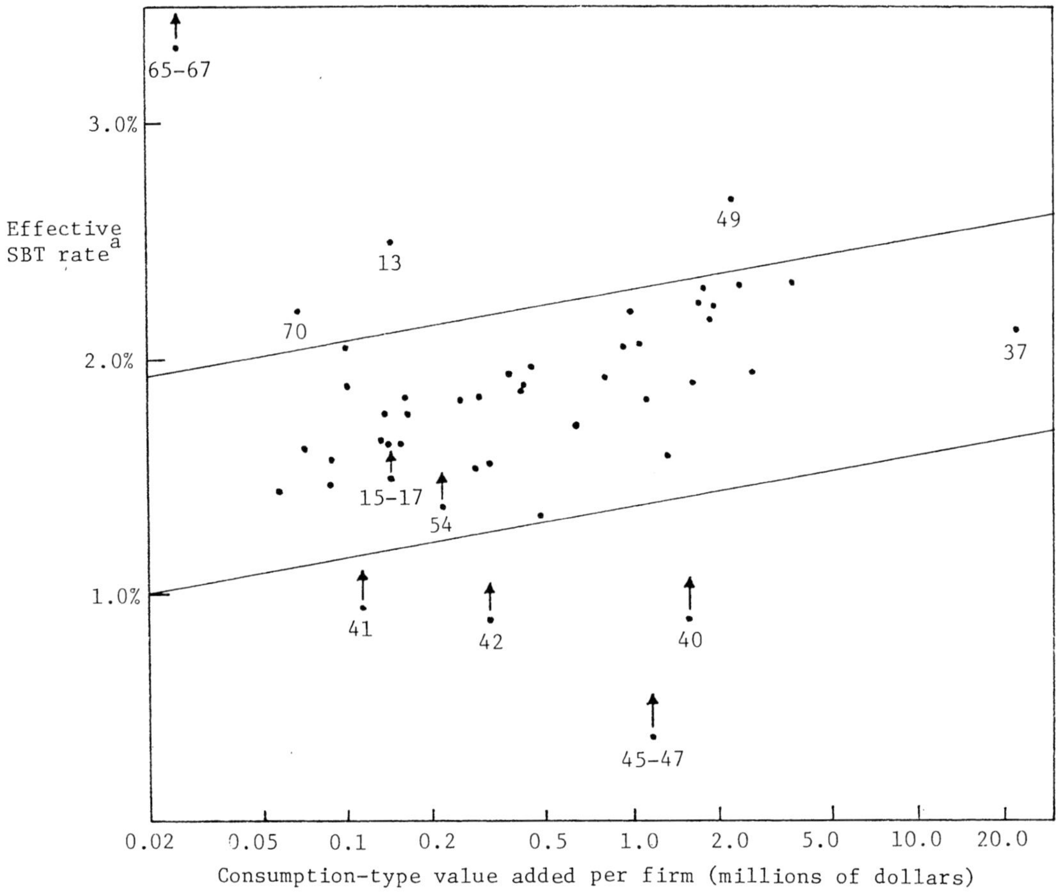

---

[a]For each sector, aggregate SBT liability (after credits) divided by aggregate consumption-type value added (aggregate Apportioned Tax Base minus aggregate Capital Acquisition Deductions, used and unused).

↑ = The sector's effective tax rate probably rises after 1977-78 due to scheduled termination of special tax relief.

Standard Industrial Classification Code	
13	Crude Petroleum & Natural Gas Mining
15 - 17	Construction
37	Transportation Equipment
40	Railroad Transportation
41	Local Transportation
42	Motor Freight Transportation & Warehousing
45 - 47	Other Transportation
49	Other Utilities
54	Food Retailing
65 - 67	Real Estate, Insurance, Loan, & Investment Office
70	Hotels & Other Lodging

Source: Michigan Department of Treasury, "SBT Annual Return Analysis" (January 1981 Printout)

merchandise retailing, and insurance carriers. The insurance carriers also benefited greatly from the gross receipts reduction, which in addition significantly lowered tax liabilities for firms in real estate, etc., miscellaneous business services, and professional services. Certain sectors also benefited from provisions giving temporary tax relief which was important in 1977-78 but which is now being phased out. This relief, lowering the effective tax rate but not reflected in the other columns of Table 22.4, principally aided the sectors of construction, transportation (all four subsectors listed), food retailing, and real estate, etc.

The variation in effective tax rates across sectors is shown graphically in Figure 22.1. This diagram also shows how the effective tax rate tends to increase as the size of the firm increases. Such a relationship is the natural result of the special provisions favoring small firms: the statutory exemption, the small business/low profit credit, and the unincorporated credit. The bias in favor of small firms is one reason, although certainly not a major one, explaining the fact that such firms, while numerically predominant, generate only a moderate fraction of total SBT revenues. In 1977-78, firms with value added in Michigan of less than $1 million accounted for 96 percent of the 148,324 SBT returns filed, but provided only 29 percent of total revenue.[10]

The central band in Figure 22.1, indicating the generally positive relationship between effective tax rate and firm size, covers the great majority of the sectors in the Michigan economy. The outlying cases can be explained by special factors. The four sectors with effective tax rates significantly lower than would be expected on the basis of average firm size were all in the field of transportation. In 1977-78 firms in this field were allowed a special deduction of 70 percent of their value added. The four sectors with effective rates significantly higher than expected all had large capital expenditures relative to value added. In those sectors, several firms had unused capital acquisition deductions (their capital acquisition deductions exceeding their apportioned tax base), and hence the denominator of the sector's effective tax rate (aggregate apportioned tax base minus aggregate capital acquisition deductions, used and unused) tended to be small relative to the numerator (aggregate SBT payments). Thus in the case of real estate, etc. we have the paradox of a sector in which many firms pay no tax at all (because their capital acquisition deductions exceed their apportioned tax base), where most of the others pay at a low effective rate (because they benefit from the features favoring small business or from the temporary relief given to rental housing enterprises), but where the sector as a whole is taxed at a high effective rate. The paradox is resolved when we understand that under a pure consumption-type VAT, the firms with capital acquisition deductions exceeding the apportioned tax base would pay a <u>negative</u> tax rather than zero tax, i.e., they would receive subsidy payments. The effective tax rate in the sector as a whole would then fall to a level reflecting the sector's special advantages.

A proposal to permit subsidies under the SBT when capital acquisition deductions exceed the apportioned tax base would be widely regarded as eccentric, but there is no doubt that such subsidies would be in the spirit of a consumption-type VAT and would act as a further stimulus to investment. The subsidies, however, would not be in the spirit of a tax imposing charges for government services rendered to business. So it must be conceded that there is an element of inconsistency in using a consumption-type VAT as a service charge.

<u>Revenue Growth</u>

Table 22.5 shows the growth of SBT revenues since FY 1977, the first year when the tax was fully applied. For the first three years, tax collections remained about the same percentage of personal income in the state, but this percentage then fell significantly in FY 1980. It is

TABLE 22.5
SBT REVENUES AND MICHIGAN PERSONAL INCOME, 1977-82

FISCAL YEAR ENDING SEPTEMBER 30	In millions of dollars		SBT REVENUE AS A PERCENT OF PERSONAL INCOME
	SBT REVENUE[1]	PERSONAL INCOME[2]	
1977	818.2	67,625	1.21%
1978	899.4	75,758	1.19
1979	1,001.3	85,001	1.18
1980	919.0[3]	88,944	1.03
1981	930.0 (est.)	-----	----
1982	1,075.0 (est.)	-----	----

[1]Source: State of Michigan, Budget Message of the Governor.

[2]Source: U.S. Department of Commerce, Survey of Current Business.

[3]Revenues reported for FY 1980 were $1,076 million. This sum included $157 million paid in October and November 1980 but owed for fiscal years ending in the twelve months before October 1980. By the cash accounting method used for FY 1979 and earlier, these payments would have been attributed to FY 1981, but the state changed to an accrual method in 1980 and assigned them instead to FY 1980. The payments must therefore be deducted from the reported revenues of FY 1980 in order to obtain a correct impression of the annual growth of revenues.

TABLE 22.6
SECTORAL ORIGIN OF SBT REVENUES, 1977-80

	PERCENTAGE DISTRIBUTION			
	1977	1978	1979	1980(est.)
Forestry & Fisheries	0.2	0.1	0.1	0.2
Mining	0.4	0.4	0.5	0.4
Construction	2.4	2.9	3.5	4.2
Manufacturing:				
primary metal industries	3.7	4.3	4.1	3.4
fabricated metal products	3.1	3.6	3.9	3.9
machinery except electrical	4.6	4.9	5.7	6.2
transportation equipment	32.0	29.0	23.4	16.7
other durable goods	6.5	7.0	7.2	7.1
nondurable goods	8.0	8.5	8.8	10.1
Transportation	1.0	1.1	1.3	1.5
Communications and Utilities	4.8	3.7	4.0	4.8
Wholesaling	3.2	3.5	3.9	4.4
Retailing	17.6	17.2	18.7	20.2
Finance, Insurance & Real Estate	3.9	4.3	4.5	4.1
Services and Others	8.6	9.5	10.5	12.9
	100.0	100.0	100.1	100.1

Data are from returns for firms' fiscal years ending in calendar year shown.

Source: State of Michigan, Budget Message of the Governor, Fiscal Years 1980, 1981, and 1982.

difficult to conclude very much about the income-elasticity of the tax from these data. During the years in question, some features of the tax base were being phased in, while others were being phased out. It does seem likely, however, that the fall in revenues in FY 1980 (both absolutely and in relation to personal income) reflects the operation of the ability-to-pay elements of the tax (like the labor intensity reduction) in conditions of business recession.

During the first few years of the SBT, there were some major shifts in the relative contributions of different sectors to total tax revenue. The details are shown in Table 22.6. Of particular note is the dramatic decline in the contribution made by "manufacturing of transportation equipment," as the automobile industry faced increasing difficulties caused by foreign imports and a nationwide recession. Even in 1980, however, the manufacturing sector as a whole still provided about half of the total SBT revenue. The rising contribution made by some other sectors, especially construction and transportation, can be explained in part by the phasing out of the tax relief which they were initially granted under the SBT.

THE VAT VERSUS THE PROFITS TAX

We now turn to an economic evaluation of the VAT in Michigan. A tax should not be evaluated in isolation, but in comparison with realistic alternatives. In the case of the VAT, the only important political alternative in Michigan seems to be the corporate income tax. On the political assumption, therefore, that some kind of major state tax on business as such will be levied, and that the choice is restricted to the VAT and the corporate income tax, we now compare the two taxes. The VAT being considered in this section is a pure version of the consumption type. We have already noted that the SBT is actually an impure VAT, containing elements of a profits tax. Hence the contrast between the profits tax and the SBT would be less stark than that between the profits tax and the VAT. The criteria for evaluating the rival taxes are those of efficiency, equity, growth, revenue stability and administrative costs.

Economic Efficiency

An economically efficient system is one which allocates the resources of land, labor and capital so as to maximize consumer satisfaction: this means using least-cost methods to produce goods which consumers want. Freely functioning markets normally yield efficient results. It follows that taxes should interfere as little as possible with the resource allocation decisions made by business firms, except where the market yields clearly inefficient results (as in the case of pollution problems). There are several areas where either the VAT or the profits tax or both are held to interfere undesirably in allocation decisions.

First, the point is made that while the VAT is a neutral tax on the use of both capital and labor, the profits tax imposes special penalties on the use of capital (the return to which essentially forms the base of the profits tax). Hence the profits tax interferes with allocation decisions by encouraging firms to substitute labor for capital, and to this extent is inferior to the more neutral VAT. However, this argument is only relevant for an income-type VAT. A consumption-type VAT like the SBT clearly introduces a bias favoring capital-intensive methods, by allowing deductions for capital expenditures. Whether the pro-capital bias of the consumption-type VAT leads to worse inefficiency than the anti-capital bias of the profits tax is an unanswerable question in the present state of empirical knowledge.

Second, it is argued that the VAT is superior to the profits tax when viewed as a charge imposed on businesses for their use of government services. Valued added, it is alleged, is more closely related to a firm's use of government services than are profits; support for this view is provided by the case of a large firm with zero profits, which would pay no profits tax even while obviously using many government services. The argument here appears to be an allocative one: the business tax, be it VAT or the profits tax, is viewed as a price being charged for certain services, and resource allocation decisions will be improved if firms are obliged to pay proper prices for the inputs which they use. The problem with this argument is that neither of the two taxes reflects actual use of government services, either at the margin or in the aggregate. At the margin, a firm's tax liability (either under VAT or under the profits tax) does not directly increase if it uses more government services, and hence it has no incentive to economize in the use of those services. In the aggregate, neither in Michigan nor elsewhere have the revenues of a general tax on business ever been designed to cover the costs of the specific services provided by government to business, because no one has ever defined those services or measured them. The SBT rate of 2.35 percent was set, not in order to cover costs of services provided to business, but in order to yield the same amount of revenue as the taxes which it replaced. They in turn had been levied at rates which had never been set on the principle of recovering the costs of relevant government services. In general, the recovery of those costs would be much better achieved by user charges than by taxation.

Third, the VAT is applied to both the incorporated and unincorporated sectors, while the profits tax is traditionally applied only to the former. Allocatively, the profits tax therefore involves a bias favoring small firms, which are able to switch without major cost from the corporate to the unincorporated form and back again depending on the tax situation. Large firms by contrast must normally remain incorporated. In this area, then, the choice between the VAT and the profits tax rests on the policy decision of whether the state should use the tax system to divert resources towards small firms.

Fourth, the pursuit of least-cost methods of production is likely to be less ardent under the profits tax than under the VAT. Under the profits tax, the hiring of an unproductive employee reduces after-tax profits by less than the amount of the employee's salary. Under the VAT, after-tax profits are reduced by more than the amount of the salary. Hence the hiring is more likely to take place under the former regime than under the latter.

Fifth, relatively unprofitable or losing firms are more lightly treated and survive longer under the profits tax than under the VAT. Allocatively, the profits tax therefore diverts resources towards firms many of which are technically inefficient, uncompetitive or unresponsive to changing market conditions. The VAT by contrast tends to hasten the demise of unprofitable firms, whose resources can then be transferred to enterprises able to make better use of them.

Equity

In this discussion, an equitable tax is defined as one which is progressive, or more precisely, one which leaves the distribution of real after-tax income among Michigan residents more equal than before. Being a tax on the return to capital, a profits tax imposed in an open economy like that of Michigan has the long-run effect of causing some capital to migrate out of the state.[11] With less capital invested in Michigan, there is a reduced demand for both labor and land in the state. Wages received by labor and rent received by landowners are both reduced. Some of the Michigan labor migrates to other states rather than accept the lower wages. Output falls in most sectors of the Michigan economy, and the curtailment of local supplies causes the prices of some goods and services to rise.[12] Hence, the groups which suffer significant reductions in real income as a result of the profits tax in Michigan are as follows:

1) Immobile labor remaining in Michigan receives lower wages.[13] Broadly speaking, this element of the tax is regressive, wage income as a fraction of total household income tending to fall as total household

income increases.

2) Michigan landowners receive lower rents. This element of the tax is probably progressive.

3) The owners of immobile capital remaining in Michigan receive a lower after-tax return.[14] This element is also probably progressive.

4) Consumers of some goods and services in Michigan must pay higher prices. This element is probably regressive.

The combined incidence of the profits tax depends upon the degree of progressivity and regressivity of these four elements of the tax, and upon the relative importance of the relevant types of income and consumption. An elaborate empirical study would be required to arrive at a quantitative estimate of the combined incidence in Michigan.

The qualitative analysis of the VAT's incidence proceeds along similar lines. Since most of the VAT base consists of payroll and profits, the VAT can be analyzed as a combination of a payroll tax and a profits tax. The long-run incidence of a profits tax in an open economy has just been discussed. As for a payroll tax in Michigan, it causes employers to reduce their demand for labor. Wages fall, some labor migrates out of the state, and the remaining workers bear part of the burden of the tax. The reduction in the Michigan labor force lowers the productivity of capital in the state, some of which therefore eventually leaves the state in search of higher returns elsewhere, and the capital remaining must accept a lower return than before the payroll tax was imposed. The decline in business activity and population in Michigan lowers the demand for land, and landowners must accept lower rents. Reductions in Michigan's output of goods and services cause some prices to rise. Hence the groups burdened by the payroll tax are the same as those burdened by the profits tax: immobile labor, landowners, the owners of immobile capital, and consumers. Doubtless the combined incidence of the payroll tax differs from that of the profits tax, but it is impossible to say whether the difference is in the progressive or regressive direction. The size and direction of the difference depend on the elasticities of supply and demand in the relevant markets, which can presently only be guessed at. Hence there is no solid basis for distinguishing between the VAT and the profits tax on equity grounds.

Economic Growth

The stimulation of economic growth is an important criterion for judging taxes in Michigan, in view of the widespread public desire to escape from the prolonged economic stagnation which the state has experienced. Economic growth in the sense of rising per capita output depends on the rate of capital investment achieved in an economy. In its effects on investment, a consumption-type VAT is superior to a profits tax on two counts. First, the tax rate applied to profits (and hence to the return generated by investment) is much lower under a VAT than under an equal-yield profits tax. This is because profits form only a relatively small part of the base of the VAT. As indicated in Table 22.2, a profits tax in Michigan would have to be levied at a rate about six times that of a VAT in order to generate the same amount of revenue. Second, the consumption-type VAT permits full deduction of investment outlays in the year when they occur, while the profits tax requires that the deduction be spread over several years into the future, as determined by the permissible depreciation schedules.[15] Although the theoretical superiority of the VAT in the area of stimulating growth seems clear enough, its superiority in practice must remain in some doubt until empirical studies of the issue are conducted.

Revenue Stability

The revenues yielded by a VAT are more stable than those of a profits tax over the course of the business cycle.[16] A tax whose revenues do not fall sharply in recession years brings an important advantage to a budgeting

TABLE 22.7
DATA FOR A HYPOTHETICAL MULTI-STATE FIRM
(in thousands of dollars)

LINE	TOTAL (1)	LOCATED IN MICHIGAN (2)	LOCATED IN OTHER STATES (3)	PERCENT LOCATED IN MICHIGAN (4)
1 Payments for labor	2,000	1,500	500	75
2 Payments for capital (profit, interest, and depreciation)[1]	1,000	500	500	50
3 Value added	3,000	2,000	1,000	67
4 Purchases from other firms	1,000	---	---	--
5 Sales	4,000	1,000	3,000	25
Property:				
6 Value at beginning of year	9,400	4,500	4,900	48
7 Acquired during year	1,200	1,000	200	83
8 Realty	200	0	200	0
9 Tangible personalty	1,000	1,000	0	100
10 Value at end of year	10,600	5,500	5,100	52
11 Average value during year	10,000	5,000	5,000	50

[1]Distributed between Michigan and other states in proportion to average property value (line 11).

TABLE 22.8
SELECTED TAXES ON BUSINESS IN MICHIGAN AND OTHER STATES, 1978
(as a percentage of personal income)

	MICH	CAL	ILL	IND	NY	OHIO	PENN	WIS
STATE TAXES:								
Corporate income	---	1.05	0.38	0.46	0.92	0.55	0.87	0.80
Value added	1.14	---	---	---	---	---	---	---
Corporate net worth	---	---	0.03	---	---	0.10	0.27	0.01
Severance	0.01	0.02	---	---	---	---	---	---
Insurance premiums	0.13	0.20	0.09	0.12	0.14	0.13	0.15	0.11
Utility receipts	---	0.01	0.39	---	0.29	0.35	0.34	0.19
Unemployment comp.	0.89	0.80	0.74	0.43	0.70	0.66	0.73	0.80
LOCAL TAXES:								
Business property	1.42	1.61	1.64	1.30	2.34	1.08	0.88	1.39
TOTAL	3.59	3.69	3.27	2.31	4.39	2.87	3.24	3.30

Sources: U.S. Department of Commerce, Statistical Abstract of the United States; Tax Foundation, Inc., Facts and Figures on Government Finance.

situation where government expenditures tend to rise automatically (with welfare programs expanding even faster during recessions), where increases in the rates of taxation are politically difficult to achieve, and where there are legal restrictions on indebtedness.

Administrative Costs

Regarding the costs of tax collection and compliance, the profits tax is superior to the VAT, because being restricted to corporations, it involves a much smaller number of taxpaying units. As for the information required on the returns, neither tax imposes very heavy burdens on the taxpayer when levied by a state government, since virtually all information in question has already been assembled for federal income tax purposes. The actual collection costs for the SBT in 1977-78 were $3.8 million, or 0.4 percent of total SBT revenue.[17] This seems a small sum to pay, but in the absence of reliable evidence about the extent of tax evasion under the SBT, there is no way of knowing how costly a program of rigorous enforcement, preventing significant evasion, would be.

In sum, our evaluation of the VAT and the profits tax suggests that the VAT is superior according to the criteria of economic growth and revenue stability, and also probably according to the efficiency criterion, that the profits tax is superior according to the criterion of administrative costs, and that as regards equity, there is no basis for preferring one tax to the other in the present state of knowledge. On balance, the evaluation therefore seems to favor the VAT.

ANALYSIS OF SPECIAL PROVISIONS

Exclusions

The exemption of government agencies, nonprofit organizations and farms from the SBT is readily explained. The government agencies are protected by the legal principle of intergovernmental immunity from taxation. The nonprofit organizations are given the same kind of tax-exempt status under the SBT that they had enjoyed under the Michigan corporate income tax. Farms are exempted because of widespread feeling that farming is excessively burdened by local property taxation. It must be pointed out, however, that if the rationale of the SBT is to impose a charge for certain services rendered by the state government to organizations as such (as distinct from individuals as such), then none of these exemptions can be justified. Federal, state, and local government agencies, nonprofit organizations and farms all make use of the services in question, and all have measurable value added. The removal of their present exemptions is not at all likely in the current political setting, but should not be dismissed as irrational. (If the exemptions were actually removed, a renaming of the SBT would be called for, since the tax would no longer apply solely to business. It could be called the organization tax, or OT.)

The Apportionment Formula

The standard three-factor formula used for determining what fraction of a multi-state firm's value added should be taxable under the SBT is a cumbersome method of arriving at the wrong answer. Since value added consists of payments to labor and to capital, whose location in both cases is relatively unambiguous, there is no reason why value added in Michigan should not be measured directly. Instead, the apportionment formula measures it indirectly and incorrectly: first, by giving equal weight to the labor and capital aspects of a firm's activities, when in fact those inputs are often very unequal, some firms being highly labor-intensive and others highly capital-intensive; second, by giving weight to sales, which do not measure the employment of a factor of production, and hence are not a component of value added.

The difference between the direct method of measuring value added in Michigan and the indirect method required by the apportionment formula is illustrated in Table 22.7. A hypothetical firm makes total payments of $3,000,000 to the factors of production which it employs. Of this total amount of value added, $1,000,000 represents payments for the use of capital. Since 50 percent of the firm's capital is located in Michigan, 50 percent of the total payments to capital can reasonably be construed as value added by the use of capital located in Michigan. To this must be added payments made to labor located in Michigan ($1,500,000). Hence value added in Michigan is 67 percent of the firm's total value added (column 4, line 3). But the three-factor formula apportions only 50 percent of total value added to Michigan. This figure is the unweighted mean of the payroll, sales and property shares, or 75 percent, 25 percent and 50 percent respectively (column 4, Lines 1, 5, and 11). In this example, the apportionment formula reduces the firm's SBT payments below what they would be if value added were measured directly.

All of the information needed for the direct measurement of value added in the state is already reported on the SBT return, and so no additional costs of administration would be incurred if the direct method were used instead of the three-factor formula. In fact, costs should be lower, because firms would not be required to report the location of sales.

It should be noted that the sales factor, although perhaps irrelevant for determining the true location of value added, does have some economic effects when incorporated into an apportionment formula. Its presence in the Michigan formula, which defines the location of a sale in terms of its destination, has the effect of encouraging Michigan firms to export their products out-of-state. It is reasonable to ask whether this kind of export promotion is a sensible objective, and if so, whether the objective is best promoted through manipulating apportionment formulas or through some other means.

The Capital Acquisition Deduction

The deduction for new capital expenditures is not

properly regarded as a form of erosion of the SBT base, but as a necessary feature of a consumption-type VAT, one of the main purposes of which is the stimulation of investment. The stimulus takes the form of a *de facto* cut in the price of capital acquisitions. The deductibility of the acquisitions has the effect of reducing their price by the rate of the SBT, or 2.35 percent. This reduction is eventually modified in the case of corporations, however, by the application of the federal corporate income tax. With lower SBT payments, taxable profits are higher. Given the typical marginal federal rate of 46 percent, the capital acquisition deduction therefore implies a net reduction in capital goods prices of only 1.27 percent (2.35 percent times the complement of 46 percent). In combination with a high rate federal tax on profits, a low-rate state tax on value added cannot achieve a very powerful stimulus to investment.

The stimulus is further weakened in Michigan by the special apportionment formula applied to acquisitions of tangible personalty (movable property like vehicles, tools, office equipment, etc.) by multi-state firms. While acquisitions of buildings in Michigan can be fully deducted under the SBT, acquisitions of tangible personalty used by the firm in Michigan in most cases are not fully deductible. This is because deductible acquisitions of tangible property are determined by applying a two-factor formula (based on payroll and property) to the firm's total acquisitions of tangible property (worldwide), the property factor being based on the location of the firm's *total* property, both realty and tangible personalty (not on the location of the property acquired during the year).

The consequences of these roundabout methods are illustrated in Table 22.7. The firm has total capital expenditures of $200,000 on realty and $1,000,000 on tangible personalty. Since the realty expenditures all occur outside Michigan, none of them are deductible under the SBT. The personalty expenditures all occur inside

Michigan, but nevertheless cannot be fully deducted. The fraction which is deductible is given by the mean of the payroll factor (column 4, line 1) and the property factor (column 4, line 11), or 62 percent. In the case of multi-state firms, both of these factors are less than 100 percent, which means that these firms can never fully deduct additional expenditures on Michigan personalty. At the same time, perversely from the standpoint of stimulating Michigan development, the two-factor formula allows such firms to obtain additional deductions under the SBT when they acquire personalty outside Michigan. If the growth of the Michigan economy is a serious objective, it would seem better to measure the capital acquisition deduction directly (column 2, line 7). This means treating tangible personalty expenditures in the same way that realty expenditures are already treated.

The Statutory Exemption

A tax which for administrative reasons excludes very small units (firms with less than $40,000 of gross receipts in the case of the SBT) must allow some kind of exemption. Otherwise a "notch problem" will be created, confronting firms with large increases in tax liabilities as their gross receipts (in the case of the SBT) move past the filing minimum. The statutory exemption allowed by the SBT goes beyond this requirement by incorporating an ability-to-pay element. The exemption starts to diminish as profits rise above a certain level (between $40,000 and $88,000, depending on the type of ownership), and eventually disappears altogether when profits pass a second, higher level (between $60,000 and $132,000).

Hence the statutory exemption is one of several SBT features which lead high-profit firms to pay more tax than do low-profit firms with the same value added. The operation of the exemption can be illustrated with a numerical example which we can also use when discussing the other ability-to-pay features of the SBT. Suppose that there are two unincorporated businesses, each owned by two partners, and with the same value added comprised as follows:

	Firm W	Firm L
Profit	$80,000	0
Interest and depreciation	40,000	60,000
Payroll	180,000	240,000
Value added	$300,000	$300,000

The formula for the statutory exemption, described in Table 22.1, assigns a deduction of $32,000 to the profitable firm, but $64,000 to the unprofitable firm, which on that account ends up paying less tax.

The rationale for this graduated feature of the statutory exemption is the same as one often advanced in support of the profits tax and against the VAT: taxation ought to be based on the ability to pay, and unprofitable firms have less ability to pay. But serious questions can be raised about the appropriateness of the ability-to-pay concept in the case of business enterprises. The concept makes sense in the case of individuals, because it is generally agreed, as a matter of anti-poverty policy, that low-income individuals should pay a smaller proportion of their income in taxes than is required of high-income individuals. But it is not at all obvious that the state should similarly subsidize low-income enterprises. Doing so is not necessarily in accordance with individual ability-to-pay, since the owners of low-income enterprises do not necessarily have lower individual incomes than the owners of high-income enterprises. If they do, then they will be appropriately treated under an individual income tax, which Michigan already possesses.

Hence the ability-to-pay features found in the statutory exemption and some of the other special provisions of the SBT do not guarantee an equitable treatment of individual taxpayers. At the same time, they entail all of the disadvantages of profits taxation noted in the preceding section: the diversion of resources from efficient enterprises to the inefficient, the encouragement of wasteful expenditures, the deterrence to capital expansion, the sharp decline of tax revenues during recession, and so forth.

We conclude that the statutory exemption ought to be a fixed sum related to a filing minimum chosen for administrative reasons. The disappearing or ability-to-pay feature should be removed. So should the extra exemptions for business partners, since there is no good reason for the tax structure to favor unincorporated businesses as such, or within the unincorporated sector, to encourage the fragmentation of ownership.

The Labor Intensity Reduction

The special relief given to firms with a high ratio of payroll to value added, enabling them to deduct what is called "excess compensation," has two undesirable consequences. There is a strong case for the removal of this feature of the SBT. First, as between firms with the same value added, the labor intensity reduction will generally be greater for the firm with the lower profits. A further ability-to-pay element is introduced into the SBT, with the generally undesirable consequences noted above in connection with the statutory exemption. This effect of the labor intensity reduction is illustrated by the numerical example just presented. The formula for the reduction (see Table 22.1 again for the details) gives a deduction of $40,120 to Firm L, the unprofitable firm, while the profitable Firm W in view of its low ratio of payroll to value added receives no deduction at all. So as a result of the labor intensity reduction and the statutory exemption, Firm L's SBT liability before credits is $4,603, while Firm W's is $6,298.

A second regrettable consequence of the labor intensity reduction is that, by favoring the use of labor-intensive rather than capital-intensive methods of production, it effectively weakens the stimulus to investment in Michigan intended by the capital acquisition deduction. The undertaking of investment will increase the relative importance of nonlabor components of value added (profits, interest and depreciation) in future years. A firm engaging in investment will therefore find that its labor intensity reduction in future years will tend to decline, and its SBT liability will be thereby raised. In effect, the adding of the labor intensity reduction to the capital acquisition deduction moves the SBT some distance away from a consumption-type VAT and towards an income-type VAT. If the state really desires an income-type VAT, it would be better to use neither of these deductions. But it should be recognized that an income-type VAT is weaker than a consumption-type VAT in stimulating economic growth.

The Gross Receipts Reduction

Politically speaking, the gross receipts reduction responded to the demands of certain powerful interests, particularly small professional firms, for tax relief based on some apparently objective criterion. The provision, limiting the SBT base to 50 percent of gross receipts, does not belong in a pure VAT, and should be questioned. One of its effects, as Brazer has pointed out, is to insert into the SBT "the major defect of the turnover taxes that several European countries sought to avoid by adoption of the tax on value added."[18] The turnover tax, or tax on gross receipts, gives an unjustifiable advantage to an integrated firm competing with a group of unintegrated firms in the production and sale of a given final product. The integrated firms pays the turnover tax only once, at the point of the final sale, while in the unintegrated process the tax is paid at several intermediate stages, and cumulates to a larger total by the time the final sale is reached. The integrated firm is also given an unfair advantage by the gross receipts reduction under the SBT. Such a firm tends to have a relatively high ratio of value added to gross receipts, and hence qualifies for a relatively large gross receipts reduction.

The Small Business/Low Profit Credit

The small business/low profit credit brings yet another ability-to-pay element into the SBT, and is therefore of doubtful merit. In our numerical example, this credit would be worth $2,302 to Firm L, the unprofitable firm, but nothing to Firm W.

The Unincorporated Credit

Still another dubious ability-to-pay element is introduced by the unincorporated credit. This tax relief is biased in favor of small businesses, as is the case with two of the other ability-to-pay provisions, the statutory exemption and the small business/low profit credit. (By contrast, the labor intensity reduction is often claimed by very large firms.) The unincorporated credit reduces Firm L's tax by a further 20 percent in our example, while Firm W's tax is reduced by only 10 percent. As a result of the two credits plus the statutory exemption and the labor intensity reduction, the unprofitable firm pays a tax of only $1,841. The profitable firm although generating the same value added, pays a tax of $5,668, more than three times as much.

Other Provisions

Other special provisions of the SBT, which are inconsistent with the concept of a pure VAT, may be mentioned very briefly. The exclusion of part of the labor compensation paid by domestic insurance companies is difficult to justify. The credits for educational contributions and for property taxes paid by public utilities are of doubtful merit, but do not cause a large revenue loss. The special relief still existing in 1981 for firms in the fields of transportation, food retailing, private security, building maintenance, and rental housing is scheduled to be phased out over the next two years. Whatever may have been the transitional problems faced by these firms when the profits tax was replaced by the SBT, there should be no permanent place for *ad hoc* relief of that type in a general tax on business.

EFFECTS OF THE SBT ON BUSINESS LOCATION DECISIONS

Much of the discussion of the SBT in Michigan has centered on the issue of whether the tax adds unduly to the burdens borne by business in the state and causes new enterprises to be located elsewhere. The burden of the SBT and other business taxes in Michigan, relative to the size of the state's economy as measured by personal income, is shown in Table 22.8. This table also compares the burden in Michigan with those in other states which often compete with Michigan for business. It should be noted that there is some ambiguity about the concept of a "business tax." Some taxes commonly regarded as imposed on individuals, and hence excluded from Table 22.8, might nonetheless often be relevant for business decisions. For example, the top rates levied by a state individual income tax will be of interest to corporate executives contemplating the location of a new plant in the state in question. And the retail sales tax, while normally viewed as a tax on consumers, is also paid by business firms. Nonetheless, the taxes listed in Table 22.8 are generally the ones at issue in discussions about business location decisions.

We observe, first, that the SBT in Michigan imposes a burden roughly equivalent to the combined burden of profits and net worth taxes in four of the seven competing states. In the other three states (Illinois, Indiana, and Ohio), the combined burden of profits and net worth taxes is much lower than that of Michigan's SBT. Second, in six of the states under review (all except Ohio and Pennsylvania), local property taxes constitute 40 percent or more of the aggregate tax burden on business. Third, looking at the total burden of all state and local taxes on business, we note that the burden in Michigan is clearly higher than that in Indiana or Ohio, about the same as that in California, Illinois, Pennsylvania, or Wisconsin, and clearly lower than that in New York.

Whether tax differentials of the size shown in Table 22.8 have a significant influence on business location is a question which could only be answered if extensive new empirical studies were undertaken. As indicated by Wilbur Thompson in another chapter of this volume, however, there are good reasons for being skeptical about whether the differentials can have much impact.[19] For example, higher taxes on business are likely to be associated with a higher quality of public services in the state, which by itself would tend to attract rather than repel business. Furthermore, the effect which the differentials shown in Table 22.8 have on after-tax profits is approximately halved in most businesses by the existence of the federal corporation income tax.

THE VAT IN OTHER COUNTRIES

Although the VAT has not been employed in the United States outside Michigan, it should be recognized that the tax is widely used in other countries, and that studies of the SBT could profit from an examination of the similar taxes levied overseas. A comparison between the foreign versions of the VAT and the Michigan version reveals a number of important differences. First, as noted earlier, the foreign VAT is normally viewed as a tax on consumers rather than as a service charge on business enterprises. Given the principle of a consumption tax, it is a natural step to introduce modifications so that necessities will be taxed less heavily and luxuries more heavily. So in an attempt to achieve some progressivity, most of the foreign VATs are applied at multiple rates. Whatever may be the contribution of a multiple-rate structure towards an equitable redistribution of income (a contribution which must remain in some doubt owing to the uncertainties of tax shifting), it seems clear that such structures add substantially to the administrative costs of the tax.

Of course the SBT also taxes different commodities at different effective rates, as is made clear in Table 22.4.

This result, however, is achieved not by an explicit structure of multiple rates but by a system of exclusions, deductions and credits which benefits different sectors in an uneven and capricious way.

Second, the rates of the VATs levied by national governments overseas are typically much higher than that of the SBT. Most of the foreign VATs are major sources of finance for public budgets which in relation to the rest of the economy are much larger than the budget of the State of Michigan. Tax rates exceeding 10 percent are common. A rate of 40 percent has been levied in a multiple-rate structure by the government of Peru.[20]

Third, on the administrative side, most of the foreign VATs are collected by the "invoice method," a variant of the subtraction method. Under the invoice method, a firm applies the VAT rate to its sales, showing on its sales invoices the amount of tax collected. In filing its periodic VAT return, the firm then remits to the government these tax collections _minus_ a credit for the taxes which it paid on its own purchases and which are evidenced by the invoices prepared by its suppliers. The invoice method is relatively simple, and gives the tax an element of self-enforcement. It would not work well in Michigan, because it would require that all out-of-state firms shipping supplies to Michigan firms pay the SBT and file periodic returns in Lansing. The tasks of administering and enforcing the tax would become much more difficult. This problem does not arise with a national VAT because a national VAT can be integrated into an already existing system of customs duties. The government can tax imports at the same rate as is applied to sales by domestic firms. The domestic firms then claim credits for the import taxes they have paid, as evidenced on invoices, when they file their VAT returns.

SUMMARY OF FINDINGS AND RECOMMENDATIONS

Findings

1) At the state level, a consumption-type value-added

tax is probably superior on balance to a tax on corporate profits. The criteria used in comparing the two taxes were those of economic efficiency, equity, growth, revenue stability and administrative cost.

2) The SBT approximates a consumption-type value-added tax, but differs from it by allowing several important exclusions, adjustments, reductions and credits. These forms of erosion of the tax base cause major differences in effective rates between economic sectors. The erosion has generally harmful effects on efficiency, growth, and revenue stability.

3) The revenues generated by the SBT remained steady at about 1.2 percent of personal income in normal business years, but fell significantly to 1.0 percent in the recession year of 1980.

4) It is not likely that the SBT has placed Michigan at a general disadvantage in competing with other states for new business.

Recommendations

Our study suggests that the following policy recommendations should be given serious consideration:

1) The SBT should not be replaced by a corporate profits tax.

2) In view of our conclusion that the VAT is superior to the profits tax, the elements in the SBT reflecting the principle of profits taxation or "ability-to-pay" should be abolished. These elements include the labor intensity reduction, the small business/low profit credit, the unincorporated credit, and the disappearing feature of the statutory exemption.

3) The statutory exemption should not permit additional deductions for business partners.

4) The gross receipts reduction discriminates against nonintegrated firms, and should be abolished.

5) Value added by government agencies, nonprofit organizations, and farms should be included in the SBT base. So should the presently excluded compensation paid by domestic insurers.

6) Value added in Michigan by multi-state firms should be measured directly rather than by the three-factor apportionment formula.

7) For purposes of the capital acquisition deduction, expenditures on depreciable personalty located in Michigan should be measured directly rather than by the two-factor apportionment formula.

8) The special privileges given to firms in the fields of transportation, food retailing, private security, building maintenance and rental housing should be allowed to expire on schedule.

Besides promoting efficiency, growth, and revenue stability, these recommendations would greatly simplify the SBT. The data in Table 22.3 suggest that their adoption would permit the tax rate to be lowered from 2.35 percent to about 1.5 percent, without any loss of aggregate revenue.

NOTES, CHAPTER 22

[1]For invaluable assistance, the authors are indebted to Robert J. Kleine and Richard W. Willitts of the Office of Revenue and Tax Analysis, Department of Management and Budget, Lansing. Their assistance does not necessarily imply agreement with the statements contained in this chapter.

[2]The others are Nevada, South Dakota, Texas, Washington and Wyoming.

[3]For a discussion of alternative bases for the VAT in terms of national accounting definitions, see Harvey E. Brazer, "Michigan's Single Business Tax--Theory and Background," Proceedings of the Sixty-Ninth Annual Conference on Taxation, 1976 (National Tax Association - Tax Institute of America), pp. 62-69.

[4]For analyses of the BAT, see Richard W. Lindholm, "The Business Activities Tax," in Harvey E. Brazer (ed.), _Michigan Tax Study Staff Papers_ (Lansing: House of Representatives, 1958), pp. 259-75, and James A. Papke, "Michigan's Value-Added Tax After Seven Years," _National Tax Journal_ 13 (December 1960), pp. 350-63.

[5]To compensate local governments for their loss of inventory tax receipts, part of the SBT revenue is earmarked for distribution to municipalities and counties. Another part is earmarked by the State Revenue Sharing Act for cities, villages, and townships. Under these two formulas, 15 percent of the total SBT revenue was distributed to localities in FY 1979.

[6]But in the case of rental equipment companies and rental housing companies, rent received is obtained from the sale of the firm's product, and therefore should not be subtracted from the tax base.

[7]Except in the case of financial institutions, where the SBT requires neither the inclusion of interest paid nor the exclusion of interest received. The theory behind this provision, which seems defensible enough, is that since the principal productive activity of financial institutions consists of obtaining money from one group and lending it out to another, the interest received from the second group is akin to "sales receipts" and interest paid to the first group is akin to "cost of goods sold." Hence for such an institution, value added is measured by interest received minus interest paid. This amount will be equal (roughly) to the sum of profit, wages, and depreciation reported by the institution, and this latter sum therefore does not need to be adjusted for interest paid and interest received in order to yield a measure of value added.

[8]Out-of-state insurance companies continue to pay Michigan's insurance premiums tax, and are excluded from the SBT.

[9]This range ignores the case of metal and coal mining, which was characterized by negative consumption-type value added (aggregate capital acquisition deductions exceeding the aggregate apportioned tax base), and whose effective tax rate was therefore formally negative. At the other extreme, a sectoral effective tax rate exceeding the nominal rate of 2.35 percent is possible if the sector as a whole has a positive consumption-type value added, but if many individual firms in the sector have unused capital acquisition deductions (exceeding their apportioned tax base). The high effective tax rate in real estate, etc. reflects this situation. The sector's aggregate capital acquisition deductions (used and unused) amounted to 69 percent of its aggregate apportioned tax base in 1977-78.

The phenomenon of a sectoral effective tax rate exceeding 2.35 percent can perhaps be clarified by a numerical example. Suppose that a sector consists of two firms, A and B, each with an apportioned tax base of $1,000,000, with capital acquisition deductions of $200,000 and $1,200,000 respectively, and with no other deductions. Firm A will pay a tax of $18,800 (2.35 percent of $800,000), Firm B will pay no tax, and the sector as a whole will be taxed at an effective rate of 3.13 percent ($18,800 divided by the difference between the aggregate apportioned tax base of $2,000,000 and the aggregate capital acquisition deductions of $1,400,000).

[10]Source: Michigan Department of Commerce. The value added figure is before subtraction of the capital acquisition deduction.

[11]Note that the capital migration occurring in the long run does not mean a physical exodus of buildings and equipment, but rather that as old capital located in Michigan wears out, new capital will tend to be placed outside the state. Our analysis of the incidence of the profits tax and the VAT assumes that the spending of the tax revenues has no effect on business location decisions. The conclusions reached about the difference between the two taxes in their effects on the distribution of income are not changed if some other assumption is made about the expenditure effects.

[12]In general, prices rise in those markets dominated by goods or services produced in Michigan, and remain unchanged in those markets dominated by goods imported from other states.

[13]This result rests on the assumption that the quantity of labor supplied in Michigan is an increasing function of Michigan wage rates (relative to wage rates elsewhere).

[14]This result rests on the assumption that the capital supplied to Michigan is an increasing function of the after-tax rate of return in Michigan (relative to returns elsewhere). A more common assumption in modern analyses of tax incidence is that of a perfectly elastic supply of capital to Michigan (at the nationally prevailing after-tax rate of return), in which case the Michigan profits tax imposes no significant long-run burden on the owners of capital located in Michigan. But it seems more likely that after the imposition of a Michigan tax, some owners of Michigan capital will accept a lower return rather than move their capital out of the state. This kind of behavior could be explained by inertia, loyalty, or fear of the unfamiliar.

[15]Suppose that a corporation is considering an investment of $1,000,000 which would yield annual gross profits (before depreciation) of $300,000 over a five-year life. Under a 2.35 percent consumption-type VAT, the present value of the additional taxes over the five-year period would be only $5,891 (using a 10 percent discount

rate). Under a profits tax levied at a 14.10 percent rate (six times the VAT rate) and requiring straight-line depreciation, the present value of the additional taxes would be $58,153, about ten times as much.

[16]For a comparison of the revenue stability of a profits tax and a hypothetical VAT in Michigan in 1969-74, see Robert J. Kleine, The Michigan Single Business Tax: A Different Approach to State Business Taxation (Washington, D.C.: Advisory Commission on Intergovernmental Relations, 1978), p. 21.

[17]Michigan Department of Treasury, Report of the Treasurer for the Period October 1, 1977 to September 30, 1978, p. 51.

[18]Ibid., p. 67.

[19]Wilbur Thompson, "Industrial Location: Causes and Consequences."

[20]Alan Tait, "Is the Introduction of a Value Added Tax Inflationary?" Finance and Development (June 1981), pp. 38-42.

Chapter 23

The Michigan Liquor Control Commission and the Taxation of Alcoholic Beverages

by

Barbara Weinstein

The University of Michigan

INTRODUCTION[1]

Proceeds from the sale and taxation of alcoholic beverages have provided revenue for the State of Michigan since 1934. In fiscal year 1980 these sources together yielded $164 million.[2] The net revenues were disbursed to the General Purpose-General Fund ($129 million), to the Restricted-General Fund ($19 million),[3] to the School Aid Fund ($18 million) and to the Liquor Purchase Revolving Fund ($7 million).[4] Contributions to the General Fund amounted to 3.1 percent of that Fund.

Taxation and Control of Alcoholic Beverages

As revenue sources for Michigan, alcoholic beverage taxation and control are appealing for several reasons. In the first place, taxation of alcoholic beverages is widely accepted. Federal liquor excise taxation dates from the eighteenth century and constituted one of the leading sources of revenue until the imposition of the income tax in 1913. Although tax increases may be fought by consumers and sellers there is no effectively organized opposition to their existence. Second, advocates of temperance view liquor excises as appropriately sumptuary. Third, in the realm of control, Michigan currently receives the proceeds of a profitable monopoly enterprise. Finally, the fact that approximately 80 percent of liquor-derived revenues are earmarked for general purposes means that a great deal of flexibility is permitted in the disposition of funds from this source.

When welfare considerations are included in an analysis of alcoholic beverage revenues, the case for control and taxation becomes less clear. The often-cited goals of generating revenue, discouraging consumption and exercising control are ambiguous and conflicting. Alcohol taxation is expected to achieve the goals of effectively discouraging consumption and of generating lots of revenue. Liquor taxes have been viewed both as regressive and progressive. Alcohol is seen both as a harmful substance in need of strict control and as a consumer "good." Strict control and licensing are deemed necessary to guarantee that spirits are of good quality; yet this type of control is not deemed necessary for most other consumer goods. This inconsistency of goals is reflected in the politics of liquor control and consequently within the liquor laws themselves.

In spite of these inconsistencies, the desires to generate revenue and discourage consumption are ever present; so regulation persists. Our analysis will treat liquor control from the revenue standpoint but it will also include evaluation of the impacts on consumers, producers and the state as a whole.

Liquor Control in the United States

Current liquor control methods in the U.S. date from the repeal of prohibition in 1933. At this time states assumed the authority for regulating the liquor trade within their boundaries. Two generic systems of regulation emerged: the "control" or "monopoly" system and the "license" or "open" system. Michigan, the first state to ratify the twenty-first amendment, took the lead in establishing a control system.

The common distinguishing feature of the control systems is the state monopoly for the wholesale distribution of distilled spirits. In other respects there is variation across the eighteen monopoly states.[5] At the wholesale level, many of them monopolize the distribution of some classes of wine, beer or other liquors. In Michigan, the monopoly distributes wine with over 16 percent alcoholic content. At the retail level variation occurs in the mix of monopoly and private selling, the per capita number of

TABLE 23.1
KEY FEATURES OF SELECTED STATES LIQUOR REGULATION SYSTEMS

STATE	CONTROL or LICENSE	LOCAL OPTION FOR RETAIL SALES	ADVERTISING RESTRICTIONS	MANDATORY SPIRITS MARK-UP	SPIRITS TAXES[1]	BEER TAXES per barrel	WINE TAXES per gallon	NUMBER OF RETAIL OUTLETS (1979) On-Premise total	On-Premise per 1000 pop.	Off-Premise total	Off-Premise per 1000 pop.	PER CAPITA CONSUMPTION OF SPIRITS 1979 gallons
Calif.	License	No	lenient	none	$2.00/gal	$2.48	1¢-2¢	13,577	.60	11,043	.49	2.55
Fla.	License	Yes	Lenient	none	$4.75	$12.40	$1.75-$2.43	2,827	.32	501	.06	2.79
Ill.	License	Yes	essentially none	none	$2.00/gal	$2.17	23¢-60¢	20,596[3]	1.83	20,596[3]	1.83	2.24
Ind.	License	No	Lenient	none	$2.62/gal	$2.95	45¢	1,174	.22	1,724	.32	1.45
Mich.	Control: Spirits & Wine>16%	Yes	restrictive	51%	9.85% of retail price	$6.30	50¢ (4¢ in-state)	8,986	.98	3,508	.38	1.95
N. Y.	License	Yes	essentially none	wholesale: none retail: 12% min	$3.63/gal	$1.38	89¢	24,030 (1978)	1.36	4,459 (1978)	.25	2.24
Ohio	Control: Liquor>21%	Yes	resrictive	42.9%	--[2]	$2.50	24¢-60¢	11,737	1.09	423	.04	1.39
Penna.	Control: Spirits & Wine	Yes	restrictive	48%	18% of retail price	$2.48	5¢ unit proof wine gal	19,455	1.66	710	.06	1.45
Wis.	License	Yes	Fairly Lenient	Wholesale: min 3% retail: min 6%	$2.60/gal	$2.00	20¢-39¢	12,813	2.71	1,644	.35	2.41

Notes: [1]In many cases these are selections or averages. See DISCUS Public Revenues for details.

[2]In Ohio the formula is ($2.25 weight tax)x(5% special tax)x(4.5 or 5.5% sales tax).

[3]In Illinois the same type of license is issued for on- and off-premise consumption.

Sources: DISCUS Summary of State Laws and Regulations Relating to Distilled Spirits, 1981. For markup and taxes, also the Liquor Handbook Gavin-Jobson Associates, 1980. For taxes, also DISCUS Public Revenues from Alcohol Beverages 1978. Also see DISCUS Apparent Consumption of Distilled Spirits, 1975-1979.

retail outlets, the extent of price regulation and the restrictions on advertising. In Michigan and several other states, most off-premise sales are made by private businesses, retail prices are administered, and the state does some retail selling. In two of the states retail sale is done solely by private businesses with no retail price maintenance and in the remaining states all package sale is done by the state monopoly.

In all states except Oklahoma some sale by the drink is permitted by private licensees.

In contrast with the control states, the open states permit all wholesale and retail trade to be undertaken privately. There are, however, great differences among these states and the District of Columbia with respect to licensing, price maintenance and advertising restrictions. Table 23.1 summarizes some key features of selected states' systems.

Authority and Jurisdiction of the Liquor Control Commission

The Michigan Liquor Control Commission is vested with the "sole power and duty to control alcoholic beverage traffic in Michigan."[6] In this capacity the Commission serves as sole wholesale distributor of liquor*;[7] it controls retail trade through participation, uniform price setting, licensing and enforcement; and it collects tax revenues on liquor, beer and wine.

There are three main classes of retail sellers of liquor*: the state, specially designated distributors (SDDs), and on-premise licensees. Since the institution of Michigan's control system, SDDs have been utilized to assist the state with off-premise selling.[8] These agents sell liquor* at LCC-determined uniform prices and make wholesale purchases from the Commission at a discount. As the system has evolved, the state has dwindled in importance as a retail seller, from 21 percent of sales in 1936 to approximately 0.5 percent in 1980. SDDs are responsible for almost all of the rest of package sales.[9] Sale by the drink is made exclusively by private establishments. There is no retail on-premise price maintenance, but the licensee gets a discount from the uniform retail package price for its wholesale purchases.

The LCC administers licenses for the sale and manufacture of liquor, beer and wine. It is responsible for enforcing the provisions of the Liquor Control Act (LCA), including those pertaining to the administration and collection of alcoholic beverage excise taxes.

In the policy-making arena, the LCC has a significant voice. Proposed changes in the Liquor Control Act are frequently funneled through the Commission for input and feedback. The Commission maintains working relationships with the legislature and with the interest groups representing retailers, wholesalers of beer and wine*, manufacturers, consumers, and those concerned about alcohol abuse.

Although the LCC is responsible for revenue generation, its focus is on control and regulation. In its liquor business it aims for a "satisfactory" rate of return, not the maximization of profits or revenues. It is noteworthy that although the LCA specifies both minimum and maximum mark-ups for liquor*, the Commission has traditionally chosen the lowest mark-up permitted under the act. Since active encouragement of alcohol consumption is largely prohibited by the LCA, the Commission avoids using marketing techniques to stimulate consumption and hence to increase revenues.[10]

STRUCTURE OF THE STATE MONOPOLY

The Liquor Control Commission operates a business which grossed $405 million in fiscal year 1980 and yielded $58 million in net profits for the state.[11] Virtually all of the business revenues arose from wholesale sales of liquor* to various classes of retailers (SDDs, on-premise licensees and hospital and military sellers), while a tiny fraction arose from the state's own retail sales. Sales to SDDs and

TABLE 23.2
HISTORY OF SPIRITS* MARK-UPS AND DISCOUNTS IN MICHIGAN

MARK-UP HISTORY

Effective Date	Mark-up Percentage	
January, 1934	45	
August, 1937	55	
July, 1940	50	
October, 1941	46	
July, 1952	44	
March, 1956	46	
January, 1975	48	
July, 1980	51	
(November, 1981)	(48)	(tentative)

DISCOUNT HISTORY

	Discount Percentages		
Effective Date	Specially Designated Distributor	On-premise	
January, 1934	NA	NA	
April, 1945	10	15	
July, 1947	10	12.5	
February, 1967	11.5	12.5	
January, 1975	15	15	
July, 1980	17	17	
(November, 1981)	(15)	(15)	(tentative)

Source: Michigan Department of Commerce, LCC Report to T. Schwiegert, Dec., 1980.

on-premise licensees alone accounted for over 99 percent of gross revenues.

Pricing

Under Michigan's uniform pricing structure the LCC determines a basic retail mark-up for liquor* and uses discounts to arrive at wholesale prices. The basic retail mark-up is currently equal to 51 percent[12] and is applied to the delivered cost of goods to the Commission, inclusive of the federal distilled spirits tax of $10.50 per proof gallon. On special orders, which account for approximately 6 percent of total sales, the mark-up is 55 percent. The uniform price to consumers is obtained from the basic price by adding first the state excise taxes[13] and then the four percent sales tax. At the wholesale level SDDs and on-premise licensees are permitted 17 percent discounts.

Since the institution of the present system the retail mark-up has changed slightly, moving from 45 percent in 1934 to the present level. (Unless the legislature intervenes, the mark-up will revert back to 48 percent in November, 1981.[14]) Discounts have similarly changed, and until 1975, on-premise sellers received slightly higher discounts than SDDs. Table 23.2 gives a history of mark-ups and discounts.

Michigan, as a wholesaler, is the world's largest single purchaser of distilled spirits and has the potential for exerting monopsony power in its dealings with distilleries. In practice, the explicit exercise of monopsony power is limited, however. Due to various price affirmation laws and agreements the distilleries are prohibited from engaging in overt price discrimination.[15] Because of this the state must exert its influence over price in less explicit ways. It can do so by purchasing in advance of distilleries' posted price increases,[16] by product selection,[17] and by the temporary withholding of payments, especially at the end of the fiscal year.[18]

State Stores

Michigan's seventy-six state liquor stores serve

chiefly as wholesale warehouses and distribution centers and secondarily as retail package outlets. At the wholesale level they form the second part of a two tier distribution system. They receive merchandise from the state's three main warehouses (in Lincoln Park, Lansing, and Escanaba) and distribute directly to SDDs and on-premise retailers. Each store also serves as a retail package outlet.

Although the state's retail sales amounted to a miniscule 0.5 percent of total sales in fiscal year 1980, the stores are profitable. Still, the desirability of operating state stores must hinge on their ability to fulfill functions more thoroughly or efficiently than SDDs can. The only respect in which certain state stores may have this ability is in the area of product selection. In some of the sparsely populated, rural or resort areas of Michigan, demand limitations result in SDDs offering more narrow product selections than they do in highly populated urban areas. In these regions the state, by relying on the merchandise which is routinely stocked in the state store, can offer a larger product selection at no additional inconvenience.[19]

The continuation of state retail sales may become an active point of controversy in the event that retail prices are deregulated and retailers are permitted to choose their own profit margins. In this event, the state, as retail seller, could be placed in unfair price competition with private enterprise. On the other hand, it could serve as a price leader, particularly in those areas where SDDs are sparsely located and have a great deal of location-induced monopoly pricing power.

<u>Licenses and Fees</u>

The LCC is responsible for issuing licenses to and collecting fees from all alcoholic beverage retailers, wholesalers, and manufacturers operating in Michigan. In fiscal year 1980, $9.1 million in revenue was generated from this source.

In Michigan, the number of licenses available for alcoholic beverage trade is a function of population, local option, geography and mutual agreement.[20] Individual licenses are easily transferable. Over 95 percent of license fees arise from retail sales, with most collections coming from SDDs, class "C" bars, and specially designated merchants selling beer and wine* for off-premise consumption.

License fee determination can potentially serve any of several objectives. Fees can be designed to restrict the number of licenses, to capture monopoly rents resulting from license ownership, and to generate revenue for the state. The first objective is intimately tied to license issue and may be redundant if adequate criteria for awarding licenses are already specified. Further, its implementation requires detailed knowledge of the demand for licenses. Although a resale market for licenses does exist in Michigan, little is known about its structure or about the value of licenses to those who choose not to enter the market.[21] For these reasons license fees are better suited for the latter purposes. As long as licenses are not simply available on demand, some degree of monopoly power may be associated with ownership. By expropriating any monopoly rents that arise, the state can try to redress the distributional inequity created by the license system. In the process of doing so, it can generate public revenues.[22]

A description of the license fee schedules for SDDs and class C bars can provide some insight into the potential of Michigan's fee structure for eliminating monopoly rents. SDDs are assessed $150 per year plus $3.00 for every $1,000 of the basic retail value of goods purchased from the LCC during the previous calendar year.[23] An SDD with basic retail sales of $200,000 would have a liability of $675, or 0.34 percent of retail sales. Class C bars pay $600 per year regardless of sales, except that owners of more than one bar pay $350 per year for each additional bar.[24] An average class C establishment taking in $100,000 would be assessed 0.6 percent of sales.

It is noteworthy that in each of the retail fee schedules, the proportion of sales paid in fees declines as sales increase. In addition, it is frequently the case that as net income rises the proportion of income paid in fees falls. This "regressivity" is further exacerbated by the fact that class C licensees are charged lower fees for additional bars regardless of the volume of sales in each. These features can work together to the relative disadvantage of the smaller retailer. It is also true that with the exception of Sunday sales fees, there is no variation in fees according to geographical location or hours of operation. Finally, it is significant that less than one percent of the sales of an average-volume SDD or class C establishment are paid in annual fees. These observations cast serious doubt as to the ability of Michigan's present fee structure to reduce, eliminate or redistribute any existing monopoly rents.

Ideally, the computation of optimal license fees should consist of a determination of the amount of excess returns[25] earned by representative SDDs and class C bars of various sizes, broken down by hours and seasons of operation. An alternative to this kind of detailed estimation is the use of average data, say over all SDDs or classes. This approach was used by Finnel, et al. (1980) in their report for the Pennsylvania legislature. Using some cost estimates from Michigan, together with an assumption that a 12 percent rate of return on invested capital was normal, they estimated off-premise license fees under several scenarios relevant to Pennsylvania. Their one-time fee estimates of $0 to $240,000 were quite sensitive to per capita consumption and the total number of outlets.

Despite the lack of precise estimates of optimal license fees, it is probable that the state could reduce inequities and generate more revenue by making fees more responsive to sales or profits. Also, since location and hours of operation can be important determinants of profitability, the state might achieve the same goals by varying fees according to location or hours of operation.

ANALYSIS OF THE OBJECTIVES OF THE LCC

Optimal choices of mark-ups, discounts, taxes, and state share of retail sales obviously depend upon the objectives of the liquor control system. Here we will examine choices of the LCC with a view towards actual objectives as well as towards other possible revenue or economic welfare goals.

Actual Objectives

The LCC deliberately purports not to be a revenue or profit maximizing agency. Instead it attempts to "make alcoholic beverages available while regulating...in order to protect the...interests of all Michigan citizens."[26] The implicit belief is that the welfare of Michigan citizens is greatest when alcoholic beverages are made available but consumption is not encouraged.

Analyzing the Commission's actual behavior in light of its professed purpose is difficult, as the purpose itself is ambiguous. It is not clear what is meant by, and what decisions are appropriate for, permitting availability but not encouraging consumption.

One possible interpretation is that alcoholic beverage consumption affects social welfare nonnegatively up to a certain level (or level of increase) and that thereafter it has a negative effect. According to this view, maximization of social welfare with a minimum revenue requirement would yield a rule which would either place consumption where it first begins to affect welfare negatively, or balance marginal welfare losses from increased consumption with marginal revenue gains.

Another behavioral interpretation is that the Commission acts more passively, accepting a "satisfactory" profit level and not letting revenue prospects induce it to actively encourage consumption. This "satisficing" behavior will not in general lead to optimal revenue or welfare attainment, but a model which incorporates this view might shed some light on actual decision making.

Revenue and Welfare Objectives[27]

How should the LCC choose prices and rates if explicit revenue or welfare concerns are paramount?

Suppose that the Commission is responsible for just one product, liquor, and that consumers face the basic retail price without excise or sales taxes. The Commission's optimal choices may be interpreted by means of the price elasticity of demand for liquor, which is a measure of the sensitivity of liquor demand to changes in retail price.[28]

Maximization of net revenue requires the mark-up to be chosen so that the price elasticity of demand is equal to the ratio of retail price to mark-up. Thus, demand must be elastic at the net revenue maximizing mark-up.

If the state's goal is the maximization of profits, net of operating costs, optimal mark-ups will be associated with higher demand elasticities. Here the optimal choice of mark-up involves a demand elasticity which is larger than in the net revenue maximizing case by the factor: marginal revenue/marginal profit.

If more than one type of liquor is sold the net revenue maximizing mark-up will in general not be uniform. As consumer demand varies across products, so will optimal mark-ups and associated demand elasticities. The way in which demand for each liquor product varies with the prices of other liquor products will be of significance, and no universal maximization rule will emerge. However, in the special case where the Commission sells just two substitute products, demand elasticities associated with optimal mark-ups will necessarily be higher than in the single or independent product cases.

The analysis can be generalized to include consideration of social welfare. Suppose that alcoholic beverages affect social welfare through the utility of consumers, the social costs of alcohol consumption, and the discount to retailers. The state's optimization problem becomes: Choose a retail mark-up and wholesalers' discount to maximize social welfare subject to the constraint that net revenue reach some specified level.

In general, the effect of social costs on optimal-choice demand elasticities is ambiguous. This is because of the conflict between revenue goals and social costs of consumption. If revenue objectives are not binding, the effect becomes unambiguous, with higher marginal costs of alcohol consumption necessarily associated with higher demand elasticities.

The discount should be set as low as possible unless increasing it increases social welfare. In this case, it should be set at a level where the gain in social welfare from increasing it further is exactly offset by the attendant loss in state revenue.

Conditions for the selection of optimal retail mark-ups have been couched in terms of liquor demand elasticities. To summarize the results: Net revenue maximization requires the selection of mark-ups which will cause liquor demand to be in the elastic ranges. At optimal choices, demands will be more elastic if profits rather than revenues are to be maximized or if different mark-ups are to be chosen for different substitute types of liquor. The introduction of welfare considerations complicates matters, but in the special case where only social welfare is important and there are high marginal social costs of alcohol consumption, optimal choice elasticities will be high.

With these results, policy makers can adopt guidelines for determining optimal mark-ups. Specifically, if demand elasticities are lower than desired, the retail mark-up can be increased, and vice versa. (Empirical estimation of liquor demand elasticities will be treated later in this chapter.)

Analytically, selection of a net-revenue-maximizing

mark-up is equivalent to selection of a revenue-maximizing *ad valorem* tax rate.[29] In practice, the use of *both* kinds of decision variables in lieu of just one may be desirable. It may be easier to change the mark-up than the tax rate (or vice versa) and there may be legal constraints which restrict possible values of the decision variables in different ways. Under the current system, the LCC has the authority to choose a mark-up within the range 51-65 percent, but it has no autonomous power to change rates of excise taxation. This is probably due to legislative intent in imposing the taxes and to the fact that excise tax revenues tend to be earmarked whereas liquor monopoly revenues are not. Because of this the use of both the tax rate and the mark-up does provide additional revenue-generating flexibility.[30]

ALTERNATIVE METHODS OF OPERATION

Since Michigan's control system is by no means the only available method of regulating liquor traffic in the state, questions arise as to the comparative qualities of alternative systems. In particular, it is useful to consider the respective advantages and disadvantages of systems which feature competitive retail pricing, private licensed wholesaling, and differential pricing or taxation. Each of these alternatives will be considered in turn.

Competitive Retail Pricing

In order to compare and contrast the features of a competitive retail pricing system with those of Michigan's system, consider a situation in which the state is the sole wholesale distributor but all retailing is done privately in the absence of price controls. (Mississippi and Wyoming currently operate in this way, Pennsylvania is planning to move to this type of system, and in Michigan there is a movement afoot to switch.) Since price advertising can enhance competition, its legality is assumed.[31] Of concern are the effects of this type of system on prices, liquor consumption, state revenue, and the profits of retailers.

TABLE 23.3
COMPARISON OF LIQUOR PRICES FOR SELECTED STATES

STATE	WHISKEY				VODKA	RUM	GIN	9 BRAND AVERAGE[1]	STATE SALES TAX
	SEAGRAM 7 Blend 80 pf.	OLD GRAND-DAD Bonded 100 pf.	DEWAR'S Scotch 86.8 pf.	CANADIAN CLUB Canadian 80 pf.	SMIRINOFF 80 pf.	BICARDI Silver 80 pf.	BEEFEATER 94 pf.		
California	$6.03	$9.33	$9.52	$7.62	$5.84	$5.71	$8.89	$7.05	6%
Florida	6.38	9.18	10.11	8.40	6.24	6.32	9.07	7.48	4
Illinois	5.54	8.65	9.56	7.51	5.14	5.35	8.16	6.69	5
Indiana	6.27	9.79	11.02	8.14	6.07	6.11	9.61	7.73	4
New York	6.56	9.32	10.10	8.41	6.09	6.13	9.05	7.46	8
Ohio	6.18	9.95	10.15	8.24	5.73	5.83	9.24	7.43	4
Pennsylvania	6.48	10.83	11.08	8.94	5.97	5.83	9.92	7.90	6
Wisconsin	6.09	9.16	10.00	8.09	5.60	6.03	8.28	7.12	4
MICHIGAN	5.83	9.77	9.98	8.02	5.35	5.48	8.97	7.14	4
Control state average	$6.12	$9.75	$10.30	$8.18	$5.64	$5.70	$9.22	$7.36	4.73%
License state average	$6.37	$9.63	$10.41	$8.27	$6.17	$6.13	$9.33	$7.57	3.83%
U.S. AVERAGE	$6.29	$9.67	$10.37	$8.24	$5.98	$5.98	$9.29	$7.50	4.15%

Notes: All prices are for fifths, at the indicated proofs, or estimated from similar items.

[1]The 9 brand average also includes Old Crow Straight 80 pf. whiskey, and Seagrams Extra-Dry, 80 pf. gin.

Source: DISCUS Distilled Spirits Retail Bottle Price Survey, 1980.

Prices. In this context, prices are determined by two types of decision makers: the state and individual firms. Choice of the wholesale mark-up continues to be a state policy variable and affects consumer prices in the same way it does now. (Note that the effective wholesale mark-up is currently 34 percent.) Increases in the wholesale mark-up would be accompanied by consumer price increases unless retailers chose gross profit margins below the current 17 percent.

Evidence concerning the effects of competition on retail liquor prices is inconclusive. Overall, there is no appreciable difference between license and monopoly state prices. Generally, control state average prices are lower than license state prices, but insignificantly so. As a typical example, the 1980 average prices for a fifth of Seagram's 7 blended whiskey were $6.12 for control states and $6.37 for license states.[32] Fair trade laws and the repeal thereof might provide some basis for prediction of the effects of deregulation, but here again no clear answers emerge. Some interstate price comparisons appear in Table 23.3.

One effect is fairly certain, however. Deregulation of prices tends to result in price variations across firms, products and locations. This suggests that in response to deregulation retailers choose different profit margins and use their increased flexibility to offer sales or price leaders on different products at various times. Price deregulation may also result in the appearance or private or special brands and labels which are sold by retailers at reduced prices.

Consumption. It is noteworthy that despite the lack of significant price differentials, per capita consumption of distilled spirits is appreciably higher in license states than in monopoly states (2.17 gallons and 1.70 gallons respectively in 1979).[33] Although the reasons for this are open to debate, likely explanations include easier access (more, or more convenient outlets),[34] greater product selection, fewer advertising restrictions, and more price differentiation in license states than in control states.[35] Michigan's per capita consumption is high for a monopoly state (1.95 gallons in 1979); still, it is likely that consumption would be increased under a competitive pricing system by the last two factors mentioned above.

State revenue. The level of state liquor revenue is determined by prices, consumption, and taxes. Regarding taxes, the state is currently able to collect the tax on liquor at the time of sale to retailers and, by virtue of the discount system, it is still able to compute the tax on the retail price base. Under a competitive system it would be necessary either to change the tax base from retail to wholesale price, thereby reducing state revenue,[36] or to change the method of collection so as to allow the tax to be collected at the time of retail sale.

Profits. For reasons discussed above under pricing and consumption, it is not clear how the average profits of retailers would change as a result of competition. The determinants of this are the extent to which the retail trade is inherently competitive, retailers' optimizing prices relative to state-imposed prices, and the elasticities of demand for liquor. But regardless of average profit changes, particular concern has been expressed about the plight of the small package dealer under a competitive pricing system. The fear is that large volume stores or chains will be so successful in under-cutting smaller stores that the latter will cease to be profitable. This, of course, is a potential problem in any industry in which some scale economies can be realized,[37] though the problem may be slightly mitigated by the ability of small businesses to offer convenience and service to patrons. If protection of small business is deemed to be in the interests of the state and its residents, the state can use the retail licensing and fee system to discriminate on behalf of small liquor stores. As noted above, the license system presently discriminates against such firms.

In summary, competitive retailing would likely result in increased consumption and in price differentiation, but the effect of such a system on average prices, state revenues, and average retail profits is uncertain.

Private Licensed Wholesaling

How would Michigan fare under a license, as opposed to control set-up? Structurally, change to a license system would mean dismantling Michigan's wholesale distribution system and replacing it with a private wholesale system. Fiscally, the change would involve exclusive reliance on excise taxation and fees. Raising revenues comparable to those currently realized would require a tax rate on liquor of around 20 percent.[38]

Changing Michigan's system into one featuring private wholesaling and retailing would entail major changes in licensing, enforcement, and revenue collections, and the final impact on state revenues is uncertain.[39] In the area of licensing it would be necessary to determine appropriate fees and restrictions for wholesalers. This, of course, would involve a trade-off between the desire for regulation and the encouragement of competition.[40] It is clear that the wholesale liquor business can be highly profitable. If the number of licenses were restricted, possession of a license would confer monopoly power on firms. Since monopoly rents generated as a result would represent potential losses of state revenue, the state might want to consider the use of fees to attempt to control their size.

The role of the LCC in enforcing provisions of the Liquor Control Act (as amended) would be complicated if the monopoly were eliminated. Fears have been expressed about increased LCA violations, corruption and the introduction of organized crime into the liquor business.[41]

It is uncertain as to the direction in which wholesale prices would go if the monopoly were dissolved. Both the number of licenses issued and the nature of the distribution networks would have an impact on this. The effect of the system on retail prices is also unclear. They would be influenced by the factors discussed in the previous section as well as by decisions of wholesalers and the relationships between retailers and wholesalers. Retailers would probably find dealing with private wholesalers to be significantly different from dealing with the LCC. On one hand, they would likely be inconvenienced by having to deal with more than one wholesale firm.[42] On the other hand, private wholesalers might be more amenable to making special delivery and service arrangements. Also, even if quantity discounts continued to be prohibited it would be easier to circumvent those restrictions if sales were made exclusively on a private basis.

It is interesting that no state, control or license, has yet (since prohibition) changed its basic distribution system.[43] The implications of this are that the systems are simply too entrenched and the perceived benefits of switching are insufficiently great to balance associated uncertainties and administrative costs. At this point there is not enough evidence regarding the relative efficiency of public and private liquor distribution systems to shed much additional light on the subject.[44]

Differential Pricing or Taxation

In general, maximization of revenue or welfare requires mark-ups and tax rates to vary across liquor products, as consumers respond differently to price changes on different items. As an example, net revenue maximization requires the use of higher mark-ups for types of liquor with lower demand elasticities.[45] Presently, the state employs different excise tax rates for liquor, beer and wine, but within those categories uniform rates are used; and a single percentage mark-up is used for liquor* pricing by the monopoly.

Theoretically, the use of "differential" mark-ups or tax rates can provide a way for the state to realize its objectives within the context of any type of alcoholic beverage distribution system. In practice there are serious economic, administrative, and political obstacles to the use of differential price or tax formulae, particularly within the context of the present monopoly system. Economically, implementation is rendered difficult by the fact that general formulae for differentiated prices are complicated and by the fact that elasticity estimation is so imprecise.[46] Thus it may be impossible to translate maximization criteria into useable pricing or taxing rules. Administratively, there can be lags in implementation and accounting problems. Politically, there may be objections on the part of producers to mark-ups or tax rates which generate differentially higher prices for their products.[47]

The use of different mark-ups for different products becomes easier if retail prices are not controlled. If retailers are completely free to choose prices, they can routinely mark different products up by different amounts and they can offer sales on selected items. Such practices can potentially work to increase revenues and improve economic efficiency.

To conclude the discussion of alternatives: The introduction of price competition can potentially improve economic efficiency; the extent to which it succeeds is a function of industry structure and any external costs or benefits. For the liquor industry, important factors include the state's choice of wholesale mark-up, the extent to which the retail industry is inherently competitive, and the social costs of alcohol consumption. Potential advantages of license systems over control systems depend upon the structure of the wholesale industry and the nature of licensing and enforcement. The use of differential prices or taxes can contribute to efficiency but may be impractical or unfeasible to implement on a centralized basis.

EXCISE TAXES

By constitutional amendment in 1932, the State of Michigan authorized the legislature to provide for excise taxes on the sale of alcoholic beverages. Excises were initiated on beer in 1933, on wine in 1937, and on liquor in 1957. For purposes of taxation, the liquor base is taken to be distilled spirits of at least 22 percent alcoholic content, while the wine base is taken to be all wine. The Michigan liquor tax is *ad valorem*, whereas the wine and beer taxes are specific. (The effects of specific and *ad valorem* taxes are discussed later in this section.)

The Liquor Tax

Presently, there are three categories of excises imposed on the price of liquor. These are: A 4 percent tax earmarked for the School Aid Fund (dating from 1957), a 4 percent tax earmarked for the General Purpose-General Fund (dating from 1962) and a 1.85 percent "alcoholism" tax which goes to the Liquor Purchase Revolving Fund and dates from 1973 with a rate change in 1978.[48] The 4 percent taxes apply to all liquor sales while the 1.85 percent tax applies only to off-premise sales.

The base of each tax is the basic retail price of liquor, exclusive of state sales tax but inclusive of the full federal tax. Since tax liabilities are computed *before* the allowance of discounts, revenues are unaffected by discount size.[49] The tax is collected at the time of sale by the Commission.

Each of the four percent taxes yielded $18.6 million in fiscal year 1980 and the alcoholism tax yielded $7 million.

There are wide variations in liquor taxation across states. Unfortunately, direct interstate rate comparisons are of limited use since bases as well as rates differ and because in monopoly states revenues derive from sales as well as taxation. More meaningful comparisons may be based upon the computation of net state revenue from taxation *and* sales.[50] Among the fifty states and the District of Columbia, Michigan ranks twelfth in net state liquor revenues per gallon sold and fifteenth in revenue generated per $1,000 of personal income.[51] In general, monopoly states rank higher than license states in these categories.

The revenue potential of the liquor tax depends upon elasticities of revenue with respect to both tax rate and income. As long as the tax rate elasticity of revenue is positive, the state can realize additional revenues by raising the rate, and as long as the income elasticity of revenue is positive, increases in state income will result in increases in tax yield.[52]

Tax rate elasticities of revenue can either be computed from demand elasticities or can be estimated directly. We directly estimated tax rate elasticities for Michigan and found them to be significantly positive, in the range 0.41-0.83. Income elasticities were estimated as positive, but insignificantly different from zero in most cases.[53] These results suggest that in the absence of taste changes, increases in the tax rate would increase revenue, but changes in personal income would have little impact.

The Beer Tax

Beer intended for consumption in Michigan is taxed at the rate of $6.30 per thirty-one gallon barrel. The tax is paid by means of prepaid stamps and crowns respectively affixed by the brewer if the beer is domestic and by the wholesaler if the beer is imported. Beer brewed in Michigan for out-of-state consumption is subject to a tax refund when proof of exportation is provided.[54]

Although the beer tax yield has grown from $4.6 million in 1936 to $44 million in 1980, tax rate changes have been infrequent, and the tax rate as a percentage of price has fallen.

As indicated in the liquor tax discussion, revenue potential depends upon tax rate and income elasticities of revenue. Based upon price elasticities of demand and revenue, we estimated the tax rate elasticity of beer revenue to be around 0.5, implying that tax increases would raise revenue. As in the case of liquor, the income elasticity was insignificant.

The fact that beer prices are increasing over time

means that revenues could be further enhanced by a switch to an *ad valorem* method of taxation.

The Wine Tax

Wine sold in Michigan is taxed at the specific rate of \$0.50 per gallon if it is imported and at the reduced rate of \$0.04 per gallon if it is produced from Michigan grapes.[55] Based upon sales of 14.6 million gallons in fiscal year 1980 the yield was \$6.8 million. The imported rate is equivalent to about 3.3 percent of price at an assumed average price of \$15 per gallon and the domestic rate is a mere 0.26 percent.

The fact that wine from Michigan grapes is taxed at a drastically reduced rate means that Michigan vintners are afforded economic protection. In 1980 the protection amounted to \$414,000 based upon sales of 0.9 million gallons by Michigan wineries.

Since imported wine is almost a perfect substitute for Michigan wine, the latter's price elasticity of demand is probably high. This implies that increases in the Michigan wine tax rate would be borne chiefly by producers.

Specific Versus Ad Valorem Tax Rates

Only eleven states, including Michigan employ *ad valorem* tax rates for liquor. The rest of the taxing states and the federal government use *specific* rates for liquor; and, with the exception of Hawaii, all (taxing) states levy specific beer taxes. A discussion of the relative effects of the two types of taxes follows.

For any particular product, at any given time, an *ad valorem* tax rate can be converted into a specific rate, and vice versa. The equivalence is given by s=ap where s is the specific rate, a is the *ad valorem* rate and p is the (before tax) price. Because of this equivalence, any differences in the effects of the two types of taxes must result from application of the rates to different products and from relative changes in yields over time.

Consider first the application of specific and *ad valorem* tax rates to different products (e.g., different brands or types of liquor) with prices and quantities demanded held constant for each. As a particular example, consider the relative effects of the rates on consumers of a high-priced, "premium" brand of bonded whiskey versus consumers of a more popular, lower priced blend. Under a specific formula, tax revenue from each product is the tax rate multiplied by total quantity sold and the more popular brand necessarily generates more revenue than the premium brand. Under an *ad valorem* system, the revenue yield is a percentage of sales and so depends directly upon both price and quantity. The difference in yields under the two schemes is the weighted sum of effective rate differentials multiplied by quantities sold. With the specific tax each consumer has the same tax liability per unit of purchase regardless of the type of purchase (low or high priced) whereas under the *ad valorem* tax consumers of the premium brand necessarily pay a higher per unit tax.

Of interest from an equity standpoint is the relative regressivity or progressivity of the two kinds of taxes as applied to high and low priced products.[56] With *equal yield* specific and *ad valorem* tax formulae, the specific tax will be more regressive than the *ad valorem* tax exactly when the income elasticity of demand for the premium product exceeds that for the popular, lower-priced product.

As prices and quantities demanded change over time so do the relative effects of specific and *ad valorem* taxes. Beginning at a point where equivalent tax rates ($s=ap$) are applied to a particular product, the growth of *ad valorem* tax revenues will exceed those of specific revenues exactly when the retail price of the product increases over time.

Empirical Estimates of Elasticities

From the preceding analysis it is clear that estimates of demand and revenue elasticities are crucial for policy purposes. This section is devoted to a discussion of liquor demand estimation and to a presentation of some demand and revenue elasticity estimates.

Various problems plague attempts to estimate liquor demand elasticities. First and foremost, data on sales trends indicate that the demand for liquor is highly volatile.[57] Changes in tastes resulting from such factors as changes in life style, the relative price of leisure, culture, demographic composition of the population, the drinking age, religion and morality, and availability of substitutes affect both the demand for alcoholic beverages as a whole and the demand for various components such as beer, wine and generic categories of liquor. The fact that pronounced taste changes occur both over time and across geographical areas poses problems both for time-series and for cross-sectional analyses. The use of specific variables to control for taste variations may be limited both by the fact that elasticities need not be constant over time, and, in the case of cross-sectional studies, by possible causal relationships between prices and taste parameters.

A second type of problem concerns the choice between considering alcoholic beverages as a single commodity versus treating it as a bundle of separate commodities.[58] The use of alcoholic beverages as a single commodity is undesirable in that it tends to obscure the effects of price-induced substitution among the various types of alcohol and can in turn lead to inconsistencies in the estimation of revenue elasticities. Consumers may well respond to price increases by switching to cheaper alcoholic beverages rather than by reducing their physical consumption. If this is the case, alcoholic beverage demand will be found to be price-inelastic; however expenditures and tax revenues might be quite sensitive to prices and tax rates because of the substitution of cheaper products.

It is necessary to treat alcoholic beverages as separate commodities in order to investigate possibilities for differential pricing and taxation. For this purpose it is important to assess how demand for each alcoholic beverage product depends upon its own price and upon prices of related (alcoholic beverage) products. Unfortunately, estimation of these influences may be hampered by the correlation of product prices over time. In the case of subcategories of liquor, pricing methods themselves may result in perfect collinearity of prices.

Other estimation and data problems include those of constructing price indices and averages and the lack of substate data for intra-state cross sectional analysis.[59]

We estimated demand and revenue elasticities for Michigan over the period 1968-79, using quarterly data from a study by Haas (1980), supplemented when needed.[60] We found liquor demand to be significantly price-inelastic, with values in the range -0.04 to -0.35. Beer price elasticities ranged from -0.48 to -0.52, and wine price elasticities from -2.2 to -2.4; both were found to be significantly different from zero. Income elasticities were generally found to be insignificant.

We also estimated the elasticity of demand for liquor with respect to prices of liquor, beer and wine. The results showed wine is a significant substitute for liquor, and beer is of indeterminate influence.

Some elasticity estimates from various studies have been included in Table 23.4. From the wide ranges of values that are covered, it is difficult to draw any overall conclusions about the nature of alcoholic beverage demand. All of the estimates must be taken with a grain of salt. However, insofar as estimates for Michigan provide a better indication of demand within the state than do studies of other regions, our results and those from Haas' study suggest that, in Michigan, liquor and beer demand are price-inelastic and wine demand is price-elastic.

SUMMARY AND CONCLUSIONS

As a result of historical precedent, revenue needs, and the desire of various groups to discourage consumption, the regulation of alcoholic beverage trade is an ubiquitous

TABLE 23.4
SELECTED ESTIMATES OF ALCOHOLIC BEVERAGES
DEMAND ELASTICITIES

PRODUCT	REGION OF STUDY	PRICE ELASTICITY	INCOME ELASTICITY	AUTHOR	TIME PERIOD
Liquor:	U.S.	-2.1 to -1.4	.21 to .33	Niskanen	1934-60
	U.S.	-.79	---	Simon	1955-61
	Canada	-1.13	.10	Johnson and Oksanen	1956-70
	Michigan	-.15 to -.21	.21 to .31	Haas	1968-79
	Michigan	-.04 to -.35	.1	Weinstein (this study)	1968-79
Beer:	U.S.	-.62 to -.70	-.33	Niskanen	1934-60
	Canada	-.25 to -.27	-.02	Johnson and Oksanen	1956-70
	U.S.	-.09	.4	Hogarty and Elzinga	1956-69
	Michigan	-.82	-.27	Haas	1968-79
	Michigan	-.48 to -.52	-.15	Weinstein (this study)	1968-79
Wine:	U.S.	-.56 to -.98	.61	Niskanen	1934-60
	Canada	-.67	.01	Johnson and Oksanen	1956-70
	Michigan	-4.1 to .1	-.79 to 2.8	Haas	1968-79
	Michigan	-2.4 to -2.2	-.57 to .27	Weinstein (this study)	1968-79

feature of our economy. In Michigan this regulation takes the form of a state monopoly over the wholesale distribution of liquor*, regulation of private liquor trade, and excise taxation of all alcoholic beverages.

Although the state monopoly is profitable, it fails to exploit all of its available revenue possibilities. Based upon estimates of elasticities of demand for liquor, increases in the retail mark-up would result in increases in state revenue.

Michigan's system of license fees appears to be ineffectual in capturing monopoly rents which emerge as a result of the ownership of licenses. The system is insufficiently sensitive to factors such as volume of sales, profits, geographical location, and hours of operation.

Alternative methods of operation for the LCC include the use of competitive retail pricing, change to a license system of operation, and the use of differential pricing or taxation. It is likely that consumption would increase with a switch to any of these methods, but there are no clear verdicts on the effects of alternative systems on average prices, revenue or welfare.

Examination of the structure of excise taxation indicates that there are increased revenue possibilities for the liquor and beer taxes. Both would probably generate more revenue from rate increases, and beer tax revenues could be further increased by a switch to ad valorem taxation.

The estimation of alcoholic beverage demand and revenue elasticities is quite problematic. This is unfortunate since the efficient use of alcoholic beverage sales and taxation for the state depends closely upon various elasticities. The estimation problems stem mainly from the inconsistency of liquor demand and from problems with aggregation and disaggregation.

According to our estimates of demand and revenue elasticities for Michigan, liquor and beer are demand-inelastic and wine is demand-elastic at prevailing prices. This means that retail price or tax rate increases could generate additional state revenue in the cases of liquor and beer.

NOTES, CHAPTER 23

[1]I would like to thank Therese Mendola for her valuable research assistance.

[2]The source of this and other LCC data is: Annual Financial Report of the Liquor Control Commission, 1980 (and previous years).

[3]The restricted funds go mainly to local governments and to licensing and enforcement.

[4]The Liquor Purchase Revolving Fund is the LCC's operating fund. Revenues from the 1.85 percent alcoholism tax (discussed under excise taxation in this chapter) are placed here until they are appropriated by the legislature for substance abuse programs.

[5]Alabama, Idaho, Iowa, Maine, Michigan, Mississippi, Montana, New Hampshire, North Carolina, Ohio, Oregon, Pennsylvania, Utah, Vermont, Virginia, Washington, West Virginia, and Wyoming.

[6]Public Act Number 8 of 1933 (Section 1).

[7]"Liquor*" will be used throughout this chapter to denote distilled spirits and wine of over 16 percent alcoholic content. "Wine*" will refer to wine of no more than 16 percent alcoholic content. Without the asterisk, liquor will refer to distilled spirits, generally of at least 22 percent alcoholic content; and wine will refer to all wine.

[8]SDDs must be established merchants or hotels (LCA, Section 436.14).

[9]Military sales are the exception.

[10]There is an inconsistency here. The commission does not consider the use of prohibitive pricing to restrict consumption.

[11]Net profits are defined as gross liquor* sales less discounts less the cost of liquor* to the LCC less all operating and administrative costs. The gross revenue figure of $405 million is gross liquor* sales less discounts.

[12]The current maximum is 65 percent (LCA, Section 436.16).

[13]These are discussed under excise taxation in this chapter.

[14]And 51 percent for special orders.

[15]Price affirmation laws and agreements typically require manufacturers to affirm that the prices charged to the given customer (say the State of Michigan) are no higher than the lowest prices charged at that time to <u>any</u> wholesaler in any state. The control states use affirmation agreements, while most of the license states operate with affirmation laws.

[16]Distilleries post prices every ninety days.

[17]The LCC has the power to include or exclude any particular product on its list of regularly stocked items.

[18]At any one time the LCC might have as much as $50 million tied up in unpaid inventory. Federal law requires liquor purchases to be made on thirty day accounts or "according to common practices." Because of this and because of "tier" rules (preventing the wholesale buyer from colluding with the manufacturer), late payment can be risky. To date distilleries have not seriously pressured the LCC in this regard. This in itself may be testimony to the state's monopsony power.

[19]The special order system can help to alleviate the product selection problem.

[20]The first three criteria apply to retail licenses and the last two to wholesale licenses.

[21]The LCC charges only a nominal fee for license transfer. The actual transfer payment is included as "goodwill" in the transfer documents. The amount of "goodwill" is not restricted, and no careful account of amounts has been recorded.

[22]The situation is complicated by the fact that gross profit margins are prespecified by the state. Thus the discount is also a determinant of profit levels. The state could use both variables to control rents by letting the discount determine a minimum or average profit rate and letting license fees reflect distributional objectives.

[23]Precisely, it is $3.00 for every $1,000 or <u>major portion thereof</u>, with the first $25,000 exempted from the $3.00 fee.

[24]Publicly owned or supported facilities pay just $100 per year.

[25]"Excess returns" may be defined as net profits in excess of those necessary to keep the licensee in its present business.

[26]Preface to the Liquor Control Act booklet.

[27]A technical appendix containing derivations of the rules in this section is available from the author upon request.

[28]In general an elasticity is the ratio of one proportionate change to another with which it is related. The price elasticity of demand is the ratio of the proportionate change in quantity demanded to the associated proportionate change in (retail) price. At a given price, demand is said to be elastic (inelastic) as the elasticity has magnitude greater than (less than) unity. Movement along a demand curve from an inelastic region to an elastic one may be thought of as associated with a price increase.

[29]An *ad valorem* tax rate is a percentage of price. See the section under excise taxation in this chapter.

[30]Also, the fact that taxes are paid before discounts are taken means that the tax rate and the mark-up affect net revenue in slightly different ways. Formally, revenue=$(1-d+t)\cdot m\cdot p\cdot L$ where d=discount, t=tax rate, m=mark-up, p=price to the Commission and L=quantity sold.

[31]Of the two states with this type of system, Mississippi severely restricts advertising; Wyoming is more permissive.

[32]DISCUS *Annual Price Survey*, 1980.

[33]DISCUS *Apparent Consumption of Distilled Spirits*,1978.

[34]Michigan has the highest per capita number of off-premise outlets of any monopoly state, and has a higher number than the majority of license states. Its per capita consumption of distilled spirits (1.95 gallons in 1979) is just below the national figure of 2.03.

[35]Finnel, et al. discuss these influences in some detail.

[36]Given the same tax rate.

[37]Scale economies are chiefly limited in this type of industry to the areas of finance and merchandising, over a relatively small range.

[38]This figure assumes that prices and consumption remain constant, and is based only on distilled spirits revenues.

[39]The change could be made with varying degrees of retail price maintenance but it seems most useful to discuss the consequences in the context of a retail system with no price maintenance, few advertising restrictions and an unchanged number of retail package outlets.

[40]The assumption is that the desire to regulate will persist.

[41]Michigan's system has been remarkably free of corruptive influences.

[42]License states vary widely in the types of wholesale distribution jurisdictions that are permitted. Some require nonoverlapping jurisdictions for each brand (as Michigan does for beer), while others permit competition among distributors of a single brand in the same geographical area. Some allow wholesalers to have exclusive rights to a brand over the whole state.

[43]A couple of states waited awhile after prohibition to become "wet."

[44]It is true that, on average, monopoly states obtain more alcoholic beverage revenues per capita than license states.

[45]Ignoring cross-price effects, which could be quite significant.

[46]Nice inverse elasticity rules disappear when there are cross-price effects. See the author's technical appendix.

[47]This may be one reason why the LCC only runs product sales when the product in question is being discontinued.

[48]From one percent.

[49]Except insofar as discount size indirectly affects consumption.

[50]Net state revenue = net state monopoly profits (note 10) + excise tax revenues from alcoholic beverages.

[51]When necessary, an average price of thirty dollars per gallon was used for conversion.

[52]A limitation to the potential for increases to generate more revenue is the problem of "bootlegging" across states borders. Little is known about the seriousness of this problem in Michigan, given current prices and tax rates.

[53]See the discussion of elasticity estimation in this chapter.

[54]The refund constitutes a "tax expenditure" which amounted to $35 million in 1980. This is probably a necessary implicit expenditure. The beer tax is designed as a tax on consumption, not production of beer. If exported beer was taxed it would interfere with the ability of other states to levy similar taxes.

[55]Although the commerce clause of the U.S. Constitution prohibits discriminatory trade practices, this appears to have been superceded in the case of alcoholic beverages by the twenty-first amendment.

[56]An excise tax applied to a single product at a point in time will be regressive if the income elasticity of demand for the product is less than unity.

[57]For example, over the period 1964-79, U.S. consumption of American whiskey declined 30 percent while consumption of rum increased 420 percent. (The Liquor Handbook, 1980.)

[58]Including, say, liquor, beer, and wine or their subcategories.

[59]Some researchers have tried to deal with demand estimation problems. Johnson and Oksanen (1974, 1977) estimated alcoholic beverage demand in Canada, using pooled time-series and cross-sectional data. One of their main goals was to account for the effects of ethnic background, religion and schooling on alcoholic beverage consumption. The use of cross-sectional data (across the ten provinces) enabled the noneconomic variables to display needed observational variation. All three factors turned out to be significant. Liquor demand was found to be price elastic and wine and beer demands were found to be price inelastic. Niskanen (1960, 1962) got the same qualitative elasticity results in his study of U.S. liquor demand, over the period 1934-60. He used both demand and supply equations for his estimates.

Haas (1980) estimated alcoholic beverage demand in Michigan, making extensive use of "dummy" variables to account for taste parameters. Of the variables he used, only age composition of the population and the wage rate were found to be significant determinants of alcoholic beverage consumption. Liquor and beer were found to be price inelastic and wine was found to be price elastic.

[60]Elasticity estimation: Per capita consumption of liquor, beer and wine were regressed on own relative price indices and on real per capita Michigan personal income. The observations were quarterly, so seasonal dummies were used. Liquor was also regressed on lagged liquor consumption in addition to the other variables. This variable turned out to be quite significant and had a negative sign. Finally, liquor per capita consumption was regressed on the relative price indices for liquor, beer and

wine, on Michigan per capita personal income, and on the seasonal dummies. The wine coefficient was positive and significant; the beer coefficient was negative and insignificant.

Price indices were obtained from U.S. Bureau of Labor Statistic consumer price indices. Income (and population) figures are from the Census Bureau. Unfortunately, it seems to be impossible to obtain a chronology of liquor, beer and wine prices in Michigan. The BLS does not have those categories for Detroit SMSA, and other records are either not kept or unavailable.

REFERENCES, CHAPTER 23

Can Manufacturers Institute. Beer And Soft Drink Retail Prices. Surveys #2, #3. Washington, D.C., undated.

Distilled Spirits Council of the United States. Annual Statistical Review. Washington, D.C., 1979.

___. Apparent Consumption of Distilled Spirits by Month and by State, 1975-79. Washington, D.C., 1980.

___. Distilled Spirits Retail Bottle Price Survey, 1973-80. Washington, D.C.

___. Public Revenues from Alcohol Beverages, 1978. Washington, D.C.

___. Summary of State Laws and Regulations Relating to Distilled Spirits. 23d ed. Washington, D.C., 1981.

Finnel, Arthur; Harmon, Marcie; and Adams, F. Gerard. A Study to Evaluate the Financial Consequences of Converting the Pennsylvania State Store System to a Private Retail System. Wharton Research Center, University of Pennsylvania. Unpublished, 1980.

Gavin-Jobson Associates. The Liquor Handbook, 1980. New York, N.Y.

Haas, Mark P. Alcoholic Beverage Demand and Taxation in Michigan. Office of Revenue and Tax Analysis, State of Michigan. Unpublished, 1980.

Hogarty, Thomas F. and Elzinga, Kenneth G. "The Demand for Beer." Review of Economics and Statistics, 1972. 59: 195-198.

Johnson, James A. and Oksanen, Ernest. "Estimation of Demand for Alcoholic Beverages in Canada From Pooled Times Series and Cross Sections." Review of Economics and Statistics, 1977. 59: 113-118.

___. "Socioeconomic Determinants of the Consumption of Alcoholic Beverages." Applied Economics, 1974. 6: 293-301. 1974.

Johnston, J. Econometric Methods. New York: McGraw Hill, Inc., 1972.

Navin, Leo. An Analysis of the Demand for Liquor in Michigan. Unpublished Ph.D. dissertation, Michigan State University, 1968.

Simon, Julian. "Economic Effects of State Monopoly of Package Liquor Retailing." Journal of Political Economy, 1966. 74: 188-194.

Smith, Rodney T. "The Legal and Illegal Markets for Taxed Goods: Pure Theory and an Application to State Government Taxation of Distilled Spirits." Journal of Law and Economics, 1976. 19: 393-427.

State of Michigan, Department of Commerce, Liquor Control Commission. Annual Financial Report. Lansing, Michigan, 1968-80.

___. Financial Report. Monthly. Lansing, Michigan, 1968-80.

___. Liquor Control Act and Rules. Lansing, Michigan, 1977.

State of Michigan, Department of Management and Budget. A Liquor Deregulation Proposal. Unpublished, 1980.

Theil, Henri. Principles of Econometrics. Santa Barbara, California: John Wiley and Sons, Inc., 1971.

United States, Bureau of Labor Statistics. Consumer Price Indices, 1968-80.

Wales, T. J. "Distilled Spirits and Interstate Consumption Effects." American Economic Review, 1968. 58: 853-863.

Chapter 24

Miscellaneous Taxes

by

Harvey E. Brazer and Mary Walz

The University of Michigan

The three state taxes that are the subject of this chapter are anomalies in a tax system that is otherwise in reasonably close conformity with widely accepted notions of good tax policy. The cigarette and foreign insurance company premiums tax and the tax on telephone, telegraph, and railroad company property are commendable only by reason of the fact that together they are expected to yield $366 million in fiscal year 1982.[1] In the sections that follow each of these three taxes is discussed in turn.

THE CIGARETTE TAX

Rates and Revenues

The cigarette tax is one of a very few taxes that are levied by all fifty states. With the exception of Hawaii's *ad valorem* tax rate of 40 percent of wholesale price, all states impose a specific tax rate expressed in terms of cents per package of twenty. Rates, which have changed little since 1975, range from North Carolina's two cents to twenty-one cents in Connecticut, Florida, and Massachusetts. Nationwide, these taxes yielded $3.7 billion in 1980 at an average rate of thirteen cents.[2]

In Michigan the tax was initially imposed in 1947 at the rate of three cents per package of twenty cigarettes. The rate was raised to 5 cents in 1957, with the added 2 cents earmarked to the School Aid Fund. In 1959, as part of a "nuisance tax" package aimed at eliminating a huge budget deficit and staving off enactment of an income tax, the rate was increased to six cents. Under legislation enacted in 1962 and 1970 the rate was raised again, to seven cents and then to its present level of eleven cents.[3]

Over the years the cigarette tax has produced an almost constant flow of revenue. The estimated yield for fiscal year 1981, $142 million, is less than 1 percent higher than it was in 1978.[4] As the rate has increased each additional cent in that rate has produced approximately $13 million.

Michigan's 11 cent rate is 2 cents below the national average and below that imposed in the neighboring states of Illinois (12 cents), Ohio (15 cents), Pennsylvania (18 cents), and Wisconsin (20 cents). The only adjacent state with a lower rate is Indiana at 10.5 cents.

It is interesting to observe that the reported average retail prices of cigarettes in Michigan and its neighboring states do not closely reflect differences in tax rates. In 1980, for example, the average price per package was 61.4 cents in Ohio and 61.8 cents in Michigan, even though Ohio's tax was 4 cents higher. And the average price in Indiana was 3.5 cents lower than Michigan's while its tax rate was only 0.5 cents lower. Although we would not make too much of it because a number of other factors enter into the determination of the level of cigarette consumption, we note that per capita sales of cigarettes appear to be quite highly correlated with the tax rate. For the six states here subject to comparison the rank order correlation between cigarette sales and tax rate is -1, higher than it is for sales volume and average price.[5]

When the question of whether or not the cigarette tax rate should be raised is discussed, it is often alleged that a higher tax rate will lead to an increase in bootlegging from low-rate states and reduced sales for Michigan wholesalers and retailers. The raw data on sales and tax rates among the states do not cast adequate light on this issue, but they do suggest that the price elasticity of demand for cigarettes in any state is appreciably greater (absolutely) than zero. Thus if the tax in Michigan now yields $13 million per penny in the rate, we should expect that an increase in the rate of 1 cent would increase revenue by somewhat less than this amount. If, as has been suggested by one study, the price elasticity of demand for cigarettes is about -0.30,[6] and if it is assumed that a 1 cent increase in the tax rate would add 1 cent to the 1980 average price of 61.8 cents, quantity sold would fall off by 0.5 percent and the tax yield would increase by over $12.94 million. Allowing for an increase in bootlegging might bring the yield below this level, but probably by no more than the error inherent in the estimate.

Equity and Efficiency

Historically the cigarette tax has been justified by the view that, as the U.S. Surgeon General says, "Cigarette smoking is dangerous to your health," and the tax may discourage it. But the low price elasticity of demand noted above suggests that this sumptuary objective is not attained. Alternatively, therefore, the tax would appear to "punish" smokers for their misbehavior. And to the extent that it does not affect behavior patterns the cigarette tax can be held to be an "efficient" tax, one that does not impose a substantial "excess burden."[7]

The cigarette tax may be said to be efficient in another sense. There are relatively few tobacco wholesalers in the state and the tax base is extremely simple. Thus administration and compliance are easy and very low in cost. Bootlegging might be a major problem but it is discouraged under federal law that prohibits interstate shipment of cigarettes through the mails, and Michigan cigarette packages are easy to spot. Unlike those sold in all other states, they do not carry tax stamps. It seems unlikely that cigarette bootlegging into Michigan is a source of much revenue loss. With higher tax rates in all surrounding states except Indiana the bootlegger haul is a long one.

Offsetting the efficiency of the cigarette tax, however, is its failure to meet any reasonable test of vertical or horizontal equity. With respect to vertical equity, it has been estimated that the average ratio of cigarette taxes paid to income in Michigan ranges from 1.00 percent at incomes below $3,000 to 0.14 percent for those with incomes above $35,000.[8] Thus it is a tax that treats the poor most harshly while tapping middle and upper income groups very lightly.

Horizontal equity requires that people similarly circumstanced in terms of income, wealth, or total consumption expenditure be required to contribute equally to the support of government. Since some people at all levels of income, wealth, or consumption smoke cigarettes and some do not, and some smoke heavily and others only occasionally, the tax is capricious in its distribution among people and fails utterly any reasonable standard of equity. In fact it resembles a head or poll tax levied at rates that vary with people's cigarette consumption habits.

Conclusions

From the standpoint of equity, few existing taxes can be held to be more reprehensible than the cigarette tax. On the other hand its attractiveness lies in its ease of collection and compliance and its efficiency in terms of the economist's welfare loss minimization criterion. It is a reliable, stable source of revenue with little growth potential at the existing tax rate.

Clearly if the legislature were looking for additional revenue the cigarette tax, capable of yielding close to $13 million for each penny in the rate, would be a tempting target. But, given the alternatives, the pursuit of such temptation would be difficult to justify. Tax-bearing cigarette smokers typically do not smoke less when rates go up; they and their families consume less of other things.

FOREIGN INSURANCE COMPANY PREMIUMS TAX

Insurance, more than any business activity, is subject to protective taxation by the states. Foreign insurance companies, defined as those incorporated outside of the home state, are generally subject to a tax on their gross premiums. The states' laws contain reciprocity and/or retaliatory provisions under which, if state A's companies are taxed at a higher rate by state B than A levies on B's companies, state A will raise its rate to that of state B with respect to B's companies. At the same time domestic companies' premiums may be either exempt or taxed at a lower rate. That such tax provisions do not involve regulation of commerce "among the several states," an activity reserved to the U.S. Congress under the commerce clause of the Constitution,[9] is surprising to the lay observer. The revenue yield of this tax, at about $3 billion for all states in 1980 is not trivial. Nor are Michigan's 1982 expected receipts of $140 million, fully 5 percent of total state tax revenue.[10]

Structure of the Tax

Michigan conforms quite closely to this long established pattern of state insurance taxation. The present law has been essentially unchanged for over sixty years and the tax was first imposed in 1861.[11] All foreign insurance companies are taxed on the gross premiums received under policies covering risks having a Michigan status. Life insurance premiums are taxed at the rate of 2 percent, while casualty insurance premiums carry a 3 percent rate. Amounts paid under annuity contracts are exempt and mutual companies are permitted to deduct dividends paid. Premiums received by fraternal benefit societies, nonprofit companies, and cooperative associations are fully exempt. The foreign insurance company premiums tax is in lieu of all other taxes except the local property tax.

Domestic Insurers

Domestic insurance companies are taxed in Michigan essentially like all other business firms. They pay the single business tax and the local property tax but, along with foreign companies, are exempt under the intangibles tax.

Data assembled by the Michigan Insurance Bureau, covering all domestic insurers, provide some insights into the relative tax position of domestic and foreign insurers.[12] Of the ninety-seven domestic insurers doing business in Michigan in 1978, twenty-five were exempt from the SBT because they are fraternal societies, farm mutuals, nonprofit associations, cooperatives, or funds and pools, For the remainder SBT liabilities amounted to $3.8 million. The Insurance Bureau estimated that if these companies had paid the in lieu tax on premiums at a rate of 2 percent[13] their tax liabilities would have been $41.8 million. Thus domestic insurers saved $38 million in the one year.

It is not clear what the State of Michigan gains in return for this strong tax discrimination in favor of domestic insurers. Foreign companies account for approximately three-quarters of the volume of premiums paid in the state. Competition and regulation together would make it unlikely that tax savings are passed on to policy holders. Thus domestic companies enjoy a cost advantage that may result in somewhat larger employment in the industry in the state than would otherwise obtain. But it is difficult to imagine that the net gain in earnings can be worth as much as $38 million per year.[14]

Undoubtedly some small domestic insurers that now pay little or nothing under the SBT because of allowable deductions of costs related to insurance claims would be especially hard hit by the imposition of the premiums tax. With respect to these companies there remains the question as to whether or not the tax laws should subsidize firms which, for whatever reason, are otherwise unable to remain successfully competitive.

Conclusions

The Michigan foreign insurance company premiums tax is both an anomaly and an anachronism. It is a tax that is unsupportable on the basis of all widely accepted norms of taxation because it meets neither equity nor efficiency criteria. Even if it uniformly applied to all insurance premiums one would be hard pressed indeed to produce an underlying sensible rationale for the tax. About all that may be said in its favor is that it does yield $142 million for the General Fund. And to the extent that insurers, regulatory authorities, and insurance markets in general have adjusted to its existence, its consequences may be of no great significance. It is an old tax and major changes in it would give rise to windfall gains and losses that, conceivably, could result in more inequities and economic distortions than its continuing imposition will entail.

Nevertheless, serious consideration should be given to amendments to the law that would make for a more even handed application of the tax, reduction in arbitrary discrimination among insurers, and a more efficient allocation of resources in the industry. These amendments might encompass taxing domestic and foreign insurers alike under a uniform 2 percent premiums tax, subjecting currently exempt insurers to tax, and including payments for annuities in the tax base. If all insurance companies were exempted under the SBT the net revenue gain to the state would approximate $80 million per year, or $35 million if Blue Cross-Blue Shield premiums were to continue to be exempt.

STATE-ASSESSED UTILITY PROPERTY TAXES[15]

Under Act No. 282 of the Public Acts of 1905, as amended, and Article IX, Section 5 of the constitution property owned by telephone, telegraph, and railroad companies is exempt from local property taxation. It is subject to an in lieu tax levied by the state on the value of real and tangible personal property as assessed by the State Board of Assessors. The tax rate in the current year is the statewide average rate levied on locally assessed property in the preceding year, 53.42 mills for 1981. The tax base is 50 percent of market or "true cash" value.

In fiscal year 1982 telephone and telegraph companies are expected to pay $102.5 million and railroad companies $1.5 million.[16] The communications companies are contributing more now to the state's General Fund than ever. The railroads, however, have been enjoying a very nearly free ride since 1978. In 1977 the state-levied tax on railroad property yielded $10.5 million.[17] In that year the legislature passed Public Act No. 290, under which (as amended by Public Act No. 322 of 1980) railroad companies are permitted a credit against their property tax liabilities equal to 25 percent of their expenditures for maintenance and improvement of rights of way. The immediate result was a drop in revenue to less than $0.5 million for 1978. There has been only a modest recovery since.

Issues

The principal issue involved in this tax is the question as to why railroads and telephone and telegraph companies are treated differently under the property tax from all other business enterprises in general and gas and electric utilities in particular. Obviously when this differential treatment was initiated at the turn of the century railroads and telephone and telegraph companies owned property that extended across many local taxing jurisdictions, as they do now. No one of these jurisdictions could assess more than a small fraction of the companies' property, and it could well be argued that the value of a railroad or telephone company's property was its value as part of a going concern, a value that could only be reached by applying a "unit rule" to the enterprise as a whole. But in 1981 the multi-plant firm is a common phenomenon in many industries, not least the gas and electric utilities. Thus there is no longer a clear case for differential taxation of railroad and communications companies' property. And a tax subsidy of the order of at least $9 million to the railroads seemed a high price to pay for a dubious return.

The assessed value of all taxable railroad property in the state is not much more than $200 million, which, given its concentration in the lower part of the state, seems modest indeed. The corresponding tax base in the case of the telegraph and telephone companies approaches $2 billion. Because these properties do not change hands in a market, however, it is impossible to judge how close to or how far from 50 percent of true cash value the assessed values are.

The difficulties involved in assessing industrial as well as utility property argue for centralized assessment of all such property. And the location of a plant need not coincide with the place of residence of employees whose children's education gives rise to the largest part of local property tax rates. Thus there is much to be said as well in favor of treating all industrial, public utility and transportation property alike - assessing and taxing it at the state level. The disposition of the resulting revenue, however, is an issue that requires far more study than we have been able to give it and it remains for us, therefore, an open question. We believe that this antiquated feature of the state's tax system should be closely examined at the earliest opportunity.

NOTES, CHAPTER 24

[1]*Budget Message of the Governor*, 1982, p. 72. All but $25.7 million, from two cents of the eleven cent cigarette tax, is available to the General Fund for general purposes. The $25.7 million is earmarked to the School Aid Fund.

[2]Data are from Tobacco Tax Council, *Tax Burden on Tobacco*, vol. 15, 1980.

[3]Public Act No. 265 of 1947, 312 of 1957, 274 of 1959, 218 of 1962, and 11 of 1970.

[4]*Budget Message*, 1982, p. 72.

[5]*Tax Burden on Tobacco*, 1980, Table 11.

[6]Alexander C. Wiseman, "The Demand for Cigarettes in the U.S.: Implications for State Tax Policy" (Doctoral dissertation, University of Washington, 1968).

[7]The excess burden of a tax is the loss in welfare or utility attributable to the tax, over and above the loss associated exclusively with the amount of tax paid, itself seen as a reduction in income or spending power equal to that amount.

[8]Donald Phares, *Who Pays State and Local Taxes?*, 1980, p. 182. It is assumed that the cigarette tax, imposed on the wholesale distributor, is shifted forward to and is borne by the consumer.

[9]Article I, Section 8 (3).

[10]U.S. Bureau of the Census, State Tax Collections in 1980; Budget Message, 1982, p. 72.

[11]The detailed analysis presented in Robert R. Gilliat, "Taxation of Insurance Premiums," Michigan Tax Study Staff Papers, is still essentially valid and may be commended to the interested observer.

[12]Memorandum dated April 1, 1981 provided by Ms. Jean Carlson, Deputy Commissioner.

[13]If domestic insurers were taxed exactly like foreign companies fire, marine, and auto premiums would be taxed at 3 percent. The estimated premiums tax receipts are, therefore, substantially understated.

[14]The gain associated with added employment in Michigan is the difference between the amount that the additional Michigan resident workers earn and the amount they would have earned if the additional employment opportunities had not been available. Only in the unlikely event that these workers would otherwise have been unemployed can the gain be valued at their earnings less the cost to them of going to work.

[15]As in the case of the insurance premiums tax, little has changed since 1958 and we refer the interested reader to a detailed analysis of this tax by John A. Gronouski, "The Taxation of Utilities," Michigan Tax Study Staff Papers.

[16]Budget Message, 1982, p. 72.

[17]Budget Message, 1979, p. 76.

Chapter 25

User Charges as Revenue Sources

by

John Goddeeris

Michigan State University

INTRODUCTION[1]

In discussions of the proper size of government and the ideal tax system for financing its activities, the fact that there may be alternative sources of revenue available in addition to taxes is sometimes overlooked. Users of particular government services may in some cases be assessed charges designed to cover all or part of the associated cost, thus easing the burden on the general taxpayer. Many such user charges are already in place, and they take a wide variety of forms. Fares for public transportation, tolls for bridge crossings, admission charges at parks and other recreational facilities, tuition fees at institutions of higher education, inspection fees, and license fees required for the pursuit of some activity all have the character of charges for particular government services. It is therefore quite appropriate that we examine the current and potential role of user charges in the context of a study of Michigan's fiscal and economic structure.

The Functions of User Charges

Since user charges are, in fact, prices for publicly provided goods, they perform much the same functions that prices do in the private sector. The most obvious function of charges is as a source of revenue for the government involved. Unlike a private firm, a government can resort to taxes to cover the costs of services it provides, so it need not charge prices sufficiently high to cover costs. But the choice between taxes and charges is not a meaningless one, even if the level of expenditures to be financed is the same in either case. Taxes generally distort incentives in undesirable ways, discouraging productive activity. Thus, to the extent that revenues raised through user charges reduce the need to rely on taxes, such charges perform a useful function. The choice between tax and charge finance will of course also affect the distribution of the burden involved in providing public services. It may be argued that charges distribute the burden more fairly, since they ensure that, as in the private sector, services are paid for by those who use them. Whether this is the fairest distribution of the burden will be discussed at greater length below.

In addition to this revenue producing function, user charges can play a valuable role in guiding the allocation of resources. For a service financed by taxes rather than charges, so that there is no direct link between use of the service and payment for it, the question of whether or not the service is worth its cost is not easily answered. It is similarly difficult to know whether a little less (or a little more) of the service should be offered. These questions arise frequently. Depending on the nature of the service, user charges may provide useful information on these issues. The total amount raised in user charges, for example, is a lower bound estimate of the value of the service to its users. If this amount exceeds the full cost of providing it, there is evidence that the service is worthwhile.

Another allocative function that user charges can perform is to ration the available supply of a good or service among consumers. For a good that is fixed in supply (at least temporarily), for example the number of campsites in a state park or spaces in a local parking lot, the number of potential users may exceed the supply if no price is charged. In the absence of charges, the available supply must then be allocated on a first-come, first-served basis, or by some other form of nonprice rationing. Alternatively, a charge can be used and set at the level at which demand equals supply. This approach has the advantage of allocating the supply to those who are willing to pay the most to get it; that is, to those who value it most highly.

User Charges in the Context of the Demand for Lower Taxes

The tax limitation movement going on in Michigan and elsewhere has aroused interest in the potential of user charges as substitutes for taxes. If government were required to finance certain services entirely through charges, this would serve as a constraint on the amount of resources devoted to such services. Such a constraint might seem attractive to those who favor tax limitation because they believe government is too large and wasteful. On the other hand, there are those who do not wish to see the size of government reduced, who believe that the tax limitation movement derives from the failure of individuals to perceive the link between taxes paid and public services received. If this view is correct, the use of charges might provide a natural way to strengthen that link and perhaps defuse any movement toward smaller government arising from that source.

THE THEORY OF USER CHARGES

We have emphasized the analogy between user charges for government services and prices in the private sector. But as we examine more closely when user charges are appropriate and at what levels they should be set, it is important to keep in mind that the kinds of goods and services provided by government are *different* in important ways from those provided by private firms. In fact, the traditional view of the economic role of government holds that government should get involved in precisely those areas where private markets *fail* to satisfy our objectives adequately. If government is providing the things that private firms cannot or will not provide well, then perhaps the price-setting methods of private firms are not the best model for government to follow. It will be useful to sort out conceptually the kinds of goods and services that governments do provide.

It is clear that user charge finance is infeasible or inappropriate for a large portion of government expenditures in Michigan. For one thing, considerable amounts are spent in assistance to low income individuals. With respect to activities benefiting all residents, user charges are only feasible if nonpayers can be excluded from the benefits of the services in question. But the absence of excludability is an important reason why some services are provided by government rather than private firms. The state and local prison system, for example, might be thought of as providing benefits (or preventing costs) to the general population, but supporting it through voluntary charges is clearly infeasible. So too, the general overhead costs of government--the salaries of legislators, judges, and so forth--must largely be covered through taxes rather than charges. Frequently, however, exclusion is not technically impossible but is costly. Users of city streets, playgrounds, and sewer systems can conceivably be charged for their use, but it is an important question whether the benefits of charge finance justify the additional costs of collecting charges and excluding nonpayers.

Governments, particularly at the local level, do provide some services that are not purely redistributive and for which exclusion is quite feasible. Refuse collection, bus systems, campgrounds, zoos and golf courses are a few examples. To decide how such services should be priced (if at all), we must first ask why they are provided by government rather than left to the private sector. Probably the most valid arguments for government provision of excludable goods have to do with natural monopoly and external benefits. We will examine each of these in turn.

<u>Natural Monopoly and User Charges</u>

In the natural monopoly case, cost and demand conditions are such that one firm can supply the total quantity of services desired more cheaply than could a large number of smaller firms, each providing a small fraction of the total. Since a private monopoly would be expected to restrict output and charge an unnecessarily high price, public provision is sometimes seen as desirable.

Characteristic of natural monopolies--a bus system is a

good example--are high fixed costs and relatively low marginal costs of taking on additional users. This creates a conflict in pricing. A price set at average total costs will by definition cover the full costs of the system, but it will discourage some potential beneficiaries from using it. The system is used efficiently if price is set at marginal cost, but such a strategy generates deficits that must be covered out of other revenues.[2] An important consideration in making the choice is the elasticity of demand for the service. If demand is very inelastic (unresponsive to changes in price) then setting a price above marginal cost leads to little reduction in use; that is, little efficiency cost. Alternatively, if demand is very elastic, increases in price lead to large reductions in quantity, which in addition to being inefficient also reduce revenue.

Slightly more complicated pricing schemes can sometimes combine the advantages of average and marginal cost pricing. One possibility is to split the charge for the service into two or more parts. A bus system, for example, might require a monthly pass for which a fee is charged, and an additional fee per ride (with perhaps an alternative, higher, per ride charge for those without passes). The intent is to cover part or all of the fixed costs of running the system through the monthly fee while retaining marginal cost pricing to encourage efficient use. It must be recognized, however, that some potential users may find the monthly fee unattractive, and stop using the system entirely (or use it less frequently at the higher per unit fee). Another possibility is charging different prices to different types of consumers. If different types can be readily identified (say, by age), it makes sense from an efficiency point of view to charge a higher price to groups with relatively inelastic demands.

In practice the demand for many government services varies by time of day, day of week, or for other reasons, while at least some portion of costs does not vary with use.

Buses run full during rush hours but less so at other times. Campsites in parks are full to capacity on weekends, only partially full during the week. Efficiency in use still calls for a charge equal to short run marginal cost when excess capacity exists. But the users in peak demand periods ought to pay a higher charge, equal to the full long run marginal costs of expanding the system, and the system's size should be set at the point at which they are just willing to do so.[3] If a price below long run marginal cost is charged at times when the system is fully used, the case for raising the charge is rather strong. Doing so can increase revenue without losses in efficiency; in fact, efficiency may be increased as the higher price rations the available supply to those who value its use most highly. Raising the charge also provides useful information on the value of the service to users. If a charge designed to cover long run marginal costs restricts demand to the point where the system is never fully used, this suggests that the system has already been overexpanded and reductions in its size might be considered. These considerations are relevant to the pricing of transit systems, parks and other recreational facilities, and parking lots, among other services.[4]

<u>Services Involving External Benefits or Costs</u>

Another possible reason for government provision of a good or service is the presence of external benefits. External benefits are said to exist when the benefits of consuming a commodity accrue to others in addition to the direct consumer. Vaccinations against infectious diseases provide a good example. When any particular individual is vaccinated everyone benefits, since the risk of contracting the disease from that person is reduced. Goods involving external benefits may be provided at an inefficiently low level in the absence of government action, because individuals are likely to consider only private benefits in deciding how much to purchase. The traditional prescription given by economists in this case is that individuals be subsidized to purchase such goods, with the subsidy per unit equal to the marginal value of external benefits. Alternatively, such goods may be provided by government, with the subsidy in the form of below cost pricing.

If external benefits do justify a subsidy to some activity, we should be careful to direct the subsidy at the activity that produces the externality. It is frequently argued that the provision of primary and secondary education involves significant external benefits; we all benefit from living in a society where people possess basic knowledge and skills. Even if this argument is accepted, however, one may ask whether it applies to musical training or sports, for example. If not, then perhaps charges are appropriate for at least those latter aspects of education.

For services that benefit the poor, might not charges below marginal cost be desirable as a means of redistribution? We have largely skirted this issue thus far, but it is clearly an important one in discussions of public prices. Placing the argument in an externality framework, one might contend that everyone is better off when the welfare of the poor is increased, and that therefore a subsidy to those things consumed by the poor is called for. A standard response by economists to this argument is that to the extent that redistribution is justified, it ought to be done in the form of cash, not subsidies to specific goods. The subsidization of particular goods distorts consumption expenditure patterns. The recipients can be made better off (at least in terms of their own preferences) if the cost of such subsidies is given to them in the form of cash, allowing them to decide how best to spend it.

This argument for the superiority of cash to in-kind transfers (or price subsidies) is an important one, but it is not entirely persuasive. It may be that those from whom the assistance is coming--the taxpayers in general--are more willing to subsidize particular goods than to simply transfer purchasing power. That is, they may wish to make the transfer conditional on consumption of some particular goods. Several reasons for such an attitude are possible. It may be felt that those in need of a particular service--for example, medical care--are more deserving of transfers than others of similar income. Or there may be a deliberate attempt to interfere with the recipients' consumption patterns, directing them towards goods believed to be meritorious.

Where, then, do these considerations leave us? Our earlier discussion of the natural monopoly case produced some suggestions on how to price services so that they will be used efficiently, and so as to obtain information on the value of such services to the public. The basic message may be summarized by saying that where feasible, prices ought to be set so as to cover at least the relevant marginal costs, and perhaps somewhat more if marginal cost pricing does not cover the full costs of the service. We have now suggested that distributional considerations may make pricing at less than marginal cost desirable. How are we to decide in any particular case?

The question is difficult, but several points can be made with respect to it. We should bear in mind, first, that pricing below cost provides no free lunch; the resulting deficits must be made up in taxes. If the pattern of use matches the pattern of incidence of the taxes collected, pricing below cost has no desirable distributional effect. It is thus important to examine the pattern of use of the service in question across income classes, to see whether the distributional consequences of a particular pricing strategy do go in the desired direction. We should also ask in each case whether we really do want to redistribute income in this way. That is, we should ask whether we want to favor the consumers of this particular good relative to those who choose not to consume it. A further point is that subsidizing a commodity for one group may not require subsidizing it for everyone, and in some cases a blanket subsidy may not be the best solution. A belief that higher education ought to be available to everyone, for example, does not necessarily imply that price should be below cost to everyone; marginal cost pricing with aid on the basis of financial need might be more sensible. One other point worth making is that if the choice is between marginal cost pricing and some _higher_ price (say, an average cost price), and the service is one that does primarily benefit the poor, both efficiency and distributional considerations would appear to support the lower price.

The Issue of Deductibility

An important factor working against reliance on user charges at both the state and local levels is the deductibility of taxes paid to lower levels of government from income taxed at higher levels. For individuals who itemize deductions, state and local _taxes_ paid are deductible from income before federal income tax is computed; user charges are not deductible.[5] In this sense the federal government subsidizes state and local government expenditures financed by taxes. Greater reliance on user charges would reduce this subsidy to the State of Michigan. In addition to the federal subsidy, local expenditures financed by property taxes are substantially subsidized by the state through the homestead property tax credit (examined in detail in Chapter 17). This situation seriously limits the incentives of local governments to move toward greater reliance on user charges.[6]

USER CHARGES IN MICHIGAN

State Level

Despite the attention afforded recently to user charges, their use by state governments has actually declined relative to other revenue sources, both in Michigan and the U.S. generally. Nor does significant further substitution of charges for taxes appear likely. A possible exception is in the area of higher education, which will be examined below.

TABLE 25.1
CHARGE RELATED REVENUES FOR STATES,
U.S. AND MICHIGAN FOR SELECTED FISCAL YEARS

	1962	1967	1972	1977	1979
U.S.					
Charge Related Revenue (millions of dollars) .	8,532	12,658	20,410	29,005	33,054
Per Capita: nominal . . .	45.91	63.97	98.02	134.04	150.18
1979 Dollars[1]	110.32	139.26	170.30	160.77	150.18
Percent of General Revenue	27	24	17	17	16
Percent of Own Source General Revenue .	36	34	29	24	22
MICHIGAN					
Charge Related Revenue (thousands of dollars) .	366,224	547,164	910,459	1,269,157	1,591,197
Per Capita: nominal . . .	45.61	63.74	101.00	138.94	172.82
1979 Dollars[1]	109.59	138.76	175.48	166.65	172.82
Percent of General Revenue	25	23	19	16	16
Percent of Own Source General Revenue .	32	30	29	22	22

Note: [1]Using U.S. Consumer Price Index as deflator.

Sources: U.S. Census Bureau, State Government Finances, various years.

TABLE 25.2
STATE CHARGE RELATED REVENUES PER CAPITA BY TYPE,
U.S. AND SELECTED STATES, FISCAL 1979

	U.S.	MI	CA	IL	IN	NY	OH	PA	WI
Total Charge Related	150.62	172.82	126.39	123.66	163.30	96.98	155.49	158.37	153.50
Percent of General Revenue	13	14	9	12	19	9	15	15	12
Motor Vehicle Related	74.57	84.29	61.26	78.93	75.85	55.63	71.19	82.14	61.22
Motor Fuel Excise	45.48	55.11	39.56	37.80	51.30	28.65	39.34	44.80	38.92
Motor Vehicle and Operators Licenses	23.49	28.27	18.36	32.28	18.90	18.34	26.55	28.21	21.88
Charges for Highways	5.60	0.91	3.34	8.85	5.65	8.64	5.30	9.13	0.42
State Institutions of Higher Education	36.87	54.41	29.24	27.62	60.23	15.46	46.33	24.56	53.14
State Hospitals	13.83	20.28	16.53	5.63	14.40	3.65	21.51	10.55	24.01
Other Licenses	13.94	6.71	7.58	6.08	5.27	8.74	14.14	35.57[1]	10.24
Other Current Charges	11.41	7.13	11.78	5.40	7.55	13.50	2.32	5.55	4.89
Other Licenses and Charges as a Percent of General Revenue	2.3	1.1	1.4	1.1	1.5	2.0	1.5	3.8	1.1

Note: [1]32.63 is for corporations, public utilities, and other occupations and businesses.

Source: U.S. Census, State Finances in 1979.

Table 25.1 presents some aggregate data on the use of charges over time by the State of Michigan and in the nation as a whole. Classified as charge-related revenues here are motor vehicle fuel excise taxes (which are closely linked to the use of highways and are typically earmarked to their finance), all license fees,[7] and all current charges. Looking at the total of these as a percentage of general revenue and as a percentage of own source general revenue, it is clear that the U.S. and Michigan follow very similar patterns over time.[8] In Michigan and in the nation as a whole, charge-related revenue has declined rather substantially as a proportion of both revenue measures since the 1960s. This decline is probably less the result of reduced reliance on charges for specific services than of relatively rapid growth of expenditures on items for which charges have always been relied on very little. Examination of the U.S. Census Bureau data (again for both Michigan and the U.S.) suggests that for functions for which comparisons can be made, user charges have not declined as a percentage of expenditure. Conversely, over the same period, direct expenditure on public welfare has grown as a share of total state expenditure (from eight to twenty-two percent for Michigan, seven to fourteen percent for the U.S.)

Charge related revenues still account for 16 percent of the state general revenues, about $1.6 billion in Michigan in fiscal 1979. It is important to recognize, however, that a very large fraction of this revenue comes from charges related to only three types of activities. In order of amounts of revenue raised these are: the use of motor vehicles and highways, higher education, and hospitals. This point is brought out in Table 25.2 which gives a breakdown of charge related revenues per capita in the U.S., Michigan, and several other states in 1979. In Michigan over 90 percent of charge related revenues fall into one of the above three categories; for the U.S. as a whole it is almost 85 percent. Although there are differences among states in reliance on various charges, the data in Table 25.2 suggest that charges other than for those three categories represent a relatively minor portion (one to two percent) of state general revenues in most states comparable to Michigan.

For the most part charges other than in those three categories probably should not be regarded as potentially important substitutes for other state revenue sources.[9] Table 25.2 suggests that they are not used in that way by other states. Furthermore, the activities they are associated with generally are not at present heavily subsidized by the state. This is not to say that such charges should be eliminated or that they are already set at optimal levels. For services with well-defined beneficiaries (and which are not intentionally redistributive), charges should be examined to see whether the beneficiaries are indeed bearing the appropriate marginal costs. Examples are the provision of documents and records, and the rental of state buildings. In the case of licenses and fees associated with regulated industries and occupations, the most important question in each instance is whether regulation provides net benefits to the residents of the state. If not, it should be abandoned. If the regulatory process does provide benefits to the consumers of the services of those regulated, it seems reasonable to set the licenses and fees so as to cover the costs of regulation. If the benefits of regulating a particular industry accrue to others in addition to the consumers of its services, the case for covering the full costs of regulation through license fees is weaker.

The potential for the State of Michigan to further substitute charges for taxes is limited by the nature of current expenditures. An examination of state expenditures (see Chapter 12) reveals the importance in the state budget of such redistributive programs as financial assistance and medical assistance to the poor, the provision of mental health services, and aid to local units for the finance of primary and secondary education. Other functions providing largely nonexcludable benefits include general government overhead, the state corrections system, the state police, and public health. The state highway system, another major expenditure area, is already financed through charge related taxes (the Department of Transportation received no General Fund subsidy in fiscal 1981).

Charges for higher education. Charges for some particular state functions are discussed elsewhere in this volume; user taxes for the state park system and fish and game management are discussed in Chapter 26. We will consider here one other area, that of higher education, though space does not permit the depth of analysis this subject warrants.

Higher education is one service with identifiable beneficiaries that is heavily subsidized by the state. Appropriations to state colleges and universities were $673.8 million in fiscal 1980, and $134.6 million was appropriated to community colleges in that year. The total of $808.4 million represents about 42 percent of the net revenue raised by the state income tax in that year, and is several times the total amount of the state charge revenues aside from the three main categories.

If state appropriations to institutions of higher education are simply divided by the number of full-time students (thus ignoring any services other than student instruction that such institutions provide), figures on state subsidy per student can be calculated. In Table 25.3, this is done for two groups of colleges and universities and for community colleges for selected years. For the colleges and universities, these subsidies are compared with tuition levels.[10] These subsidy levels are clearly large, and large relative to tuition. The largest subsidies go to students at Group I universities (The University of Michigan, Michigan State, and Wayne State), and the smallest to those at community colleges. Even at the latter, however, state subsidization amounted to more than a thousand dollars per student in 1981. Tuition levels have been growing even faster than state appropriations, but they are still only about half the size of the subsidies.

TABLE 25.3
AVERAGE RESIDENT UNDERGRADUATE TUITION
AND STATE APPROPRIATIONS
PER FISCAL YEAR EQUATED STUDENT,
MICHIGAN PUBLIC INSTITUTIONS
OF HIGHER EDUCATION, SELECTED FISCAL YEARS

STATE COLLEGES AND UNIVERSITIES		1962	1967	1972	1977	1981
GROUP I	(A)	288	342	636	987	1494
	(B)	1173	1400	1764	2616	3386
	(C)	.20	.20	.27	.27	.31
GROUP II	(A)	225	308	508	733	1041
	(B)	601	876	1155	1695	2121
	(C)	.27	.26	.31	.33	.33
COMMUNITY COLLEGES	(B)		388	628	902	1056

Notes: Group I: University of Michigan (Ann Arbor), Michigan State University, Wayne State University.

Group II: All other state four year institutions.
(A): Average resident undergraduate tuition.
(B): State appropriations/Fiscal year equated students (total student credit hours divided by 31 semester credit hours).
(C): (A)/ (A)+(B)

Sources: Michigan Department of Management and Budget, and State of Michigan Executive Budget: Fiscal Year 1982.

TABLE 25.4
CHARGE RELATED REVENUES FOR LOCAL GOVERNMENTS,
U.S. AND MICHIGAN FOR SELECTED FISCAL YEARS

	1962	1967	1972	1977	1979[1]
U.S.					
Charge Related Revenue (millions of dollars) .	4,235	6,497	11,352	19,526	25,121
Per Capita: nominal . . .	22.79	32.84	54.52	90.27	113.16
1979 dollars[2]	54.76	71.49	94.72	108.27	113.16
Percent of General Revenue	11	11	11	11	12
Percent of Own Source General Revenue .	16	17	17	19	21
MICHIGAN					
Charge Related Revenue (thousands of dollars) .	174,933	300,997	586,974	950,909	1,268,500
Per Capita: nominal . . .	21.79	35.06	64.63	103.95	137.78
1979 dollars[2]	52.35	76.32	112.29	124.68	137.78
Percent of General Revenue	10	11	12	12	13
Percent of Own Source General Revenue .	15	19	19	21	23

Notes: [1]Estimated.

[2]Using U.S. Consumer Price Index as deflator.

Sources: U.S. Census Bureau, Compendium of Government Finances, various years, and Preliminary Data on State and Local Government Finances in 1978-79.

Substantial state support for higher education is by no means unique to Michigan. In fact Michigan appears relatively high in the extent of its reliance on charges. For fiscal 1979, charge revenues were 39 percent of expenditures for Michigan institutions of higher education, only 33 percent for state institutions in the U.S. on average.[11] Tuition levels in Michigan are also relatively high. State universities in California, Illinois, New York and Wisconsin, for example, all had tuition levels below $1,000 in fiscal 1981.

Can such subsidies be defended, or is higher education an area where user charge finance ought to be relied on more extensively? The natural monopoly argument does not seem relevant here, but the case for subsidies may be made on several grounds. One argument is that the state is buying research and public service in addition to the education of students. The case for public subsidy of research as a nonexcludable good seems strong (Nerlove 1972), although it is not clear that the state level is the most appropriate level of government to provide it. The differential in subsidies between the Group I and Group II colleges and universities might be regarded as largely a subsidy to research, but surely a large subsidy to student instruction remains. Another argument for subsidies to higher education is that education of students itself generates significant external benefits, so that low tuition is desirable in order to encourage more students to attend than otherwise would. To some the existence of these external benefits is apparently self-evident, but virtually no hard evidence exists with respect to their magnitude (see the discussions in Nerlove 1972, and Friedman and Friedman 1981).

Perhaps the most widely accepted argument for low tuition at public colleges and universities is that such a policy helps equalize opportunities for individuals from different economic backgrounds. But it is important to realize that the net subsidy to students attending institutions of higher education comes about because part of the cost is borne, through taxes, by families who will never make use of the system. The likelihood of attending college is strongly correlated with family income, and evidence from other states (Hansen and Weisbrod 1969) suggests that even among individuals who attend college, those from families with higher incomes are more likely to attend the more heavily subsidized institutions, and for longer periods of time.

A case can be made, then, for substantially reducing public subsidies to higher education and relying more heavily on tuition as a source of funds.[12] Even if one believes, however, that this is a good policy for the nation to adopt, whether it is advisable for one state to adopt it unilaterally is a different question. If Michigan's higher educational institutions were to double or triple tuition levels while subsidies continued in other states, the state would certainly become far less attractive to families anticipating sending children to college. The tax relief that this policy would make possible would likely make the state more attractive to others, but if the former group is considered a particularly desirable one, the effect on its incentives should be considered. There is also a transitional equity problem to be considered. The current system of financing higher education is a kind of social contract, in which families contribute to the education of others, with the understanding that the education of their children will also be subsidized (although, as already noted, many families contribute but never benefit directly). To end this system suddenly might seem unfair to families who have contributed over a long period of time through taxes but have not yet enjoyed the benefits.[13]

Local Level

To a greater extent than the state, local governments do provide a variety of services that have identifiable beneficiaries (exclusion is possible) and that are not purely redistributive. Local governments provide sewage services, refuse collection, water, parking facilities, and

TABLE 25.5

LOCAL GOVERNMENT CHARGES PER CAPITA AND AS A PERCENT OF DIRECT EXPENDITURES, BY FUNCTION, U.S. AND SELECTED STATES, FISCAL 1977

	U.S.	MI	CA	IL	IN	NY	OH	PA	WI
PER CAPITA CHARGES									
Total	88.26	103.93	103.13	71.07	76.53	116.36	81.22	59.47	86.58
Education	16.03	22.46	11.79	18.88	12.66	19.08	19.30	17.27	14.49
Hospitals	28.32	37.98	31.15	15.32	38.74	20.25	17.99	1.32	24.00
Sewerage	11.32	16.55	11.60	6.19	11.47	6.39	17.91	16.66	10.34
Other Sanitation	4.08	1.36	4.56	0.93	0.49	1.43	1.89	1.54	0.41
Parks and Recreation	2.93	3.13	5.22	5.58	1.83	2.71	3.00	1.57	3.63
Housing and Urban Renewal	4.08	1.95	2.22	4.34	2.08	15.11	3.03	3.89	2.26
Airports	5.14	4.31	6.75	6.61	1.97	13.47	2.55	4.21	1.72
Parking	1.24	1.64	1.23	1.89	0.62	2.72	1.17	2.06	1.58
Water Supply	23.06	26.13	34.98	27.62	10.72	20.98	20.73	15.45	17.12
Transit Systems	7.78	3.84	7.56	15.72	1.26	43.40	4.01	10.27	4.85
CHARGE REVENUE AS A PERCENT OF DIRECT EXPENDITURE									
Education	5	6	3	5	4	4	5	5	4
Hospitals	67	84	58	52	87	32	57	10	61
Sewerage	34	52	41	16	45	15	68	53	30
Other Sanitation	27	13	51	8	11	6	20	17	4
Parks and Recreation	16	19	18	21	17	13	20	14	17
Housing and Urban Renewal	27	20	16	31	23	43	18	25	26
Airports	96	81	89	130	54	121	48	88	62
Parking	90	82	84	88	94	113	114	90	83
Water Supply	78	91	70	94	88	98	90	95	98
Transit Systems	34	29	28	52	33	54	39	36	67

Source: U.S. Census Bureau, Compendium of Government Finances 1977.

in some cases airports, bus systems, golf courses, swimming pools, zoos, and cemeteries. In all these cases charge finance is quite feasible and indeed is frequently applied to cover at least part of the costs of these services. Furthermore the trend in the use of charges relative to other revenue sources appears to be upward. In Table 25.4 we use U.S. Census Bureau data to look at the trend in the use of charges by local governments in Michigan and in the nation as a whole. Charge related revenues include the same components as in Table 25.1. We can see that as was true at the state level, the relative importance of charges in the revenue structures of Michigan local governments is and has been fairly similar to the national averages. Between 1962 and 1979, charge related revenues increased slightly as a share of local government revenues, and more substantially as a portion of own source local revenues. Local revenues in general increased rather rapidly during this period (somewhat more rapidly in Michigan than in the U.S.), so that charge related revenues more than doubled in real per capita terms.

Table 25.5 breaks down current charges by function, and compares per capita charges and charges as a percent of direct expenditures for local governments in Michigan with those in several other states and with national averages, all for 1977. Included are charges for water supply and transit systems, which the Census Bureau treats separately as local utilities. Michigan appears to make relatively heavy use of charges on a per capita basis, compared with neighboring states, although California's are about as high and New York's are higher. Looking across states, there is considerable variance in per capita charges for particular functions. In part this reflects differences among states in the importance of those functions in local government budgets. Differences by state exist in charges as a percent of expenditure, but these tend not to be as great. Charges generally cover a large fraction of expenditures for hospitals, airports, parking, and water, and a much smaller fraction for education, sanitation other than sewerage, and parks and recreation. The most important charges at the local level in terms of revenue raised are those for education, hospitals and sewerage.

User charge finance is, of course, not a realistic option for all locally provided services. Local schools remain the largest local government expenditure, and it seems unlikely that charges will be used very extensively in the finance of primary and secondary education. If we add expenditures for public welfare, police and corrections, and general government administration, the total amounted to about 57 percent of total local government expenditure in Michigan in 1977 (59 percent for the U.S.). Still, there is probably considerable potential for further expansion on the use charges by local governments.[14] Where charges are not already used for sewerage systems, for example, this can frequently be done with relatively little additional administrative cost by linking the charge to the household's water consumption. Much greater reliance on charges for refuse collection is feasible.[15] Tuition levels can be increased at community colleges. Local transit systems can rely more heavily on fares. Where they exist, subsidies to golf courses, swimming pools, parking lots, airports and cemeteries can be eliminated. Greater use of charges for local parks is possible.

But feasibility is not the only relevant issue here. We have already observed that the deductibility of local taxes and the existing homestead property tax credit program together imply that tax finance of local services is substantially subsidized for at least some taxpayers. This situation provides some disincentive to the use of charges. Even more importantly, feasibility of user charge finance does not imply desirability. User charges should not be regarded as an entirely painless way of raising revenue that should always be substituted for taxes where possible. Residents who suddenly must pay an explicit charge for refuse collection or for the use of a local park will not find such charges painless. The appeal of user charges is not that they eliminate the burden of paying for local services, but rather that they allocate the burden to the beneficiaries, and that they provide valuable information. Used properly, they can provide governments with information on the value of services to their constituents, and users with information on the costs, discouraging overuse. Used improperly--as in the case of a flat fee for refuse collection that is identical for all households--they may seem even less fair than tax finance, without providing appropriate signals to users. The desirability of user charge finance of local services should be assessed on a case by case basis, taking into consideration the kinds of factors discussed earlier.[16] As was noted, prices that do not cover full costs may be desirable to encourage efficient use of some services (if average cost exceeds marginal costs). Where significant externalities exist, prices that cover either more or less than full costs can be optimal.

SUMMARY OF FINDINGS

User charges are an attractive alternative to tax finance for some services provided by state and local governments. At the state level, Michigan's reliance on charges relative to taxes seems fairly comparable to that of other states. The potential for further substituting charges for taxes by the State of Michigan is probably limited, due to the nature of most of the state government's expenditures. One possible exception is in the area of higher education, which is currently heavily subsidized by the State of Michigan (and by state governments generally). Local governments provide a larger variety of services for which the use of charges is appropriate, and their use at the local level has generally been on the upswing. On average, local units in Michigan also rely on charges about as intensively (relative to taxes) as those in other states. But the use of charges varies considerably among local governments, and further expansion is surely feasible. One factor limiting the incentives for state and particularly local governments to substitute charges for taxes is the deductibility situation. State and local taxes are deductible from income for federal tax purposes, and local property taxes are subsidized by the State of Michigan through the homestead property tax credit.

Charge finance is no panacea for all government revenue problems. User charges impose burdens on the payers, just as taxes do, and the substitution of charges for taxes is not <u>always</u> desirable. The proper role of charges is in providing information to aid governments in making resource allocation decisions, in giving incentives to individuals to economize on the use of public services, and in spreading the burden of financing government programs in a more equitable manner.

NOTES, CHAPTER 25

[1]Research assistance by Karen Bole is gratefully acknowledged.

[2]Other prices are possible but generally less attractive. A price above average cost may sometimes raise additional revenue that can be used to finance other services, but it is equivalent to an excise tax on the service in question. Providing the service free of charge encourages overuse as long as marginal cost is positive.

[3]For a more complete analysis of "peak-load" pricing see Williamson (1966) and Mohring (1970).

Many public facilities and services become "congested" before absolute capacity is reached; beyond some point additional users reduce the enjoyment of others --for example, at a swimming pool or park. In such cases a "congestion toll" added to the fee can raise additional revenue while improving efficiency. See Oakland (1972) for a rigorous discussion.

[5]This argument does not apply to businesses, for whom charges as well as taxes are deductible.

[6]It has also been argued that federal and state revenue sharing formulas, by making revenue sharing funds dependent on <u>tax</u> effort, have also created an incentive for the use of tax rather than charge finance. See Reischauer (1975).

[7]We exclude corporation franchise fees for Michigan from 1962 to 1972. These were a fairly important revenue source for the state in those years, but were more in the nature of a net worth tax on corporations franchised in Michigan than a user charge. These fees were virtually eliminated with the introduction of the single business tax.

[8]The revenue definitions (what constitutes general revenue, and so forth) used here are those of the U.S. Census Bureau, which differ somewhat from those of the State of Michigan.

[9]See Michigan Department of Management and Budget (1980) for some additional detail on the nature and magnitude of these charges.

[10]Tuition levels given are for resident undergraduates. Nonresident tuition is typically about three times as high.

[11]U.S. Census Bureau, State Government Finances in 1979.

[12]Many of those who support reductions in subsidies to higher education (e.g., Friedman and Friedman 1981) simultaneously favor special loan programs for educational finance, on the grounds that otherwise many students for whom higher education is a good investment would be unable to attend.

[13]This discussion is far from complete. Other options that might be explored further include combining general tuition increases with more extensive financial aid based on need, and greater use of tuition differentials reflecting differences in cost among types of programs (professional schools versus liberal arts, for example).

[14] The experience of California local governments after Proposition 13 cut back local property tax revenues may be instructive. A study by the U.S. General Accounting Office (1979) found that in the first fiscal year after Proposition 13, local governments raised an additional $334 million in charges. This amounted to about 5 percent of the total reduction in property tax revenues, and about 18 percent of the $1.8 billion not offset by increased state aid. About two-thirds of the total increase in fees was by enterprise special districts, providing such services as water, waste disposal, and electric power. These more than offset reduced property tax revenues through increased charges. Other increased charges included the following; business permits and licenses, parks and recreation fees, library use fees, ambulance fees, and animal control fees.

[15]Charges by government for refuse collection are still uncommon in Michigan, but Grand Rapids and Lansing collect refuse only in bags sold by the city at a price designated to cover a substantial portion of the costs of collection and disposal. This system does create a link between payment for service and benefits received, and involves at least some incentive to economize on refuse created.

[16]For studies of pricing policies for local services in general and for specific service types, see Mushkin (1972) and Downing (1977). See also Advisory Commission on Intergovernmental Relations (1974).

REFERENCES, CHAPTER 25

Advisory Commission on Intergovernmental Relations. Local Revenue Diversification: Income, Sales Taxes, and User Charges. Washington D.C., 1974.

Downing, Paul, ed. Local Service Pricing Policies and Their Effect on Urban Spatial Structure. Vancouver: University of British Columbia, 1977.

Friedman, Milton and Friedman, Rose. Free to Choose. New York: Avon, 1981.

Hansen, W. Lee and Weisbrod, Burton. Benefits, Costs, and Finance of Public Higher Education. Chicago: Markham, 1969.

Michigan Department of Management and Budget. State of Michigan Annual Financial Report. Lansing, 1980.

Mohring, Herbert. "The Peak-Load Problem with Increasing Returns and Pricing Constraints." American Economic Review 60 (1970): 693-705.

Mushkin, Selma, ed. Public Prices for Public Products. Washington D.C.: Urban Institute, 1972.

Nerlove, Mark. "On Tuition and the Costs of Higher Education: Prolegomena to a Conceptual Framework." in Investment in Education, edited by Theodore Schultz. Chicago: University of Chicago, 1972.

Oakland, William. "Congestion, Public Goods, and Welfare." Journal of Public Economics 1 (1971): 339-57.

Reischauer, Robert. "General Revenue Sharing--the Program's Incentives." in Financing the New Federalism, edited by Wallace Oates. Baltimore: Johns Hopkins, 1975.

U.S. General Accounting Office. Proposition 13--How California Governments Coped with a $6 Billion Revenue Loss. Washington D.C.: GPO, 1979.

U.S. Census Bureau. Compendium of Government Finances. Washington D.C.: GPO, various years.

_____. Preliminary Data on State and Local Government Finances in 1978-79. Washington D.C.: GPO, 1980.

_____. State Government Finances. Washington D.C.: GPO, various years.

Williamson, Oliver. "Peak-Load Pricing and Optimal Capacity Under Indivisibility Constraint." American Economic Review 56 (1966): 810-27.

Chapter 26

The Public Management of Michigan's Natural Resources

by

Richard C. Porter

The University of Michigan

INTRODUCTION[1]

Michiganders have always been proud of the state's natural beauty and natural resources. Increasingly, the state's public policies are reflecting this pride and concern. The purpose of this chapter is to display and discuss the economic criteria necessary for a sensible development of resource policies. Specifically, we focus on the pricing, taxing, and public management of the state's resources.

Just listing the ways in which the state's fiscal and Department of Natural Resources (DNR) activities affect the use of its natural resources could fill a number of pages. Here, we will focus on a few; those where the fiscal and allocative interactions are, or could be, large. In the next section, we examine the way the state generates public revenue from the exploitation of its principal nonrenewable resource, oil and gas. Then we look at the pricing and management decisions of the most important public outdoor-recreation activities, the state park system and fisheries and wildlife management. Finally, we analyze the operation and potential of the state forest system. A brief overview of the issues raised concludes the paper.

MICHIGAN'S NONRENEWABLE RESOURCES

Much of Michigan's economic history has been drawn from beneath its surface and there are strong indications of the renewed importance of the extraction of nonrenewable resources. Copper and iron have given way to oil and gas and, while hydrocarbons will never play the role in Michigan's economy that minerals did in earlier times, their importance is currently accelerating dramatically. Production of oil and gas (see Table 26.1) has more than tripled in the 1970s and values have increased even more rapidly. The executive budget suggests that oil and gas revenues will exceed $100 million in 1982.[2]

The State of Michigan directly owns the rights to the minerals under six million acres of public land. Through the DNR, the state regulates the subsurface development of all twenty-nine million acres of private lands. Moreover, the state controls the resources under its part of the Great Lakes--another twenty-five million acres--although its official policy is to neither explore nor exploit these at this time. Since by tradition, the state does not itself extract its subsurface resources, the DNR's task is to construct policies of authorization, regulation, and taxation so as to achieve an optimal process of withdrawal of its nonrenewable resources.

The determination of this optimal process depends upon the goals that the state is trying to attain. There are basically two. One, the state seeks to maximize the present value of the economic rent attributable to these resources that is actually acquired by its citizens. And two, the state seeks to constrain the path and means of this extraction so as to be consistent with Michiganders' concerns for the environment, community stability, and equity, both intragenerational and intergenerational equity.

The problem is to translate these goals into implementable rules, regulations, procedures, and taxes. (Here, we shall concern ourselves only with oil and gas policies, since this resource is of overriding quantitative importance at this time, but much of the discussion of what is being done, and what might or should be done, is applicable to other metals and minerals.) Currently, on the land it administers, the DNR determines what new acreage is to be leased for oil and/or gas exploration and extraction. Each such lease, ranging in size up to 640 acres (chosen to promote the efficient extraction of the underlying resource

TABLE 26.1
OIL AND GAS PRODUCTION IN MICHIGAN

YEAR	QUANTITY OF OIL (millions of bbls)	QUANTITY OF GAS (millions of cubic feet)	VALUE OF OIL AND GAS[1] (millions of 1980 $)
1955	10.4	9.8	104.1
1960	16.7	27.3	140.7
1965	14.7	35.7	135.5
1970	11.7	39.3	98.8
1971	11.9	25.9	92.8
1972	13.0	33.6	106.4
1973	14.5	43.7	142.3
1974	18.1	69.8	317.6
1975	24.4	102.7	501.1
1976	30.4	120.2	632.6
1977	33.0	133.2	698.5
1978	34.7	150.5	749.4
1979	35.4	161.7	885.9[2]

Notes: [1]At wellhead prices.

[2]Currently about 1/3 gas and 2/3 oil.

Sources: _Michigan Statistical Abstract_, and _A Study of Michigan Tax Structure_, Office of Revenue and Tax Analysis, Department of Management and Budget.

pool), is let at auction to the highest "bonus bid." The winning bidder then has seven years to locate and extract the oil and gas, paying a "royalty rate" to the state of one-sixth of the gross wellhead value of the production.[3] The DNR also levies a "severance tax" of 5 percent (for gas) and 4 to 6.6 percent (for oil) on the gross wellhead value of production and oversees the drilling process. All of the revenue except the severance tax is earmarked to trust funds that are used to purchase lands for, or to provide, public recreational activities.

This brief description of current procedures suggests the policy questions that are raised:

1. At what rate and on what public lands should leases be offered?

2. To what extent should the state rely on the "royalty rate" and to what extent the "bonus bid" in its effort to achieve efficient extraction and to maximize its acquisition of the economic rent?

3. By what means and rules should the state award the lease rights on its lands to private drilling operations?

4. Given that the state decides to continue to rely extensively on the "royalty rate" and given the dramatic changes of oil and gas prices in the 1970s, should the "royalty rate" be changed?

5. Should the "severance taxes" on oil and gas removed from private lands be changed?

6. Should the various revenues that the state collects in the process of nonrenewable resource exhaustion be earmarked for limited purposes, and if so, for what purposes?

These six questions are discussed in the six subsections below.

<u>When and Where to Lease</u>

The rule for the optimal time-shape of the state's oil and gas leasing is easily found, in principle. The state should offer leases at the rate that maximizes the present value of its revenues - that is, its share of the economic rents. This means that the present value of the state's real revenue from its last lease each year should be equalized over time. It is difficult to put this rule into operation, primarily because both the quantity and the price of the oil and gas under any given lease are uncertain at the time of the lease contract.

A clue about the extent of the divergence of actual from the optimal leasing rate in the past is offered by Table 26.2. The highest real winning bonus bids per acre occurred around the time that OPEC was becoming effective and have declined since then. Neither the size of the lease offering nor a dry-hole trend seems to explain this decline, although recent leases may well have been thought to be of lower quality. Data on the actual oil extractions from these leases are unhelpful for an understanding of the trend for two reasons: (1) the lease histories are not yet complete, and (2) the ex-post production may not tell us much about the ex ante expectation that motivated the bidding.

In fact, the solution to the optimal rate of leasing problem is probably simpler than the theoretical rule suggests, for two reasons. One, Michigan's fiscal need and U.S. ("new") oil prices are currently so high that a fine-tuning marginal adjustment may be unnecessary; maximization of current "bonus bid" revenues may closely approximate the equal-marginal rule. And two, there are only a small number of potential bidders and drillers currently ready to take up and execute Michigan oil and gas leases. As a result, maximization of current lease revenues in no way means maximization of the numbers of acres leased. At some point, long before leases go unbid-for, an additional lease offered dilutes the competition for other acres, and hence their bonus prices, so much as to lower the state's total bonus revenue. The actual total number of producing oil wells has remained about constant at 4,000 in Michigan over the past

TABLE 26.2
RECENT MICHIGAN OIL AND GAS LEASING

YEAR	ACRES OFFERED (thousands)	ACRES LEASED (thousands)	BONUS BID PER ACRE (1980 dollars)	DRY HOLES (percent)
1965	113	50	1.11	60
1966	158	78	0.61	71
1967	162	99	1.19	68
1968	700	672	4.22	68
1969	153	113	17.60	69
1970[1]	---	---	----	65
1971[1]	---	---	----	47
1972	681	594	33.74	54
1973[1]	---	---	----	44
1974	348	217	54.71	49
1975	170	58	13.39	58
1976	102	34	16.88	59
1977	155	119	4.08	57
1978[1]	---	---	----	54
1979	335	319	4.94	--[2]

Notes: [1]No lease auctions were held in these years.

[2]Not available.

Sources: DNR Land Division records; Michigan Statistical Abstract.

thirty years, so despite all the changes in that period it would seem that until now new leases have been bid for and new wells opened only when old wells were discontinued.

On the issue, on what state lands to permit drilling, it comes down to a matter of environmental and aesthetic concerns, since rarely is there much opportunity cost in foregone output in other productive activities when drilling and extraction occur. Although little quantifiable environmental damage has ever resulted from drilling in Michigan,these concerns are not taken lightly by Michigan's citizenry, as evidenced by the decade-long dispute over the Pigeon River country. In the end, it was not the DNR but direct negotiation between an environmental group and the lease-holders that cleared the way to drilling, albeit with more environmental safeguarding than the existing DNR rules required. Beyond the obvious lesson of Pigeon River, that stricter DNR rules about the environmental aspects of drilling are being urged where forest, wildlife, and recreation are involved, there are two points that need to be noted. One, negotiation between environmentalists and developers, under threats of a time-consuming, uncertain, costly court battle is unlikely to lead to either an efficient set of environmental safeguards or a socially desirable drilling decision.[4] The DNR must always play the lead role in this process. And two, decisions about drilling on environmentally fragile or valuable areas should not be procrastinated, except where environmentally safer drilling technology is expected. The fragility of such areas will not disappear and their environmental value, the opportunity cost of drilling, will almost surely increase over time.

Bonus Bid Versus Royalty Rate

Michigan gathers a share of the oil and gas removed from public lands principally in two ways, through the initial payment of the high bidder for the lease (the "bonus bid") and the fraction of the extracted value paid to the state (the "royalty rate"). Except for the two big lease years, 1972 and 1974, most of the state's oil and gas revenue has derived from the royalty payments (see Table 26.3),[5] and the fossil-fuel price rises of the 1970s are only reflected in those royalty revenues.

What strikes the economist immediately is that neither the bonus nor the royalty is levied directly on what the state should be trying to collect, namely, the economic rent. Ideally, the state would extract from each oil or gas lease all the wellhead revenues minus the costs, where the costs would include an amortization for expected dry holes and a reasonable rate of return on the invested capital. Just to state that ideal is to see its difficulties. Costs are hard to know, for multi-state drillers especially; and the drillers' incentives to husband capital, explore wisely, and minimize costs are seriously eroded by taxes levied on an inaccurately calculated rent. The result is that Michigan, like most states in the United States (and most countries in the world), attempts to approximate the direct 100 percent taxation of rent by an indirect system of bonus and royalty.

Why both? It would seem that the right to a given pool of valuable resources would be worth so much, and both the bidder and the state would be indifferent between a lump-sum "bonus" payment and a comparable series of "royalty" payments as the pool was removed. This indifference quickly disappears, however, once we consider a more realistic world that incorporates uncertainty, costs of extraction, time preference, imperfect factor markets, and the distortions of taxation. In reality, there is a serious danger that, in the process of collecting its share of the economic rent, the state will employ fiscal means that discourage the optimal extraction of the resource and hence diminish the size of that rent.

Royalty rates most clearly provide disincentives to the private driller, three of which are particularly worth noting.[6]

Premature abandonment. As a well (or mine) nears

TABLE 26.3
SOURCE OF STATE REVENUE FROM OIL AND GAS
ON STATE LAND
(millions of 1980 dollars)

YEAR	ROYALTY RATE[2]	BONUS BIDS	OTHER[2]	TOTAL[2]
1955[1]	1.7	0.2	1.2	3.1
1960[1]	1.0	0.3	0.4	1.7
1965[1]	0.7	0.2	0.6	1.6
1970	0.9	0.0	2.0	2.9
1971	1.5	0.0	1.7	3.3
1972	1.9	20.0	1.6	23.5
1973	3.6	0.0	2.3	6.0
1974	9.7	11.9	2.1	23.8
1975	14.7	0.8	2.0	17.5
1976	19.3	0.8	1.9	22.0
1977	18.2	0.4	1.6	20.2
1978	23.0	0.0	1.4	24.4

Notes: [1]Five year averages.

[2]These figures do not include the severance taxes levied.

Source: Michigan Statistical Abstract.

exhaustion, the costs of extraction generally rise. Optimally, extraction continues until (and only until) the resource cost of extracting the next unit of the resource equals its price.[7] But the private operator will abandon the undertaking when the marginal cost reaches the after-royalty price, which is lower and hence occurs sooner.

Postponed extraction. Royalty rates are essentially taxes paid at the moment of extraction. This gives the operator an incentive to postpone tax payments by postponing extraction.

Discouraged exploration. On "marginal" lands where the cost of drilling or extraction is high or where the probability of success or the anticipated resource discovery is low, the anticipated after-royalty revenues may be inadequate to induce positive lease bids even where the before-royalty revenues, the social benefits, make exploration socially desirable.

How important in fact these distortions are is a difficult empirical question. But these theoretical considerations do make a prima facie case for greater, and perhaps sole, reliance on the lump-sum bid.

There are, on the other hand, a number of advantages to the retention of fixed royalty rates, theoretically less tidy but perhaps quite important.

Risk-sharing. The state, by accepting some of the risk for itself--as it does with the royalty rate and does not with a single ex-ante bonus bid--may induce small, risk-averse entrepreneurs into the lease-bidding process, thereby increasing the state's expected total revenues.[8]

Bonus-bid distortions. The bonus is not quite a lump-sum payment because the explorer is able to write it off immediately for tax purposes if the lease is "dry." Because earlier tax deductions are in effect larger deductions, this may induce a socially premature cessation of exploration on an initially discouraging lease. Thus, the bonus shares with the royalty the distorting property of all "second-best" taxation techniques.[9]

Few bidders. The bonus-only system relies heavily on the ability of the state to select the correct rate of lease offerings. The royalty provides a backup to prevent the economic (and political) disaster of an excessive number of minimum-bid giveaways.[10]

Collusion. Although there has been no evidence of collusion in Michigan's lease auctions, the existence of the fixed royalty rate insulates the treasury from its potential effects and thereby reduces the incentive for bidders to collude.

Where general considerations provide no clear guide and the quantitative evidence is sparse, it is wise to postpone any dramatic restructuring of the system.

The Lease Auction

In most auctions, the seller offers a known quantity and the potential buyers differ among themselves in their maximum willingness to pay for that quantity. A successful auction, from the seller's point of view, is one that locates the buyer with the highest willingness to pay and extracts a sale price at, or near, that willingness to pay. Such auctions have been fairly well, if not yet definitively, studied through theory, econometrics, and experimentation.[11] Unfortunately, what the state of Michigan is offering at auction is not a known quantity of oil and/or gas but a right to seek and extract an uncertain quantity. Auctions with intrinsic uncertainty are much less understood at this time.[12]

With auctions of known quantities, there are two critical areas of concern: whether the seller gains more by selling at the first or second price[13] or with oral or sealed-bid auction. We look briefly at each.

First or second price. Within a sealed bid auction, the seller delivers to the highest bidder at a price of either that high bid or the highest losing bid.[14] Once the bids are proferred, the state would, of course, be simply forgoing rent to use a second-price settlement. But the bids themselves are affected by the system employed. With first-price auctions, bidders offer less than their maximum willingness to pay, weighing the probability of regrettably losing the auction against the additional profit if they do win; with second-price auctions, intelligent strategy clearly dictates that the maximum willingness to pay be bid. This second-price system may well earn the state a higher revenue and is recommended by many.[15] But the evidence supporting this recommendation comes from Treasury Bill auctions, with many bidders for many identical auctioned items, and is probably not transferable to the institutionally very different situation of oil and gas leases.

Oral or sealed-bid auction. In principle we would expect the oral auction to be equivalent to the second-price auction in that there, the winner only has to pay the maximum willingness to pay of the second highest bidder (or a very small amount above it). There are, however, a number of other considerations. Collusion among bidders may be easier with oral auctions; on the other hand, the direct competition of an oral auction may stimulate higher bidding (that another bidder thinks a tract is valuable may reinforce one's own belief in the tract's value). How important these considerations are is difficult to evaluate. There is evidence from federal timber auctions that sealed first-price bids give significantly greater revenue than oral auctions.[16]

Once uncertainty enters, bidders face a new problem: they must first estimate what the object of the auction is worth to them, and the more they overestimate, the more likely they are to win the bid. Bidders who are to survive must continually bid less than their estimates of their own willingness to pay. This additional complication makes the choices between first and second prices and between oral and sealed-bid auctions more fuzzy. In short, the received literature about the lease auction is not yet clearly helpful, except as a way of sorting out the arguments.

The Royalty Rate

Economic theory warns us persistently that any royalty rate will distort the driller's incentive to allocate efficiently, and it is difficult to derive from it much advice about the correct royalty rate in the actual, second-best world. Nevertheless, since the royalty rate is retained largely because one believes that the bonus bid fails to capture for the state a sufficiently large portion of the ex post rent, we can get some insight from a theory of royalty without bonus. The royalty rate then becomes the sole means of dividing up the excess of revenues over costs between the state and the lease-holder. To leave the lease-holder with a given rate of return, one should charge a higher royalty rate: (1) the higher the price of the extracted resource, (2) the lower the probability of dry holes, (3) the greater the anticipated resource pool, and (4) the lower the costs. The first and third of these considerations suggest a higher rate for Michigan at this time.[17]

Examination of the practices of other states is instructive. The five largest oil-producing states all charge royalty rates of at least one-sixth, and almost all other states charge one-eighth.[18] Not only is this rate structure consistent with the theory outlined above, but it suggests that Michigan, eleventh and rising in the ranking, has not placed itself at too great a competitive disadvantage by raising its royalty rate to one-sixth.

Oil and gas leases negotiated with private landowners in Michigan generally contain lower bonuses[19] and higher royalty rates[20] than on public lands. If one presumes that these terms reflect the mutually preferred distribution of risk between lessor and lessee, and if the state of Michigan is more able to bear risk than its individual citizens, then this private-land information suggests that the public-land royalty rate is too low.

It has sometimes been suggested that royalty rates should be lower for lower grades of land ("wildcat acreage") or wells in the final stages of their economic life.[21] The idea is sound in principle, in that it alleviates the allocative distortions of royalty rates where and when they are most likely to impinge, but it does raise the spectre of asymmetry of information. The advantage of the auction system over one of direct individual negotiation of terms is that the DNR is not required to match the bidder's technical expertise. This expertise is not cheaply gained. For such areas and wells, an extension of the bidding system, whereby the royalty rate itself were made the object of the bid, would be better.[22]

The Severance Tax

This tax ranges from four percent to 6.6 percent of gross wellhead values for various kinds of oil and gas (and is about 3 percent for iron).[23] For oil and gas and all minerals, Michigan's real severance tax revenues rose at 37 percent per annum during the 1970s.[24] Since tax assessments for local property tax purposes specifically exclude subsoil values, the severance tax is the principal means by which the state shares in the economic rent of its privately owned mineral resources.

Any examination of the proper level of severance taxes must begin by answering two questions. The first question is, why does the state demand a share of the economic rents of minerals? The answer is not that it is a handy source of revenue transferred from the profits of "foreign" corporations, since the ultimate incidence of the tax is largely on the Michigan landowners. Rather, the answer rests uneasily on one or more of the following five rationales:

Externalities. Mineral extraction often imposes unpaid external costs on the community, and special taxation is a recognized way of internalizing those costs. The argument has more validity in a boomtowning, landscarring, stripmining context than for most of Michigan's extractive operations. But even in Michigan, oil drilling, for example, poses such environmental risks and costs as oil spills, well fires, subsurface blowouts, noise, and odor, none of which is fully internalized into the driller's costs.

Myopia. It is sometimes claimed that "people" are short-sighted, failing to provide for the needs of their late years and, even more, of their heirs. To the extent that mineral taxation retards an over-rapid rate of extraction, it may help to correct this failing.

Capital gains. Discovery of exploitable minerals means capital gains and these are widely held as a fit target for special taxation beyond the usual taxes on the income yielded.

Unearned income. In many jurisdictions, it is deemed correct to tax nonwage income at special, higher rates.

Revenue needs. Treasuries must raise revenues and land rents are especially inviting because they offer so few opportunities for distortionary tax-avoidance activities.

The second question is why, among the possible means of taxation, a severance tax is selected. It is subject to all the criticisms of distorting disincentives rehearsed earlier for royalty rates. Such distortions may be socially desirable, as with the externalities and myopia reasons for taxation; but for the other three rationales, the distortions are an unfortunate byproduct. Notwithstanding, there remains the fact that it is an easy tax to calculate and to collect, compared with the less distorting alternatives of taxes on property, subsoil rent, or net mineral income. And the distortions may be smaller for private-land severance taxes than for public-land royalty rates because increased severance taxes may ultimately be offset by lower private-land royalty rates so that the drillers' overall (severance-plus-royalty) payment per extracted dollar's worth of mineral may be little affected.

Michigan's choice of the rate of severance tax is,

then, quite a different one than the choice of bonus-plus-royalty on public lands. The severance tax represents a decision as to how to split the economic rent among Michiganders--i.e., between the landowners and the citizenry as a whole--whereas on public lands the bonus/royalty choice is intended to prevent the rent from accruing to "foreigners." Since the severance tax may ultimately be without serious allocative implications, it can be set by the political process according to the weight given to the five "uneasy rationales" listed above.

Earmarking

The Michigan Legislature has earmarked the flow of public revenues from oil and gas in so curious a way that one can only conclude that it has not yet decided what to do with them. About half goes directly to the General Fund; and the rest is directed into a trust fund to purchase land for hunting, fishing, and other recreational purposes. Because the trust fund will receive a rapidly increasing share of the rapidly increasing revenues, it would appear to represent a major commitment to turn one public asset, oil and gas, into another, land. But the expenditure of the trust fund is limited to $2.5 million per year plus interest, and the fund begins to revert back to the General Fund when it reaches $150 million. Thus, almost all that has been done in the end is to lock $150 million of treasury receipts into a bank deposit.

Despite this convolution, the issue remains whether the economic rents of minerals on public lands should be earmarked, and if so, for what? Economics generally has little favorable to say about earmarking, and almost nothing favorable when the source and the use of the funds are unrelated. The present earmarking basically suggests two indefensible assertions. One, the current (and future) generations of fishers and hunters should be subsidized because past generations of fishers and hunters were excessively taxed or because the land purchased to enhance their fishing and hunting happens to have oil or gas under it.[25] And two, the proceeds of the sale of property belonging to all Michiganders should be transferred to those who heavily consume the services of recreational land. From the viewpoint of the present generation of Michiganders, no case can be made for earmarking the revenues from the sale of the assets of all citizens to expenditures that subsidize the consumption of some citizens.

But the present generation is not the only one involved. The current, and near-future, removal and consumption of the oil and gas under Michigan means, in itself, that all future generations are being made poorer while we are enriching ourselves. Basic ideas of inter-generational equity strongly suggest that we should collectively take care to leave behind more of other assets to offset the reduction of this hydrocarbon asset. One way to insure this is to earmark part of the revenues to the formation of public assets for the future. The question then becomes what kind of assets. Since we cannot know the preferences of future generations and can only crudely estimate the future productivity of different kinds of assets, the correct selection is not easy. My own opinion is that land is a good choice - both urban open space for city dwellers and the consolidation of the state forests for outdoor recreation or, more generally, for some kind of renewable resource production. But the limit currently placed on land acquisition means that Michigan is not officially preparing to provide much (of land or anything else) to replace the oil and gas assets it is using up.

MICHIGAN'S RESOURCE-BASED RECREATIONAL ACTIVITIES

Indoor recreation in the United States has traditionally been left to private markets (or nonmarket mechanisms), but the provision of outdoor recreation has long been a concern of public policy, partly because it is very intensive in its use of public land and partly because its social costs diverge from private costs in critical ways. In this section, we examine two important areas of public, resource-based outdoor recreation, the state parks and fishery and game management. The purpose is to indicate where and how economic criteria could be better applied in the search for optimal pricing, management, and capacity decisions.

State Parks

The Michigan state park system consists of eighty parks, ranging in size from 32 to 58,332 acres and in number of campsites from none to 500. The total acreage is 245,595 and the total number of campsites is 13,900. Total attendance in 1980 was 21 million people, with 403 thousand camping overnight and 102 thousand vehicles being turned away for lack of space. If this park demand had occurred smoothly over time, on, say, the 90 days of June through August, and smoothly over space, these attendance figures would have meant that only one-third of the campsites were filled and that park visitors enjoyed one acre per person during their attendance. In fact, however, the state parks are not homogeneous with respect either to the nature of the acres supplied or to their demand across time or space.

What is supplied and demanded differs importantly across two broad dimensions. With respect to demand, some of the parks, mostly in the southern part of the Lower Peninsula, are heavily demanded and frequently filled to capacity. For example, just two parks (Holland and Warren Dunes) provided 13 percent of the total system attendance and 22 percent of the total turnaways in 1980; but these two parks together comprise less than one percent of the total park acreage. What is supplied also differs among parks. Not only are recreation opportunities supplied at different densities, as a result of the demand structure, but also a range of facilities is provided, from "rustic" to "modern." About one-fifth of the parks offer no electricity, flush toilets, or showers, and in these there are few campers and large areas. Of the parks that do offer "modern" facilities, many also provide a park store and a sanitation station.

TABLE 26.4
STATE PARK USE IN 1979

Annual permits (millions of cars)	0.34
Daily permits (millions of cars)	0.65
Total attendance (millions of people)	21.40
Estimated auto attendance (millions of cars)	7.13[1]
Percent second or greater use on an annual permit	86%

Notes: [1]Total attendance divided by an estimated three people per car.

Sources: Michigan Statistical Abstract; Park Division records.

TABLE 26.5
RECENT PATTERN OF MICHIGAN STATE PARK FINANCING
(figures are percentages of total operating costs)

YEAR	SOURCE[1]		
	GENERAL FUND	VEHICLE ENTRY PERMITS	CAMPING FEES AND CONCESSIONS
1975	67%	--[2]	33%
1976	56	--[2]	40
1977	57	--[2]	42
1978	59	--[2]	38
1979	52	8%	35
1980	44	10	43
1981	31	16	50

Notes: [1]Where the totals do not add to 100%, the difference is largely accounted for by federal funds.

[2]Vehicle entry permit revenues were not used for operating costs until 1979.

Source: Parks Division records.

Although the actual state park system does not divide itself into two extremes in terms of available facilities, it is instructive to examine the proper pricing for the stereotypes. In parks with large acreage, with few or no facilities, and where the campsites are rarely filled, the appearance of a marginal camper involves practically no marginal social cost. On the universal rule of publicly provided services, that use should be proffered as long as the marginal social benefit exceeds the marginal social cost, the entry price at these parks should be kept low, perhaps even lower than the current two dollars per camp night.[26]

On the other hand, in frequently congested parks, where extensive "modern" facilities are provided, the marginal visitor adds two kinds of costs. Not only are there heavy operating costs there, but there are congestion externalities. Indeed, when people are turned away, it is the official recognition that excessive congestion costs are being incurred. Here the base price should be high and, if political considerations do not prevent it, a peak-demand surcharge should be added at certain parks and at certain times. How high the base price should be is partly a function of park costs, but it is also essential that it be kept comparable to private-market modern campgrounds, lest the parks invite excessive congestion through substitution.

To what extent does the actual Michigan state park pricing structure conform to these general precepts? For camping, fairly well, with fees ranging from two dollars to six dollars, according to the facilities provided. But for daily visits, not at all, with the same two dollars fee being charged everywhere, regardless of the facilities. Moreover, as Table 26.4 indicates, only about one-seventh of the daily users pay any fee at all, purchasing instead an annual permit (currently at ten dollars) that makes the effective cost, after the first entry, zero for all parks and all times. Finally, for neither camping nor daily use is there any alteration of price in response to congestion, either the periodic congestion of almost all parks at some times or the continual congestion of some parks at almost all times.

The rationale for the annual permit for state parks is presumably rooted in the "golden age" of low-cost low-congestion parks when a multi-part tariff might have been an appropriate means of collecting revenue for the park system while charging the zero marginal social cost for marginal use.[27] The contemporary result, however, has been effectively an admission policy of zero marginal price to the state parks since some 86 percent of the visitors enter on an annual permit for the second or greater time. The annual permit no longer serves either the purpose of correct marginal pricing or the purpose of gathering enough revenue for the state park system. In the absence of an income redistribution rationale - and it is well established that the state parks, unlike urban parks, are not much used by the poor[28] - there really remains no economic justification for the annual state park permit.

The discussion so far has been concerned with pricing for Michigan residents. It is not unduly xenophobic for this state to take the attitude that its state parks should be made available to nonresidents only to the extent that the revenue they provide covers the costs of serving them. This means that the resident optimal pricing rule, price equal to marginal cost, must be changed for nonresidents to the rule, <u>marginal revenue</u> equal to marginal cost. For any given level of usage, therefore, the optimal fee structure requires that the resident price equal the nonresident marginal revenue. Thus, the nonresident <u>price</u> should be higher than the resident price by a factor of $(e/(e-1))$, where e is the absolute value of the price elasticity of demand for Michigan's state parks by nonresidents.[29] In only one of Michigan's parks, however, is such a fee differential established--in Warren Dunes, where a nonresident pays a three dollar daily fee (but can, curiously, purchase the ten dollar annual permit). Higher nonresident fees are both an efficient means of discriminating against "foreigners" and a costless source of added DNR revenue, and they should be considered throughout the state park system.

The "concession" operations in the state park system raise different pricing issues. Currently, the DNR offers monopoly concession rights of various kinds for one, three, or five years to the highest bidders, where what is bid is the percentage of the gross concession revenue after sales tax that is turned over to the DNR. The procedure raises a number of issues. One,it can be demonstrated that, for risk-neutral concessionaires, the prices charged to campground users would be lower and the revenues of the DNR higher if the bidding were on a one-time annual "bonus" basis rather than on a percentage "royalty" basis; it is not clear that potential concessionaires are so risk-averse as to warrant the present system. Two, under either bidding system, the concession prices charged Michiganders in their own state parks end up above not only the marginal cost but also the average total cost of their purchases; it may be politically necessary to raise funds for the park system wherever they can be located - and especially if they happen to come from park users' pockets - but it should also be recognized that this is an inefficient means. And three, the duration of the monopoly concession must be carefully balanced: if too short, low-quality, fly-by-night concessions will enter; if too long, obsolete contract terms will abound, to the detriment of either the state or the concessionaires.

The state park system is not self-supporting, as Table 26.5 shows. While camping (and other) fees now cover a larger portion of the operating expenses, and some of the daily and annual permit revenues are now earmarked to current expenses, General Fund assistance is still required.[30] The inability to cover costs with marginal cost pricing is an old problem for public enterprise economics, and there are several not wholly satisfactory solutions.

Fortunately, these need no rehearsal here. With congestion and peak-demand pricing, and with the discontinuance of annual permits, all of which are necessary for correct marginal-cost pricing, the state park system would almost certainly be self-supporting, even with much of the daily permit revenue earmarked, as it is now, to the state park capital account.

This brings us to the final question, how much should the state spend on park improvements and new acquisitions? Currently, five dollars of each annual permit and one dollar of each daily (resident) permit is earmarked to a fund whose sole use is financing expansion of, and construction in, the state park system. In 1979 this fund contained $6.7 million, received $1.3 million, and spent $2.2 million. It would appear that the state park system is irrationally self-expanding and that basic policy decisions are needed to prevent it from over-expansion. Actually, this is not so serious a problem as it seems at first glance. As Michigan's system grows and as private campgrounds proliferate, both the number of visitors per park and the congestion surcharges will fall, and one can picture a reasonable equilibrium being attained, with equality of state park revenues and costs. This is not to counsel laissez-faire, for we ought not to rely wholly on this dynamic benignity, and there remain important allocative issues such as which types of parks to expand and whether old parks should be enlarged or improved or new ones created. But the legislature's only critical role is gradually to reduce the General Fund support.

<u>Fish and Game Management</u>

In the United States, the fish and wildlife within the (water as well as land) boundaries of a state belong to the people of the state. It has been long recognized that this ownership would invite an overhunting of the faunal "commons" if free access were permitted. Accordingly, most states have restricted the privilege of taking, or seeking to take, from this commons. The initial restrictions involved regulation about seasons, numbers, means, etc., but in this century a price for entering the commons has also come to be charged. This price is almost always higher for nonresidents of the state than for residents. While the revenues so derived went originally to a variety of public uses, such as schools or jails, they have increasingly become earmarked to fish and wildlife "funds" to be used for the management and improvement of the state's fish and wildlife populations.

This brief review of state fish and game policies in the United States is sufficient to indicate the key areas where Michigan policies are needed, explicitly or implicitly. One, what is the correct fee to charge residents who fish or hunt? Two, what is the correct degree of discrimination to practice against nonresidents? And three, how much should the state of Michigan spend on fish and game management? We examine each of these questions in turn.[31]

Economists are fond of designing fee structures to achieve almost any collection of allocative outcomes. But tradition - nurtured by biologists, not economists - dictates that most of the allocation decisions concerning fish and game are constrained by direct regulation. Thus, those residents who wish to fish or hunt must first accept nonmarket restrictions as to where, when, how, and what they may fish or hunt and as to how much they may harvest. Only then do fees begin to matter. The real resident fees (1980 prices) have risen from $8.73 to $13.50 for fishing (including trout) and fallen from $12.16 to $9.25 for hunting (deer only) over 1950-80. These levels and changes are too small compared to the overall cost of these activities to have had much impact on demand.[32]

Although the fee is not used as a demand-management tool, there is no shortage of debate about the correct level at which fishing and hunting fees should be set. While there are extreme arguments that involve morality, rights, or public revenue needs, most people agree that the benefit principle is applicable here and that fees should cover costs. Unfortunately, "there are few well-documented studies of costs of producing wildlife."[33] Moreover, the very concept of costs is unclear: economists have not thought nearly so much about the recreational harvesting of renewable resources as they have about the management of nonrenewable resources or such renewable resources as forests or commercial fishing. Where renewable resources are unmanaged, their harvest up to maximum sustained yield may involve no costs beyond those borne by the recreationist. Where they are managed, as in Michigan for both fish and deer, the determination of the correct fee is then a byproduct of the bigger decision about the correct extent of management (to be discussed shortly). Moreover, a significant part of the costs is that of law enforcement, and it is not at all clear why those who fish and hunt legally should cover the entire cost of detecting and apprehending those who fish and hunt illegally.[34]

In fact, it is nearly impossible to say to what extent fishing and hunting revenues cover the public costs of these activities. Much of the fish and game revenue is spent on items that have little to do directly with fishing or hunting. Aside from the enforcement activities--to which little other resource-related, user-fee revenue is earmarked--the fish and game revenues support general DNR administration and provide grants to counties, neither of which has a very direct relation to fish and wildlife. And much of the benefit of the fish and wildlife management is derived by people who do not fish or hunt, giving rise periodically to the suggestion that a "lookers'" license be demanded of hikers, photographers, birdwatchers, etc. In general, so many of these activities of the DNR are so "public-good" in nature that it is impossible to allocate costs with any precision. If "covering costs" is the criterion, then fees of half or double present levels could be easily justified. As long as demand for these licenses is not price elastic, the level of fees has little short-run allocative significance.

While the license fees of Michigan residents probably represent mostly transfers among different citizens, the same is not true of the license fees of nonresidents. Here, as with the state parks, the total numbers of people fishing and hunting should be divided so that the price to residents equals the marginal revenue contributed by nonresidents. The ratio of resident to nonresident fees are shown in Table 26.6, along with the implied estimates of nonresident price elasticity of demand, on the assumption that the resident price does, in fact, equal the nonresident marginal revenue. These implied estimates range from one to two with no intuitively clear pattern. If the nonresident price elasticity of demand for any of these licenses is less than the value shown in Table 26.6, then the (relative) nonresident fee should be raised. My guess is that the elasticities are indeed less and that research on how to price Michigan's resource-based recreation "exports" could be profitable.

Just as there is general agreement that license fees should cover costs, so also is it widely accepted that the fee revenues should be devoted completely to fish and wildlife management. In fact, however, much of it gets diverted into other programs, some quite peripheral to fish and game. Although changes in budgetary classifications over time make it difficult to establish the absence of a trend, it appears that just over half of the license revenues are traditionally directed to the fishery and wildlife management programs.

There is, however, no sound economic reason for either complete or partial earmarking. Rather, one should expand such management - as all publicly operated activities - only to the point where an additional dollar of expenditure yields an additional dollar of recreational benefits. It can be shown that the equality of marginal hunter benefit and management costs may imply that optimal total management expenditures should be greater or smaller than license revenues depending upon the relative efficiency with which

TABLE 26.6
RATIO OF MICHIGAN RESIDENT TO NON-RESIDENT LICENSE FEES[1]

YEAR	HUNTING[2]			FISHING	
	Small Game	Deer		Excluding Trout	Including Trout
		General	Bow & Arrow		
1930	0.10	0.05	--[3]	0.00[4]	0.33
1940	0.07	0.09	0.09	0.25	0.25
1950	0.14	0.10	0.35	0.51	0.63
1960	0.16	0.15	0.34	0.32	0.51
1970	0.16	0.15	0.34	0.52	0.57
1980	0.19	0.12	0.18	0.46	0.61
Average	0.14	0.11	0.26	0.34	0.48
Implied Price Elasticity for Non-Residents[5]	1.16	1.12	1.35	1.52	1.92

Notes: [1]Annual fees for those who do not qualify for lower rates (e.g., wives, senior citizens, etc.)

[2]License that is not territorially restricted.

[3]Not issued.

[4]Resident fee zero.

[5]See text for explanation.

Source: DNR.

TABLE 26.7
MICHIGAN STATE FOREST TREATMENT
(figures in thousands of acres treated)

YEAR	TIMBER SALES	PLANTING AND DIRECT SEEDING	TIMBER STAND IMPROVEMENT[4]
1973	71.1	1.8	1.6
1974	75.8	1.0	8.6
1975	51.5	2.0	16.7
1976[1]	49.6	2.6	19.7
1977	39.6	3.4	16.6
1978	41.5	2.5	16.4
1979	41.0[2]	0.0[3]	18.4
1980	41.0[2]	2.7[3]	9.5

Notes: [1]Fiscal year 1976 contained five quarters.

[2]Data not yet reported. These figures are estimates of acreage from the volume-cut data.

[3]Data for these years are not given on a fiscal year basis but for "fall" and "spring."

[4]Not including management for improved game habitat.

Source: DNR, Biennial Reports, various issues.

hunters harvest and management produces the relevant fauna.[35] This is not operational advice since the empirical work needed to derive this optimal management effort does not yet exist; but it does warn us against thoughtlessly perpetuating time-honored rules of thumb.[36]

MICHIGAN'S STATE FOREST SYSTEM

Nearly half of the land acreage of Michigan is forested, and its state forest system is the largest in the nation. And yet, "their potential...economic value is largely unexploited," concluded a recent consultant's report to the DNR.[37] In this section, we will examine the potential for the state forests and the kinds of long-run policies needed to move toward its realization.[38] But first, it is necessary to understand how the current situation has come about.

Michigan began exporting timber in 1847 and, by 1869, was the biggest timber producer in the United States. Along with Wisconsin and Minnesota, it dominated U.S. timber production for the remainder of the nineteenth century. Once the stands of pine and hardwoods were cut, the land became vulnerable to forest fire, and much of it proved inadequately productive for agriculture. Gradually, parcels were forfeited to the state for nonpayment of taxes. The depression of the 1930s completed the process, with 2.2 million acres reverting to the state in 1938 alone. Today's 3.8 million acre state forest system was essentially completed by World War II.[39]

In essence, Michigan acquired its immense state forest system by accident. There are good reasons for public ownership and operation of forests: many of the recreational services they provide are in the nature of a public good, and unremunerated positive externalities may be generated in forest fire control and research activities. But these reasons were never weighed, except implicitly, by Michiganders. Perhaps because of this unconscious acquisition, the legislature has failed to recognize the potential for revenue generation through investment in, and cultivation of, the state forests, never providing an annual budget as large as two dollars per acre (in 1980 prices). Moreover, because of its low level, most of the forestry budget must go to routine management and planning;[40] in 1980, only $935,500 was devoted to forest improvement treatments in immature stands, roughly twenty-five cents per acre.[41]

The result of this neglect is that Michigan's state forests have "just growed" for the past half century. Nevertheless, they are now "growing up in striking form"[42] and contain more than one thousand cubic feet of growing stock per acre.[43] Unfortunately, because of the low level of cultivation and management, many of the trees are of poor quality and of less desirable species. This, plus a low rate of harvest, means that Michigan currently earns less than $3 million per year from its public timber assets - in 1980, for example, the total revenue was seventy-three cents per acre.

One must not forget that the objective of a public forest system is not only timber. These forests are operated for "multiple use," and the "key value" has been officially denoted timber growth and harvest on only about one-fourth of the state forest acres.[44] Nevertheless, many of the other uses are thoroughly compatible with periodic timber harvesting,[45] and it is the timber side of the state
1560 forest operation that we will examine in the rest of this section.

The potential for Michigan's forests, if fully converted to carefully managed stands, is well known in both its theoretical and empirical aspects. The chief of the Forest Management Division of the DNR has stated that "...stand improvement practices, when concentrated in high value forest types on high-productivity sites, can return financial rewards up to 12 to 14 percent per year."[46] The Jaako Poyry consultant report noted that "a forest management program...[to] insure prompt, full regeneration of cut-over stands and maintain regularly scheduled thinning operations" would yield at the end of thirty years "three to seven times current removals."[47] Studies of particular species at particular sites, by the DNR and the Forest Industries Council, show real internal rates of return to managed stands in Michigan almost always above nine percent. With currently known forest cultivation technology, the real rate of return is sufficiently high that all the state Forest acreage whose "key value" is already designated as timber, and probably other acreage as well, could be profitably placed under more intensified management.

At what pace should the conversion take place is the next question. While the economic theory of managed forests is over a century old and well worked out, the theory of converting mature, unmanaged stands to regularly rotated, managed stands is still being developed. Essentially, it views the mature "old-stand" timber as a nonrenewable resource to be "mined" in once-and-for-all fashion and then replaced with a renewable resource. There is no need to review the theory in detail since it is not exactly applicable to Michigan - our state forests are neither fully mature nor totally unmanaged. But the conclusion nevertheless applies: if there are no constraints to the pace of conversion, the welfare of both present and future generations could be improved by converting too-little-managed acreage to optimally managed acreage in the course of the next optimal-length rotation.[48]

The two-pronged strategy for Michigan's state forests, harvesting existing stock and then managing superior replacement stands, is being in fact undertaken in only the most modest way. As Table 26.7 indicates, harvesting usually occurs on only about one percent of the state forest acreage each year. Planting and direct seeding is still quite rare, and less than one half of one percent of the state forests undergo timber stand improvement activities in a typical year. Not only are the management activities modest but they are also, as the 1980 figure shows, highly

TABLE 26.8
DESIRABLE VERSUS ACTUAL HARVEST OF MICHIGAN'S STATE FORESTS
(1975-77 averages)

STATE FOREST	ACTUAL HARVEST AS A PERCENTAGE OF DESIRABLE HARVEST							
	PULPWOOD				SAWLOGS			
	Aspen	Other Hardwood	Pine	Other Softwood	Aspen	Other Hardwood	Pine	Other Softwood
Upper Peninsula								
Copper Country	48%	30%	53%	40%	8%	35%	19%	0%
Escanaba River	43	37	125	45	--[1]	39	57	0
Lake Superior	20	23	93	34	5	68	140	0
Lower Peninsula								
Ausable	26%	103%	67%	29%	11%	71%	167%	0%
Pere Marquette	52	101	73	12	100	108	11	0
Mackinaw	29	55	158	58	11	22	75	0
All State Forests	34%	61%	90%	39%	11%	44%	56%	0%

Notes: [1]Desirable cut zero.

Source: Calculated from data in DNR, "Lands and Resources by Forest Management District," memo, 13 March 1979.

susceptible to the fiscal pressures felt by the legislature.

We look first at the low rate of timber harvest. Sustained-yield, static-technology forestry often suggests - against the advice of economic theory - that the timber harvest should equal the net annual volume of growth of the forests. Michigan state forest timber sales usually are about one-third of net growth.[49] Put differently, the DNR Forest Management Division "prescribed" ninety-four thousand acres for cut in 1981,[50] but no more than half those acres will probably be successfully auctioned for actual harvest. The success ratio varies across location, species, and timber size, as Table 26.8 shows, which indicates that it is to a great extent a matter of demand.

The problem of low demand for low quality timber is not insoluble, and the DNR is thinking small and big about it. The small aspect is the encouragement of firewood use of state forest; the large is the encouragement of voracious wood-product factories.[51] But there is another side to the problem that must not be ignored. Unmarketable timber poses an opportunity cost if it clutters a site that could be profitably converted to a superior managed stand. Timber removals that do not earn net revenues, but rather involve net costs (i.e. "noncommercial" harvesting), may simply represent part of the "site preparation" costs of an optimal program.

The low ratio of actual to desirable harvest is also partly due to the sale procedures of the Forest Management Division. Manpower shortages there, flowing from inadequate budgets, mean that barely half of the desirable annual cut is actually processed to the stage where an offer of "stumpage" is made to bidders. Much of the time of preparation is occupied making a volume and value appraisal of the timber involved. Some sort of volume appraisal--although probably one that is cheaper and less accurate than the present one--is desirable since, if it were not done, each potential bidder would have to make his own estimate of timber volume, a wasteful duplication of effort that would ultimately reduce timber sale revenues by more than the budget saved. But the value appraisals serve no purpose at all. While no bid may be made below the appraised value, the appraisals are negotiated downward on offerings for which no bids are made, so it does not, in fact, provide a floor. And most winning bids are well above the appraised value - generally 28 percent above on average according to one analysis,[52] 45 percent above in 1980, and 50 percent above in 1981,[53]--so value appraisal does not seem necessary to prevent noncompetitive bidding. Something must be done to streamline the offering process: in 1980, it cost $39 per acre to offer and administer the sale of timber[54] and the winning bids only averaged $106 per acre.[55] One suggestion that addresses this problem is that the DNR accept bids per cord cut, but this opens up a new set of problems, namely, the distortions of a severance tax or royalty bid already discussed.

All of the above discussion of the rate of harvest, however, fails to go to the real long-run problem of Michigan's state forests. Even those acres whose "key value" will be timber production are not, after harvest, being converted to fully managed stands. To do that would require a budget not just marginally greater but many times the present legislative allocation for reforestation and timber stand management. Exactly how many times we cannot now be sure since, to my knowledge, the Forest Management Division of the DNR has not prepared the necessary research for so large a program.

Perhaps a crisis-responsive legislature is inherently unable to think in terms of investments that pay off in half a century, no matter how profitably. But as long as present investment is tied to present receipts, the result is a "low-level trap" for Michigan's state forests. The only way out may be for the DNR to explore other avenues for funding. Long-term timber management by, and sale contracts with, private forestry firms is one possibility. Or, if it is important to keep the state forests under public management, the possibility of DNR issue of long-term indebtedness could be explored. The danger with both routes is that nontimber uses of the forests will be subordinated to the search for timber profit. Nevertheless, until something is done, Michiganders are implicitly deciding not even to examine the potential for productive use of a large part of the state's land area.

OVERVIEW

With respect to natural resources, as elsewhere, economic analysis is better at organizing issues and providing criteria than in giving specific answers to questions about pricing, taxing, and public management. This shortcoming is most evident in the discussion of Michigan's nonrenewable oil and gas resources on public lands. Current economic thinking does not offer strong advice on the best bidding procedure or the optimal mix of bonus and royalty payments.

For the pricing and capacity decisions in publicly provided outdoor recreation, economic analysis is more helpful. The general rule, to price lower and expand faster wherever marginal social benefit exceeds marginal social cost, forces an appropriate focus on the decisions of state parks and fish and game management. Difficulties arise here because costs in these areas are not always straightforwardly measured: for state parks, congestion costs are hard to quantify; and for fish and game management, the basic concept of cost of production is complicated by the fact of natural reproduction.

With the state forest system, however, basic economic analysis is most applicable. Once areas have been designated as primarily for timber growth, the necessary benefit-cost or capital-budgeting methodology can be readily applied for the maximization of social profit. The absence of such application in Michigan has left the state forests in a "low-level trap" where long-run social profit considerations have been implicitly ignored.

While the problem shows up most clearly in the forests, it affects the public management of all Michigan's natural resources. The legislature treats these resources as a short-run budgetary concern rather than a long-run productive resource. While the increasing application of user charges is often appropriate, it has two unfortunate concomitants. The first is earmarking, which constrains expenditure to a fixed relation with revenues generated; as we have seen, such constraint is generally irrational in natural resource management. And the second is the lumping together of current maintenance expenditure and capital investment outlays; when this is done, the correct criteria for the determination of user charges, management activities, and capacity expansion can become obscured.

NOTES, CHAPTER 26

[1]I am indebted to many in the Michigan state government, especially in the Department of Natural Resources, for their time and cooperation, to Carl Sawyer for research assistance, and to the following for comments on an earlier draft: D. A. Arnold, R. Barlow, W. B. Botti, W. O. Cornish, E. M. Gramlich, G. C. Loury, T. M. Reuschel, G. J. Thiede, and H. H. Webster.

[2]Budget data refer to fiscal years throughout.

[3]There are other payments - principally a "rental" rate of $1 per acre leased and a "privilege" fee of 0.2 percent of the gross wellhead value to cover the monitoring of drilling activities - but these do not warrant separate analysis.

[4]See R. C. Porter, "Environmental Negotiation and Economic Efficiency," Mimeographed, 1981.

[5]The "other" revenues in Table 26.3 are largely the land rental charges. Although these revenues have not been insignificant in the past, they seem destined to become token payments in the future; and for all practical purposes, they are simply part of the bonus for the original lease.

[6]These disincentives also apply to the "severance taxes" levied on oil and gas removed from private lands (discussed in subsection five). On these disincentives, see R. O. Jones, W. J. Mead, and P. E. Sorensen, "The Off-shore Continental Shelf Lands Act Amendments of 1978," <u>Natural</u>

Resources Journal, December 1979; and Chapter 12, P. S. Dasgupta and G. M. Heal, Economic Theory and Exhaustible Resources, (Cambridge University Press, 1979).

[7]The price is a measure of its social benefit in a willingness-to-pay sense.

[8]The risk aversion may reside not in the entrepreneur but in the operation of an imperfect capital market. The bonus bid may require too much "up front" borrowing for small-scale operators.

[9]See S. McDonald, "Federal Energy Resources Leasing Policy," Natural Resources Journal, December 1978.

[10]Politically also, the royalty rate prevented the post-OPEC price increases from entirely becoming private-sector windfalls. See Table 26.3.

[11]The classic studies are W. Vickrey, "Counterspeculation, Auctions, and Competitive Sealed Tenders," Journal of Finance, March 1961; V. L. Smith, "Experimental Studies of Discrimination versus Competition in Sealed Bid Auction Markets," Journal of Business, January 1967; and W. J. Mead, "National Resource Disposal Policy - Oral Auction versus Sealed Bids," Natural Resources Journal, April 1967.

[12]Although research is in progress, spurred by the great amounts of money at stake in the U.S. offshore oil leases. In fact, the Offshore Continental Shelf Lands Act of 1978 expressly required that such sales be varied so as to yield experimental evidence about the bid-maximizing procedure.

[13]By "second" price is meant the offer of the second highest bidder (i.e., the highest losing bid).

[14]This choice is absent in an oral auction. There, the high bidder pays the second-high bid price (plus an iota).

[15]E.g., A. Brimmer, "Price Determination in the U.S. Treasury Bill Market," Review of Economics and Statistics, May 1962.

[16]R. N. Johnson, "Oral Auction versus Sealed Bid: An Empirical Investigation," Natural Resources Journal, April 1979.

[17]Assuming the current rate was optimal in the past. The rate has recently been, in fact, raised from one-eighth to one-sixth.

[18]Texas, Louisiana, Alaska, California, and Oklahoma, in that order (1978 data), are the largest. Each has a variable-rate system with higher royalty rates being either placed on "proven" lands or the object of the bid

(D. P. Tierney, Report to the Director of the Michigan DNR of the Special Task Force on the Oil and Gas Hearing Program, 19 May 1980, Table 7).

[19]"...less than $5 per acre" (Ibid. p. 28), as compared to an average of $32.76 per acre in the state's last (1974) major lease sale (DNR, Oil and Gas Hearing Procedure and Environmental Overview, 25 January 1979, p. 7).

[20]From one-eighth to one-fourth (Ibid. [The same page as the preceding note.]), to which must be added the 4.0-6.6 percent severance tax to get the total public-plus-private royalty rate.

[21]See, e.g., Ibid. Table 7 and p. 35.

[22]Since bids of one dimension are considerably easier to conduct, the bonus for such leases would have to be fixed, presumably at zero.

[23]To the percentages for oil and gas should be added a 0.2 percent "privilege fee." The oil and gas severance tax was raised from 2 percent in 1979.

[24]From $2.0 million in 1970 to $47.0 million in 1980 (1980 dollars). The latter figure is a forecast from the executive budget. The rate of real growth over 1970-79 was 26 percent per annum.

[25]The assertion would make some sense if the mineral extraction process irreparably destroyed the fishing or hunting values of the land, but this does not apply here.

[26]These observations apply also to the state forest system, which supplies some 3,500 rustic campsites in 171 campgrounds at three dollars per camp night.

[27]I say "might have been" because the annual permit still represents a price - a high one - for the first use and hence inefficiently discourages infrequent users.

[28]See 1979 Michigan Recreation Plan (Lansing, 1979), p. 62.

[29]e is of course, not necessarily the same for all parks. In fact, the optimal markup for foreigners is likely to be higher for parks further from neighboring state borders since travel costs are higher to these for nonresidents. There is no necessary inconsistency between a particularly low resident fee and a particularly high nonresident fee.

[30]$4.3 million in 1981.

[31]There is a fourth question, rarely raised in Michigan (and only in this note here) but which may become increasingly important: How should we divide the Great Lakes fishery between commercial and recreational use? Commercial fees and revenues are quite small: about $120 per boat per year (for residents - the nonresident fee is some five times higher) and a total state revenue of less than $20 thousand per year (1979).

[32]See, e.g., R.H. Giles, Wildlife Management (W. H. Freeman, 1978), p. 21.

[33]Giles, Ibid. p. 201.

[34]The Michigan legislature lengthily debated this question most recently in another context; whether or not those who obey air pollution regulations should be required to pay for their own surveillance.

[35]The benefit to the marginal hunter, the willingness to pay to hunt (in excess of privately borne costs), is the license fee paid. The public cost of the marginal hunter is the product of two things: (1) the additional animals harvested by the marginal hunter; and (2) the additional management costs necessary to provide each additional animal. The equality of marginal benefit and cost, in the optimal steady state, then requires that the ratio of license fees to management costs be equal to a ratio: the elasticity of animal harvest with respect to number of hunters, divided by the elasticity of animal production with respect to management expenditures. There is no reason to suspect that this latter ratio is one; it may well be larger or smaller than one.

[36]All of this ignores, and should not, the issue of the quality of recreational fishing and hunting. Increased management effort produces more game--that, after all, is what it is supposed to do--but as the effort comes closer to animal husbandry, the fishing and hunting may come closer to commercial slaughter.

[37]By a Finnish consultant group, Jaako Poyry, 2: 10.

[38]Although we shall focus here on the state forests, it must not be forgotten that Michigan has over fifteen million acres of forest outside this system (2.7 million acres of National Forests, 2.0 million acres of timber-industry forests, and 10.5 million acres of nonindustrial private forests. Much of what will be said in this section about the unfulfilled potential of the state forests applies with greater force to the nonindustrial private forests. (The question of tax incentives for private forests is treated in Chapter 29 of this volume.) To the extent that the development of private forests requires state forest assistance, on public-good and externality grounds, the

budget inadequacies of the state forest system are even more serious than suggested by the discussion in the rest of this section.

[39]Some purchases, sales and swaps continue to occur, but these rarely amount to more than a few thousand acres per year.

[40]And to a cooperative forestry program with nonindustrial private forest owners.

[41]T. M. Reuschel, "Division Time and Cost Distribution," Memorandum, 20 April 1981.

[42]DNR, "Improving Management and Planning for Michigan's Vitally Important State Forests" (Lansing, October 1976).

[43]U.S. Department of Agriculture Forest Service estimate for 1978.

[44]DNR, Commission Policy 2207, 11 May 1979. The process of "key value" selection is not yet complete.

[45]Indeed some, such as deer management, require it.

[46]H. H. Webster _et al._, "Improved State Forestry for a More Productive and Attractive Michigan" (Lansing, August 1975), p. 8.

[47]Jaako Poyry, a Finnish consultant group. This report noted that yields would be even higher if fertilization and genetically improved stock were added. Professor G. R. Gregory, forest economist at the University of Michigan, maintains that the multiple is much higher - that Michigan forest growth rates could, with optimal management, be "perhaps as much as ten times the present rate" (interview).

[48]The optimal degree of management and the optimal rotation are determined by the usual maximization of present value calculus. Both vary across sites and across species. The optimal rotation derivation must also consider nontimber values of the forest. For example, where hiking/camping is an object, a longer rotation is appropriate, and where deer management is an objective, a shorter rotation. See W. F. Hyde, "Resources for the Future," in _Timber Supply, Land Allocation, and Economic Efficiency_, 1980.

[49]DNR, "Michigan's Forest Resources - A Recommended Program," draft, February 1981, p. 11.

[50]DNR, "Timber Sales, Fiscal Year 1980" (Lansing, February 1981), Table 6.

[51]Recent investments indicate some success: Champion International's pulp mill ($477 million), Mead Corporation's expansion ($260 million), and Weyerhauser's particleboard mill ($60 million). The possibility of large-scale, wood-fired, electric power generation is also being explored.

[52]Audit Report on the Forest Management Division, 20 November 1980.

[53]DNR, "Timber Sales." The gap is increasing because the appraised value is based on previous years' prices and hence is further off the faster nominal timber prices are rising.

[54] Reuschel, "Division Time and Cost Distribution." $1.36 million and 34.8 thousand acres.

[55]DNR, "Timber Sales," $3.69 million and 34.8 thousand acres.

Chapter 27

Gambling as a Source of Revenue

by

Daniel B. Suits

Michigan State University

INTRODUCTION

Gambling has long been a part of state revenue systems in the United States, largely in the form of taxation of pari-mutuel gambling at horse or dog races. Today, a total of thirty-two states derive revenue from such pari-mutuel taxation. But during the past eighteen years, state sponsored gambling and gambling taxation have greatly expanded.

Beginning with New Hampshire in 1963, lotteries became an acceptable revenue source, and today there are lotteries in operation in thirteen states. The state lottery began as a system in which winners were determined by drawings made once a month or in some cases quarterly, but has now evolved to encompass "instant" games where winners are determined on the spot, and in some states to a legal version of the old illegal numbers game accompanied by televised daily drawings of winning numbers.

Other forms of state operated gambling flourish as well. New York and Connecticut operate off-track betting parlors. Pari-mutuel betting at jai-alai frontons has expanded from Florida to invade New England. Casino gambling is featured in Atlantic City, and the State of Delaware has experimented with a sports-betting pool. At the extreme, the State of Nevada, having legalized all forms of gambling, now derives half of its total revenue from taxation of the resulting action.

The recent growth of gambling stems from increasing budgetary stringency at the state and local levels and rising taxpayer resistance to tax increases. It is facilitated by recent trends toward moral codes and life-styles in which gambling has gained widespread acceptance. In short, gambling revenues that contributors appear to enjoy paying constitute an almost irresistible opportunity to hard-pressed legislatures and fiscal officers. Yet proposals to extend legalized gambling meet with strong resistance from many segments of the community, and are often among the most controversial social issues in the public view.

While not in the forefront of the trend, Michigan has followed close behind, both in the legalization of gambling and in public controversy. Pari-mutuel racing has been legal in this state since 1933. A state lottery began operation in 1973. But proposals to legalize dog racing and gambling casinos, although strongly pressed, have met with vigorous opposition and have so far failed to attract sufficient support to carry.

This chapter is devoted to a systematic analysis of gambling as a source of revenue to Michigan. The existing lottery and the pari-mutuel tax on horseracing will be examined, along with the proposed legalization of gambling casinos in Detroit. In each case, an attempt will be made to analyze the patrons of the activity, particularly with regard to how the tax burden is apportioned among income groups.

The history of the lottery and of pari-mutuel gambling are examined together with other information to assess the revenue potential of the respective taxes. An estimate of the revenue potential of proposed Michigan casinos is derived by reference to experience in Nevada and Atlantic City.

The analysis throughout addresses the fiscal aspects of the taxes. No attempt is made to broach the broader issues surrounding gambling nor the question of whether it constitutes an appropriate source of state revenue.

THE MICHIGAN LOTTERY

The Michigan lottery was instituted by Public Act 239 of 1972 which established a Bureau of State Lottery to operate lottery games. The law provided that 45 percent of receipts were to be paid out in prizes to winning tickets, but left the task of designing the particular forms of game to be offered and the pattern of prize allocation up to the bureau.

At the present, three general types of game are offered. The most popular, accounting for about two-thirds of all ticket sales in the state is the "daily" lottery. This game, introduced in June 1977, is a legal version of the hitherto illegal numbers or policy game. Wagering is done on a 3-digit number of the player's own choice, and prizes are paid daily on the basis of a number produced by a random drawing. A winning number pays $500 on a $1 ticket. Since the chances of winning are only one in 1,000, the game returns half of all wagers to ticket buyers in prizes.

Second in popularity, accounting for 30 percent of ticket sales, is the "instant" lottery. This game, introduced in Michigan in 1975, involves purchase of a ticket on which the prize is revealed when the player rubs away covering material that conceals the payoff, if any. Prizes for a $1 ticket range from receipt of a free ticket to $10,000, with certain tickets eligible for larger prizes in subsequent drawings.

Least patronized these days is the weekly lottery in which pre-numbered tickets are sold, with winners determined weekly by drawing. This is the only type of game that was offered during the first two years of operations in Michigan, but now makes up only 3.8 percent of ticket sales in the state.

The history of ticket sales and revenue is given in Table 27.1. Lottery tickets worth $137 million were sold during the first year of operation, producing $63 million in state revenue after payment of prizes and deduction of the 9

TABLE 27.1
LOTTERY TICKET SALES BY GAME, FISCAL YEAR 1972-73 TO 1979-80
(millions of dollars)

FISCAL YEAR	WEEKLY GAME[1]	SPECIAL GAMES[2]	INSTANT $1 GAME	DAILY GAME	TOTAL	ESTIMATED REVENUE[3]
1972-73	83.1	-	-	-	83.1	38.2
1973-74	137.4	-	-	-	137.4	63.2
1974-75	84.1	51.7	-	-	135.8	62.5
1975-76[4]	65.1	25.5	182.4	-	273.0	125.6
1976-77	40.3	5.3	178.4	27.2	251.2	115.6
1977-78	37.2	-	157.5	131.8	326.5	150.2
1978-79	24.7	-	131.6	253.1	409.4	188.3
1979-80	18.4	-	143.7	321.4	483.5	222.4

Notes: [1]Fiscal Years 1972-73 to 1975-76: the Green Game; Fiscal Years 1976-77 and after: the Michigame.

[2]Fiscal Year 1975: Jackpot $1, Triple Play, $1. Fiscal Year 1976: Triple Play $1. Bicentennial $5, 76 Game $1. Fiscal Year 1977: Winter Wonderland $1.

[3]Estimated at 46 percent of sales.

[4]Fiscal Year 1975-76 contained 15 months.

Source: Data Supplied by Jay Wortley, Office of Revenue and Tax Analysis.

TABLE 27.2
LOTTERY TICKET PURCHASES BY FAMILY INCOME BRACKETS
AVERAGE OF ALL STATES WITH LEGAL LOTTERIES, 1974

FAMILY INCOME	AVERAGE PER CAPITA TICKET PURCHASE	PERCENT OF INCOME SPENT ON TICKETS
Under $5,000	$ 7.48	0.30
$5,000-$9,999	16.91	0.23
$10,000-$14,999	16.84	0.13
$15,000-$19,999	11.15	0.06
$20,000-$29,999	14.23	0.06
$30,000 and over	8.72	0.02
All Families	12.71	0.08

Source: A survey of American gambling habits conducted by the Survey Research Center, The University of Michigan, as reported in _Survey of American Gambling Attiitudes and Behavior_, Appendix 2 of the _Final Report_, Commission on the Review of the National Policy Toward Gambling, Washington, D.C., U.S. Government Printing Office, 1976.

percent operating cost. This amounted to an average of over $15 per Michigan resident in total sales and almost $ 7 per capita in revenue.

With the introduction of the instant game in 1975, sales expanded to $273 million or nearly $30 per capita. Another leap in sales occurred upon the introduction of the daily game in 1977, when sales climbed to $327 million or $36 per capita during fiscal year 1977-78.

Overall, the growth rate of both total and per capita ticket sales has averaged 21 percent per year, but after adjustment for inflation, per capita ticket sales have almost exactly doubled since introduction of the lottery. This amounts to an average annual growth rate of about 12 percent per year, compounded. However, most of the stimulus for this growth has been the popularity of the instant and daily lotteries, and since all three games have become available, sales adjusted for inflation have shown a growth rate of only about 6 percent per year.

The Patrons

According to a national survey conducted by the Survey Research Center of The University of Michigan, at least 50 percent of all adults residing in states where legal lotteries were offered bought lottery tickets during the year 1974 (Kallick et al., 1977). At that time, however, the daily lottery, the most popular form of the game, was not yet legally available, nor had the instant game yet been devised. For this reason, it is likely that a similar survey taken today would indicate considerably greater participation. In fiscal year 1979-80, 6.4 million Michigan residents purchased an average of more than $75 in tickets each. If participation in the Michigan lottery includes half to three-quarters of all adults in the state, this would represent an average yearly outlay of $100 to $150 per ticket buyer, or about $2 to $3 a week. In any event, this wide popularity of the lottery makes it difficult to characterize lottery patrons as distinct from the public at large. They come from all walks of life and are found in all economic strata and among all social and ethnic groups.

But if all participate, not all participate to the same extent. Analysis of Michigan sales by county reveals that ticket buying varies widely in response to a number of factors. Rural residents spend much less on the lottery than people in urban areas. This is markedly the case with the daily game, although part of the reason is the absence of daily ticket agencies in many rural counties. Ticket buying is somewhat higher among black than among white adults.

Family Income and the Lottery

The survey of American gambling behavior revealed the relation of lottery ticket purchases to family income shown in Table 27.2. Although these data apply to residents of all states operating legal lotteries in 1974, comparison shows the figures match closely those for Michigan. For example, as reported by the sample, nationwide purchase of lottery tickets amounted to $12.07 per capita of residents of lottery states. This compares with $15.04 per capita in Michigan during the fiscal year 1973-74, and to $14.63 during fiscal year 1974-75.

As another comparison, examination of per capita income and ticket sales among zip-code areas of Michigan shows that the proportion of family income spent on lottery tickets tends to decline about 12 percent for every 10 percent rise in per capita income (Haas 1981). If anything, this is a somewhat steeper rate of decline in proportion of income spent on lottery tickets than was shown by the national sample.

Incidence of the State Lottery

Since low-income people tend to spend a greater fraction of their incomes on lottery tickets than high-income people do, the lottery is a regressive source of state revenue. Measured on the S-scale, the lottery shows a value of -0.30 to -0.40. This shows the lottery to be more than twice as regressive as the state sales tax.[1] In other words, as a revenue source, the state lottery is one of the most regressive taxes known and imposes by far the heaviest relative burden on those least able to pay.

Is the Lottery a Tax?

Despite this disproportionate burden on poor people, it is often argued that regressivity is not an issue "because the lottery is not a tax." Taxation, so this reasoning goes, is revenue that taxpayers turn over to the government under coercion whereas people buy lottery tickets only when they want to.

But this argument confuses a difference in form with one of economic substance. People also buy liquor only when they want to, but the tax on alcoholic beverages is nevertheless a tax for all that. Nor does the situation change in those states where liquor sales are a state monopoly and the revenue is incorporated directly in the monopoly price.

Exactly the same consideration governs receipts from the state lottery. Unlike horse racing where revenue is raised by an excise tax on wagering at privately-operated tracks, funds from the lottery are derived from a monopoly price yielding revenue directly to the state. That one is reported in the State of Michigan Financial Report as tax receipts and the other as receipts from the lottery is merely a difference in language and labels. In both cases, people contribute revenue to the state in proportion to the amount they gamble.

The State Lottery and Illegal Gambling

The monopoly aspect of the state lottery has an important bearing on another proposition often advanced. It is often said that one purpose of the legal lottery is to "curb illegal gambling." But this proposition is confused both logically and in terms of economic reality.

In terms of its logic, it is important to start by recognizing that without laws prohibiting it, gambling would not be a crime in the first place. The argument for such laws is presumably that gambling is in some important way contrary to the public interest and must be eliminated. But if this is the case, the state clearly has no business providing and advertising the same practices. To be sure, pursued vigorously enough at low enough prices, the state might be able to wipe out illegal operations by attracting all their customers to itself, but it is by no means clear what would be gained thereby. Gambling would flourish and would presumably still be contrary to the public interest, state operation or no. The direct way to accomplish the same thing is merely to repeal the laws that make gambling illegal.

In terms of economic reality, it must be recognized that when the state prohibits any activity greatly in demand, illegal operators find it profitable to create a supply to satisfy that demand. This illegal supply is profitable, not because there is anything intrinsically profitable about illegal activity, but because competitive forces, deprived of the protection of law, cannot operate in normal fashion and the illegal supply becomes a monopoly. Lottery is profitable to the state only insofar as the state can succeed in transferring this monopoly to itself. But precisely to the degree this monopoly is profitable to the state, it provides an umbrella under which illegal suppliers can operate profitably in competition with the state. In the absence of vigorous enforcement to maintain its own monopoly position, the only way the state can seriously interfere with the illegal supply is to compete it out of existence. It could, indeed, divert demand from illegal operations by active price competition, making prizes a greater and greater proportion of the price of the ticket until operations were no longer profitable to the private operator. But this would undermine the lottery as a source of revenue. The state could no more derive revenue from a truly competitive lottery than it could from selling groceries in competition with private supermarkets.

TABLE 27.3
MICHIGAN LOTTERY TICKET SALES
PER CAPITA AND PER $1,000 OF PERSONAL INCOME,
FISCAL YEARS 1973-74 TO 1979-80

FISCAL YEAR	TOTAL SALES (millions of dollars)	SALES PER CAPITA		SALES PER $1,000 OF PERSONAL INCOME
		(current dollars)	(1980 dollars)	
1973-74	136.4	15.04	24.76	2.77
1974-75	133.2	14.64	21.93	2.54
1975-76	272.8	29.98	42.00	4.92
1976-77	251.1	27.56	35.52	3.95
1977-78	326.5	35.68	44.16	4.55
1978-79	411.0	44.77	50.84	5.12
1979-80	486.0	52.83	52.83	5.52

Sources: Sales per capita: current dollars, total sales divided by average population per fiscal year as estimated from average population per calendar year reported in Michigan Statistical Abstract.

Constant dollars, sales per capita deflated by the Detroit CPI, fiscal year basis as estimated from calendar year data in the U.S. Bureau of Labor Statistics, Handbook of Labor Statistics 1980.

Sales per $1,000 of personal income: total sales divided by Michigan personal income, fiscal year basis as estimated from calender year data in Michigan Statistical Abstract.

TABLE 27.4
ATTENDENCE, WAGERING HANDLE, AND
STATE TAX REVENUE AT MICHIGAN RACE TRACKS, 1975-80

	1980	1979	1978	1977	1976	1975
ATTENDANCE						
Thoroughbred	1,327,686	1,401,593	1,350,756	1,466,517	1,741,323	1,765,283
Harness	1,685,661	1,611,403	1,659,900	1,760,389	1,829,989	2,064,977
Quarter horse	16,910	22,907	13,471	23,901	-	-
WAGERING HANDLE						
Thoroughbred	178,760,736	202,054,383	183,461,640	180,973,217	200,270,912	192,300,257
Harness	216,842,656	221,971,577	214,312,964	205,846,675	195,432,869	202,625,238
Quarter Horse	792,925	1,164,944	900,074	783,268	-	-
TAX REVENUE						
Thoroughbred	13,974,027	15,265,010	13,894,654	13,296,849	15,417,566	16,334,875
Harness	13,175,688	13,008,985	12,694,263	12,232,072	11,644,196	12,056,747
Quarter Horse	49,346	72,148	55,938	48,749	-	-

Source: Annual Report of the Michigan Racing Commissioner, years 1975-1980.

Revenue Prospects for the Lottery

During the first two years of operation, lottery ticket sales averaged about $15 per Michigan resident, or about $2.77 per $1,000 of state personal income. With increased advertising, and particularly with the introduction of the instant lottery and the daily game, by 1980 total ticket sales had reached $5.52 per $1,000 of personal income. How much more growth can be expected?

One answer to this question can be based on projections compiled from the survey of gambling behavior conducted in 1974. At the time that survey was conducted, legal daily lotteries were available only in New Jersey where they had been in operation for just two or three months. Consequently there was little information about the probable reception that would be accorded a legal version of the game. The gap could be filled, however, by reference to participation in the illegal numbers game as widely reported by respondents to the survey. On the basis of betting reported, and by conjecturing that participation in the legalized numbers game would reach at least the level of participation in the already legal lotteries, it was estimated that a maximum potential ticket sales of about $62 per capita could be expected in terms of 1974 prices and incomes. Transferring this estimate to Michigan, we find it would have amounted to about $11 per $1,000 of 1974 Michigan personal income, a figure about double that currently being experienced.

In arriving at this maximum estimate, however, the projected sales of tickets on the daily game were merely added to the known rate of sale of tickets on the weekly games already available in 1974. In other words, no allowance was made for people who would abandon the weekly game in favor of the new one. Yet it is plain that a substantial fraction of the Michigan lottery fans who patronized the weekly lottery when it was the only game available shifted much of their participation to the instant game when it was introduced, and have now shifted most of their action to the daily game. Indeed, in contrast to the sale of $137 million tickets in 1973-74, sale of tickets on the weekly game amounted to only the $18 million in 1979-80. This is less than 14 percent of the earlier figure, even before any allowance is made for inflation.

This shift of patronage, plus the significant decline in the share of income devoted to ticket buying with rising income shown in the study of Michigan zip-code areas, makes it appear likely that participation in the lottery will fall considerably short of the earlier estimate. Although there is no evidence that the upward trend in popularity of the lottery has reached its limit, it is probably optimistic to expect future ticket sales to exceed about $8 per $1,000 of state personal income. This would represent revenue of about $3.68 per $1,000 of state personal income, or about 45 percent more than is currently being realized.

HORSE RACING

Horse racing was established in Michigan in 1933 with a schedule of 31 racing days and total attendance of barely more than 100,000 patrons. Since then it has grown steadily to become the most popular spectator sport in the state. The 1980 racing season involved 703 racing days and over 3 million total attendance, distributed among two thoroughbred race tracks, five harness tracks, and one small quarter horse track. A total of nearly $400 million was wagered at pari-mutuel windows, from which the state collected nearly $28 million in horse racing taxes.

Attendance, total wagering handle, and state tax revenue derived from Michigan tracks are shown in Table 27.4 Of the average annual attendance of 3 to 4 million, slightly less than half attend thoroughbred races and slightly more than half patronize harness tracks. Quarter horse races, introduced in 1977 at Glendale Downs in Hillsdale, attract a small following.

Under the Racing Law of 1980 (P.A. 327 of 1980), Michigan race track operators are permitted to retain a gross commission equal to 17 percent of the total pari-mutuel handle plus half of all breakage.[2] From this commission, operators are required to pay a state tax of six percent of all wagering at thoroughbred tracks and at all harness tracks located in counties with population over 200,000. Harness tracks in smaller counties pay a tax rate of five percent of all wagers. In addition, the law imposed a nine percent tax on daily double wagering at harness tracks until October 1, 1981, after which the tax rate on the daily double is to revert to the same six percent imposed on other wagers.

Previous to passage of the 1980 law, the tax at thoroughbred tracks had been 5.5 percent on wagering on straight bets and on the daily double, but 10 percent on other multiple bets. Since the latter constitute 40 to 45 percent of all wagering on thoroughbred races, the tax rate averaged out to about 7.3 percent of handle. The shift to a six percent tax rate on all forms of betting therefore amounted to about an 18 percent tax reduction for thoroughbred racing.

At harness tracks, on the other hand, the tax had been 5.5 percent on all betting, so the increase to 6 percent provided in the 1980 law represented an increase of about 9 percent in the tax on wagering at harness tracks in large counties. Since the daily double constitutes about 6 percent of betting at harness tracks, the one-year rate of 9 percent imposed on the daily double brought the increase to 12 percent for the 1981 racing season. For the Jackson Harness Raceway, located in a county of fewer than 200,000 population, the 1980 law represented about a 10 percent reduction in tax rate.

The Racing Law of 1980 also provided for a "special sweepstakes" to be taxed at 10 percent of wagering, the funds to be used for capital improvements and promotion of the racing industry. The idea was to profit from the special multiple betting device that had proved popular in California, but it has been poorly received in Michigan.

In addition to the pari-mutuel tax, the state receives half of all breakage. This brings the state's share of handle to about 6.35 percent under the 1980 law.

The state also receives as revenue certain license fees, fines, and all unclaimed winnings. Details of state revenue under the new law will be unavailable until the end of the 1981 racing season, but the sources of state revenue under the 1980 tax rates are shown in Table 27.5. It may be seen that the tax on pari-mutuel betting accounts for almost 93 percent of total revenue of about $28 million.

Earmarked Revenues

In any evaluation of the equity or revenue potential of the tax on horse racing, account must be taken that a substantial portion of the funds raised by the tax are earmarked for specific purposes and are unavailable for General Fund expenditures. Earmarked funds include rebates to local governments where tracks are located, supplements to purses won by Michigan-bred horses, special awards to breeders of Michigan-bred winners, provision of purses for races at county and certain other fairs, and a stadium rental subsidy that now provides $800,000 annually to support the Pontiac Silverdome.

During 1980, a total of $9,549,913, or about 35 percent of total revenues from horseracing were distributed as earmarked outlays. Although this is a substantial fraction, it is well short of the maximum potentially required. If all provisions of the law were funded at the maximum level, somewhat more than 50 percent of state revenue would be applied to designated outlays.

The Patrons

Horse racing patrons come from all strata of society and are found at all income levels and among all ethnic, racial, and religious groups. The most detailed information about racing fans comes from the 1974 nationwide sample survey conducted by the Survey Research Center of The University of Michigan (Kallick et al., 1977). Analysis of

TABLE 27.5
STATE REVENUE FROM THE 1980 PARI-MUTUEL RACING PROGRAM

	AMOUNT	PERCENT OF TOTAL
Total State Revenue	$27,828,645	100.0
Mutuel tax	25,829,676	92.8
Breakage	1,389,376	5.0
Occupational licenses	67,854	0.3[1]
Track licences	1,800	---
Unclaimed winnings	526,992	1.9
Fines	12,945	---[2]

Notes: [1]Occupational and track licences combined.

[2]Less than 0.1 percent.

Source: Annual Report of the Michigan Racing Commissioner, 1980

TABLE 27.6
TRACK ATTENDANCE AND WAGERING IN RELATION TO FAMILY INCOME
ALL U.S. FAMILIES, 1974
(all money figures are in dollars of 1974 purchasing power)

FAMILY INCOME	PERCENT THAT ATTENDED TRACK	AVERAGE ANNUAL BET PER BETTOR	AVERAGE BET AS PERCENT OF INCOME	TOTAL WAGERING PERCENT OF INCOME OF ALL FAMILIES
Under $5,000	8.7	$187.50	7.5	0.63
$5,000-$9,999	15.5	293.51	3.9	0.61
$10,000-$14,999	11.2	395.75	3.1	0.35
$15,000-$19,999	17.2	577.48	3.3	0.57
$20,000-$29,999	20.9	294.20	1.2	0.22
$30,000 or over	20.3	435.87	1.1	0.22
ALL FAMILIES	15.9	$512.70	2.1	0.50

ource: Survey of American Gambling Attitudes and Behavior, Appendix 2 of Gambling in America, Final Report of the Commission for the Review of the National Policy Toward Gambling. Government Printing Office, Washington D.C., 1976.

the returns indicated that 14 percent of all adults residing in states with legal horseracing reported visiting a race track at least once during the survey year. As might be expected, patronage was heaviest among those closest to tracks, and included 30 percent of all adults living within a short ride of the track, compared to ten percent of those living in areas without a conveniently located track.

The survey also showed that racing was somewhat more popular among men (16 percent) than among women (12 percent). Moreover, the proportions interested in racing were found to rise with education. For example, among those with no more than a high school diploma, only 8 percent reported visiting a track during the year, compared to 23 percent among college graduates.

Wagering and Income

Participation in racing is strongly influenced by household income. As summarized in Table 27.6, the proportion of adults attending a track at least once a season rose from less than 9 percent of people in the lowest income bracket to over 20 percent of those with income over $30,000. Likewise, the total amount wagered over a racing season rose from $187.50 per low-income bettor to $435.87 per bettor in the highest bracket.

Although the figures from the survey apply to the U.S. as a whole, they are quite consistent with what is known about Michigan. For example, in 3,030,257 visits to Michigan tracks in 1980, racing fans wagered a total of $397,397,317, or an average of $131 per visit. It is estimated that the average bettor visits the track six to seven times per season, which at an average of $131 per visit, works out to an average wager per bettor of $787 to $918 per season. When the 1974 U.S. average of $435.87 is raised to allow for inflation since then, it becomes the equivalent of about $872 in dollars of 1980 purchasing power, a figure well within the limits provided by the Michigan experience.

Incidence of the Pari-mutuel Tax

Despite higher track attendance and heavier wagering among higher income people, total betting does not rise in proportion to income. Bettors in the lowest income bracket wagered an average of 7.5 percent of family income over the course of a racing season, compared to little more than 1 percent among those with the highest incomes.

Even when allowance is made for the smaller proportion of racing fans among lower income families, average wagering, including even those who do not bet, constitutes a higher fraction of family income in low brackets than in high brackets. As a result of this declining relationship of betting to income, the pari-mutuel tax is regressive; that is, the burden of the tax falls disproportionately on low-income families. Measured on the S-scale, the pari-mutuel tax shows a value of S=-0.17, about the same as the sales tax.

Revenue Prospects

Analysis of past performance reveals that horse racing in Michigan is subject to cycles of popularity. Annual attendance at Michigan tracks has trended upward, both in total numbers and in relation to population, but in a series of cycles with peaks in 1953, 1965 and again in 1971. Since the 1971 peak, however, attendance has been in a serious decline. As a percent of state population, yearly attendance figures, which stood at nearly 47 percent in 1971, have slid to less than 38 percent in 1980. This is the lowest level since the year 1968.

Average bet per patron-day appears to fluctuate around an average of about $171.80 (in dollars of 1980 purchasing power). A peak of $181 was reached in 1953, and levels above $190 were sustained during the years 1965-69. But since that time, per capita betting declined to $162 by 1979, and to $130 in 1980, the lowest level in more than thirty years.

Since racing patronage varies with both population and

income, probably the best measure of demand is the proportion of state personal income that is wagered at the track. Over the last thirty years, this has varied around an average of $7.36 wagered per $1,000 of state personal income, reaching peaks in 1953, 1966 and 1971 before sliding to record lows of $4.91 in 1979 and an estimated $4.30 in 1980.

To some extent, the Michigan experience is part of a general nation-wide trend toward reduced participation in racing. Total U.S. pari-mutuel wagering, measured in dollars of 1980 purchasing power, stood at $12.30 billion in 1970, but only $11.67 billion in 1975 and $11.63 billion in 1979. In view of the national picture, it appears unlikely that Michigan racing will, in the near future, attract the proportions of state personal income that it did in the past. Even with return to normal prosperity, we can hardly expect total betting handle to exceed $5 to $6 per $1,000 of state personal income. At tax rates legislated in the Racing Law of 1980, this implies tax revenues on the order of 30 to 40 cents per $1,000 of state personal income.

<u>Changes in Tax Rates</u>

Could revenue be improved by increasing tax rates beyond those called for in the 1980 law? This question has several important aspects. Under the present law, the track share of wagering is limited to 17 percent of handle. With the volume of wagering falling seriously behind the rate of inflation, any significant increase in tax rate would have to be accompanied by a corresponding increase in the take-out rate permitted to the track.

But the take-out rate represents the price of wagering on races. Like any other price increase, a rise in take-out rate tends to discourage participation, and, other things equal, to reduce total betting handle. It has been estimated that demand for pari-mutuel racing is characterized by elasticity of about -1.6 (Suits 1979). That is, a 10 percent increase in total take-out rate (a rise from 17 to 18.7 percent of handle) tends to reduce the total volume of wagering by about 16 percent. Given this high elasticity, any attempt to increase tax revenues by raising tax rates would yield the state a larger share of a sharply reduced betting pool. The net result would be little additional revenue for the state, but drastically reduced gross receipts for the tracks.[3]

In other words, the state is already extracting about the maximum possible revenue from pari-mutuel racing. Attempts to gain more through increases in tax rates are likely to prove self-defeating. Indeed, the national trend is quite in the other direction. Rather than increase, pari-mutuel tax rates have been reduced in a number of states in an effort to reduce the burden on the racing industry. Whether we will reach a similar position in Michigan is an open question, but in any event, the pari-mutuel tax is unlikely to prove an important source of net revenue for general fund purposes.

CASINO GAMBLING

The movement to install casino gambling in Michigan derives its force from the desire to help revitalize downtown Detroit. Its promise is based on the experience in Nevada and Atlantic City. Revenues from gambling casinos pay nearly half of the expenses of the State of Nevada, and indirectly account for a substantial portion of the remainder.

Yet the prospect for legalization in Michigan is not bright. Bills introduced into the legislature in 1976, 1978 and 1980 were defeated, as was an advisory referendum on the question of casinos in Detroit. Aside from vigorous campaigning by the Mayor of Detroit and representatives of the casino industry, the proposition seems to have little support, and the governor of the state has promised to veto any legislation that might be passed.

The question of legalized casino gambling involves a number of complex issues, including questions of the effect of casinos on the moral climate of the city and its probable environmental impact on living conditions, traffic, crime and rents. Discussion of such topics extends beyond the purpose of this analysis. The following discussion deals with only two questions: How much revenue could be expected from legalization of casinos in Detroit? And who would bear the revenue burden?

<u>The Prospective Patrons</u>

Data collected and analyzed for casino gambling as part of the 1974 survey of gambling indicated that 40 percent of all American adults, or a total of about 58 million people had visited a casino at one time or another during their lives, and 9.5 percent, or about 14 million had done so at least once during the survey year. Those who visited a casino reported an average of 2.3 trips made during the year. The games reported by the respondents are shown in Table 27.7. As can be seen, nearly all who visited casinos played slot machines, almost double the percentage who said they had played blackjack or Keno. Craps and roulette were somewhat less popular. Figures in the table total more than 100 percent, since many respondents reported several games.

Table 27.8 gives the participation in casino gambling by income bracket. Among the poorest part of the population, barely more than 4 percent of adults visited a casino during 1974, compared to well over 20 percent of those in the highest income bracket. The steep graduation of participation by income is, of course, no surprise, for at the time of the survey the nearest casino gambling was available only in Nevada, Puerto Rico, or the Bahamas, and the cost of travel acted as a deterrent to lower income people.

Amounts bet at casinos are difficult to evaluate. Unlike lotteries and horseracing where wagering consists of the purchase of a ticket that can be easily accounted for, casino games involve more or less continuous play with winnings sometimes drawn out of the game and sometimes rewagered. As a consequence, nobody, including the patrons themselves, keeps track of the total number of dollars

TABLE 27.7
GAMES REPORTED BY CASINO VISITORS, U.S. AND NEVADA ONLY

GAME	PERCENT OF CASINO VISITORS WHO REPORT PLAYING	
	TOTAL U.S. VISITORS	NEVADA RESIDENTS
Slot Machines	87	93
Blackjack	47	31
Roulette	37	10
Keno	43	70
Craps	29	14

Source: Kallick and others.

TABLE 27.8
PARTICIPATION IN CASINO GAMBLING BY INCOME BRACKET OF VISITOR

FAMILY INCOME	PERCENT OF ADULTS VISITED A CASINO	AVERAGE BET PER VISITOR	PERCENT OF TOTAL BRACKET INCOME WAGERED AT CASINOS
Under $5,000	4.1	$ 586.57	0.98
$5,000-$9,999	8.1	193.17	0.20
$10,000-$14,999	6.2	124.33	0.06
$15,000-$19,999	12.3	336.57	0.24
$20,000-$29,999	12.3	261.70	0.13
$30,000 and over	20.6	1,293.93	0.67
All Families	9.5	448.26	0.27

Source: Kallick and others.

actually wagered during the course of the play. Because of this difficulty, respondents to the survey were asked how much money they took on each visit to buy chips or play slot machines, and these are the amounts indicated in Table 27.8.

Although relative to income, the heaviest wagering was reported by those in the lowest income bracket, by far the greatest total betting was done by those in the highest bracket. As a result, despite the heavy participation of those in the lowest income bracket, taxes imposed on casino gambling tend to be borne by high income people out of proportion to their high incomes. That is, taxes on Nevada gambling are highly progressive, imposing the heaviest relative burden on those most able to pay. On the scale of the S-index, the Nevada casino tax measures S=+0.26. This makes the Nevada casino tax strongly progressive, about twice as progressive as the U.S. personal income tax (S=+0.16).

Because of the cost of travel to the action, the high progressivity of the Nevada casino tax is hardly surprising. Plane fare, the cost of hotel rooms and meals, not to mention the need for enough free leisure time to make the trip, all combine to act like a high admission charge to minimize participation of poor people in the activity.[4]

But casinos located in Detroit would not be subject to these barriers to participation by poor people. A better idea of the probable result can be had by analysing the special sub-sample of the gambling survey that consisted exclusively of Nevada residents. In drawing the sub-sample, people who were, in any way, directly connected with the gambling industry in the state were excluded, so the resulting responses represent gambling participation by the "ordinary citizen" where gambling is readily available. Analysis of the Nevada subsample revealed that for people who live where access to casinos is easy and slot machines are ubiquitous, casino taxes are about as regressive as the lottery tax in Michigan, with an S-index of -0.4. (Kallick et al. 1977.)

In other words, in the absence of distance or other special discriminatory devices to prevent poor people from playing, taxation of casino games is two to three times as regressive as the Michigan sales tax, and imposes a greatly disproportionate share of state financing on low income groups.

Revenue Potential

Proponents of casino gambling have projected $125 million additional revenue for Detroit to be derived from legalized casino operation (Detroit Free Press, February 18, 1981). Since the projected revenue for Detroit would amount to half of the proposed 10 percent tax on gross casino revenues, revenue to the city of $125 million would require gross casino revenues of $2.5 billion per year.

Expectation that gross revenues would reach this figure are unrealistic. If casinos manage to win as much as 20 percent of the money people bring in with them, gross revenues of $2.5 billion a year would require casino players to bring $12.5 billion to the tables of Detroit casinos every year. To reach this would require total attendance of 13 million adults who would bring an average of $1,000 each to bet at the tables!

A more realistic estimate can be based on current experience in Atlantic City. As recently reported, gross revenues of Atlantic City casinos totaled $63.5 million for the month of January, 1981 (Wall Street Journal, February 12, 1981). This would imply an annual rate in the neighborhood of $800 million which, subject to a 10 percent tax would yield only $80 million, of which the Detroit share would be $40 million.

To be sure, Detroit would also gain income tax from salaries paid by the casino industry, and property tax and other revenues indirectly generated by the casinos, but if the $40 million figure is doubled, it is still considerably short of the projected revenue figures. In addition, allowance must be made for the heavy additional cost of crime prevention in the casino area, and for fire protection and other city services necessitated by the presence of the industry.

Moreover, it would be difficult for Detroit to duplicate the Atlantic City experience. Atlantic City has two substantial advantages as a location for casino gambling. In the first place, it is well situated in the Eastern metropolitan corridor, close to a number of large population centers. Secondly, like Las Vegas, but completely unlike Detroit, Atlantic City is, and always has been, primarily a resort area with no important commercial or industrial base. Given these differences, it is unreasonable to expect the performance of casinos in Detroit to match, let alone exceed, those in Atlantic City.

Finally, it should be noted that the apparent success of Nevada and Atlantic City as gambling centers is largely the result of the restricted number of places where legal casinos are available. Given this restriction, those places that offer casino facilities can draw clientele from a wide area, far outside their own jurisdictions. Tax burden and regressivity are minor issues because somebody else is paying, and total receipts are swollen by the contributions of visitors. But this happy state of affairs is short-lived. Others want to get in on the perceived bonanza. Indeed, proposals to legalize casino gambling are now current in New York and Pennsylvania, and the Michigan proposal, itself, is motivated by the same desire.

As legal casinos proliferate, the volume of play at each location is correspondingly reduced, and with it the prospect for large tax revenues. Whatever gain there might be from legalization of casinos is, therefore, subject to substantial erosion in the long run.

In summary, the revenue promised by casino gambling is considerably short of what has been set forth as expectations. Contrary to the views of many, there is simply not a vast untapped reservoir of revenue that can painlessly be diverted to state and city coffers by legalization and taxation of casinos. Moreover, once removed from the restrictions imposed by expensive travel, casino gambling revenues are as regressive as state lotteries as a revenue source.

CONCLUSIONS

Gambling taxation plays a minor role in Michigan's fiscal system. The lottery and pari-mutuel tax combined currently produce revenues of slightly more than $250 million annually, or 2.5 percent of total state revenues. Moreover the future is unlikely to see any substantial growth.

Increasing public familiarity with the lottery, advertising, and most especially introduction of the instant and daily games, have raised annual ticket sales from $2.77 per $1,000 of personal income to $5.52. Some further growth can be expected, but it is unlikely that participation will again double, although another 50 percent increase is not beyond possibility.

Horseracing revenues are 30 to 40 cents per $1,000 of personal income, and are heavily earmarked for promotion, development and advancement of the Michigan racing and horse raising industry. Nationwide, racing patronage is in a decline, and a return to its former popularity is not likely. Nor can higher tax rates be imposed without seriously jeopardizing the industry itself. If any change is likely in this regard, it is lower tax rates in the interest of relief from declining demand.

Casino gambling could produce additional revenue for the state and for the City of Detroit, but it does not constitute the potential revenue bonanza that some believe it to be. The revenue potential of casinos located in Detroit is probably considerably short of that generated in Atlantic City. At a 10 percent tax rate, the $800 million gross gaming revenue per year now realized in Atlantic City would yield $80 million in revenue, of which half would accrue to the City of Detroit under the proposed division.

Detroit could, of course, expect something more than this because of income taxes on casino salaries and property taxes. On the other hand, casinos are accompanied by changes in environment that require additional outlays for police and other city services.

In any event, gambling taxes are remarkably regressive. The pari-mutuel tax on horseracing is about as regressive as the state sales tax. Lottery receipts and taxes on casinos in metropolitan areas are two to three times more regressive than the sales tax. Such revenues as are available from these are obtained from those least able to bear the burden of supporting state services.

NOTES, CHAPTER 27

[1]The progressivity or regressivity of a tax can be precisely measured by an index, S, that ranges between the limiting values -1 and +1. Regressive taxes, that is those that impose a disproportionate burden on poor people, are characterized by negative values of S, and the more regressive the tax, the larger the negative value. At the extreme limit where the entire tax burden would fall on the poorest segment of the community, S would have the value -1.

Taxes that extract revenue exactly in proportion to income have S=0. Progressive taxes, that impose a disproportionate burden on rich people are characterized by positive values of S and the more progressive the tax, the larger the positive value. At the extreme limit where the entire tax burden would fall only on the very richest segment of the community, S would have the value +1.

Most taxes are characterized by values of S that fall well within the extremes. The state sales tax is characterized by S=-0.15; the U.S. personal income tax has S=0.16. With S=-0.3 to S=-0.4, therefore, the lottery is a remarkably regressive tax. See Suits 1977.

[2]According to the racing law, amounts paid on a winning ticket are rounded back to the next lower multiple of ten cents on the dollar wagered. Breakage is the money left over after rounding back, and amounts to about 0.7 cents per dollar of handle.

[3]The principle can be illustrated with figures roughly corresponding to Michigan experience. Under the 1980 law, the total take-out rate (including breakage) is 17.7 percent, divided into 6.35 percent in state tax, and 11.35 percent retained by the tracks. When these figures are applied to a total handle of $400 million (comparable to Michigan's 1980 experience) the result is $25.4 million tax revenue and $45.4 million left to the tracks to cover

operations.

If the tax rate were now raised by one percentage point to 7.35, it would be necessary to raise the total take-out rate to 18.7 percent to maintain 11.35 percent for track operations. This constitutes a 5.6 percent rise in total take-out rate. In keeping with elasticity of -1.6, this rise in take-out rate would tend to reduce total betting handle by almost 9 percent, or to about $364 million. The 7.35 percent tax rate applied to this handle would yield $26.8 million in revenue to the state, an increase of only $1.4 million. In contrast, the operator's share would fall to $41.3 million, a reduction of $4.1 million.

[4]The same thing is accomplished in England by restricting casino facilities to "clubs" with relatively high membership fees. In Europe it is done by restricting casinos to spas and similar resorts, and sometimes by the requirement of evening dress for admission to the premises. See Skolnick 1979.

REFERENCES, CHAPTER 27

Haas, Mark. An Economic Analysis of the Michigan Lottery. Dissertation in progress, Michigan State University, 1981.

Kallick, Maureen; Suits, Daniel; Dielman, Ted; and Hybels, Judy. Survey of American Gambling Attitudes and Behavior. Appendix 2 of Gambling in America. Final Report of the Commission on the Review of the National Policy Toward Gambling. Washington, D.C.: U.S. Government Printing Office, 1977.

Michigan Racing Commissioner. Annual Report of the Michigan Racing Commissioner. Plymouth, Michigan.

Michigan Statistical Abstract

Skolnick, Jerome H. "The Dilemmas of Regulating Casino Gambling." Journal of Social Issues 35, no. 3 (1979): 129-143.

State of Michigan Financial Report. Lansing, Michigan.

Suits, Daniel B. "Elasticity of Demand for Gambling." Quarterly Journal of Economics 93, (February 1979): 155-162.

______"Measurement of Tax Progressivity. " American Economic Review 67 (1977): 747-52.

Chapter 28

Fiscal Problems and Policies of the Cities

by

Ronald C. Fisher and Janet E. Kohlhase

Michigan State University

INTRODUCTION[1]

Michigan is an urban state. Over three-quarters of its population is located in the eleven major metropolitan areas of the state. Nearly fifteen percent of Michigan's residents are in the City of Detroit alone, the sixth largest city in the United States. The cities and metropolitan areas in Michigan, as those in other states, are presented with specific, difficult fiscal issues that arise from their urban character, and the fiscal condition of local governments in these metropolitan areas is an important concern to the state.

In this chapter, we address the fiscal problems and policies of the major cities in the state. Our goals are (1) to identify the major metropolitan areas and cities in Michigan, (2) to present a statistical picture of major city finances and economic conditions and associated changes over the last decade, (3) to review some potential government policies to improve city fiscal conditions, and (4) to present a specific discussion of the fiscal problems of Detroit and the fiscal issues in the Detroit metropolitan area. We shall concentrate on the largest cities and those policies not examined in detail in other chapters of this volume.

DEFINING THE MAJOR METROPOLITAN AREAS OF THE STATE

There are eleven Standard Metropolitan Statistical Areas (SMSA) in Michigan spread out over the southern half of the lower peninsula. In 1980, 78 percent of the state's population was in these eleven SMSAs. These metropolitan areas vary greatly in size, from the Detroit SMSA with a

1980 population of over 4.4 million to the Bay City SMSA with a population of about 120,000.

In 1980, there were twenty-two cities in Michigan with a population of more than 50,000, fifteen in the Detroit SMSA and all in one of the seven largest SMSAs. These seven, all with a population greater than 225,000, are Detroit, Grand Rapids, Flint, Lansing, Kalamazoo, Ann Arbor, and Saginaw. In 1980, these sMSAs accounted for 72 percent of the state's population. We elected to limit our presentation in this chapter to these seven SMSAs and twenty-two cities. We recognize that many of the smaller cities in the state may face problems similar to those of the larger cities, including population decreases, reductions or very small increases in tax bases, greater costs of providing basic city services, and others. Although we will not include these smaller cities in the statistical analysis, many of the findings and conclusions developed in this chapter may apply to them.

SOURCES OF CITY REVENUE

The fraction of general revenue derived from the major revenue sources for the Michigan cities in our sample is reported in Table 28.1. The two most important taxes available to cities in Michigan are the general property tax and city income tax. Sixteen cities in Michigan have adopted a city income tax under the authority granted to them by statute in 1964. Six of the cities are in our sample. In Table 28.1, the column labeled other taxes includes, in addition to the city income tax, such small taxes as taxes in lieu of property tax on grain, iron ore, and mobile homes, the accommodations tax, and for Detroit, the sales tax on utility charges.[2]

Property Tax

Municipalities in Michigan generated about 23 percent of general revenue in 1979 from the property tax, exactly the same as all municipalities in the United States on average.[3] There is great variation in property tax

TABLE 28.1
CITY REVENUE SOURCES, 1975 AND 1979

Jurisdiction	PERCENT 1975 GENERAL REVENUE FROM:					PERCENT 1979 GENERAL REVENUE FROM:				
	Property Tax	Other Taxes	Charges and Miscellaneous	State Aid	Federal Aid	Property Tax	Other Taxes	Charges and Miscellaneous	State Aid	Federal Aid
Ann Arbor	37%	1%	28%	19%	15%	32%	1%	27%	20%	20%
Dearborn	57	1	24	12	6	41	1	26	17	15
Dearborn Heights	40	4	12	34	4	38	1	16	28	11
Detroit	24	20[1]	16	15	2	16	17[1]	18	22	22
Farmington Hills	32	5	26	32	4	30	6	33	23	2
Flint	11	10[1]	47	16	16	7	13[1]	33	18	24
Grand Rapids	14	16[1]	20	20	28	11	15[1]	23	19	30
Kalamazoo	35	1	28	26	11	27	1	28	25	18
Lansing	15	13[1]	35	14	23	12	18[1]	32	16	22
Livonia	38	2	33	21	6	37	2	24	24	13
Pontiac	15	8[1]	50	8	18	13	12[1]	48	12	14
Roseville	38	1	22	27	8	38	2	21	28	9
Royal Oak	48	2	15	29	5	39	1	22	24	13
Saginaw	20	14[1]	22	15	29	14	19[1]	24	20	23
St. Clair Shores	46	2	12	33	8	39	1	20	23	17
Southfield	52	3	26	15	4	53	2	23	15	6
Sterling Heights	42	4	28	20	5	38	2	33	17	10
Taylor	46	3	22	24	5	41	1	23	22	7
Troy	na	na	na	na	na	44	3	30	14	6
Warren	46	1	23	21	9	37	1	21	24	17
Westland	37	1	30	26	6	38	1	18	30	13
Wyoming	27	2	43	19	7	23	1	34	26	8
MI Municipalities	28	10	27	18	16	23	10	24	22	18
MI Local Governments	39	3	18	32	7	32	3	17	30	10
US Municipalities	27	17	19	27	12	23	18	20	22	15
US Local Governments	34	8	16	35	7	30	9	17	35	10

Notes: [1]These cities use a city income tax.

Sources: U.S. Bureau of the Census, City Government Finances, 1975, 1979; U.S. Bureau of the Census, Governmental Finances, 1975, 1979.

reliance among the cities we examined, ranging from 7 percent of general revenue in Flint to 44 percent in Troy. It is apparent that those cities which have adopted a city income tax collect a much smaller fraction of revenue by property taxation than the other cities. The fraction of revenue provided by the property tax in the six income tax cities is about half the fraction for all municipalities in the state.

Per capita property taxes, reported in Table 28.2, are lower in those cities that use a city income tax. The per capita property taxes in Flint, Grand Rapids, Lansing, and Saginaw are much lower than in all the other cities even though per capita total taxes in those cities are higher. This casual evidence is consistent with econometric evidence reported by ACIR (1977) and Inman (1979) which indicate that the use of local sales or income taxes does reduce property tax burdens. Inman concludes that "Access to a local income tax seems particularly effective in reducing property tax burdens."[4]

The relative reliance on the property tax by Michigan cities has decreased substantially since 1975. For all municipalities in Michigan the fraction of revenue from property taxes fell from 28 percent in 1975 to 23 percent in 1979 which is consistent with a similar decrease for all U.S. municipalities. In fact, only two cities in our sample, Southfield and Westland, increased their reliance on the property tax over this four year period.

Other Taxes

Sixteen cities in Michigan have adopted a city income tax since that authority, subject to voter approval, was granted by the state in 1964. In our sample, Detroit, Flint, Grand Rapids, Lansing, Pontiac, and Saginaw use the city income tax.[5] Under this tax, city residents are taxed at one percent on all income received, nonresidents at 0.5 percent on income earned in the city only, and corporations at one percent on corporate income earned in the city and determined by formula. In Detroit, the tax rate has been

TABLE 28.2
PER CAPITA AMOUNTS OF FINANCIAL ITEMS FOR MICHIGAN CITIES, 1979

CITY	REVENUE				EXPENDITURE							
	General Revenue	Inter.-gov. Revenue	Taxes	Charges & Misc.	General Expenditure Total	Highways	Police Protect.	Fire Protect.	Sewerage	Sanita. (Non-Sewer.)	Parks & Recr.	HUD[1]
Ann Arbor	436.40	175.54	141.78	119.09	341.40	42.38	45.25	29.53	31.57	22.11	22.21	25.15
Dearborn	567.00	183.67	238.36	144.98	535.66	44.35	83.80	49.23	48.58	21.20	56.62	23.18
Dearborn Heights	232.64	104.24	91.45	36.95	223.68	35.37	46.92	25.82	16.14	15.51	5.87	5.18
Detroit	816.24	401.07	268.08	147.09	766.98	36.93	140.70	38.44	85.77	25.23	68.18	54.98
Farmington Hills	238.35	76.28	84.14	77.93	253.81	49.93	42.30	20.44	4.40	18.84	9.85	-
Flint	945.84	450.20	187.42	308.22	1,039.89	36.74	104.54	65.17	28.82	14.38	31.06	28.88
Grand Rapids	473.72	239.26	124.19	110.28	503.78	36.69	56.20	42.06	185.15	11.24	30.25	9.89
Kalamazoo	412.00	180.38	115.29	116.33	410.57	46.31	75.81	60.78	72.37	4.05	19.78	12.44
Lansing	575.63	220.25	169.36	186.03	564.61	56.50	62.67	43.98	31.87	14.73	64.74	52.23
Livonia	297.78	111.18	115.06	71.55	309.78	55.84	48.48	27.37	6.23	17.46	20.39	.41
Pontiac	1,136.42	304.89	284.28	547.25	1,213.97	62.84	110.63	66.44	32.44	36.44	107.84	19.84
Roseville	279.39	110.97	110.39	58.02	228.04	30.63	47.98	23.41	22.96	18.81	8.44	-
Royal Oak	301.16	113.96	119.53	67.66	241.04	39.22	39.30	26.99	19.28	20.21	6.17	-
Saginaw	487.54	211.42	159.33	116.78	429.41	56.94	65.02	38.16	49.40	9.19	27.42	10.07
St. Clair Shores	250.85	102.38	99.05	49.41	234.11	28.81	41.19	25.55	27.56	13.72	20.74	11.65
Southfield	417.83	92.49	227.15	98.19	386.77	33.12	73.42	41.45	23.25	9.03	31.03	-
Sterling Heights	327.16	88.12	129.89	109.16	275.11	25.81	66.31	30.67	25.21	14.12	17.68	5.23
Taylor	296.92	106.17	123.40	67.35	260.87	23.67	37.83	19.41	17.29	25.90	11.20	-
Troy	398.43	89.16	188.25	121.01	381.62	49.40	64.10	13.27	37.39	14.47	47.96	-
Warren	295.28	122.17	111.83	61.28	246.01	25.75	53.59	32.25	22.08	17.72	11.49	.81
Westland	205.15	87.31	80.40	37.37	216.15	28.41	37.71	17.41	14.44	17.23	13.18	6.32
Wyoming	310.93	131.29	74.18	105.46	222.42	38.55	43.22	12.70	35.30	.87	15.91	-
ALL U.S. CITIES	507.57	199.17	207.58	100.81	473.43	38.15	53.84	29.47	33.27	22.73	18.62	-

Note: [1]Housing and Urban Development.

Source: U.S. Bureau of the Census, City Government Finances, 1979.

two percent on residents and corporations. By vote in June, 1981, the tax rates in Detroit were increased to three percent for residents and corporations and 1.5 percent for nonresidents. A personal exemption of at least $600 is allowed although itemized deductions are not allowed. There is a resident credit for taxes paid to another city.

Because only a few Michigan cities use an income tax, the reliance on nonproperty taxes by local governments in Michigan is much less than for all local governments in the U.S. It is more instructive to compare the fraction of revenue from all taxes among cities in Michigan and the U.S. Michigan municipalities get about 33 percent of general revenue from taxes, significantly less than the 41 percent for all U.S. municipalities. There is also great difference in tax reliance among Michigan cities. Taxes provide 55 percent of Southfield's general revenue compared to only 20 percent of Flint's. In total, Michigan municipalities have decreased their reliance on local taxes since 1974, with taxes falling from 38 percent of general revenue in 1975 to 33 percent in 1979.

Charges and Miscellaneous Receipts

Municipalities in Michigan rely upon charges and miscellaneous revenue sources to about the same degree as municipalities nationwide, although there is a substantial amount of variation from city to city. Pontiac and Flint are cities where unusually high reliance on charges is shown by the statistics, although this is explained by some special services offered in those cities. There has been little overall change in reliance on charges and miscellaneous revenues in these years in Michigan or the U.S. There have been some substantial changes in individual cities although no pattern is apparent. Reliance on charges and miscellaneous revenues rose in ten of the sample cities in this period, fell in ten others, and remained constant in one.[6]

Federal and State Aid

Between 1975 and 1979 federal aid as a fraction of general revenue increased for Michigan cities by a small amount similar to the increase for all U.S. cities. Only four cities in the sample showed decreased reliance on federal aid and three of those had relatively great reliance on federal aid in 1975. By 1979, federal aid comprised only two percent of general revenue in Farmington Hills, as high as 30 percent in Grand Rapids, and averaged 15 percent for all Michigan cities. Obviously these data do not reflect the severe reductions in federal aid to cities in the last two years.

A somewhat different pattern emerges from examining changes in state aid over these four years. Reliance on state aid by Michigan municipalities increased significantly from 18 percent to 22 percent of general revenue, while at the same time state aid decreased as a fraction of general revenue for all local governments in Michigan. State aid to local governments was increased substantially in Michigan during this period and apparently was targeted more to municipalities than other local government types. By 1979, state aid comprised 30 percent of general revenue in Westland but only 12 percent in Pontiac. Reliance on state aid increased in twelve sample cities over this period with the largest gain to Detroit where state aid rose from 15 percent of general revenue to 22 percent.

Because some federal aid directed to the state is "passed on" to local governments and because some state aid programs may be a substitute for federal programs, overall reliance on intergovernmental revenue is best shown by combining state and federal aid. Nine of the twenty-two sample cities receive more than 40 percent of general revenue from intergovernmental aid, including Grand Rapids (49 percent), Detroit (44 percent), Kalamazoo, Saginaw, and Westland (43 percent), Flint (42 percent), Warren (41 percent), and Ann Arbor and Saginaw (40 percent). All Michigan municipalities together average 40 percent of general revenue from intergovernmental aid, up from 34 percent in 1975. Throughout the U.S., municipalities average 37 percent of general revenue from intergovernmental aid, down from 39 percent in 1975. Thus, cities in Michigan receive a slightly greater share of general revenue from intergovernmental aid than all U.S. cities. During the years from 1975 to 1979, intergovernmental aid became more important to Michigan cities and somewhat less important, on average, in U.S. cities. Again, this occurred in large part because Michigan increased state aid to cities significantly in this period.

Revenue Sources for Detroit

Because Detroit is, by a factor of about seven, the largest city in the state and because the fiscal difficulties of Detroit are so apparent, it may be useful to focus on the revenue sources of that city. In 1979, Detroit collected about 33 percent of general revenue from taxes, 44 percent from intergovernmental aid and 24 percent from charges and miscellaneous sources. While Detroit relied on taxes to the same degree as all Michigan municipalities on average, Detroit relied much more on the income tax and less on the property tax than other cities. As we shall see in the next section, this follows the relative strength of the two tax bases. Between 1975 and 1979, the fraction of Detroit general revenue from taxes fell from 44 percent to 33 percent while the fraction from intergovernmental aid rose from 36 percent to 44 percent, an increase fueled in large part from by state aid. To put it another way, over these four years, taxes rose slower than the total city budget while intergovernmental aid rose faster.

USES OF CITY FUNDS

Per capita 1979 expenditures for selected city functions for the twenty-two Michigan cities in our sample are shown in Table 28.2.[7] Per capita expenditure and revenue data have been used in an attempt to standardize this budget data for cities of very different sizes, although they are not a perfect adjustment. Differences in per capita expenditures do not necessarily indicate different amounts of service.

Expenditure Categories

Michigan cities do not, in general, have major responsibilities for education, public welfare or, excepting Detroit, Flint, and Pontiac, health and hospitals. Thus, the per capita city expenditures for these functions shown in Table 28.2 are very small or zero.

The primary functional expenditure categories of Michigan cities are, therefore, highways, police protection, fire protection, sewerage, sanitation, parks and recreation, housing and urban development, and general administration. Within each of these functions, expenditures are made for labor, materials and utilities, and capital goods and maintenance.

In terms of per capita expenditures on these six major functions, Michigan cities are, on average, not much different than all U.S. cities. For example, per capita police expenditures are between 10 percent and 24 percent of total expenditures for our Michigan cities compared to a 15 percent average for all U.S. cities.[8] In dollar terms, per capita police expenditures vary from $141 to $26 in the Michigan sample and average $54 for the U.S. A similar situation applies to the other expenditure categories as well. For the U.S., the fractions of total per capita expenditures on each function are: highways, 11 percent; fire protection, 8 percent; sewerage and sanitation, 14 percent; parks and recreation, 6 percent; and housing and urban development, 5 percent.

The variation both in per capita expenditures on these different functions and the share of total expenditures for each function among Michigan cities is, therefore, the more interesting issue. In addition to the figures on police protection above, the comparable data for the other functions are:

Fire Protection: $66 to $13 and 15 percent to 3 percent.

Highways: $63 to $24 and 20 percent to 5 percent.

Sewerage and Sanitation: $198 to $23 and 39 percent to 7 percent.

Parks and Recreation: $108 to $6 and 15 percent to 3 percent.

Housing and Urban Development: $55 to 0 and 8 percent to 0 percent.

Therefore, there does appear to be some considerable variation in per capita expenditures on similar functions and variation in relative importance among Michigan cities.

These variations in per capita expenditures can occur because of(1) differences in input prices, primarily labor prices, (2) the existence of scale economies or diseconomies in the production of public services, (3) city characteristics that influence production costs, and (4) differences in amount or quality of service provided. Within a metropolitan area, one expects variation in input prices to be small. Therefore, among cities of similar size, differences in per capita expenditures are likely to reflect either some special circumstance in that city (older or more densely located buildings increasing fire protection costs, for example) or a different amount of service.

To measure this dispersion in expenditures, we calculated the coefficient of variation for 1979 total per capita expenditures and those for police and fire.[9] The coefficient of variation for total per capita expenditures (excluding health and hospitals in Detroit, Flint, and Pontiac) is 0.42, for police 0.42, and for fire 0.45. Thus, while there is considerable variation in per capita expenditures among large Michigan cities, the variation is nearly identical for total expenditures and these two specific functions.

To capture a potential source of these variations, we used per capita employment and comparative salaries in these cities, reported in Table 28.3, to calculate the

TABLE 28.3
EMPLOYMENT AND SALARIES IN MICHIGAN CITIES

JURISDICTION	ALL FUNCTIONS: Employees per 10,000 Pop. 1975	ALL FUNCTIONS: Employees per 10,000 Pop. 1979	POLICE: Employees Per 10,000 Pop. 1975	POLICE: Employees Per 10,000 Pop. 1979	POLICE: Police Office Salary, 1981[1]	POLICE: % Change Since 1977	FIRE: Employees Per 10,000 Pop. 1975	FIRE: Employees Per 10,000 Pop. 1979	FIRE: Firefighter Salary 1981[1]	FIRE: % Change Since 1977
Ann Arbor	116	147	18	17	$15,494	43%	11	11	$18,000	40%
Dearborn	136	180	23	33	16,497	14	11	14	17,491	34
Dearborn Heights	39	61	13	18	17,958	30	7	10	19,492	41
Detroit	150	193[4]	40	51	19,041[3]	35	12	15	19,041[3]	35
Farmington Hills	na	62	na	12	16,500	17	na	4	14,780	-
Flint	243	291[4]	26	31	16,375	10	16	17	19,207	56
Grand Rapids	126	132	20	20	15,594	18	15	15	14,588	1
Kalamazoo	138	145	26	28	12,872	13	20	19	13,105	24
Lansing	191	196	26	31	13,869	30	21	16	15,352	38
Livonia	69	87	16	17	20,612	30	10	9	20,612	32
Pontiac	363	370[4]	33	35	17,305	34	17	16	17,930	66
Roseville	68	57	17	16	12,847	19	9	8	12,621	17
Royal Oak	68	82	14	16	20,522	32	11	12	19,269	24
Saginaw	152	120	30	25	18,411	62	17	17	16,956	43
St. Clair Shores	60	64	14	13	16,448	25	7	8	18,026	40
Southfield	108	113	23	21	14,880	26	12	13	13,910	18
Sterling Heights	62	62	20	21	16,000	43	9	9	14,982	27
Taylor	60	57	14	14	11,057	8	6	7	11,473	21
Troy	na	83	na	19	13,653	15	na	1	na	na
Warren	68	77	16	18	18,512	43	7	11	17,055	44
Westland	50	50	11	13	21,840[2]	25	7	7	11,000	8
Wyoming	88	91	19	19	16,317	33	6	5	14,693	34
U.S. Cities	162	158	-	-	13,086[3]	-	-	-	12,648[3]	-
U.S. Cities >50,000	208	206	-	-	-	-	-	-	-	-

Notes: [1]Minimum salary (not including fringe benefits) for this employee class.

[2]Maximum salary.

[3]1980.

[4]Includes employees in hospitals and health category.

Sources: U.S. Bureau of the Census, City Employment, 1975, 1979; Michigan Municipal League, Salaries and Wages in Michigan Municipalities over 4,000 Population, 1977, 1981.

coefficients of variation for employment and salaries for the common functions of police and fire protection:

Category	Coefficient of Variation	
Police Officer	Min. Salary: 0.16;	Max. Salary: 0.07
Police Lieutenant	Min. Salary: 0.15;	Max. Salary: 0.12
Police Employment	0.42	
Firefighter	Min. Salary: 0.17;	Max. Salary: 0.09
Fire Lieutenant	Min. Salary: 0.14;	Max. Salary: 0.11
Fire Employment	0.43	

Obviously, some caution is necessary in interpreting these data because fringe benefits are not included and employee mix may vary.[10] There is substantially more variation of per capita employment, at least for these two functions, than variation in basic police officer or firefighter salaries. The intercity variation of both salaries and per capita employment do not differ for these two functions.

It appears that the observed variation of per capita expenditures for these functions among cities may be due more to variations of per capita employment than differences in salaries. There are reasons other than salary differences for cities to use different numbers of employees per capita in police and fire protection. City characteristics may require different inputs to produce the same result or cities may provide different quantities of service. The substantial variation of per capita employment in these categories provides some evidence, at least for cities similar in other respects, of large differences in quantities of police and fire protection.

Detroit City Expenditures

After adjusting for expenditures on health and hospitals, Detroit has the second highest per capita city expenditures in Michigan, second to Pontiac. Among the ten largest U.S. cities, per capita city expenditures in Detroit, adjusted for functional differences, are less than in New York or Baltimore, about the same as Philadelphia, and more than in the others (including Chicago).[11] Comparing the Michigan cities in our sample for common functions, the per capita expenditure in Detroit is relatively high for police protection (ranks first), parks and recreation (ranks second), and housing and urban development (ranks first). In contrast, expenditures on highways, fire protection, sewerage and sanitation are not much different in Detroit than the other cities (Detroit provides sewerage services to the entire metropolitan area).

SOCIOECONOMIC CHARACTERISTICS OF THE CITIES

The following characteristics are often cited or suggested as evidence that cities bear unusual economic burdens compared to other local jurisdictions or regions of the state.

Unemployment Rate

With the exception of the Ann Arbor SMSA, the unemployment rate in the major central city of the seven largest SMSAs is generally greater than that for the entire SMSA. For example, in 1980 the unemployment rate in Detroit was about 25 percent higher than in the metropolitan area, about 13 percent higher in Flint, Grand Rapids, and Kalamazoo and about 16 percent higher in Saginaw. On the other hand, there has been remarkable consistency between the unemployment rate in these central cities and the corresponding SMSAs. Since 1975, there have been no significant variations of that ratio.

Since 1975, there have, however, been major changes in the unemployment condition of the major SMSAs compared to the entire state. Comparing 1975 and 1980, the ratio of SMSA to state unemployment rates rose for the Detroit, Flint, and Saginaw SMSAs and fell in Ann Arbor, Grand Rapids, Lansing, and Kalamazoo. Moreover, the 1980 unemployment rates in the Detroit, Flint, and Saginaw SMSAs are 4 percent, 41 percent, and 16 percent higher than the 1980 rate for Michigan. These three metropolitan areas--and their corresponding central cities--have suffered disproportionately in the current economic difficulties.

Total Employment

The central city's share of SMSA employment fell between 1975 and 1980 from 34 to 31 percent in Detroit, from 32 to 29 percent in Lansing, from 34 to 32 percent for Kalamazoo, and remained constant in the other four major cities. Therefore, total employment in these larger cities moves together with total employment in the region. While there is evidence of a worsening relative employment position for three of these cities, it is not as large as one might expect.

Housing

Michigan's total stock of housing grew at close to the U.S. rate from 1960 to 1970. However, it grew substantially slower than the U.S. rate in the next decade. Both the U.S. and Michigan housing stocks grew somewhat faster than their corresponding populations from 1960 to 1970 and much faster during the next decade. From 1970 to 1980, the U.S. population growth of 11.5 percent was surpassed by a 30.6 percent housing stock growth. In Michigan the population increased by only 4.3 percent yet the housing stock grew by 26.2 percent. This pattern held true for most local jurisdictions.

All counties in the seven SMSAs showed an increase in housing stock over these two decades, ranging from 0.6 percent from 1970 to 1980 in Wayne County to 88 percent in Livingston county for the same period. The only three cities to experience losses in their year round housing stocks were the declining central cities of Detroit, Saginaw and Flint. For example, Detroit lost 4 percent of its housing stock from 1960 to 1970 (and 9 percent of its population) and another 11 percent from 1970 to 1980 (and 20 percent of its population). Saginaw's population and year round housing stock declined by 6 and 0.3 percent from 1960 to 1970 and accelerated to 12 and 3 percent losses in the next decade. For these cities, housing stock declines over the past twenty years have not been as dramatic as their population losses.[12]

The quality of the existing housing stock is difficult to measure. Nevertheless, according to the census definition, only a small proportion of housing in the seven SMSAs can be classified as substandard, ranging from 0.6 percent in Livonia to 5.1 percent in Clinton County. Although these figures probably underestimate the actual substandard housing stock, the incidence of measurable substandard housing has greatly declined in the past twenty years. From 1960 to 1970 most Michigan places reported a 40 to 60 percent decline in the incidence of inadequate housing. Thus federal and local housing programs seem to have been successful in reducing the incidence of measurable housing inadequacies since 1960.

THE NATURE OF THE FISCAL PROBLEMS OF THE CITIES

In this section, we discuss some symptoms and sources of city fiscal problems and evaluate the existence and seriousness of each problem for cities in Michigan. Some of these problems arise primarily from the structure of metropolitan areas, especially the results of intrametropolitan resident and firm migration, and others are due more to regional or national difficulties. This division suggests that both the traditional city-suburb conflicts and problems that apply more to entire metropolitan regions may be major sources of city fiscal problems and may require very different solutions.

Population Changes

In a 1976 paper on city finance, George Peterson noted that "probably the most salient fact about central cities is that, on balance, people are moving out of them."[13] This trend has been noted for the largest U.S. cities and applies in Michigan as well. During the decade of the 1970s, population declined in fifteen of the twenty-two Michigan cities with population greater than 50,000. Those with declining population included all of the older central cities except Ann Arbor.

Because fifteen of these twenty-two large cities are in the Detroit metropolitan area, the pattern of population change there is most significant. Three facts stand out. First, the population decreases are not restricted to the City of Detroit, but apply also to many smaller cities in the central region of the metropolitan area. During the 1970s, population decreases were the rule for localities in Wayne County, the central county of the SMSA. These decreases occurred not only in Dearborn, Dearborn Heights, and Livonia, but also in smaller cities such as Allen Park, Garden City, Hamtramck, Highland Park, Inkster, Lincoln Park, Southgate, and Wyandotte. Similarly, population decreases were also recorded in the older or central localities of Macomb and Oakland counties. As Peterson also noted, "Where central city boundaries have been most tightly and rigidly drawn, as in the eastern and north-central industrial states, the first ring of suburbs is, for all practical purposes, largely indistinguishable from the central city."[14]

Second, the population decreases in this central area were large enough so that the population of the entire central county, Wayne County, also fell since 1970. This is the only county in these seven SMSAs to show a population decline between 1970 and 1980. Although all the other counties of the Detroit SMSA gained population in these years, the decline in the central region was so large that the entire SMSA also declined in population since 1970, the only one of the SMSAs to do so.

Third, this trend of population decline in the central region of the SMSA is not new. Detroit has been declining in population for many years, and other cities, such as Dearborn, have been declining in size since 1960. In fact, there has been no significant gain in population in all of Wayne County since 1960.

One component of population change in these urban areas

is net migration. Of the eighteen counties that comprise these seven larger SMSAs, seven experienced net out-migration between 1970 and 1979.[15] These seven counties are Genessee, Ingham, Kalamazoo, Kent, Saginaw, Washtenaw and Wayne. Each of these includes the older central city of the corresponding metropolitan area. In all of these counties, the number of births was greater than the number of deaths during these years. Therefore, the population decline that did occur in the central region of these major SMSAs was due to large outmigration.

Racial Composition of the Population

Michigan's black population has grown more rapidly than that of the nation. From 1960 to 1970, Michigan's black population grew at about double the rate for blacks in the nation and about a quarter faster from 1970 to 1980. This reflects migration of blacks to the state.

Several Michigan SMSAs are disproportionately black relative to the racial composition of the state. In 1960 the Saginaw and Detroit SMSAs had a higher proportion of blacks than did the state, and by 1970 and 1980 Flint also had a larger share. Moreover, in 1980 the Detroit SMSA was 20.5 percent black, while one of its constituent counties, Wayne, was 35.5 percent black, and Detroit (in Wayne County) was 63 percent black.

Blacks are concentrated in the major central cities and central counties of the SMSAs. More than one-half of each SMSA's black population lives in the corresponding central cities and 63 to 99 percent live in the central county. Only the Ann Arbor SMSA does not follow this pattern: in 1980 about 35 percent of its blacks lived in the central city. Since 1970, the proportion of all blacks in the metropolitan areas who live in the central cities has tended to remain constant or to decline slightly.

All SMSAs experienced an increase in the proportion of their total population that was black over the last two decades. Detroit experienced the most dramatic shift in its racial structure over time. From 1960 to 1970 to 1980, its black population grew from about 480,000 to 660,000 to 760,000 and from 29 to 44 to 63 percent of total population. Saginaw and Flint experienced shifts in racial structure that were nearly as strong. Both cities' black populations almost doubled between 1960 and 1980; and Saginaw's black population grew to 36 percent and Flint's to 41 percent of their total populations.

Cities that are declining in total population are the biggest gainers in black population. Detroit, Flint, and Saginaw lost total population since 1960, yet gained more blacks than did other jurisdictions. In the 1960s Detroit, Flint, and Saginaw lost total population at rates of -9, -2 and -6 percent while their black population growth rates jumped to 37, 57 and 35 percent respectively. Total population losses for the three cities accelerated to rates of -20, -17 and -12 percent from 1970 to 1980 while the black populations grew at rates of 15, 22 and 24 percent. In the 1970s several older suburbs in the Detroit SMSA and the cities of Grand Rapids, Kalamazoo and Lansing experienced similar changes.

Firm Location

Population and employment have become more decentralized in most U.S. metropolitan areas since World War II. Employment subcenters abound in urban areas as industrial parks, regional malls, and other noncentral city nuclei develop. The fiscal implication for older central cities is a loss of their commercial and industrial tax base. As employment disperses, former city residents may find it increasingly desirable to follow the jobs and move outward. The suburban job pull on central city population may exacerbate the central cities' population losses and the cities may lose actual as well as potential residential tax base.

The seven SMSAs accounted for approximately three-quarters of Michigan's businesses and employment in manufacturing, retailing and selected services in 1972 and

1977. While the number of firms and total employment have increased in the manufacturing and service sectors for Michigan, the total number of retail firms actually declined from 1972 to 1977 as retail employment rose.

Although central cities still claim the largest share of SMSA firms and establishments (shares range between 30 and 60 percent), their shares are declining over time. Detroit, Grand Rapids, Flint, Lansing, Kalamazoo and Saginaw central cities all lost relative shares of employment and establishments in retail and manufacturing industries. Only Ann Arbor gained in the proportion of retail firms and establishments within its boundaries. Results for the service sector are mixed; Detroit, Grand Rapids and Saginaw lost employment and firm shares while Flint, Lansing and Ann Arbor all gained in the share of service employment within their boundaries. Although declining shares do not necessarily imply an actual loss in employment and number of firms, Detroit[16] and Saginaw lost firms and employment in all three sectors between 1972 and 1977 and Flint only gained in service employment over the same time period.

It is in the retail sector that declines in growth rates in the number of firms have been most closely correlated with population declines. The central cities of Detroit, Grand Rapids, Flint, Lansing, Kalamazoo and Saginaw had the largest negative growth rates for number of firms and number of employees in the retail sector. The older surrounding areas of Detroit also lost retail establishments and or employment.

Expansion of Expenditures

Within metropolitan areas, individuals have a substantial choice about residential location. There are many separate jurisdictions that differ in tax level, amount and type of public goods or services provided, and other physical characteristics. Changes in the fiscal variables may cause individuals or firms to change location.

It is clearly true that individuals have been moving

out of central cities. One hypothesized cause of this migration is that central cities have increased expenditures so fast that individuals have fled to avoid rising city taxes. An alternative hypothesis is that individuals have moved in response to other economic forces and because of the advantages available in the newer, smaller, more suburban jurisdictions. To shed some light on this debate regarding Michigan metropolitan areas, we examine here the growth of per capita expenditures in Michigan cities.

As shown in Table 28.4 per capita city expenditures in Michigan have increased substantially in the last fifteen years. These high rates of growth in per capita expenditures continued in the recent period from 1975 to 1979. During these years, the GNP deflator for state-local goods and services increased 32 percent, while per capita expenditures rose faster in seventeen cities and more slowly in only three. While there is some evidence that recent growth rates of local government expenditures are lower than in the past (see Chapter 2), real per capita expenditures (after inflation) for these largest cities did continue to grow.

Increasing per capita city expenditures in Michigan are not due entirely to rising costs, but are also affected by employment changes. Public employees per 10,000 population rose between 1975 and 1979 in fifteen of these cities, fell in three and stayed the same in two. Perhaps more important, per capita employment also rose in twelve of the fourteen cities that declined in population during the 1970s. Therefore, one important reason why per capita expenditures increased in recent years in these cities is that city employment has not decreased proportionally with city population. Of course, even if per capita employment remains constant, as in Sterling Heights and Westland, per capita expenditures can rise due to rising costs.

There are several reasons why it may be difficult or impossible for cities to decrease government employment as population declines. First, the population decline may

TABLE 28.4
EXPENDITURE GROWTH IN MICHIGAN CITIES

JURISDICTION	PER CAPITA GENERAL EXPENDITURE				GROWTH RATE		
	1965	1970	1975	1979	1965-70	1970-75	1975-79
Detroit SMSA	$282.65	$466.54	$788.51	$1,129.08	65%	69%	43%
Lapeer County	-	-	796.98	813.76	-	-	2
Livingston County	-	-	536.92	810.36	-	-	51
Macomb County	252.61	440.53	758.46	905.28	74	72	19
Oakland County	-	470.15	737.63	1,045.17	-	57	42
St. Clair County	-	-	710.37	1,260.42	-	-	77
Wayne County	287.70	471.40	825.36	1,238.28	64	75	50
Dearborn	121.52	216.69	333.73	535.66	78	54	61
Dearborn Heights	-	84.43	143.76	223.68	-	70	56
Detroit	143.05	233.86	448.77	766.98	63	92	71
Farmington Hills	-	-	124.44	253.81	-	-	104
Livonia	108.36	305.03	165.21	309.78	181	-46	88
Pontiac	187.08	344.40	718.89	1,213.97	84	109	69
Roseville	-	94.05	188.03	228.04	-	100	21
Royal Oak	73.60	94.82	158.18	241.04	28	67	52
St. Clair Shores	55.73	83.58	159.67	234.11	50	91	47
Southfield	-	128.22	283.06	386.77	-	121	37
Sterling Heights	-	96.10	183.40	275.11	-	91	50
TAYLOR	-	149.54	148.89	260.87	-	-4	75
TROY	-	-	-	381.62	-	-	-
WARREN	170.75	99.97	216.28	246.01	-41	116	14
WESTLAND	-	71.78	156.19	216.15	-	118	38
GRAND RAPIDS SMSA	-	390.66	626.68	938.52	-	60	50
KENT COUNTY	-	404.20	638.31	930.70	-	58	46
OTTAWA COUNTY	-	347.18	591.16	961.62	-	70	63
GRAND RAPIDS	116.52	168.29	267.94	503.78	44	59	88
Wyoming	-	194.40	181.27	222.42	-7	23	23
Flint SMSA	-	564.55	839.86	1,123.69	-	49	34
Genessee County	-	583.04	877.84	1,169.13	-	51	33
Shiawassee County	-	-	587.22	832.49	-	-	42
Flint	155.53	303.09	617.37	1,039.89	95	104	68
Lansing SMSA	-	-	-	-	-	-	-
Clinton County	-	-	-	-	-	-	-
Eaton County	-	-	-	-	-	-	-
Ingham County	-	462.08	872.50	1,120.55	-	89	28
Ionia County	-	-	-	-	-	-	-
Lansing	143.25	201.12	404.56	564.61	40	101	40
Kalamazoo	-	-	-	-	-	-	-
Kalamazoo County	-	-	587.03	776.86	-	-	32
Van Buren County	-	-	-	-	-	-	-
Kalamazoo	99.36	143.39	272.85	410.57	44	90	50
Ann Arbor SMSA	-	462.70	619.44	834.71	-	34	35
Ann Arbor	118.87	162.87	282.88	341.40	37	74	21
Saginaw SMSA	-	376.81	671.24	909.70	-	78	36
Saginaw	108.21	187.41	322.10	429.41	73	72	33

Sources: U.S. Bureau of the Census, City Government Finances, 1965, 1970, 1975, 1979; U.S. Bureau of the

itself increase the inputs required to maintain current services. For example, if more buildings are vacant, fire protection may be more difficult. Second, at least in the short run, the city has a fixed capital stock that limits the potential for change in the way services are provided. Third, the production of some city goods and services may exhibit increasing returns to scale so that the production technology may not allow inputs to decline proportionately as quantity produced declines. Fourth, the city may be limited by contractual arrangements and fifth, there may be political pressure for city government to become a stabilizing force in a declining local economy.

The revenue data in Table 28.1 showed that since 1975, total taxes of Michigan cities have grown slower than total revenue while total intergovernmental aid has grown faster. Thus the major source of revenue growth to these cities in this period was increased aid, particularly state aid. While it may not be correct to say that the increases in aid caused these expenditure increases, it does seem that at least the state aid increases allowed city per capita expenditures to continue to grow in real terms.

In conclusion, the per capita expenditures of the larger Michigan cities continue to increase at a rapid rate partly because of rising costs, but also because per capita city government employment is rising.

<u>Detroit City Expenditures</u>

Detroit city expenditures rose 40.6 percent from 1977 to 1980, about the same as the Consumer Price Index. The Budget Planning and Stabilization Committee concluded that "the pressures on the City's budget are more a result of revenue shortfalls than they are of failure to control expenditures."[17] Over these years city population declined about two percent annually. Per capita expenditures in Detroit grew 71 percent from 1975 to 1979; the CPI about 35 percent.

From 1975 to 1979, per capita city government

TABLE 28.5
TAX BASE GROWTH IN MICHIGAN CITIES

JURISDICTION	PROPERTY TAX				INCOME TAX				SALES TAX		
	Real SEV($mil) 1980	Per Capita SEV 1980	Growth Rate Per Capita SEV		Income' ($mil) 1977	Per Capita Income' 1977	Growth Rate Per Capita Income'		Retail Sales 1977 ($1000)	Per Capita Retail Sales 1977	Growth Rate Sales 1972 to 1977
			1972-77	1977-80			1969-72	1972-77			
Detroit SMSA	$33,325	$7,656	36%	38%	$30,026	$6,805	19%	55%	15,846,014	$3,611	52.0%
Lapeer County	562	8,027	77	35	331	5,102	22	55	159,360	2,310	72.9
Livingston County	970	9,676	56	42	526	6,056	19	54	225,970	2,283	103.8
Macomb County	5,838	8,405	58	40	4,578	6,661	19	56	2,702,797	3,823	77.1
Oakland County	10,614	10,490	49	48	8,200	8,284	19	55	4,528,678	4,440	67.9
St. Clair County	1,346	9,695	45	37	716	5,427	18	52	394,258	2,942	53.1
Wayne County	13,994	5,988	20	30	15,673	6,394	20	53	7,834,951	3,321	35.4
Dearborn	1,209	13,334	39	44	772	8,230	20	56	778,779	8,465	84.8
Dearborn Heights	494	7,292	29	48	527	7,215	18	57	173,825	2,519	60.1
Detroit	4,271	3,549	-1	12	7,338	5,689	18	50	2,968,783	2,360	9.7
Farmington Hills	697	12,000	-	63	555	9,655	24	57	178,093	2,920	-
Livonia	1,200	11,451	43	49	819	7,558	20	60	616,067	5,867	54.5
Pontiac	447	5,831	12	28	423	5,341	20	56	305,080	3,862	35.8
Roseville	342	6,289	49	34	346	6,075	19	56	303,646	5,422	35.2
Royal Oak	542	7,650	40	42	558	7,315	18	46	338,555	4,575	57.6
St. Clair Shores	555	7,280	48	49	602	7,039	18	58	245,257	2,920	64.6
Southfield	1,004	13,286	34	34	788	10,439	18	49	778,169	10,376	85.6
Sterling Heights	1,064	9,761	72	40	659	6,819	18	56	373,721	3,628	201.1
Taylor	477	6,154	38	28	473	5,971	18	59	345,266	4,426	77.2
Troy	993	14,796	55	58	541	8,668	-	-	568,439	8,613	81.6
Warren	1,466	9,101	49	34	1,132	6,655	18	55	702,221	4,205	55.3
Westland	498	5,886	37	36	563	6,349	19	58	340,877	3,918	59.3
Grand Rapids SMSA	4,324	7,187	49	49	3,320	5,760	19	51	2,142,317	3,594	57.2
Kent County	3,073	6,914	45	40	2,525	5,863	19	51	1,733,723	3,931	54.8
Ottawa County	1,251	7,961	62	41	795	5,456	19	53	408,594	2,653	68.1
Grand Rapids	1,017	5,591	22	40	1,041	5,627	18	50	756,703	4,113	41.9
Wyoming	435	7,297	39	41	333	5,706	22	55	269,479	4,646	34.9
Flint SMSA	3,702	7,097	40	31	3,316	6,412	21	63	2,021,227	3,880	64.4
Genessee County	3,227	7,163	38	31	2,931	6,552	21	64	1,817,915	4,031	63.9
Shiawassee County	475	6,675	62	33	385	5,518	18	55	203,312	2,864	61.6
Flint	1,019	6,383	24	22	1,039	6,352	20	64	688,143	4,222	35.1
Lansing SMSA	3,117	6,768	42	37	2,694	5,934	20	52	1,592,443	3,810	57.5
Clinton County	378	6,760	78	20	290	5,379	18	50	114,306	4,763	54.2
Eaton County	687	7,774	55	30	494	6,232	19	57	337,887	4,022	77.2
Ingham County	1,742	6,395	30	37	1,678	6,183	21	50	1,000,941	3,694	50.2
Ionia County	310	5,981	53	48	231	4,692	18	51	139,309	2,843	75.3
Lansing	788	6,044	22	24	773	6,081	28	41	628,893	5031	44.2

Kalamazoo SMSA	2,069	7,411	40	38	1,552	5,770	17	54	957,740	3,534	63.6
Kalamazoo County	1,587	7,473	36	37	1,252	6,067	17	54	798,370	3,838	66.6
Van Buren County	482	7,215	55	43	299	4,792	18	51	159,370	2,570	50.5
Kalamazoo	523	6,571	19	45	455	5,756	17	52	397,155	5,089	46.0
Ann Arbor SMSA	2,403	9,076	46	34	1,650	6,581	18	48	981,126	3,863	62.0
Ann Arbor	917	8,548	42	38	725	6,869	19	46	499,241	4,755	77.8
Saginaw SMSA	1,691	7,415	42	35	1,388	6,103	23	59	848,317	3,754	64.3
Saginaw	439	5,655	26	24	468	5,696	21	58	254,217	3,138	26.5
MICHIGAN	72,500	8,169	-	45	56,304	6,130	19	53	31,912,356	3,492	55.3

Notes: [1]Money income as defined by the U.S. Census.

Sources: Computations based on L-4023 computer printouts from the State Tax Commision; State Tax Commission, Factors, Assessed Valuation and Units Portion of State Equalized Valuation (various years); State Tax Commission, "State of Michigan, Final Report of State Equalization," May 1977 and May 1980; U.S. Bureau of the Census, Current Population Reports, Series P-25, Nos. 5-67, 670, 761, 835; U.S. Bureau of the Census, 1980 Census of Population and Housing, Michigan, PHC-80-V-24, U.S. Census of Retail Trade, Geographic Area Series, 1972 and 1977.

employment grew about 25 percent, despite large decreases in total city employment. Although the fiscal year 1980 and 1981 budgets called for additional layoffs and reductions in city employees, city government employment per 10,000 residents rose from 194 in 1978 to 209 in 1980.[18]

Detroit also experienced large increases in costs, particularly labor costs. Police and fire employees received salary increases of about 36 percent for 1978-81, partly as the result of arbitration awards. These increases in costs coupled with the inability to reduce employment as fast as population is declining guarantees that per capita expenditures will rise.

Tax Base Changes

Concomitant with population and firm geographic distribution is the related tax base distribution. If businesses and residents are suburbanizing, it is expected that tax bases are too. Table 28.5 illustrates the recent growth of local tax bases.

Real property and income bases are growing in almost all jurisdictions. Only Detroit experienced a small decline; its total state equalized valuation (SEV) of real property declined by eight percent from 1972 to 1977 and its per capita SEV declined by one percent.

Money income growth appears to be more uniform over all jurisdictions than does real SEV growth. From 1969 to 1972 total and per capita money income averaged about a 20 percent growth rate and about a 60 percent increase from 1972 to 1977. Per capita property tax base growth varied from -1 to 77 percent for the latter time period. The coefficients of variation for the 1972-77 growth rates were 0.42 for per capita SEV and 0.09 for per capita money income.

It is to be expected that central cities' tax bases would be declining relative to the tax bases in their associated suburbs. In fact, from 1974 to 1980, all central cities' shares of industrial and residential real property declined dramatically. Shares of commercial property found in the central cities also fell, with the only exception being Lansing which had a mere one percent increase in its share. As expected the most precipitous declines occurred in the Detroit, Flint, and Saginaw SMSAs. For example, Detroit's shares of commercial, industrial and residential real SEV in 1974 were 25, 37 and 21 percent, but fell to only 15, 16 and 13 percent respectively by 1980.

Like the property tax base, money income tax bases for the most part grew more slowly in the older central cities than in their associated suburban communities. The growth in central city tax base per capita from 1972 to 1977 often fell short of the suburban rates:

Exhibit: Ratio of Central City Per Capita Tax Base Growth, 1972-77 to the Rest of the SMSA

SMSA	Per Capita Real SEV	Per Capita Money Income
Detroit	-0.02	0.61
Grand Rapids	0.34	0.94
Flint	0.55	1.01
Lansing	0.53	0.84
Kalamazoo	0.39	0.97
Ann Arbor	0.77	1.02
Saginaw	0.46	0.88

The central cities are more disadvantaged in terms of property base growth. From 1972 to 1977 Detroit's ratio is negative. At the high end, the Ann Arbor central city experienced a growth rate in per capita real property SEV equal to about three-quarters of the rate found in its suburbs. The central cities' per capita income growth more nearly equals the suburban growth and is slightly greater in the Flint and Ann Arbor SMSAs.

The relative deterioration of the central cities' ability to raise revenue has forced the central cities to raise tax rates and/or to rely more heavily on intergovernmental aid to support their increasing expenditures. In view of the Reagan administration's desire to curtail federal grant programs, it is imperative that local governments investigate the possibilities of local revenue diversification. It is to some of these possibilities that we now turn.

APPROACHES TO AMELIORATION OF THE FISCAL POSITION OF THE CITIES

In a 1974 report, the U.S. Advisory Commission on Intergovernmental Relations recommended that "when equipped with proper safeguards, local income and sales taxes should be viewed as one of several appropriate means for achieving a more balanced use of property, income, and sales taxes."[19] Local income taxes are now used by sixteen cities in Michigan and are available to all other cities while sales taxes are not authorized for direct use by local governments in the state. In the next two sections, we examine local income and sales taxes to determine their revenue potential, the strength and effects of any resulting locational incentives, and whether these taxes, directly or utilized as part of a tax sharing program, have the potential to improve the fiscal prospects of the major cities in Michigan.

Local Sales Taxes

ACIR reports that by 1979 about 5,500 local governments in the U.S., including more than 4,500 municipalities, used a local sales tax. These local governments are located in twenty-six states, while three other states have authorized local sales taxes although they are not used. Seven of these states restrict use of the sales tax to municipalities only, five to counties only, while sixteen allow use in both. Nine states allow various special districts use of the sales tax, often along with more general local jurisdictions. Among comparable states, local sales taxes are used in Illinois (municipalities, counties, and transit districts), Ohio (counties and transit authorities), and New York (municipalities and counties), while Wisconsin counties have authority to use a local sales tax but have not done so.

The rates of these local sales taxes vary from 0.5 percent to 3.0 percent, although the great majority are levied at 1 percent. In Illinois, all counties and most municipalities tax at 1 percent, in Ohio, counties tax at 0.5 percent, while in New York, the tax rates vary from 1 percent to 3 percent. These local sales taxes are administered by the state government in twenty states while in four others, local governments have the option to request state administration. State administration usually means that the local sales tax base conforms to that of the state and that the state government collects all sales tax revenue and returns the local component to each appropriate jurisdiction.

The most recent source of data on potential city sales tax bases in Michigan is the 1977 Census of Retail Sales. Assuming that the tax would exclude sales of groceries, prescription drugs and most services, both total city retail sales, reported in Table 28.5, and retail sales excluding sales of food stores (SIC 54) and drug and proprietary stores (SIC 591) can serve as a rough approximation to the potential tax base. The first is most likely an upper bound and the second a lower bound to the actual base.[20]

Based on the census data, there is substantial revenue potential for these major cities from a one percent local sales tax. Potential revenue for 1977 was on the order of \$21 to \$30 million in Detroit, \$6 to \$7 million in Flint and Grand Rapids, and \$5 to \$6 million in Lansing. In per capita terms the comparison figures are \$17 to \$24 for Detroit, \$34 to \$42 for Flint, \$34 to \$41 for Grand Rapids, and \$43 to \$50 in Lansing.[21]

Would a local sales tax improve the fiscal position of the older, central cities relative to others in the SMSA? Per capita retail sales in the central city in 1977 were greater than per capita sales for the SMSA in Flint, Grand Rapids, Lansing, and Ann Arbor, while central city per capita sales were less than for the SMSA in Detroit and Saginaw. In other words, if the local sales tax were adopted by <u>all cities</u> in these SMSAs, Detroit and Saginaw would collect less revenue per capita than the newer, more suburban cities in the SMSA while Flint, Grand Rapids,

Lansing, and Ann Arbor would collect more.

Even in those SMSAs where the central city would enjoy a fiscal advantage from a local sales tax, the relative advantage may be declining. In all of these SMSAs except Ann Arbor, retail sales from 1972 to 1977 grew more slowly in the central city than for the entire metropolitan area. In Detroit, for example, retail sales grew only 9.7 percent in these five years, only about 2.0 percent a year, while retail sales in the Detroit SMSA grew 52 percent during this time. The central city share of total SMSA retail sales declined between 1972 and 1977 for these six metropolitan areas. Among cities in the Detroit SMSA, the city's share of total retail sales also fell in Pontiac, Roseville and Warren. If one expects this trend to have continued since 1977, as seems reasonable, then the central city's share of retail sales has declined further.

If the local sales tax was not used by all local governments in a metropolitan area or if different tax rates were levied, then there is an incentive for individuals to shift purchases to the lower tax jurisdictions. This potential effect of sales tax rate differentials within a metropolitan area has been evaluated in a number of studies.[22] The remarkably consistent result of these studies is that a sales tax rate differential in a metropolitan area does result in a decrease (increase) in retail sales in the higher (lower) tax jurisdictions. It appears that on average, each one percentage point difference in sales tax rate translates into about a six percent or seven percent change in retail sales. Of course, the possibility of tax induced sales losses depends on such area characteristics as size, the transportation network, location of retail establishments (at least in the short run), and the pattern of employment location in the region.

The inherent conflict about local sales taxes and city finances has been noted by Stocker (1976).

> They have a significant revenue potential for central cities. But unless they are confined to the largest

> cities, they result in... fiscal disparities.... if they are imposed only by large central cities they tend to accelerate the movement out of downtown.[23]

One potential solution to this difficulty is to allow or require sales tax adoption only by more broadly defined local jurisdictions than municipalities, such as a county or even a metropolitan area. Because the tax would apply to all jurisdictions in a wider area, the incentive to change the location of purchases would be reduced. The revenue collected could then be distributed among the municipalities according to retail sales or population. In that way, the tendency for the sales tax to create central city relative fiscal disadvantages could be reduced.

If a local sales tax were imposed county wide and the revenue allocated to the municipalities according to population, each city would receive the same sales tax revenue per capita. The tax would not create any fiscal disparities. The county-wide sales tax base is shared on a per capita basis.

Of course, some cities would receive more revenue from this plan than if each city separately adopted its own sales tax. If the per capita retail sales in a city are less than the county-wide per capita retail sales, this city would gain from the tax sharing arrangement compared to separate local taxes. For example, in 1977, 53 percent of Wayne County's population was in Detroit but only 37 percent of retail sales occurred there.

In Wayne County, Dearborn Heights and Detroit would do better with per capita sharing than separate local taxation. In Oakland County, Farmington Hills and Pontiac would gain, and in Macomb County, St Clair Shores and Sterling Heights gain. Among the central cities in the other SMSAs, Flint and Grand Rapids, Lansing, Kalamazoo and Ann Arbor have higher per capita retail sales than in the corresponding county and thus would not gain from per capita allocation of a county wide sales tax, at least in 1977. Only Saginaw would benefit from such a plan. Those jurisdictions with

TABLE 28.6

LOCAL NET INCOME TAXES[1] FOR SELECTED MICHIGAN CITIES

CITY	1973		1975		1977		1980		GROWTH RATE		
	Total ($000)	% Non-res.	Total ($000)	% Non-res.	Total ($000)	% Non-res.	Total ($000)	% Non-res.	1972-77	1977-80	19774-75
Detroit	$109,865	11%	$101,909	13%	$128,340	14%	$130,248	15%	32%	2%	-6%
Flint	12,641	12	9,179	30	18,260	30	15,595	36	83	-15	-17
Grand Rapids	8,052	20	8,599	21	10,689	23	14,570	23	47	36	5
Lansing	7,460	n.a.	7,033	n.a.	9,212	33	11,430	35	42	24	1
Pontiac	5,672	24	4,062	22	9,014	24	8,385	24	78	-7	-24
Saginaw	5,050	20	4,066	36	6,752	39	5,728	42	50	-15	-18

Note: [1]Rate on resident income 1% (2% in Detroit), on non-residents, 5%. As of 9-81, Detroit is authorized to tax residents at 3% and non-residents at 1.5%.

Source: Michigan Department of Treasury, State Tax Commission.

high per capita retail sales would still receive substantial new revenue that could be used, for example, to provide property tax relief.

Local Income Taxes

By 1979, 4,456 local governments including cities, counties and school districts, had imposed local income taxes.[24] Although local income taxes are permitted in fewer states (thirteen) than are local sales taxes (twenty-six), there are much greater differences among the local income taxes. Tax rates may be uniform (most common) or increase with income (New York). Moreover, flat rates vary from 0.25 percent in some local jurisdictions in Ohio, Kentucky, or Pennsylvania to over 4.3 percent in Philadelphia. Tax bases may include some or all of personal wage income, dividends, interest, other nonlabor income and corporate profits. And the administration of the tax varies widely. Most localities offer no personal exemptions for income taxes although they are allowed in Michigan, New York, Iowa, Maryland, and Indiana. In addition, treatment of commuter income varies. In most places nonresidents must pay taxes on their earnings where they work, while in Maryland and Iowa local income taxes revert entirely to the place of residence.

Table 28.6 shows net local income tax collections in 1973, 1975, 1977 and 1980 for the six relevant cities in our sample. Clearly the tax revenues are sensitive to conditions in the regional and national economy. Growth rates of income tax revenues were negative in three of these cities during the 1979-80 Michigan downturn and in four during the 1974-75 national recession.

If the other sixteen cities included in this study levied income taxes, a significant increase in their own-source revenue could be expected. Assuming $600 personal exemptions, that all payees are residents, and a one percent tax rate, potential revenue gains for 1977 range from about $3 million in Wyoming to $10 million in Warren, or $51 and $60 per capita respectively. These are more than three-quarters of local property tax revenues in 1977.

As indicated in Table 28.6, all six cities collect a significant portion of their income tax revenue from nonresidents, varying in 1980 from 15 percent in Detroit to 42 percent in Saginaw. The share of local income taxes borne by nonresidents has been increasing over time in the six sample cities, due partly to population suburbanization and higher average earnings of suburban commuters. Thus like a local sales tax, a local income tax may offer central cities the chance to tax commuters into the city.

As for the local sales tax, there may be some potential incentive to exit from the local income taxing jurisdiction to nearby tax-free jurisdictions. Gruenstein (1980), based on Sternlieb (1977) and Grieson (1980), estimated that in Philadelphia a 1 to 2.5 percent job loss could be expected for each 10 percent tax increase in the local income tax. However, this effect has not been well documented and there may be little basis for generalization of these results to other cities and regions.

In order to minimize any potential tax base loss due to intrametropolitan area migration, a SMSA wide local income tax could be instituted and collections shared according to a population or income base formula. As with the local sales tax, this sharing approach would not create fiscal disparities. However, some cities would receive less revenue under this plan than if each city separately adopted its own city income tax while, of course, others would gain. If per capita money income in a city were greater than the SMSA-wide per capita money income, then the city would lose under the tax sharing plan.

With such a large revenue potential and property tax relief seemingly possible under local income tax sharing schemes, it may seem surprising that only sixteen cities in Michigan have adopted income taxes. Perhaps this is due to political inertia and the view that all taxes are undesirable, especially new ones. Another reason may be that the Michigan state income tax circuit-breaker program provides sufficient property tax relief to individuals, so that the traditional property tax gains in its attractiveness to Michigan residents.[25] Finally, those individuals or groups who would lose if an income tax were substituted for the property tax may be able to block that change.

CONCLUSIONS

It seems apparent from this analysis that current or near future fiscal problems are not restricted only to Detroit or the larger cities. Many medium or small cities located in the central region of the metropolitan areas share the characteristics of fiscal distress. These cities are losing population, their property tax base is declining or increasing only very slowly, unemployment is higher in these cities than the metropolitan area in general, and incomes are lower. These cities and the state should recognize these similarities. And if programs to aid city fiscal health are considered, they should be directed to all the cities with these difficulties.

Additional increases in state aid may not be a desirable way to improve major city finances in Michigan. Michigan cities already rely on intergovernmental aid more than U.S. cities on average. Moreover, total intergovernmental aid rose from 34 percent of total revenue for Michigan municipalities in 1975 to 40 percent in 1979. Most of the older central cities rely on aid to an even larger extent. New state aid programs may not address the fundamental fiscal problems of cities and may even mask those problems by allowing additional increases in city expenditures. These cities may risk losing some independence if they become too reliant on aid. Moreover in view of the Reagan administration's desire to reduce federal aid to local governments, they should look to other sources for revenue.

It is sometimes suggested that some city services be assumed by the state or a metropolitan government to ease city fiscal problems. The information in this paper contributes two points about that idea. First, Michigan cities do not have responsibility for education or welfare, two functions most commonly suggested for more centralized provision. Second, there is evidence of considerable variation in the amount or type of standard services provided by different cities, even in the same metropolitan area. Therefore, centralization may lead to dissatisfaction if all cities received the same type or quantity of service. Unless, therefore, there are substantial economies to be realized by centralization, this seems a marginal solution at best.

A local sales tax would provide substantial new revenue to cities in Michigan, including most of the larger, older, central cities. If the tax were used only by these cities, however, the tax differentials would cause further decreases in central city retail sales.

One possibility is a county-wide or metropolitan-wide sales tax allocated to municipalities on a per capita basis. Per capita sales tax revenue would be equal in all municipalities. Because the tax would apply to all jurisdictions in a wider area, any incentive to change the location of purchases would be reduced. In effect, this program is a way for communities to share equally the county or metropolitan sales tax base.

City income taxes are a significant source of revenue to sixteen Michigan cities and a potential revenue source to other cities in the state. As for the local sales tax, a metropolitan-wide tax sharing program would be likely to reduce fiscal disparities between central and suburban cities.

Thus cities and SMSAs have several potential sources for local revenue diversification. Potential local tax sources include the property base, income base, and retail sales base. Each has desirable and undesirable political and economic characteristics. These advantages and disadvantages must be traded off in the design of a local tax system, one that most likely will be called on to provide increasing proportions of local revenues in the near future.

NOTES, CHAPTER 28

[1]We would like to thank Ruth Beier and Karen Bole for valuable research assistance. Special thanks also go to the State Tax Commission and State Demographer's Office for help in data gathering. More detailed tables are available from the authors upon request.

[2]For more discussion of these taxes, see Citizens Research Council, 1979.

[3]These data slightly overstate local government reliance on property tax in Michigan because a state income tax credit is available for many property taxpayers. This circuit-breaker program effectively converts property taxes into a type of state aid. For detailed discussion of this program, see Chapter 17 in this volume.

[4]Inman, 1979, p. 164.

[5]The other income tax cities are Albion, Battle Creek, Big Rapids, Grayling, Hamtramck, Highland Park, Hudson, Jackson, Lapeer and Port Huron.

[6]For more discussion of user charges, see Chapter 25.

[7]The per capita data in Table 28.2, calculated by the U.S. Bureau of the Census, are based on 1979 fiscal data and 1977 population. Differences in per capita expenditures depend also on differences in input prices, economies of scale, and functional responsibility. By using this data, comparisons between these Michigan cities and U.S. cities of similar size can be made.

[8]Total per capita expenditures for U.S. cities are adjusted to exclude expenditures on education, public welfare, health, and hospitals. Thus, these data are comparable to that for Michigan cities.

[9]The coefficient of variation is the standard deviation divided by the mean.

[10]This is based on data collected by the Michigan Municipal League. The results hold for different jobs, in different years.

[11]Citizens Research Council of Michigan, 1981.

[12]This occurred during the decade 1970-80 in the cities of Dearborn, Pontiac, Roseville, Royal Oak, Warren, Westland, Grand Rapids, Lansing, and Kalamazoo, as well as St. Clair County and the whole Detroit SMSA.

[13]Peterson, 1976, p. 43.

[14]Ibid., 1976, p. 116.

[15]See Michigan Statistical Abstract, 1980, pp. 33-36.

[16]Dun and Bradstreet's Monthly Failure Report includes figures on business failures and their associated liabilities. For the City of Detroit, a slowing trend in failures was experienced from 1972 to 1978 and a reacceleration from 1979 through the first two months of 1981. In 1972, 151 failures valued at $77,420 million were reported and only 35 valued at $10,900 million in 1978. For 1979 the failures and liabilities climbed to 49 and $12,340 million and jumped to 60 at $14,290 million in 1980.

[17]Report of the Budget Planning and Stabilization Committee, 1981, p.3.

[18]See the State of the City Message of Mayor Young, 1981.

[19]See ACIR, 1974, p.2

[20]These data are only a rough approximation to the actual tax base because not all retail sales may be taxable, some sales of the excluded stores may be taxable, some services (some admissions) that are taxed are excluded, and business purchases at wholesale are excluded. We also assume that tax liability is determined by the location of retail sale (rather than point of delivery).

[21]Retail sales in Detroit are unexpectedly low compared to these other large cites. However, the relative sales figures correspond closely to relative retail employment in these cities. From 1972 to 1977, retail sales in Detroit rose only 10 percent, but 35 percent in Flint and 57 percent in Grand Rapids and Lansing.

[22]Mikesell, 1970, provides a general cross-section analysis. See Fisher, 1980, for a short review of the previous research and detailed evidence about the District of Columbia metropolitan area.

[23]Stocker, 1976, p. 319.

[24]For further description of local income taxes see ACIR (1974) and Gold (1979).

[25]See Fisher and Rasch, "Incidence and Incentive Effects," 1980.

REFERENCES, CHAPTER 28

Advisory Commission on Intergovernmental Relations, Local Revenue Diversification: Income, Sales Taxes, and User Charges. Report A-47. Washington, D.C.: October, 1974.

Advisory Commission on Intergovernmental Relations, State Limitations on Local Taxes and Expenditures. Report A-64. Washington, D.C.: February, 1977.

Advisory Commission on Intergovernmental Relations, Significant Features of Fiscal Federalism 1979-80 Edition. Report M-123. Washington, D.C.: October 1980.

Citizens Research Council of Michigan. Outline of the Michigan Tax System. Detroit, Michigan: March, 1979.

Citizens Research Council of Michigan. Unpublished fiscal analysis and data for Detroit, 1981.

City of Detroit. Report of the Budget Planning and Stabilization Committee, April, 1981.

Fisher, R. "Local Sales Taxes: Tax Rate Differentials, Sales Loss, and Revenue Estimation." Public Finance Quarterly 8 (April 1980): 171-188.

Fisher, R. and Rasche, R. "The Incidence and Incentive Effects of Property Tax Credits: Evidence from Michigan." Econometrics Workshop Paper No. 7912, Michigan State University, April 1980.

Gold, Steven David. Property Tax Relief, Lexington Books, 1979.

Grieson, R. E. "Theoretical Analysis and Empirical Measurements of the Effects of the Philadelphia Income Tax." Journal of Urban Economics (July 1980): 123-37.

Gruenstein, J. "Jobs in the City: Can Philadelphia Afford to Raise Taxes?" Business Review. Federal Reserve Bank of Philadelphia (May-June 1980): 3-11.

Inman, R. "Subsidies, Regulations, and the Taxation of Property in Large U.S. Cities." National Tax Journal. Supplement 32 (June, 1979): 159-168.

International City Management Association. Urban Data Service Report 12 (July, 1980).

Michigan Employment Security Commission. Civilian Labor Force and Wage and Salary Employment Estimates. Detroit, 1975-1981.

Michigan Municipal League. _Salaries and Wages in Michigan Municipalities Over 4000 Population_. Ann Arbor, February 1981.

Michigan State Tax Commission. _Final Report of State Equalized Valuation_. Lansing, May 1977 and May 1980.

Michigan Statistical Abstract, D. Verway, ed., Graduate School of Business Administration, Michigan State University, September, 1980.

Mikesell, J. "Central Cities and Sales Tax Rate Differentials: The Border City Problem." _National Tax Journal_ 23 (June 1970): 206-214.

Peterson, G. "Finance," in _The Urban Predicament_. W. Gorham and N. Glazer, eds., The Urban Institute, 1976.

Sternlieb, G.; Clark, T.; and Ford, K. "The Impact of Local Taxation on the Economy of Philadelphia." Rutgers: Center for Urban Policy Research, March 1977.

Stocker, F. "Diversification of the Local Revenue System: Income and Sales Taxes, User Charges, Federal Grants." _National Tax Journal_ 29 (September, 1976): 312-321.

U.S. Bureau of the Census. _City Government Finances_. Washington, D.C. 1965, 1970, 1975, 1979.

U.S. Bureau of the Census. _Census of Retail Trade, Geographic Area Series_. Washington, D.C. 1972, 1977.

U.S. Bureau of the Census. _City Employment_. Washington, D.C. 1975, 1979.

U.S. Bureau of the Census. _Government Finances_. Washington, D.C. 1975, 1979.

U.S. Bureau of the Census. _1980 Census of Population and Housing, Final Population and Housing Unit Counts, Michigan_. Washington, D.C. 1981.

U.S. Bureau of the Census. _U.S. Statistical Abstract_. Washington, D.C. 1980.

U.S. Bureau of the Census. _Current Population Reports_. Series P-25, nos. 567, 670, 761.

U.S. Bureau of the Census. _1970 Census of Population, General Population Characteristics, Michigan_. Washington, D.C. 1970.

U.S. Bureau of the Census, _Plumbing Facilities and Estimates of Dilapidated Housing_. Vol. 6, Washington, D.C.

Young. C., "State of the City Message," City of Detroit, February, 1981.

Chapter 29

Taxation of Agriculture and Forestry in Michigan

by

Raleigh Barlowe

Michigan State University

INTRODUCTION

Farms and forests provided the principal underpinning for Michigan's tax base until the early decades of this century. Together, they accounted at various times for 90 percent or more of the privately owned land in the state. With the rise of cities, industries, and rural nonfarm developments, and with the acceptance of new types of taxes, their overall significance as a source of tax revenues has declined substantially. But they still account for three-fourths of the privately-owned land area of the state and represent a major portion of the property tax base of the state's rural and suburban townships.

Farming in Michigan

The 1978 Census of Agriculture indicates that Michigan had 68,158 farms covering a total area of 11.4 million acres (Census 1980). More than 80 percent of this farmland area is found in the southern forty-one counties of the state. Some 8.7 million acres, almost 76 percent of the farmland, was classified as cropland and 7.0 million acres as cropland harvested in 1978. Farm real estate had a total market value of $11.2 billion, an average of $975 an acre. Total farm assets had a value of more than $20 billion in 1980 (Wright 1981).

Almost 94 percent of the farms were operated by owners or part-owners and more than nine out of ten were managed as individual or family farms. The average farm had 168 acres; but farms varied considerably in size as is indicated by the fact that 4,374 operating units, 6.4 percent of the total number, had 500 or more acres while 20,146 units, almost 30 percent, contained less than 50 acres. These farms provided employment for around 100,000 people, about 2.4 percent of the state's labor force (Wright 1981).

Farmers as a class face the double problem of high capital investment costs and relatively low net annual returns. The average farm in Michigan in 1978 represented an investment of $163,748 in real estate. In addition to land and buildings, farm operators must also have substantial investments in livestock, machinery, equipment, and supplies. Typical average farm operators often think in terms of minimum capital investments of $250,000 to $400,000.

Farm incomes, on the other hand, have not been high. Proprietor incomes from farming came to $760 million in 1980 and farm wages to $185 million (Michigan 1981). Together, they accounted for slightly over one percent of the personal incomes reported for the state. The Census of Agriculture indicates that only 17.8 percent of the operators had farm product sales of $40,000 or more in 1978 while 59.0 percent reported sales receipts of less than $10,000. Gross farm incomes, including allowances for the rental value of farm dwellings, value of farm-grown produce, government payments, and other farm income, averaged $33,140 per farm (Wright 1981). Average production expenses took $26,447 of this amount, leaving operators with an average net income, including interest on their business equities and payments for operator and family labor and management, of $6,693 in 1978. This average net income ranks below the averages for 1974 ($7,391) and 1979 ($7,170) as the third highest average for the 1960-79 period and compares favorably with the average of $6,059 for the 1975-79 period.

Many farm families receive reasonably good incomes and enjoy a good living from their farms. Most operators, however, cannot look to incomes from farming as a source of individual or family affluence. Large numbers of operators counted as farmers in 1978 supplemented their receipts from farming with incomes from off-farm employment. More than 61 percent of the operators reported some days of off-farm employment in 1978, while 53.3 percent worked 100 or more days off their farms (Census 1980). Eighty-two percent of the operators lived on the farms they were operating but only 45.3 percent indicated that they regarded farming as their principal occupation.

Ownership and Management of Forestlands

Far less information is available concerning the private ownership of forestlands in the state. Around 52 percent of Michigan's land area is forested. Of this total, 6.6 million acres are included in federal, state, and local government-administered forests; 1.5 million acres are in federal and state parks, recreation, game, and wildlife areas; and 1.6 million acres represent farm woodlands. This leaves approximately 9.2 million acres of privately owned forest and wooded recreation areas (Forest Conference 1978; Land Resources Conference 1981).

Michigan's forest resources are concentrated mostly in the Upper Peninsula and in the northern counties of the Lower Peninsula. Approximately 90 percent of the land area of the Upper Peninsula is forested as compared with 70 percent of the twenty-seven northern counties of the Lower Peninsula and 22 percent of the forty-one southern counties (Forest Conference 1978). Most of the areas administered by the state and federal governments involve large contiguous tracts. The area of these lands is almost equally divided between the Upper and Lower Peninsulas. Around 2.2 million acres, about 24 percent, of the privately owned forests are managed in sizeable commercial holdings of 5,000 acres or more. Approximately 97 percent of this area is in the Upper Peninsula.

The remaining 7.0 million acres are held by a mixed group of owners. Some are interested in managing their lands for commercial timber production. Most of the wooded area held in small ownerships of less than 200 acres, however, is subject to indifferent management. Trees grow and forest products are harvested from time to time because this is nature's bounty. But the typical owner is holding the land primarily for development, recreation, speculation, or some other purpose and is little inclined to invest in commercial timber production practices. It is with these small ownerships that the state has its greatest opportunities for increasing timber production (U.S. Forest Service).

The forested area of northern Michigan includes a wide assortment of land types. Some areas are well-suited for timber production while others are sandy or swampy and offer little prospect for productive management. A recent prime forestland identification study indicates that 7.1 million acres, 68.5 percent of the area of the Upper Peninsula, can be classified as prime timberland that has the soil and other characteristics needed to grow eighty-five cubic feet or more of wood per acre per year (U. P. Identification Project 1981). Most of these lands, together with some unique timberlands of less inherent productive capacity and a comparably large area of forestland in the Lower Peninsula, probably find their long run highest and best economic use in commercial timber management.

Developers, recreationists, and wilderness enthusiasts often have other objectives for the use of certain areas. Public policies and programs can accommodate many of these conflicting demands and at the same time emphasize the promotion of intensive forest management practices. Programs of this order are needed both because they provide a means for shifting large areas of underutilized land to more effective economic use and because they can add to the economic base needed to support several northern communities.

Individual forestland owners can contribute to this goal by adopting intensive management practices such as forest thinning, fertilization, and the substitution of genetically superior trees for the natural forest regrowth now found on their lands. In so doing, many operators can raise their annual forest yields from current averages of up to 30 cubic feet of wood per acre to yields of 200 cubic feet or more (Chase 1970). Shifts of this order can make forestry a profitable enterprise and have important implications for the economy of northern Michigan. Tax and other cost and risk considerations associated with the long term nature of forest production, however, often discourage private investments in forestry.

Scope and Objectives

As the foregoing comments indicate, farming and forestry are important enterprises in Michigan. Both have unique characteristics and problems that pose special difficulties in taxation. These are explored in more detail in the discussion that follows.

Emphasis is given in this chapter to the nature and application of the principal state and local taxes that affect agriculture and forestry in Michigan. Primary emphasis is on the operation of the property tax and some alternative taxing arrangements associated with it. Consideration also is given to the operation of other taxes such as the income, sales, single business, motor fuels, and inheritance taxes as they affect farms and forests. This discussion is followed with an evaluation from an overall perspective of the problems of farm and forest taxation in the Michigan economy.

TAXATION OF FARM AND FOREST PROPERTIES

Ad valorem property taxes based on the assessed value of real and personal property are among the oldest, most commonly accepted, and at the same time most criticized taxes we have in Michigan and the United States. Property taxes provided most of the state and local revenues in Michigan until fifty years ago, and they still account for most of the locally-collected tax revenues used to support local government. An understanding of the current operation of these taxes as they affect farms and forests calls for a brief discussion of property tax law together with separate examinations of their impacts on agriculture and on forest properties and also of two closely associated programs that represent modifications of the usual property tax.

Property Tax Law[1]

Farm and forest real properties are taxed in the same manner under Michigan law as other properties. Properties in every township are supposedly assessed at 50 percent of their true cash values on the last day of December each year. These values, which are subject to local review and county and state equalization during the early months of the ensuing year, provide the base on which taxes are levied. The total millage rates used in determining the tax levies represent the sum of the separate millage levies needed to support county, township, school district, and other local government programs. Provisions exist for the possible levying of some taxes during the summer months, but most rural townships make their tax levies and send out their property tax bills once each year on December 1.

Township supervisors normally handle the responsibility for making property tax assessments in rural areas. Training or aptitude for property appraisal is not a qualification for election to the position of supervisor. Those individuals who are elected, however, must take classes on property appraisal and pass an examination administered by the State Tax Commission before they can be certified to sign their assessment rolls.

Local assessment has been identified by many observers in the past as the weakest link in the property tax system. Tremendous progress has been realized in recent decades in improving the quality of local assessments. Part of this success can be credited to the assessor training programs and part to the existence in every county of an office of tax equalization. The county equalizers assist the county board of equalization and work with local supervisors and assessors to secure equity between taxing jurisdictions in the levying of county and other interdistrict taxes.

Despite increasing amounts of supervision, it is common

practice for many supervisors to assess properties at levels far below the 50 percent level stipulated by state legislation. An examination of the 1980 assessments for a sample of sixty rural townships that will be discussed later shows that thirty-one assessed farm properties at between 45 and 51 percent of the true cash value levels determined by the State Tax Commission while eleven assessed values at 35 to 44.9 percent of true cash value, twelve at between 25 and 34.9 percent, three at between 15 and 24.9 percent, and three at less than 15 percent.

Rapidly increasing market (true cash) values since 1972 have been a common cause of failure by supervisors to keep their assessments up to date. Some possible problems associated with these differences have been averted by a requirement that local governments use the state equalized values in their determinations of taxes levied on individual owners. This practice yields higher revenues for most local governments and at the same time shifts much of the blame for rising taxes from local officials to the State Tax Commission.

In theory, all farm and forest properties, both real and personal, should be assessed and counted for property taxation. With these classes of property as with others, however, a substantial portion of the tax base has been removed by a series of exemptions. Exemptions of household goods and motor vehicles are provided by legislation affecting all property owners. Specific provisions have been made for exemptions of the properties owned by fair boards, 4-H clubs, and agricultural societies. Until 1966, $1,000 of value of farm livestock and equipment was exempt. This exemption was expanded by P.A. 205 of 1966 to include all personal property used by farmers in agricultural production.

Other specific exemptions include the value of farm tools, farm products designed for human or animal consumption held in storage (beer, wine and alcoholic beverages excepted), and all deciduous and evergreen trees,

TABLE 29.1

FARM PROPERTY TAXES LEVIED, STATE EQUALIZED VALUATIONS OF AGRICULTURAL AND TIMBER CLASSES OF PROPERTY, AND AVERAGE PROPERTY TAX MILLAGE RATES, MICHIGAN, 1965-1980
(all dollar values in millions)

YEAR	TOTAL PROPERTY TAXES LEVIED ON FARMS	STATE EQUALIZED VALUES BY CLASS			AVERAGE MILLAGE RATE
		Agriculture Real Property	Agriculture Personal	Timber, Cut Over Real Property	
1965	37.5	$1,782.3	$150.6	$120.9	38.35
1966	40.4	1,865.4	147.3	121.5	40.03
1967	43.0	1,948.8	1.0	121.5	43.11
1968	47.5	2,034.1	0.3	131.9	46.03
1969	52.1	2,259.8	0.1	142.8	47.32
1970	55.4	2,430.1	0.1	152.2	48.62
1971	63.8	2,631.6	0.1	166.4	49.54
1972	69.4	2,768.0	0.1	198.4	49.07
1973	78.6	2,966.6	0.1	230.4	50.84
1974	91.1	3,253.5	0.2	259.9	51.08
1975	105.2	3,680.7	0.2	289.7	51.12
1976	121.3	3,931.3	0.2	339.3	53.37
1977	122.9	4,410.3	0.3	382.0	53.89
1978	137.7	5,050.1	0.3	422.6	53.73
1979	157.0	5,766.4	0.3	466.5	53.64
1980	179.3(est.)	6,328.1	0.3	687.8	53.42

Source: Property tax levies on Michigan farms from Jerome Stram and Eleanor Courtney, _Revised Estimates of Taxes Levied on Farm Property 1960-73_, ERS, USDA Statistical Bulletin, No. 538, and _Economic Indicators of the Farm Sector: State Income and Balance Sheet Statistics_, 1979. ESS, USDA Statistical Bulletin, No. 661, 1980. Estimate for 1980 assumes an increase in taxes between 1979 and 1980 equal to increase in state equalized values of classes of agricultural properties between 1978 and 1979. Data on state equalized values of classes of property and average millage rates from reports of the Michigan State Tax Commission.

shrubs, bushes, and vines growing on agricultural lands. Growing timber is excluded from this exemption. Prior to 1960, farm personalty was often assessed at ten percent or more of the value of farm realty. Since 1967, however, exemptions have almost totally removed agricultural personalty from the tax rolls (See Table 29.1).

Except for the exemption of business inventories that became effective in 1977, forest owners and operators have not benefited from special exemptions to the same extent as farmers. An important exception to this situation exists with the 1.46 million acres classified under the commercial forest reserve program. These properties are exempt from general property taxation and are taxed separately under an alternative arrangement that will be described later.

Farm and forest owners enjoy the same opportunities as other taxpayers to receive homestead property tax credits. The circuit-breaker provisions of the state income tax law permit taxpayers to receive credits against their income taxes or cash refunds of up to $1,200 for 60 percent of property tax payments they make on their residential properties over 3.5 percent of their household incomes. The homestead tax credits have a leveling effect in reducing the regressivity of property taxes (Governor's Report 1976). They also have special significance for farmers because: (1) the value of farm products produced for home consumption is not included in the calculation of household income, and (2) farmers who participate under the state's farmland preservation program with its credit for property taxes paid in excess of seven percent of the operator's net household income are eligible for tax credits from both programs.

Trends in Taxation of Farm Properties

Farm real estate property taxes rose almost five-fold in Michigan between 1960 and 1980. An estimated $179 million in property taxes were levied on farm real estate in 1980 as compared with $105.2 million in 1975, $55.4 million in 1970, and $37.5 million in 1965 (Table 29.1). This represents an average increase of slightly more than 12 percent annually between 1970 and 1980.

This dramatic increase is a product of steadily increasing assessed valuations and an upward trend in average millage rates. Detailed information is not available concerning the property taxes levied on farm properties in the state or on the tax rates applied to farmlands. It is known, however, that the value of Michigan farm real estate, as reported by the U.S. Department of Agriculture, rose from $3.1 billion in 1965 to $11.4 billion in 1980 (U.S. Dept. of Agriculture 1981). Meanwhile, the true cash value of agricultural real property (twice the state equalized value), as determined by the State Tax Commission, rose from $3.56 billion in 1965 to $12.66 billion in 1980 (Michigan 1981). Average millage rates in the townships with farm properties were lower than for the state as a whole; but these rates were affected by an upward trend that saw the average millage rate for the state increase from 38.35 mills in 1965 to 53.42 mills in 1980.

A major factor contributing to higher property taxes has been the upward spiral of farmland values. Reports on the farm real estate market supplied by the U.S. Department of Agriculture indicate that farmland values in Michigan rose from averages of $194 an acre in 1960, $237 an acre in 1965, $326 an acre in 1970, and $553 an acre in 1975 to $1,113 an acre in 1980 (Table 29.2). This upward movement reflects a nationwide trend that has been fueled more by inflationary pressures and urban and other nonfarm demands for farmland than by the profitability of farming as a business.

With the increase in farmland values and tax assessed values, average taxes paid per acre also increased. As Table 29.3 indicates, these averages rose steadily from $2.21 per acre in 1960 to $2.66 in 1965, $4.36 in 1970, $9.15 in 1975, and $15.73 in 1980. Inflation had an important impact on these increases; but even when the averages are stated in terms of constant 1970 dollars, they are $2.89 in 1960, $4.36 in 1970, and around $7.55 for 1980.

TABLE 29.2
TRENDS IN MICHIGAN FARM REAL ESTATE VALUES, 1950-1981

YEAR	MARKET VALUE OF FARM REAL ESTATE (in millions of $)	AVERAGE VALUE PER ACRE	INDEX OF REAL ESTATE VALUES (1967=100)	AVERAGE VALUES PER ACRE IN CONSTANT 1970 DOLLARS
1950	$1,701	$99	41	$160
1955	2,241	136	55	197
1960	2,922	194	72	254
1965	3,149	237	84	292
1966	3,280	252	89	302
1967	3,505	275	100	320
1968	3,663	294	103	328
1969	3,854	317	110	336
1970	3,883	326	113	326
1971	4,022	331	115	317
1972	4,551	370	127	343
1973	5,328	444	150	388
1974	6,096	521	174	410
1975	6,525	553	184	399
1976	7,067	604	201	412
1977	8,897	776	256	497
1978	9,804	874	287	520
1979	10,123	975	319	522
1980	11,434	1,113	364	524
1981	13,036(prelim)	1,268(prelim)	415	N.A.

Source: Farm Real Estate Market Developments, ESCA, USDA, CD-77, Supplement July 1973; CD85, August 1980, and CD-85 Supplement, March 1981, and earlier issues. Values in 1970 dollars determined by dividing average market value by current Consumers Price Indexes.

TABLE 29.3

PROPERTY TAXES LEVIED ON FARMS, AVERAGE TAX PER ACRE, TAXES PER $100 OF PROPERTY VALUE, AND PROPERTY TAXES AS A PERCENTAGE OF NET FARM INCOME BEFORE PAYMENT OF TAXES, MICHIGAN, 1960-1980

YEAR	PROPERTY TAXES LEVIED ON FARM PROPERTIES (millions of $)	AVERAGE TAX PER ACRE	AVERAGE TAX PER $100 OF PROPERTY VALUE	PROPERTY TAXES AS A PERCENT OF NET FARM INCOME BEFORE PAYMENT OF TAXES
1960	$34.1	$2.21	$1.21	12.8
1961	34.6	2.29	1.22	11.0
1962	35.9	2.43	1.24	12.3
1963	35.8	2.45	1.20	11.8
1964	37.0	2.57	1.20	12.4
1965	37.5	2.66	1.20	13.5
1966	40.4	2.91	1.23	11.5
1967	43.0	3.16	1.23	15.8
1968	47.5	3.57	1.30	16.9
1969	52.1	4.04	1.36	16.8
1970	55.4	4.36	1.43	18.6
1971	63.8	5.10	1.62	25.4
1972	69.4	5.64	1.60	17.6
1973	78.6	6.55	1.53	13.8
1974	91.1	7.79	1.48	13.2
1975	105.2	9.15	1.51	17.6
1976	121.3	10.64	1.61	25.5
1977	122.9	10.78	1.38[1]	21.4[1]
1978	137.7	12.08	1.40[1]	21.1[1]
1979	157.0	13.77	1.55[1]	23.8[1]
1980	179.3[1]	15.73	1.57[1]	22.6[1]

Notes: [1]Unofficial estimates.

Average taxes per acre represent the totals for property taxes assessed divided by the acreages of farmland reported by the Michigan Department of Agriculture. These figures differ slightly from those reported by the USDA becasue of differing assumptions concerning farmland acreage.

The figures reported for average taxes per $100 of property value and property taxes as a percentage of farm net income before payment of taxes for 1960 through 1976 are from _Revised Estimates of Taxes Levied on Farm Property 1960-1973_, _Farm Real Estate Taxes 1975_, ERS, USDA RET-16, _Farm Real Estate Taxes 1976_, ERS, USDA, RET-17. Estimates for these two categories for the 1977-80 period have been determined by dividing the amount of property taxes levied by the reported value of farm properties for the various years and by calculating the percentages that property taxes represented of total reported net farm incomes before payment of taxes.

Source: Figures on property taxes levied on Michigan farms between 1960 and 1974 are those reported by Jerome Stram and Eleanor Courtney, _Revised Estimates of Taxes Levied on Farm Property 1960-1973_, ERS, USDA State Bull. No. 538; and _Economic Indicators of the Farm Sector, State Income and Balance Sheet Statistics_, 1979. ESS, USDA State. Bull. No.661,1980. The estimate for 1980 assumes an increase in farm property taxes between 1979 and 1980 commensurate with the increase in state equalized values of agricultural properties between 1978 and 1979.

State equalized values, the standard of assessed value used in the determination of individual property taxes since 1954, have been closely correlated with current farm real estate market values.[2] This situation caused the amount of tax levied per $100 of farm property value to remain relatively constant between 1960 and 1967 and then rise as local millage rates climbed. In 1976, the last year for which regional and national comparative data are reported, Michigan's average tax of $1.61 per $100 of farm property value was the highest rate for the six-state region made up of Michigan, Ohio, Indiana, Illinois, Wisconsin, and Minnesota and compared with averages of ninety-seven cents for the region and seventy-six cents for the nation (Bailey 1977).

The higher levels of property taxes per farm and per acre have not been accompanied by comparable increases in reported net farm income. Farm property taxes took less than five percent of average net farm incomes before payment of taxes in the thirteen years extending from 1940 through 1952 (Heneberry 1958). They then rose to statewide averages of 12.8 percent in 1960, 18.6 percent in 1970, and 22.6 percent in 1980. (Table 29.3.) They exceeded 25 percent in 1971 and 1976 and have been above 20 percent in each of the last five years. This increase explains the growing unrest among farmers with this tax. It also shows that while higher tax levies are associated with increasing property values, a farmer's higher net worth may seem rather hollow when it is not associated with a commensurately higher operating income from farming. Interstate comparisons for 1976 indicate that Michigan farmers paid a higher percentage of their net incomes in property taxes than farmers in any other state in the region and that their percentage was three times higher than the national average of 8.6 percent (Bailey 1977).

Tax assessment records for 1965, 1970, 1975, and 1980 were studied for a sample of sixty rural townships to see if some classes of property have shown larger increases in assessed valuation than others. The total sample was divided into subsamples of twelve townships each for five classes of townships. Four of the five classes involved townships with considerable agricultural land located in (1) prime agricultural areas, (2) specialty crop (fruit, potatoes, truck crop) areas, (3) urban growth zones, and (4) other townships. A fifth class involved townships with large assessed values of timberland.

Analysis of the records for the sample townships indicates that assessed valuations have increased for all classes of property, and that average millage rates are higher and have tended to increase faster in the urban growth areas than in the more rural townships and that they are higher in the southern agricultural townships than farther north. Comparisons of the five classes of townships showed that the total assessed value of agricultural land increased most rapidly in the prime agricultural area townships. Total state equalized value of agricultural real property increased 316 percent in these twelve townships between 1965 and 1980 while the S.E.V. for all properties increased 368 percent. Slightly lower rates of increase occurred in the "other" and the speciality crop townships where the S.E.V. for agriculture and all properties increased by 292 and 423 percent and 263 and 369 percent respectively.

For the urban growth townships, the value of the agriculture class rose 150 percent while all property values rose 505 percent. The increase in S.E.V. for agriculture was higher in these townships than any other group except the prime agricultural townships, but the percentage rate of increase was lower than it would have been without the shifting of considerable acreages of farmlands to urban uses. Timberland values increased 230 percent within the forested group of townships, while all property values increased 278 percent. Valuation trends for these townships were complicated by timber harvesting operations in some years and the possible listing of forestlands under the commercial forest reserve program.

Tax Incentives for Protecting Farmlands

Michigan adopted a unique program under the Farmland and Open Space Preservation Act, P.A. 116 of 1974, that grants special tax benefits to farm owners who enter into contractual arrangements with the state to retain their lands in agricultural use. This program was born of a joint effort to secure tax relief for farmers and at the same time promote a program of farmland protection. Census reports indicated that the total area of farmland in the state had dropped from 18.4 million acres in 1945 to 10.8 million acres in 1974. Much of this loss of farmland occurred in the northern counties where numerous operators discontinued marginal farming operations. But considerable areas also were lost to expanding urban and suburban developments around the growing cities. Analyses of these losses indicated that the state was losing important segments of its agricultural production capacity and that action was needed to protect essential agricultural areas for future agricultural use (Barlowe 1966; Frazier 1979; Land Resources Conference 1981; Taxation Seminar 1971).

Proposals calling for use-value assessment of farmlands, tax rollback arrangements that would require farm owners to repay tax benefits realized in some final number of years if they withdrew from the program, and possible contracts under which owners would agree not to use their land for nonfarm uses for specified minimum periods were considered by the legislature during the late 1960s and early 1970s. The final format that emerged with P.A. 116 provided a new tax incentive arrangement.

Farm owners who enrolled under the program were granted an offset against their state income taxes (with cash rebates for any excess payment) of the amounts by which their property taxes exceed seven percent of their household income. In exchange for this tax benefit, participating owners enter into contracts in which they grant their land development rights to the state for periods of ten or more years and agree to repay the benefits they receive plus interest for the last seven years of enrollment should they develop or sell their land for nonfarm uses. Use-value assessments were called for with lands enrolled under the open space phase of the program.[3]

Unlike the use-value assessment programs already adopted by most other states, Michigan's farmland protection program was the first to accept the premise that the program costs represented by foregone tax revenues should be borne by the state[4] (Barlowe 1976). The actual cost of the program to the state varies with annual levels of farm income. Individual tax rebates can be high in years when farm incomes are low and should be somewhat lower in years when farm incomes are higher. Enrollments under the program have increased from 100,000 acres in 1975 to around 800,000 acres in 1978, 1.2 million acres in 1979, and almost 2.0 million acres at the end of 1980. Total costs to the state for the tax rebates rose from $953,000 in 1977 and $1.5 million in 1978 to $7.5 million in 1979 and $15.6 million in 1980. Costs of $21.4 and $23.1 million have been projected for the 1981 and 1982 fiscal years (Michigan 1982).

Enrollment under the farmland preservation program has brought tangible tax relief for many farm operators. In 1977, for example, 90 percent of those enrolled enjoyed some tax credits while 57 percent received credits in combination with their homestead property tax credits that equalled 100 percent of their property tax payments. Sixty percent of the enrolled owners in 1978 realized benefits equal to all of their tax payments. This tax benefit experience has popularized the program among farm groups and has enticed many who were initially skeptical about the development right feature to enroll. As one farm leader has observed, the program has provided a means "by which farmers can secure tax relief with honor."

P.A. 116 has brought tax relief for participating farmers, but nagging questions remain concerning the extent to which it has actually contributed to the protection of farmlands. Unlike its Wisconsin counterpart, the program contains no provisions for local (or state) designation of permanent agricultural protection districts. Very few enrollees have thus far attempted to withdraw their land from the program; but as long as owners keep their lands in the program for the duration of their contracts, there is nothing to prevent them from using the program to secure tax benefits and long-term loans of the amounts of their last seven years of benefits until they are ready to sell or develop their land for nonfarm uses.

Many of the owners who have enrolled under the program have a sincere and genuine interest in keeping their lands in their present use. Indeed, a large number of applicants since 1978 has requested contracts for twenty years or more and sometimes as much as eighty or ninety-nine years. At the same time, however, studies of the location of the enrolled lands show that they lie for the most part in strictly rural areas where there is little prospect of demand for their development for nonfarm uses (Frazier 1979). Enrollments are sparse in the urban growth zones around cities and, when farmlands are enrolled in these areas, owners often withhold strips of land along major roads from enrollment.

Farmers in urban growth areas have two good reasons for not enrolling lands under P. A. 116. Many are interested in selling their holdings for a good price as soon as a suitable opportunity arises. Enrollment under the program might only complicate the interests of these owners, particularly if they plan to sell their properties within ten years. A second reason is related to the basing of the owner's tax credits on household income. Part-time farming is more prevalent around cities than in more strictly rural areas and part-time farm operators who live near cities have opportunities to secure larger proportions of their total household incomes from nonfarm work than is usually the case in more strictly rural areas. With higher household incomes, these operators have less incentive for enrolling their lands under the farmland protection program.

A modification of the law to permit owners in urban growth areas to base their tax credits on agricultural rather than household income has been suggested as a possible means for encouraging more of these owners to participate in the program.[5] A change of this order was opposed by farm leaders in 1979 on the grounds that tax benefits under P.A. 116 should be based on an ability-to-pay criterion and that no loopholes should be provided that would allow owners with high nonfarm incomes to realize benefits from holding land under a farmland protection program (Smith 1980). This view supported the feature of the law that provided tax benefits for farmers but quite overlooked the fact that when farmland protection is stressed as a goal, emphasis should be placed on measures for saving farmland regardless of the income status of the owners.

Taxation of Forestlands

Forestland taxation has had a colorful history in Michigan. Rising property taxes were frequently cited during the exploitive lumbering period as compelling reasons for owner acceptance of "cut out and get out" practices. High property taxes on cutover lands, along with the low productive potential of many of these lands for agricultural development, contributed in later years to the tax delinquency and tax forfeiture of millions of acres during the 1920s and 1930s (Barlowe 1951). By 1940, property taxes on most of the remaining privately-owned forestlands had dropped to relatively low levels; but since then tax levels have risen steadily along with timber prices and the growth of new timber on much of the cutover land.

From an equity point of view, forest ownership and forestland management have always fared poorly under the property tax for the simple reason that they do not match the basic assumptions of the *ad valorem* property tax system. Annual taxes based on the market value of property appear reasonable because it is assumed that properties have annual flows of real or imputed income that correlate with their market values. Businessmen may turn their inventories over several times during a year, and farmers normally expect to have a new crop to harvest and sell each year. Forestland owners, however, deal with a product that has a growing cycle of twenty to eighty years. Taxation of the growing forest on the basis of its true cash value each year can have definite anti-conservational impacts in encouraging premature cutting practices and may easily make the private holding of forests an uneconomic operation.

Specific data are not available for Michigan on average taxes per acre of forestland or taxes per $100 of forestland investment. State figures indicate that the class of property described by the State Tax Commission as "timber-cutover" had a true cash value of $687.8 million in 1980 as compared with $289.7 million in 1975, $152.2 million in 1970, and $120.0 million in 1965 (Michigan 1982). The reported true cash value of this class increased 569 percent between 1965 and 1980 as compared with an increase of 355 percent in the value of the agriculture class and a 346 percent increase in the value of the other classes of real property.

The trend in true cash values for "timber-cutover" is probably indicative of what has happened to assessed values for forestlands. These value figures can be misleading though because the classification includes swamps, sandy areas, and some wastelands as well as forestlands, while it does not include public forests, private lands entered under the commercial forest reserve program, farm woodlands counted as "agriculture," or forested properties that may be counted as "residential," "commercial," or "industrial" because of developments on their legal descriptions.

An alternative approach was used by the present author in a 1978 study in determining the average assessed values of forestlands (Land Use Conference 1978). Letters were sent to the county equalization officers of all of the Upper Peninsula counties and the twelve northern Lower Peninsula counties with the largest acreages of private forest lands. These officials were asked to indicate the ranges of assessed values accepted in determinations of the county equalized values of forestlands. Twenty-two officials responded with data that indicated general equalized value ranges of $25 to $50 an acre in the western Upper Peninsula, $60 to $250 an acre in the eastern counties of the Upper Peninsula, and $150 to $350 an acre in the northern Lower Peninsula. Weighting of these data suggested a median assessed value of around $160 an acre.

Examination of the millage rates used in the twenty-seven counties showed that 70 percent of the townships had millage rates in the thirty to thirty-nine mill range in 1976 and that the median rate for the rural townships was thirty-five mills. Application of this rate to the median assessed valuation of $160 indicated an average tax of around fifty-six cents per acre on forestland. This calculated rate is lower than the averages reported by owners and managers of productive forestlands and it is low by 1980 valuation standards.

Low as the fifty-six cent tax figure probably is, it does provide a suitable base for comparison with the average forestry income streams of forest owners. Studies conducted in 1954, 1966 and 1970 indicated average annual forest growth rates of 0.201 cords, 0.234 cords, and 0.36 cords of wood per acre per year, respectively (Chase 1970). If one assumes an average growth rate of 0.4 cords (fifty-one cubic feet) of wood per acre per year and an average market value of $4.00 a cord, which is slightly higher than the average price paid for all species of wood in northern Michigan in 1977, it would appear that the new forest growth on the average acre of forestland in northern Michigan had a market value of around $1.60 per acre in 1976 and 1977. Of this total, fifty-six cents, or 35 percent, was needed to pay property taxes. This is an annual charge against gross, not net, income and shows that forest owners had more reasons to complain about property taxes than farmers who paid out 25 percent of their net income before payment of taxes as property taxes in 1976.

Some forest owners are in a better position, some in a worse position, than this example indicates. The example, however, highlights the fact that a more enlightened system that better correlates the forest owner's annual taxes to value of the annual tree growth is needed if progress is to be realized in selling investors on the profitability of long term forest management. When consideration is given to the necessary long term nature of forest investments and to the risks and costs associated with holding forests for these periods, it is easy to identify annual property taxes as a major barrier to the desired adoption of long term forest management practices.

Operation of the Commercial Forest Reserve Act

Michigan's legislature recognized the anti-conservational impacts of property taxation on forest management in 1925 when it enacted the Commercial Forest Reserve Act.[6] This law provides an alternative approach to forestland taxation under which qualifying owners pay a nominal annual tax on their forestland and pay a yield or severance tax on the stumpage value of any timber they harvest.

Tracts with appreciable quantities of merchantable timber and tracts with little or no forest cover were specifically excluded from classification at first; but the law was amended to permit the listing of selectively logged lands in 1939. As amended by P.A. 393 of 1980, the law now authorizes special classification of forest lands under the program upon the request of individual owners and after examination by representatives of the Department of Natural Resources:

> of land containing no material natural resources other than forest growth, no portion of which is used for agricultural, mineral extraction, grazing, industrial, developed recreational or resort purposes, and upon which the owner proposes to develop, maintain, and actively manage a forest

> through planting, natural reproduction, or other forestry practices.

To be eligible for listing, forestlands should have sufficient productive potential "to give assurance that a stand of merchantable timber will be developed within a reasonable time" but "nonproductive land which occurs intermixed with productive land and which is an integral part of a managed forest" is eligible for listing.

The annual land tax was initially set at five cents an acre for pinelands and ten cents for lands with hardwood tree cover. This rate was raised to a uniform ten cents per acre in 1927, reduced to five cents in 1935, changed to a sliding scale rate ranging from five to ten cents in 1958, increased to fifteen cents in 1970, and boosted to thirty cents an acre in 1980. P.A. 393 provides that the annual acreage tax will now be readjusted at ten year intervals beginning in 1990. The annual land tax is paid and allocated in the same way as property taxes.

A yield tax of 25 percent of the value of timber harvested was specified in the original law. This rate was reduced to the present ten percent yield tax rate in 1931. Yield taxes were shared by the state and the local governments until 1970 when provisions were made for the entire tax to go to the state's General Fund. Since the 1980 amendments, all yield taxes are returned to the local units by the Department of Natural Resources. This payment is balanced by a state commitment to make annual payments on all listed lands to the local governments. Annual state payments of five cents an acre were scheduled in 1925. This payment rate was raised to ten cents an acre in 1927 and fifteen cents an acre in 1956. Payments at a sliding scale based on local millage rates were provided for in 1958; and later legislation raised the annual state acreage payments to twenty-five cents an acre in 1970 and seventy cents in 1980. Like the annual land tax, the state's acreage payment rates are now scheduled for readjustment at ten year intervals.

Owners are expected to apply good managerial practices to their lands, but no provisions are made for establishing or enforcing forest management or cutting standards. Cutting permits must be secured from the Department of Natural Resources. Listed lands also must be open for public hunting and fishing unless they are closed by action of the Natural Resources Commission or the legislature. Owners do not have a contract with the state for any given period and are accordingly subject to such changes in the law as the legislature may make.

Forestlands can be withdrawn from classification at the request of owners. A withdrawal fee of five cents an acre for every year of classification was charged under the 1925 law. This charge has been increased and now calls for payment

> ...of a penalty equal to the product of the current average ad valorem property tax on timber cutover real property within the township in which the land is located, as determined by the township assessor, times the number of years, not to exceed seven, the land was subject to this act, together with a fee equivalent to ten percent of the full stumpage value of the merchantable forest products on the land

on tracts classified for less than twenty years. The withdrawal fee on lands listed for twenty years or more is limited to a charge equal to ten percent of the stumpage value of the forest products on the land. The Department of Natural Resources can cancel listings and order the payment of withdrawal fees if owners violate the provisions of the act.

Forestland owners showed only limited interest in participation under the program during the 1920s. Some 233,507 acres were offered for classification during the first seven years. Of these, only 92,948 were accepted for classification and 3,410 were soon withdrawn leaving a total of only 89,538 acres under the program in 1932. Enrollments remained relatively constant at around 100,000 acres from 1938 to 1950. An upward trend in property taxes after 1950 brought increases in enrollments to 425,418 acres in 1958,

TABLE 29.4
STATE PAYMENTS TO COUNTIES AND REVENUES WITH THE COMMERCIAL FOREST RESERVE ACT, 1926-1980
(thousands of dollars)

YEARS	STATE PAYMENTS TO COUNTIES	REVENUES FROM	
		Yield Taxes	Withdrawal Fees
1926-30	$ 18.0	$ ----	$ 0.1
1931-35	43.3	0.9	2.5
1936-40	49.4	2.2	3.3
1941-45	49.4	2.4	2.8
1946-50	53.1	4.6	7.4
1951-55	73.6	6.7	6.1
1956-60	195.6	36.4	9.5
1961-65	232.9	90.0	2.5
1966-70	308.8	142.9	18.9
1971-75	1,090.6	286.1	37.8
1976	270.8	78.6	8.4
1977	301.0	114.8	4.2
1978	313.6	142.8	10.1
1979	322.1	154.0	13.4
1980	343.3	213.4	10.1
TOTALS	3,665.5	1,275.7	137.1

Source: Reports of Lands Division, Michigan Department of Natural Resources.

890,737 acres in 1970, 1,254,260 acres in 1977, and 1,457,697 acres at the beginning of 1981.

Examination of the data on forestlands classified at the end of 1980 shows that 1,170,524 acres, 80.3 percent of the total, is located in the nine western counties of the Upper Peninsula. Another 247,179 acres is found in the six eastern counties of the Upper Peninsula while 36,253 acres are located in twenty-one of the twenty-seven northern counties and 3,743 acres in twenty-three of the forty-one southern counties of the Lower Peninsula.

Seven corporation owners with listings of between 99,663 and 262,789 acres each account for 78.7 percent of the total listings. Eight other owners have between 10,000 and 99,000 acres listed, 31 between 1,000 and 9,999 acres, 31 between 500 and 999 acres, 65 between 200 and 499 acres, and 194 less than 100 acres. A total of 104 owners had single quarter-quarter sections (around forty acres) of land listed under the law. These data indicate that large industrial owners are the principal participants in terms of acreage classified but that a significant number of small tract owners, many of them farmers in the southern counties of the state, are using the law as a forestland protection program.

The state's financial balance relative to the operation of the Commercial Forest Reserve Act is summarized in Table 29.4. Throughout the first fifty-five years of the program, the state paid $3,665,517 in annual acreage payments to the counties while it received $137,116 in withdrawal fees and $1,275,706 in yield taxes. Altogether, its revenues from the program have equaled only 38.5 percent (65.1 percent in 1980) of its costs. Revenues have increased rapidly in recent years, but the raising of the state's annual acreage payment rates to twenty-five cents an acre in 1970 and seventy cents in 1980 have greatly reduced the prospect that the state will receive yield taxes commensurate with its costs anytime soon. This tabulation tells only part of the story, however, as the state has acquired a ten percent equity in a growing forest and the existence of the forest reserve program has undoubtedly had positive effects in helping to support the economic viability of many northern Michigan communities.

OTHER TAXES AFFECTING FARMS AND FORESTS

While the property tax is often viewed as the most important tax affecting agriculture and forestry, other taxes also have significant impacts. Farmers and forestland owners pay state and federal income taxes. Sales taxes are paid on their purchase of items other than food and medicine. Farmers have an exemption from the single business tax but this tax applies to forest operations. Several special commodity taxes affect farm products. Farmers can qualify for special treatment under the state inheritance tax; and the forest industry sometimes complains that it is penalized by the insurance rates applied to logging operations under the state's workmen's compensation laws.

Income and Sales Taxes

Only limited information is available concerning the payments farmers and forest owners make on state or federal income taxes. With an average reported net farm income of only $6,693 in 1978, the outlay of most farmers for taxes on farm income was relatively low. Indeed, with a farm net income of only $6,693, the average operator would have had no federal or state income tax liability if he or she had three dependents, had no other income, and paid $300 or more of property taxes during the year.

Michigan does, of course, have many farm owners and forestland owners who enjoy above average incomes. A general and admittedly very incomplete measure of the taxes paid by these individuals is provided by the Department of Treasury printout on state income tax withholding for the 1979-80 fiscal year. This tabulation shows that $3.9 million in state income taxes were withheld from agricultural sources while $155,774 were withheld from forestry sources. The income taxes withheld for these two groups represented 1.77 percent of the withheld taxes reported for all categories of taxpayers in the state.

Sales and use tax information is reported for different types of commodities and services but not for occupational groups of buyers. The basic legislation for both the sales tax and the use tax provides for exemptions on tangible properties used and consumed in agricultural production. Even with these exemptions, farmers do pay sales taxes on the purchase of some supplies along with sales taxes on automobiles, clothing, furniture and other goods and services that may be acquired by anyone. Treasury printout data for the 1979-80 fiscal year shows that $2.6 million in sales taxes and $155,657 in use taxes could be attributed to agriculture. The comparable figures for forestry were $18,748 and $6,899, respectively. Together, these tax payments represented 1.78 percent and 0.7 percent of the sales and use taxes reported for the state.

Single Business Tax

Agriculture and forestry were both treated as enterprises subject to taxation under the Single Business Tax at the time of its enactment in 1975, but operators with gross incomes of less than $40,000 were exempt from the tax. Experience soon showed that the reporting process provided an unwelcome burden for those farmers who were affected and that the net tax return from farming operations was small. The law was amended in 1976 to exempt that part of the tax base attributable to the production of agricultural products. Agricultural marketing and retailing activities are still subject to taxation as is forestry. The primary impact on forestry falls on forest industries that own and manage forestlands in association with their processing of forest products.

Special Agricultural Commodity Taxes

P.A. 87 of 1939 established a Michigan Apple Commission and provided for an assessment of one cent per bushel (two cents per hundredweight) on all apples grown and sold in the state to pay the cost of operating the commission and administering its advertising and quality control programs. Comparable legislation with specific taxes on agricultural commodities were used to establish a Michigan Cherry Commission in 1947, an agricultural seal of quality program in 1961, a Michigan Bean Commission in 1965, a Michigan Potato Commission in 1970, a Michigan Beef Industry Commission in 1972, and to authorize agricultural marketing and bargaining associations in 1972.

These programs enjoy the support of the farmers who are involved in them because it is felt that they help secure a wider market for the products of Michigan farms. It may be noted, however, that a law of 1973 calling for a specific tax on oil of peppermint and oil of spearmint has been repealed. Two other laws calling for specific taxes on malt syrup (1931) and the grain held in storage by processors, dealers, and warehousemen (1945) also have been repealed. The grain tax, repealed in 1980, was an in lieu of property tax arrangement and provided little in tax revenue.

Motor Fuel Taxes

Considerable amounts of gasoline and diesel fuel are used by farmers and loggers in their normal operations. The interests of these and other similar operators are recognized by a provision in the tax law that authorized refunds of taxes paid on gasoline for purposes other than the operations of motor vehicles on public roads, streets, or highways. Refunds totaling $130,283 were paid to agricultural (including forestry) operators in the 1978-80 fiscal year. This total was down from $199,255 in the previous fiscal year.

The decrease in refunds indicates a reduction in gasoline consumption. Some of this reduction may be attributed to economies dictated by rising prices, but much of it involved a shift to the use of lower cost diesel fuel. Tax refunds are not paid with diesel fuel as a tax is collected only on sales of diesel fuel sold for motor vehicle use on public roads.

Inheritance Taxes

With the rapid increase in property values of recent years, state inheritance and federal estate and gift taxes have acquired new significance. Heirs often find themselves in higher tax brackets than they would have been in with the same properties some years earlier. Higher taxes must be paid and sales of significant properties may be required to meet the tax obligations. This situation has particular significance for farmers and forest owners because payment of estate and inheritance taxes may force the breaking up of going concerns while good farm or forest management may dictate a need for retaining property units at their present size or even adding to the scale of operation.

This problem was recognized by P.A. 628 of 1978 which updated the state's inheritance tax structure by increasing the specific exemption for surviving spouses from $30,000 to $65,000 and the exemption of Class I (close relative) heirs from $5,000 to $10,000. Even with these higher exemptions, inheritance taxes in combination with the federal estate and gift taxes can have serious implications for farm and forest owners. P.A. 628 specifically recognized this problem as it affects farmers by providing a unique set of exemptions for those farm properties enrolled under the Farmland and Open Space Preservation Act.

Farms enrolled or that heirs agree to enroll under P.A. 116 are eligible for a 50 percent reduction in the normal inheritance tax on the market value of the farm real estate (Craig 1980). Heirs also may request a ten year interest- and penalty-free deferment of inheritance tax payments on the remaining 50 percent of the tax on real property values. Inherited properties must be held in the farmland preservation program for a full ten years to qualify for this exemption and deferment. Probate court records indicate that several farm heirs have elected to enroll lands not earlier enrolled once they have learned about these inheritance tax benefits.

Workmen's Compensation Insurance

The accident insurance premiums that forest operators have been required to pay for their logging operations are viewed by many operators as a discriminatory tax. Provisions are made in the Workmen's Compensation Act of 1969 for a self-supporting accident compensation fund which is financed by insurance payments based on a rating of industrial establishments and employers according to probable risk. The rating for logging operations in 1980 was $46.00 per $100 of payroll. Forest operators have complained that this rate is unduly high, that it is above the $34.55 rate used by the Michigan Association of Timbermen (an independent self-insuring group), and that it is far above the rate of fifteen to sixteen dollars which some Upper Peninsula operators pay with their logging operations in northern Wisconsin.

Legislative action was taken with P.A. 357 of 1980 to transfer responsibility for compensating logging industry injuries involving claims of $12,500 or more to the Silicosis, Dust Disease, and Logging Injury Compensation Fund. This transfer will greatly reduce the premiums forest operators pay to the Workmen's Compensation Accident Fund though it leaves questions concerning their liabilities for the operation of the new fund.

OVERALL EVALUATION

Evaluations of the impacts, merits, and workability of tax systems on agriculture and forestry vary with the points of view and the criteria of the evaluators. A comprehensive evaluation of the Michigan tax system as it affects these two industries calls for consideration of the views of the individuals and firms that pay the taxes, the attitudes of local government officials who look to taxes for their major sources of revenues, and the general position of the larger community or society represented by the state (Land Use Conference 1978).

Farm and forest owners frequently disagree with each

other on issues of tax policy because as individuals they tend to accept and support varying combinations of the views represented by the above three different poles of interest. Insofar as they operate as economic men, they can be expected to have a natural interest in minimizing their individual tax costs and opposing any tax or increase in taxes that does not promise them tangible benefits that have a value at least equal to their cost.

Local governmental officials and citizen groups interested in schools and other public services tend to view taxes not as costs but rather as necessary public revenues. The typical farming or forested rural community has a relatively limited tax base per capita. Those people who feel pressures for financing existing public services or for providing additional services see higher taxes as necessary, and their emphasis on getting additional revenues now can easily cause them to favor tax policies that may undermine rather than strengthen the future economic base of their taxing jurisdictions.

A third point of view is represented by the state which acts as the agent for society at large. As the representative of the interests of the larger community and of the long-run interests of society, including the interests of citizens yet unborn, the state has a responsibility for maintaining and enhancing its economic base and for securing equity in the tax system. It has an obligation to promote long-run environmental, resource conservation, and land-use goals while encouraging continued economic growth of communities and enterprises.

Individual farmers and forest owners have had good reasons for complaining about the upward spiral of property taxes in recent years. This has been the principal tax many have paid; and it has indeed taken an inordinate share of the average operator's income as it has climbed above the level of 20 percent of net income before payment of tax for average farmers and to still higher levels for forest owners. Yet as community-minded citizens, the individuals who have paid these taxes have often joined with their neighbors in voting for higher local millage rates to finance desired local governmental services.

Farm organizations have utilized citizen concern about the adequacy of food supplies and data concerning the disadvantaged position of the average farmer to political advantage in securing major tax benefits for agriculture. The exemptions they have secured under the sales tax, the single business tax, and the personal property phase of the general property tax speak well for the political power of agriculture in Michigan. P.A. 116 has effectively removed most, and sometimes all, of the burden of the property tax for those farm owners who are willing to enroll in the farmland preservation program. Added benefits under the inheritance tax place these operators in a favored position.

Sales and motor fuel taxes are now the principal taxes that many average farmers with no off-farm income pay. Taxes are still a problem for high-income operators in agriculture; but for equity reasons, these individuals should be treated on much the same basis as high income operators in other enterprises. Similarly, tears need not be shed for those owners who fail to enroll their lands under P.A. 116. These owners often have speculative objectives that do not merit special tax consideration.

Forest owners fall generally into two classes: large industrial owners and owners of smaller tracts. Industrial forests are operated largely as an adjunct to wood processing industries. These companies own and operate forests to guarantee access to the raw materials they must have in their principal operations. Many of them would prefer to leave the business of growing trees to others if they could be certain that they could get the wood they need at a reasonable price when they need it. These operators have strong economic reasons for favoring lower taxes on timber production. But as responsible citizens of local communities, they have accepted higher property taxes because they understand the needs of local governments for higher tax revenues.

Forestland owners have not secured tax benefits commensurate with those received by agriculture. They do not benefit from comparable exemptions under the sales, single business, property or inheritance taxes. With the revision of the Commercial Forest Reserve Act in 1980, they accepted a doubling of their annual land taxes in return for minor concessions on handling of cutting permits. The rising tax costs of holding industrial forests can be charged off as necessary costs for wood processing industries. This situation does not exist, however, for the small owners who hope to make a living from their forest operations or who are willing to invest in forest management if they can be convinced that it is a paying proposition. These owners need a program especially designed for their needs, perhaps an adaptation of P.A. 116 to permit the enrollment of forest as well as farmlands, that will reduce their tax liabilities while encouraging the acceptance of long term forest management practices. Lacking such a program, 259 owners of forests of less than 200 acres have had their holdings enrolled under the commercial forest reserve program.

The concerns of the state in the taxation of agriculture and forestry go beyond the interests of individual taxpayers and the local communities in which they live. The state has an obligation to make certain that the overall tax system is equitable, that farmers and forest owners are treated fairly relative to each other and other groups of taxpayers. Agriculture seems to be well cared for relative to forestry at the present time.

As the agent of society, the state also has an obligation to make certain that tax policies promote rather than undermine the long run interests of the larger community. Michigan has not yet taken action to identify its essential areas of farm or forestland. Once these areas are identified, tax policies should favor their retention and further development for farming and forest production.

Justification could be advanced, if need be, for the state paying 90 percent or all of the property taxes on farms and forests, as was recently proposed in Ontario, to keep them in their present use (Ontario Commission 1977). Measures of this nature may or may not be needed, but careful consideration should be given to constructive uses of tax policy that will help protect and enhance the physical and economic base on which the state will depend for its agricultural and forest production in the future.

NOTES, CHAPTER 29

[1]See also Chapter 16 in this volume.

[2]Michigan's Supreme Court held in School District Number 9, Pittsfield Township, Washtenaw County v. Washtenaw County Board of Supervisors, 341 Mich. 388 (1954) that state equalized values of property must be used by local governments for tax computation purposes.

[3]Privately owned open space lands can be enrolled under the program and be assessed at their current use values. The state reimburses local governments for any revenues lost on areas that the state designates as open space but no reimbursement is paid for nondesignated lands. About 6,000 acres were enrolled under this phase of the P. A. 116 program in 1980.

[4]Local governments bear the cost of lost revenues in all of the use-value assessment states except New York where the state reimburses local governments for one-half of the tax losses on lands included in agricultural districts (Barlowe 1976). Wisconsin enacted a farmland protection law with a circuit-breaker provision similar to the Michigan arrangement in 1977. Wisconsin's law goes further than that of Michigan to limit enrollments after 1982 to farmlands that are officially designated by local officials as being located within areas zoned for exclusive agricultural use.

[5]Questions exist as to whether any system of tax credits can provide enough economic incentive to protect farmlands from development in urban growth pressure zones. Programs for the public acquisition of development rights may be needed if farmlands are to be retained in their current use over time in these areas. One Michigan legislator observed in 1979 that the state could probably get more farmland protection where it is needed if it would take the funds used for P.A. 116 tax credits and use them to purchase the development rights for farmlands that are subject to urban development pressures.

[6]A farm woodlot law that authorized assessment of woodlots at $1 per acre for up to forty acres of woodland and required payment of a five percent yield tax on timber harvested was passed earlier in 1911 and revised in 1917. This law has been seldom used. Only 601 acres were known to be enrolled under it in 1975.

REFERENCES, CHAPTER 29

Bailey, Mary L. Farm Real Estate Taxes, 1976. Economic Research Service, U.S. Department of Agriculture, RET-17, 1977.

Barlowe, Raleigh. Administration of Tax-Reverted Lands in the Lake States. Michigan Agricultural Experiment Station Technical Bulletin 225, 1951.

Barlowe, Raleigh. Use of Land and Water Resources in Michigan. Project 80 Report, Michigan Agricultural Experiment Station Research Report 52 - Natural Resources, 1966.

Barlowe, Raleigh and Alter, Theodore R. Use-Value Assessment of Farm and Open Space Lands. Michigan Agricultural Experiment Station Research Report 308, 1976.

Chase, C. D.; Pheifer, R. E.; and Spencer, J. S., Jr. The Growing Timber Resource of Michigan. North Central Forest Experiment Station, U.S. Forest Service, 1970.

Commission on the Reform of Property Taxation in Ontario. Report. Ontario Government Bookstore, 1977.

Craig, Robert G. Michigan's Taxation of Farm Inheritances. Michigan Farm Bureau Research Report 80-1, 1980.

Forests and Michigan's Future. Proceedings of Michigan's Sixth Land Use Policy Conference, Michigan State University, June 1, 1978.

Frazier, Donald N. Locational Analysis of Participants in Michigan's Farmland and Open Space Preservation Program. Master's degree technical paper, Department of Resource Development, Michigan State University, 1979.

Governor's Advisory Task Force on Property Tax Revision. Interim Report to Governor. State of Michigan, 1976.

Heneberry, William H. and Barlowe, Raleigh. *Property Tax Trends Affecting Michigan Farmers*. Michigan Agricultural Experiment Station Special Bulletin 421., 1958.

"Land Resources Role in the Michigan Economy". *Proceedings of Natural Resources Outlook Conference*, Michigan State University, April 15-16, 1981.

Smith, Elton R. "It's Your Land They Are Talking About." *Farm News* (March 1980) Michigan Farm Bureau.

State of Michigan. *Budget Message of the Governor for Fiscal Year 1982*.

State of Michigan. *Economic Report of the Governor, 1981*.

Stram, Jerome and Courtney, Eleanor. *Revised Estimates of Taxes Levied on Farm Property, 1960-73*. Economic Research Service, U.S. Department of Agriculture Statistical Bulletin No. 538, 1975.

Taxation of Agricultural and Other Open Land. Proceedings of Seminar, Michigan State University Cooperative Extension Service. April 1-2, 1971.

U.S. Bureau of the Census. *Census of Agriculture, Michigan 1978*. Preliminary state report, 1980.

U.S. Department of Agriculture. *Real Estate Market Developments*. Economics, Statistics, and Cooperatives Service, U.S.D.A. CD 85, August 1980, and CD 85 Supplement, March 1981.

U.S. Department of Agriculture. *Economic Indicators of the Farm Sector: State Income and Balance Sheet Statistics, 1979*. Economics and Statistics Service, U.S.D.A. Statistical Bulletin No. 661, 1980.

U.S. Forest Service. *RPA: A Recommended Renewable Resource Program, 1977 to 2020*.

Upper Peninsula of Michigan Prime Forestlands Identification Project. *Final Report, 1981*.

Wright, Karl T. and Ferris, John N. *Michigan Agriculture Going Into the Eighties*. Cooperative Extension Service, Michigan State University, 1981.

Chapter 30

A Summary of Findings and Policy Options

by

Harvey E. Brazer

The University of Michigan

This chapter begins with some general observations on the current Michigan fiscal scene, then moves to a summary of the principal findings of each of the substantive chapters, and concludes with a statement of policy options with respect to taxation. The findings and policy options presented are based on the facts and analyses contained in the relevant chapters of this volume. But I alone am responsible for their selection and interpretation, neither of which have been endorsed or approved by the authors of those chapters.

GENERAL OBSERVATIONS

In terms of purchasing power, as measured by the Gross National Product deflator for state and local government purchases, the General Fund-General Purpose Budget of the State of Michigan has declined by at least 20 percent in the past three years. It is not apparent, in these circumstances, that the budget for fiscal year 1982 should be balanced exclusively by reducing expenditures below appropriations by as much as $500 million to $700 million. The well-being of the people of Michigan, the quality of life in the state, may be better served by means of an appropriate selection of adjustments in taxes and other revenue sources. The results of surveys, voting on referenda, and millage elections, all indicate that the majority of Michigan residents do not favor cutting the level of public services.

Statements on the alleged widespread demand for property tax reduction do not square with the results of elections on school millage renewals. Voter rejections of increased millages indicate a difference of opinion on the size of the school budget, not necessarily a demand for property tax reduction. With school levies currently accounting for 68 percent of total property taxes, these taxes must be seen in the context of school finance as a whole. Under the present formula for state school aid, for districts such as Alpena, Pontiac, Romulus, and Taylor, each dollar of local property tax attracts between twenty-five cents and one dollar of general state aid. Moreover, for most homeowners that dollar in property tax will cost, at the margin, only forty cents after deduction of the Homestead Property Tax Credit. Thus the voters of Taylor school district may realize a dollar in school revenue at a cost to them of only approximately twenty cents. If the voter itemizes deductions under the federal income tax the net cost is even substantially less than that.[1]

The property tax in Michigan is a purely local tax (except for certain utility property). It is now within the authority of local taxing jurisdictions to reduce their tax levies and, through periodic elections on extra-voted millage, local electorates now have the option of cutting their property taxes. A statutory or constitutional requirement that all property taxes be reduced would deny local autonomy and prohibit the expression of local preferences in fiscal matters. It seems perfectly appropriate for voters in Alpena to determine their school millage; it does not make sense to permit those same voters to participate in the decision as to the level of school millage to be levied in other Michigan communities.

Reducing the tax bill for business in Michigan will undoubtedly improve the state's image in the business community and may even bring some new jobs to the state. But it is not enough that the expected benefits be positive. We must be confident that those benefits will exceed the costs in terms of public services curtailed and/or additional taxes borne by those who are asked to make up the revenue lost.

In sum, the foregoing observations are meant simply to suggest that further reductions in the state's General Fund budget may or may not constitute the optimal set of policy measures. Seeking additional revenues to offset at least part of the budgetary shortfall may be the preferred alternative; whether or not property taxes are to be cut seems an issue that is most appropriately settled by local electorates with respect to their own levies. And tax reduction that is good for business may or may not be good for the state.

A SUMMARY OF FINDINGS

In less than fifteen years Michigan's tax system has been drastically revised. These years have seen the adoption of a modest flat rate personal income tax, exemption of food and prescription drugs under the sales tax, the introduction of property tax relief for homeowners, renters, and farmers through the homestead property tax credit and the farmland preservation program, and the substitution of the single business tax for the property tax on inventories, the corporate income and franchise taxes, and other less important business taxes. The result is a far more equitable distribution of taxes among people, far less reliance on taxes initially borne by business, and a revenue system that rests broadly on income, consumption, and wealth.

The Economy

The Michigan economy continues to be characterized by a high level of industrialization, as indicated by the fact that manufacturing accounts for fully one-third of total employment. Moreover, an extraordinarily large proportion of manufacturing employment is in durable goods industries and 55 percent of that employment is directly related to the auto industry. That figure contrasts with a corresponding 11 percent for the U.S. as a whole. And, while one-third of employment is in manufacturing, in the recession of 1979-80 manufacturing accounted for 84 percent of the decline in jobs.

Heavy concentration in employment in durable goods industries contributes substantially both to high wages and relatively high income in Michigan and also to the large amplitude of cyclical fluctuations in employment in the state.

In May 1981 average hourly earnings in the motor vehicles industry were $10.95, 38 percent higher than the $7.92 hourly rate for all manufacturing industries. This differential grew rapidly during the past decade, having been only 26 percent in 1970.

Given Michigan's concentration in durable goods manufacturing, it is not surprising that wage rates are high here. In fact they are 32 percent higher in manufacturing in Michigan than in the U.S. About one-sixth of this difference is attributable to our concentration in durables, but <u>within</u> the durable goods sector, the average wage in Michigan is 27 percent higher than it is in the nation as a whole. Relative to those states with which Michigan competes most directly, wage rates range from 10 to 33 percent higher here.

Wages in both manufacturing and nonmanufacturing industries are highest in southeastern Michigan. In such labor market areas as Grand Rapids, Muskegon, Kalamazoo, and most of the rest of the state, however, wage rates are not appreciably different from those found in the rest of the nation. Thus, while high labor costs may be a deterrent to diversification and expansion of the economy in the Ann Arbor, Detroit, Flint, Lansing, and Saginaw areas, the same cannot be said for other parts of the state.

Given the fact that unemployment rates in Michigan tend to be higher than they are in the nation, it is to be expected that unemployment insurance taxes will be relatively high here. Actually, in 1978 (latest available data) unemployment insurance costs averaged 1.38 percent of total payrolls in the U.S. and 1.65 percent in Michigan.

Benefit levels are not high in Michigan, but our rules governing eligibility tend to be lenient compared with those in other states. This factor is likely, however, to be less important following the 1980 amendments to the statutes governing qualification for benefits.

Workmen's compensation costs tend to be high in Michigan in part because of the industrial structure of the state. Prior to the taking effect of the 1980 legislation that brought some major reforms in the area of W.C., Michigan had been among the most generous states in terms of providing benefits to retirees, benefits for nonwork-related injuries, and permitting an individual to receive both W.C. and U.I. benefits from the same employer's account. Further study is undoubtedly needed on this subject, in order to develop fully plans for bringing Michigan W.C. costs more closely into line with those of other heavily industrialized states while providing adequately for those who suffer injuries or work-related illnesses that impair their earning capacities.

The auto market in the U.S. has undergone a major change in the past few years. In the past, American automotive manufacturers profited from the low substitutability between large and small cars. But the dramatic change in the price of gasoline has brought about a breakdown of the separation of the market into two segments, and the newly competitive market that has emerged makes the high U.S. wage level a major obstacle to the recovery of American producers' share of the market. In addition, the Japanese appear to enjoy a basic material cost advantage which, when added to their labor cost advantage, gives them the ability to deliver automobiles to the American market at prices variously estimated at between $1,000 and $1,800 less than comparable American units.

Industrial Location

State and local taxes have generally not been found to be a major factor in industrial location decisions, particularly when they are viewed as part of the overall public sector, including the quality and quantity of public services. Observation of growth and change in the American economy suggests an "industrial filtering" theory that leads to the conclusion that state and local jurisdictions may find that policies directed toward attracting new firms and industries may prove more effective than those aimed at trying to hold existing ones.

A review of recent studies of factors affecting location decisions indicates that Michigan frequently gets a low rating for wage costs and degree of unionization of the labor force and a high rating for the level and structure of business taxes (excluding W.C. and U.I.).

Thus far Michigan has enjoyed only limited success in attracting or developing high technology industry. We have had many promising starts, but as firms have grown and matured they have tended to move out, frequently following a merger with a large conglomerate. Close observation of successful experience in attracting and keeping growing employment in high technology industries in such locations as "Silicon Valley" in the San Francisco Bay area, the North Carolina Research Triangle, and St. Paul-Minneapolis suggests that success requires strong, able leadership, an outstanding university science program, ready availability of suitable sites, venture capital, and a high "quality of life."

Michigan is now one of thirty-one states that offer tax abatement in one form or another to new firms or old firms that expand or renovate existing plants. By 1981 virtually all new industrial construction and substantial renovations of obsolete plants in Michigan get property tax abatements offered by some 400 local jurisdictions. Through 1980 some 2,100 projects had been approved for tax abatement, at a total foregone tax cost of $1.7 billion through the end of the eligible period. About 80 percent of this cost is borne by the state.

Available evidence suggests that tax abatement under Public Act 198 has had little effect on job creation.

However, each Michigan municipality or township appears to feel compelled to offer abatements, knowing that its neighbors are doing so. Thus a very large part of the revenue lost is foregone because of competition for industry among Michigan jurisdictions.

All but three states now permit local governments to issue Industrial Revenue Bonds in behalf of private industrial and commercial firms. The volume of such tax exempt bonds issued in 1980 exceeded $8 billion nationally. In Michigan the estimated annual gain to beneficiary firms amounts to $10 million. Since, as in the case of tax abatement, a special concession granted by all is of advantage to none, it is unlikely that Industrial or Commercial Development Bonds have a major effect on new job creation. They may increase local governments' borrowing costs. But otherwise their cost to Michigan residents is very small, and the issuing of these bonds cannot be sensibly stopped here unless it is simultaneously stopped in the nation as a whole.

Public Expenditures

During the past decade state government expenditures do not appear to have grown excessively. They remained more or less constant as a proportion of personal income through the 1970s. But the mix of expenditures did change sharply. In general, there was a shift away from services to the general population toward services to specifically targeted groups. Thus aid for elementary and secondary education dropped from 40.4 to 29.1 percent of total state expenditures, higher education's share of the total dropped as well, as did the share of several other categories. But during the decade the state's share of AFDC increased at the rate of 13 percent per year, medicaid at 14 percent, general assistance 19 percent, juvenile services 20 percent, and corrections 19 percent.

In keeping with Michigan's position as a high wage state, civil service salaries are 24 percent higher than the U.S. average, and AFDC benefits for a family of four in 1979 were third highest in the nation, at 52 percent above the national average.

Except for a series of ad hoc grants to Detroit for special purposes, state aid to cities, villages, townships, and counties is not highly responsive to such criteria as need, equalization, or effort. The system appears to function without reference to any logical set of goals or objectives. It relies mainly on head counts of population for determining the distribution of a large and growing amount of state tax receipts.

The past eight years have witnessed a major structural change in the system of distributing state aid to local school districts. The new system has as its central objective the equalization of fiscal capacity among school districts. Unfortunately, however, the system has not been adequately funded, with the result that the state share of school revenues has been permitted to fall from approximately half at peak to about one-third now, and school property taxes have risen from less than half of the total levy to 68 percent. Each year since 1974 additional school districts go "out-of-formula" and receive no general aid at all; such districts now number about 171. The state's failure to maintain its share of elementary and secondary education revenues has contributed in large measure to pressures for property tax relief.

A review of contemporary experience with tax and/or expenditure limitations suggests that, when approved, they build into the constitution rigid constraints on legislative bodies for long periods of time. Generally these tend to be very complex and poorly understood, typically containing detailed legislation-like provisions rather than simple rules designed to provide a framework within which legislative bodies may act.

As an alternative to the referenda that have confronted the Michigan voter in the past four years, it is suggested that local (or state) electorates might be offered the opportunity periodically to vote on the level of real expenditures. They might, for example, be asked to express a preference among levels of change from existing budgetary outlays ranging, say, from -4 percent through 0 to +4 percent.

The Revenue System

The property tax, yielding $4.4 billion, continues to be the principal source of tax revenue for local governments in Michigan. Only sixteen cities supplement it with an income tax, levied at the rate of 1 percent (1/2 percent on commuters), except in Detroit where it is now 3 percent (1 1/2 percent for commuters). School districts now receive 68 percent of total property taxes levied, with the remainder going to municipalities, counties, townships, and various special districts.

The property tax in Michigan amounted to 5.3 percent of personal income in 1972. By 1980 the net (after credits) property tax bill amounted to 3.8 percent of income. Over the same period the share of the tax base accounted for by residential property rose from 49.2 to 56.5 percent, while that of industrial and commercial property fell from 39.7 to 31 percent. These changes are attributable in part to the increasing exemptions afforded to industry and trade for inventories and tools and dies, in part to tax abatement for industry, and in part they are attributable to the higher rate of inflation in the market for residential property compared with industrial and commercial realty.

The Homestead Property Tax Credit (circuit breaker) provides a substantial offset to the larger share of the tax base that is now accounted for by residences. For the fiscal year 1982 (1981 property tax payments) it is estimated that this credit will reduce homeowners', renters', and farmers' net property tax burdens by $531 million, or by about one-sixth. The average net property tax liability of homeowners, after taking account of the circuit breaker and deductibility under the federal income tax, is estimated at 1.5 percent of income. On industrial property the tax amounts to approximately 1.5 percent of value added.

Unfortunately the circuit breaker is one of the state's best kept secrets. It is estimated that less than 60 percent of all eligible households filed for the credit in 1978. And of those who do file, few seem to understand that it is, in fact, a property tax credit. It is found to be substantially more effective in terms of vertical equity than such alternatives as reduction in assessed value, exemption of a portion of assessed value, or a credit equal to a percentage of tax paid. The circuit breaker approach is particularly appealing as a means of providing relief for the poor and the elderly.

The Michigan personal income tax is now the most productive of all state taxes. Its virtues include its simplicity and a modest degree of progression. It is, however, not as equitable as it might be by reason of the exclusion of 60 percent of realized capital gains, lottery winnings, military pay and pensions, and general pension benefits. Failure to allow a deduction for interest results in some taxation of gross rather than net income. Furthermore, the tax is being increasingly eroded by credits, in particular those for local income and property taxes paid, agricultural property taxes on farms participating in the farmland preservation program, contributions to institutions of higher education and public radio stations, and home heating costs. The last increase in the personal exemption was enacted in 1974. Since then inflation has reduced the real value of the $1,500 exemption by about two-thirds. Thus one of its central purposes, to shield those with incomes below the poverty level from the income tax, is no longer being realized. In addition, with inflated incomes, the contribution of the fixed exemption to progression in a flat-rate income tax has declined substantially.

The sales and use taxes are generally regarded as taxes on consumption. The Michigan taxes, however, like those of other states, are inconsistent in that they apply to business purchases other than for re-sale or direct use in production, and do not apply to household expenditures on services. The exemption of food for home consumption and prescription drugs is widely regarded as necessary for the attainment of equity objectives.

The Michigan intangibles tax is essentially a vestigial remain left over from an earlier era in state and local taxation. With most of its revenue coming from taxation of individuals' dividends and interest income, it is highly progressive; certainly the most progressive tax levied by the state. But it is highly capricious in what it does and does not tax and from the standpoint of horizontal equity it fails badly. There appears to be little effort exerted by the state to enforce payment of the tax except when estates are subject to probate. It appears that between one-sixth and one-half of those who should file intangibles tax returns are, in fact, not doing so. This in itself renders the tax very inequitable and may mean that as much as $20 million in revenue is being lost each year.

Taxes on gratuitous transfers of wealth at death or by gift are not major contributors to public revenues. In Michigan the inheritance tax yields less than one percent of total state tax receipts. The importance of the tax lies in its contribution to vertical equity in the tax system. But in the absence of a gift tax in Michigan, and with the exclusion of insurance proceeds paid to a named beneficiary, all jointly-owned property, and much of the value of farm property, the taxation of wealth transfers is ineffectual and productive of much less revenue than might be warranted. Moreover, the tax is highly capricious in its impact, depending as it does on the nature of assets held by the decedent, the number of heirs and their relationship to the decedent, the extent to which the estate had been distributed through _inter vivos_ gifts, and the form in which ownership was held.

The single business tax, third largest source of state tax revenue, is, unfortunately, riddled with special concessions that reflect the log-rolling that was needed to gain its passage in the legislature in 1975. Many of the features of the business activities tax, repealed in 1967, features that produced distortions of the value-added base, were carried forward into the SBT. They include the labor intensity reduction, permitting deduction of labor costs exceeding 63 percent of the tax base; the gross receipts deduction, which limits the SBT base to a maximum of 50 percent of gross receipts; and the three factor allocation formula that assigns much of the value added produced in Michigan to other states. Using a similar two factor formula to allocate deductible investments in machinery and equipment results in some investment in other states being deductible while portions of investment wholly in Michigan may not be deductible.

On balance, however, the SBT is found to be preferable, as a business levy, to the principal alternative, the corporate income tax. It does not appear to have an adverse affect on Michigan's competitive position. But erosion of the tax base does seriously impinge on equity and efficiency and on revenue growth and stability.

The Michigan Liquor Control Commission is placed in an ambivalent position. Since it is charged with both control and revenue-raising functions, it may be seen as neither effectively exploiting in full the revenue potential of its liquor monopoly nor protecting the social interest by restricting liquor consumption. Under these circumstances it is difficult to evaluate its functioning.

License fees paid by liquor vendors do not appear to be adequately sensitive to differences in the value of licenses.

The specific tax on beer has become an increasingly small fraction of its price. It represents, moreover, an increasingly smaller part of the price for premium and imported beers than for the lower-priced beers. On both counts, there is much to be said for moving to an _ad valorem_ tax based on wholesale price. Such a move would be consistent with the fact that the tax on liquor is _ad valorem_.

Taxation of the insurance industry appears to be governed far more by a determination to emulate the practices of other states than by concern for equity or efficiency. The result is that "foreign" companies are taxed on their premiums while Michigan companies pay the far lower SBT instead. The merits of strongly favoring this particular "domestic" industry are elusive.

The distinctive tax treatment of telephone, telegraph, and railroad companies that exempts them from local property taxation and subjects them, instead, to a state-levied tax at the average statewide property tax rate may once have been highly sensible. There is now little or no reason why these taxpayers should be treated differently from other utilities or firms in other industries.

Like the beer tax, Michigan's specific cigarette tax has fallen relative to the price of the product as inflation has carried that price up in recent years. The Michigan tax rate is now substantially below that of several neighboring states and it is little more than half as high as the highest rates in the nation. Clearly, however, in terms of both vertical and horizontal equity, it is among the worst taxes we have. Nor is it likely that a modest increase in the tax rate would discourage consumption appreciably, while an increase large enough to do so would undoubtedly lead to major bootlegging problems.

As a means of financing the supply of public services, the capacity of user charges to serve as allocative devices, much like private prices, makes them very appealing. This is especially true at the local level, where there is ample room for their expanded use. A deterrent to this expansion, however, lies in the loss of the federal deductibility feature when financing is shifted from property, income, or sales taxes to user charges. Nevertheless, charges provide important information regarding decisions on resource allocation to service-supplying governments, they encourage consumers to economize in the use of the public services they finance, and they allot the costs of services to specific beneficiaries rather than to the public at large.

In general it would seem clearly desirable that the state's natural resources should be viewed as a long-run productive investment, rather than as a short-run budgetary drain. It is the latter viewpoint that seems to prevail, however, particularly with regard to the now inadequately productive and relatively neglected state forests.

Our state parks are not now priced rationally. In partial consequence of this they are not self-supporting. Present pricing practices permit most people to use the parks at a zero marginal price and no distinction in pricing is drawn between residents and nonresidents of the state.

Revenues from oil and gas production have been increasing rapidly as petroleum and gas prices have risen sharply. But the present system of earmarking much of these revenues to a land purchase fund has the effect of tying up some $150 million that cannot be spent either for land acquisition or anything else.

Legal gambling in Michigan now yields about $250 million per year in revenue to the state and its local subdivisions, through the tax on pari-mutuel wagering and the state lottery. Gambling taxes are found to be highly regressive. Given recent years' decline in the pari-mutuel take at the horse tracks, it is difficult to justify seeking additional revenues from this source. Nor can the lottery be expected to yield rapidly increasing revenues in the foreseeable future.

Reasonable estimates of the revenue potential of casino gambling in Detroit fall far short of some projections of as much as $125 million per year for the city. Long-range prospects are seen as unpromising as legalized gambling sites proliferate.

During the past decade expenditures of the major cities in Michigan have continued to increase at a rate in excess of the rate of inflation. Detroit, through 1980, continued to experience an increase in the number of people employed by the city per 1,000 of its population, in large part because service demands have not declined as rapidly as has the population, which fell 20 percent from 1970 to 1980.

The fiscal distress being experienced by Detroit is, increasingly, being shared by many other central cities in the state and by the older, close-in suburbs. Current large cuts in federal programs are bound to exacerbate existing difficulties in circumstances in which state aid is being curtailed as well in budget balancing maneuvers in Lansing. The outlook for many cities is bleak indeed, and there are no easy solutions.

In recent years the Michigan legislature has taken major steps to lighten the tax load carried by farmers. All personal property used on the farm is now exempt. Farmers are entitled to the Homestead Property Tax Credit on the same terms as nonfarm homeowners and renters. And those farmers who choose to do so may place their properties under the farmland preservation program that ensures that as long as they refrain from selling their land for development their property taxes will not exceed seven percent of household income. A large proportion of the owners of the two million acres of farmland now in the preservation program pay little or no net property taxes. The two property tax credits combined now return over $26 million of property taxes per year to farmers.

Property taxes on privately held forest lands may inhibit long-term investment in forest management. But owners may choose to be taxed instead under a severance or stumpage tax under the terms of the Commercial Forest Reserve Act. Forestry, however, is not nearly as highly favored under state and local tax laws as agriculture.

SOME POLICY OPTIONS

In this section the intent is to offer, not a set of recommendations, but a recapitulation of the major tax policy measures suggested by the analyses contained in the relevant chapters. Changes in tax bases, aimed at improving equity and efficiency, may offer the opportunity either to realize more revenue as an alternative to further budget cuts, or to reduce tax rates and/or increase income tax exemptions or property tax credits. Thus no judgment is implied as to the "proper" level of either total budget expenditures or revenues.

It is important to note, however, that under the Headlee amendment to the constitution, the state revenue limit is 10 percent of personal income in the year preceding the beginning of the current fiscal year. Personal income in Michigan in 1980 has been estimated by the U.S. Department of Commerce at $92.3 billion.[2] Thus the maximum revenue for fiscal year 1982 is $9.23 billion, compared with likely actual receipts subject to the limitation of less than $8 billion. There is, therefore, ample room to increase revenues should the legislature wish to do so.

The Property Tax

If property tax relief is to be provided, the most efficient means for doing so, in terms of the goal of targeting relief to those who are most heavily burdened relative to income, is through liberalization of the existing circuit breaker. This may be achieved by reducing the income threshold in the formula from the current 3.5 percent to 3.0 or 2.5 percent, increasing the maximum credit from $1,200 to perhaps $2,000, and by raising the income levels at which the sliding scale threshold applies for the elderly and selected others. The revenue loss will depend, of course, on how far liberalization is taken. At a cost of under $300 million, however, it would be possible to attain a large part of the objectives of those who wish to offer relief in this area.

Deserving of a higher priority than changes in the circuit breaker is a concentrated effort to ensure that everyone entitled to the credit actually gets it and that the public is thoroughly acquainted with its terms. This will require an effective education campaign and "front-loading." The latter may be achieved in a number of ways. One of these would involve sending each household entitled to the circuit breaker credit, a voucher redeemable in payment of property taxes or a portion of the annual rent in the case of renters. This approach would have the effect of separating the homestead property tax credit from the income tax, and increasing public awareness of the credit and availability of property tax relief amounting now to about one-sixth of the tax on residential property. It would also have the incidental effect of solving a major part of the state's cash flow problem because more than $500 million would be paid out in August through October in redemption of vouchers, instead of February through June in income tax refunds and reduced income tax payments.

The Income Tax

Inflation in the past eight years has eroded the effectiveness of the $1,500 exemption in shielding the poor from the income tax and in providing an element of progression in the tax. It would take an increase to $2,500 to restore the role of the exemption to its 1974 position. This would entail a revenue loss of about $350 million, a loss that could be offset by raising the tax rate from the present 4.6 to 5.2 percent.

The Sales Tax

From the standpoint of equity and efficiency a major shortcoming of the sales tax as a tax on consumption expenditure is its failure to reach the purchase of services. For a variety of reasons, including administrative feasibility, compassion, and political realities, not all services can be taxed. Those excluded would be housing, educational, religious, medical and hospital services, mortuary services and those that are now subject to special taxes, such as pari-mutuel wagering and insurance. If all other services were subject to the sales or use tax, the net revenue gain would amount to between

$150 million and $200 million. Among the principal components of the more than $4 billion addition to the tax base would be the following: services of barbershops, beauty parlors, and health clubs; auto repair, parking, etc.; local transit and taxi services; radio and TV repair; admissions and amusements; cleaning, storage, and repair of clothing; legal services to households; and household operation services.

The Single Business Tax

The tax that is most thoroughly riddled with special concessions to various groups of taxpayers is the single business tax. Among these are the low-income reduction, the small business/low profit credit, the unincorporated business credit, the extra exemption for partners, the gross receipts reduction, the high labor intensity reduction, and the favored treatment afforded to firms in transportation, food retailing, private security services, building maintenance, and rental housing. At 1978 levels of activity, removing all of these features of the SBT would yield $440 million per year in additional revenue or permit reducing the tax rate from 2.35 to 1.5 percent. The indicated changes would make the SBT an evenhanded, effective tax on value added.

Other Taxes

Modest efforts to enforce the filing requirements under the intangibles tax could bring improvements in equity and provide additional annual revenues in the range of $10 million to $20 million.

The inheritance tax in Michigan is far less productive of revenue than the equivalent taxes in comparable states. Its base is so poorly defined that the tax is a source of injustice rather than a means of adding an element of equity to the revenue system of the state. Obvious changes called for include the replacement of the present tax with an integrated tax on gifts and bequests or, alternatively, an accessions tax, changing the treatment of insurance proceeds and jointly-owned property to conform to the federal estate and gift tax rules, and excluding transfers between spouses from the tax base. These changes, together with appropriate rate adjustments, could reasonably be expected to yield about $30 million per year in new revenue.

A reading of the relevant chapters of this volume will suggest other possible or desirable changes in tax policy and in other areas such as workmen's compensation, unemployment insurance, and school finance. It is not our objective to set out a reform "package" or to offer a "blueprint" for change. It is hoped, rather, that the contents of this volume may help to inform the ongoing debate on fiscal policy in the state. The policy options discussed are offered in the spirit of illustrations or demonstrations of changes that might reasonably be pursued, rather than in a spirit of advocacy.

NOTES, CHAPTER 30

[1]With a 1980 state equalized value per pupil of about $26,000, Taylor school district would receive close to one dollar from the state for each dollar of local property tax levied. Thus one dollar in school revenues initially costs taxpayers fifty cents. This fifty cents is subject to 60 percent reduction under the terms of the Homestead Property Tax Credit, 100 percent for people over age sixty-five. As a consequence, the net cost of the fifty cents in property tax and one dollar in school revenue may be as little as twenty cents or even zero.

[2]Survey of Current Business, July, 1981.

Glossary

Effective tax rate. Generally this expression means the amount of tax paid expressed as a percentage of the taxpayer's total income.

Efficiency. This term is used throughout the book in a special sense that has its origins in the field of welfare economics. For the most part efficiency is a concept that refers to the extent to which a tax does or not induce economic actors to change their behaviour relative to what it would have been in the absence of the tax. Thus a tax that leads people to work less is inefficient, whereas a tax that results in little or no change in behavior is said to be efficient.

Horizontal equity. Equity is always an elusive, subjective concept. Horizontal equity is generally interpreted to require the equal treatment of similarily (equally) circumstanced persons. It may refer to equal treatment with respect to income or wealth, or equal treatment with reference to the subject of taxation. Thus, for example, the intangibles tax may be horizontally inequitable because it does not tax people with equal total income or wealth equally, but in the narrowest sense it may be held to be equitable if it taxes all people with equal dividend and interest income equally.

Income effect. This term refers to the change in the quantity of a good or service demanded as a result of a change in real income. Since a decrease (increase) in the nominal price of a good results in an increase (decrease) in real income, a price change has an income effect.

Price effect. The price effect is the change in the quantity of a good or service demanded resulting from a change in the relative price of the good, holding real income constant.

Proportional. A tax is said to be proportional if it takes the same percentage of income from all relevant households.

But, if so specified, it may refer to equal proportions of specific tax bases, such as wealth or expenditure.

Progressive. With provisos similar to those suggested for "Proportional," a tax is progressive if it takes an increasing percentage of household income as that income rises.

Regressive. This is the opposite of progressive. A tax is regressive if households with higher income pay a smaller percentage of that income in tax than do households with lower incomes.

Vertical equity. Vertical equity is even more difficult to define than horizontal equity. It refers to justice or fairness in the distribution of tax liabilities among persons or households with different levels of income. Whether or not a tax is vertically equitable is a matter of subjective value judgment and relates more clearly to ethics than to economics. The authors of the chapters of this volume ordinarily regard a tax that has the effect of increasing income inequality as vertically inequitable and vertical equity as requiring either that a tax or tax system be neutral with respect to income distribution (proportional) or that it reduce income inequality.